ACCOUNTING An Introduction

ACCOUNTING An Introduction

KENNETH W. PERRY, Ph.D., C.P.A.
Professor of Accountancy, University of Illinois

McGraw-Hill Book Company

New York
St. Louis
San Francisco
Düsseldorf
Johannesburg
Kuala Lumpur
London
Mexico
Montreal
New Delhi
Panama
Rio de Janeiro
Singapore
Sydney
Toronto

ACCOUNTING An Introduction

Library of Congress Catalog Card Number 70-141923

07-049425-8

234567890 VHVH 7987654321

This book was set in Baskerville by York Graphic Services, Inc., and printed on permanent paper and bound by Von Hoffmann Press, Inc. The designer was Merrill Haber; the drawings were done by John Cordes, J. & R. Technical Services, Inc. Cover photo by Zvonko Glyck. The editors were Jack R. Crutchfield, Hiag Akmakjian, and Sonia Sheldon. Les Kaplan supervised production.

Contents

Loss on Realization with a Capital Deficiency   376
  Capital Deficiency: Partner Has Sufficient Personal Assets   Capital Deficiency:
  Partner Has No Personal Assets   Capital Deficiency: Partner Has Some Personal
  Assets

PART FIVE
ACCOUNTING FOR FEDERAL INCOME TAXES

Preface

This text is an introduction to accounting, designed for a full-year beginning course at the college level. It is intended for use both by students planning to become professional accountants and by those desiring to utilize accounting as a tool in other areas of specialization or for personal use.

Financial and Managerial Accounting

The scope of *Accounting: An Introduction* is consistent with the current trend of dividing the first year's work in accounting between the financial and managerial areas. Chapters 1 through 18 provide the background for both areas; Chapters 19 and 20 are essentially financial in nature; and Chapters 21 through 26 carry a managerial orientation.

Student-oriented

Generally, as we all know, there are two important people involved in the learning process: the student and the teacher. Although *Accounting: An Introduction* is essentially student-oriented, it was written with both the student and the teacher in mind. As an aid to both, every effort has been made to present the material in a clear, concise, and readable manner and to eliminate the fancy, opaque prose which so often obscures the learning process. The reader should not be misled by the simplicity of style, however; nothing essential to a beginning course in accounting has been omitted. The student who masters the material in this text will have an adequate background for any future accounting study he might wish to undertake. The author's chief concern was to provide sufficient coverage and support for the student and at the same time to permit maximum teaching flexibility.

Teaching Flexibility

The author recognizes that while many teachers will prefer an in-depth study of certain areas, others will wish to cover them in less detail. *Accounting: An Introduction* has been designed to accommodate both approaches. For example, although the author is of the opinion that a thorough knowledge of the way accounting data flow through the accounts is essential to a proper understanding of the total accounting process, others may not agree. Those teachers who do not wish to become too involved in the flow of data through the accounts may spend as few as two to three classroom hours on Chapter 4, a chapter in which the entire accounting cycle is covered. Other teachers may spend as many as eight to ten classroom hours on this chapter and not lack for material. The problem material is specifically designed to meet these differences. At the end of each chapter, the most important areas discussed in the text are first covered by short discussion questions and problems; then, in order of increasing complexity, a large number of more advanced problems are provided. (As an additional aid to the teacher, lecture guides for each chapter are provided elsewhere, in which the problems applicable to given areas of study are indicated.) Thus, by judicious selection of the questions and problems, a teacher can go into as much depth in a particular area as he wishes. As another example, in Chapter 22 the basic tools of capital budgeting may be covered without the student becoming overly involved in the decision-making process; however, by selecting problems of increasing complexity, the teacher can place considerable emphasis on this aspect of the subject. Teaching flexibility is further provided for in Chapters 11, 12, and 13 by the inclusion of computer problems for depreciation accounting, payroll accounting, and long-term debt.

Basic Mathematical Tools Emphasized

Because an understanding of certain fundamental mathematical procedures is essential to the accountant in this age of the computer, the appropriate "math tools" are introduced and utilized in this text as the occasion arises. Compound interest, for example, is introduced in Chapter 13 when long-term debt is studied, and it is employed again in Chapter 22 when capital budgeting is covered. In addition, because much of advanced accounting is mathematically oriented, Chapter 26, "Mathematical Techniques Essential to the Accounting Process," is included for those who may require a brief refresher before progressing further with their studies. Basic arithmetic, algebra, and probability theory are included in the review. All three areas are tied together as they relate to inventory management.

Instructional Aids

A comprehensive set of instructional aids is provided, all prepared and integrated with the text by the author. The set consists of:

1 An instructor's manual ("solutions manual") containing:
   a A lecture guide for each chapter
   b A checklist of key figures
   c Estimated times for answering questions and problems
   d Solutions to questions and problems in the text
   e Solutions to achievement tests
   f Solutions to practice sets
2 Transparencies of selected problem solutions and text material
3 Working papers for the question and problem material
4 A workbook of study guides
5 A checklist of key figures for the student
6 Achievement tests
7 Two practice sets

Acknowledgments

The author expresses his grateful appreciation to the American Institute of Certified Public Accountants for permission to use questions and problems from past CPA examinations as well as various materials copyrighted by the Institute. All questions and problems borrowed from the Institute are identified by the notation "AICPA adapted."

The author also wishes to express his thanks to his colleagues and students at the University of Illinois for their many suggestions and assistance in the development and preparation of this text. Special appreciation is expressed to Professor Donald H. Skadden for helping to mold the material on federal income taxes into a workable status.

Sincere thanks are also extended to the many reviewers who read either the manuscript or the solutions manual in various stages of completion for their painstaking reviews and valuable suggestions. Especially helpful was the advice received from Professors Clarence G. Avery, Northern Illinois University; Robert W. Clark, University of Idaho; Roy E. Crossno, Sacramento City College; Fred T. Gilson, Eastern Michigan University; John P. Klingstedt, The University of Oklahoma; Gary McCombs, Eastern Michigan University; Eugene McNeil, University of Houston; Edwin Pinto, San Jose State College; J. Everett Royer, University of Miami (Florida); Nelson G. Sullivan, North Texas State University; Mathilda M. Tassin, Portland State University; Lee C. Wilson, Eastern Michigan University; and Dorsey E. Wiseman, California State College at Fullerton. Finally, the author gratefully acknowledges the invaluable editorial assistance of Hiag Akmakjian, Glen Johnson, and Sonia Sheldon.

Most of the author's colleagues will undoubtedly argue that this book should be dedicated to his wife, Shirley, in appreciation for her constant assistance and encouragement throughout its preparation. However, she and the author are in complete agreement that it should be dedicated to Professor R. R. Richards, whose early inspiration and motivation made its writing possible.

Kenneth W. Perry

Part One
The Accounting Environment

1
Accounting: The Language of Business

The maxim "knowledge is power" is nowhere better illustrated than in the operation of a modern business organization. In a competitive society such as we traditionally have had in the United States, well-informed management is a necessity if an organization is to survive. Management must have access to information regarding all activities related to the enterprise; it must have the right information at the right place in the right format at the right time. Thus, economic reality must be translated into business data or, as these data are generally termed, **business information.** Accounting is the vehicle employed by business organizations for this conversion process. As a result, it has come to be known as "the language of business."

ACCOUNTING AND MANAGEMENT

Accounting may be defined simply as the **collection, classification,** and **interpretation** of the financial information relevant to the operation of an organization.

It is an indispensable tool in the effective management of all organizations involved in the earning or spending of money, regardless of size and whether they are business firms, governments, churches, schools, or other. Accounting is particularly useful to management in such areas as the:

1 Determination of the basic objectives of the organization
2 Development of plans of action and the projection of their results
3 Provision of controls over activities
4 Determination of the costs of activities
5 Establishment of prices for goods and services
6 Evaluation of results of operations
7 Formulation of policies for future guidance of the organization

Accounting and the Business Unit

Accounting is principally associated with the individual business unit, or, as it is frequently termed, the **enterprise entity.** This association has been both a helpful and a deterring factor in the natural evolution of accounting. On the one hand, it has contributed to the remarkable growth of specialized techniques and practices requisite to the recording of day-by-day transactions within the individual enterprise. Considered solely from this point of view, progress in the field has been generally satisfactory. Viewed in another light, however, the enterprise entity relationship has to a certain extent limited inquiry into the broad social implications of accounting. These have only recently begun to be investigated, with the result that accounting is now being considered by some individuals in a perspective quite distinct from its traditional associations and responsibilities.

Need for Accounting Data

In earlier times, when the business enterprise was small and its activities local, the owner, who was also usually the manager, could easily obtain the information he needed to conduct his business. This is still true in some cases. The owner or operator of a neighborhood grocery, for example, with only the simplest accounting records, is able to plan his sales campaign, determine the nature and extent of the advertising to be done, select the goods to be purchased, secure the necessary funds from sources which he chooses, and actively direct, if not actually perform, all the operations of the business. He can do this because the information upon which he bases his actions is usually obtainable in the daily routine of business and can be correlated and interpreted with little difficulty.

However, when business organization grows complex and the business enterprise becomes large and its activities widespread, it is generally impossible for management to obtain in the daily routine of business reliable, timely, and adequate information upon which to base business policies and decisions. Therefore, the accountant's periodic reports—the means by which the financial condition and results of operations of a business organization are summarized—become managerial tools for obtaining the necessary information.

Users of Accounting Data

In addition to the operating management, many other interested individuals and groups require, for various purposes, financial reports prepared from an organization's accounting data. Regulatory agencies, for example, such as the Securities and Exchange Commission, the Federal Power Commission, and the Interstate Commerce Commission, as well as federal, state, and local taxing authorities, frequently need detailed accounting data, often in specialized form. On the other hand, an organization's employees and the general public may need only broad general information presented in the simplest terms. Still others, such as the knowledgeable stockholder or potential investor, along with his advisers, may require a highly sophisticated presentation of the financial facts. Although not exhaustive, the following list is indicative of the wide range of users of accounting data:

1 Management (at all levels)
2 Owners
3 Creditors
4 Employees
5 Regulatory agencies
6 Taxing authorities
7 Consumers
8 General public

Management Process

Management has been defined as the science of employing the three M's—men, material, and machines—in the effective and economical accomplishment of a given task. Its primary functions, as identified by the French industrialist Henri Fayol as early as 1916, consist of:

1 Planning
2 Organizing
3 Directing
4 Coordinating
5 Controlling

These five broad functions are not necessarily separate and distinct, to be accomplished in a prescribed order, but are instead often interrelated and may at any time be applied simultaneously. When considered collectively, they form the **management process.** Needless to say, no task of any degree of complexity can be efficiently accomplished without being wisely planned, properly organized, judiciously directed, suitably coordinated, and effectively controlled.

Accounting aids management in all the above functions. However, while it may be of value in the organizing, directing, and coordinating phases of a business operation, its greatest usefulness is in the areas of planning and control.

THE ACCOUNTING PROCESS

Accounting for business transactions is as old as business itself. Early references to the subject may be found in the works of certain ancient oriental writers, but accounting as we know it today probably originated in the thirteenth century. In 1494, Luca Paciolo, a Franciscan monk living in Italy, published his now well-known work, *Summa de Arithmetica, Geometria, Proportioni et Proportionalita,* which was primarily a study of mathematics but also included a section on accounting methods. In it he set forth essential principles which have remained relatively unchanged to the present day.

Ever-changing Scope and Methodology

Although the basic principles have not changed substantially since Paciolo's time, the scope and methodology of accounting are in a constant state of evolution. By its very nature, accounting adapts itself to the business environment—it responds to business stimuli. Much of its progress has been related either directly or indirectly to the constantly changing economic environment and the ever-increasing use of mathematical tools by the accountant. It is important that we have an appreciation for the relationship of economics and mathematics to accounting before we begin our study of the basic process.

Accounting and Economics The science of economics deals largely with the social aspects of production and distribution, while accounting is concerned chiefly with the problems of the individual enterprise. Nevertheless, the two fields treat of similar subject matter. Both are concerned with property and with the human activities related to its production, exchange, and consumption. In general, it is the point of view that differentiates one from the other. Whereas economics treats of society as a whole, of wealth in general, of the wants of people, and of the satisfaction of those wants, accounting deals with individual units of society and their property, requirements, efforts, and accomplishments.

Accounting is presently developing rapidly in the area of statistical methodology; as a consequence, the accountant is reaching more and more into areas hitherto mainly the habitat of the economist. At the same time, in many fields of economic investigation, the economist must deal directly with data which can be supplied to him only by the accountant. Thus, it is perhaps obvious that if their respective missions are to be accomplished satisfactorily, accountants and economists must have a mutual appreciation for their interdependence.

Accounting and Mathematics In his impressive contribution to the study of world history, *The Decline of the West*, Oswald Spengler, in the chapter "The Meaning of Numbers," points out that every culture has had not only its own philosophy, religion, music, architecture, and economics, but also its own mathematics. Classical culture, for example, had its plane surface geometry, Arabian culture created a science from the letter notations of algebra, while Western culture evolved the dynamics of calculus, which has led to ever more abstractions of variable quantities. "It is," wrote Spengler, "by means of names and numbers that the human understanding obtains power over the world."[1]

There has been no other period in world history when mathematics has represented the concepts of all action and thinking as it does today. The continual advances in science, the discoveries of the innermost secrets of nature, the operations of businesses in their tremendous diversity are all founded on advances in applied mathematics. Thus, the accountant lives and works in a mathematical world. If he is to be capable of measuring properly the economic phenomena with which he deals, he must have at least a basic understanding of the mathematics involved.

Fields of Accounting Specialization

Accounting, like the professions of medicine and law, offers many opportunities for specialization. The professionally trained accountant may elect to practice in one of three major fields: (1) private accounting, (2) public accounting, or (3) governmental accounting. Each of these in turn permits further specialization in such areas as auditing, budgeting, cost control, and tax accounting. Most of these areas will be discussed in this text, and all are developed further in advanced accounting study.

Private Accounting Accountants engaged in **private accounting** generally are employed by individual business organizations. These enterprises may range in size from the small, perhaps family-owned, business to the large corporation employing thousands of persons. Positions occupied by accountants in private accounting include those of financial vice president, treasurer, controller, chief accountant, general auditor, and budget director.

Public Accounting This is practiced by individual accountants or independent accounting firms of varying size. Like the lawyer and the doctor, the public accountant offers his services to the general public for a fee. His clients range

[1]Oswald Spengler, *The Decline of the West*, Alfred A. Knopf, New York, 1926, p. 57.

from individuals to large business enterprises and governments. Leaders in the field of public accounting hold the certificate of certified public accountant (CPA). To become a CPA, an accountant must meet certain educational and other qualifications, pass comprehensive written examinations, and obtain certification from the state in which he intends to practice. While many CPAs practice in the field of public accounting, numerous others are employed in both private and governmental accounting.

Governmental Accounting Accountants employed by the various branches of federal, state, and local governments are engaged in **governmental accounting.** As a general rule, the work performed by the governmental accountant is similar in nature to that of the private or public accountant.

Shift to General Management Although accounting is ordinarily a richly satisfying career in itself, it is not uncommon for accountants to move from this field into top positions in general management. For example, accountants have become presidents and chief executive officers of such major organizations as Chrysler, Crucible Steel, Ford, General Electric, General Motors, Prudential Insurance, Sun Oil, TWA, U.S. Steel, and Western Union.

Steps in the Accounting Process

Simply stated, the accounting process is the means by which raw economic data are transformed into intelligent business information. In general, it consists of three steps, or subprocesses, namely:

1 Collection and tabulation

2 Collation and modification

3 Reporting and interpretation

Collection and Tabulation The collection and tabulation process consists of collecting, authenticating, recording, and to a certain extent, classifying accounting data. To **collect** simply means to bring together the raw data from their various sources of origin. These sources are extensive and varied; they may range all the way from sales slips to written or oral promises.

To **authenticate** is to determine that the data originated from an unquestioned source; that is, that they are valid.

From an accounting standpoint, **recording** and **classifying** consist of setting down the raw data in writing or the like and then grouping together related items. Proper recording and classifying make subsequent collation, modification, reporting, and interpretation easier. Needless to say, the recording method employed in a particular situation must be adequate to handle the volume of raw data collected and to serve the needs of those who will eventually have access to the data.

Collation and Modification   To **collate** accounting data is to further classify them in some predetermined sequential order and to combine like items so that they may be compared for points of agreement or difference.   To **modify** accounting data is to adjust them whenever necessary in order to reflect changes in an organization's financial status.

Reporting and Interpretation   **Reporting** is the dissemination of the refined data to those who require it.   Inherent in the reporting process is the idea that the information must be pertinent, concise, clear, reliable, and timely.   The user of the data should not be burdened with irrelevant details or illogically presented information.

Interpretation, the final step in the accounting process, consists of bringing out the meaning of the reported data.   Sound interpretation of accounting data is the result of logical judgment based upon analysis, integration, and deduction.

In sum, to be most useful, accounting data must be collected, collated, modified, and reported within a suitable time period and then placed in the hands of the ultimate user so that he may evaluate and interpret them, formulate plans, and initiate action while the information is still relevant.

Systemization of the Accounting Process

In this era of the so-called "information explosion" or "knowledge revolution,"[1] it is imperative that business data be collected, assimilated, and at least partially digested by some kind of system.   The need for systemization becomes obvious when we consider some of the more important characteristics of the information explosion, such as the:

1 Availability of incredible quantities of previously unavailable data
2 Phenomenal speed with which such data can be processed and communicated to their ultimate users
3 Increasing use of the scientific method in the decision-making process

Characteristics of an Accounting System   An accounting system may be operated primarily manually or with key-driven machines, punched card equipment, electronic data processing devices, or some combination thereof.   The modern system usually may be characterized as follows:

1 It is man-made; that is, it is not created by nature but is constructed by man from equipment (frequently referred to as "hardware").
2 It has integrity; all its components contribute to a common purpose, the production of maximum output from a given input.

[1]It has been estimated that by the year 1800 the sum of human knowledge was doubling every 50 years; by 1950, every 10 years; and by 1970, about every 5 years.

3 It is semiautomatic; mechanical or electronic equipment performs some of its functions, while others are performed manually.

You will note that neither the completely manual nor the completely automatic system is considered here, the reason being that the former is generally inefficient except for use in the simplest economic entity, and the latter probably does not exist.

To be effective, an accounting system must be sufficiently **comprehensive** to supply the users of its data with all the information they require. It must be internally **consistent;** the various components must be so integrated that there is no conflict in the data produced. It must be **flexible;** the system must be sufficiently elastic to meet future changes in the structures of both the enterprise and the system. Finally, it must be **practical;** the usefulness of the information it produces must be balanced against the cost of providing it.

It makes little difference whether accounting data are carried in the hip pocket of the owner of an enterprise, kept in a loose-leaf binder, entered on punched card equipment, or integrated into a highly sophisticated electronic system; the basic principles of all sound accounting systems are the same.

Principles of Organization and Systems Design   The principles of organization, as applied to a sound accounting system, provide for:

1 Centralized direction

2 Decentralized execution

3 Standard operating procedures

While these principles are particularly applicable to accounting systems in large enterprises, they also apply in varying degrees to all accounting systems.

Centralized direction is essential for the effective control of men and machines throughout the accounting process.

Decentralized execution is desirable because, as a general rule, no individual can effectively control the detailed actions of a large number of persons; this limitation is usually referred to as the **span of control.** Many authorities on management maintain that no one individual can adequately supervise more than seven subordinates and that he needs at least three to keep him busy.

The establishment of **standard operating procedures** is essential for mutual understanding among all involved in the system so that timely and effective actions can be taken routinely. These procedures are generally predicated upon what are commonly known as the **basic concepts and principles of accounting,** which in turn are formulated upon the so-called **basic assumptions, or postulates, of accounting.**

The remaining chapters in this text are devoted primarily to the development of an understanding of the basic concepts and principles; therefore, before we continue, it is important that we become familiar with the basic assumptions which underlie them.   Regarding the concepts and principles, it should suffice to say at this time that they are developed from theory and practice, that they represent the best available thought that can be defended by reason, and that they are taught authoritatively as guidance but require judgment in application.

Basic Assumptions of Accounting

While no one set of accounting assumptions has been accepted as authoritative, the following list, which was developed by a special study group at the University of Illinois under the sponsorship of its Center for International Education and Research in Accounting,[1] has gained fairly widespread recognition:

1 Usefulness
2 Entity
3 Transaction
4 Quantifiability
5 Continuity
6 Periodicity

The assumptions may be summarized briefly as follows:

Usefulness Assumption   Accounting data have validity and usefulness for widely differing purposes.

Entity Assumption   Economic activity is engaged in by identifiable enterprises (entities) which constitute units of accountability and centers of interest for accounting analyses and reports.

Transaction Assumption   Accounting is concerned chiefly with the effect on an enterprise of its exchange transactions with other enterprises or individuals and with events which produce results essentially the same as those produced by exchange transactions.   Thus, the entity assumption, in conjunction with the transaction assumption, tends to fix the boundaries of accounting interest and service.

Quantifiability Assumption   Transactions in which an enterprise engages are consummated in terms of a stated or implied money price, and this money price provides an appropriate basis for accounting measurement and analysis.

Continuity Assumption   An enterprise will continue without significant change of environment and activities unless there is persuasive evidence to the contrary.

[1] *A Statement of Basic Accounting Postulates and Principles,* Center for International Education and Research in Accounting, Urbana, Ill., 1964, pp. 8–11.

Needless to say, in analyzing transactions and reporting their effects upon an enterprise, accountants must make some assumption with respect to the future of the enterprise. A continuance of approximately the present conditions and trends has generally proved to be the most reasonable solution.

Periodicity Assumption Implicit in present accounting practice is the assumption that the economic activities of an enterprise can be allocated among successive periods of time on a reasonable and useful basis.

The influence of these assumptions upon the basic concepts and principles of accounting will become evident as we move through the remainder of the text. However, recognition at this time that they do exist and that they are relied upon is essential to a real understanding of the accounting process.

Manual System as a Model

Although the completely manually operated accounting system is seldom used today, it does have value as a model in the study of the accounting process. A **model** is a representation of an object, or an explanation of a system, a process, or a series of related events. Thus, a globe may be employed as a model of the earth; a set of equations may be formulated for use as a model of a sector of an economy; and by the same token a manually operated accounting system may serve as a model for any type of accounting system. Models, however, are not intended to be anything more than useful approximations of reality; a globe, for example, merely duplicates the salient features of its massive counterpart. In like manner, the manual accounting system, as outlined in the following chapters, will be employed simply to illustrate the more important aspects of all types of accounting systems.

SUMMARY

Accounting is the collection, classification, and interpretation of financial data. It is a major aid to management in the operation of an enterprise. In addition, many other individuals and groups require accounting data for various purposes.

Three primary fields of accounting specialization are (1) private accounting, (2) public accounting, and (3) governmental accounting.

The accounting process consists of three steps: (1) collection and tabulation, (2) collation and modification, and (3) reporting and interpretation. In order to facilitate this process, most organizations set up some kind of accounting system.

The six basic assumptions of accounting, upon which the principles and concepts of accounting are based, are the usefulness, entity, transaction, quantifiability, continuity, and periodicity assumptions.

PREVIEW

Our chief objective in Part One of this text has been to establish the background for our subsequent study. This we have done by examining the role and function of accounting within the framework of the management process. In the sections which follow we shall examine step by step both the theoretical and practical aspects of the basic accounting process. In Part Two we shall study the collection and tabulation process, and in Part Three the collation and modification process. In Part Four we shall cover different forms of business organization and in Part Five examine income taxes as they relate to accounting. In Part Six we shall study the dissemination and interpretation process, and in Part Seven the role and function of accounting in the planning and controlling of manufacturing operations. Finally, in Part Eight we shall review the basic mathematical tools relative to the accounting process.

QUESTIONS

1-1 Briefly define **accounting.** In what ways is it useful to management?

1-2 Discuss the relationship of accounting to the enterprise entity.

1-3 What are the primary functions of the management process?

1-4 What differentiates public accounting from private accounting?

1-5 List and discuss the three basic steps in the accounting process.

1-6 What is meant by systemization of the accounting process? Why is it important?

1-7 Why is accounting often called "the language of business"?

1-8 What is meant by the term **model** as used in the study of accounting?

1-9 Creditors, employees, regulatory agencies, and taxing authorities are ordinarily listed among the numerous users of a business organization's accounting data. What kind of information do you think each of these would be most interested in?

1-10 What kind of information based on a business organization's accounting data do you think consumers and the general public would be most interested in?

1-11 In which functions of the management process is accounting apt to be of most use?

1-12 Why should the accountant have an appreciation for the relationship of economics and mathematics to accounting?

1-13 It is not uncommon for accountants to move out of accounting into top positions in general management. How do you account for this?

1-14 What is meant by the **span of control** in the management process?

1-15 Briefly discuss the entity assumption.

1-16 Briefly discuss the quantifiability assumption.

1-17 Briefly discuss the transaction assumption.

1-18 Briefly discuss the continuity assumption.

1-19 Briefly discuss the periodicity assumption.

1-20 Discuss in general terms the basic characteristics of a modern accounting system.

Part Two
The Collection and Tabulation of Accounting Data

2

Accounting Transactions and the Basic Equation

The basic assumptions of accounting which were introduced in Chapter 1 are interwoven throughout the accounting process. Some, logically, are of more significance in certain phases of the process than others. In the first step, the collection and tabulation of accounting data, the accountant collects and records **useful** information concerning the particular **entity** for which he is accounting. His primary interest, however, is accounting **transactions** and their **quantification** into monetary terms.

ACCOUNTING TRANSACTIONS

The typical business organization engages in hundreds and sometimes thousands of activities each day. Those which meet the criteria for entering the accounting system are known as accounting transactions; they are the source of an organization's accounting data.

As indicated by the transaction assumption, accounting is concerned primarily with the effect on an entity of its exchange transactions with other organizations or individuals and with events which produce results essentially the same as those produced by exchange transactions. The accounting concept of a transaction, then, must be broad enough to include both exchange transactions and events commonly known as nonexchange transactions.

Typical Accounting Transactions

An **exchange transaction** is an economic event which results in an exchange of value between two or more independent parties. Typical examples in a business organization are:

1 Purchase of merchandise for cash or on credit

2 Sale of merchandise for cash or on credit

3 Payment of debts

4 Collection of debts

5 Purchase of equipment for cash or on credit

6 Borrowing of money

A **nonexchange transaction** is an economic event which has much the same effect on an enterprise as an exchange transaction but which does not result in an exchange of value. For example, the physical destruction of a business resource by fire, flood, or wind results in a loss of value to the enterprise, but no exchange as such takes place. Other examples of nonexchange transactions are:

1 Payment of taxes

2 Collection of taxes (such as state sales taxes)

3 Day-to-day accumulation of interest

4 Physical wear and tear on machinery and equipment

Business Activities Which Are Not Accounting Transactions

It is important to recognize that many activities which are essential to the operation of an organization—for example, opening and sorting mail, filing business documents, corresponding with customers and creditors, and the like—are not accounting transactions, and thus are not entered into the organization's accounting records.

Certain other business activities, however, such as the planning of research and development projects, the negotiation of labor contracts, and the hiring of new employees may not as yet meet the requirements for entering the accounting system but may eventually qualify as transactions. Activities of this nature often provide the accountant with information which enables him to be of assistance to management in solving related problems, for example, whether a proposed project is necessary or desirable and how it can be financed.

Business Papers and Source Data

Accounting transactions are usually (and preferably should always be) evidenced by business papers. These papers, ordinarily referred to as **underlying, supporting,** or **source documents,** furnish the raw, or source, data for the accounting process. In addition to providing a certain degree of validity to the accounting data, source documents are also useful for reference and as verification in cases of misunderstanding or legal controversy. Typical examples are:

1 Sales invoice
2 Purchase invoice
3 Cash register tape
4 Canceled check
5 Memorandum issued by a bank to adjust a bank account
6 Memorandum issued by a seller reducing the amount owed by the buyer
7 Bank deposit slip
8 Rental lease
9 Contract covering the purchase of equipment
10 Insurance policy
11 Utility bill
12 Payroll record

Data Collection Systems

Organizations employ various methods of collecting source data, ranging from manual collection in small accounting systems to the use of electronic devices in complex systems. Data concerning an employee's work record, for example, may be collected manually by a timekeeper, semiautomatically as a result of his punching a time clock, or automatically by a sophisticated device which "senses" his identification badge for his ID number. We shall not examine these methods in detail here, as our main concern is with the concepts and principles basic to the accounting process; we should, however, be aware of their existence and importance.

Transaction Analysis

The primary objective of the accounting process is to bring order out of a seemingly chaotic mass of raw data by classifying them into pertinent categories and then compressing them into understandable information. The logical starting point in this process is the transaction itself. Proper understanding of a transaction can result only from analysis—the breaking down of the transaction into its various elements. For example, who were the parties involved, what were their intentions, what kinds of things were involved, what amounts, prices, and dates were agreed upon?

Transaction Analysis Illustrated Transaction analysis in perhaps its simplest form may be illustrated by the following example. Let us assume that the Northside Grocery buys merchandise for resale from the Southside Wholesale House for $1,000 cash. What has happened? From Northside's point of view, it has merely exchanged something it owned (cash) for something else that it now owns (merchandise). From Southside's point of view, a similar event has taken place. It has exchanged something it owned (merchandise) for something else it now owns (cash).

If we assume that Northside buys the merchandise from Southside under an agreement that it will pay Southside within 30 days rather than pay cash at the time of purchase, transaction analysis becomes a little more involved. First, at the date of purchase, Northside increases what it owns and at the same time increases what it owes. Southside, on the other hand, decreases one thing it owns (merchandise) while it increases something else it owns (a claim against Northside). Second, at the date of payment, Northside decreases one thing it owns (cash) and at the same time decreases what it owes. On the other hand, Southside increases something it owns (cash) and decreases something else it owns (the claim against Northside).

Transaction analysis can become even more involved. Let us assume that Northside resells the merchandise to Eastside for $1,200 cash. Northside has now exchanged something it owned which cost $1,000 for something it now owns (cash in this case) worth $1,200. Northside, of course, has gained $200. We now have three elements involved in the transaction, namely: something owned, something owed, and a residual something. In general terms, an enterprise owns **assets,** owes **liabilities,** and its residual something is usually referred to as **owner equity.**

You are probably familiar with the term **equity.** An equity in a house, for example, is the cost of the house minus the amount owed on the mortgage. Similarly, when an individual purchases an automobile on a contract basis, paying a certain amount down and so much per month, the cost of the automobile minus the unpaid balance on the contract is generally considered as his equity in the automobile. It is in this sense that the term "owner equity" is used in accounting.

Transaction Duality Since an accounting transaction is primarily an exchange of value, it is composed of dual elements and "both sides of the coin," so to speak, must be recognized in the accounting process. Thus, if a particular transaction results in an increase in an asset, there will be at the same time either a compensating decrease in another asset, an increase in a liability or in owner equity, or some combination of these changes. The various possibilities may be expressed either positively or negatively as follows:

Positive Approach	Negative Approach
An asset **increase** may result in:	An asset **decrease** may result in:
1 Decrease in another asset	**1** Increase in another asset
2 Increase in a liability	**2** Decrease in a liability
3 Increase in owner equity, or	**3** Decrease in owner equity, or
4 Some combination of the above	**4** Some combination of the above
A liability **increase** may result in:	A liability **decrease** may result in:
1 Increase in an asset	**1** Decrease in an asset
2 Decrease in another liability	**2** Increase in another liability
3 Decrease in owner equity, or	**3** Increase in owner equity, or
4 Some combination of the above	**4** Some combination of the above
An owner equity **increase** may result in:	An owner equity **decrease** may result in:
1 Increase in an asset	**1** Decrease in an asset
2 Decrease in a liability	**2** Increase in a liability
3 Decrease in another form of owner equity, or	**3** Increase in another form of owner equity, or
4 Some combination of the above	**4** Some combination of the above

Accounting Transactions and Financial Reports

Once the transaction is analyzed, the resulting data are recorded as a preliminary step to further processing. The end product of the accounting process, relevant information, is disseminated by means of financial reports, two of the most common being the balance sheet, also known as the statement of financial condition or position, and the income statement, often called the profit and loss statement. The **balance sheet** summarizes the business enterprise's financial position as of a particular moment in time; it is a listing of what the enterprise owns and what it owes, and thus indicates how things stand on a given date. The **income statement,** on the other hand, reports what has happened in the enterprise over a period of time; it reflects the way things have been moving during a particular period.

THE BASIC EQUATION

Because the idea of duality in transaction analysis is so fundamental to the accounting process, it is usually expressed in mathematical language in the form of an equation. This equation is generally known as the **basic accounting equation,** and in its simplest form is frequently referred to as the **balance sheet equation.** However, as we shall see later in this chapter, it can be expanded to include the income statement as well as the balance sheet.

The basic equation is usually stated as:

$$\text{Assets} = \text{liabilities} + \text{owner equity}$$

or merely as:

$$A = L + OE$$

As in any other algebraic equation, its terms may be transposed from one side to the other, for example: $A - L = OE$, or $A - OE = L$. In addition, the terminology employed in the equation may vary. "Owner equity" is used in accounting synonymously with such terms as "proprietorship," "capital," and "net worth." Thus, the equation could be expressed as:

$$A = L + P$$

or

$$A = L + C$$

or

$$A = L + NW$$

The effects of all transactions properly entered into the accounting system are ultimately reflected in the basic equation; it thus becomes the mathematical model upon which the entire superstructure of accounting is developed. This tool is ancient in derivation, as Paciolo included it in his treatise in 1494. All accounting systems, no matter how sophisticated, are predicated upon the basic equation.

Basic Equation and the Balance Sheet

The reason for the basic equation in its simplest form being referred to as the balance sheet equation becomes obvious when we recall that the purpose of the balance sheet is to show how an enterprise stands at a particular moment of time in relation to what it owns (assets), what it owes (liabilities), and what is left over (owner equity).

Basic Balance Sheet Format The relationship of the basic equation to both the form and content of the balance sheet may be simply illustrated. Let us assume that Ralph Pendery invested $8,000 cash in a clothing business on April 1, 1972, and prepared a balance sheet as of that date to conform to the basic equation. In its simplest form the balance sheet would appear as follows:

Assets _____ $8,000 = Owner equity _____ $8,000

Generally, however, the equality sign is placed in a vertical position ($\parallel$) instead of in the usual horizontal position ($=$); often it is shown as a single vertical line ($|$), or omitted. In the vertical position the sign serves two purposes: (1) It indicates equality, and (2) it is a dividing line between the asset side and the liability and owner equity side of the statement. The simple balance sheet now appears as:

Assets _____ $8,000 $\parallel$ Owner equity _____ $8,000

An essential element of all financial statements is a proper heading. The heading of the balance sheet, like the headings of most financial statements, is usually composed of three parts: (1) the name of the enterprise or of its proprietor, (2) the name of the statement, and (3) the date. Pendery's balance sheet would now appear as:

RALPH PENDERY
Balance Sheet, April 1, 1972

| Assets _____ $8,000 | Owner equity _____ $8,000 |

The heading frequently appears in three lines instead of two. Also, the date of the balance sheet is often written "as of" the particular date. These variations would appear as follows:

RALPH PENDERY
Balance Sheet
As of April 1, 1972

| Assets _____ $8,000 | Owner equity _____ $8,000 |

The balance sheets that we have examined thus far are technically correct but considerably simplified. As a rule, it is desirable that they be more detailed and descriptive. Pendery's balance sheet will be more informative to its ultimate users if we classify and describe the items appearing on it as follows:

RALPH PENDERY
Balance Sheet
As of April 1, 1972

Assets		Liabilities and Owner Equity	
		Owner equity:	
Cash	$8,000	Ralph Pendery, capital	$8,000

Transaction Analysis and the Balance Sheet   As Pendery conducts his business, he will spend some of the $8,000 cash for various goods and services needed in the business.   He will, in addition, buy and sell merchandise on credit, pay expenses, and engage in various other transactions.   In order to see exactly what effect individual transactions have on a balance sheet, let us assume the following facts about Pendery's business during the first month of operation:

Apr. 2   Pendery purchases furniture and equipment for $800 from Central Supply Company, paying $500 cash, the balance to be paid in 90 days.

Apr. 3   Pendery purchases merchandise for resale, paying $2,000 cash.

Apr. 4   Pendery purchases $1,500 worth of merchandise for resale from the T. Scott Company, paying $1,000 cash, the balance to be paid in 60 days.

The effects of the individual transactions are reflected in chronological order on the following three balance sheets.   (Remember that Pendery started his business on April 1 with $8,000 cash.)

RALPH PENDERY
Balance Sheet
As of April 2, 1972

Assets		Liabilities and Owner Equity	
Cash	$7,500	Liabilities:	
Furniture and equipment	800	Owed to Central Supply Company	$ 300
		Owner equity:	
		Ralph Pendery, capital	8,000
	$8,300		$8,300

RALPH PENDERY
Balance Sheet
As of April 3, 1972

Assets		Liabilities and Owner Equity	
Cash	$5,500	Liabilities:	
Merchandise	2,000	Owed to Central Supply	
Furniture and equipment	800	Company	$ 300
		Owner equity:	
		Ralph Pendery, capital	8,000
	$8,300		$8,300

RALPH PENDERY
Balance Sheet
As of April 4, 1972

Assets		Liabilities and Owner Equity	
Cash	$4,500	Liabilities:	
Merchandise	3,500	Owed to Central Supply	
Furniture and equipment	800	Company	$ 300
		Owed to T. Scott	
		Company	500
		Owner equity:	
		Ralph Pendery, capital	8,000
	$8,800		$8,800

Periodic Preparation of the Balance Sheet Needless to say, it would be impracticable to prepare a balance sheet after each transaction, particularly in organizations having hundreds or thousands of transactions a day. As a consequence, balance sheets are usually prepared on a periodic basis determined by the needs of management. Some organizations, for planning and control purposes, require that they be prepared monthly, while others have them prepared quarterly, and still others annually; and in many organizations they are prepared monthly, quarterly, and annually. The time period reported upon is usually referred to as the fiscal (financial) period.

To illustrate the periodic preparation of the balance sheet, let us assume the following information regarding Pendery's assets and liabilities as of April 30:

1 Cash on hand, $4,397.

2 During the month he sold merchandise on account as follows: George Carrell, $90; Richard Greenwell, $50; Otwell Rankin, $130. During the month of April Rankin paid $45 on his account.

3 Pendery took inventory of the merchandise he purchased for resale during the month and found that he had $3,700 worth still on hand at the end of the month.

4 As indicated in the April 2 transaction, Pendery purchased furniture and equipment for $800 from the Central Supply Company. As of the end of April he still owed $300 to Central Supply.

5 As indicated in the April 4 transaction, Pendery purchased $1,500 worth of merchandise for resale from the T. Scott Company. As of the end of April he still owed Scott $350.

6 During the first week of April, Pendery paid six months' rent at $100 a month.

7 On April 10 Pendery paid $108 for insurance on the contents of the store for one year.

8 During the month Pendery purchased $40 worth of store supplies but at the end of April he had used only $10 worth.

9 On April 14 Pendery borrowed $1,000 from the bank, giving a 90-day promissory note (a written promise to pay).

The balance sheet which follows has been prepared from this information. It is important to bear in mind that at this time we are concerned primarily with

RALPH PENDERY
Balance Sheet
As of April 30, 1972

Assets		Liabilities and Owner Equity		
Cash	$4,397	Liabilities:		
Owed by G. Carrell	90	Owed to Central Supply		
Owed by R. Greenwell	50	Company	$	300
Owed by O. Rankin	85	Owed to T. Scott Company		350
Merchandise on hand	3,700	Owed on note to bank		1,000
Rent paid in advance	500*			$1,650
Insurance paid in advance	102*			
Store supplies on hand	30	Owner equity:		
Furniture and equipment	800	Ralph Pendery, capital		8,104
	$9,754			$9,754

*The computations of these amounts are explained in detail on pages 28 and 29.

the relationship of the balance sheet and the basic equation; thus no attempt has been made to use precise terminology. This will be stressed in Chapter 3 when we study further classification of the various assets and liabilities.

If we compare this balance sheet with Pendery's beginning balance sheet on page 24, we can see that the total assets are greater by $1,754 at the end of April than they were at the beginning of the month. Similarly, the total of the liabilities and owner equity has increased by the same amount. By carefully studying the beginning and ending balance sheets, we can account for the changes in the assets and liabilities during the month. However, the balance sheets do not reflect the cause of the change in owner equity. In this case the $104 increase was the net income from the operation of Pendery's clothing store for the month of April. Owner equity changes of this kind are reported in the income statement rather than on the balance sheet.

Basic Equation and the Income Statement

The net income of a business enterprise is determined by deducting negative items called expenses from positive items known as revenues. In general, **revenues** result from the sale of goods and rendering of services; they are measured by the amounts charged for such goods and services. **Expenses,** in their broadest sense, include all costs which are deductible from revenues for the purpose of determining net income. Revenue and expense items are periodically summarized in the income statement.

Since net income is ultimately reflected as an increase in owner equity, to include it in the basic equation we must expand the equation to read:

$$\text{Assets} = \text{liabilities} + (\text{owner equity} + \text{net income})$$

or

$$A = L + (OE + NI)$$

Moreover, if we are to reflect both the form and content of the income statement in the basic equation, we must further expand it by substituting "revenue minus expense" for "net income." The equation will then read:

$$A = L + [OE + (R - E)]$$

Income Statement Preparation When we prepared Pendery's balance sheet as of April 30, we were primarily concerned with his assets and liabilities. In order to prepare his income statement for April, we must examine his revenue and expense transactions for the period. Let us assume that during the month he:

1 Sold merchandise on credit for $270 and for cash, $935.

2 Purchased merchandise on credit for $1,550 and for cash, $3,000. (Remember, he had $3,700 worth on hand at the end of the month.)

3 Paid expenses as follows: sales salary, $60; miscellaneous expenses, $75.

4 Purchased $40 worth of store supplies. ($30 worth of these were still on hand as of April 30.)

5 Paid rent for 6 months at $100 a month.

6 Paid $108 for insurance on the contents of the store for 1 year. The insurance policy was effective as of April 10.

The income statement which follows was prepared from these data.

RALPH PENDERY

Income Statement

For the Month of April, 1972

Revenues:		
Sales		$1,205
Expenses:		
Cost of goods (merchandise) sold	$850	
Sales salary	60	
Store supplies used	10	
Insurance used	6	
Rent used	100	
Miscellaneous	75	1,101
Net income		$ 104

Explanation of Pendery's Income Statement Although Pendery's income statement for April is a relatively simple one, its format is typical of income statements in general. Note that the heading, unlike that of the balance sheet, refers to a definite period of time rather than to a particular moment of time. Another important feature is the segregation of revenues and expenses. As was true of the assets and liabilities on Pendery's balance sheet, most of the revenue and expense items are more or less self-explanatory; a few, however, require further explanation regarding their computation, and one, the cost of goods sold, merits more detailed discussion.

Only revenues and expenses which pertain to the month of April are included in the April income statement. Pendery's one source of revenue for the month is sales totaling $1,205. This includes $270 in credit sales and $935 in cash sales.

The amount of store supplies used during April is listed as an expense. The amount remaining on hand at the end of the month appeared on the balance sheet as an asset.

The amount of insurance used (the amount that expired during the month) is computed by determining the cost of the insurance per month and then taking two-thirds of that amount. The $108 total cost of insurance for a year when divided by 12 results in a cost of $9 per month; two-thirds of this is $6, the insurance expense for the last two-thirds of April. The $102 of unexpired insurance remaining on April 30 appeared on the balance sheet as an asset, just as the unused supplies did.

Pendery's rent is $100 a month, and he paid six months in advance during the first week of April. On the last day of April, one-sixth, or $100, of this had been used up; the remaining $500, which pertains to the future, appeared on the balance sheet as an asset.

The miscellaneous expenses of $75 include small expense items which normally are not large enough to categorize in detail, for example, postage due on mail received or small contributions to local fund-raising drives.

Cost of Goods Sold This is a major expense of merchandising concerns. In Pendery's case it is the amount which the merchandise he sold during the month of April cost him when he originally purchased it from the manufacturer, wholesaler, or jobber. Because the computation of the cost of goods sold sometimes proves difficult, we shall at this time examine some of the more important problems which may be involved in its determination.

First, let us assume that Pendery started business on April 1 with cash only, that he purchased merchandise for resale, and that during the month he sold all the merchandise he purchased. If he bought the merchandise for $4,550 and sold the entire lot for $6,400, he would realize a **gross margin** (the difference between the amounts for which the merchandise was purchased and sold) of $1,850, as illustrated in the following partial income statement.

Sales	$6,400
Cost of goods sold:	
Purchases	4,550
Gross margin	$1,850

It is unlikely, however, that every month Pendery will sell all the goods he purchases during the month. As we saw in the illustration of his April income statement, he purchased $4,550 worth of merchandise, sold some of it for $1,205, and had $3,700 worth remaining. This $3,700 is known as the "ending merchandise inventory." In the computation of the cost of goods sold, it is handled as follows:

Sales		$1,205
Cost of goods sold:		
Purchases	$4,550	
Less: Merchandise inventory, Apr. 30	3,700	
Cost of goods sold		850
Gross margin		$ 355

If Pendery had been in business prior to April 1, he probably would have had some merchandise on hand at the beginning of the month. To illustrate a situation of this kind, let us assume that:

1 Sales during April amounted to $3,000.

2 Merchandise on hand (beginning merchandise inventory) on April 1 amounted to $1,500.

3 Purchases during April amounted to $4,500.

4 Merchandise on hand (ending merchandise inventory) on April 30 amounted to $3,700.

In the partial income statement that follows, note that purchases are added to the beginning inventory to obtain the cost of goods available for sale and that the ending inventory is deducted from the cost of goods available for sale to obtain the cost of goods sold.

Sales		$3,000
Cost of goods sold:		
Merchandise inventory, Apr. 1	$1,500	
Purchases	4,500	
Goods available for sale	$6,000	
Less: Merchandise inventory, Apr. 30	3,700	
Cost of goods sold		2,300
Gross margin		$ 700

The importance of a thorough understanding of the cost of goods sold section of the income statement cannot be emphasized too strongly, as this section is the source of many errors by beginners. Remember that the beginning inventory is **added** to the purchases and the ending inventory is **subtracted** from the total of the beginning inventory and purchases. In other words, using purchases as a base, add the beginning inventory and "strip out" the ending inventory.

INTERRELATIONSHIP OF BALANCE SHEET AND INCOME STATEMENT

The balance sheet and the income statement are closely interrelated and thus interdependent. For example, when Pendery bought supplies he acquired an asset, but as he used the supplies they became expenses. The same was true of merchandise bought for resale, and of insurance and rent.

Pendery's net income ($104) for the month of April was exactly equal to the increase in the owner equity section of the balance sheet, as reflected in Pendery's capital. Thus, although it is reported in the income statement, the ultimate effect of operations is also reflected in the owner equity section of the balance sheet. It is possible, therefore, to determine the amount of an enterprise's profit or loss during a fiscal period from an analysis of the balance sheet, if the amount of capital at the beginning of the period is known. Of course, if there were additions to or withdrawals from capital during the period, these would also have to be taken into consideration.

To illustrate the determination of net income by an analysis of the owner equity section of the balance sheet, assume first that Pendery's capital at the beginning of the accounting period was $8,000, that his capital at the end of the period was $9,000, and that he made no additional contributions to or withdrawals from capital during the period. In this case his net income would be $1,000 ($9,000 − $8,000).

However, if Pendery's beginning capital was $8,000 and his ending capital $9,000, but he added $600 to the business during the period from his personal savings, the net income of his business would be $400, determined as follows:

Ending capital		$9,000
Less: Beginning capital	$8,000	
Plus: Capital added during the period	600	8,600
Net income		$ 400

Similarly, if Pendery's beginning capital was $8,000 and his ending capital $9,000, but he added $600 from his personal savings early in the period and withdrew $200 later in the period, the net income of his business would be $600, determined as follows:

Ending capital		$9,000
Less: Beginning capital	$8,000	
Plus: Capital added during the period	600	
Minus: Capital withdrawn during the period	200	8,400
Net income		$ 600

While numerous variations of this type of owner equity analysis are possible, one other example will perhaps suffice at this time. If we assume that Pendery's beginning capital was $8,000 and his ending capital $9,000, but that he added $2,000 and withdrew $600 during the period, the result of operations of his business would be a $400 loss, determined as follows:

Ending capital		$9,000
Less: Beginning capital	$8,000	
Plus: Capital added during the period	2,000	
Minus: Capital withdrawn during the period	600	9,400
Net income (loss)		$ (400)*

*Parentheses are frequently employed in accounting to depict negative amounts.

The relationship between net income for a period and changes in owner equity during the same period can be expressed mathematically as follows:

NI = net income
OE_b = owner equity as of beginning of period
OE_e = owner equity as of end of period
WD = withdrawals during period
AI = additional investments during period

Then,

$$NI = OE_e - OE_b + WD - AI$$

or

$$OE_b = OE_e - NI + WD - AI$$

or

$$OE_e = OE_b + NI - WD + AI$$

Although it is possible to determine the amount of an organization's profit or loss by analyzing the owner equity section of the balance sheet, the formal income statement is more informative. In addition to showing the amount of profit made or loss incurred during a period, it also indicates the sources of revenue and gives detailed information regarding the various expenses of the business. This type of information is vital for control and planning purposes.

SUMMARY

Accounting transactions are the source of accounting data. They include exchange transactions, which result in an exchange of value, and nonexchange transactions, in which no exchange of value takes place.

An organization's accounting system is the vehicle by which transactions are collected and processed into useful information. Such information is disseminated by means of financial reports, the two major ones being the balance sheet and the income statement.

When a transaction first enters the accounting system, it must be analyzed and classified into pertinent categories. Transaction analysis results in a two-sided action. This concept of duality is so fundamental to the accounting process that it is usually expressed in mathematical terms in what is known as the **basic accounting equation.**

The basic equation in its simplest form may be expressed in several different ways, such as: $A = L + OE$, $A = L + P$, or $A = L + C$. It is also referred to as the balance sheet equation, because in its simplest form it provides the mathematical model upon which the balance sheet is built.

The basic equation can also be expanded to include the income statement merely by expressing it as: $A = L + [OE + (R - E)]$. The expanded equation illustrates the close mathematical relationship between the balance sheet and the income statement.

QUESTIONS AND PROBLEMS

2-1 Describe briefly the accountant's concept of a transaction.

2-2 What is meant by **transaction analysis?**

2-3 What is meant by **transaction duality?**

2-4 Accounting transactions are ordinarily evidenced by source documents. What are the major functions of source documents?

2-5 What is a **balance sheet?** An **income statement?**

2-6 Balance sheet headings, like the headings of most financial statements, are ordinarily composed of three parts. What are they?

2-7 What three items are essential to the proper computation of the cost of goods sold of a merchandising concern?

2-8 **Instructions** The following numbered transactions pertain to the operation of John Johnson's Supermarket for the month of December. Match each one with its correct lettered analysis.

1 Johnson invested an additional $100,000 in his market.

2 He purchased merchandise on account for $40,000.

3 He paid sales salaries for December of $8,000.

4 He paid creditors $22,000.

5 Johnson withdrew $600 from the supermarket for his personal use.

6 He received $3,000 from customers to apply on their accounts.

7 He borrowed $5,000 from the bank.

8 He paid the local television station $1,600 for advertising.

9 He returned some of the merchandise purchased in (2) above because it did not come up to his expectations. The merchandise had not been paid for at the time it was returned.

10 $10,000 in cash was stolen from the market.

Transaction Analysis

A Increase in one asset, decrease in another

B Increase in an asset, increase in a liability

C Increase in an asset, increase in owner equity

D Decrease in an asset, decrease in a liability

E Decrease in an asset, decrease in owner equity

2-9 Instructions To illustrate transaction analysis, match each of the following numbered transactions with the appropriate lettered effects.

1 Purchase of merchandise on account

2 Purchase of merchandise for cash

3 Collection from a credit customer

4 Payment to a creditor

5 Purchase of equipment on account

6 Return of the equipment purchased in (5) because it did not meet specifications

7 Borrowing of money from the bank

8 Payment of interest on the money borrowed in (7)

9 Loss of merchandise to shoplifters

10 Sale of merchandise at a profit

Transaction Effect

A Increase in an asset

B Decrease in an asset

C Increase in a liability

D Decrease in a liability

E Increase in owner equity

F Decrease in owner equity

2-10 Instructions Match each of the following numbered transactions, which apply to the operations of the A and B Department Store for the month of June, with the appropriate lettered effects.

1 Sale of merchandise at its cost

2 Sale of merchandise at a profit

3 Sale of merchandise at a loss

4 Sale of an asset other than merchandise at its cost

5 Sale of an asset other than merchandise at a profit

6 Sale of an asset other than merchandise at a loss

7 Loss of merchandise in a fire

8 Wear and tear on delivery truck

9 Donation of merchandise to charity

10 Return of part of the merchandise donated in (9)

Transaction Effect

A Increase in an asset

B Decrease in an asset

C Increase in a liability

D Decrease in a liability

E Increase in owner equity

F Decrease in owner equity

2-11 Instructions Determine the amount of net income (or loss) for the period in each of the following unrelated cases.

	Case 1	Case 2	Case 3	Case 4
Beginning capital	$30,000	$40,000	$60,000	$75,000
Ending capital	40,000	30,000	75,000	60,000
Withdrawals during period	4,000	6,000	12,000	12,000
Additional investment during period	3,000	8,000	8,000	14,000

2-12 Instructions Fill in the missing amounts in the following data. (The individual cases are not related.)

	Case 1	Case 2	Case 3	Case 4	Case 5
Beginning capital	$50,000	$70,000	$ (?)	$30,000	$44,000
Ending capital	60,000	(?)	40,000	45,000	36,000
Withdrawals during period	6,000	8,000	9,000	(?)	17,000
Additional investment during period	10,000	15,000	20,000	13,000	(?)
Net income	(?)	22,000	18,000	16,000	6,000

2-13 Instructions Fill in the missing amounts in the following data. (The individual cases are not related.)

	Case 1	Case 2	Case 3	Case 4	Case 5
Beginning capital	$40,000	$60,000	$ (?)	$46,000	$42,000
Ending capital	50,000	(?)	36,000	20,000	32,000
Withdrawals during period	2,000	6,000	5,000	(?)	13,000
Additional investment during period	20,000	13,000	16,000	9,000	(?)
Net loss	(?)	(24,000)	(14,000)	(12,000)	(4,000)

2-14 Instructions Fill in the missing amounts in the following data which pertain to the owner equity sections of J. B. Smith's balance sheets over a 5-year period.

	Year 1	Year 2	Year 3	Year 4	Year 5
Beginning capital	$80,000	$ (b)	$85,000	$86,000	$ (f)
Ending capital	(a)	85,000	86,000	(e)	90,000
Withdrawals during year	6,000	5,000	8,000	11,000	9,000
Additional investment during year	2,000	8,000	(d)	9,000	12,000
Net income (loss)	11,000	(c)	(12,000)	14,000	(g)

2-15 Instructions Fill in the missing amounts in the following data. (The individual cases are not related.)

	Case 1	Case 2	Case 3	Case 4
Beginning inventory	$10,000	$20,000	$ (?)	$15,000
Merchandise purchased	30,000	(?)	40,000	60,000
Ending inventory	5,000	10,000	6,000	(?)
Cost of goods sold	(?)	60,000	70,000	45,000

2-16 Instructions Fill in the missing amounts in the following data. (The individual cases are not related.)

	Case 1	Case 2	Case 3	Case 4	Case 5
Sales	$80,000	$70,000	$ (?)	$64,000	$72,000
Beginning inventory	13,000	(?)	8,000	16,000	24,000
Merchandise purchased	60,000	50,000	48,000	(?)	56,000
Ending inventory	10,000	5,000	11,000	9,000	(?)
Gross margin	(?)	10,000	13,000	17,000	21,000

2-17 The following data pertain to the operations of the Joe Guy Company for the month of August:

Beginning capital	$40,000
Ending capital	58,000
Beginning inventory	10,000
Ending inventory	15,000
Merchandise purchased	26,000
Amount owed to creditors, Aug. 1	8,000
Amount owed to creditors, Aug. 31	13,000
Amount owed by customers, Aug. 1	12,000
Amount owed by customers, Aug. 31	14,000
Expenses other than the cost of goods sold	16,000
Cash on hand, Aug. 1	26,000
Cash on hand, Aug. 31	42,000
Sales	(to be computed)

Instructions Assuming that all sales and purchases of merchandise during the month were made on account and that all expenses other than the cost of goods sold were paid as incurred, prepare:

(1) A balance sheet as of August 1

(2) A balance sheet as of August 31

(3) An income statement for the month of August

2-18 The following data pertain to the operations of the Pat Delaney Company for the month of March:

Sales	$80,000
Beginning capital	60,000
Beginning inventory	17,000
Cash on hand, Mar. 1	40,000
Amount owed to creditors, Mar. 1	15,000
Amount owed by customers, Mar. 1	18,000
Merchandise purchased during month	44,000
Ending capital	(to be computed)
Ending inventory	26,000
Amount owed to creditors, Mar. 31	21,000
Amount owed by customers, Mar. 31	23,000
Expenses (paid as incurred)	25,000
Cash on hand, Mar. 31	(to be computed)

Instructions Assuming that all sales and purchases of merchandise during the month were made on account, prepare:

(1) A balance sheet as of March 1

(2) A balance sheet as of March 31

(3) An income statement for the month of March

2-19 J. B. West began business on April 1 with a cash investment of $25,000. The following information was taken from his accounting records as of April 30:

Amount owed to creditors for merchandise	$10,000
Amount paid to creditors for merchandise	12,000
Amount owed by customers	15,000
Expenses (paid as incurred)	3,000
Merchandise on hand as of Apr. 30	6,000
Net income for the month	2,000

Instructions Assuming that all sales and purchases of merchandise during the month were made on account, prepare:

(1) A balance sheet as of April 30

(2) An income statement for the month of April

2-20 B. J. East began business on June 1 with a cash investment of $50,000. The following information was taken from his accounting records as of June 30:

Amount owed to creditors for merchandise	$15,000
Amount paid to creditors for merchandise	18,000
Amount owed by customers	22,500
Expenses (paid as incurred)	4,500
Expenses (not paid as of June 30)	1,500
Merchandise on hand as of June 30	7,500
Net loss for the month	2,600

Instructions Assuming that all sales and purchases of merchandise during the month were made on account, prepare:

(1) A balance sheet as of June 30

(2) An income statement for the month of June

3

Transaction Analysis and the Account

Management seldom requires information about individual transactions in order to make operating or policy decisions, as it can obtain a better overall view of a situation by examining the summarized data of a group of transactions. For this reason, and because it generally is not feasible to prepare financial statements following each transaction, the accountant must have a means of compressing data and storing them until they are needed. The device employed for this purpose is known as an **account.** Increases and decreases in an organization's assets, liabilities, and owner equity components are recorded in accounts, and financial statements are prepared periodically from these records.

STRUCTURE OF THE ACCOUNT

The physical form of an account will vary depending upon the accounting system in operation. In a relatively simple manual system it may be kept on a sheet of paper in a loose-leaf binder, on a page in a bound book, or on a card in a filing cabinet, while in a more sophisticated system it may exist only in the memory of an electronic computer.

Even though an accounting system may be almost completely automated and the accountant never lays eyes on an account as such, he must be able to picture it in his mind. Therefore, we need an account model which will permit us to visualize the operations of an account in much the same way that a mathematician visualizes a function on a graph or a map reader visualizes a point on a map. For this purpose we shall employ the T account, so-called because in its simplest form it resembles the capital letter T.

T Account as a Model

In order to reflect properly the dual elements of a transaction, an account must be capable of reflecting both increases and decreases in the item being recorded. The T account is made to order for this purpose. The vertical line of the T partitions the account into the two necessary cells—one for increases and one for decreases. In accounting terminology, the left cell is referred to as the **debit** side of the account and the right cell is known as the **credit** side. An item is said to be **debited,** or **charged,** to the account when it is entered on the left side, and **credited** to the account when it is entered on the right side. A simple illustration of the T account is shown below.

Account Title	
Debit side	Credit side

Although the terms **debit** and **credit** have been commonly accepted and used throughout the business world for centuries, even predating the time of Paciolo, they are not always employed in a precise fashion. From the standpoint of the T account, however, the terms refer to one thing and one thing only—**debit** means the **left** side of the account and **credit** means the **right** side.

Account Balances

In Chapter 2 when we prepared Pendery's financial statements at the end of April, we were concerned primarily with the balances of the accounts, although they were not identified as such at that time. The term **balance** is used here in the sense of a remainder, that is, the excess of the debits over the credits, or vice versa, the excess of the credits over the debits. If the debits in an account exceed the credits, we refer to the balance as a **debit balance;** similarly, if the credits exceed the debits, we have a **credit balance.**

For example, the debits ($8,935) in the following Cash account exceed the credits ($2,500) by $6,435. Thus, the account has a debit balance of $6,435.

Cash

8,000	500
935	2,000

Although the left side of an account is always the debit side and the right side is always the credit side, increases and decreases in an item cannot be precisely categorized in this manner. The side on which an increase or a decrease will be recorded (debited or credited) depends on the nature of the item being accounted for. For example, increases in assets are debited and decreases are credited, but increases in liabilities are credited and decreases are debited. Probably the best way to remember whether increases and decreases in the various items are debited or credited in the accounts is to recall their positions in the expanded version of the basic equation $A = L + [OE + (R - E)]$. If we remove the brackets and parentheses and transpose the negative E to the positive position, the equation will read:

$$A + E = L + OE + R$$

Assets and expenses will then appear on the left side of the equation. Therefore, if we are to be consistent with the equation, increases in assets and expenses will be debited and decreases will be credited. Liabilities, owner equity, and revenue appear on the right side of the equation; thus, increases in these items will be credited and decreases will be debited. These rules may be summarized as follows:

Debit indicates:	**Credit** indicates:

Asset increase | Asset decrease

Expense increase | Expense decrease

Liability decrease | Liability increase

Owner equity decrease | Owner equity increase

Revenue decrease | Revenue increase

As a general rule, the sum of the increases in an account will be equal to or greater than the sum of the decreases. It follows that the **normal balance** of an account will appear on the positive, or increase, side. Thus, asset and expense accounts normally have debit balances, whereas liability, owner equity, and revenue accounts ordinarily have credit balances. This may be illustrated as follows:

42

Positions of Normal Account Balances

Any Asset Account		Any Liability Account	
+	−	−	+

Any Expense Account		Any Owner Equity Account	
+	−	−	+

		Any Revenue Account	
		−	+

You will note that we have not used precise account titles in the illustration. "Any Asset Account," for example, could be Cash, Store Supplies on Hand, Furniture and Equipment, or the like.

CLASSIFICATION OF ACCOUNTS

In most organizations of any size, accounts are classified in some manner in order to make them more useful to the accountant and more meaningful to their users. Before we discuss the operation of the account in detail, it is important that we become familiar with some of the more common methods of classification. Three of the major ones are:

1 Basic equation classification
2 Real, nominal, and mixed classification
3 Financial statement classification

Basic Equation Classification

A study of the classification of accounts can perhaps best be approached by beginning with the broad categories inherent in the expanded version of the basic equation, namely:

1 Assets
2 Liabilities
3 Owner equity
4 Revenues
5 Expenses

Asset Accounts   In Chapter 2 assets were defined as anything of value owned by an individual or a business organization.   Some of the more common asset accounts are Cash, Accounts Receivable, Notes Receivable, Merchandise Inventory, Supplies, Land, Buildings, and Furniture and Equipment.

Cash, as used in accounting, includes not only coins and paper currency but also checks, money orders, bank drafts, and demand deposits in banks (also referred to as "checking accounts").   Such items as postage stamps, IOU's, dishonored checks (also known as NSF—not sufficient funds—checks), and deposits in closed banks should *not* be included in the Cash account.

The term **accounts receivable** refers to amounts owed to an entity which are not evidenced by formal written promises to pay.   Accounts receivable usually result from the sales of goods or services.   For example, when a business organization sells merchandise "on account," the amount owed by the buyer becomes an accounts receivable to the seller.   In like manner, when a person goes to a doctor or dentist for professional services and asks him to "charge it," the patient becomes an accounts receivable.

The term **notes receivable** refers to amounts owed to an entity as evidenced by formal written promises to pay at some definite or determinable future date.   Such promises, or "notes," commonly bear interest and are ordinarily transferable from one person or business organization to another.   For example, if a student buys an automobile, paying one-third down and the balance in equal monthly installments, the usual procedure is for him to "sign a note" for the balance.   His written promise to pay becomes a note receivable to the automobile dealer.   If the dealer should decide not to wait for the monthly payments, he can transfer, or "sell," his claim against the student to someone else, frequently a bank.

Merchandise inventory is the amount of merchandise on hand at a particular moment of time.   The term **merchandise,** as used in accounting, pertains to goods purchased for resale (also called "stock-in-trade")—for example, clothes in a clothing store, books in a bookstore, groceries in a grocery store.

Supplies is the term used in accounting to describe various consumable items which are essential to the operation of a business organization but which are not sold to customers, for example, office supplies such as stationery, pencils, and ink, and store supplies such as sacks, boxes, and wrapping paper.   As was noted in the Pendery illustration, supplies on hand represent an asset, whereas those used represent an expense.

Land is ground owned by the enterprise which is used for the conduct of business.

Buildings are structures owned by the enterprise which are used in the conduct of business operations.

Furniture and equipment includes such items as cash registers, chairs, desks, filing cabinets, and similar articles necessary for the efficient operation of a business.

Liability Accounts   Liabilities were defined in Chapter 2 as anything of value owed by an individual or business organization.   Business liabilities, then, are debts of an enterprise to its creditors. Some of the more common liability accounts are Accounts Payable, Notes Payable, Mortgages Payable, and Bonds Payable.

The term **accounts payable** refers to amounts owed by an entity which are not evidenced by formal written promises to pay. They usually result from the purchase of goods or services. The similarity and difference between accounts receivable and accounts payable should be noted. The term **accounts payable** is associated with purchases, whereas **accounts receivable** is associated with sales.

The term **notes payable** refers to amounts owed by an entity as evidenced by written promises to pay at some definite or determinable future date. Like notes receivable, notes payable usually bear interest and are transferable. Generally, they are created by an entity when it borrows money from a bank or when a creditor demands a written instead of an oral promise to pay.

The term **mortgage payable** refers to an amount owed by an entity as evidenced by a written promise to pay which is accompanied by a conditional conveyance of the title to property as security.

Bonds payable are forms of long-term notes issued under formal legal procedure and secured either by the pledge of specific properties or revenues or by the general credit of the entity. Bonds are ordinarily issued by an organization for the purpose of borrowing from the general public when the amount of money it needs is too large for a small number of lenders to supply. When we study the three basic forms of business organization—proprietorships, partnerships, and corporations—we shall see that the issuance of bonds is peculiar to the corporate structure.

Owner Equity Accounts   **Owner equity,** frequently referred to as **net worth,** is the excess of assets over liabilities and represents the ownership interest in a business enterprise. Stated another way, it represents the residual claim against the assets of a business, whereas liabilities represent the priority claim. Needless to say, under normal conditions the owner equity should exceed the liabilities; otherwise, the creditors could conceivably gain control of the business.

Asset and liability accounts, with the exception of Bonds Payable, apply equally well to proprietorships, partnerships, or corporations. Owner equity accounts, however, must be viewed from the standpoint of the particular form of business organization. Some of the more common owner equity accounts are Capital, Drawing, Capital Stock, and Retained Earnings.

Capital accounts reflect the amount of capital contributed on a more or less permanent basis by the owner in a proprietorship or by the owners in a partnership.

Drawing accounts are employed in proprietorships and partnerships to reflect changes in owner equity such as withdrawals or additional investments. The net income (or loss) from operations is also ordinarily transferred to drawing accounts until a decision is made either to leave it in the business as permanent capital or to withdraw it. Drawing accounts are often referred to as **personal** or **current** accounts.

Capital stock is the legal evidence of the more or less permanent investment of the owners of a corporation. It is divided into equal shares represented by stock certificates held by the owners (known as **stockholders** or **shareholders**) and reflected as a total in the Capital Stock account.

Retained earnings consists of the accumulated earnings or profits of a corporation which have not been distributed to stockholders or transferred to other owner equity accounts. Thus, the amount shown in a Retained Earnings account is a cumulative amount representing the portion of past earnings retained for subsequent use in the business. The functions of both the Retained Earnings and Capital Stock accounts will be discussed in detail in Chapters 16 and 17.

Revenue Accounts Revenue results from the sale of goods and the rendering of services and is measured by the amounts charged for them. It also includes gains from the sale or exchange of assets other than stock in trade, and interest and dividends earned on investments in other organizations. Revenue from ordinary sales or from other transactions in the normal course of business is often called **operating revenue.** Some of the more common revenue accounts are Sales Revenue, Service Revenue, and Interest Revenue.

Sales revenue results from transactions in which revenue recipients exchange merchandise for cash, promises to pay, other assets, or any combination of these. For example, an automobile dealer sells automobiles, a clothing store sells clothes, a real estate agent sells real estate.

Service revenue results from transactions in which revenue recipients sell services for cash, promises to pay, other assets, or some combination of these. For example, a doctor sells medical services, a dentist sells dental services, a carpenter sells his services as a craftsman.

Interest revenue is income of an entity resulting from the lending of money or the granting of credit. For lenders, interest is a source of revenue, whereas for borrowers it is an expense.

Expense Accounts Expense, which was defined in a broad sense in Chapter 2, may be defined more precisely as a cost which has expired in the process of producing revenue or with the passage of time. The term **cost** as used here means the sum of all applicable expenditures made and charges incurred in providing a good or service in the condition and location in which it is sold or used. Cost incurrence initially produces an asset or provides a service, the benefits of which are expected to contribute to the production of present or future revenues. As the benefits are used up, the portion of the cost applicable to the revenue realized becomes an expense.

For example, when Pendery insured the contents of his store for one year at a cost of $108, the effective date of the insurance was April 10. As of April 10, Pendery had a $108 asset. However, as of April 30 (two-thirds of a month later) he had an asset of only $102 on his balance sheet and an expense of $6 in his income statement. Thus, with the passage of time, $6 ($\frac{2}{3} \times \frac{1}{12} \times$ $108) of the cost expired and became an expense. As we shall observe throughout this text, the proper identification and measurement of expired costs and the appropriate matching of them with applicable revenues is fundamental to the accounting process.

Some of the more common expense accounts are Cost of Goods Sold, Advertising, and Interest.

The **cost of goods sold** is the cost of the merchandise which is marketed (sold) during a period. As was emphasized in Chapter 2, the operation of this account can sometimes be quite complicated.

Advertising expense is the cost of obtaining publicity through the various news media such as newspapers, magazines, radio, and television, and through similar activities which have as their ultimate purpose the increasing of sales.

Interest expense is the cost of borrowing money and, in some cases, of obtaining credit.

Real, Nominal, and Mixed Classification of Accounts

Another major classification of accounts categorizes asset, liability, and owner equity accounts as **real** accounts and revenue and expense accounts as **nominal** accounts. Although related to the expanded version of the basic equation, this grouping is more closely related to the basic financial statements and its use makes for convenience in their preparation.

Real and Nominal Accounts The term **real,** as used in account classification, indicates permanency, whereas **nominal** carries the idea of temporariness. Thus, the balance sheet accounts (assets, liabilities, and owner equity) are categorized as real because they represent items which are of a more or less permanent nature. For example, their balances at the end of one accounting period are carried over as the beginning balances for the next period. The income statement accounts (revenue and expense), however, are summarized and transferred to the owner equity accounts at the end of the fiscal period. Thus, since they are of a somewhat temporary nature, they are categorized as nominal accounts.

Mixed Accounts At the close of an accounting period, some accounts may be **mixed,** that is, part real and part nominal. Before financial statements can be prepared, mixed accounts must be segregated into their real and nominal elements. For example, the account in which Pendery's insurance policy was reflected on April 10 was a real account with a balance of $108. However, on April 30 part of the $108 was real ($102) and part was nominal ($6). Carrying the illustration forward for another month, we would have a real account with a balance of $102 on May 1. As the month passed, however, the account would again become mixed, and on May 31 the $102 balance in the account would be composed of a real element of $93 ($102 − $9) and a nominal element of $9 ($\frac{1}{12} \times$ $108).

Financial Statement Classification

A third method of account classification is one used to categorize the various accounts on the basic financial statements, the balance sheet and income statement. Although this classification is very detailed in its entirety, we shall examine only the major categories. However, it is important to remember that each category can be further subdivided as the need arises.

Balance Sheet Classification Assets and liabilities each are subdivided on the balance sheet into two broad categories: current and noncurrent.

   Current assets is the balance sheet category used to designate cash and other resources which can reasonably be expected to be converted into cash or consumed during the current operating cycle of the business.[1] Current assets are usually listed on the balance sheet in the order of their liquidity, with the most liquid asset first. The current asset category typically includes the following accounts:

1 Cash	**5** Store Supplies
2 Accounts Receivable	**6** Office Supplies
3 Notes Receivable	**7** Prepaid Rent
4 Merchandise Inventory	**8** Prepaid Insurance

   In comparison to current assets, **noncurrent assets** are relatively long-lived. They are necessary to the continued operation of a business and thus are not readily convertible into cash. The noncurrent asset category typically includes the following accounts (listed in the relative order of their permanency):

1 Land

2 Buildings

3 Machinery

4 Furniture and Equipment

   Current liabilities are debts of an entity which must be satisfied within the current operating cycle or one year, whichever is longer. The current liability category typically includes the following accounts (listed in the relative order of their due dates):

1 Wages Payable

2 Accounts Payable

---

[1]An operating cycle in a trading concern is the amount of time required to buy merchandise, sell it, convert the receivable into cash, and purchase new merchandise. In a manufacturing concern it is the amount of time needed to acquire raw materials, produce the product, sell the product, collect the receivable, and purchase new material. In either case, if the operating cycle is less than a year, we use one year as the basis for classification.

3 Notes Payable

4 Taxes Payable

Noncurrent liabilities are debts of an entity, the maturity dates of which fall beyond the current operating cycle or one year, whichever is longer. The noncurrent liability category includes the following accounts (again listed in the relative order of their due dates):

1 Mortgages Payable

2 Bonds Payable

Income Statement Classification   Revenues and expenses are often classified in the income statement into the following categories:

1 Revenues (frequently referred to as the **revenue section**)

2 Cost of goods sold (often called the **cost of goods sold section**)

3 Selling expenses

4 General and administrative expenses

The **revenue section** of the income statement typically includes the following accounts:

1 Sales Revenue, or simply, Sales

2 Service Revenue

3 Rental Revenue, or Rental Income

4 Interest Revenue, or Interest Income

The **cost of goods sold**[1] **section** of the income statement may contain any or all of the following accounts:

1 Merchandise Inventory (both beginning and ending)

2 Purchases

3 Purchase Discounts

4 Purchase Returns and Allowances

5 Transportation Costs (on incoming purchases)

Selling expenses are expenses directly associated with the marketing of merchandise or services.   Typical selling expense accounts include:

---

[1] The term **cost of sales** is often used in the income statement in lieu of cost of goods sold.

1 Advertising

2 Delivery Expense

3 Transportation Costs (on outgoing sales)

4 Sales Salaries

General and administrative expenses include all operating expenses except those directly associated with the sale of merchandise or services. Typical general and administrative expense accounts include:

1 Office Salaries

2 Rent

3 Heat, Light, and Power

4 Office Supplies

THE LEDGER

An organization's accounts are generally grouped together in one or more ledgers. A **ledger** may be a book, a filing cabinet, the memory unit of a computer, or a similar device in which related accounts are kept. For our ledger in our manual accounting system, we shall simply use sheets of paper with the accounts depicted thereon in T account form.

Chart of Accounts

The accounts selected for use in a particular accounting system make up what is known as the organization's **chart of accounts**. The chart of accounts provides a framework for the collection and recording of the raw data as well as for their subsequent processing and reporting.

Coding of Accounts

In accounting systems which utilize large numbers of accounts, as well as in systems which are highly automated, a symbolic method of referring to accounts is ordinarily used; that is, the ledger accounts are usually coded in some fashion. Although many types of codes have been developed and put into use, the one employed most frequently is the straight numerical system.

In a numerical coding system the position of each digit in a numbered account, as well as the value of the digit, has a definite meaning. While we shall not undertake a detailed study of numerical coding, it is important that we have a general understanding of the way it operates. In a typical system the accounts may be grouped and numbered somewhat as follows:

100–199 Asset accounts
200–299 Liability accounts
300–399 Owner equity accounts
400–499 Revenue accounts
500–599 Expense accounts

It is not uncommon for the individual accounts in a chart of accounts to be arranged in the ledger and coded somewhat in the order of their appearance in the financial statements. However, this is not a hard and fast rule. This procedure is illustrated below.

100 Assets
   101 Cash
   111 Accounts Receivable
   121 Notes Receivable

200 Liabilities
   201 Accounts Payable
   211 Notes Payable
   221 Mortgage Payable

300 Owner Equity
   301 Capital
   311 Drawing

400 Revenue
   401 Sales
   411 Rental Revenue
   421 Interest Revenue

500 Expense
   501 Advertising—Newspapers
   502 Advertising—Radio
   503 Advertising—Television
   504 Delivery Expense

OPERATION OF ACCOUNTS

To illustrate further the operation of accounts, we shall continue the Pendery illustration. The accounts which follow reflect the transactions first introduced in Chapter 2 and are "keyed" for identification according to the number of the transaction. Remember that two or more accounts are always affected by a transaction. For example, transaction (1) is reflected as a debit (increase) in the Cash account and as a credit (increase) in Pendery's Capital account.

For practice, analyze each transaction and then trace it into the ledger accounts. In Chapter 2 we assumed that Pendery:

1 Invested $8,000 cash in a clothing business on April 1, 1972.

2 Purchased furniture and equipment for $800 from Central Supply Company, paying $500 cash with the balance to be paid in 90 days.

3 Purchased merchandise for resale, paying $2,000 cash.

4 Purchased $1,500 worth of merchandise for resale from the T. Scott Company, paying $1,000 cash with the balance to be paid in 60 days.

5 Sold merchandise for $935 cash.

6 Sold merchandise on account to George Carrell, $90; Richard Greenwell, $50; Otwell Rankin, $130.

7 Purchased $50 worth of merchandise for resale on account. (Although this transaction was not specifically identified in Chapter 2, the merchandise was purchased on credit from G. Smith and was paid for during the month.)

8 Collected $45 from Otwell Rankin.

9 Paid G. Smith in full.

10 Paid 6 months' rent at $100 a month.

11 Paid the T. Scott Company $150 to apply on account.

12 On April 10 paid $108 for insurance on the contents of the store for one year.

13 Paid $40 cash for store supplies.

14 Paid expenses as follows: sales salary, $60; miscellaneous expenses, $75.

15 Purchased $1,000 worth of merchandise for resale, paying cash.

16 Borrowed $1,000 from the bank as of April 14, giving a 90-day promissory note.

17 Took inventory of the merchandise purchased for resale during the month and found that $3,700 worth was still on hand at the end of the month.

18 Took inventory of store supplies and found that $30 worth was still on hand at the end of the month.

19 Checked the insurance policy and found that it had expired in the amount of $6 during the month.

20 Realized that one month's rent had expired.

Comments on Pendery's Ledger

You will note that the Purchases of Merchandise and G. Smith accounts as they now stand have no balances; that is, the debits and credits total the same amount. An account with no balance (a zero balance) is known as a **closed** account, whereas an account with a balance is called an **open** account. The Purchases of Merchandise account has a zero balance because purchases costing $850 were sold and their cost was transferred to the Cost of Goods Sold account; the remaining purchases are still on hand and their cost ($3,700) is reflected in the Merchandise Inventory account.   Smith's account has a zero balance because Pendery made only one purchase from him and later paid him in full.

RALPH PENDERY
Ledger

Cash

(1)	8,000	(2)	500
(5)	935	(3)	2,000
(8)	45	(4)	1,000
(16)	1,000	(9)	50
		(10)	600
		(11)	150
		(12)	108
		(13)	40
		(14)	135
		(15)	1,000

George Carrell

(6)	90	

Richard Greenwell

(6)	50	

Otwell Rankin

(6)	130	(8)	45

Purchases of Merchandise

(3)	2,000	(17)	850
(4)	1,500	(17)	3,700
(7)	50		
(15)	1,000		

Merchandise Inventory

(17)	3,700		

Store Supplies

(13)	40	(18)	10

Prepaid Rent

(10)	600	(20)	100

Prepaid Insurance

(12)	108	(19)	6

Furniture and Equipment

(2)	800		

Central Supply Company

		(2)	300

T. Scott Company

(11)	150	(4)	500

G. Smith

(9)	50	(7)	50

Notes Payable

		(16)	1,000

Ralph Pendery, Capital

		(1)	8,000

Sales

		(5)	935
		(6)	270

Cost of Goods Sold

(17)	850	

Sales Salary

(14)	60	

Miscellaneous Expense

(14)	75	

Store Supplies Used

(18)	10	

Rent Expense

(20)	100	

Insurance Expense

(19)	6	

TRIAL BALANCE

Since the proper recognition of the duality concept of an accounting transaction results in "offsetting" debits and credits in the ledger accounts, it follows that the total of all the debit items entered into the accounts must equal the total of all the credit items. The accountant periodically tests the accuracy of his work by either (1) listing the totals of all the debits and credits and adding them, or (2) listing only the debit and credit balances and adding them; in either instance, the procedure is ordinarily known as **taking a trial balance.**

A trial balance based on totals is referred to as a **trial balance of totals,** whereas one based only on account balances is known as a **trial balance of balances.** The following example prepared from Pendery's ledger is a trial balance of balances. The Cash account has total debits of $9,980 and total credits of $5,583, but instead of using both totals we have used only the debit balance of $4,397. In studying the trial balance, note that we list the **debit** balances on the **left** and the **credit** balances on the **right.** This, of course, is consistent with the theory of debits and credits.

RALPH PENDERY
Trial Balance
As of April 30, 1972

Account	Debit	Credit
Cash	$ 4,397	
George Carrell	90	
Richard Greenwell	50	
Otwell Rankin	85	
Merchandise inventory	3,700	
Store supplies	30	
Prepaid rent	500	
Prepaid insurance	102	
Furniture and equipment	800	
Central Supply Company		$ 300
T. Scott Company		350
Notes payable		1,000
Ralph Pendery, capital		8,000
Sales		1,205
Cost of goods sold	850	
Sales salary	60	
Miscellaneous expense	75	
Store supplies used	10	
Rent expense	100	
Insurance expense	6	
	$10,855	$10,855

Uses and Limitations of the Trial Balance

The trial balance is used by the accountant to test the accuracy of his work. The word "test" should be emphasized, because the trial balance merely shows whether or not the debits in the ledger are equal to the credits. It is not conclusive proof that all the data reflected in the accounts have been handled correctly. For example, the trial balance would still balance even though:

1 A transaction was omitted entirely.
2 A fictitious transaction was included.
3 An incorrect amount was recorded for both the debit and the credit in a transaction.
4 "Offsetting" errors were involved.
5 The wrong account was debited or credited in a particular transaction.

In addition to being used to test the mathematical accuracy of the ledger, the trial balance is employed by the accountant as a basis for the preparation of the financial statements. We shall study its use for this purpose in Chapter 4. The close correlation between Pendery's trial balance and his balance sheet and income statement should, however, be noted at this time.

SUMMARY

Because of the multitude of transactions engaged in by modern business organizations, it is not practical to prepare new financial statements following each one. As a consequence, we employ a vehicle called an **account,** in which changes in the various assets, liabilities, and residual equities are recorded and summarized.

The T account, which is divided into two cells—one for increases and one for decreases—is employed in this text as an account model. From a terminology standpoint, the left side of the account is called the debit side, and the right side is the credit side. The expanded version of the basic equation, when stated as $A + E = L + OE + R$, assists us in remembering whether increases and decreases in items are debited or credited.

The three major ways by which accounts may be classified in order to increase their usefulness in an organization are (1) basic equation classification, (2) real, nominal, and mixed classification, and (3) financial statement classification.

A group of related accounts is known as a **ledger.** Most organizations also employ a chart of accounts, which is a list of accounts selected for use in a particular accounting system. In large systems, as well as in those that are highly automated, the accounts are usually coded in some manner.

In order to test the accuracy of his work and also to provide a basis for the preparation of financial statements, the accountant takes a trial balance. However, even though the trial balance balances, this does not mean that all the data reflected in the accounts have been handled correctly. It only shows that the debits and credits in the ledger are equal.

QUESTIONS AND PROBLEMS

3-1 In accounting terminology, what is the difference between an **account** and a **ledger?**

3-2 What is the primary function of the T account in the study of accounting?

3-3 Do the following types of accounts normally have debit or credit balances? (a) Asset, (b) Liability, (c) Owner equity, (d) Revenue, (e) Expense.

3-4 What is meant by the terms **real, nominal,** and **mixed,** as they apply to account classification?

3-5 What is meant by the term **operating cycle?**

3-6 What is a **chart of accounts?**

3-7 Why are accounts frequently coded numerically or by the use of symbols?

3-8 What is a **trial balance?** What are its major uses?

3-9 The accounts listed below appear in the ledger of the Midwest Sales Company. Classify them in accordance with the expanded version of the basic equation, that is, as assets, liabilities, owner equity, revenues, or expenses. Further classify the assets and liabilities into current and non-current categories.

Cash	Land
Sales	Office Supplies
Interest (with a debit balance)	Retained Earnings
Rent Expense	Merchandise Inventory
Prepaid Rent	Cost of Goods Sold
Accounts Receivable	Bonds Payable
Accounts Payable	Notes Payable
Capital Stock	Salaries Payable
Buildings	Income Taxes Payable

3-10 Instructions Set up five T accounts, labeling them as follows: Any Asset Account, Any Expense Account, Any Liability Account, Any Owner Equity Account, and Any Revenue Account. Enter the following transactions in the appropriate accounts and take a trial balance to prove that the equation $A + E = L + OE + R$ holds.

1 Investment of $20,000 cash by the owner

2 Purchase of merchandise on account, $4,000

3 Purchase of merchandise for cash, $3,000

4 Payment of one month's rent, $400

5 Sale of merchandise on account, $1,500

6 Sale of merchandise for cash, $800

7 Payment of $300 to creditors

8 Collection of $400 from customers

9 Receipt of a $35 telephone bill from the telephone company

10 Withdrawal of $500 by the owner

3-11 Instructions Set up five T accounts, labeling them: Any Asset Account, Any Expense Account, Any Liability Account, Any Owner Equity Account, and Any Revenue Account. Enter the following transactions into the accounts and take a trial balance to prove your work.

1 Investment of $30,000 cash and a delivery truck worth $5,000 by the owner

2 Purchase of merchandise for cash, $10,000

3 Borrowing of $15,000 from the bank

4 Sale of merchandise on credit, $3,000

5 Sale of merchandise for cash, $4,000

6 Purchase of a building with a payment of $10,000 cash and a mortgage for $50,000

7 Collection of $1,000 from a customer

8 Payment of $2,000 to the bank—see transaction (3)

9 Payment of a $200 advertising bill

10 Investment of an additional $10,000 by the owner

3-12 Instructions Analyze the following transactions, which pertain to Bandy's TV Sales and Service, in terms of debits and credits and the accounts to be debited and credited. (Example: The sale of $1,000 worth of merchandise for cash would be analyzed as a debit of $1,000 to the Cash account and a credit to the Sales account for the same amount.)

1 Bandy invested $30,000 cash in the business.

2 Purchased merchandise on credit from the Reed TV Sales Company for $30,000.

3 Purchased equipment for cash, $5,000.

4 Sold a television set to A. B. See for cash, $625.

5 Sold a television set to A. C. Moyer on credit, $700.

6 Collected $100 from A. C. Moyer—see transaction (5).

7 Received $90 in cash for servicing and repairing a television set.

8 Paid the Reed TV Sales Company $800—see transaction (2).

9 Withdrew $100 for his personal use.

10 Paid $100 in cash for local advertising.

3-13 Instructions Analyze the following transactions, which pertain to J. Cook's Southside Grocery, in terms of debits and credits and the accounts to be debited and credited. (Example: The purchase of $1,000 worth of merchandise for cash would be analyzed as a debit of $1,000 to the Purchases account and a credit to the Cash account for the same amount.)

1 Cook invested $40,000 cash in a small retail business.

2 Purchased merchandise on credit from the J. Jones Company, $10,000.

3 Purchased equipment for cash, $8,000.

4 Purchased store supplies on credit from the Aztec Company, $500.

5 Purchased store supplies for cash, $200.

6 Purchased office supplies for cash, $150.

7 Purchased land and buildings for $100,000. A cash payment of $20,000 was made and a mortgage was given for the balance. The land was valued at $10,000.

8 Paid the J. Jones Company $1,500—see transaction (2).

9 Paid the Aztec Company $200—see transaction (4).

10 Paid off one-fifth of the mortgage given in transaction (7), plus $1,500 interest.

3-14 Instructions Prepare a trial balance from the following data, which pertain to the D. Colbert Drugstore as of April 30, 19X1.

D. Colbert, capital	$34,000
Cash	18,000
Sales	24,566
Buildings	30,000
Purchases	15,506
Returned purchases	260
Furniture and equipment	7,200
J. Johnson (a customer)	310
B. Smith (a creditor)	420
Store supplies	460
Prepaid insurance	320
Prepaid rent	1,800
C. Jones (a creditor)	580
Notes receivable	2,200
B. Baker (a creditor)	970
Notes payable	5,000
Mortgage payable	10,000

3-15 Instructions Prepare a trial balance from the following data, which pertain to the Fisher Corporation as of May 31, 19X2.

Cash	$ 35,000
Accounts receivable	52,000
Notes receivable	11,000
Land	60,000
Buildings	150,000
Equipment	35,000
Accounts payable	30,000
Bank loans	20,000
Notes payable	40,000
Mortgage payable	50,000
Capital stock	100,000
Retained earnings	(to be computed)
Sales	200,000
Returned sales	6,000
Purchases	170,000
Returned purchases	15,000
Transportation costs	8,000
Selling expenses	36,000
General and administrative expenses	18,000

3-16 The following transactions pertain to the first month's operations of the W. C. Jones Market.

1 Jones invested $90,000 cash in the market.

2 Borrowed $10,000 from the Last National Bank, giving a 60-day promissory note.

3 Rented a building, agreeing to pay rent at the rate of $300 per month.

4 Purchased $5,000 worth of furniture and equipment from the Baker Supply House, paying $1,000 cash with the balance to be paid in 90 days.

5 Purchased merchandise for $12,000 cash.

6 Sold merchandise on account to B. Beals, $150; to C. Seals, $120; and to Z. Zimmerman, $200.

7 Paid Baker Supply House $200—see transaction (4).

8 Paid expenses as follows: sales salaries, $600; rent, $300; heat, light, and power, $110; miscellaneous, $76.

9 Collected $50 from B. Beals; $20 from C. Seals; $10 from Z. Zimmerman—see transaction (6).

10 Jones withdrew $500 cash for his personal use.

Instructions

(1) Enter the transactions in T accounts, keying them for ready identification.

(2) Prove your work by preparing a trial balance.

3-17 The following transactions pertain to the first week's operations of A. B. Smith's Southside Pharmacy.

1 Smith invested $40,000 cash in the pharmacy.

2 Rented a building, agreeing to pay rent at the rate of $600 per month.

3 Paid 6 months' rent in advance.

4 Purchased $10,000 worth of furniture and equipment from the Miller Supply House, paying $4,000 cash and giving a 90-day promissory note for the balance.

5 Purchased merchandise on credit from Drugs Unlimited, $7,000.

6 Purchased merchandise for cash from Drugs Limited, $3,000.

7 Sold drugs to J. Jensen on credit, $200.

8 Sold drugs to various customers for cash, $2,000.

9 Paid expenses as follows: sales salaries, $200; heat, light, and power, $150; 3 years' insurance, $600.

10 Was robbed of $2,000 cash by burglars.

Instructions

(1) Enter the transactions in T accounts, keying them for ready identification.

(2) Prove your work by preparing a trial balance.

3-18 The following information pertains to the operations of the Kimball Flower Shop for the month of June, 19X3.

June Transactions

1 Purchased merchandise on credit from Floral Supply, $375.

2 Collected $30 from John Ward, $40 from Sam Spade, and $75 from Sue Wardman.

3 Sold merchandise for cash, $2,800.

4 Sold merchandise on credit to Sam Spade, $115.

5 Purchased store supplies on credit from Floral Supply, $160.

6 Paid the rent for June, $350.

7 Paid Floral Supply $300 and Y. Z. Flowers $450 to apply on account.

8 Received a bill of $100 from the *Gazette* for local advertising. Had not paid the bill as of June 30, 19X3.

9 Paid expenses as follows: sales salaries, $600; heat, light, and power, $120.

10 Kimball withdrew $800 for his personal use.

Trial Balance
June 1, 19X3

Cash	$17,000	
John Ward	110	
Sam Spade	60	
Sue Wardman	125	
Merchandise inventory	3,160	
Furniture and equipment	9,000	
Floral Supply		$ 3,200
Y. Z. Flowers		960
T. Kimball, capital		25,295
	$29,455	$29,455

Instructions

(1) Open T accounts and enter the beginning account balances therein.

(2) Enter the June transactions in the T accounts, opening additional accounts as necessary.

(3) Prove your work by preparing a trial balance as of June 30.

3-19 Instructions From the trial balance on page 63, which pertains to the operations of Mac Smith's Westside Body Shop for the year 19X2, prepare:

(1) A balance sheet as of December 31, 19X2.

(2) An income statement for the year 19X2.

Other data as of December 31, 19X2:

Merchandise on hand	$12,000
Store supplies on hand	190
Unexpired insurance	500

WESTSIDE BODY SHOP
Trial Balance
December 31, 19X2

Cash	$ 4,490	
William Sawtell	1,400	
Joel Berger	500	
L. C. Rubin	1,200	
Merchandise inventory, Jan. 1, 19X2	8,000	
Furniture and equipment	10,000	
Land	6,000	
Buildings	35,000	
A. Portelli		$ 3,200
C. Roth		2,900
Notes payable		10,000
Mac Smith, capital		32,000
Mac Smith, drawing	3,000	
Sales		40,000
Purchases	18,000	
Advertising	600	
Prepaid insurance	750	
Store supplies	360	
Sales salaries	4,800	
	$91,100	$91,100

3-20 The following information pertains to the operations of the J. Franz Specialty Shop for the month of June, 19X4 (Franz's first month in business).

1 Franz invested $10,000 in the business.
2 Purchased $6,000 worth of merchandise on credit from C. Seefeldt.
3 Sold merchandise for cash, $800.
4 Paid June rent, $250.
5 Had $5,500 worth of merchandise on hand on June 30.

Instructions

(1) Enter the above data in T accounts.
(2) Take a trial balance.
(3) Prepare financial statements (balance sheet and income statement).

4
Books of Original Entry and the Accounting Cycle

Although ledger accounts compress input data to a certain extent, they are primarily classification and storage units.   When they were first introduced, we entered each element of a transaction directly into an account.   This, however, is generally impractical in modern business organizations, just as it is impractical to prepare a balance sheet or an income statement following every transaction.   For example, in the Pendery illustration we had four debit entries and ten credit entries in the Cash account (see page 52) and we dealt with only a few transactions.   If we multiply Pendery's operations by tens, hundreds, or thousands, it becomes obvious that we need some means by which we can start the compression process before the elements of a transaction reach the accounts in the ledger.   For this purpose the accountant employs **books of original entry,** commonly referred to simply as **journals.**

BOOKS OF ORIGINAL ENTRY

The primary function of books of original entry is to serve as formal connecting links between the source data from business transactions and the ledger accounts.

In addition they:

1 Provide a chronological history of the transactions engaged in by an organization.

2 Make possible a better division of labor in an accounting system. (When data are entered directly into the ledger accounts, only a limited number of employees can work efficiently, because in many situations only one person can work with one ledger at one time.)

3 Provide more information about the transactions. (The direct entry of data into ledger accounts limits the amount of explanatory information that can be provided. Situations frequently arise—for example, a dispute with a customer or creditor—when detailed explanation of a transaction is needed.)

4 Permit errors to be located more easily. (The direct entry of data into ledger accounts makes it extremely difficult to locate certain types of errors such as the omission of a debit or credit from the accounts, the entering of a debit or credit in the wrong account, the entering of a particular debit or credit on the wrong side of an account, or the entering of the wrong amount in an account.)

Before we proceed with our study of the books of original entry, two important points should be emphasized. First, the journals do not replace the ledger. In fact, their use does not alter the major function of the ledger in any way. Second, when journals are utilized, no transaction should ever be entered in the ledger without first being recorded in a book of original entry.

Basic Terminology

To understand the way in which books of original entry are employed in an accounting system, we must first become familiar with certain basic terms. These include:

1 Journalize

2 Journal entry

3 Posting

Journalize This is the recording of the various elements of a business transaction in one or more books of original entry.

Journal entry A journalized transaction is generally known as a **journal entry.** Although its form may vary in different accounting systems, each journal entry should contain the following information:

1 Date of the transaction

2 Names of the accounts to be debited and credited

3 Amounts to be debited and credited

4 Explanation of the transaction

Posting   The process of transferring the essential facts of a journal entry from a book of original entry to the ledger is called **posting.**   It should be done in such a way that we can look at a ledger account and determine from which book of original entry a given debit or credit came, and conversely, look at a book of original entry and determine the place in the ledger to which an item was posted. For this purpose we employ what is known as a **posting reference,** also called **ledger folio.**   In our model we shall use an abbreviation and a page number to identify the book of original entry from which an item is posted and an account number to identify the ledger account to which the item is posted.   The posting procedure will be illustrated in detail when we study the use of each of the books of original entry.

Basic Books of Original Entry

Just as it would be possible, but as a general rule not practical, to enter all transactions directly into the ledger accounts without using any books of original entry, it would also be possible, but generally not practical, to use only one book of original entry to record all transactions before they are posted to the ledger. In any accounting system, the number and types of books of original entry in use will depend chiefly upon the volume and kinds of transactions to be recorded and the availability of mechanical devices for the recording process.   However, certain kinds of transactions occur so frequently that a few books of original entry are common to many organizations.   They are:

1 Cash receipts journal

2 Cash disbursements journal

3 Purchases journal

4 Sales journal

5 General journal

The **cash receipts journal** records *all* cash received by an organization regardless of its source.

The **cash disbursements journal** records *all* cash paid out by an organization.

The **purchases journal** records *all* purchases of merchandise on account. (Cash purchases of merchandise are recorded in the cash disbursements journal.)

The **sales journal** records *all* sales of merchandise on account.   (Cash sales are recorded in the cash receipts journal.)

The **general journal,** commonly referred to simply as **the journal,** is used to record transactions of a general nature, as its name implies. It contains all transaction data which cannot be recorded in any of the other books of original entry employed in an accounting system. For example, in our system any transaction which does not represent a receipt of cash, a payment of cash, a purchase of merchandise on credit, or a sale of merchandise on credit must be recorded in the general journal.

ILLUSTRATIONS OF THE USE OF BOOKS OF ORIGINAL ENTRY

The illustrations presented in this section are based upon the data from the Pendery illustration in Chapters 2 and 3. You will recall that in Chapter 3 we entered all transactions directly into the ledger accounts without using any books of original entry. In Illustration 4-1 we shall record the transactions in the general journal and then post them to the ledger, whereas in Illustration 4-2 we shall record the transactions in the five basic books of original entry before posting them to the ledger. The ledger accounts in these illustrations are somewhat more formal both in form and content than the skeleton T accounts introduced in Chapter 3.

Basic Data

Ralph Pendery opened a clothing store on April 1, 1972, and during the month engaged in the following transactions:

Apr. 1 Invested $8,000 cash in the clothing business.

1 Paid rent for 6 months at $100 a month.

2 Purchased furniture and equipment for $800 from Central Supply Company, paying $500 cash, the balance to be paid in 90 days.

3 Purchased merchandise for $2,000 cash.

4 Purchased $1,500 worth of merchandise from the T. Scott Company, paying $1,000 cash with the balance to be paid in 60 days.

10 Paid $40 cash for store supplies.

10 Paid $108 for insurance on the contents of the store for 1 year.

14 Borrowed $1,000 from the bank, giving a 90-day promissory note.

15 Sold merchandise on credit to George Carrell for $90.

15 Sold merchandise on credit to Richard Greenwell for $50.

15   Sold merchandise on credit to Otwell Rankin for $130.

15   Purchased merchandise for $1,000 cash.

15   Paid the T. Scott Company $150 to apply on account.

15   Purchased $50 worth of merchandise from G. Smith on account.

15   Sold merchandise for $235 cash.

21   Received $45 from Otwell Rankin to apply on his account.

30   Sold merchandise for $700 cash.

30   Paid sales salary of $60.

30   Paid miscellaneous expenses amounting to $75.

30   Paid for merchandise purchased on April 15 from G. Smith.

Information for adjustments, April 30, 1972:

Merchandise inventory on hand	$3,700
Store supplies on hand	30
Prepaid rent	500
Prepaid insurance	102

Illustration 4-1   Use of General Journal and Ledger

The general journal entry ordinarily serves as a model for all journal entries. Therefore, we shall first journalize the Pendery illustration using only the general journal, so that we may become thoroughly familiar with journal entry form. Remember, however, that the general journal is seldom employed as the only book of original entry in an accounting system.

Two-column General Journal   The form of general journal used in this text is generally known as the two-column general journal, or simply as the two-column journal (the two columns being the debit and credit columns). As you study the illustration, give particular attention to the way in which each journal entry is written. Note that it includes all the required elements, namely: the date, the names of the accounts debited and credited, the amounts debited and credited, and an explanation of the transaction. Note also that the idea of debits on the left and credits on the right is carried out. For example, the name of the credit account is indented to the right of the name of the debit account, and the debit amount is placed in the left money column and the credit amount in the right money column.

Recording in the General Journal   If we use the basic data for the month of April and employ only one book of original entry (the general journal), the transactions for the month will be recorded as shown.

ILLUSTRATION 4-1

General Journal   *Page 1*

Date		Account Titles and Explanation	PR	Debit	Credit
1972					
Apr.	1	Cash	101	8,000 00	
		Ralph Pendery, Capital	301		8,000 00
		Investment in clothing store.			
	1	Prepaid Rent	151	600 00	
		Cash	101		600 00
		Paid rent for 6 months.			
	2	Furniture and Equipment	171	800 00	
		Cash	101		500 00
		Central Supply Company	201		300 00
		Purchased for use in store.			
	3	Purchases	505	2,000 00	
		Cash	101		2,000 00
		Purchased merchandise for cash.			
	4	Purchases	505	1,500 00	
		Cash	101		1,000 00
		T. Scott Company	202		500 00
		Purchased merchandise to be paid for in 60 days.			
	10	Store Supplies	141	40 00	
		Cash	101		40 00
		Purchased for use in store.			
	10	Prepaid Insurance	161	108 00	
		Cash	101		108 00
		Paid insurance for 1 year on the contents of the store.			
	14	Cash	101	1,000 00	
		Notes Payable	211		1,000 00
		Gave 90-day note at the bank and received credit in checking account.			
	15	George Carrell	111	90 00	
		Sales	401		90 00
		Sold merchandise on credit.			
	15	Richard Greenwell	112	50 00	
		Sales	401		50 00
		Sold merchandise on credit.			
	15	Otwell Rankin	113	130 00	
		Sales	401		130 00
		Sold merchandise on credit.			

ILLUSTRATION 4-1

General Journal   *Page 2*

Date		Account Titles and Explanation	PR	Debit		Credit	
Apr.	15	Purchases _____	505	1,000	00		
		Cash _____	101			1,000	00
		Purchased merchandise for cash.					
	15	T. Scott Company_____	202	150	00		
		Cash _____	101			150	00
		Paid on account.					
	15	Purchases _____	505	50	00		
		G. Smith_____	203			50	00
		Purchased merchandise on account.					
	15	Cash _____	101	235	00		
		Sales _____	401			235	00
		Sold merchandise for cash.					
	21	Cash _____	101	45	00		
		Otwell Rankin_____	113			45	00
		Rankin paid on his account of April 15.					
	30	Cash _____	101	700	00		
		Sales _____	401			700	00
		Sold merchandise for cash.					
	30	Sales Salary_____	507	60	00		
		Cash _____	101			60	00
		Paid sales salary for April.					
	30	Miscellaneous Expense_____	508	75	00		
		Cash _____	101			75	00
		Paid miscellaneous expense for April.					
	30	G. Smith_____	203	50	00		
		Cash _____	101			50	00
		Paid in full of account.					

Posting to the Ledger   The transactions recorded in our two-column general journal are next posted directly to the ledger accounts (see pages 71 to 73). Each amount appearing in the debit column opposite an account title is posted as a **debit** to that account in the ledger, and each amount appearing in the credit column opposite an account title is posted as a **credit** to that account. To familiarize yourself with the procedure, follow the posting of each journal entry to the proper ledger accounts. For example, Pendery's transactions during April required five general journal entries debiting the Cash account and eleven crediting it. You will find each of these entries posted to the Cash account in the ledger. Note that for each amount posted to the Cash account, the number "101" is inserted in the PR (posting reference) column in the journal. This indicates that the amount has been posted to account number 101, the number assigned to the Cash account in our chart of accounts. The "J numbers" which appear opposite the amounts in the money columns of the ledger accounts show from which pages in the general journal the amounts were posted. Note also that dollar signs are not used in either the journal or the ledger.

ILLUSTRATION 4-1

Ledger   **Cash**   *Account No. 101*

Apr.	1		J1	8,000	00	Apr.	1		J1	600	00
	14		J1	1,000	00		2		J1	500	00
	15		J2	235	00		3		J1	2,000	00
	21		J2	45	00		4		J1	1,000	00
	30		J2	700	00		10		J1	40	00
							10		J1	108	00
							15		J2	1,000	00
							15		J2	150	00
							30		J2	60	00
							30		J2	75	00
							30		J2	50	00
							30	Balance	√	4,397	00
				9,980	00					9,980	00
May	1	Balance	√	4,397	00						

George Carrell   *Account No. 111*

| Apr. | 15 | | J1 | 90 | 00 | | | | | | |

Richard Greenwell   *Account No. 112*

| Apr. | 15 | | J1 | 50 | 00 | | | | | | |

Otwell Rankin   *Account No. 113*

| Apr. | 15 | | J1 | 130 | 00 | Apr. | 21 | | J2 | 45 | 00 |

Store Supplies   *Account No. 141*

| Apr. | 10 | | J1 | 40 | 00 | | | | | | |

Prepaid Rent   *Account No. 151*

Apr.	1		J1	600	00				

Prepaid Insurance   *Account No. 161*

Apr.	10		J1	108	00				

Furniture and Equipment   *Account No. 171*

Apr.	2		J1	800	00				

Central Supply Company   *Account No. 201*

					Apr.	2	J1	300	00

T. Scott Company   *Account No. 202*

Apr.	15		J2	150	00	Apr.	2	J1	500	00

G. Smith   *Account No. 203*

Apr.	30		J2	50	00	Apr.	15	J2	50	00

Notes Payable   *Account No. 211*

					Apr.	14	J1	1,000	00

Ralph Pendery, Capital   *Account No. 301*

					Apr.	1	J1	8,000	00

Sales   *Account No. 401*

					Apr.	15	J1	90	00
						15	J1	50	00
						15	J1	130	00
						15	J2	235	00
						30	J2	700	00

Purchases   *Account No. 505*

Apr.	3		J1	2,000	00				
	4		J1	1,500	00				
	15		J2	1,000	00				
	15		J2	50	00				

				Sales Salary				*Account No. 507*	
Apr.	30		J2	60	00				

				Miscellaneous Expense				*Account No. 508*	
Apr.	30		J2	75	00				

Balancing and Ruling Ledger Accounts The Cash account in our ledger illustrates the proper balancing and ruling of an account in a manual accounting system. (In automated systems accounts are ordinarily balanced automatically after each entry.) The net effect of the strictly optional procedure of balancing and ruling an account is to combine algebraically all the debits and credits into one amount known as the **balance.**

To balance an account manually we merely obtain a total of all the debits posted to the account and one of all the credits and subtract the smaller total from the larger. We then enter the difference on the side having the smallest total. This puts the account in balance. For example, the total debits ($9,980) in Pendery's Cash account exceed the total credits ($5,583) by $4,397. The account is balanced by entering the $4,397 on the credit side. This amount is then brought down to the debit side of the account as the May 1 beginning balance. When an account is balanced in this fashion, the word "balance" is inserted opposite the balancing amount and a check mark ($\vee$) is placed in the posting reference column to indicate that the amount has not been posted from a book of original entry.

Accounts with only one entry are not formally balanced and ruled (see George Carrell's account). Likewise, it is generally not necessary to balance and rule an account containing only a few entries. For instance, we can tell by simple inspection that the debit in Otwell Rankin's account exceeds the credit by $85. G. Smith's account has a zero balance and is thus illustrative of a closed account.

Illustration 4-2. Use of Five Basic Books of Original Entry and Ledger

Illustration 4-2 demonstrates the use of a set of books consisting of the five basic books of original entry and the ledger. When studying the illustration, give particular attention to the way the transactions are recorded as well as to the way the entries are posted. You will note that the column headings in the various journals are indicative of the procedures to be followed. Again, each recorded entry, regardless of the book of original entry involved, includes all the required elements, namely: the date, the accounts debited and credited, the amounts debited and credited, and an explanation of the transaction.

Recording in the Cash Receipts Journal The five transactions involving the receipt of cash during the month of April are recorded in a single-column cash receipts journal as shown.

ILLUSTRATION 4-2

Cash Receipts Journal   *Page 1*

Date		Account Credited	Explanation	PR	Cash Debit
1972					
Apr.	1	Ralph Pendery, Capital	Investment	301	8,000 00
	14	Notes Payable	90-day note	211	1,000 00
	15	Sales	Cash sales	401	235 00
	21	Otwell Rankin	On account	113	45 00
	30	Sales	Cash sales	401	700 00
	30	Total			9,980 00
					(101)

Posting from the Cash Receipts Journal Each amount appearing in the cash debit column opposite an account listed in the account credited column in Pendery's cash receipts journal is posted as a **credit** to that account in the ledger (see the ledger on pages 77 to 79). However, the accounts are not all credited for the same reason. The Capital account is credited because the $8,000 investment increases an owner equity account. The Notes Payable account is credited because the act of borrowing money results in the increase of a liability. The Sales account is credited because the increase side of a revenue account is the credit side. When Otwell Rankin paid $45 on his account, this reduced an asset and, as you recall, the decrease side of an asset account is the credit side.

The total of the cash debit column is posted as a **debit** to the Cash account, as it represents an increase in an asset account. The individual amounts in the cash debit column are ordinarily posted daily, whereas the column is usually totaled and the total posted monthly. Note that the equality of the ledger is maintained by the posting of each individual item as a credit and the total as a debit.

The use of posting references in the cash receipts journal should be noted. For example, the number "301" in the PR column opposite Ralph Pendery, Capital, tells us that the $8,000 amount in the cash debit column was posted to account number 301 in the ledger. Likewise, the "101" below the total of the cash debit column tells us that the $9,980 amount was posted to account number 101 in the ledger. If we turn either to account number 101 or 301 in the ledger, we will see "CR1" used as a posting reference. This means that the item came from page 1 of the cash receipts journal.

Recording in the Cash Disbursements Journal The eleven transactions involving the payment of cash during the month of April are recorded in a single-column cash disbursements journal as shown.

ILLUSTRATION 4-2

Cash Disbursements Journal   *Page 1*

Date		Account Debited	Explanation	PR	Cash Credit
1972					
Apr.	1	Prepaid Rent	Paid rent for 6 months	151	600 00
	2	Furniture and Equipment	For use in store	171	500 00
	3	Purchases	Merchandise purchased	505	2,000 00
	4	Purchases	Merchandise purchased	505	1,000 00
	10	Store Supplies	For use in store	141	40 00
	10	Prepaid Insurance	Insurance on store contents	161	108 00
	15	Purchases	Merchandise purchased	505	1,000 00
	15	T. Scott Company	Paid on account	202	150 00
	30	Sales Salary	Salary for April	507	60 00
	30	Miscellaneous Expense	Misc. expense for April	508	75 00
	30	G. Smith	Paid on account	203	50 00
	30	Total			5,583 00
					(101)

Posting from the Cash Disbursements Journal Each amount appearing in the cash credit column opposite an account listed in the account debited column in Pendery's cash disbursements journal is posted as a debit to that account in the ledger. Again, however, the accounts are not all debited for the same reason. The Prepaid Rent, Furniture and Equipment, Store Supplies, and Prepaid Insurance accounts are debited because each item involved is an asset. The Purchases account is debited because the merchandise purchased is an asset. The T. Scott Company and G. Smith accounts are debited because the payments to these creditors result in decreases in liabilities. The Sales Salary and Miscellaneous Expense accounts are debited because the payments reflect expense increases.

The total of the cash credit column is posted as a credit to the Cash account in the ledger, as it represents a decrease in an asset account. The individual amounts in the column are ordinarily posted daily, whereas the column is usually totaled and the total posted monthly. Again, it should be noted that the equality of the ledger is maintained by the posting of each individual item as a debit and the total as a credit.

Posting references are employed in the cash disbursements journal in the same way as in the cash receipts journal. The abbreviation "CD" is used in the ledger to refer to the cash disbursements journal.

Recording in the Purchases Journal Pendery's credit purchases for April are recorded in a single-column purchases journal as shown. The columns "Invoice No." and "Terms" are customarily included in the purchases journal and are self-explanatory.

ILLUSTRATION 4-2
Purchases Journal   Page 1

Date		Account Credited	Invoice No.	Terms	PR	Purchases Debit
1972						
Apr.	4	T. Scott Company	500	60 days	202	500 00
	15	G. Smith	501	On account	203	50 00
	30	Total				550 00
						(505)

Posting from the Purchases Journal Each amount appearing in the purchases debit column opposite an account listed in the account credited column in Pendery's purchases journal is posted as a **credit** to that account in the ledger. The total of the purchases debit column is posted as a **debit** to the Purchases account in the ledger. Again, by posting the individual items as credits and the total as a debit, we have preserved equality in the ledger. As you study the posting process, note that the abbreviation "P" is used as a posting reference in the ledger to identify items posted from the purchases journal.

Recording in the Sales Journal Pendery's credit sales for April are recorded in a single-column sales journal as shown. As in the purchases journal, the columns "Invoice No." and "Terms" are included.

ILLUSTRATION 4-2
Sales Journal   Page 1

Date		Account Debited	Invoice No.	Terms	PR	Sales Credit
1972						
Apr.	15	George Carrell	100	On account	111	90 00
	15	Richard Greenwell	101	On account	112	50 00
	15	Otwell Rankin	102	On account	113	130 00
	30	Total				270 00
						(401)

Posting from the Sales Journal Each amount appearing in the sales credit column opposite an account listed in the account debited column in Pendery's sales journal is posted as a **debit** to that account in the ledger. The total of the sales credit column is posted as a **credit** to the Sales account in the ledger. Again, by posting the individual items to the ledger as debits and the total as a credit, we have maintained the equilibrium of the ledger. As you study the posting process, note that the abbreviation "S" is used in the ledger as a posting reference to identify items posted from the sales journal.

Recording in the General Journal Inasmuch as cash receipts, cash disbursements, purchases, and sales journals were used to record Pendery's transactions for April, only one general journal entry is necessary. It appears as follows:

ILLUSTRATION 4-2

General Journal   *Page 1*

Date		Account Titles and Explanation	PR	Debit	Credit
1972 Apr.	2	Furniture and Equipment _____ Central Supply Company_____ Purchased furniture and equip- ment to be paid for in 90 days.	171 201	300 00	 300 00

Posting from the General Journal The one transaction recorded in Pendery's general journal during the month of April represents the purchase of an asset (not merchandise) on credit. When the transaction is posted, the Furniture and Equipment account is **debited** and the Central Supply Company account is **credited.** J numbers are used in the ledger as posting references to identify items posted from the general journal just as they were in Illustration 4-1.

ILLUSTRATION 4-2

Ledger

Cash   *Account No. 101*

Apr.	30		CR1	9,980 00	Apr.	30		CD1	5,583 00
						30	Balance	√	4,397 00
				9,980 00					9,980 00
May	1	Balance	√	4,397 00					

George Carrell   *Account No. 111*

Apr.	15		S1	90 00	

Richard Greenwell   *Account No. 112*

Apr.	15		S1	50	00						

Otwell Rankin   *Account No. 113*

Apr.	15		S1	130	00	Apr.	21		CR1	45	00

Store Supplies   *Account No. 141*

Apr.	10		CD1	40	00						

Prepaid Rent   *Account No. 151*

Apr.	1		CD1	600	00						

Prepaid Insurance   *Account No. 161*

Apr.	10		CD1	108	00						

Furniture and Equipment   *Account No. 171*

Apr.	2		CD1	500	00						
	2		J1	300	00						

Central Supply Company   *Account No. 201*

						Apr.	2		J1	300	00

T. Scott Company   *Account No. 202*

Apr.	15		CD1	150	00	Apr.	2		P1	500	00

G. Smith   *Account No. 203*

Apr.	30		CD1	50	00	Apr.	15		P1	50	00

Notes Payable   *Account No. 211*

						Apr.	14		CR1	1,000	00

Ralph Pendery, Capital   *Account No. 301*

						Apr.	1		CR1	8,000	00

Sales   *Account No. 401*

						Apr.	15		CR1	235	00
							30		CR1	700	00
							30		S1	270	00

Purchases   *Account No. 505*

Apr.	3		CD1	2,000	00					
	4		CD1	1,000	00					
	15		CD1	1,000	00					
	30		P1	550	00					

Sales Salary   *Account No. 507*

Apr.	30		CD1	60	00					

Miscellaneous Expense   *Account No. 508*

Apr.	30		CD1	75	00					

Comments on Illustrations 4-1 and 4-2

A comparison of the ledger accounts in Illustrations 4-1 and 4-2, after all transactions for the month have been posted, will show that the account balances are exactly the same. This is as it should be because the ultimate effect of a transaction is the same regardless of the number of books of original entry employed in an accounting system. However, the use of several books of original entry makes possible a division of duties among the accounting personnel, thus promoting efficiency in the handling of large numbers of transactions and also providing for a certain degree of internal control, because no one employee is allowed to perform too many functions in the accounting process.

ADJUSTING AND CLOSING THE BOOKS

Now that the transactions for the month of April have been analyzed, journalized in the books of original entry, and posted to the ledger (often called the **book of final entry**), we are ready to complete the accounting cycle for the month by preparing financial statements. As a general rule, however, before we can do this, it is necessary to adjust and close the books.

Adjusting the Books

Accounting transactions are ordinarily journalized and posted daily as they occur throughout the accounting period. It is, however, often impractical to record the day-to-day changes in certain accounts; as a consequence, some ledger accounts are not up to date at all times. The process of bringing the ledger up to date at the end of an accounting period is known as the **adjusting process, adjusting**

the books, or simply as **adjusting.** The entries involved in the process are called **adjusting entries.**

A comparison of the appropriate accounts in Pendery's ledger in Illustration 4-2 with the "information for adjustments" included in the basic data for the illustrations (see page 68) emphasizes the need for the adjusting process. For example, the Store Supplies account shows that $40 worth of store supplies was bought during the month of April, but according to the information for adjustments only $30 worth of the supplies is on hand at the end of April. This account, as well as the accounts reflecting merchandise on hand, prepaid rent, and prepaid insurance, must be brought up to date before we can prepare accurate financial statements as of April 30.

Closing the Books

As indicated in Chapter 3, the income statement accounts (revenue and expense accounts) are summarized and transferred to an owner equity account at the end of the fiscal period in order to reflect the results of operations in the owner equity section of the balance sheet. The formal process is known as the **closing process, closing the books,** or simply as **closing.** The revenue and expense accounts are summarized in a ledger account referred to variously as the Revenue and Expense Summary account, the Income Summary account, the Profit and Loss Summary account, the Profit and Loss account, or simply as the P & L account. As the title "Revenue and Expense Summary" is somewhat more descriptive of the closing process than the other captions, it will be used in this text; however, any of the titles would be equally satisfactory.

The Work Sheet

Accountants ordinarily use a device known as a **work sheet** to simplify the process of adjusting and closing the books. The accountant employs work sheets, also known as **working papers,** in much the same way that the mathematician uses "scratch paper"; that is, he first solves problems on work sheets and then incorporates the solutions into the accounting records. Work sheets are *not* part of the accounting records as such and have no standardized format. Most, however, are similar in form as well as in arrangement of content.

In our study of the adjusting and closing process, we shall employ initially what is commonly known as an **eight-column work sheet** (see page 81). The first two columns contain a trial balance taken as of the end of the fiscal period before adjusting and closing entries have been made. (This trial balance is ordinarily known as an **unadjusted trial balance.**) The required adjustments are entered in the next two columns, with the debit and credit entries keyed with a letter notation for ready reference. The income statement account balances are entered in the fifth and sixth columns, and the balance sheet account balances in the seventh and eighth columns. (On some work sheets the income statement debit and credit columns are labeled "Expense" and "Revenue" respectively, and the balance sheet debit and credit columns are labeled "Assets" and "Liabilities and Owner Equity.")

RALPH PENDERY

Work Sheet

For the Month Ended April 30, 1972

Account	Trial Balance		Adjustments		Income Statement		Balance Sheet	
	Debit	Credit	Debit	Credit	Debit	Credit	Debit	Credit
Cash	4,397						4,397	
George Carrell	90						90	
Richard Greenwell	50						50	
Otwell Rankin	85						85	
Store supplies	40			(b) 10			30	
Prepaid rent	600			(c) 100			500	
Prepaid insurance	108			(d) 6			102	
Furniture and equipment	800						800	
Central Supply Company		300						300
T. Scott Company		350						350
Notes payable		1,000						1,000
Ralph Pendery, capital		8,000						8,000
Sales		1,205				1,205		
Purchases	4,550			(a) 4,550				
Sales salary	60				60			
Miscellaneous expense	75				75			
	10,855	10,855						
Merchandise inventory			(a) 3,700				3,700	
Cost of goods sold			(a) 850		850			
Store supplies used			(b) 10		10			
Rent expense			(c) 100		100			
Insurance expense			(d) 6		6			
			4,666	4,666	1,101	1,205	9,754	9,650
Net income					104			104
					1,205	1,205	9,754	9,754

The adjustments in Pendery's work sheet may be explained as follows:

(a) The Purchases account in Pendery's trial balance shows a debit balance of $4,550. According to the information for adjustments, however, only $3,700 worth of purchases is still on hand. This indicates that purchases costing $850 have been sold. To bring the records up to date, these facts must be reflected in the accounts. The adjustment is made by debiting the Merchandise Inventory account for $3,700, debiting the Cost of Goods Sold account for $850, and crediting the Purchases account for $4,550. Since the trial balance contains only open account balances, the Merchandise Inventory and Cost of Goods Sold accounts do not appear in the account column of the work sheet; therefore, they must be entered therein and in addition must be opened in the ledger when the items are posted. The effect of the adjustment upon the ledger accounts is shown (for explanatory purposes only) as follows:

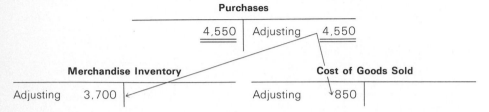

(*b*) The trial balance shows the Store Supplies account with a debit balance of $40. The information for adjustments, however, shows that there is only $30 worth of supplies on hand. Thus, we must adjust the Store Supplies account by decreasing (crediting) it by $10 and at the same time we must reflect the portion used by debiting the Store Supplies Used account, another new account which is added to the work sheet.

(*c*) The trial balance reflects a debit balance of $600 in the Prepaid Rent account. The information for adjustments, however, indicates that $100 of this expired during the month of April. Therefore, we must adjust the Prepaid Rent account by crediting it for $100, and also debit another new account, Rent Expense.

(*d*) The Prepaid Insurance account in the trial balance has a debit balance of $108. The information for adjustments, however, indicates that $6 of this expired during the month of April. Therefore, we must adjust the Prepaid Insurance account by decreasing it to $102, and we must also reflect an expense of $6 in another new account, Insurance Expense.

The adjustments required to bring Pendery's accounts up to date are only a few of many which may be necessary in the accounts of organizations which regularly engage in large numbers of transactions. For example, adjusting entries are ordinarily required for expenses that have been incurred but not reflected in the accounts, as well as for revenues that have been earned but not reflected in the accounts. In addition, it is often necessary to adjust for the allocation of the cost of a noncurrent asset over its useful life as depreciation. These and other types of adjustments will be discussed in more detail in Chapters 9 through 13.

Once the adjustments have been made, the balances of the revenue and expense accounts are extended to the appropriate income statement debit and credit columns, and the balances of the asset, liability, and owner equity accounts to the appropriate balance sheet debit and credit columns. Finally, to complete the work sheet, we total these columns. In Pendery's work sheet, the total of the income statement credit (revenue) column exceeds the total of the debit (expense) column by $104, showing that he has a net income, or profit, of $104. If the expense column total had exceeded the revenue column total, he would, of course, have had a loss.

The total of the balance sheet debit (asset) column in Pendery's work sheet exceeds the total of the credit (liability and owner equity) column by $104, again showing a net income of that amount. If Pendery had sustained a loss for the period, the credit column total would have exceeded the debit column total.

Recording Adjusting and Closing Entries

Since no item is ever entered into a ledger account without first being recorded in one of the books of original entry, adjusting and closing entries must be journalized before they can be incorporated into the accounts. The general journal is used for this purpose. The adjusting entries are ordinarily recorded immediately following the last regular journal entry, and the closing entries follow the adjusting entries.

To journalize adjusting entries from a work sheet, we simply copy the entries from the work sheet into the general journal. Adjustment (*a*) in our illustration, for example, would be journalized in simplified form as follows:

Merchandise Inventory _____ 3,700
Cost of Goods Sold _____ 850
    Purchases _____ 4,550

To journalize closing entries from a work sheet, we proceed as follows:

1 Debit the income statement accounts which have credit balances and credit the Revenue and Expense Summary account. This closes the revenue accounts.

2 Credit the income statement accounts which have debit balances and debit the Revenue and Expense Summary account. This closes the expense accounts.

3 Close the balance in the Revenue and Expense Summary account to an owner equity account (in Pendery's case, his Capital account).

The adjusting and closing journal entries for Ralph Pendery's April transactions are shown on the following page. As we have not used a Revenue and Expense Summary account in the Pendery illustration prior to this time, it will be necessary to open this account along with the new expense accounts mentioned earlier.

General Journal *Page 1*

Date	Account Titles and Explanation	PR	Debit	Credit
1972 Apr. 2	Furniture and Equipment	171	300 00	
	Central Supply Company	201		300 00
	Purchased furniture and equipment to be paid for in 90 days.			
	Adjusting Entries			
30	Merchandise Inventory	131	3,700 00	
	Cost of Goods Sold	506	850 00	
	Purchases	505		4,550 00
	To record merchandise inventory and cost of goods sold.			
30	Store Supplies Used	509	10 00	
	Store Supplies	141		10 00
	To adjust the Store Supplies account for supplies used.			
30	Rent Expense	510	100 00	
	Prepaid Rent	151		100 00
	To adjust the Prepaid Rent account for rent used.			
30	Insurance Expense	511	6 00	
	Prepaid Insurance	161		6 00
	To adjust the Prepaid Insurance account for insurance used.			
	Closing Entries			
30	Sales	401	1,205 00	
	Revenue and Expense Summary	310		1,205 00
	To close the revenue account.			
30	Revenue and Expense Summary	310	1,101 00	
	Cost of Goods Sold	506		850 00
	Sales Salary	507		60 00
	Miscellaneous Expense	508		75 00
	Store Supplies Used	509		10 00
	Rent Expense	510		100 00
	Insurance Expense	511		6 00
	To close the expense accounts.			
30	Revenue and Expense Summary	310	104 00	
	Ralph Pendery, Capital	301		104 00
	To close the Revenue and Expense Summary account.			

Posting the Adjusting and Closing Entries

After the adjusting and closing entries have been recorded in the general journal, they are then posted to the ledger accounts as shown in the ledger appearing on pages 85 through 87. As you study the ledger, note that after the revenue and expense accounts have been closed—that is, after their balances have been transferred to the Revenue and Expense Summary account—they have zero balances. The same thing is true of the Revenue and Expense Summary account once its balance has been transferred to the Capital account.

ILLUSTRATION 4-2

Ledger

(After adjusting and closing entries have been posted)

Cash *Account No. 101*

Apr.	30		CR1	9,980	00	Apr.	30		CD1	5,583	00
							30	Balance	√	4,397	00
				9,980	00					9,980	00
May	1	Balance	√	4,397	00						

George Carrell *Account No. 111*

| Apr. | 15 | | S1 | 90 | 00 | | | | | | |

Richard Greenwell *Account No. 112*

| Apr. | 15 | | S1 | 50 | 00 | | | | | | |

Otwell Rankin *Account No. 113*

| Apr. | 15 | | S1 | 130 | 00 | Apr. | 21 | | CR1 | 45 | 00 |

Merchandise Inventory *Account No. 131*

| Apr. | 30 | Adjusting | J1 | 3,700 | 00 | | | | | | |

Store Supplies *Account No. 141*

| Apr. | 10 | | CD1 | 40 | 00 | Apr. | 30 | Adjusting | J1 | 10 | 00 |

Prepaid Rent *Account No. 151*

| Apr. | 1 | | CD1 | 600 | 00 | Apr. | 30 | Adjusting | J1 | 100 | 00 |

Prepaid Insurance *Account No. 161*

| Apr. | 10 | | CD1 | 108 | 00 | Apr. | 30 | Adjusting | J1 | 6 | 00 |

Furniture and Equipment — Account No. 171

Date			Ref	Debit					Ref	Credit	
Apr.	2		CD1	500	00						
	2		J1	300	00						

Central Supply Company — Account No. 201

Date						Date			Ref	Credit	
						Apr.	2		J1	300	00

T. Scott Company — Account No. 202

Date			Ref	Debit		Date			Ref	Credit	
Apr.	15		CD1	150	00	Apr.	2		P1	500	00

G. Smith — Account No. 203

Date			Ref	Debit		Date			Ref	Credit	
Apr.	30		CD1	50	00	Apr.	15		P1	50	00

Notes Payable — Account No. 211

Date						Date			Ref	Credit	
						Apr.	14		CR1	1,000	00

Ralph Pendery, Capital — Account No. 301

Date			Ref	Debit		Date			Ref	Credit	
Apr.	30	Balance	√	8,104	00	Apr.	1		CR1	8,000	00
							30	Closing	J1	104	00
				8,104	00					8,104	00
						May	1	Balance	√	8,104	00

Revenue and Expense Summary — Account No. 310

Date			Ref	Debit		Date			Ref	Credit	
Apr.	30	Closing	J1	1,101	00	Apr.	30	Closing	J1	1,205	00
	30	Closing	J1	104	00						
				1,205	00					1,205	00

Sales — Account No. 401

Date			Ref	Debit		Date			Ref	Credit	
Apr.	30	Closing	J1	1,205	00	Apr.	15		CR1	235	00
							30		CR1	700	00
							30		S1	270	00
				1,205	00					1,205	00

Purchases — Account No. 505

Date			Ref	Debit		Date			Ref	Credit	
Apr.	3		CD1	2,000	00	Apr.	30	Adjusting	J1	4,550	00
	4		CD1	1,000	00						
	15		CD1	1,000	00						
	30		P1	550	00						
				4,550	00					4,550	00

Cost of Goods Sold   *Account No. 506*

Apr.	30	Adjusting	J1	850	00	Apr.	30	Closing	J1	850	00

Sales Salary   *Account No. 507*

Apr.	30		CD1	60	00	Apr.	30	Closing	J1	60	00

Miscellaneous Expense   *Account No. 508*

Apr.	30		CD1	75	00	Apr.	30	Closing	J1	75	00

Store Supplies Used   *Account No. 509*

Apr.	30	Adjusting	J1	10	00	Apr.	30	Closing	J1	10	00

Rent Expense   *Account No. 510*

Apr.	30	Adjusting	J1	100	00	Apr.	30	Closing	J1	100	00

Insurance Expense   *Account No. 511*

Apr.	30	Adjusting	J1	6	00	Apr.	30	Closing	J1	6	00

FINANCIAL STATEMENT PREPARATION

In addition to serving as a device to simplify the adjusting and closing process, the work sheet is also a useful tool in the preparation of financial statements. All the information necessary for the preparation of Pendery's income statement can be found in the income statement columns of his work sheet, and all the required balance sheet data can be found in the balance sheet columns. The statements which follow were prepared from the data in Pendery's work sheet. Note that the accounts are classified and arranged on the statements in accordance with the financial statement method of account classification introduced in Chapter 3.

RALPH PENDERY
Income Statement
For the Month Ended April 30, 1972

Revenues:
  Sales _____ $1,205
Expenses:
  Cost of goods sold_____ $850
  Sales salary _____ 60
  Miscellaneous expense _____ 75
  Store supplies used _____ 10
  Rent expense _____ 100
  Insurance expense _____ 6   1,101
Net income _____ $ 104

RALPH PENDERY
Balance Sheet
As of April 30, 1972

Assets		Liabilities and Owner Equity	
Current assets:		Current liabilities:	
Cash	$4,397	Central Supply Company	$ 300
George Carrell	90	T. Scott Company	350
Richard Greenwell	50	Notes payable	1,000
Otwell Rankin	85	Total current liabilities	$1,650
Merchandise inventory	3,700		
Store supplies	30	Owner equity:	
Prepaid rent	500	Ralph Pendery, capital	8,104
Prepaid insurance	102		
Total current assets	$8,954		
Noncurrent assets:			
Furniture and equipment	800	Total liabilities and	
Total assets	$9,754	owner equity	$9,754

POSTCLOSING TRIAL BALANCE

To make sure that the ledger is in balance for the start of the next accounting period, the accountant frequently takes a trial balance after the adjusting and closing entries have been posted. Note that the postclosing trial balance illustrated contains only real accounts (asset, liability, and owner equity accounts); all the other accounts in Pendery's ledger have been closed as of the end of the accounting period. Thus, our basic equation $A = L + OE$ is the mathematical model for the postclosing trial balance as well as for the balance sheet.

RALPH PENDERY
Postclosing Trial Balance
As of April 30, 1972

Cash	$4,397	
George Carrell	90	
Richard Greenwell	50	
Otwell Rankin	85	
Merchandise inventory	3,700	
Store supplies	30	
Prepaid rent	500	
Prepaid insurance	102	
Furniture and equipment	800	
Central Supply Company		$ 300
T. Scott Company		350
Notes payable		1,000
Ralph Pendery, capital		8,104
	$9,754	$9,754

SUMMARY

The basic books of original entry were introduced in this chapter, and the entire accounting cycle was illustrated. We started with the raw transactions, analyzed them, recorded them, posted them, took a trial balance, adjusted the accounts, closed the accounts, prepared a balance sheet and an income statement, and took a postclosing trial balance. After the books have been closed and their accuracy tested by means of the postclosing trial balance, they are in readiness to receive the transactions of the next accounting period.

A thorough understanding of the accounting cycle is essential to the successful study of accounting, because the same procedures are followed in each fiscal period. However, these procedures should not be memorized blindly. The cycle consists of steps which follow one another in a logical order; consequently, it should be studied and reviewed until each step is understood in relation to every other step. The accountant must know why he does something as well as when and how to do it.

The flow chart which follows illustrates in a somewhat summarized form both the function of the basic books of original entry and the flow of data through the accounting system during an accounting cycle.

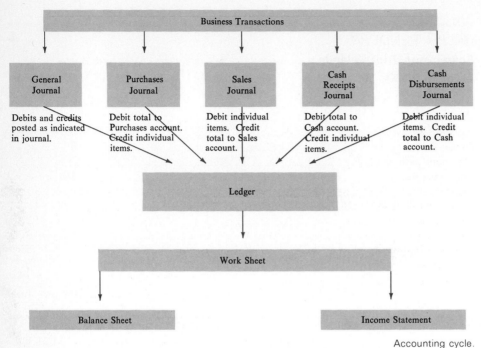

Accounting cycle.

QUESTIONS AND PROBLEMS

4-1 What is the primary function of a book of original entry?

4-2 List the five basic books of original entry and indicate the type of transaction recorded in each.

4-3 What is a **journal entry**? What type of information should it normally contain?

4-4 Distinguish between **journalizing** and **posting**.

4-5 How is each of the five basic books of original entry posted?

4-6 Distinguish between **adjusting** the books and **closing** the books.

4-7 Describe briefly the way in which the accountant employs work sheets.

4-8 List the steps in the accounting cycle in their proper sequence.

4-9 Assuming that the five basic books of original entry discussed in this chapter
are in use, name the book or books in which each of the following types of
transactions would initially be recorded.

1 Investment of cash by the owner

2 Purchase of merchandise on account

3 Purchase of merchandise for cash

4 Payment of 1 month's rent

5 Payment of 6 months' rent

6 Sale of merchandise on account

7 Sale of merchandise for cash

8 Payment to creditors

9 Collection from customers

10 Receipt of a telephone bill

4-10 Assuming that the five basic books of original entry are in use, name the
book or books in which each of the following types of transactions would
be recorded.

1 Investment of cash and equipment by the owner

2 Purchase of merchandise for cash

3 Purchase of equipment on account

4 Sale of merchandise for cash

5 Sale of a noncurrent asset on account

6 Purchase of a building for cash

7 Purchase of a building for part cash and a mortgage for the balance

8 Borrowing of money from the bank

9 Payment of an advertising bill

10 Withdrawal of merchandise by the owner

4-11 **Instructions** Assuming that the five basic books of original entry are in
use:

(1) Journalize the following transactions.

(2) Set up T accounts and post.

(3) Take a trial balance.

Transactions

Jan. 1 D. Palmer invested $10,000 cash in a small retail business to be known as the Palmer Company.

    1 Purchased merchandise for $1,200 cash.

    1 Purchased $1,400 worth of merchandise from the Midwest Supply Company on account.

    1 Paid rent for 3 months at $250 per month.

    2 Paid $60 cash for store supplies.

    3 Sold merchandise on credit to J. Scott for $200.

    6 Sold merchandise for $250 cash.

  10 Received $50 from J. Scott to apply on his account.

  15 Sold merchandise on credit to M. Tenner for $600.

  20 Gave the Midwest Supply Company a $500 note to apply on account.

  25 Sold merchandise on credit to S. Lampert for $800.

  31 Purchased furniture and equipment on credit from the Midwest Supply Company for $2,800.

4-12 Instructions Assuming that the five basic books of original entry are in use and that the books are adjusted and closed monthly, complete the entire accounting work for the month of October from the following information.

Transactions

Oct. 1 Frank Nelson invested $50,000 cash in the garage business.

    1 Paid rent for 4 months at $300 a month.

    1 Purchased merchandise for $3,000 cash.

    1 Purchased equipment for $1,900 on credit from the Newman Company.

    1 Purchased merchandise for $1,050 on credit from the Dorna Company.

    1 Paid $144 for an insurance policy on the contents of the garage for 1 year.

    2 Purchased store supplies for $90 cash.

    2 Purchased $600 worth of merchandise on credit from the Griffitt Company.

4 Sold merchandise to Jack Nicholson on credit for $350.

5 Purchased store supplies on credit from the Ballew Company for $20.

6 Paid for the merchandise purchased from the Griffitt Company on October 2.

9 Sold merchandise for $200 cash.

10 Sold merchandise on credit to Ed Tackett for $250.

11 Sold merchandise for $215 on credit to M. Maddox.

11 Sold merchandise on credit to Rose Collins for $150.

14 Received payment in full from Jack Nicholson. (See October 4 transaction.)

16 Purchased merchandise on credit from the Herr Company for $790.

16 Purchased merchandise on credit from the Heucke Company for $595.

18 Received $50 from Ed Tackett to apply on his account.

21 Paid $240 for advertising.

31 Paid miscellaneous expense of $120.

Information for adjustments on Oct. 31:

Merchandise on hand	$5,610
Rent expired	300
Store supplies used	50
Insurance expired	12

4-13 Instructions From the following information, prepare an income statement for the H. Kaplan Company for the month of June, the first month of the company's operations.

The company's credit sales totaled $9,000 and cash sales amounted to $11,350. H. Kaplan Company purchased $5,500 worth of merchandise on credit and paid cash for $34,500 worth. On June 1, the company paid $6,000 for 1 year's rent, $360 for a 3-year insurance policy, and $150 for store supplies. On June 30, approximately 60 percent of the store supplies are still on hand. The company's salesclerks earned $2,000 during the month. Merchandise inventory on hand on June 30 cost $24,500.

4-14 Instructions From the following information, prepare a balance sheet for the J. Wright Company as of September 30, 19X4, the end of the company's first month of operations.

The company has $13,100 in cash, and merchandise on hand which cost $12,200. Accounts receivable (debts owed to the company) are as follows: Roy Bezold, $900; Richard Brown, $800; Elmer Farris, $550. On September 1, Wright paid $1,800 for 3 months' rent, $192 for a 1-year insurance policy, and $100 for store supplies. (On September 30, Wright estimates that he used approximately one-fourth of the supplies during the month.) The company's accounts payable (debts owed by the company) are as follows: Cottle Company, $1,800; Floyd Company, $1,400; Myers Company, $700. Furniture and equipment purchased on September 1 cost $10,600.

4-15 Having reason to believe that his accounting records are not being kept properly, D. Tremblay, president of the D. Tremblay Company, retains you to examine his records as of January 1, 19X5, the beginning of the company's second year. Your examination reveals that the books were closed as of December 31, 19X4. In addition, you find that the procedures followed during 19X4 included the following:

1 Sales on account were not recorded in the books until cash was collected, at which time the Cash account was debited and the Sales account credited. During the year:

Actual cash sales totaled _____	$26,000
Credit sales totaled_____	22,000
Collections from credit customers amounted to_____	15,000

2 A new office desk was purchased for $400 on December 31, 19X4, at which time the Purchases account was debited and the Cash account was credited.

Instructions Journalize the entries necessary to correct the company's accounts as of January 1, 19X5.

4-16 **Instructions** Based on the data contained in the following T accounts, which represent only a few of the accounts found in a company's general ledger after its books have been adjusted and closed, journalize to the extent possible (1) the adjusting and (2) the closing entries reflected therein.

Purchases		Sales		Sales Salary	
6,000	6,000	7,000	7,000	450	450

Advertising		Rent		Insurance	
105	105	420	420	14	14

Revenue and Expense Summary		John Jones, Capital	
6,189	7,000		14,000
811		14,811	811
7,000	7,000	14,811	14,811
			14,811

4-17 Instructions From the following unadjusted trial balance and information for adjustments, which pertain to the first month's operations of the Ferguson Company:

(1) Prepare an eight-column work sheet.

(2) Journalize the adjusting entries.

(3) Journalize the closing entries.

FERGUSON COMPANY

Trial Balance
As of March 31, 19X4

Cash	$ 5,000	
Notes receivable	2,000	
Prepaid rent	2,100	
Prepaid insurance	288	
Store supplies	80	
Furniture and equipment	1,500	
Notes payable		$ 3,000
S. Ferguson, capital		10,000
Sales		4,758
Purchases	6,000	
Sales salaries	750	
Miscellaneous expense	40	
	$17,758	$17,758

Information for adjustments, March 31, 19X4:

Merchandise on hand	$2,600
Store supplies on hand	25
Rent expired during March	$\frac{1}{12}$
Insurance expired during March	$\frac{1}{36}$

4-18 Instructions From the following unadjusted trial balance and information for adjustments, which pertain to the first month's operations of the Mappa Company:

(1) Prepare an eight-column work sheet.

(2) Journalize the adjusting entries.

(3) Journalize the closing entries.

MAPPA COMPANY
Unadjusted Trial Balance
As of May 31, 19X4

Cash	$ 9,000	
Notes receivable	2,000	
Store supplies	110	
Prepaid rent	900	
Prepaid insurance	144	
Notes payable		$ 3,500
P. Mappa, capital		10,000
Sales		3,474
Purchases	4,350	
Sales salary	380	
Miscellaneous expense	90	
	$16,974	$16,974

Information for adjustments, May 31, 19X4:

Merchandise on hand	$1,300
Store supplies on hand	36
Rent expired during May	$\frac{1}{3}$
Insurance expired during May	$\frac{1}{12}$

4-19 Instructions From the following trial balances of the Santow Company, which pertain to its first month of operations, journalize (1) the adjusting and (2) the closing entries.

SANTOW COMPANY
Trial Balances
As of April 30, 19X4

	Unadjusted Trial Balance	Postclosing Trial Balance
Debits		
Cash	$10,000	$10,000
Notes receivable	4,000	4,000
Merchandise inventory		1,800
Store supplies	320	235
Office supplies	180	115
Prepaid rent	1,500	1,000
Prepaid insurance	360	345
Sales salaries	800	
Advertising	260	160
Miscellaneous expense	35	
Purchases	6,260	
	$23,715	$17,655
Credits		
Notes payable	$ 5,000	$ 5,000
M. Santow, capital	12,000	12,655
Sales	6,715	
	$23,715	$17,655

4-20 Instructions From the following work sheet:

(1) Journalize the adjusting entries.

(2) Journalize the closing entries.

(3) Prepare an income statement.

(4) Prepare a balance sheet.

(5) Prepare a postclosing trial balance.

D. MISENER COMPANY

Work Sheet

For the Month Ended November 30, 19X4

Account	Trial Balance Debit	Trial Balance Credit	Adjustments Debit	Adjustments Credit	Income Statement Debit	Income Statement Credit	Balance Sheet Debit	Balance Sheet Credit
Cash	500						500	
Notes receivable	5,800						5,800	
Furniture and equipment	430						430	
Prepaid rent	225			25			200	
Prepaid insurance	72			6			66	
D. Misener, capital		8,652						8,652
Sales		4,640				4,640		
Purchases	6,725			6,725				
Store supplies	30			20			10	
Sales salary	50				50			
Miscellaneous expense	35				35			
Notes payable		575						575
	13,867	13,867						
Merchandise inventory			2,300				2,300	
Cost of goods sold			4,425		4,425			
Rent expense			25		25			
Insurance expense			6		6			
Store supplies used			20		20			
			6,776	6,776	4,561	4,640	9,306	9,227
Net income					79			79
					4,640	4,640	9,306	9,306

5
Subsidiary Ledgers, Controlling Accounts, and Credit Transactions

In Chapter 4 it was pointed out that although it is possible to maintain a complete and accurate set of accounting records using only one book of original entry and a ledger, many organizations employ several books of original entry in order to expedite the recording process. Similarly, in order to expedite the posting process, many businesses utilize more than one ledger.

SUBSIDIARY LEDGERS AND CONTROLLING ACCOUNTS

The use of only one ledger, like that of only one book of original entry, is practicable only in relatively small organizations. When the business unit increases in size, it ordinarily becomes necessary to supplement the principal or **general ledger** with additional ledgers. This is accomplished by grouping like accounts in supplementary or **subsidiary ledgers.** The two subsidiary ledgers most frequently maintained are the **accounts receivable ledger,** which contains customers' accounts and the **accounts payable ledger,** which contains creditors' accounts.

When subsidiary ledgers are used, **controlling accounts** are employed in the general ledger to summarize the accounts in the subsidiary ledgers. Thus, the subsidiary ledgers contain the detailed transaction data, while the controlling accounts reflect the data in the aggregate.

An important advantage of using subsidiary ledgers and controlling accounts in an accounting system is that the number of accounts in the general ledger can be greatly reduced. It is estimated that 85 to 95 percent of all business transacted in the United States is done on a credit basis. Department stores in medium-sized cities often have from 5,000 to 15,000 credit customers, and in large metropolitan areas it is not unusual for a single department store to have more than 100,000 credit customers. It is also commonplace for a manufacturing company to have from 20,000 to 30,000 suppliers or creditors. In such organizations one controlling account, typically entitled "Accounts Receivable," may take the place of as many as 100,000 or more customers' accounts; similarly, one controlling account, typically entitled "Accounts Payable," may substitute for 20,000 to 30,000, or even more, creditors' accounts.

Subsidiary Ledgers, Controlling Accounts, and the Pendery Illustration

If subsidiary ledgers and controlling accounts for "receivables" and "payables" had been employed when the Pendery illustration for April was introduced, the accounts of Carrell, Greenwell, and Rankin would not have appeared in the general ledger at all but instead would have been entered in an accounts receivable ledger; the aggregate of their balances would then have been reflected in an Accounts Receivable account in the general ledger. Similarly, the accounts with Central Supply Company and the T. Scott Company would not have appeared in the general ledger but instead would have been entered in an accounts payable ledger. The total of their balances would have been reflected in an Accounts Payable account in the general ledger. This relationship can be illustrated diagrammatically in T-account form as shown below.

Relationship between Controlling Accounts and Subsidiary Ledgers

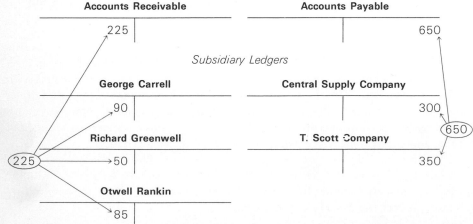

Basic Data for Continuation of the Pendery Illustration

In order to illustrate the operation of subsidiary ledgers and controlling accounts in detail, we shall continue the Pendery illustration for a second fiscal period, the month of May. The transaction data which follow will also be employed in our discussions of credit transactions in the remainder of this chapter, cash transactions in Chapter 7, the voucher system in Chapter 8, and the adjusting process in Chapter 9.

Pendery engaged in the following transactions during the month of May:

May 1 Invested an additional $3,000 cash in his business.

1 Paid $100 for advertising in the *Times*.

1 Purchased merchandise for $800 cash.

1 Purchased $700 worth of merchandise from The Long Company. Terms: 2/10, n/30.

2 Sold $400 worth of merchandise to George Myers. Terms: 2/10, n/30.

4 Purchased store supplies for $30 cash.

5 Sold merchandise for $200 cash.

6 Sold $500 worth of merchandise on account to C. Bond.

6 Purchased $900 worth of merchandise from The Sparks Company. Terms: 30 days eom.

7 Purchased $250 worth of merchandise on account from The Davis Company.

10 Paid The Long Company account of May 1 in full, less discount.

12 Received payment in full, less discount, from George Myers (see May 2 transaction).

13 Purchased $80 worth of office supplies on account from The Wyan Company.

13 Sold $100 worth of merchandise on account to Wilson Ashby.

14 Purchased $450 worth of merchandise on account from The Hart Company.

16 Received payment in full from Wilson Ashby (see May 13 transaction).

16 Sold $300 worth of merchandise to R. Lawson. Terms: 1/5, n/20.

17 Purchased $200 worth of merchandise from The Graham Company. Terms: 1/5, n/20.

18 Paid The Hart Company in full (see May 14 transaction).

19 Purchased $400 worth of furniture and equipment on account from Central Supply Company.

20   Received payment in full, less discount, from R. Lawson (see May 16 transaction).

21   Paid The Graham Company in full, less discount (see May 17 transaction).

22   Sold $175 worth of merchandise on account to Harold Hall.

31   Paid sales salary of $60.

31   Paid freight of $70 on incoming merchandise.

31   Paid $40 for miscellaneous expense.

Credit Terminology

Two words which are used in a somewhat specialized fashion in credit terminology appear in the list of Pendery's May transactions, namely, "discount" and "terms." The word **terms,** as it applies to credit transactions, refers to the conditions of payment in a sale or purchase. The word **discount** refers to an amount which is deducted or deductible for prompt payment or other special reasons.

It is customary in many business organizations to offer terms which permit a cash discount if the buyer pays within a specified period. For example, the terms "2/10, n/30" mean that a 2 percent discount on the sale price will be allowed if the buyer pays within 10 days, or that the net (total) price must be paid if payment is delayed beyond 10 days. The terms also mean that the seller expects the buyer to delay payment no longer than 30 days.

On occasion, credit terms are stated in relation to the end of the month (eom). For example, "30 days eom" means that payment must be made within 30 days from the end of the month in which the purchase or sale was made.

Credit Purchases and Controlling Accounts

As you recall from Chapter 4, **purchases** is the name given to transactions in which the merchandise, or stock-in-trade, of a business is bought by the business either for cash or on credit. The purchases journal in our model serves as a record of the credit purchases of merchandise, while cash purchases are recorded in the cash disbursements journal. When controlling accounts are employed, the purchases journal must be designed in such a way that postings can be made not only to the subsidiary ledger but also to the controlling account, Accounts Payable, in the general ledger.

Recording in the Purchases Journal   Using the basic data for May, we would record credit purchases for the month in a single-column purchases journal as follows:

Purchases Journal   *Page 2*

Date		Account Credited	Invoice No.	Terms	PR	Purchases Debit
1972						
May	1	The Long Company	502	2/10, n/30	204	700 00
	6	The Sparks Company	503	30 days eom	205	900 00
	7	The Davis Company	504	On account	206	250 00
	14	The Hart Company	505	On account	207	450 00
	17	The Graham Company	506	1/5, n/20	208	200 00
	31	Accounts Payable			200	2,500 00
						(505)

Posting from the Purchases Journal   The purchases journal shows that $2,500 worth of merchandise was purchased on credit during the month of May.   This total is posted as a debit to the Purchases account and as a credit to the controlling account, Accounts Payable, in the general ledger.   The individual amounts are posted to the corresponding creditors' accounts in the subsidiary ledger, the accounts payable ledger.   Posting in this fashion keeps the debits and credits of the general ledger equal, and at the same time keeps the algebraic sum of the accounts in the accounts payable ledger equal to the balance of the Accounts Payable account in the general ledger.   Only the transactions recorded in the purchases journal during the month of May are reflected in the accounts which follow.

General Ledger

Accounts Payable   *Account No. 200*

| | | | | | May | 31 | | P2 | 2,500 00 |

Purchases   *Account No. 505*

| May | 31 | | P2 | 2,500 00 | | | | | |

Accounts Payable Ledger

The Long Company   *Account No. 204*

| | | | | | May | 1 | | P2 | 700 00 |

The Sparks Company   *Account No. 205*

| | | | | | May | 6 | | P2 | 900 00 |

The Davis Company   *Account No. 206*

| | | | | | | May | 7 | | P2 | 250 | 00 |

The Hart Company   *Account No. 207*

| | | | | | | May | 14 | | P2 | 450 | 00 |

The Graham Company   *Account No. 208*

| | | | | | | May | 17 | | P2 | 200 | 00 |

Columnar Purchases Journal   Multicolumn, or "columnar," purchases journals are often employed in preference to single-column journals by organizations wishing to categorize their purchases according to some predetermined classification scheme.   In a retail store, for example, it may be desirable to classify purchases according to department.   Thus, Pendery could have classified and recorded his purchases in a columnar purchases journal as shown.   (Note that the Purchases account is simply broken down into several smaller accounts, three in this case.)

Columnar Purchases Journal

						Credit		Debits		
Date		Account Credited	Invoice No.	Terms	PR	Accounts Payable	Purchases Dept. A	Purchases Dept. B	Purchases Dept. C
1972									
May	1	The Long Company	502	2/10, n/30		700	100	400	200
	6	The Sparks Company	503	30 days eom		900	600	200	100
	7	The Davis Company	504	On account		250	50	100	100
	14	The Hart Company	505	On account		450		450	
	17	The Graham Company	506	1/5, n/20		200	150		50
	31					2,500	900	1,150	450

Posting from a Columnar Purchases Journal   To post from a columnar purchases journal, we credit the individual creditors' accounts in the subsidiary ledger and the controlling account (Accounts Payable) in the general ledger.   Then we debit the various purchases accounts in the general ledger (in this case, Departments A, B, and C) with the total purchases of the month.

Credit Sales and Controlling Accounts

The term **sales,** as used in accounting, is the title given to transactions in which the merchandise, or stock-in-trade, of a business is sold either for cash or on credit. The sales journal in our model is used to record credit sales of merchandise, while cash sales are recorded in the cash receipts journal. When controlling accounts are employed, the sales journal must be designed so that postings can be made not only to the subsidiary ledger but also to the controlling account (Accounts Receivable) in the general ledger.

Recording in the Sales Journal Using the basic data from the Pendery set for May, we would record the credit sales in a single-column sales journal as follows:

Sales Journal   *Page 2*

Date		Account Debited	Invoice No.	Terms	PR	Sales Credit
1972						
May	2	George Myers	103	2/10, n/30	114	400 00
	6	C. Bond	104	On account	115	500 00
	13	Wilson Ashby	105	On account	116	100 00
	16	R. Lawson	106	1/5, n/20	117	300 00
	22	Harold Hall	107	On account	118	175 00
	31	Accounts Receivable			110	1,475 00
						(401)

Posting from the Sales Journal The sales journal shows that credit sales of $1,475 were made during the month. This total is posted as a debit to the controlling account, Accounts Receivable, and as a credit to the Sales account in the general ledger as shown. Since both of these accounts are maintained in the general ledger, the debits and credits therein are kept equal. The individual items in the sales journal are posted to the corresponding customers' accounts in the subsidiary ledger, the accounts receivable ledger, an excerpt from which is shown. Posting in this fashion, as with the purchases journal, again keeps the debits and credits equal in the general ledger and also keeps the algebraic sum of the customers' accounts in the subsidiary ledger equal to the balance of the Accounts Receivable account in the general ledger. Again, for illustrative purposes, only the transactions recorded in the sales journal during the month of May are reflected in the accounts at this time.

General Ledger

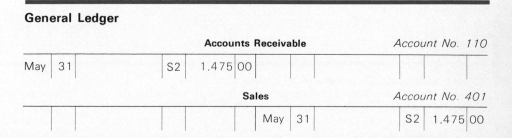

				Accounts Receivable						Account No. 110	
May	31		S2	1,475 00							

				Sales						Account No. 401	
						May	31		S2	1,475 00	

Accounts Receivable Ledger

George Myers   Account No. 114

May	2		S2	400	00					

C. Bond   Account No. 115

May	6		S2	500	00					

Wilson Ashby   Account No. 116

May	13		S2	100	00					

R. Lawson   Account No. 117

May	16		S2	300	00					

Harold Hall   Account No. 118

May	22		S2	175	00					

Columnar Sales Journal A columnar sales journal may be used instead of a single-column journal when it is desirable to categorize sales according to some predetermined scheme such as classification by department. Thus, Pendery could have classified and recorded his sales in a columnar sales journal as shown. (Again, note that the Sales account is merely subdivided into several accounts, three in this case.)

Columnar Sales Journal

			Invoice			Debit	Credits		
Date		Account Debited	No.	Terms	PR	Accounts Receivable	Sales Dept. A	Sales Dept. B	Sales Dept. C
1972									
May	2	George Myers	103	2/10, n/30		400	100	300	
	6	C. Bond	104	On account		500	50	200	250
	13	Wilson Ashby	105	On account		100		50	50
	16	R. Lawson	106	1/5, n/20		300	100	100	100
	22	Harold Hall	107	On account		175	25	50	100
	31					1,475	275	700	500

When posting from a columnar sales journal, we debit the individual customers' accounts in the subsidiary ledger and the controlling account in the general ledger. The individual sales accounts (in this case, Departments A, B, and C) in the general ledger are credited.

TRANSACTIONS RELATED TO PURCHASES AND SALES

In the preceding discussion we handled sales and purchases as if they were isolated transactions, unrelated to any others. However, many businesses frequently engage in transactions which relate directly to prior sales or purchases. For example, merchandise which is bought or sold generally must be delivered. On occasion, part of the invoice price of a sale or purchase may be canceled because merchandise is returned or some kind of allowance is granted. The custom of offering discounts for prompt payment may reduce the amount of cash subsequently received. In addition, there is always the possibility that a credit customer's account will turn out to be uncollectible, regardless of earlier expectations.

While it is difficult to classify precisely those transactions that are specifically related to purchases and sales, for our purposes they can perhaps best be categorized as follows:

1 Transportation transactions
2 Cash discount transactions
3 Transactions involving returns and allowances
4 Uncollectible transactions

General Journal as a Model

Throughout the remainder of our text journal entries will often be made in general journal form for illustrative purposes, even though they normally would be made in one of the other books of original entry. It is important to recognize that when this is done, the general journal entry is employed only as a model. In a specific situation the transaction would be recorded in the appropriate book of original entry.

Transportation Transactions

When a business organization buys merchandise from or sells merchandise to another business organization, transportation (freight) is usually involved. Either business may be required to bear the transportation charges, depending upon the terms of the sale. If the seller is to bear the freight, the transaction is ordinarily reflected in an account entitled "Transportation Out"; if the buyer is to bear the charges, the account is called "Transportation In."

Transportation Terminology   The invoice covering a purchase or sale customarily includes the term **f.o.b.** (free on board) **shipping point,** which means the buyer must bear the transportation cost, or **f.o.b. destination,** which means the seller must bear the cost.

Merchandise is shipped either **freight prepaid** (the transportation agency being paid when it picks up the merchandise) or **freight collect** (the transportation agency being paid when it delivers the merchandise).   Prepaid freight, therefore, is paid by the seller, whereas freight collect is paid by the buyer.

Problems in Accounting for Transportation Transactions   As a general rule the business which is to bear the transportation cost pays the transportation agency; the transaction is then handled routinely in the accounts either as transportation in or transportation out.   However, on occasion the organization which is *not* responsible for the transportation cost may pay it in order to satisfy the requirements of the delivery agency.   (The latter may insist upon payment at either end of the delivery process regardless of who is to bear the cost.)   In this event a problem arises.   It may be simplified, however, if we ask and answer two questions: Who is to bear the freight?   Who actually pays the freight?   The following cases illustrate the various possibilities.   Let us assume a transportation charge of $50 in each case.

CASE 1   The sales invoice reads "f.o.b. shipping point," and the merchandise is shipped freight collect.   Thus, the buyer is to bear the freight, and since he must also pay the transportation agency, the transaction is routine. The buyer will merely charge the payment to his Transportation In account.

Buyer			*Seller*
Transportation In	50		(No entry)
Cash		50	

CASE 2   The sales invoice reads "f.o.b. destination" and the merchandise is shipped freight prepaid.   Thus, the seller is to bear the freight, and since he must also pay the transportation agency, the transaction is routine.   The seller will merely charge the payment to his Transportation Out account.

Buyer	*Seller*	
(No entry)	Transportation Out	50
	Cash	50

CASE 3   The sales invoice reads "f.o.b. shipping point" and the merchandise is shipped freight prepaid.   In this case the buyer is to bear the freight, but the seller will actually pay the transportation agency.   Thus, the seller

must charge the buyer for the freight. The buyer in turn will charge his Transportation In account and increase the amount he owes the seller.

Buyer		Seller	
Transportation In	50	Accounts Receivable	50
Accounts Payable	50	Cash	50

CASE 4 The sales invoice reads "f.o.b. destination" and the merchandise is shipped collect. In this case, the seller is to bear the freight, but the buyer will actually pay the transportation agency. Thus, the buyer must reduce the amount he owes the seller. The seller in turn will charge his Transportation Out account and also reduce the amount owed him by the buyer.

Buyer		Seller	
Accounts Payable	50	Transportation Out	50
Cash	50	Accounts Receivable	50

Financial Statement Classification of Transportation Costs When financial statements are prepared at the end of a fiscal period, transportation out is classified in the income statement as a selling expense.

When the buyer bears the freight, the cost of delivered merchandise rightfully includes the transportation charges. Therefore, transportation in is added to the purchases in the cost of goods sold section of the income statement in order to determine the cost of goods available for sale. The following partial income statement illustrates this procedure.

Partial Income Statement

Sales			$100,000
Cost of goods sold:			
Beginning inventory		$20,000	
Purchases	$60,000		
Transportation in	1,000	61,000	
Goods available for sale		$81,000	
Less: Ending inventory		25,000	
Cost of goods sold			56,000
Gross margin			$ 44,000

Cash Discount Transactions

A **cash discount** is an allowance that is deductible from the selling price of merchandise if payment is made within a specified period of time. The amount of the discount is determined by multiplying the invoice price by the rate specified in the terms on the invoice.

Let us assume that Pendery sells merchandise with an invoice price of $1,000 and terms of 2/10, n/30 (read 2 percent in 10 days; net (total) in 30 days). If payment is made within 10 days, Pendery will receive [$1,000 − (.02 × $1,000)], or $980. On the other hand, if Pendery purchases merchandise with an invoice price of $1,000 and terms of 3/10, n/30 and pays within 10 days, he will pay [$1,000 − (.03 × $1,000)], or $970. Note that there is no time element in the computations; the only consideration is whether or not payment is made within the discount period.

Purchase Discount (or some variation) is the title of the account generally used to reflect discounts on purchases, while a Sales Discount account is commonly employed to show discounts on sales. A purchase discount to the buyer, of course, is a sales discount to the seller.

Accounting for Purchase Discounts The method of accounting for purchase discounts depends upon whether purchases are recorded in the accounting system at **net purchase price** (invoice price less discount) or at **gross purchase price** (full invoice price). Under the net approach, discounts not taken are looked upon as losses, whereas under the gross approach, discounts taken are treated as reductions of cost. Although both methods are used, many accountants maintain that the spotlighting of losses when discounts are not taken is a more effective control device for management than the mere reporting of reductions in cost.

To illustrate both approaches, let us assume that Pendery purchases merchandise with an invoice price of $1,000 and terms of 1/10, n/20. If he makes payment within 10 days, he will pay [$1,000 − (.01 × $1,000)], or $990. The entries for each approach, both at the date of purchase and the date of payment, are shown in general journal form.

Methods of Accounting for Purchase Discounts			
	Net Approach	*Gross Approach*	
Date of purchase	Purchases ——— 990	Purchases ——— 1,000	
	Accounts	Accounts	
	Payable — 990	Payable — 1,000	
Date of payment (discount taken)	Accounts Payable — 990	Accounts Payable 1,000	
	Cash ——— 990	Purchase	
		Discount— 10	
		Cash ——— 990	
Date of payment (discount not taken)	Accounts Payable — 990	Accounts Payable 1,000	
	Purchase Discount	Cash ——— 1,000	
	Lost ——— 10		
	Cash ——— 1,000		

Accounting for Sales Discounts Sales may be recorded at either the net or gross sales price. Under the net approach, sales discounts not taken are looked upon as revenue gains; under the gross approach, those taken are treated as reductions of revenue.

To illustrate both approaches, let us assume that Pendery sells merchandise with an invoice price of $1,000 and terms of 3/10, n/60. If payment is made within 10 days, he will receive [$1,000 − (.03 × $1,000)], or $970. Again, the entries for the net and gross approaches at both the date of sale and date of payment are shown in general journal form.

Methods of Accounting for Sales Discounts				
	Net Approach		*Gross Approach*	
Date of sale	Accounts Receivable ____	970	Accounts Receivable ____	1,000
	Sales ____	970	Sales ____	1,000
Date of payment (discount taken)	Cash ____	970	Cash ____	970
			Sales Discount ____	30
	Accounts Receivable ____	970	Accounts Receivable ____	1,000
Date of payment (discount not taken)	Cash ____	1,000	Cash ____	1,000
	Sales Discount Not Taken ____	30	Accounts Receivable ____	1,000
	Accounts Receivable ____	970		

Financial Statement Classification of Cash Discounts Financial statement presentation of cash discounts is also dependent upon the method used to record purchases and sales. If purchases are recorded at net, discounts not taken are treated as losses in the income statement; if they are recorded at gross, discounts taken are treated as reductions of cost and are deducted from purchases in the income statement.

If sales are recorded at net, discounts not taken are treated as revenue gains in the income statement; if they are recorded at gross, discounts taken are treated as reductions of revenue and are deducted from sales in the income statement.

Trade Discounts Another form of discount frequently associated with purchases and sales is the **trade discount,** an amount allowed as a deduction from a catalog or list price in the determination of the actual price. Trade discounts are used to quote different prices to different classes of buyers. For example, one discount may be offered to wholesalers and quantity buyers, another to small-lot buyers, and still another to retailers. The amount allowed as a trade discount may be stated either as a percentage or in the form of a numerical series such as 10/10/5 (read 10 percent, 10 percent, and 5 percent, and applied successively to the declining balances).

If a trade discount of 10/10/5 is allowed on an item with a published list price of $1,000, the invoice price will be $769.50, computed as follows:

$$\$1,000 - (.10 \times \$1,000) = \$900$$
$$\$900 - (.10 \times \$900) = \$810$$
$$\$810 - (.05 \times \$810) = \$769.50$$

Trade discounts are not to be confused with cash discounts, which are employed as incentives for prompt payment. Trade discounts are used merely as a means of quoting prices; unlike cash discounts, they are not recorded in the accounts.

Transactions Involving Returns and Allowances

It is not unusual for a part of an invoice price to be canceled because merchandise is returned or an allowance is granted for some reason. For example, the delivered merchandise may not be exactly the kind, style, or size ordered, or it may have been damaged in shipment. Returns and allowances associated with purchases are referred to as **purchase returns and allowances**; those associated with sales are known as **sales returns and allowances**.

Accounting for Purchase Returns and Allowances Although an organization's purchase returns and allowances are often accounted for in separate accounts for control purposes, for instructional purposes they are usually combined into one account and will be so treated in this text. Let us assume that Pendery (1) returned $50 worth of merchandise to the seller because it was not as ordered, and (2) received an allowance of $20 because of a minor defect in merchandise purchased but not returned. The following journal entries show how the transaction would be accounted for both on a cash and a credit basis.

Cash Transaction

Cash	70	
Purchase Returns and Allowances		70

Credit Transaction

Accounts Payable	70	
Purchase Returns and Allowances		70

Accounting for Sales Returns and Allowances Like purchase returns and allowances, sales returns and allowances are often accounted for in separate accounts for control purposes, but for instructional purposes are generally combined into one account. Assume that Pendery (1) allowed a customer to return $60 worth of merchandise because it was the wrong color, and (2) granted an allowance of $50 to another customer because the merchandise delivered did not meet the customer's specifications. Again, both cash and credit transactions are reflected in the journal entries.

Cash Transaction

Sales Returns and Allowances	110	
Cash		110

Credit Transaction

Sales Returns and Allowances	110	
Accounts Receivable		110

Debit and Credit Memorandums A return or an allowance is ordinarily evidenced by either a **debit** or a **credit memorandum** (often referred to simply as a **memo**).

A debit memorandum issued by a buyer is notification to the seller that his account (an account payable) is being debited. When issued by a seller, a debit memo is notification to the buyer that his account (an account receivable) is being debited. A credit memorandum issued by a buyer notifies the seller that his account (an account payable) is being credited. When issued by a seller, it notifies the buyer that his account (an account receivable) is being credited. In each instance the two parties involved record the transaction in their records in the opposite sense.

In sum, the issuer of a debit memorandum **debits** the recipient's account, while the issuer of a credit memorandum **credits** the recipient's account. The recipient of a debit memorandum **credits** the issuer's account, and the recipient of a credit memorandum **debits** the issuer's account.

Financial Statement Classification of Returns and Allowances Purchase returns and allowances are generally deducted from, or offset against, the Purchases account in the income statement. Sales returns and allowances are deducted from, or offset against, the Sales account in the income statement. The following partial income statement illustrates this procedure as well as the treatment of cash discounts and transportation in.

Partial Income Statement

Revenue from sales:			
Sales			$100,000
Less: Sales returns and allowances		$ 1,000	
Sales discount		1,980	2,980
Net sales			$ 97,020
Cost of goods sold:			
Beginning inventory		$20,000	
Purchases	$60,000		
Transportation in	1,000		
Delivered cost of purchases	$61,000		
Less: Purchase returns and allowances	$ 500		
Purchase discount	1,190	1,690	
Net purchases		59,310	
Goods available for sale		$79,310	
Less: Ending inventory		25,000	
Cost of goods sold			54,310
Gross margin			$ 42,710

Accounting for Uncollectible Transactions

The average user of credit in the United States is a very good risk. Some buyers, however, grossly neglect payment, and still others end up as "no-pays." Needless to say, the various credit applicants cannot be precisely categorized; if this were possible, the granting of credit would present far fewer problems than it now does.

Since the risks cannot be completely eliminated, there is always a possibility that once a credit sale is made, the receivable will prove to be uncollectible. In this event, the loss ordinarily can be accounted for by one of two methods: the **direct write-off method** or the **allowance method.** Under the direct write-off method, losses arising from uncollectibles are recognized in both the accounts and the financial statements in the periods in which they are determined to be uncollectible. Under the allowance method, provisions ordinarily based upon estimates are made for potential losses, prior to the time that specific receivables are actually determined to be uncollectible.

Methods of Estimating Uncollectibles When anticipating potential losses from uncollectibles, the accountant must estimate the probability of collecting the receivables, or, more to the point, the probability of *not* collecting them. He must then convert this probability into monetary terms in order to reflect the uncollectibles in the accounts and the financial statements.

Most of the methods for estimating potential uncollectibles are based on an average of the losses experienced by an organization over several years' time. For example, average losses for 5 years may be correlated with the average ending balance of the Accounts Receivable controlling account, the average total sales, or the average credit sales for the same number of years. The data in the table below illustrate this procedure.

Estimation of Losses from Uncollectible Accounts				
Year	*Receivables*	*Total Sales*	*Credit Sales*	*Losses*
1	$ 80,000	$ 460,000	$ 380,000	$ 4,200
2	85,000	480,000	390,000	4,300
3	75,000	475,000	385,000	3,900
4	105,000	455,000	305,000	5,200
5	110,000	405,000	360,000	5,150
Total	$455,000	$2,275,000	$1,820,000	$22,750
Average	$ 91,000	$ 455,000	$ 364,000	$ 4,550
Percentage of losses	5%	1%	1.25%	

From a study of these data, it can be concluded that losses from uncollectible transactions will average 5 percent ($4,550 ÷ $91,000) of the balance in the Accounts Receivable controlling account at the end of the year, 1 percent ($4,550 ÷ $455,000) of total sales, and 1.25 percent ($4,550 ÷ $364,000) of credit sales.

Writing Off Uncollectible Accounts   Under the direct write-off method, when a particular receivable is determined to be uncollectible, it is merely written off the books by debiting an expense account (frequently titled Loss on Uncollectible Accounts) and crediting the individual customer's account along with the controlling account.   For example, if John Smith's account of $100 proves uncollectible, it would be written off as follows:

Loss on Uncollectible Accounts _____ 100
        Accounts Receivable (John Smith) _____ 100
To write off Smith's account as uncollectible.

When the allowance method is used, the accounting treatment is somewhat different.   Anticipated or estimated losses are recorded periodically, something not done under the direct write-off method.   The periodic entry is made by debiting an expense account (often titled Estimated Loss on Uncollectible Accounts) and crediting an allowance account (frequently titled Allowance for Uncollectible Accounts).   If at a later date a specific receivable is determined to be uncollectible, it is written off the books, since the loss has already been anticipated and charged to an expense account.   This is done by debiting the allowance account and crediting the individual customer's account along with the controlling account.

Thus, under the allowance method, Smith's account would be written off as follows:

Allowance for Uncollectible Accounts ——————————————————— 100
       Accounts Receivable (John Smith) ——————————————— 100
To write off Smith's account as uncollectible.

Adjusting the Allowance Account When the allowance method is employed, the periodic entry made to record the anticipated losses is an **adjusting entry.** The amount of allowance provided for depends upon the method used to estimate losses from uncollectibles. The following entries, which are based on the data for the fifth year in the table on page 115, record the adjustments necessary if we assume (1) that the estimate is based on a percentage of the balance in the receivable account and that the allowance account has a credit balance of $1,200 at the end of the fifth year, (2) that the estimate is based on a percentage of total sales, and (3) that the estimate is based on a percentage of credit sales.

(1)
Estimated Loss on Uncollectible Accounts ——————————————— 4,300
    Allowance for Uncollectible Accounts ———————————— 4,300
[($110,000 × .05 = $5,500) − $1,200 = $4,300]

(2)
Estimated Loss on Uncollectible Accounts ——————————————— 4,050
    Allowance for Uncollectible Accounts ———————————— 4,050
($405,000 × .01 = $4,050)

(3)
Estimated Loss on Uncollectible Accounts ——————————————— 4,500
    Allowance for Uncollectible Accounts ———————————— 4,500
($360,000 × .0125 = $4,500)

Financial Statement Classification of Uncollectible Transactions The provision for the actual loss under the direct write-off method or the estimated loss under the allowance method is handled in one of three ways in the income statement. It may be (1) deducted from gross sales, (2) classified as a selling expense, or (3) classified as a general and administrative expense. Theoretically, it would be justifiable to deduct it from gross sales. However, as a matter of practicality, this item is usually classified as either a selling expense or a general and administrative expense. If the business has adopted a liberal credit policy in order to "push" sales, the classification of the provision as a selling expense would be warranted. On the other hand, if the credit department has the primary responsibility for determining who is, or is not, to be granted credit, the provision properly should be considered a general and administrative expense, as the credit department is a unit of the general and administrative function.

Under the allowance method, the balance of the Allowance for Uncollectible Accounts account is deducted from the balance of the Accounts Receivable account on the balance sheet in order to reflect the net realizable value of the receivables.

To illustrate, let us assume that a company has a balance of $110,000 in its Accounts Receivable account and $5,500 in its Allowance for Uncollectible Accounts account. The accounts would appear on the balance sheet as shown.

Partial Balance Sheet

Current assets:

Cash		$120,000
Accounts receivable	$110,000	
Less: Allowance for uncollectible accounts	5,500	104,500

Collection of a Written-off Account Occasionally an account that has been written off is later collected in full or in part. When this happens, the previous write-off should be reversed and the collection then handled in the routine fashion in order that the true picture regarding the customer's account will be reflected in the records. To illustrate, let us assume that under the allowance method John Smith's account was written off as worthless by the following entry.

Allowance for Uncollectible Accounts	100	
Accounts Receivable (John Smith)		100

Smith subsequently pays the $100. We must now (1) reverse the write-off, and (2) record the collection in the usual way.

(1)

Accounts Receivable (John Smith)	100	
Allowance for Uncollectible Accounts		100

(2)

Cash	100	
Accounts Receivable (John Smith)		100

If Smith's account had been written off as worthless under the direct write-off method instead of the allowance method, the subsequent reversal and collection would have been recorded as follows:

(1)

Accounts Receivable (John Smith)	100	
Loss on Uncollectible Accounts		100

(2)

Cash	100	
Accounts Receivable (John Smith)		100

Double-posted Transactions

It has been emphasized repeatedly in this chapter that when controlling accounts are used for credit transactions, we must remember to post the data not only to the controlling account in the general ledger but also to the individual customers' and creditors' accounts in the subsidiary ledger. As a general rule, the books of original entry are designed to take care of this problem automatically; however, there are exceptions. For example, our two-column general journal does not permit us to post totals; each item must be posted individually. Thus, only individual items may be posted from the general journal to a controlling account (either Accounts Receivable or Accounts Payable). Since we must also post the same item to the subsidiary ledger, the individual item is posted twice. This is known as **double posting.**

To illustrate, let us refer back to the transportation transactions on page 108. In Case 3 the buyer was to bear the freight but the seller actually was to pay the transportation agency. Since we were emphasizing the transportation problem at that time rather than controlling accounts, we simply used a skeleton entry. Now, however, let us assume that controlling accounts are in use and that the seller is John Jones. The general journal entry in the buyer's books would be:

Transportation In	50	
Accounts Payable (John Jones)		50

In Case 4 of the transportation transactions, let us assume that Sam Smith is the buyer. The general journal entry in the seller's books would be:

Transportation Out	50	
Accounts Receivable (Sam Smith)		50

A similar situation arises in the case of returns and allowances unless a book of original entry designed specifically to handle such transactions is employed. While books of original entry designed for these purposes do exist and are feasible when an organization engages in many transactions of this kind, the five basic books used in our illustrations include neither a purchase returns and allowances journal nor a sales returns and allowances journal. We must, therefore, record returns and allowances in the general journal and then double-post them. For example, if Adam Smith had been the seller when purchase returns and allowances were accounted for on page 112, Pendery's entry for the credit transaction would have been:

Accounts Payable (Adam Smith)	70	
Purchase Returns and Allowances		70

Double posting will also be necessary when uncollectible accounts are written off, if the book of original entry employed is not designed to handle such transactions. The amount of the write-off must be posted to the controlling account in the general ledger and also to the customer's account in the subsidiary ledger. Note that the entry to write off John Smith's account on page 115 was set up for double posting.

SUMMARY

Many business organizations employ more than one ledger in order to expedite the posting process. When this is done, like accounts such as receivables and payables are taken out of the general ledger and placed in subsidiary ledgers. They are replaced in the general ledger by controlling accounts which summarize the accounts in the subsidiary ledgers. Subsidiary ledgers are most useful in organizations which transact a large amount of business on credit.

Certain business transactions which relate directly to purchases and sales require special treatment in the accounting records. These include transactions in which transportation, cash discounts, returns and allowances, or uncollectible accounts are a major factor. In order to determine the amount of revenue earned during a fiscal period, as well as the expenses incurred in earning the revenue, the accountant must give due consideration to such transactions.

QUESTIONS AND PROBLEMS

5-1 Discuss briefly the role and function of subsidiary ledgers and controlling accounts.

5-2 Distinguish between the terms **f.o.b. shipping point** and **f.o.b. destination;** between **freight prepaid** and **freight collect.**

5-3 Distinguish between a cash discount and a trade discount.

5-4 What is a debit memorandum? A credit memorandum?

5-5 What is meant by the term **double posting?**

5-6 Which of the following transactions would require double posting if controlling accounts for accounts receivable and accounts payable along with the books of original entry discussed in this chapter are in use?

    1 Purchase of merchandise on account

    2 Purchase of store supplies on account

    3 Payment for store supplies purchased on account

    4 Return of merchandise which had been sold on credit

    5 Return of merchandise which had been sold for cash

6 Collection of cash from a customer within the discount period

7 Payment of freight charges on merchandise shipped f.o.b. destination

8 Payment of freight charges on merchandise shipped f.o.b. shipping point

9 Payment of freight charges upon the receipt of merchandise which had been shipped f.o.b. destination

10 Payment of freight charges upon the receipt of merchandise which had been shipped f.o.b. shipping point

5-7 Instructions Assuming that the books of original entry discussed in this chapter are in use,

(1) List the journal in which each of the following transactions (shown in general journal form) should be entered.

(2) Give a brief explanation of each transaction.

(a)

Cash	970	
Sales Discount	30	
Accounts Receivable (J. Jones)		1,000

(b)

Transportation In	40	
Accounts Payable (H. Henry)		40

(c)

Purchases	850	
Accounts Payable (I.Ison)		850

(d)

Transportation Out	60	
Accounts Receivable (K. King)		60

(e)

Accounts Receivable (L. Long)	90	
Furniture and Equipment		90

5-8 Instructions Journalize the following related transactions in general journal form, assuming, first, that purchases are recorded under the **net approach** and, second, under the **gross approach.**

1 Purchase of merchandise with an invoice price of $10,000 and terms of 2/10, n/30

2 Payment of $4,900 cash within the discount period

3 Payment of the balance after expiration of the discount period

5-9 Instructions Journalize the following related transactions in general journal form, assuming, first, that sales are recorded using the **net approach** and, second, using the **gross approach**.

1 Sale of merchandise with an invoice price of $5,000 and terms of 3/10, n/30

2 Receipt of $3,104 cash within the discount period

3 Receipt of the balance after expiration of the discount period

5-10 The balance of the Accounts Receivable controlling account in the general ledger of the Ogundele Company as of May 1 was $1,085. The subsidiary ledger contained the following account balances: Briscoe, $198; Granat, $207; Shobe, $269; Taylor, $411. During the month of May, transactions relative to the company's accounts receivable were as shown in the following books of original entry:

Sales journal Sales to Briscoe, $203; Shobe, $218; Taylor, $334; Hardy, $400; Romano, $379.

Cash receipts journal Cash received from Briscoe, $150; Granat, $207; Shobe, $218; Hardy, $390. (Hardy was allowed a $10 discount for prompt payment.)

General journal The company granted a $60 allowance to Briscoe; Shobe returned $90 worth of merchandise.

Instructions

(1) Using T accounts, set up the controlling and subsidiary ledger accounts and enter the May 1 balances.

(2) Post the data from the various books of original entry. (Post the data as individual items or as totals, whichever is appropriate.)

(3) Prove the balance in the controlling account as of the end of May by preparing a list of account balances from your subsidiary ledger.

5-11 The balance of the Accounts Payable controlling account in the general ledger of the Tunde Company as of June 1 was $3,573. The subsidiary ledger contained the following account balances: Burns, $1,205; Center, $916; Ross, $850; Warren, $602. During the month of June, transactions relative to the company's accounts payable were as shown in the following books of original entry:

Purchases journal Purchases from Burns, $308; from Center, $469; from Warren, $388; from Resser, $1,300; from Young, $1,450.

Cash disbursements journal Cash paid to Burns, $1,205; Center, $1,116; Ross, $833 (Ross allowed the Tunde Company a $17 discount); Warren, $388; Resser, $500.

General journal The Tunde Company received a $50 allowance from Center and returned $30 worth of merchandise to Resser.

Instructions

(1) Using T accounts, set up the controlling and subsidiary ledger accounts and enter the June 1 balances.

(2) Post the data from the various books of original entry (either as individual items or as totals, whichever is appropriate).

(3) Prove the balance in the controlling account as of the end of June by preparing a list of account balances from your subsidiary ledger.

5-12 Instructions Determine the invoice price in each of the following cases:

	List Price	Quantity Discount
Case 1 _____	$2,000	10/10/10
Case 2 _____	3,000	10/10/5
Case 3 _____	4,000	15/10/5
Case 4 _____	5,000	20/10/5
Case 5 _____	6,000	20/20/5

5-13 Instructions Prepare as complete an income statement as possible from the following data.

Purchase returns and allowances_____	$ 3,200
Sales returns and allowances _____	4,300
Purchase discount _____	1,100
Sales discount_____	3,600
Purchases _____	66,000
Sales_____	98,000
Beginning inventory _____	20,200
Ending inventory _____	26,400
Transportation in _____	1,200

5-14 Instructions From the following data, determine the amount of merchandise purchased during the period.

Gross margin _____	$30,000
Purchase returns and allowances_____	1,400
Sales returns and allowances _____	6,000
Purchase discount _____	5,000

Sales discount	4,200
Sales	90,000
Beginning inventory	18,400
Ending inventory	14,600
Transportation in	800

5-15 Instructions Assuming that the Kelly Company uses the books of original entry discussed in this chapter and records purchases at gross:

(1) Record each of the following transactions in the appropriate journal.

(2) Post to T accounts.

(3) Prove the balance in the controlling account at the end of May by preparing a list of account balances from your subsidiary ledger.

May 1 The Kelly Company purchases $500 worth of merchandise on account from the Darling Company; terms 2/10, n/30, f.o.b. shipping point.

2 Purchases $800 worth of merchandise on account from the Yinger Company; terms 2/10, n/30, f.o.b. destination.

6 Purchases $1,200 worth of merchandise on account from the Tinnell Company; terms 30 days, f.o.b. shipping point.

8 Receives a memo from the Darling Company that freight of $28 was prepaid on the merchandise purchased from them.

10 Receives a memo from the Yinger Company that freight of $40 was prepaid on the merchandise purchased from them.

12 Receives a memo from the Tinnell Company that freight of $70 was prepaid on the merchandise purchased from them.

14 Returns $200 worth of merchandise to the Darling Company because it is not up to standard.

16 Receives a $100 allowance from the Yinger Company for damaged merchandise.

31 Receives an $80 credit memo from the Tinnell Company as the result of an error in billing.

5-16 Instructions Assuming that the Barr Company uses the books of original entry discussed in this chapter and records sales at gross:

(1) Record each of the following transactions in the appropriate journal.

(2) Post to T accounts.

(3) Prove the balance in the controlling account at the end of June by preparing a list of account balances from your subsidiary ledger.

June 1 The Barr Company sells $1,000 worth of merchandise on account to R. Turner; terms 2/10, n/30, f.o.b. shipping point.

3 Sells $2,000 worth of merchandise on account to C. Shearer; terms 2/10, n/30, f.o.b. destination.

5 Sells $1,800 worth of merchandise on account to C. Park; terms 30 days, f.o.b. shipping point.

8 Receives a memo from Turner that freight of $60 was paid collect on the merchandise he purchased.

10 Receives a memo from Shearer that freight of $88.20 was paid collect on the merchandise he purchased.

12 Receives a memo from Park that freight of $75 was paid collect on the merchandise he purchased.

15 Turner returns $150 worth of the merchandise he purchased from the Barr Company because it is not up to standard.

24 Shearer is given a $40 allowance because part of the merchandise he purchased was damaged.

30 The Barr Company sends Park a $90 credit memo, because an error was made in billing.

5-17 Instructions Journalize the following miscellaneous transactions of the Hoffman Company in general journal form, assuming that controlling accounts for accounts receivable and accounts payable are in use and that the company uses the gross approach when recording both purchases and sales.

Jan. 2 The Hoffman Company sells $2,000 worth of merchandise to J. Holt on account; terms 2/10, n/30, f.o.b. destination.

4 Pays $60 freight on the January 2 sale to J. Holt.

5 Sells $1,000 worth of merchandise to W. Duke on account; terms 2/10, n/30, f.o.b. shipping point.

6 Pays $35 freight on the January 5 sale to W. Duke.

8 Purchases $3,000 worth of merchandise from the Abrams Company; terms 2/10, n/30, f.o.b. shipping point.

9 Pays $80 freight on the purchase from the Abrams Company.

10 Purchases $4,000 worth of merchandise from the Baker Company; terms 2/10, n/30, f.o.b. destination.

12 Pays $245 freight on the January 10 purchase from the Baker Company.

14 Receives a check from W. Duke in full of account.

17 Sends the Abrams Company a check in full of account.

19 Sends the Baker Company a check in full of account.

20 Receives a check from J. Holt in full of account.

25 Receives a $120 check from C. Grider in payment of his account, which had been written off the previous year under the direct write-off method.

5-18 Instructions Journalize the following miscellaneous transactions of the Stallman Company in general journal form, assuming that controlling accounts for accounts receivable and accounts payable are in use and that the company uses the gross approach when recording both purchases and sales.

Jan. 1 The Stallman Company sells $1,000 worth of merchandise to J. Jones on account; terms 2/10, n/30, f.o.b. shipping point.

2 Pays $40 freight on the January 1 sale to J. Jones.

3 Purchases $2,000 worth of merchandise from the Adams Company; terms 2/10, n/30, f.o.b. destination.

4 Pays $147 freight on the January 3 purchase from the Adams Company.

8 Sends the Adams Company a check for $1,323 to apply on account.

9 Returns $100 worth of merchandise to the Adams Company as it was not the type ordered.

9 Grants J. Jones an allowance of $50 on Jones's purchase of January 1 because the merchandise was damaged in shipment.

10 Receives a check from J. Jones in full of account.

12 Sends the Adams Company a check in full of account.

15 Receives a $300 check from P. Burks in payment of his account, which had been written off the previous year by a charge to the allowance account.

5-19 As of December 31, 19X1, Blanchard and Southard, retail clothiers, had accounts receivable amounting to $35,000. As of that date, they set up an allowance for estimated uncollectibles equal to 5 percent of the accounts receivable. During 19X2 they wrote off the following accounts: Richard Diamond, $115; Johnny Dollar, $130; and Sam Spade, $190.

Instructions Assuming that as of December 31, 19X2, the accounts receivable amount to $40,000 and that the allowance for estimated uncollectibles is to be maintained at 5 percent of the accounts receivable:

(1) Journalize the adjusting entry necessary at the end of 19X1.

(2) Journalize the write-offs which took place during 19X2.

(3) Journalize the adjusting entry necessary at the end of 19X2.

(4) Journalize the adjusting entry necessary at the end of 19X2, assuming that the write-offs during the year totaled $2,200 instead of $435.

5-20 Average annual credit sales of the Royer Company amount to $4,824,600. A cash discount of 3 percent is allowed all customers who pay their bills on or before the twentieth of the month following the month in which the sale is made. Cash discounts allowed customers average $57,895.20 per year.

Instructions Assuming that the average time taken to pay by customers who take advantage of the discount is 30 days and the average time taken by those who do not take advantage of the discount is 60 days, compute the average amount owed by customers as of the end of any month.

6

Accounting for Credit Instruments

In many credit transactions, goods or services are bought or sold on "open account." This means that the buyer and seller have reached an oral agreement or simply have a mutual understanding that the seller's terms regarding payment will be met. In Chapter 5, we dealt primarily with this kind of transaction. In other credit transactions, however, formal written documents are employed. In this chapter, we shall concern ourselves chiefly with transactions which are evidenced by such documents.

NEGOTIABLE INSTRUMENTS

Many financial documents, usually known as **instruments,** are negotiable; that is, they may be transferred from one person to another by endorsement. Both the Uniform Negotiable Instruments Law and the Uniform Commercial Code[1] define a **negotiable instrument** as an unconditional promise in writing, made by one person to another, signed by the maker, agreeing to pay on demand or at a fixed or determinable future time, a sum certain in money to order or bearer. Thus, in order to be negotiable, an instrument must be:

1 An unconditional promise or order to pay a certain sum of money

2 In writing

3 Payable on demand or at a fixed or determinable future date

4 Payable to a designated person on his order or to the bearer of the instrument

5 Signed by the maker or drawer

Negotiable instruments fall into one of two categories: those which serve as substitutes for money, and those employed as credit instruments. While our primary concern at this time is with the latter classification, we shall be dealing with the former in Chapter 7. Hence, a brief discussion of negotiable instruments which serve as substitutes for money is included here.

Negotiable Instruments as Substitutes for Money

Negotiable instruments commonly employed as substitutes for money include:

1 Checks

2 Certified checks

3 Cashier's checks

4 Bank drafts

Check This is an unconditional order in writing signed by the person giving it, known as the **drawer**, requiring the person to whom it is addressed, known as the **drawee**, to pay on demand a sum certain in money to the order of a named **payee** or to bearer. Thus, the parties to a check are the drawer, the drawee, and the payee.

In the check illustrated, Pendery is the drawer, the National Bank of Monticello is the "person" drawn upon, or the drawee, and the T. Scott Company, to whom the check is made payable, is the payee.

---

[1] The Uniform Negotiable Instruments Law is a uniform act in effect in all states except those which have adopted the Uniform Commercial Code. The latter repeals the former and updates, clarifies, and simplifies the law in this area.

Check.

Certified Check This is a regular check that has been presented to the drawee bank for "certification," that is, a guarantee that the check is good. By certifying a check, the bank says in effect that:

1 The depositor had the amount of the check on deposit at the time the check was written.

2 The bank has taken the amount of the check out of the depositor's account and is holding it for payment when the check is presented.

3 The bank guarantees the signature of the drawer.

Certified check.

Cashier's Check This is a check drawn by a bank upon its own funds and signed by its cashier. Cashier's checks are issued chiefly for the payment of obligations of the bank. They also are sold to persons wishing to use them as means of payment, in preference to personal checks or other instruments. Since cashier's checks have the resources of a bank behind them, they are generally more readily accepted than personal checks.

NATIONAL BANK OF MONTICELLO   436
MONTICELLO, ILLINOIS

MONTICELLO, ILL.   April 15, 1972   70-2143
711

PAY
TO THE
ORDER OF   T. Scott Company $150.00

One hundred fifty and no/100 -------------------------------- DOLLARS

CASHIER'S CHECK

Tom Kimball

⑆0711⑈21431⑉

Cashier's check.

Bank Draft   This is a check drawn by one bank against funds it has on deposit in another bank.   When payments must be made in distant cities, bank drafts are often preferable to personal checks.

2-1
710

NATIONAL BANK OF MONTICELLO
MONTICELLO, ILLINOIS

April 15, 1972 No.   61337

PAY TO THE
ORDER OF   T. Scott Company $150.00

One hundred fifty and no/100 -------------------------------- DOLLARS

TO THE FIRST NATIONAL BANK
OF CHICAGO
CHICAGO, ILL.   CASHIER

Tom Kimball

⑆0710⑈0001⑉   10 14420⑈

Bank draft.

Negotiable Instruments as Credit Instruments

From an accounting standpoint, negotiable credit instruments ordinarily fall into one of three broad categories, namely: promissory notes, mortgages, or bonds.

Promissory Note   This is an unconditional promise in writing made by one person, called the **maker,** to another. It is signed by the maker, engaging to pay on demand or at a fixed or determinable time, a sum certain in money to the order of a named payee or to bearer.

Promissory notes have been commonplace in business for many years. They are particularly useful to:

1 Sellers in making definite the amounts and dates of payments of obligations due from customers

2 Banks and other financial institutions when granting loans to borrowers

Mortgage This is a conveyance (transfer) of title to property given by a debtor to a creditor as security for the payment of a debt, with the provision that the conveyance is void if interest payments are made and the debt is paid as promised. The debt itself is evidenced by a promissory note which is essentially the same as any other promissory note, except that it includes a reference to the accompanying mortgage.

The property mortgaged as security for an indebtedness may be **real property** such as land and buildings or **personal property** such as merchandise, machinery, or equipment. A mortgage is therefore usually classified as a real estate mortgage (a mortgage on real property), or a chattel mortgage (a mortgage on personal property).

Bonds A **bond** is essentially a long-term promissory note issued in accordance with corporate legal procedure and secured either by a mortgage on specific property or by the general credit of the issuer. Although more formal in nature than promissory notes and mortgages, from an accounting viewpoint bonds involve the same problems, namely, the payment of interest and the payment of a definite sum of money at some time in the future.

Negotiation by Endorsement

According to the Uniform Negotiable Instruments Law, an instrument is negotiated when it is transferred from one person to another in such a manner as to constitute the transferee (the person receiving the instrument) the holder thereof. According to the law, an instrument payable to bearer is negotiated by **delivery,** whereas an instrument payable to order is negotiated by **delivery** accompanied by **endorsement.**

Although an instrument payable to bearer can be negotiated legally without an endorsement, in actual practice banks, businesses, and individuals receiving negotiable instruments from a person other than the maker usually require the bearer to endorse it. An endorsement consists of the signature of the holder plus, in some cases, specific wording placed on the back of the instrument. An endorsement may take one of several forms, for example:

1 Blank endorsement
2 Special endorsement
3 Restrictive endorsement
4 Qualified endorsement

Blank Endorsement This consists merely of the signature of the endorser on the back of the instrument. Since negotiable instruments endorsed in blank can, if lost or stolen, be negotiated without further endorsement, blank endorsements are not always desirable.

Special Endorsement This specifies the person to whom, or to whose order, the instrument is payable. If a negotiable instrument having a special endorsement is lost or stolen, it cannot be further negotiated without the signature of the person to whom, or to whose order, it is endorsed.

Restrictive Endorsement This prohibits the further negotiation of the instrument. When a restrictive endorsement is used, the endorser retains title to the instrument and the endorsee becomes his agent or representative in connection with the instrument. Restrictive endorsements are frequently used when bank deposits are made by mail.

Qualified Endorsement This constitutes the endorser a mere assignor of title to the instrument and relieves him of any liability. He is in effect saying: "Here it is. Take it for what it is worth." Note in the illustration that the words "without recourse" are added to the endorsement to negate the endorser's liability.

Examples of Endorsements

Blank Endorsement	*Restrictive Endorsement*
Constance Muehlhauser	For deposit only in Madison National Bank John Giles
Special Endorsement	*Qualified Endorsement*
Pay to the order of State Bank & Trust Co. Jennifer Warfel	Pay to the order of Highland Wiseman Harry Price without recourse

Credit Instrument Terminology

The terms defined below are commonly associated with credit instruments.

Interest is the charge made for the use of money or credit.

The **rate of interest** is the charge made for the use of money or credit stated as a percentage, usually on an annual basis. Thus, a rate of interest of 6 percent is assumed to be 6 percent per year unless stipulated otherwise.

Bank discount is interest deducted in advance. In accounting parlance, bank discount is commonly referred to simply as "discount."

The **rate of discount** is bank discount stated as a percentage. Like the rate of interest, the rate of discount is generally stated on an annual basis.

The **face value** of an instrument is the amount stated on its face, exclusive of interest.

An **interest-bearing instrument** is one that stipulates on its face that a certain rate of interest will be paid.

A **non-interest-bearing instrument** is one that does not stipulate a rate of interest on its face.

The **maturity date** is the date on which the instrument becomes due.

The **maturity value** is the amount the instrument will be worth at maturity. For an interest-bearing instrument, the maturity value is the face value plus interest. For a non-interest-bearing instrument, the maturity value and the face value are the same.

The **proceeds** of an instrument is the difference between the maturity value and the bank discount.

Mathematics of Credit Instruments

In accounting for credit instruments, we must be able to compute mathematically several major items. These include:

1 Maturity dates
2 "Time"
3 Interest
4 Maturity values
5 Discount
6 Proceeds

Determining a Maturity Date In accordance with the Uniform Negotiable Instruments Law, the maturity date must be stated on the instrument or it must be determinable from facts stated thereon. Most instruments indicate the time of maturity as:

1 A specified date, such as June 15, 1975

2 A specified number of months after the date of the instrument, for example, "2 months after date"

3 A specified number of days after the date of the instrument, for example, "90 days after date"

When the maturity date is stated specifically, we have no problem. When the time of maturity is stated as a certain number of months after the date of the instrument, we simply determine the appropriate month, and the maturity date is the same day of the month as the date of the instrument. For example, an instrument dated March 15, payable "three months after date," would be due on June 15.

When the time of maturity is stated as a specific number of days after the date of the instrument, we must make an exact computation based on the number of days. For example, an instrument dated March 15, payable "90 days after date," would be due on June 13, determined as follows:

Days remaining in March (31 − 15)_____ 16
Days in April _____ 30
Days in May _____ 31
Days needed in June _____ 13
   Total number of days _____ 90

It is important to note that we *exclude* the date of the instrument but *include* the maturity date in the computation. The date of the instrument is automatically excluded when it is deducted from the total number of days in the month.

Determining "Time" The term **time,** as used in relation to credit instruments, refers to an element in the computation of interest, that is, the number of days between two dates. It is computed in essentially the same way as the maturity date. For example, in determining time we again exclude the first date and include the last date. Thus, the time between March 15 and June 15 is 92 days, determined as follows:

Days remaining in March (31 − 15)_____ 16
Days in April _____ 30
Days in May _____ 31
Days in June _____ 15
   Total number of days _____ 92

Determining Interest The determination of interest is based upon three factors, namely, the principal (the amount of money borrowed or credit used), the rate of interest charged, and the time involved. The formula for computing interest may be stated as follows:

$$\text{Principal} \times \text{rate} \times \text{time} = \text{interest}$$

or simply as

$$P \times R \times T = I$$

Although there are exceptions, it is common business practice to compute interest on the basis of 360 days per year, as we shall do in this text. Thus, interest for 30 days will be computed as 30/360 of a year.

Using the preceding formula, we would compute the interest on a 60-day, 6 percent, $1,000 promissory note as follows:

$$\$1,000 \times .06 \times \frac{60}{360} = \$10$$

When using a 360-day year and a 6 percent rate of interest, accountants frequently employ a short-cut method of determining interest known as "the 6 percent method." As you can see in the above computation, 6 percent for 60 days is the equivalent of 1 percent for 360 days, since the ultimate effect of the computation is to move the decimal point two places to the left. Thus, whenever the rate of interest is 6 percent and the number of days involved is either a fraction or a multiple of 60, we can readily determine the amount of interest. For example, the interest on $1,000 at 6 percent for 30 days is $5 ($\frac{1}{2} \times \$10$); the interest on $1,000 at 6 percent for 90 days is $15 ($1\frac{1}{2} \times \$10$); the interest on $1,000 at 6 percent for 45 days is $7.50 ($\frac{3}{4} \times \$10$); and the interest on $1,000 at 6 percent for 36 days is $6 [($\frac{1}{2} \times \$10$) + ($\frac{1}{10} \times \$10$)].

The 6 percent method can also be used when the rate of interest is something other than 6 percent. Interest is first computed at 6 percent, and an adjustment is then made for the difference between 6 percent and the actual rate. For example, the interest on $1,000 at 7 percent for 60 days is $11.67 ($\frac{7}{6} \times \$10$) and the interest on $1,000 at 5 percent for 60 days is $8.33 ($\frac{5}{6} \times \$10$).

Determining Maturity Values   The maturity value of an interest-bearing instrument is the face value plus interest. Thus, the maturity value of a $1,000, 6 percent, 90-day promissory note would be $1,015, determined as follows:

$$MV = P + I$$

$$MV = \$1,000 + \left(\$1,000 \times .06 \times \frac{90}{360} \right)$$

$$MV = \$1,015$$

Since no rate of interest is stipulated on the face of a non-interest-bearing instrument, the maturity value and the face value are the same. Thus, the maturity value of a $1,000, non-interest-bearing, 90-day promissory note is $1,000.

Determining Discount In the determination of discount, three factors are involved, namely, the maturity value, the rate of discount, and the time. The formula may be stated as:

$$\text{Maturity value} \times \text{rate} \times \text{time} = \text{discount}$$

or simply as

$$MV \times R \times T = D$$

The computation for discounting a $1,000, non-interest-bearing, 60-day promissory note at 6 percent would be:

$$\$1,000 \times .06 \times \frac{60}{360} = \$10$$

Since the amount of discount on $1,000 for 60 days at 6 percent is the same as the amount of interest on $1,000 for 60 days at 6 percent, we might incorrectly conclude that interest and discount are the same. It is important to remember, however, that discount is deducted in advance, whereas interest is paid after the passage of time. According to our computations, discount of $10 would be paid in advance for the use of only $990 for 60 days, while interest of $10 would be paid for the use of $1,000 for 60 days. As a matter of fact, if we were to convert the rate of discount in the computation to a rate of interest, the resulting rate would not be 6 percent, but 6.06 percent (that is, $10/990 \times 6$). All other things being equal, the payment of discount will result in a higher rate being paid for the use of money or credit than the payment of interest.

Determining Proceeds The formula for determining proceeds may be stated as:

$$\text{Maturity value} - \text{discount} = \text{proceeds}$$

The proceeds of a $1,000, non-interest-bearing, 60-day promissory note discounted at 6 percent would be $990, determined as follows:

$$\$1,000 - \left(\$1,000 \times .06 \times \frac{60}{360}\right) = \$990$$

Whereas the determination of the proceeds of a discounted non-interest-bearing instrument is a simple arithmetic problem, the determination of the proceeds of a discounted interest-bearing instrument may not be as simple. The procedure, however, is exactly the same. The difficulty lies in the quantity of work involved rather than in its complexity. For example, the proceeds of a $1,000, 6 percent, 90-day promissory note, discounted at the bank at 7 percent, 60 days before maturity, would be $1,003.16, determined as follows:

$$\text{Proceeds} = \text{maturity value} - \text{discount}$$
$$\text{Maturity value} = \text{principal} + \text{interest}$$
$$\text{Maturity value} = \$1,000 + \left(\$1,000 \times .06 \times \frac{90}{360}\right)$$
$$\text{Maturity value} = \underline{\underline{\$1,015}}$$
$$\text{Discount} = \$1,015 \times .07 \times \frac{60}{360}$$
$$\text{Discount} = \$11.84$$
$$\text{Proceeds} = \underline{\underline{\$1,003.16}} \ (\$1,015 - \$11.84)$$

ACCOUNTING FOR PROMISSORY NOTES

A promissory note was defined as an unconditional promise, in writing, to pay a definite sum of money at a specified time. From an accounting standpoint, promissory notes logically fall into two broad categories, notes receivable and notes payable.

Accounting for Notes Receivable

The entries to record the **receipt** of a note and those to record its **collection** are the major factors in accounting for notes receivable. The form of these entries depends on whether the note is interest-bearing or non-interest-bearing.

For illustrative purposes, let us assume that in each of the following cases we, as owners of an appliance store, receive a note from Jack Wollman, a customer, to apply on his account. Let us also assume that the note is:

CASE 1 Interest-bearing (a $1,000, 6 percent, 60-day instrument)

CASE 2 Non-interest-bearing (a $1,000, 60-day instrument, which we accept at a 6 percent discount)

The entries which follow record the **receipt** of the note in each case.

Interest-bearing Note

Notes Receivable	1,000	
Accounts Receivable (Jack Wollman)		1,000

Non-interest-bearing Note

Notes Receivable	1,000	
Accounts Receivable (Jack Wollman)		990
Interest Revenue*		10

*The accounts Interest Revenue and Interest Expense are ordinarily used to record discount as well as interest.

The entries to record the **collection** of the note would appear as shown.

Interest-bearing Note

Cash	1,000	
Notes Receivable		1,000
Interest Revenue		10

Non-interest-bearing Note

Cash	1,000	
Notes Receivable		1,000

Accounting for Notes Payable

When accounting for notes payable, our primary consideration is the entries which record the issuance and the payment of a note. As was true of entries for notes receivable, the form taken by entries for notes payable depends on whether the instrument is interest-bearing or non-interest-bearing.

Let us assume that in each of the following cases we issue a note to Ace Supply, a creditor, to apply on our account. Let us also assume that the note is:

CASE 1 Interest-bearing (a $1,000, 6 percent, 60-day instrument)

CASE 2 Non-interest-bearing (a $1,000, 60-day instrument which Ace Supply accepts at a 6 percent discount)

The entries which follow record the **issuance** of the note in each case.

Interest-bearing Note

Accounts Payable (Ace Supply)	1,000	
Notes Payable		1,000

Non-interest-bearing Note

Accounts Payable (Ace Supply)	990	
Interest Expense	10	
Notes Payable		1,000

The entries to record the **payment** of the note would appear as shown.

Interest-bearing Note

Notes Payable	1,000	
Interest Expense	10	
Cash		1,010

Non-interest-bearing Note

Notes Payable	1,000	
Cash		1,000

Notes Receivable Discounted

It is not uncommon for the holder of a promissory note to negotiate the instrument before maturity. That is, he may transfer it by endorsement either to a bank or other financial institution for cash, or to a creditor to apply on account. Because such notes are ordinarily negotiated at amounts less than their maturity values, the procedure is commonly known as the **discounting of notes receivable.**

When a note receivable is discounted, the required computations involve the determination of:

1 Maturity value $(P + I)$

2 Time (the days the instrument has yet to run, stated as a fraction of a year)

3 Discount $(MV \times R \times T)$

4 Proceeds $(MV - D)$

To illustrate, let us assume that 30 days before maturity we discount at 7 percent a $1,000, 6 percent, 90-day note at the bank for cash. The computation would be:

Maturity value [$1,000 + $15($1,000 $\times$ .06 $\times$ 90/360)]	$1,015.00
Less: Discount ($1,015 $\times$ .07 $\times$ 30/360)	5.92
Proceeds	$1,009.08

This transaction would be recorded in general journal form as shown.

Cash	1,009.08	
Notes Receivable		1,000.00
Interest Revenue		9.08

If the proceeds in our illustration had been *less* than the face value of the note, the difference would have been debited to the Interest Expense account instead of credited to the Interest Revenue account.

If the note being discounted had been a non-interest-bearing instrument instead of an interest-bearing one, the proceeds would be $994.17, determined as follows:

Maturity value (face of the instrument)	$1,000.00
Less: Discount ($1,000 × .07 × 30/360)	5.83
Proceeds	$ 994.17

This transaction would be recorded in general journal form as follows:

Cash	994.17	
Interest Expense	5.83	
Notes Receivable		1,000.00

If the note in our illustration had been taken originally at a discount, the difference between the face value and the proceeds would be debited to the Interest Revenue account to the extent of the amount originally recognized; any excess would then be charged to the Interest Expense account.

When a note receivable is discounted, the endorser becomes contingently liable. Thus, if the maker of the instrument fails to pay at maturity, the endorser becomes responsible to the bank or other endorsee for its payment. The contingent liability arising from the discounting of notes receivable is ordinarily reported on the balance sheet either as a notation in the liability section or as a footnote at the bottom of the statement. The following notation is typical:

Note: As of December 31, 19X4, the company was contingently liable for notes receivable discounted in the amount of $10,000.

Notes Receivable Dishonored

If the maker of a promissory note fails to pay it when it becomes due, the note is commonly known as a **dishonored note.** The accounting treatment of a dishonored note depends upon whether it is still on hand or has been discounted.

If the instrument is still on hand, it is usually reclassified from a note receivable to an account receivable. This is appropriate, inasmuch as the instrument is no longer negotiable. Assuming that a $1,000, 6 percent, 120-day promissory note given us by John Jones is dishonored at maturity, we would make the following entry:

Accounts Receivable (John Jones)	1,020	
Notes Receivable		1,000
Interest Revenue ($1,000 × .06 × 120/360)		20

If, instead of keeping Jones's note on hand, we had discounted it at the bank or other financial institution or with a creditor, at the time of dishonor we would become obligated to pay and would make the following entry:

| Accounts Receivable (John Jones) _____ | 1,020 | |
| Cash _____ | | 1,020 |

End-of-period Adjustments

A promissory note acquired or given in one accounting period may not mature until a subsequent period. When this happens, it becomes necessary to make an end-of-period adjustment in order to apportion the interest (either revenue or expense) to the period in which it belongs. For example, when interest is not paid until the note matures, it is necessary to adjust for the amount that has accumulated, or **accrued.** Similarly, when interest (discount) is paid in advance, the recognition of that portion which pertains to the future must be postponed, or **deferred.** We shall examine adjusting entries in detail when we study accruals and deferrals in Chapter 9.

ACCOUNTING FOR MORTGAGES AND BONDS

Promissory notes such as those we have been studying are generally classified as short-term credit instruments, because the time elapsing between their issue and maturity is relatively short. Mortgages and bonds, however, are ordinarily considered to be long-term instruments.

On the whole, the process of accounting for mortgages and bonds is the same for both the issuer and the holder, the only major difference being that the instruments are liabilities to the former and assets to the latter. For this reason, we shall examine the accounting treatment of long-term credit instruments from the issuer's viewpoint only.

Accounting for Mortgage Notes Payable

The issuance of a mortgage is one of the simplest forms of long-term borrowing, and the accounting problems involved are also relatively simple. The debt is evidenced by a promissory note, which is essentially the same as any other promissory note except that it includes a reference to the accompanying mortgage, which is security for it. The entries to record the issuance of the mortgage, the payment of periodic interest, and the eventual retirement of the mortgage are the chief factors to be considered.

To illustrate the entries involved, let us assume that the Smetana Lumber Company borrows $100,000 from the Southern Loan Company in order to build a new warehouse. Let us also assume that the lumber company gives the loan company a mortgage note as of January 1, 1972, which carries an interest rate of 5 percent per year, payable annually on December 31, and that the mortgage is for 10 years.

The Smetana Lumber Company's entry to record the issuance of the mortgage on January 1, 1972, would be:

Cash _____ 100,000
     Mortgage Notes Payable_____   100,000

Its entry to record the annual payment of periodic interest would be:

Interest Expense_____ 5,000
     Cash _____   5,000

Finally, the entry to record the retirement of the mortgage on December 31, 1981, would be:

Mortgage Notes Payable_____ 100,000
     Cash _____   100,000

Accounting for Bonds Payable

When business organizations require more money for operations than they can obtain from their usual lending sources, they frequently sell bonds to the investing public. Bonds are bought and sold on the bond market in much the same way that stocks are traded on the stock market.

The use of bonds as a means of long-term financing results in transactions that must be reflected in the accounting records. In accounting for bonds payable, entries are required to record the issuance of the bonds, the payment of periodic interest, and the retirement of the bonds at maturity.

Bonds are sold either at their **par value** (face value), **below par,** or **above par.** Although the borrower (issuer of the bonds) stipulates both a par value and a rate of interest for the bonds before they are issued, he has no way of predicting precisely what they will sell for when they are put on the market or what the actual rate of interest will be. These factors will be determined by the interplay of supply and demand and depend primarily upon the rate of interest offered on the bonds and the prevailing rate offered for comparable bonds. We shall study the pricing of bonds in more detail in Chapter 13.

The entries required at both the date of issuance and date of payment of periodic interest are dependent upon the price received when the bonds are issued; however, the liability incurred by their issuance is ordinarily reflected in the Bonds Payable account at par, because this is the amount that must be repaid at maturity.

Bonds Issued at Par   To illustrate the entries involved when bonds are issued at par, let us assume that a $100,000, 10-year bond issue, bearing interest at 6 percent and payable annually on December 31, is issued at par on January 1, 1974, by the Carter Storage Company in order to finance the purchase of a fleet of trucks.

The company's entry to record the issuance of the bonds on January 1, 1974, would be:

Cash _____ 100,000
    Bonds Payable _____   100,000

Its entry to record the annual payment of interest would be:

Interest Expense _____ 6,000
    Cash _____   6,000

Its entry to record the retirement of the bonds on December 31, 1983, would be:

Bonds Payable _____ 100,000
    Cash _____   100,000

Bonds Issued at a Discount When bonds sell for less than par, they are said to sell at a **discount.** This happens when the prevailing market rate of interest for comparable bonds is greater than the rate stipulated on the bonds being sold. For example, if a particular bond issue stipulates a 6 percent interest rate but the prevailing rate for comparable bonds is 7 percent, the 6 percent bonds will sell only at a discount because investors will be unwilling to buy the bonds at par. When bonds are issued at a discount, the total interest cost to the borrower over the life of the bonds consists of the total of the periodic interest payments plus the amount of the discount. Thus, in reality discount is interest paid in advance.

To illustrate the entries involved when bonds are issued at a discount, let us assume the same information used in the preceding illustration except that the bonds are issued by the Carter Storage Company at 98 percent of par, or for $98,000. The company's entry to record the issuance of the bonds on January 1, 1974, would be:

Cash _____ 98,000
Discount on Bonds Payable_____ 2,000
    Bonds Payable _____   100,000

The entries to record the annual payment of periodic interest and the allocation of discount would be:

Interest Expense _____ 6,000
    Cash _____   6,000
Interest Expense _____ 200
    Discount on Bonds Payable ($\frac{1}{10} \times \$2,000$)_____   200

The entry to record the retirement of the bonds on December 31, 1983, would be:

Bonds Payable _____ 100,000
    Cash _____   100,000

    Note that in the illustration the discount is allocated over the life of the bonds on a straight-line basis; that is, one-tenth of the total is allocated to each year. There are other ways in which this allocation, usually called **amortization,** may be made; some of these will be discussed in Chapter 13.

Bonds Issued at a Premium   When bonds sell for more than par, they are said to sell at a **premium.** This happens when the rate of interest stipulated on the bonds is greater than the prevailing market rate for comparable bonds. For example, if a particular bond issue stipulates a 6 percent interest rate, but investors are willing to settle for only 5 percent on their investments, the bonds, in order to yield 5 percent, will sell at a premium. When bonds are issued at a premium, the total interest cost to the borrower over the life of the bonds is equal to the total of the periodic interest payments minus the amount of the premium. Thus, the investor's payment of bond premium actually results in a reduction in the borrower's interest expense.

    Bond premium is allocated over the life of the bonds in the same way as bond discount, except that it has the opposite effect on the Interest Expense account. That is, the amortization of bond discount has an increasing effect on the Interest Expense account, whereas the amortization of bond premium has a decreasing effect on it.

    To illustrate the entries involved when bonds are issued at a premium, let us assume the same facts employed in the preceding illustrations except that the bonds are issued at 102 percent of par, or for $102,000. The entry to record the issuance of the bonds on January 1, 1974, would be:

Cash _____ 102,000
    Premium on Bonds Payable_____   2,000
    Bonds Payable _____   100,000

The entries to record the annual payment of periodic interest and the allocation of premium would be:

Interest Expense_____ 6,000
    Cash _____   6,000
Premium on Bonds Payable_____ 200
    Interest Expense ($\frac{1}{10} \times \$2,000$)_____   200

Finally, the entry to record the retirement of the bonds on December 31, 1983, would be:

Bonds Payable _____ 100,000
    Cash _____   100,000

SUMMARY

When goods or services are bought or sold on "open account," there is simply an oral agreement or mutual understanding between the buyer and seller that the seller's terms regarding payment will be met. At times, however, these agreements are replaced by formal written documents, often referred to as **credit instruments.** Typical credit instruments are promissory notes, mortgage notes, and bonds.

From an accounting standpoint, the problems associated with credit instruments are those involved in (1) the issuance of the instrument, (2) the payment of periodic interest, and (3) the payment of the instrument at maturity. These problems may become somewhat complicated because a promissory note may be either interest-bearing or non-interest-bearing, and bonds may be issued at a discount or a premium, as well as at par.

QUESTIONS AND PROBLEMS

6-1 What is a **negotiable instrument?**

6-2 List the negotiable instruments which most often serve as substitutes for money.

6-3 What is a **promissory note?** A **mortgage?** A **bond?**

6-4 What is a **blank endorsement?** A **special endorsement?** A **qualified endorsement?** A **restrictive endorsement?**

6-5 Distinguish between (1) interest and bank discount, (2) face value and maturity value, (3) an interest-bearing and a non-interest-bearing note.

6-6 Distinguish between a cashier's check and a certified check.

6-7 **Instructions** Determine the maturity date of each of the following notes:

	Date of Note	Term of Note
(1)	January 5, 19X1	30 days
(2)	March 16, 19X1	60 days
(3)	April 22, 19X1	120 days
(4)	July 6, 19X1	90 days
(5)	July 6, 19X1	3 months

6-8 Instructions Determine the number of days between the following dates:

    (1) March 19, 19X1, and July 1, 19X1

    (2) June 3, 19X1, and July 14, 19X1

    (3) July 6, 19X1, and November 5, 19X1

    (4) October 10, 19X1, and January 3, 19X2

    (5) December 1, 19X1, and February 1, 19X2

6-9 Instructions State the basic formula for computing interest, and determine the amount of interest on each of the following principal amounts.

	Principal Amount	Time, Days	Rate of Interest, %
(1)	$10,400	90	3
(2)	9,600	60	4
(3)	14,400	102	5
(4)	8,400	87	6
(5)	7,600	99	7

6-10 Instructions Determine the amount of interest on each of the following principal amounts, using the 6 percent method.

	Principal Amount	Time, Days	Rate of Interest, %
(1)	$1,235	60	6
(2)	2,610	66	6
(3)	4,500	69	6
(4)	7,200	87	6
(5)	9,570	58	6

6-11 Instructions Determine the maturity value of each of the following notes:

	Face Value of Note	Time, Days	Rate of Interest, %
(1)	$2,500	90	4
(2)	3,200	80	5
(3)	3,800	48	6
(4)	4,500	36	7
(5)	5,600	120	8

6-12 Instructions Determine the proceeds of each of the following non-interest-bearing notes, assuming that they are discounted on the dates and at the rates indicated.

	Face Value	Terms, Days	Date of Note	Date of Discount	Rate of Discount, %
(1)	$5,400	30	Mar. 1, 19X1	Mar. 1, 19X1	3
(2)	4,800	60	Apr. 5, 19X1	Apr. 5, 19X1	4
(3)	7,200	40	June 10, 19X1	June 10, 19X1	5
(4)	4,200	80	July 15, 19X1	July 20, 19X1	6
(5)	3,800	90	Aug. 5, 19X1	Aug. 23, 19X1	7

6-13 Instructions Determine the proceeds of each of the following notes, assuming that they are discounted on the dates and at the rates indicated.

	Face Value	Terms, Days	Date of Note	Date of Discount	Rate of Discount, %
(1)	$6,600	4%, 60	Mar. 5, 19X1	Mar. 5, 19X1	6
(2)	6,000	5%, 90	Apr. 8, 19X1	Apr. 8, 19X1	8
(3)	8,300	6%, 120	June 10, 19X1	June 22, 19X1	5
(4)	5,400	6%, 50	Aug. 15, 19X1	Aug. 20, 19X1	8
(5)	4,800	5%, 30	Sept. 20, 19X1	Oct. 10, 19X1	6

6-14 On June 16, 19X5, the Nessinger Company receives a 90-day, non-interest-bearing, $6,000 note from the Odmark Company, a customer, to apply on account.

Instructions Assuming that the Nessinger Company accepts the note, which is dated June 16, 19X5, at 5 percent discount, prepare in general journal form:

(1) The Nessinger Company's entry to record the acceptance of the note

(2) The Nessinger Company's entry to record the payment at maturity

(3) The Odmark Company's entry to record the issuance of the note

(4) The Odmark Company's entry to record the payment at maturity

6-15 On September 16, 19X4, the Solomon Company receives a 120-day, 5 percent, $1,800 note from Mike Looney, a customer, to apply on account.

Instructions Assuming that the Solomon Company accepts the note, dated August 17, 19X4, at 6 percent discount, prepare in general journal form:

(1) The Solomon Company's entry to record the acceptance of the note

(2) The Solomon Company's entry to record the payment at maturity

(3) Looney's entry to record the issuance of the note

(4) Looney's entry to record the payment at maturity

6-16 Instructions Prepare in general journal form the entries necessary to record the following transactions in the books of the Kemp Company.

(1) On June 5, 19X4, James Ray gives the Kemp Company a $2,000, 4 percent, 90-day note to apply on account. The note, dated June 5, 19X4, is accepted by the company at its face value.

(2) On July 5, 19X4, the company discounts the note at the bank at a discount rate of 6 percent.

(3) On September 4, 19X4, the Kemp Company receives notice from the bank that Ray failed to pay the note at its maturity and that the bank has charged the company's account for the maturity value of the note.

6-17 The Craig Ehlen Company is in need of a short-term loan of approximately $9,800. The following three alternatives are available:

(1) Bank A will accept a $10,000, 90-day, non-interest-bearing note, discounted at 6 percent.

(2) Bank B will accept a $9,850, 90-day, 6 percent note, discounted at 7 percent.

(3) Bank C will accept a $9,850, 90-day, 6 percent note, discounted at 5 percent.

Instructions Indicate which of the alternatives you consider to be the most desirable and which the least desirable. Explain briefly.

6-18 On June 1, Don Leaf purchases $5,000 worth of merchandise from the Berger Company on terms of 2/10, n/30. Leaf is not in a position to pay for the merchandise within the discount period unless he borrows the money from the bank. The bank agrees to lend him the amount he needs if he will sign a 60-day, 6 percent note for it.

Instructions Assuming that Leaf borrows the money from the bank on their terms and that he records purchases at gross,

(1) Prepare in general journal form an:
   (a) Entry to record the issuance of the note to the bank
   (b) Entry to record the payment to the Berger Company
   (c) Entry to record the payment of the note (plus interest, if any) at maturity

(2) Prepare an analysis showing the extent to which it was profitable (or unprofitable) for Leaf to borrow the money in order to pay the Berger Company.

6-19 On March 1, Paul Duckworth purchases from the Johnson Company $5,000 worth of merchandise subject to a 2.98 percent discount if paid for within 10 days. Duckworth is not in a position to pay for the merchandise within the discount period unless he borrows the money from the bank. The bank agrees to lend him the amount he needs if he will sign a 120-day, non-interest-bearing note which, when discounted at 6 percent, will give him exactly the amount of cash he needs to pay the Johnson Company.

Instructions Assuming that Duckworth borrows the money from the bank on their terms:

(1) Prepare in general journal form an:
   (a) Entry to record the issuance of the note to the bank
   (b) Entry to record the payment to the Johnson Company
   (c) Entry to record the payment of the note at maturity

(2) Prepare an analysis showing the extent to which it was profitable (or unprofitable) for Duckworth to borrow the money in order to pay the Johnson Company.

6-20 **Instructions** In each of the following cases, prepare in general journal form the entry or entries necessary to record (1) the issuance of the bonds, (2) the payment of periodic interest, and (3) the retirement of the bonds.

CASE 1 A $200,000, 10-year bond issue, bearing interest at $6\frac{1}{2}$ percent and payable annually on December 31, is issued at par on January 1, 1973.

CASE 2 A $300,000, 10-year bond issue, bearing interest at 8 percent and payable annually on December 31, is issued at 104 percent of par on January 1, 1973.

CASE 3 A $400,000, 10-year bond issue, bearing interest at 5 percent and payable annually on December 31, is issued at $97\frac{1}{2}$ percent of par on January 1, 1973.

7

Accounting for Cash Transactions

In Chapter 5 it was pointed out that the bulk of the business transacted in the United States is done on a credit basis. Although this is true, it must be recognized that practically all of a business enterprise's credit transactions eventually affect its cash resources. Thus, the volume of transactions that flows through the Cash account is, as a general rule, much greater than that flowing through any other account.

Our primary purpose in this chapter is to study methods of accounting for cash transactions; it is important, however, that we first become familiar with the role accounting plays in the effective control of the receipt and disbursement of an organization's cash.

INTERNAL CONTROL

The procedures employed in the control of an organization's assets are usually referred to collectively as its system of internal control. **Internal control** is defined by the committee on auditing procedure of the American Institute of Certified Public Accountants[1] as the plan and all the measures employed by a business organization to safeguard its assets, check the accuracy and reliability of its accounting data, promote operational efficiency, and encourage adherence to prescribed managerial policies.

This concept of internal control is perhaps broader than the meaning sometimes attributed to the term. The AICPA's definition recognizes that a system of internal control extends beyond those matters which relate directly to the functions of the accounting and financial departments. When used in the broad sense, the term internal control includes both accounting and administrative controls.

Accounting controls are employed chiefly for the purpose of protecting assets and ensuring the reliability of the accounting records. They include systems of authorization and approval and the separation of duties concerned with record keeping from those concerned with operations or the custody of assets. **Administrative controls,** on the other hand, are established mainly to ensure operational efficiency and adherence to managerial policies, and relate only indirectly to the accounting records. They generally include statistical analyses, time and motion studies, performance reports, employee training programs, and product inspection and quality controls.

A satisfactory system of internal control, then, generally will include:

1 A plan of organization which provides for the appropriate segregation of functional responsibilities

2 A system of authorization and record procedures adequate to provide reasonable accounting control over assets, liabilities, revenues, and expenses

3 The establishment of sound practices to be followed in the performance of the duties and functions of each of the organizational departments

4 The employment of personnel of a quality commensurate with responsibilities

Internal Control over Cash

The resources of a business enterprise more often than not are entrusted to management and employees who have little, if any, ownership interest in the enterprise. Thus, to be effective, an organization's accounting system must be designed to protect against the possible mismanagement or dishonest use of these resources.

---

[1] The American Institute of Certified Public Accountants (AICPA) is the national organization of certified public accountants. Its numerous committees and publications have been influential in the development of accounting theory and practice. Prior to 1959, much of the AICPA's work in these areas was published in its *Accounting Research Bulletins.* In 1959, the AICPA created the Accounting Principles Board (APB), which has the authority to issue pronouncements, or opinions, which are commonly regarded as official written expressions of generally accepted accounting principles and practices. We shall refer to the AICPA's bulletins and the APB's opinions in this text as the occasion arises.

Because cash transactions are so numerous, it is imperative that they be handled in a systematic and routine fashion. At the same time adequate safeguards must be provided, since cash is greatly desired by many, is easily concealed and transported, and is readily converted into other types of assets. The following procedures, not all of which will be appropriate in every situation, are usually considered necessary for a satisfactory system of internal control over cash:

1 The functions of record keeping and the custodianship of cash should be kept separate.

2 The number of employees who have access to cash should be limited.

3 Persons who are to have responsibility for handling cash should be specifically designated.

4 Cash on hand should be held to a minimum, with banking facilities being utilized to the greatest extent possible.

5 Cash on hand should be protected physically by the employment of such devices as cash registers, cashiers' cages, and safes.

6 All employees having access to cash should be bonded.

7 Periodic checks of cash on hand should be made by an individual who does not handle or record cash.

8 All cash receipts should be recorded promptly.

9 All cash receipts should be deposited promptly.

10 All cash should be disbursed by check.

ACCOUNTING FOR CASH RECEIPTS

In most businesses, cash payments for goods or services are received either by mail or over the counter in the form of checks or currency. All cash received by an organization should be recorded promptly in the proper book of original entry, and unless the amount is relatively insignificant, cash receipts should be deposited intact daily.

When only a small number of transactions are involved, a simple cash receipts journal such as the single-column one illustrated in Chapter 4 will probably be adequate. However, when the volume of transactions increases and controlling accounts are installed, it frequently becomes necessary to expand the single-column journal. This is accomplished simply by adding extra columns. As was noted in Chapter 5, multicolumn journals are often referred to as **columnar journals.**

Columnar Cash Receipts Journal

The number and types of special columns in a columnar cash receipts journal will vary in different business enterprises. However, most organizations will require a journal that includes at least a cash debit column, a sales discount debit column, an accounts receivable credit column, and a general ledger credit column.

Recording in the Columnar Cash Receipts Journal   The five transactions involving the receipt of cash in the basic data for the Pendery illustration on pages 101 and 102 would be recorded in a columnar cash receipts journal as shown.

Columnar Cash Receipts Journal   *Page 3*

Date		Account Credited	Explanation	PR	Debit		Credit	
					Cash	*Sales Discount*	*Accounts Receivable*	*General Ledger*
1972								
May	1	Ralph Pendery, Capital	Investment	301	3,000			3,000
	5	Sales	Cash sales	401	200			200
	12	George Myers	On account	114	392	8	400	
	16	Wilson Ashby	On account	116	100		100	
	20	R. Lawson	On account	117	297	3	300	
	31	Totals			3,989	11	800	3,200
					(101)	(402)	(110)	(✓)

Posting from the Columnar Cash Receipts Journal   Each amount in the general ledger credit column of the columnar cash receipts journal is posted to the corresponding general ledger account in the account credited column.   Thus, the $3,000 amount opposite Pendery's name is posted to the credit side of the Ralph Pendery, Capital account.   Similarly, the $200 amount opposite "sales" is posted to the credit side of the Sales account.   The total of the general ledger credit column is not posted, since the amounts that make up the total have all been posted directly to the general ledger.   The total is checked (✓) to show that it is not posted.

Each amount in the accounts receivable credit column is posted to the credit side of the corresponding customer's account in the accounts receivable subsidiary ledger.   The total of the accounts receivable credit column ($800 in this instance) is posted as a credit to the Accounts Receivable account in the general ledger. After this posting, the controlling account and the subsidiary ledger should be in agreement.

The amounts in the sales discount debit column are not posted individually, but the total of the column is posted as a debit to the Sales Discount account in the general ledger.   It should be noted, however, that Myers and Lawson received credit for the discount, as shown by the gross amounts ($400 and $300) in the accounts receivable credit column, although they only paid $392 and $297, the net amounts.

The amounts in the cash debit column, like those in the sales discount debit column, are not posted individually, but the total is posted as a debit to the Cash account in the general ledger.

Note that the inclusion of a special column for accounts receivable credit in the columnar cash receipts journal expedites the posting of the individual amounts to the accounts receivable subsidiary ledger and the total to the Accounts Receivable controlling account in the general ledger.

Only the accounts involved when Pendery's cash receipts were recorded for the month of May are shown in the ledgers which follow.

General Ledger

Cash   Account No. 101

Apr.	30		CR1	9,980	00	Apr.	30		CD1	5,583	00
							30	Balance	$\checkmark$	4,397	00
				9,980	00					9,980	00
May	1	Balance	$\checkmark$	4,397	00						
	31		CR3	3,989	00						

Accounts Receivable   Account No. 110

May	1	Balance	$\checkmark$	225	00	May	31		CR3	800	00
	31		S2	1,475	00						

Ralph Pendery, Capital   Account No. 301

Apr.	30	Balance	$\checkmark$	8,104	00	Apr.	1		CR1	8,000	00
							30	Closing	J1	104	00
				8,104	00					8,104	00
						May	1	Balance	$\checkmark$	8,104	00
							1		CR3	3,000	00

Sales   Account No. 401

Apr.	30	Closing	J1	1,205	00	Apr.	15		CR1	235	00
							30		CR1	700	00
							30		S1	270	00
				1,205	00					1,205	00
						May	5		CR3	200	00
							31		S2	1,475	00

Sales Discount   Account No. 402

May	31		CR3	11	00						

Accounts Receivable Ledger

George Myers   Account No. *114*

May	2		S2	400	00	May	12		CR3	400	00

Wilson Ashby   Account No. *116*

May	13		S2	100	00	May	16		CR3	100	00

R. Lawson   Account No. *117*

May	16		S2	300	00	May	20		CR3	300	00

From careful observation of the postings from the columnar cash receipts journal, we can see that the debits and credits in the general ledger have been kept in balance, while at the same time the total of the balances of the customers' accounts in the subsidiary ledger has been kept equal to the balance in the controlling account in the general ledger.

ACCOUNTING FOR CASH DISBURSEMENTS

As was emphasized earlier when internal control over cash was discussed, cash should be disbursed only upon specific authorization, and whenever possible by check. When an organization engages in relatively few cash transactions, a single-column cash disbursements journal generally will be adequate for recording them. However, when there are many cash transactions and controlling accounts are employed, it usually becomes necessary to expand the single-column journal by adding special columns, thus creating a multicolumn journal designed to handle in a systematic and routine fashion the bulk of transactions entering it.

Columnar Cash Disbursements Journal

The number and types of special columns contained in a columnar cash disbursements journal will vary in different business enterprises. Most organizations, however, will require a journal that contains at least a general ledger debit column, an accounts payable debit column, a purchase discount credit column, and a cash credit column.

Recording in the Columnar Cash Disbursements Journal The nine transactions involving the disbursement of cash in the basic data for the Pendery illustration on pages 101 and 102 would be recorded in a columnar cash disbursements journal as shown.

Columnar Cash Disbursements Journal   *Page 4*

Date		Account Debited	Explanation	PR	Debit General Ledger	Debit Accounts Payable	Credit Purchase Discount	Credit Cash
1972								
May	1	Advertising	In the *Times*	501	100			100
	1	Purchases	Cash purchases	505	800			800
	4	Store Supplies	For use	141	30			30
	10	The Long Company	Paid in full	204		700	14	686
	18	The Hart Company	Paid in full	207		450		450
	21	The Graham Company	Paid in full	208		200	2	198
	31	Sales Salary	For May	507	60			60
	31	Transportation In	On merchandise	514	70			70
	31	Miscellaneous Expense	Miscellaneous	508	40			40
	31	Totals			1,100	1,350	16	2,434
					(✓)	(200)	(512)	(101)

Posting from the Columnar Cash Disbursements Journal   Each amount in the general ledger debit column is posted individually from the columnar cash disbursements journal to the corresponding general ledger account in the account debited column.   For example, the $100 amount opposite "advertising" is posted as a debit to the Advertising account in the general ledger, while the $800 amount opposite "purchases" is posted as a debit to the Purchases account in the general ledger.   The total of the general ledger debit column is not posted, since the amounts that make up the total have all been posted directly to the general ledger.   Again, as with the columnar cash receipts journal, the total is checked (✓) to show that it is not posted.

Each amount in the accounts payable debit column is posted individually to the debit side of the particular creditor's account in the accounts payable subsidiary ledger.   The total of the accounts payable debit column ($1,350 in this instance) is posted as a debit to the Accounts Payable account in the general ledger.   After these postings, the controlling account and the subsidiary ledger should be in agreement.

The amounts in the purchase discount credit column are not posted individually, but the total of the column is posted as a credit to the Purchase Discount account in the general ledger.   Note, however, that Pendery received credit for the discounts taken, as shown by the credits for $700 and $200 in the accounts payable debit column, even though he paid only the net amounts ($686 and $198).

Again, the amounts in the cash credit column are not posted individually, but the total is posted as a credit to the Cash account in the general ledger.

Note that the special column for accounts payable debit expedites the posting of the individual amounts to the accounts payable subsidiary ledger and the total to the Accounts Payable controlling account in the general ledger.

For illustrative purposes, only the accounts involved when Pendery's cash disbursements for the month of May were recorded are shown in the ledgers which follow.

General Ledger

Cash — Account No. 101

Date			Ref	Debit		Date				Ref	Credit	
Apr.	30		CR1	9,980	00	Apr.	30			CD1	5,583	00
							30	Balance		√	4,397	00
				9,980	00						9,980	00
May	1	Balance	√	4,397	00	May	31			CD4	2,434	00
	31		CR3	3,989	00							

Store Supplies — Account No. 141

Date			Ref	Debit		Date			Ref	Credit	
Apr.	10		CD1	40	00	Apr.	30	Adjusting	J1	10	00
May	4		CD4	30	00						

Accounts Payable — Account No. 200

Date			Ref	Debit		Date				Ref	Credit	
May	31		CD4	1,350	00	May	1	Balance		√	650	00
							31			P2	2,500	00

Advertising — Account No. 501

Date			Ref	Debit		Date			Ref	Credit	
May	1		CD4	100	00						

Purchases — Account No. 505

Date			Ref	Debit		Date			Ref	Credit	
Apr.	3		CD1	2,000	00	Apr.	30	Adjusting	J1	4,550	00
	4		CD1	1,000	00						
	15		CD1	1,000	00						
	30		P1	550	00						
				4,550	00					4,550	00
May	1		CD4	800	00						
	31		P2	2,500	00						

Sales Salary — Account No. 507

Date			Ref	Debit		Date			Ref	Credit	
Apr.	30		CD1	60	00	Apr.	30	Closing	J1	60	00
May	31		CD4	60	00						

Miscellaneous Expense — Account No. 508

Apr.	30		CD1	75	00	Apr.	30	Closing	J1	75	00
May	31		CD4	40	00						

Purchase Discount — Account No. 512

						May	31		CD4	16	00

Transportation In — Account No. 514

May	31		CD4	70	00

Accounts Payable Ledger

The Long Company — Account No. 204

May	10		CD4	700	00	May	1		P2	700	00

The Hart Company — Account No. 207

May	18		CD4	450	00	May	14		P2	450	00

The Graham Company — Account No. 208

May	21		CD4	200	00	May	17		P2	200	00

By studying the postings from the columnar cash disbursements journal, we can see that the debits and credits in the general ledger have been kept in balance, and that the sum of the balances of the creditors' accounts in the subsidiary ledger has been kept in balance with the controlling account in the general ledger.

PETTY CASH TRANSACTIONS

Although control over cash transactions is best maintained by making all disbursements by check, there are a few occasions when this procedure is impractical. For example, in most businesses it is necessary at times to make small, or petty, disbursements of cash for such things as the payment of a few cents' postage due on incoming mail or small purchases of supply items, usually of an emergency nature, such as thumb tacks, glue, or window cleaner.

Needless to say, a transaction such as the payment of postage due can be handled more conveniently with cash than with a check. To provide for situations of this nature, most businesses set up **petty cash funds.** Although various procedures for handling petty cash transactions are available, one of the most satisfactory is the **imprest system.** Under this method, a fund is established at a fixed amount and is periodically reimbursed for the exact amount needed to bring it back to its fixed amount.

Establishing the Petty Cash Fund

To establish a petty cash fund under an imprest system, a check is issued for the amount decided upon, payable to "Petty Cash" or to the person designated to serve as custodian and cashier of the fund. (The **petty cash cashier** may be the regular cashier, a receptionist, a switchboard operator, or any employee whose working position is conveniently located and whose regular duties are not incompatible with those of a cashier.) The check is cashed and the money placed in the petty cash box, drawer, or envelope.

The only entry required when the fund is established is one to record the issuance of the check. If we assume that the fund is to be set up in the amount of $50, the entry in general journal form would be:

Petty Cash	50	
Cash		50

Reimbursing the Petty Cash Fund

Payments are made from the petty cash fund as the need arises, but individual disbursements are not recorded in the books of original entry and posted to the ledger accounts until the cash in the fund has been reduced to a predetermined reimbursement point or until a prescribed period of time, perhaps two weeks or a month, has elapsed. At this time, the fund is reimbursed for the accumulated total of the individual payments from the fund; this should bring it up to its fixed amount. The check for reimbursement, like the one to establish the fund, is made out to "Petty Cash" or to the custodian.

Reimbursements are usually recorded in the cash disbursements journal, with the appropriate accounts being charged (debited) for the individual payments. To illustrate, let us assume a reimbursement of $45 composed of $15 freight on incoming merchandise, $10 postage, and $20 for advertising in the school paper. The reimbursement entry in general journal form would be:

Transportation In	15	
Postage	10	
Advertising	20	
Cash		45

Petty Cash Over and Short

Occasionally at the time of reimbursement the composition of the petty cash fund (the amount on hand plus evidence supporting unreimbursed disbursements) will be greater or less than the fixed amount of the fund. When this happens, the fund is ordinarily reimbursed to its fixed amount. The difference between the amount of the composition of the fund and the fixed amount is then either debited, if the amount of the composition is **short** of the fixed amount, or credited, if it is **over** the fixed amount, to an account called Petty Cash Over and Short. At the end of the fiscal period, the balance in the Petty Cash Over and Short account is treated as a miscellaneous revenue or expense item in the income statement.

To illustrate the entry to record a shortage in petty cash, let us assume that at the date of reimbursement the $50 petty cash fund illustrated previously contained evidence supporting disbursements of $45 (composed of $15 freight on incoming merchandise, $10 postage, and $20 for advertising) but only $4 in cash. In general journal form, the entry would be:

Transportation In	15	
Postage	10	
Advertising	20	
Petty Cash Over and Short	1	
Cash		46

Petty Cash Voucher

While the petty cash cashier in some organizations has the authority to both approve and make disbursements from the petty cash fund, other businesses may set up stricter controls by requiring authorization by one person and payment by another. In this case, a document called a **petty cash voucher** is generally employed to authorize the payment; it also serves as a receipt for the payment once it has been made. Vouchers will be discussed in more detail in Chapter 8.

BANK TRANSACTIONS

Organizations with sound accounting systems employ banking facilities to the greatest extent possible. This has several advantages:

1 Banks provide safe places in which to keep cash, negotiable instruments, and other important business documents.

2 Banks permit the use of checks for the disbursement of cash.

3 Banks act as agents in the collection and payment of negotiable instruments.

Bank Account

The procedure for opening a bank account varies somewhat depending upon the location of the bank. In small towns and rural communities, bank employees usually are acquainted with most residents of the area. As a consequence, when an individual or an organization wishes to open a bank account little formality is involved. Generally, the prospective depositor has only to go to the bank and tell an employee that he wants to deposit some money. The bank employee, after asking a few pertinent questions, will simply request the new depositor to fill out a signature card indicating the way that checks will be signed.

Most metropolitan banks, on the other hand, require that a prospective depositor be introduced to a representative of the bank by someone known to the bank. In addition, the depositor is expected to supply written personal references and answer specific questions regarding his personal and financial background. Needless to say, banks want only reliable persons and organizations making deposits and writing checks.

When making a deposit, the depositor lists the details of the deposit on a form provided by the bank known as a **deposit ticket,** a copy of which he retains for his own records.

The bank also provides its depositors with blank checks and check stubs, usually contained in bound or loose-leaf checkbooks. The stubs are used to record the amounts of deposits made and checks written, as well as the names of payees and the balance in the account.

Bank Statement

The bank submits a report periodically (usually monthly) to each depositor showing its record of his account. This record, called a **bank statement,** lists the bank's balance of the depositor's account at the beginning of the period, deposits made during the period, checks paid by the bank, other charges and credits, and the balance of the account at the end of the period. Checks paid by the bank are ordinarily returned to the depositor with the statement. The bank statement illustrated on page 162 is typical.

Reconciling the Bank Account

More often than not the balance on the bank statement and the balance shown in the depositor's records will not agree, because certain transactions which have been recorded by the depositor have not as yet been recorded by the bank, or vice versa. The process of accounting for the difference between the two balances is known as **reconciling the bank account.** (For purposes of simplicity we shall refer to the balance in the depositor's records as the **book balance.**)

There are basically three different methods of reconciling a bank account: One begins with the bank balance and reconciles to the adjusted book balance, another begins with the book balance and reconciles to the adjusted bank balance, and a third method first ascertains the difference between the bank balance and the book balance and then accounts in detail for the difference. Many accountants prefer the first method. Regardless of the method used, however, the object of

STATEMENT OF
ACCOUNT WITH

NATIONAL BANK
of monticello
MONTICELLO, ILLINOIS

Date of Statement
May 31, 1972

Ralph Pendery
1302 Park Place
Monticello, Illinois

CHECKS	CHECKS	DEPOSITS	NO. OF CHECKS	DATE	BALANCE
		BALANCE FORWARD	9	4/30	4,582
		3,000		5/1	7,582
60	75			5/2	7,447
50				5/2	7,397
100	800			5/3	6,497
		200		5/5	6,697
30				5/7	6,667
686		392		5/12	6,373
		100		5/16	6,473
450		297		5/20	6,320
198				5/30	6,122

PLEASE EXAMINE AT ONCE, AND REPORT ANY ERRORS

MEMBER
FEDERAL RESERVE
SYSTEM

LAST AMOUNT IN THIS
COLUMN IS YOUR BALANCE

FDIC
FEDERAL DEPOSIT INSURANCE CORPORATION
Each depositor insured to $15,000

SYMBOLS USED:

SC - SERVICE CHARGES   DM - DEBIT MEMO
EC - ENTRY CORRECTION   CM - CREDIT MEMO
CC - CERTIFIED CHECK   LS - LIST OF CHECKS
RT - CHECK RETURNED

Bank statement.

reconciling a bank account is to determine the actual amount of cash the depositor has available for future disbursements.

Reconciling Items Among the items that may have to be considered in reconciling a bank account are:

1 Outstanding checks

2 Deposits in transit

3 Bank service charges

4 NSF (not sufficient funds) checks

5 Collections made by the bank on behalf of the depositor (for example, the collection of a note receivable)

6 Payments made by the bank on behalf of the depositor (for example, the payment of a note payable)

7 Errors made by either the bank or the depositor (for example, mathematical errors or the omission of an entry)

Outstanding checks are checks which have been issued by the depositor but which were not presented to the bank for payment in time to appear on the bank statement. Outstanding checks must be **deducted** from the balance per bank statement when working toward the adjusted bank balance.

Deposits in transit are deposits which have been recorded in the records of the depositor but which were not delivered to the bank in time to appear on the bank statement. Deposits in transit must be **added** to the balance per bank statement when working toward the adjusted bank balance.

Bank service charges are charges made against the depositor's account by the bank for "servicing" the account. For example, if the balance in a depositor's account falls below a certain minimum amount, many banks charge him a fee per check written. If bank service charges have not been recorded in the records of the depositor, they must be **deducted** from the balance per books when working toward the adjusted book balance.

An **NSF check** is a check which was dishonored (not paid) when it was presented to the bank upon which it was drawn, because the maker of the check did not have sufficient funds in his account to pay it. If the bank has deducted an NSF check from the depositor's account but the depositor has not deducted it from his book balance, this must be done when working toward the adjusted book balance.

There is no one best way for a holder to handle an NSF check. It may be returned to the person who gave it with the request that cash be paid, or it may simply be held until paid. At times legal action may be the holder's best approach. In accounting, as will be shown in the illustration that follows, we usually transfer the NSF check from the Cash account to the Accounts Receivable account.

Bank Reconciliation Illustrated

For illustrative purposes, let us assume that Roger Wesley's accounting records and bank statement as of September 30, 1974, contain the following data:

1 Balance per books is $9,926.10.

2 Balance per bank statement is $12,167.50.

3 The following checks are outstanding:

No. 632	$1,256.40
654	571.70
682	870.10
704	319.60

4 There is a deposit in transit in the amount of $670.00.

5 Bank service charges for September amount to $3.00.

6 An NSF check for $207.00, given by J. C. Slicker, a customer, was returned with the bank statement.

7 The bank collected a note for Wesley on September 29 and credited his account for $103.60 ($100 note, plus $3.60 interest).

Using the method which begins with the bank balance and reconciles to the adjusted book balance, we would reconcile Wesley's bank account as follows:

ROGER WESLEY
Bank Reconciliation
September 30, 1974

Balance per bank statement		$12,167.50
Add: Deposit in transit		670.00
		$12,837.50
Deduct: Outstanding checks:		
No. 632	$1,256.40	
654	571.70	
682	870.10	
704	319.60	3,017.80
Adjusted bank balance		$ 9,819.70
Balance per books		$ 9,926.10
Add: Collection of note		100.00
Collection of interest		3.60
		$10,029.70
Deduct: Bank service charge	$ 3.00	
NSF check	207.00	210.00
Adjusted book balance		$ 9,819.70

Note that the adjusted bank balance and the adjusted book balance are the same—$9,819.70. The $9,819.70 balance represents the actual amount of cash that Wesley has available for future disbursements from this bank. Assuming that he has no other bank accounts and no additional cash on hand, the $9,819.70 is the amount of cash that would appear on his September 30, 1974, balance sheet.

Adjusting Entries Based on the Bank Reconciliation   After the bank reconciliation has been made, it is frequently necessary to make some adjusting entries in order to bring the accounting records up to date. For example, in this illustration it is necessary to adjust Wesley's books for (1) the collection of the note and interest, (2) the bank service charge, and (3) the NSF check. It can be assumed that the deposit in transit and the outstanding checks, which already appear in Wesley's records, will clear the bank with the passage of time; as a consequence no adjustments are necessary for these items. In general journal form, the entries to adjust Wesley's records would be:

(1)

Cash	103.60	
Notes Receivable		100.00
Interest Revenue		3.60

(2)

| Bank Service Charge | 3.00 | |
| Cash | | 3.00 |

(3)

| Accounts Receivable (J. C. Slicker) | 207.00 | |
| Cash | | 207.00 |

Cash Over and Short   On occasion the bank balance and the balance per books will not reconcile to exactly the same amount. In the above illustration, if the bank balance had reconciled to $9,819.70 but the book balance had reconciled to $9,821.20, the bank balance would have been "short" of the book balance by $1.50. If, on the other hand, the bank balance had reconciled to $9,819.70 but the book balance had only reconciled to $9,817.50, the bank balance would have been "over" the book balance by $2.20. When the difference cannot be accounted for, a shortage is ordinarily debited to a Cash Over and Short account, while an overage is credited to the account. If a cash shortage or overage is sizable, it is most important that the cause be determined so that corrective action can be taken.

Let us assume that the book balance in our illustration reconciles to $9,823.20 instead of $9,819.70. The following compound entry would be necessary to adjust Wesley's records:

Bank Service Charge	3.00	
Accounts Receivable (J. C. Slicker)	207.00	
Cash Over and Short	3.50	
Interest Revenue		3.60
Notes Receivable		100.00
Cash ($207.00 + $3.00 + $3.50 − $103.60)		109.90

SUMMARY

The group of procedures employed by an organization to maintain control over its assets is known as its **system of internal control;** the system consists of both administrative and accounting controls.

The minimum requirements for a satisfactory system of internal control over cash are:

1 Prompt recording of cash receipts

2 Prompt depositing of receipts intact

3 Separation of the record-keeping and custodial functions

4 Disbursement of cash by check

5 Regular reconciliation of bank accounts

Cash receipts are ordinarily recorded in a cash receipts journal and cash disbursements in a cash disbursements journal. To make for ease in posting, columnar journals are usually employed by large businesses. The cash receipts journal supports the debit side of the Cash account, while the cash disbursements journal supports the credit side.

Most businesses set up petty cash funds to handle small transactions for which it would be impractical to issue checks. Petty cash vouchers are often used to support disbursements from the fund.

Organizations with sound accounting systems employ banking facilities to the greatest extent possible. They usually reconcile their bank accounts upon receipt of their periodic bank statements. The method preferred by many accountants is to begin with the bank balance and reconcile to the adjusted book balance. After this is done, adjusting entries are often necessary to bring the accounting records up to date. If the adjusted bank balance and the adjusted book balance do not agree and the difference cannot be accounted for, a Cash Over and Short account is used to absorb the difference.

QUESTIONS AND PROBLEMS

7-1 (1) Define **internal control.**

(2) Indicate what you consider to be the major characteristics of a satisfactory system of internal control.

(3) Distinguish between accounting controls and administrative controls.

7-2 List the more important procedures ordinarily considered necessary for the maintenance of a satisfactory system of internal control of cash.

7-3 Discuss briefly what you regard as the more important deficiencies in the system of internal control in the following situation; in addition, include what you consider to be a proper remedy for each deficiency.

The cashier of the Easy Company intercepted customer A's check payable to the company in the amount of $500 and deposited it in a bank account which was part of the company petty cash fund, of which he was custodian. He then drew a $500 check on the petty cash fund bank account payable to himself, signed it, and cashed it. At the end of the month, while processing the monthly statements to customers, he was able to change the statement to Customer A so as to show that A had received credit for the $500 check that had been intercepted. Ten days later he made an entry in the cash receipts journal which purported to record receipt of a remittance of $500 from Customer A, thus restoring A's account to its proper balance, but overstating cash in bank. He covered the over-statement by omitting from the list of outstanding checks in the bank reconcilement two checks, the aggregate amount of which was $500.

7-4 Describe briefly the imprest system for operating a petty cash fund.

7-5 What is the major weakness of the following procedure, and what is the internal control principle involved that has not been observed?

A wholesale concern makes advances to its salesmen from petty cash. All advances are first approved by the sales manager. The unused portions of the advances are returned to the petty cash fund. The latter is periodically reimbursed from general cash for the net amount paid out and the expenditures of the salesmen are charged to "travel and entertainment expenses." The petty cash cashier checks the salesmen's expense statements and keeps them on file.

7-6 The sole owner of a small business is under the impression that because he has only a few employees a system of internal control is not practicable for his business. List as many control measures as you can which may be used in a small business to provide some degree of internal control of cash.

7-7 What is the amount of a deposit in transit if the balance per bank statement is $6,400, the balance per books is $5,000, outstanding checks total $1,800, bank service charges are $10, the bank statement shows a credit of $700 for a note collected for the depositor but not as yet recorded by him, and all other cash details are correct?

7-8 Instructions Match each of the numbered items, which pertain to bank reconciliations, with the correct lettered treatment.

Treatment

A Add to balance per bank statement.

B Add to balance per books.

C Deduct from balance per bank statement.

D Deduct from balance per books.

E Exclude from bank reconciliation.

Item

1 Bank service charges

2 Deposits in transit

3 Outstanding checks

4 NSF checks

5 Collections made by the bank on behalf of the depositor

6 Payments made by the bank on behalf of the depositor

7 Balance in petty cash fund

7-9 A teller in a bank draws up a daily proof of his transactions. This proof is prepared by listing on the debit side the opening cash balance as a starting figure. The amounts of the various kinds of transactions handled during the day are then entered as debits or credits as indicated by the transactions. The cash balance at the close of the day is determined by actual count and entered in the proof. The proof should balance at that point unless there is an overage or shortage. Any overage or shortage would then be entered in the proof.

Instructions The following list includes all the transactions handled by Dave Barron, head teller of the Third National Bank, on November 10, 19X5. Prepare a proof. (Assume that there is no overage or shortage.)

Opening cash balance	$1,200
Deposits received	5,800
Checks received on other banks	3,600
Checks received on depositors	4,500
Loans granted	3,000
Interest collected	200
Expenses paid	100
Cashier's checks redeemed	500
Loans collected from borrowers	5,000
Certified checks redeemed	400

7-10 Transactions of the Marchetta Company for the month of June which pertained to the petty cash fund were:

June 1 Established an imprest petty cash fund in the amount of $25.

June 30 Reimbursed the fund. The petty cash box contained the following items:

Currency and coins	$ 3.14
Receipted vouchers for:	
Postage	6.30
Telephone and telegraph	3.80
Donation to charity	5.00
Office supplies	2.14
Freight on incoming merchandise	4.62
	$25.00

Instructions Journalize the June transactions in general journal form.

7-11 The transactions of the Sharaf Company pertaining to its petty cash fund during the month of December were:

Dec. 1 Established an imprest petty cash fund in the amount of $25.

Dec. 6 Reimbursed the fund and increased it to $100. The petty cash box contained the following items:

Currency and coins	$ 1.50
Receipted vouchers for:	
Postage	6.00
Travel expense	7.50
Donation to charity	10.00
	$25.00

Dec. 31 Reimbursed the fund. The petty cash box contained the following items:

Currency and coins	$26.25
Receipted vouchers for:	
Telephone and telegraph	8.00
Postage	12.00
Office supplies	10.00
Store supplies	13.00
Travel expense	7.50
Freight on incoming merchandise	22.60
	$99.35

Instructions Journalize the December transactions in general journal form.

7-12 As of January 1, the general ledger of the Worrells Company contained the following account balances: Cash, $32,600; Accounts Receivable, $64,100; Merchandise Inventory, $18,900; Store Supplies, $3,200; Accounts Payable, $28,200; Notes Payable, $20,000; S. Worrells, Capital, $70,600.

The customers' ledger showed the following balances: Robert Smith, $19,500; Claude Howard, $18,500; William Williams, $26,100.

The creditors' ledger showed the following balances: Sparks Company, $4,700; Yancy Company, $8,200; Boggs Company, $6,600; Conn Company, $8,700.

Instructions Assuming that the Worrells Company uses a two-column general journal, a single-column purchases journal, a single-column sales journal, a four-column cash receipts journal, and a four-column cash disbursements journal:

(1) Journalize the following January transactions.

(2) Enter the beginning account balances in T accounts and post the January transactions.

(3) Take a trial balance as of January 31, and prepare a list for each subsidiary ledger to prove your controlling accounts.

Jan. 2 Worrells invested an additional $10,000 cash in the business.

2 Paid rent for 4 months at $500 per month.

2 Purchased furniture and equipment for $3,250 cash.

2 Purchased $2,910 worth of merchandise on credit from the Sparks Company, terms 2/10, n/30.

2 Purchased furniture and equipment for $1,850 on credit from the Yancy Company.

2 Purchased merchandise for $1,250 cash.

2 Paid $240 for a 1-year insurance policy on business assets.

3 Purchased store supplies for $190 cash.

4 Purchased $2,600 worth of merchandise on credit from the Boggs Company, terms 2/10, n/30.

5 Sold merchandise for $1,800 on credit to Robert Smith, terms 2/10, n/30.

6 Purchased $120 worth of store supplies on credit from the Conn Company.

6 Paid for the merchandise purchased from the Boggs Company on January 4.

9 Sold merchandise for $650 cash.

11 Sold merchandise for $900 on credit to Claude Howard, terms 2/10, n/30.

14 Received payment in full from Robert Smith for his January 5 purchase.

16 Purchased merchandise for $1,400 on credit from the Tudor Company, terms 2/10, n/30.

21 Paid $300 for advertising.

26 Sold merchandise for $1,500 on credit to Lance Kendall, terms 2/10, n/30.

31 Paid sales salary of $600.

31 Paid miscellaneous expenses of $66.

31 Received $686 from Lance Kendall to apply on his account.

31 Sold merchandise for $3,300 cash.

7-13 The Turppa Company uses a two-column general journal, single-column purchases and sales journals, and four-column cash receipts and disbursements journals. As of June 30 the company's accounts receivable ledger contained the following accounts:

Able				Baker			
6/1 Bal.	3,600	6/4 (CR)	2,100	6/1 Bal.	3,300	6/7 (CR)	3,300
6/6 (S)	2,400	6/6 (J)	1,500	6/16 (S)	2,640		
		6/9 (J)	320	6/16 (CD)	300		

Wilson				Young			
6/1 Bal.	2,880	6/6 (CR)	1,600	6/9 (S)	5,400	6/1 (CR)	2,700
6/9 (S)	4,000			6/11 (J)	240	6/13 (J)	1,600
				6/14 (CD)	80		

Instructions Using a format somewhat as follows, show how the information contained in the above accounts would be reflected in the controlling account in the Turppa Company's general ledger.

Accounts Receivable

Date	Book of Original Entry	Amount	Date	Book of Original Entry	Amount

7-14 Instructions From the following information, prepare a bank reconciliation for the Popejoy Company as of January 31, 19X2.

The company's bank statement as of January 31, 19X2, showed a balance of $24,180.24. Checks not presented to the bank for payment as of that date were as follows: No. 8022, dated January 17, 19X2, $22.14;

and No. 8095, dated January 31, 19X2, $141.12. A deposit made on January 31 in the amount of $1,729.47 had not yet been credited to the company's account. The bank charged the company a service charge of $12.12, which had not yet been recorded by the company. On January 1, 19X2, the company's Cash account showed a balance of $17,235.64. The company's cash receipts for the month amounted to $37,944.12, and its cash disbursements totaled $29,421.19.

7-15 Instructions From the following data, which pertain to the cash operations of the C. Griffin Company for the current year:

(1) Prepare a bank reconciliation as of December 31.

(2) Prepare in general journal form the entries, if any, to adjust the company's records as of December 31.

(3) Indicate the proper amount of cash to be shown on the company's balance sheet as of December 31.

Data:

(a) Balance per bank statement as of December 31: $39,977.

(b) Balance per books as of December 31: $21,940.

(c) The December 31 receipts amounting to $1,250 could not be deposited until January 2.

(d) Checks issued but not returned with the bank statement totaled $3,270.

(e) A charge slip among the canceled checks showed that the bank had charged the company's account in the amount of $15 for services rendered.

(f) A credit slip among the canceled checks showed that the bank had collected a note for the company in the amount of $2,200, plus interest of $132.

(g) A $300 check was returned marked NSF. The check had been received from T. Williams, a customer.

(h) A $14,000 deposit made by the G. Griffin Company was incorrectly credited to the C. Griffin Company's account.

7-16 Instructions From the following data which pertain to the cash operations of the J. Golemme Company for the month of December:

(1) Determine the proper amount of cash to be shown on the balance sheet as of December 31.

(2) Prepare in general journal form the entries necessary to adjust the company's records as of December 31.

Data:
(a) Balance per bank statement as of December 31: $38,510.

(b) Cash on hand on December 31: $2,000.

(c) Cash in transit on December 31: $4,321.

(d) Check No. 482 for $147 was paid by the bank during December but was not recorded in the cash disbursements journal. The check was payable to the Taylor Company for merchandise purchased on terms of 2/10, n/30. The check was issued within the discount period.

(e) The bank credited the company's account during the month for $264, the proceeds of a $250 note left with the bank for collection minus $1 collection fee. As of December 31, the company had not recorded this transaction.

(f) Checks totaling $650 were outstanding on December 31.

(g) Check No. 489 for $234 was incorrectly recorded in the cash disbursements journal as $324. The check was payable to the *Gazette* for advertising.

(h) A check issued by the J. M. Golemme Company for $150 was incorrectly deducted by the bank from the J. Golemme Company's account.

7-17 Instructions The following bank reconciliation is incorrect. From the information given, prepare (1) a corrected bank reconciliation, and (2) any adjusting entries necessary.

Bank Reconciliation
December 31, 19X3

Balance per books, Dec. 31, 19X3		$17,174.86
Add:		
Collections received on the last day of December and charged to the Cash account but not deposited		2,662.25
Debit memo for customer's check returned unpaid (check is on hand but no entry has been made on the books)		200.00
Debit memo for bank service charge for December		5.50
		$20,142.61
Deduct:		
Checks drawn but not paid by bank (see detailed list below)	$2,267.75	
Credit memo for proceeds of a note receivable which had been left at the bank for collection but which has not been recorded as collected	400.00	
Check for an account payable entered on books as $240.90 but drawn and paid by bank as $419.00	178.10	2,945.85
Computed balance		$17,196.76
Unlocated difference		200.00
Balance per bank statement, Dec. 31, 19X3		$16,996.76

Checks Drawn but Not Paid by Bank	
Check Number	Amount
573	$ 67.27
724	9.90
903	456.67
907	305.50
911	482.75
913	550.00
914	366.76
916	10.00
917	218.90
	$2,267.75

*7-18 The Sun and Sand winter resort is in operation from December through April each year. After a few weeks of the current season have passed, the manager notices that the receipts of the cigar and cigarette counter are considerably less than those of the previous season, although the receipts from other resort activities have increased. The manager asks you, the accountant for the resort, to investigate. During your investigation you collect the following information:

1 Four different employees serve customers at the counter at various times.

2 All sales are at the established selling prices.

3 All cash in excess of a $10 change fund is deposited with the cashier at the close of each day.

4 No stock was carried over at the counter from the previous season.

5 Cigars and cigarettes are brought to the counter from the general stock room in full boxes and cartons as needed.

6 No inventory records are kept at the counter.

7 The cashier's record shows $951.50 received up to date of examination.

Based upon an inventory taken under your supervision, you prepare the statement shown at the top of page 175:

Instructions Based on this data:

(1) Prepare a summary of cigar-counter transactions showing the amount of shortage, if any.

(2) Indicate any recommendations you may have for improving internal control over the cigar-counter activities.

*AICPA adapted.

Cigar* and Cigarette† Inventory				
Unit Selling Prices	Received from Stock Room	Inventory		
Cigars	Boxes	Boxes		Singles
25¢	10	3		25
2/25¢	20	4		10
10¢	30	6		40
Cigarettes	Cartons	Cartons		Packages
40¢	25	4		6
30¢	300	77		5

*Boxes of 50 cigars.
†Cartons of 10 packages of cigarettes.

*7-19 The Olson Company had poor internal control over its cash transactions. Facts about its cash position as of November 30, 19X4, were as follows:

The Cash account showed a balance of $18,901.62, which included undeposited receipts. A credit of $100 on the bank's records did not appear on the books of the company. The balance per bank statement as of November 30 was $15,550. Outstanding checks were: No. 62 for $116.25, No. 183 for $150.00, No. 284 for $253.25, No. 8621 for $190.71, No. 8623 for $206.80, and No. 8632 for $145.28.

The cashier abstracted all undeposited receipts in excess of $3,794.41 and prepared the following reconciliation:

Balance per books, Nov. 30, 19X4		$18,901.62
Add: Outstanding checks:		
8621	$190.71	
8623	206.80	
8632	145.28	442.79
		$19,344.41
Less: Undeposited receipts		3,794.41
Balance per bank, Nov. 30, 19X4		$15,550.00
Deduct: Unrecorded credit		100.00
True cash, Nov. 30, 19X4		$15,450.00

Instructions Prepare a schedule showing the amount of cash the cashier abstracted and indicate how he attempted to conceal his theft.

*7-20 The management of the Korff Company has reason to believe that some of their cash is being abstracted. You have been employed to investigate. The following information is made available to you.

*AICPA adapted.

Bank Reconciliation
As of November 30

Balance per books, Nov. 30	$2,631.74
Less: Cash on hand	210.89
	$2,420.85
Less: Bank service charge for November	9.00
	$2,411.85
Add: Outstanding checks	991.00
Balance per bank statement, Nov. 30	$3,402.85

Cash Receipts Journal

Dec.			
1	Received on account		$ 403.25
2	Received on account		1,366.40
3	Received on account		974.86
4	Received on account		4,322.47
5	Received on account		5,201.89
7	Received on account		7,310.75
8	Received on account		6,195.18
9	Received on account		8,884.46
10	Received on account		10,227.55
11	Received on account		6,698.89
12	Received on account		210.20
14	Received on account		1,426.46
16	Received on account		400.00
17	Received on account		700.00
18	Received on account		2,709.82
21	Received on account		850.00
23	Received on account		1,100.00
27	Received on account		911.35
29	Received on account		3,875.50
			$62,669.03

Cash Disbursements Journal

Dec.	1	November service charge _____	$ 9.00
	3	Paid on account _____	5,236.50
	5	Paid on account _____	3,645.21
	8	Paid on account _____	16,394.89
	10	Paid on account _____	15,873.42
	12	Paid on account _____	3,123.47
	14	Paid on account _____	475.42
	17	Paid on account _____	1,250.00
	19	Paid on account _____	3,622.83
	22	Paid on account _____	3,692.09
	26	Paid on account _____	3,456.45
	31	Paid on account _____	4,201.25
			$60,989.53

Cash on hand as of December 31 amounted to $100. The transactions per the December bank statement, which were correctly recorded by the bank, show that deposits amounted to $62,870.92; checks paid amounted to $57,952.03; service charges for the month were $10; and a charge of $100 was made against the account because an NSF check for that amount was returned. Neither the service charges nor the NSF check were recorded on the company's books. The total of outstanding checks as of December 31 was found to amount to $4,110.50.

Instructions Assuming that the November 30 reconciliation is found to be correct:

(1) Determine the amount of shortage, if any.

(2) Prepare any adjusting entries necessary.

8
Systemization and Automation of the Accounting Process

Although the principles underlying the accounting process have remained relatively unchanged since Paciolo's time, the process itself has gradually become both more systematic and more automatic. The change has come about chiefly as a result of the continuous growth of the business organization and, more recently, of the increasing technological development in the area of data processing. We shall continue to employ the manually oriented system as our model, but a brief examination of two important features of many modern accounting systems is in order at this time. They are the employment of the voucher system as a means of control and the use of automatic equipment as a processing device.

VOUCHER SYSTEM

A **voucher system** consists of records and procedures for systematically accumulating, approving, recording, and paying an organizaton's expenditures; its primary objective is to obtain maximum control over both their incurrence and their payment.   A system of this kind permits maximum segregation of duties and responsibilities related to the authorization of expenditures, the receipt of goods or services, and the ultimate payment of liabilities, thus making for a high degree of internal control.

Although voucher systems vary in different organizations, most of them utilize:

1 Vouchers

2 Voucher checks

3 A voucher register

4 A check register

Vouchers

A **voucher** is a document which authorizes the payment of an expenditure and serves as the basis of an accounting entry.   Generally, its face contains the pertinent details of the expenditure, while the reverse side contains an account distribution section which indicates the accounts that are to be debited or credited and the amounts.   The voucher illustrated below and on page 180 is typical.

Face of Voucher

THE XYZ COMPANY
Chicago, Illinois
60606

Voucher no._____

Payee_____   Date due_____

Address_____   Date paid_____

_____   Check no._____

Terms_____

Invoice Date	*Description*	*Amount*

Approved_____   Approved_____
Controller   Treasurer

Back of Voucher			

Account Distribution (Debits)	*Amounts*
Purchases	
Transportation In	
Advertising	
Store Supplies	
Delivery Expense	
Salesmen's Salaries	

Voucher no. _____

Payee _____

Address _____

_____

Invoice amount _____

Discount _____

Net ══════════════

Due date _____

Date paid _____

Check no. _____

Voucher Checks

A **voucher check** is a type of check often used by organizations to pay their liabilities. It combines the more important features of both the regular check and the voucher. In addition to containing the information ordinarily found on a check, it includes, either on the voucher check itself or on a detachable slip, information indicating to the payee the purpose for which the check was issued. The voucher checks illustrated below and on page 181 are typical.

Although voucher checks are ordinarily very useful in voucher systems, they are not absolutely essential to their operation; regular checks will also suffice. Similarly, the use of voucher checks is not restricted to organizations employing voucher systems.

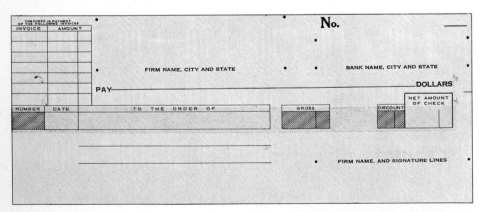

Voucher check (self-containing format).

| NAME | | | | | VOUCHER | №̲ 16778 |

D E S C R I P T I O N	DATE	INVOICE No.	INVOICE AMOUNT	DEDUCTIONS	BALANCE
				DISCOUNT	

DETACH BEFORE DEPOSITING   CHICAGO PLAYBOY CLUB, CHICAGO, ILLINOIS 60611

THE ACCOMPANYING CHECK IS IN FULL PAYMENT OF ITEMS ABOVE

CHICAGO PLAYBOY CLUB

$\frac{2\text{-}387}{710}$

116 E. WALTON STREET • CHICAGO, ILL. 60611

PAY TO THE ORDER OF   CHECK No.   DATE   GROSS   DISCOUNT   AMOUNT OF CHECK

(VOID)

CHICAGO PLAYBOY CLUB

(VOID)

THE EXCHANGE NATIONAL BANK
OF CHICAGO

Voucher check (detachable-slip format). (Playboy, Playboy Club, Rabbit Head Design and the Femlin Design are registered marks of, and used with permission of, HMH Publishing Co., Inc.)

Voucher Register

A **voucher register** is a book of original entry into which vouchers are entered after they have been properly approved. In a voucher system, the voucher register replaces the columnar purchases journal we used in the Pendery illustration in Chapter 5. The one illustrated on pages 182 and 183 is typical. Note, however, that unlike the purchases journal in our model, which records only credit purchases of merchandise, the voucher register records **all** expenditures.

Ordinarily, in a voucher system, the Accounts Payable account is replaced with a new account entitled Vouchers Payable. For this reason, a Vouchers Payable credit column is used in the illustrated voucher register instead of an Accounts Payable credit column.

Voucher Register

Voucher Number	Date 1972		Payee	Payment Date		Check Number	Vouchers Payable Cr.*	Purchases Dr.*
111	May	1	Times	May	1	109	100	
112		1	ABC Company		1	110	800	800
113		1	The Long Company		10	112	700	700
114		4	XYZ Company		4	111	30	
115		6	The Sparks Company				900	900
116		7	The Davis Company				250	250
117		13	The Wyan Company				80	
118		14	The Hart Company		18	113	450	450
119		17	The Graham Company		21	114	200	200
120		19	Central Supply Co.				400	
121		31	Payroll		31	115	60	
122		31	XYZ Company		31	116	40	
123		31	Ace Transportation		31	117	70	
							4,080	3,300
							(200)	(505)

*Cr. and Dr., the abbreviations for credit and debit, are often used on accounting forms and statements.

Check Register

The **check register** in a voucher system is merely a modification of the columnar cash disbursements journal, which it replaces. The one illustrated on page 183 is typical. You will find it helpful to study this illustration in connection with the illustrated voucher register. Both are based upon data familiar to us from the Pendery illustration.

Operation of a Voucher System

The accounting procedures in a voucher system consist primarily of preparing the vouchers, recording them, and paying them.

Preparing a Voucher Under a voucher system, a voucher is prepared for each expenditure made by the organization. All the evidence relating to an expenditure is first assembled. Generally, this will include any or all of the following: a purchase order, a purchase invoice, a receiving ticket, any document showing authorization or approval of the expenditure, and instructions regarding the accounting distribution (accounts to be debited or credited). A voucher is then

Transportation In Dr.	Advertising Dr.	Store Supplies Dr.	Delivery Expense Dr.	Sales Salaries Dr.	Other General Ledger Accounts			
					Account Title	Account Number	Debit	Credit
	100							
		30						
					Office Supplies	(142)	80	
					Furn. & Equip.	(171)	400	
				60	Misc. Expense	(508)	40	
70								
70	100	30	-0-	60			520	-0-
(514)	(501)	(141)		(507)			√	

Check Register

Check Number	Date 1972		Payee	Voucher Number	Vouchers Payable Dr.	Purchase Discount Cr.	Cash Cr.
109	May	1	Times	111	100		100
110		1	ABC Company	112	800		800
111		4	XYZ Company	114	30		30
112		10	The Long Company	113	700	14	686
113		18	The Hart Company	118	450		450
114		21	The Graham Company	119	200	2	198
115		31	Payroll	121	60		60
116		31	XYZ Company	122	40		40
117		31	Ace Transportation	123	70		70
					2,450	16	2,434
					(200)	(512)	(101)

prepared from the information on these documents and submitted, with the documents attached, to a designated individual for approval of payment.

Recording a Voucher   Upon approval, the information contained on the voucher is recorded in the voucher register.   Vouchers are entered in the register in numerical order; if they have not been prenumbered, they are assigned a number from the register.   Each entry to record a voucher ordinarily contains the voucher number, date of entry, name of the payee, and the amounts to be debited and credited to the various accounts.   (The date of payment and the check number are not recorded until the voucher is paid.) After a voucher has been recorded in the voucher register, it is filed in an unpaid voucher file where it remains until the payment date.

Posting from the voucher register is accomplished in essentially the same way as from the purchases journal, the only important difference being that the Vouchers Payable account has replaced the Accounts Payable account.

Paying a Voucher   On the date the voucher is to be paid, a check for the correct amount, accompanied by the voucher and its attached documents, is presented for signature to the individual (usually an official of the organization) authorized to sign such checks.   The check is then entered in the check register.   The entry commonly shows the check number, the date of payment, the name of the payee, the voucher number, and the amounts and accounts to be debited and credited. The date of payment and the check number are next entered in the voucher register on the line occupied by the corresponding voucher.

Posting from the check register is accomplished in basically the same way as from the cash disbursements journal, except that the data ordinarily posted to the Accounts Payable account are posted instead to the Vouchers Payable account.

Unpaid Vouchers   The sum of the unpaid vouchers on hand should be equal at all times to the balance in the Vouchers Payable account; thus, the accounts payable ledger is no longer necessary.   Unpaid vouchers, however, should be tabulated periodically to determine whether their sum agrees with the balance in the Vouchers Payable account.   This merely requires that an analytical comparison of the unpaid vouchers, the voucher register, the check register, and the Vouchers Payable account be made.   A comparison of the records in our illustration would result in the reconciliation shown on page 185.

Voucher System and Internal Control

Voucher systems are particularly applicable to large organizations, where the employment of systematic procedures makes possible a wide division of responsibilities among employees.   Because verification and approval by various individ-

Vouchers Payable

Check register	2,450	Voucher register	4,080
Balance	1,630		
	4,080		4,080
		Balance	1,630

RALPH PENDERY
Schedule of Unpaid Vouchers
As of May 31, 1972

Voucher Number		Amount
115	————————	$ 900
116	————————	250
117	————————	80
120	————————	400
Total	————————	$1,630

uals are required at different stages in the system, the opportunity for dishonest manipulations and the possibility of undetected errors are greatly reduced.

AUTOMATED DATA PROCESSING

Automated data processing, frequently abbreviated simply as **ADP,** is the term generally used to describe the processing of data by automatic equipment with minimum intervention by man. This equipment may be operated mechanically, electrically, or electronically. In systems where the data are processed by electronic computers, the term **electronic data processing** and the abbreviation **EDP** are ordinarily employed.

As the accounting process developed from the simple manually operated system to the highly sophisticated EDP system, it passed through various intermediate phases. Two of the more important of these, both of which are still employed in many business organizations, are accounting with key-driven machines and punched card accounting. Both, in a sense, are early forms of ADP. The transition may be depicted as shown on page 186.

Accounting and Key-driven Equipment

Under a manually oriented accounting system, such operations as the preparation of source documents, the recording of transactions in the various books of original

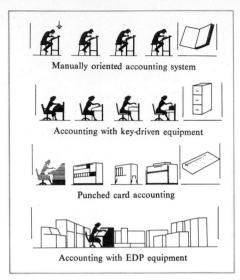

Stages in the automation of the accounting process.

entry, the posting of data to ledgers, the balancing of ledger accounts, and the taking of trial balances are all performed chiefly by hand. Needless to say, the manual processing of accounting data is both expensive and time consuming because of the cost of the human effort involved and the limitations of human capacity to process data rapidly. With the aid of key-driven equipment such as typewriters, calculators, and bookkeeping machines, many of the basic operations can be handled more or less mechanically, and thus faster and more economically. For example, source documents may be prepared on a typewriter, and calculators and bookkeeping machines may be utilized in various phases of the recording and posting processes.

The storage function in a key-driven system, as in a manually oriented system, consists mainly of manual posting or filing; however, intermediate results of arithmetic computations may be stored in the counter wheels of some of the equipment. Likewise, supervisory control in a key-driven operation, although principally human, can also be exercised mechanically by the use of control bars and other mechanical devices.

Punched Card Accounting

While the use of key-driven equipment is a step forward in the mechanization of the accounting process, even more of the basic functions can be performed mechanically by the employment of punched cards. These cards, of uniform size and shape, are made from a heavy stiff paper that is capable of being punched in a pattern that has meaning and can be handled mechanically. When the data punched on the cards are processed, the holes are sensed electrically by wire brushes, mechanically by metal fingers, or photoelectrically by photocells. Although punched cards vary in form and content, the IBM 80-column card with the standard hole pattern shown below is typical.

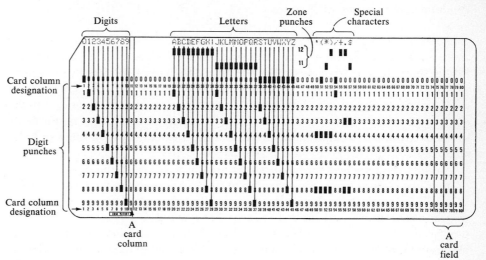

IBM punched card (standard hole pattern).

Operation of a Punched Card System In a punched card accounting system, data are transcribed from source documents onto punched cards by manually operated card-punch machines; the information is then read, or interpreted, by a machine called a **card reader.** As you will note in the illustration, IBM's card contains 80 vertical columns with 12 punching positions in each column. One or more punches in a single column denote a **character,** a symbol used to represent data. The number of columns utilized on a given card depends upon the amount of data to be coded. If more than 80 columns are needed to contain the data of a particular transaction, two or more cards will be required. In such cases, continuity between the cards is established by punching identifying information in designated columns of each card.

Historical Development of the Punched Card Concept The punched card, which has become somewhat emblematic of the age of high-speed data processing, actually has been used as a tool of automation for more than 200 years. As early as 1728, a French inventor utilized punched cards to automate the loom. In his invention, an endless chain of cards was made to rotate past the needles of the loom. As they moved by, only those needles that matched holes were able to penetrate; as a consequence, their threads determined the pattern embodied in the fabric. Still later, during the era of the player piano, the punched card principle was used in the automation of the piano. This was accomplished by employing a perforated roll of paper called a piano roll. The keys of the piano were actuated by the passage of air through the perforations, and the tune which had been punched onto the roll was then played. Today, the punched card is not only an indispensable tool of punched card accounting systems, but is also fundamental to many EDP systems.

Advantages and Limitations of Punched Card Accounting Generally speaking, more accounting operations can be performed mechanically in a punched card system than in a key-driven one. For example, although source documents in some punched card systems are prepared manually or by typewriter, in others the card itself serves as the source document. In addition, card sorting and collating equipment assemble, sort, and classify data; a variety of equipment performs the different arithmetic computations; and, to a great extent, manual filing of bulky records gives way to mechanical maintenance of files.

While the punched card system has greatly augmented the ease and speed of handling clerical loads, the extension of its use has been limited by its inability to handle exceptions mechanically (thus making manual processing necessary in certain cases), and by its limited capacity for making decisions in the course of processing operations. The practical effect of these limitations is that complex processing problems must be solved in bits and pieces rather than in one continuous operation. However, these drawbacks are overcome somewhat in systems which are essentially EDP oriented.

Accounting and EDP

Just as the key-driven accounting system is an improvement over the manually operated system and the punched card system has advantages not found in the key-driven system, the EDP system capitalizes on the major weaknesses of the punched card system. This is particularly true with regard to speed of processing, the ability to store data, the handling of exceptions to the norm, and the making of decisions simultaneously with the processing operation. These advances have been brought about by the advent of what is frequently referred to as modern technology's precocious child, the computer. Although a detailed study of the computer is beyond the scope of our work at this time, it is important that we have an appreciation for its role in the accounting process.

EDP and the Computer Although an electronic data processing system ordinarily contains many peripheral devices such as card punches, card readers, and key-driven machines, the computer is the central element of the system. Physically, it is analogous to a desk calculator, differing essentially in only three respects: It is faster, it has a memory, and it can make decisions based upon predetermined criteria. Some computers can add 250,000 sixteen-digit numbers in one second, while others can record the equivalent of a 50,000-word book in 1 second. The computer is capable of remembering both facts and instructions; unlike humans, it never forgets. Imagine how knowledgeable man would be if he could instantly recall every fact he had ever read or heard! When the decision-making capability of the computer is referred to, the implication is not that it can exercise judgment, but rather that it has the ability to evaluate data by making comparisons with predetermined criteria on a "yes" or "no" basis.

Basic EDP Configuration The basic components of an EDP system are:

1 Input unit
2 Memory (storage) unit
3 Arithmetic unit
4 Control unit
5 Output unit

Their interrelationship in the basic configuration may be depicted as follows:

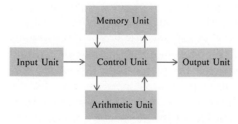

Basic EDP configuration.

As you can see in the diagram, the heart of the EDP system is composed of the control unit, the memory unit, and the arithmetic unit. The **control unit** interprets the instructions and directs the various data processing operations. The **memory unit** receives the instructions, stores intermediate results, and releases information, all as directed by the control unit. The **arithmetic unit** performs arithmetic and comparison operations upon data routed from the memory unit, again as directed by the control unit. Linked directly to the main processing units are devices which read data into the memory unit and write information out of it.

Operation of an EDP System Source documents in an EDP system are ordinarily prepared by key-driven or card-punch machines, much the same as in a punched card system. Both this step and the transfer of the data to a medium suitable for computer processing are accomplished by the input unit. The medium may be punched cards, magnetic tape, or paper tape, with transactions being reflected as punched holes or magnetic or transparent spots. At present, magnetic tape is by far the fastest. For example, it can be read into the central processing unit of the system at speeds as high as 50,000 to 60,000 characters per second, whereas the maximum speed for paper tape is about 1,000 characters per second, and for punched cards a little over 300 per second.

The output of an EDP system is ordinarily withdrawn from the central processing unit upon magnetic tape, paper tape, or punched cards, and is then fed into printers which "print out" the results. In many systems the output data are produced by direct connection between the processing units and the print-out devices, thus eliminating the need for tapes or cards in the print-out phase.

In addition to handling conventional record-keeping functions, electronic equipment has considerable potential for other important uses. The computer, for example, is now employed to identify, define, and analyze problems, as well as to suggest courses of action and evaluate alternatives. As a consequence, the employment of EDP systems in business organizations is rapidly changing decision making from what in the past has often been managerial guesswork to conclusions based upon current facts and scientific projections.

Integrated Data Processing

Since the appearance of the electronic computer upon the data processing scene, a variety of devices, many of them not electronic in principle, have been developed in an attempt to speed up the production and transmission of data. Attachments to adding machines, desk calculators, bookkeeping machines, cash registers, and typewriters, for example, make possible not only the preparation of source documents but also the simultaneous production of perforated tapes or cards for use in automatic processing. Output from these devices, sometimes unaltered or at the most easily converted, is readily acceptable to the electronic system of the computer. Thus, a number of these essentially conventional machines may be employed both in their primary function of document preparation and also to produce media compatible with the EDP system. The result is an integration of functions that eliminates the transitional operations which would otherwise be required. The utilization of this concept of integration is commonly known as **integrated data processing,** abbreviated simply as **IDP.** Needless to say, when and if input preparation equipment becomes fully electronic, the ultimate in automated data processing will have been achieved.

SUMMARY

Although the underlying concepts of accounting remain relatively unchanged, the processing of accounting data has become more systematic and automatic. Two important features of many modern accounting systems are the voucher system and the use of automatic equipment as a processing device.

A voucher system consists of records and procedures for systematically accumulating, approving, recording, and paying an organization's expenditures. It provides a considerable degree of internal control. Voucher systems are particularly effective in large business organizations.

In the progression from the simple manually operated accounting system to the sophisticated EDP system, two stages are particularly important: accounting with key-driven equipment and punched card accounting. Both are forerunners of automated data processing.

Automated data processing is the processing of data primarily by automatic equipment. With its advent, changes in the language and basic form of the recording media have occurred. Transactions are reflected as punched holes and magnetic or transparent spots, and the record form consists of such media as punched cards and paper and magnetic tape.

The computer is the central element of electronic data processing. Its main attributes are its speed of operation, its memory, and its ability to make decisions based upon predetermined criteria.

Integrated data processing results in a fusing of operational steps, so that some of the transitional operations required to prepare data for electronic data processing are eliminated.

QUESTIONS AND PROBLEMS

8-1 What is a **voucher system?** What is its primary objective?

8-2 What is the relationship between an effective voucher system and an organizaton's system of internal control?

8-3 As applied to a voucher system, what is meant by the terms **voucher, voucher check, voucher register,** and **check register?**

8-4 What kind of an account is Vouchers Payable? In which ledger is it kept?

8-5 If the balance in the Vouchers Payable account does not agree with the total of the unpaid vouchers, how is the difference reconciled?

8-6 Circle the letter or letters which would correctly complete the following statements:

(1) A voucher system
   (a) Uses vouchers as the basis for recording pertinent data about a liability.
   (b) Provides for control of cash disbursements in an orderly manner.

(c) Permits the elimination of the accounts payable subsidiary ledger.

(d) Permits the elimination of the cash disbursements journal or check register.

(2) At the end of an accounting period the balance of the Vouchers Payable account under the voucher system should

(a) Equal the total of unpaid items in the voucher register.

(b) Equal the total of the balances in the check register.

(c) Equal the total of the unpaid items in the unpaid voucher file.

(d) Be a credit balance reported as a current liability on the balance sheet.

8-7 Describe briefly the operation of a voucher system.

8-8 Distinguish between automated data processing (ADP) and electronic data processing (EDP).

8-9 What are the major limitations of the punched card accounting system?

8-10 What are the major advantages of EDP systems as compared to punched card systems?

8-11 What are the basic components of an EDP system?

8-12 What is meant by the term integrated data processing?

8-13 In general, in which areas of accounting would you expect the use of EDP equipment to be most feasible?

8-14 Although this topic was not specifically covered in our text, what avenues do you think would be open to a small business which is interested in increasing its efficiency by employing electronic data processing but whose volume of business does not warrant the purchase or rental of such equipment?

8-15 The Kessler Company's internal control procedures relating to the purchase of merchandise may be described in the following terms:

After approval by the appropriate person, purchase requisitions are forwarded to the purchasing department supervisor who distributes such requisitions to the several employees under his control. These employees prepare prenumbered purchase orders in triplicate, account for all numbers, and send the original purchase order to the vendor. One copy of the purchase order is sent to the receiving department where it is used as a receiving report. The other copy is filed in the purchasing department.

When the merchandise is received, it is moved directly to the storeroom and issued on informal requests. The receiving department sends a receiving report (with its copy of the purchase order attached) to the purchasing department and sends copies of the receiving report to the storeroom and to the accounting department.

Vendors' invoices for purchases, received in duplicate in the mail room, are sent to the purchasing department and directed to the employee who placed the related order. The employee then compares the invoice with the copy of the purchase order on file in the purchasing department for price and terms and compares the invoice quantity with the quantity received as reported by the shipping and receiving department on its copy of the purchase order. The purchasing department employee also checks discounts, footings, and extensions, then initials the invoice to indicate approval for payment. The invoice is then sent to the voucher section of the accounting department where it is coded for account distribution, assigned a voucher number, entered in the voucher register, and filed according to payment due date.

On payment dates prenumbered checks are requisitioned by the voucher section from the cashier and prepared except for signature. After the checks are prepared, they are returned to the cashier, who puts them through a check-signing machine, accounts for the sequence of numbers, and passes them to the cash disbursement bookkeeper for entry in the check register. The cash disbursements bookkeeper then returns the checks to the voucher section which notes payment dates in the voucher register, places the checks in envelopes, and sends them to the mail room. The vouchers are then filed in numerical sequence. At the end of each month one of the voucher clerks prepares an adding machine tape of unpaid items in the voucher register, compares the total thereof with the general ledger balance, and investigates any difference disclosed by such comparison.

Instructions From the standpoint of internal control, identify the weaknesses, if any, inherent in the Kessler Company's purchasing procedures. Where appropriate, suggest supplementary or revised procedures for remedying each weakness.

8-16 **Instructions** Assuming that a voucher system is in use, prepare in general journal form the entries necessary to record the following transactions:

May 1 Purchase of merchandise for $1,500 cash.

      2 Purchase of $1,000 worth of merchandise on account from the Southside Supply Company, terms 2/10, n/30.

      3 Payment of weekly payroll amounting to $2,500.

      5 Prepayment of rent in the amount of $1,200.

    6   Purchase of $3,000 worth of furniture and equipment from the Northside Supply Company, terms 90 days.

    8   Payment of $588 to the Southside Supply Company to apply on account. (See May 2 transaction.)

    9   Receipt of a bill from the *Times* for advertising, $200.

   10   Payment of $1,000 to the Northside Supply Company to apply on account. (See May 6 transaction.)

8-17 Instructions   Assuming that a voucher system is in use, journalize the following transactions in general journal form and indicate the book (or books) of original entry in which each of the transactions would ordinarily be recorded.

June 1   Purchase of $2,000 worth of merchandise on account from the Westside Supply Company, terms 3/10, n/60, f.o.b. shipping point.

    2   Purchase of merchandise for $3,000 cash.

    3   Receipt of a bill from the *Gazette* for advertising, $300.

    6   Payment of weekly payroll, $3,000.

    7   Receipt of an $80 freight bill. (See June 1 transaction.)

    8   Prepayment of insurance, $360.

    9   Payment of $1,358 to the Westside Supply Company. (See June 1 transaction.)

   10   Establishment of a petty cash fund, $100.

8-18 Instructions   Assuming that a voucher system is in use, journalize the following transactions in general journal form and indicate the book (or books) of original entry in which each of the transactions would ordinarily be recorded.

July 1   Purchase of $1,000 worth of merchandise from the Pierce Company, terms cash, f.o.b. shipping point.

    2   Purchase of $2,000 worth of merchandise from the Baird Company, terms 2/10, n/30, f.o.b. destination.

    3   Receipt of $60 freight bill on shipment from the Pierce Company. (See July 1 transaction.)

    4   Receipt and payment of $49 freight bill on shipment from the Baird Company. (See July 2 transaction.)

    6   Payment of freight bill on shipment from the Pierce Company. (See July 3 transaction.)

7 Receipt of a $100 credit memo from the Baird Company as the result of an error in billing. (See July 2 transaction.)

8 Payment to the Baird Company in full of account. (See all pertinent transactions listed above.)

8-19 Instructions Assuming that the Schlosser Company utilizes a voucher register and check register as described in this chapter:

(1) Record each of the following transactions in the appropriate register. (Number vouchers and checks consecutively, beginning with No. 101 for vouchers and No. 201 for checks.)

(2) Set up a T account for the Vouchers Payable account and post.

(3) Prove the balance in the Vouchers Payable account by preparing a list of unpaid vouchers.

The Schlosser Company engaged in the following transactions during the month of April:

Apr. 1 Purchased $800 worth of merchandise from the Shaw Company, terms 2/10, n/30, f.o.b. shipping point.

2 Purchased $1,600 worth of merchandise from the Lester Company, terms 3/30, n/60, f.o.b. destination.

4 Purchased $1,200 worth of merchandise from the Webb Company, terms 1/10, n/20, f.o.b. shipping point.

6 Paid a $72 freight bill on the April 1 purchase from the Shaw Company.

8 Sent the Shaw Company a check in full of account.

10 Purchased $5,000 worth of furniture and equipment from the North Company, terms 90 days.

11 Purchased $80 worth of store supplies from the Shaw Company for cash.

14 Paid the *Daily Bugle* $180 for advertising.

16 Paid biweekly sales salaries, $3,000.

18 Paid a $58 freight bill on the April 4 purchase from the Webb Company.

30 Paid biweekly sales salaries, $3,000.

8-20 Instructions Assuming that the McGraw Company utilizes a voucher register and a check register:

(1) Record each of the following transactions in the appropriate register.

(Number vouchers and checks consecutively, beginning with No. 201 for vouchers and No. 301 for checks.)

(2) Set up a T account for the Vouchers Payable account and post.

(3) Prove the balance in the Vouchers Payable account by preparing a list of unpaid vouchers.

Transactions for the month of May were as follows:

May 1 The McGraw Company purchases $1,000 worth of merchandise from the Rooke Company, terms 2/10, n/30, f.o.b. shipping point.

2 Pays $70 freight on the May 1 purchase from the Rooke Company.

4 Purchases $2,000 worth of merchandise from the Rolfe Company, terms 2/10, n/30, f.o.b. shipping point.

6 Pays $90 freight on the May 4 purchase from the Rolfe Company.

7 Purchases $2,500 worth of merchandise from the York Company, terms 1/10, n/20, f.o.b. shipping point.

8 Pays $80 freight on the May 7 purchase from the York Company.

10 Purchases $4,000 worth of merchandise from the Quincy Company, terms 4/10, n/90, f.o.b. destination.

12 Pays $144 freight on the May 10 purchase from the Quincy Company.

14 Purchases $1,800 worth of merchandise from the Wixon Company, terms cash, f.o.b. shipping point.

15 Pays $45 freight on the May 14 purchase from the Wixon Company.

16 Sends the York Company a check in full of account.

17 Sends the Quincy Company a check in full of account.

20 Purchases $120 worth of store supplies from the West Company, terms 30 days, f.o.b. destination.

22 Receives an advertising bill from the *Courier* for $160.

31 Pays monthly sales salaries, $2,200.

Part Three
The Collation and Modification of Accounting Data

9

Accounting for Accruals and Deferrals

In Chapter 4 we covered the entire accounting cycle, briefly examining the adjusting process prior to the preparation of financial statements. You will recall that some of the accounts in the Pendery illustration required adjustment at that time because they were not up to date. In this section we shall examine in detail some of the problems peculiar to the adjusting process.

NATURE OF THE ADJUSTING PROCESS

We learned in Chapter 1 that the accounting process as developed in this text is predicated upon six fundamental assumptions—usefulness, entity, transaction, quantifiability, continuity, and periodicity—and that some of them are more applicable to certain aspects of the process than others. The transaction and quantifiability assumptions, for example, are particularly relevant to the collection and tabulation process, while the continuity and periodicity assumptions have more bearing on the adjusting process.

In accordance with the continuity assumption, the accountant assumes, unless there is some good reason to believe otherwise, that the entity for which he is accounting will continue indefinitely without significant change in environment and activities. With respect to the periodicity assumption, he assumes that the economic activities of an entity can be allocated among successive periods of time on a reasonable and meaningful basis. Stated another way, the accountant assumes (1) that revenue and expense items can be appropriately recognized and allocated to the periods in which they apply, and (2) that assets and liabilities can be adequately recognized and measured as of a particular moment of time.

Sale Basis of Revenue Recognition

Although in an economic sense revenue is earned by production, accountants ordinarily maintain that revenue is not realized until there has been a valid sale of merchandise or services. The general rule is that revenue derived from the sale of merchandise is recognized in the period in which the sale is consummated, and revenue derived from the provision of a service is recognized in the period in which the service is furnished.

The use of the sale basis is the accountant's practical solution to the difficult problem of measuring revenue under conditions of uncertainty as to the future. The sale leads to a valid claim against the buyer and gives the seller the full support of the law in enforcing collection.

Accrual versus Cash Basis Accounting

When revenue is recognized in the period in which the sale is made or the service is furnished, regardless of when it is collected, and when expenses are recognized in the period in which they contribute to revenue, regardless of when they are paid, the procedure is called **accrual accounting,** sometimes referred to as the **accrual basis** of accounting. In contrast to the accrual basis is the system whereby revenue is recognized only when cash is received and expenses are recognized only when cash is paid out. This procedure is known as **cash basis accounting.**

Cash basis accounting is frequently used by individuals for maintaining personal or family records, also by professional people, nonprofit organizations, and some small businesses; however, most profit-oriented organizations of any size find the accrual basis the most useful. This is particularly true in businesses where inventories and long-lived assets are involved. Although we shall spend some time in Chapter 20 on a consideration of the cash basis method, the accrual basis will be our primary concern in this text.

Types of Adjustments

Ordinarily, all the revenue earned by an organization in a period will not be collected in that period; nor will all the expenses incurred in earning the revenue be paid in that period. Thus, under the accrual basis of accounting, it is generally necessary to adjust some of the revenue and expense accounts at the end of a period in order to reflect a true picture in the income statement. When this is done, the related asset and liability accounts also must be adjusted so that the financial position of the organization will be reflected properly on the balance sheet.

For study purposes, items requiring adjustment may be classified into three broad categories: accruals, deferrals, and estimated items.

Accruals Items of revenue that have been earned but not collected and expense items that have been incurred but not paid ordinarily are known as accrued items. In the adjusting process the term **accrual** is generally used to describe accrued items which have not been recorded at the time financial statements are being prepared and which thus must be adjusted for. When accruals are recognized in income statement accounts, the related assets and liabilities also must be recognized in balance sheet accounts.

Deferrals Items of revenue that have been recorded in the accounts but have not yet been earned and expense items that have been recorded in the accounts but pertain to the future are known as **deferrals.** At the time financial statements are being prepared, adjustment is necessary for any deferral appearing in the accounts. Adjustment of a deferred revenue results in the recognition of a liability, whereas adjustment of a deferred expense results in the recognition of an asset.

Estimated Items On occasion business transactions do not fit precisely into a period for which financial statements are being prepared. When this happens, the recognition, allocation, or measurement of the items involved must be based on estimates and judgment rather than on definitely ascertainable facts. For example, as we learned in Chapter 5, losses on uncollectible accounts may have to be estimated; similarly, as we shall see in Chapter 11, it is often necessary to estimate the cost of using a long-lived asset for a specific period of time. As is the case with accruals and deferrals, the recognition of estimated items also affects both the income statement and the balance sheet. For instance, the periodic provision for estimated uncollectible accounts results in an expense in the income statement, whereas the allowance account appears on the balance sheet.

Recognition and Allocation of Revenues and Expenses

The net income of an organization for a specific period is determined by matching revenues earned during the period with expenses incurred in order to earn the revenues. Under the accrual basis of accounting, an organization's revenue accounts for a period will include any or all of the following:

1 Revenue both earned and collected during the period
2 Revenue earned during the period but collected in a prior period

3 Revenue earned during the period but which will not be collected until a future period

4 Revenue collected during the period but earned in a prior period

5 Revenue collected during the period but which will not be earned until a future period

The organization's expense accounts for the period will include any or all of the following:

1 Expenses belonging in the period and paid during the period

2 Expenses belonging in the period but paid in a prior period

3 Expenses belonging in the period but which will not be paid until a future period

4 Expenses paid during the period but which pertain to a prior period

5 Expenses paid during the period but which pertain to a future period

In the above lists, items numbered 1 (revenue earned and collected during the period and expenses belonging in the period and paid during the period) create no matching problems. All other items, however, require special attention. Items numbered 2 (revenue earned during the period but collected in a prior period and expenses belonging in the period but paid in a prior period) must be pulled into the period. Since these items did not belong in the prior period, they had to be pushed off, or **deferred,** at the end of that period. Items numbered 3 (revenue earned during the period but which will not be collected until a future period, and expenses belonging in the period but which will not be paid until a future period) must be pulled into the period, or **accrued.** Similar problems are encountered with items 4 and 5, those numbered 4 being accruals at the end of the prior period and those numbered 5 being deferrals at the end of the current period. The adjusting of accruals and deferrals will be discussed in detail later in this chapter.

Recognition and Measurement of Assets and Liabilities

The recognition of assets and the recognition and measurement of liabilities ordinarily give the accountant little difficulty. The measurement of assets, however, sometimes presents problems.

Asset Recognition and Measurement   Assets have been defined as anything of value owned by an individual or an organization. Asset recognition is simply a matter of determining when legal title to something of value has passed or when a legitimate claim against another has been established.

Assets are usually measured at **cost,** the price paid or consideration given to acquire the asset in question. From the standpoint of the adjusting process, costs are classified as unexpired or expired.   **Unexpired costs** are those costs which are applicable to the production of future revenues; **expired costs** are those which have been associated with the production of past revenues.   Stated another way, unexpired costs are carried forward on the balance sheet as assets, while expired costs are included in the income statement as expenses.   The recognition and measurement of assets will be treated in detail in Chapters 10 and 11.

Liability Recognition and Measurement   Liabilities have been defined as anything owed by an individual or an organization.   Therefore, liability recognition is merely a matter of determining when a legitimate obligation has been incurred.

Liabilities are measured in accordance with contracted amounts resulting either from oral agreements or from the issuance of notes, mortgages, or bonds; thus their measurement is ordinarily a relatively simple matter.   The recognition and measurement of liabilities will be discussed further in Chapters 12 and 13.

ADJUSTING FOR ACCRUED AND DEFERRED ITEMS

When adjusting for accruals and deferrals, it is important to remember this distinction: Accruals **have not** previously been recorded in the accounts, while deferrals **have** been recorded.   Adjustment is necessary in order to pull accruals into the period and to push deferrals out.   Accruals and deferrals which require periodic adjustment may be classified as follows:

1 Accrued revenues and related assets
2 Accrued expenses and related liabilities
3 Deferred revenues and related liabilities
4 Deferred expenses and related assets

Accrued Revenues and Related Assets

Typical examples of accrued revenue are rental income (rent that has been earned but not collected) and interest income (interest that has been earned but not collected).   When adjusting entries are prepared for these items, the following accounts will be affected.   (Remember that account titles will vary from one organization to another.)

Asset Account	Revenue Account
Accrued Rent Receivable	Rental Revenue
Accrued Interest Receivable	Interest Revenue

Adjusting for Accrued Rental Income Let us assume that the Art Company has unused office space which it rents to the Ball Company for $300 a month, and that the Ball Company has paid the rent for the first 11 months of the year but has failed to pay the December rent. The adjusting entry on the Art Company's books as of December 31, when financial statements are prepared, would be:

December 31

Accrued Rent Receivable	300	
Rental Revenue		300
To record rental income for December.		

After the adjusting entry has been posted, the ledger accounts involved will appear as follows:

Accrued Rent Receivable

Dec. 31 Adjusting	300	

Rental Revenue

	Nov. 30 Balance	3,300
	Dec. 31 Adjusting	300

As a result of the adjusting entry, an asset (accrued rent receivable) will appear on the balance sheet as of December 31, and the December rent, although not collected, will be reflected as revenue in the income statement.

Adjusting for Accrued Interest Income To illustrate this procedure, let us assume that an organization holds a customer's 60-day, 6 percent, $10,000 promissory note dated December 1. The adjusting entry to reflect the accrued interest of $50 ($10,000 $\times$ .06 $\times$ 30/360) as of December 31 would be:

December 31

Accrued Interest Receivable	50	
Interest Revenue		50
To record accrued interest at 6% on $10,000 note dated December 1.		

After the entry has been posted, the ledger accounts involved will appear as follows:

Accrued Interest Receivable

Dec. 31 Adjusting	50	

Interest Revenue

	Dec. 31 Adjusting	50

As a result of the adjusting entry, an asset (accrued interest receivable) will appear on the balance sheet as of December 31, and the interest earned during December, although not collected, will be reflected as revenue in the income statement.

Accrued Expenses and Related Liabilities

Typical examples of accrued expenses are rent expense (rent that has been incurred but not paid), interest expense (interest that has been incurred but not paid), and wage expense (wages that have been incurred but not paid). When adjusting entries are prepared for these items, the following accounts will be affected:

Expense Account	Liability Account
Rent Expense	Accrued Rent Payable
Interest Expense	Accrued Interest Payable
Wage Expense	Accrued Wages Payable

Adjusting for Accrued Rent Expense In this case we are looking at adjustment for the nonpayment of rent from the viewpoint of the tenant, rather than from the landlord's side as illustrated on page 204. At that time we learned that the Ball Company rented office space from the Art Company for $300 a month and had paid the rent for the first 11 months of the year but had not paid the December rent. The adjusting entry on the Ball Company's books as of December 31, when financial statements are prepared, would be:

December 31

Rent Expense	300	
Accrued Rent Payable		300

To record rent expense for December.

After the adjusting entry has been posted, the ledger accounts involved will appear as follows:

Rent Expense

Nov. 30 Balance	3,300	
Dec. 31 Adjusting	300	

Accrued Rent Payable

	Dec. 31 Adjusting	300

As a result of the adjusting entry, rent incurred in December, although not paid, will be reflected as an expense in the income statement, and the related liability (accrued rent payable) will appear on the balance sheet.

Adjusting for Accrued Interest Expense   Let us assume than an organization issues to a creditor a 60-day, 6 percent, $15,000 promissory note dated December 1.   The adjusting entry to reflect the accrued interest of $75 ($15,000 × .06 × 30/360) as of December 31, when financial statements are prepared, would be:

December 31

Interest Expense——————————————————————— 75
    Accrued Interest Payable ——————————————————— 75
To record accrued interest at 6% on $15,000 note dated December 1.

After the adjusting entry has been posted, the ledger accounts involved will appear as follows:

Interest Expense

Dec. 31 Adjusting	75	

Accrued Interest Payable

	Dec. 31 Adjusting	75

As a result of the adjusting entry, interest incurred in December, although not paid, will be reflected in the income statement as an expense, and the related liability (accrued interest payable) will appear on the balance sheet.

Adjusting for Accrued Wages   When employees are paid on a weekly or biweekly basis, it is frequently necessary to make an adjusting entry for wages earned but not paid as of the end of the fiscal period.   If we assume that as of December 31, the end of the fiscal period, the employees of the Brace Company have earned $1,200, which they have not yet been paid, the adjusting entry will be:

December 31

Wage Expense ——————————————————————— 1,200
    Accrued Wages Payable——————————————————— 1,200
To record accrued wages as of December 31.

If we further assume that as of December 26, the last payroll date in December, the employees had already earned and received $76,800 in wages for the year, the pertinent ledger accounts will appear as follows after the adjusting entry has been posted:

Wage Expense

Dec. 26 Balance	76,800	
Dec. 31 Adjusting	1,200	

Accrued Wages Payable

	Dec. 31 Adjusting	1,200

As a result of the adjusting entry, wages incurred in December but not paid will be reflected in the income statement as an expense, and the related liability (accrued wages payable) will appear on the balance sheet.

Deferred Revenues and Related Liabilities

Unlike an adjusting entry for an accrual, an adjusting entry for a deferral is dependent upon the type of account used initially to record the item. Deferred items may be recorded either in real or nominal accounts. (You will recall that real accounts are balance sheet accounts, while nominal accounts are income statement accounts.) Although there is not complete uniformity in practice, deferrals which must be allocated over several accounting periods frequently are recorded in real accounts, whereas those pertaining to relatively short periods of time often are recorded in nominal accounts. For example, the prepayment of a 3-year insurance premium is apt to be recorded in a real account, while the advance payment of 90 days' interest is more likely to be recorded in a nominal account.

Typical examples of deferred revenue are rental income (rent that has been collected but not earned) and interest income (interest that has been collected but not earned). When adjusting entries are prepared for these items, the following accounts will be affected:

Liability Account	Revenue Account
Rent Collected in Advance	Rental Revenue
Interest Collected in Advance	Interest Revenue

Adjusting for Deferred Rental Income Let us assume that office space is rented to a tenant for $300 a month, and that the tenant paid one year's rent in advance as of November 1. The collection of the year's rent could be recorded by the use of either a real or a nominal account as follows:

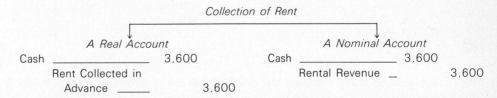

Collection of Rent

A Real Account		*A Nominal Account*	
Cash _____ 3,600		Cash _____ 3,600	
Rent Collected in		Rental Revenue _	3,600
Advance _____	3,600		

The adjusting entry as of December 31, when financial statements are prepared, will be:

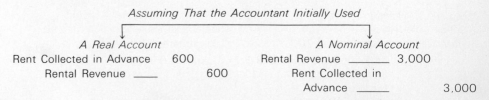

Assuming That the Accountant Initially Used

A Real Account		*A Nominal Account*	
Rent Collected in Advance	600	Rental Revenue _____	3,000
Rental Revenue ____	600	Rent Collected in	
		Advance _____	3,000

After the appropriate adjusting entry has been posted, the pertinent ledger accounts will appear as follows:

Assuming That the Accountant Initially Used

A Real Account				A Nominal Account			
Rent Collected in Advance				**Rental Revenue**			
Dec. 31	600	Nov. 1	3,600	Dec. 31	3,000	Nov. 1	3,600
Rental Revenue				**Rent Collected in Advance**			
		Dec. 31	600			Dec. 31	3,000

As a result of either adjusting entry, rent earned during November and December will be reflected as revenue in the income statement, and the liability for the future service (rent collected in advance) will appear on the balance sheet as of December 31.

Adjusting for Deferred Interest Income To illustrate this procedure, let us assume that an organization holds a customer's 90-day, $20,000, non-interest-bearing promissory note dated December 1 and taken that day at a 6 percent discount. The receipt of the note could be recorded by the use of either a real or a nominal account as follows:

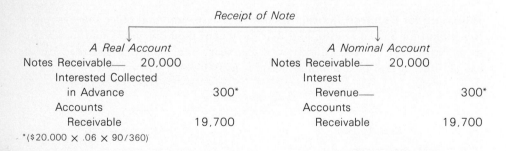

Receipt of Note

A Real Account		A Nominal Account	
Notes Receivable— 20,000		Notes Receivable— 20,000	
Interested Collected		Interest	
in Advance	300*	Revenue—	300*
Accounts		Accounts	
Receivable	19,700	Receivable	19,700

*($20.000 × .06 × 90/360)

The adjusting entry to reflect the deferred interest of $200 ($20,000 × .06 × 60/360) as of December 31 will be:

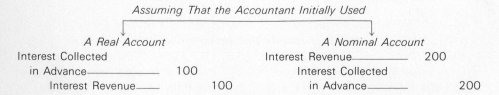

Assuming That the Accountant Initially Used

A Real Account		A Nominal Account	
Interest Collected		Interest Revenue————— 200	
in Advance————— 100		Interest Collected	
Interest Revenue—	100	in Advance—————	200

After the appropriate adjusting entry has been posted, the ledger accounts involved will appear as follows:

Assuming That the Accountant Initially Used

A Real Account | *A Nominal Account*

Interest Collected in Advance

Dec. 31	100	Dec. 1	300	

Interest Revenue

Dec. 31	200	Dec. 1	300	

Interest Revenue

Dec. 31	100

Interest Collected in Advance

Dec. 31	200

As a result of either adjusting entry, interest earned during December will be reflected as revenue in the income statement, and the liability for the service to be rendered in the future (interest collected in advance) will appear on the balance sheet as of December 31.

Deferred Expenses and Related Assets

When supplies and services are purchased in one accounting period but the supplies are not consumed or the benefits from the services are not received until a subsequent period, the costs of such supplies and services are known as **deferred** or **prepaid expenses.** Typical examples of deferred expenses are interest expense (interest which has been paid but which pertains to the future), insurance expense (insurance which has been paid but which pertains to the future), and store supplies expense (supplies which have been purchased but which will not be used until a future time). Although account titles may vary among organizations, typical accounts which would be affected in the adjusting process are:

Asset Account	**Expense Account**
Prepaid Interest Expense	Interest Expense
Prepaid Insurance	Insurance Expense
Store Supplies	Store Supplies Expense

Adjusting for Prepaid Interest Let us assume that an organization issued to a creditor a 90-day, $5,000, non-interest-bearing promissory note dated December 1 and that it was taken as of that date by the creditor at a 6 percent discount. The issuance of the note could be recorded by the use of either a real or a nominal account as follows:

Issuance of Note

A Real Account		A Nominal Account	
Accounts Payable ——— 4,925		Accounts Payable ——— 4,925	
Prepaid Interest		Interest Expense——— 75*	
Expense——————— 75*		Notes Payable—	5,000
Notes Payable—	5,000		

*($5,000 × .06 × 90/360)

The adjusting entry necessary to reflect correctly the interest expense of $25 ($5,000 × .06 × 30/360) and the prepaid interest of $50 ($5,000 × .06 × 60/360) in the financial statements as of December 31, would be:

Assuming That the Accountant Initially Used

A Real Account		A Nominal Account	
Interest Expense ————— 25		Prepaid Interest Expense——— 50	
Prepaid Interest Expense	25	Interest Expense ———	50

After the appropriate adjusting entry has been posted, the ledger accounts involved will appear as follows:

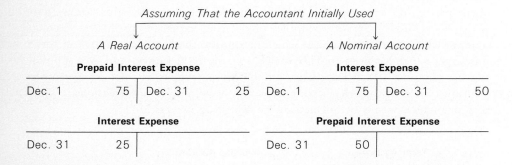

Assuming That the Accountant Initially Used

A Real Account		A Nominal Account	
Prepaid Interest Expense		**Interest Expense**	
Dec. 1 75	Dec. 31 25	Dec. 1 75	Dec. 31 50
Interest Expense		**Prepaid Interest Expense**	
Dec. 31 25		Dec. 31 50	

As a result of either adjusting entry, the $25 interest expense of December will be reflected in the income statement as an expense, and the $50 prepaid interest will be reflected on the balance sheet as an asset.

Adjusting for Unexpired Insurance Assume that an organization paid $3,600 for a 3-year insurance policy effective November 1. The purchase of the insurance premium could be recorded by the use of either a real or a nominal account as follows:

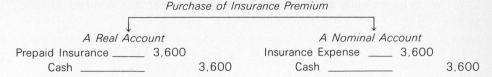

Purchase of Insurance Premium

A Real Account		*A Nominal Account*	
Prepaid Insurance _____ 3,600		Insurance Expense ____ 3,600	
Cash _____	3,600	Cash _____	3,600

When the accounts are adjusted as of December 31 (2 months later), the adjusting entry will be:

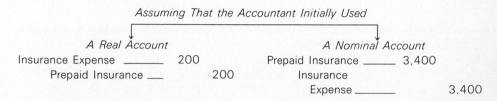

Assuming That the Accountant Initially Used

A Real Account		*A Nominal Account*	
Insurance Expense _____ 200		Prepaid Insurance _____ 3,400	
Prepaid Insurance ___	200	Insurance Expense _____	3,400

After the appropriate adjusting entry has been posted, the ledger accounts involved will appear as follows:

Assuming That the Accountant Initially Used

A Real Account		*A Nominal Account*	
Prepaid Insurance		**Insurance Expense**	
Nov. 1 3,600	Dec. 31 200	Nov. 1 3,600	Dec. 31 3,400
Insurance Expense		**Prepaid Insurance**	
Dec. 31 200		Dec. 31 3,400	

As a result of either adjusting entry, the $200 insurance expense of November and December will be reflected as an expense in the income statement, and the $3,400 of unexpired insurance will be reflected on the balance sheet as an asset.

Adjusting for Unconsumed Supplies   To illustrate this procedure, let us assume that an organization purchased $800 worth of store supplies on December 1 but has only $350 worth on hand as of December 31 when the books are adjusted and closed.   The purchase of the supplies could be recorded by the use of either a real or a nominal account as follows:

Purchase of Store Supplies

A Real Account		*A Nominal Account*	
Store Supplies _____ 800		Store Supplies Expense ___ 800	
Cash _____	800	Cash _____	800

The adjusting entry as of December 31, when financial statements are prepared, will be:

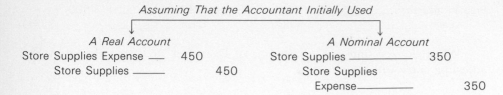

Assuming That the Accountant Initially Used

A Real Account		*A Nominal Account*	
Store Supplies Expense —— 450		Store Supplies ———— 350	
Store Supplies ———	450	Store Supplies Expense———	350

After the appropriate adjusting entry has been posted, the ledger accounts involved will appear as follows:

Assuming That the Accountant Initially Used

A Real Account — *A Nominal Account*

Store Supplies				**Store Supplies Expense**			
Dec. 1	800	Dec. 31	450	Dec. 1	800	Dec. 31	350

Store Supplies Expense			**Store Supplies**		
Dec. 31	450		Dec. 31	350	

As a result of either adjusting entry, $450 will be reflected in the income statement as an expense, and $350 will appear on the balance sheet as an asset.

READJUSTING PROCESS

You will recall from Chapter 4 that after adjusting entries have been made and posted, the nominal accounts (income statement accounts) are closed to the Revenue and Expense Summary account, which in turn is closed to the Capital account. Thus, accruals and deferrals are reflected at this time only in real accounts (balance sheet accounts). Accountants, however, tend to establish procedures which permit them to handle transactions of a similar nature in a consistent and systematic manner; therefore, it is convenient at the beginning of a new accounting period to have accrued and deferred items reflected in the accounts in which they customarily are entered initially. For example, if the collection of interest is usually recorded in the Interest Revenue account, any interest collected in advance as of the end of a fiscal period preferably should be transferred from the Interest Collected in Advance account back to the Interest Revenue account as of the beginning of the next period.

Entries pertaining to this transferring process are called **readjusting,** or **reversing,** entries because they are the exact opposite of adjusting entries. To readjust an adjusting entry we simply reverse it, or "turn it around," that is, we "debit the credit and credit the debit."

Although adjusting entries usually are made for accrued, deferred, and estimated items, readjusting entries are necessary only for accruals and for some deferrals. Deferred items initially recorded in nominal accounts will require readjusting, whereas those initially recorded in real accounts will not. Estimated items do not require readjusting because they are initially reflected in real accounts. For example, in Chapter 5 when we were considering estimated uncollectible accounts, we set the provision up in a real account, Allowance for Estimated Uncollectibles. The same approach will be noted in subsequent chapters when we consider other estimated items such as the depreciation of long-lived assets and the depletion of natural resources.

To summarize, if we use readjusting entries, we should:

1 **Always** readjust accrued items

2 **Never** readjust estimated items

3 Readjust **some** deferred items (those initially recorded in nominal accounts)

Readjusting Accrued Items

To illustrate the readjusting of accruals, we shall employ the same data we used when adjusting for accrued interest receivable and accrued interest payable.

Readjusting Accrued Interest Receivable When we adjusted for accrued interest receivable, we assumed that an organization held a 60-day, 6 percent, $10,000 promissory note upon which $50 of interest had accrued as of the end of the fiscal period. After both adjusting and closing entries have been posted, the ledger accounts involved will appear as follows:

Accrued Interest Receivable

Dec. 31	Adjusting	50		

Interest Revenue

Dec. 31	Closing	50	Dec. 31	Adjusting	50

When we made the adjusting entry, we debited the Accrued Interest Receivable account and credited the Interest Revenue account. When readjusting, we "turn the entry around" and debit the Interest Revenue account and credit the Accrued Interest Receivable account as follows:

Interest Revenue _____ 50
    Accrued Interest Receivable _____ 50

After the readjusting entry has been posted, the ledger accounts involved will appear as follows:

Accrued Interest Receivable

Dec. 31	Adjusting	50	Jan. 1	Readjusting	50

Interest Revenue

Dec. 31	Closing	50	Dec. 31	Adjusting	50
Jan. 1	Readjusting	50			

Note that after the readjusting entry is posted, the real account (Accrued Interest Receivable) is closed, whereas the nominal account (Interest Revenue) has a negative (debit) balance. When the interest of $100 ($10,000 $\times$ .06 $\times$ 60/360) is collected at maturity, it will be reflected as a debit in the Cash account and as a credit in the Interest Revenue account. The Interest Revenue account will then have a $50 credit balance representing the interest earned in January, as shown in the following T account:

Interest Revenue

Dec. 31	Closing	50	Dec. 31	Adjusting	50
Jan. 1	Readjusting	50	Jan. 31	Collection	100

Readjusting Accrued Interest Payable When we adjusted for accrued interest payable, we assumed that an organization issued a 60-day, 6 percent, $15,000 promissory note upon which $75 of interest had accrued as of the end of the fiscal period. After adjusting and closing entries have been posted, the ledger accounts involved will appear as follows:

Interest Expense

Dec. 31	Adjusting	75	Dec. 31	Closing	75

Accrued Interest Payable

			Dec. 31	Adjusting	75

When we made the adjusting entry, we debited the Interest Expense account and credited the Accrued Interest Payable account. Thus, when readjusting we simply "turn the entry around" by debiting the Accrued Interest Payable account and crediting the Interest Expense account, as follows:

Accrued Interest Payable	75	
Interest Expense		75

After the readjusting entry has been posted, the ledger accounts involved will appear as follows:

Interest Expense

Dec. 31	Adjusting	75	Dec. 31	Closing	75
			Jan. 1	Readjusting	75

Accrued Interest Payable

Jan. 1	Readjusting	75	Dec. 31	Adjusting	75

After the readjusting entry is posted, the real account (Accrued Interest Payable) is closed, while the nominal account (Interest Expense) has a negative (credit) balance. When the interest of $150 ($15,000 × .06 × 60/360) is paid at maturity, it will be reflected as a credit in the Cash account and as a debit in the Interest Expense account. The Interest Expense account then will have a $75 debit balance representing the interest expense for January, as shown in the following T account:

Interest Expense

Dec. 31	Adjusting	75	Dec. 31	Closing	75
Jan. 31	Payment	150	Jan. 1	Readjusting	75

Readjusting Deferred Items

To illustrate the readjusting of deferrals we shall employ the same data we used earlier when we adjusted for rent collected in advance and unconsumed store supplies.

Readjusting for Rent Collected in Advance When adjusting for rent collected in advance, we assumed that office space was rented to a tenant for $300 a month and that the tenant had paid 1 year's rent in advance as of November 1. After both adjusting and closing entries have been posted as of December 31, the pertinent ledger accounts will appear as follows:

Assuming That the Accountant Initially Used

A Real Account	A Nominal Account

Rent Collected in Advance

Dec. 31		Nov. 1	
Adjusting	600	Collection	3,600

Rental Revenue

Dec. 31		Nov. 1	
Adjusting	3,000	Collection	3,600
Dec. 31			
Closing	600		
	3,600		3,600

Rental Revenue

Dec. 31		Dec. 31	
Closing	600	Adjusting	600

Rent Collected in Advance

		Dec. 31	
		Adjusting	3,000

Observe that regardless of whether a real or a nominal account was used initially, after the adjusting and closing entries are posted the amount of deferred rent income is reflected in the real account (Rent Collected in Advance). If the real account is ordinarily used to record the collection of rent, no readjusting entry is necessary. However, if the nominal account generally is employed for this purpose, the following readjusting entry will be required:

Rent Collected in Advance	3,000	
Rental Revenue		3,000

After the readjusting entry has been posted, the ledger accounts involved will appear as follows:

Rental Revenue

Dec. 31	Adjusting	3,000	Nov. 1	Collection	3,600
Dec. 31	Closing	600			
		3,600			3,600
			Jan. 1	Readjusting	3,000

Rent Collected in Advance

Jan. 1	Readjusting	3,000	Dec. 31	Adjusting	3,000

Readjusting for Unconsumed Supplies When we adjusted for unconsumed supplies, we assumed that an organization purchased $800 worth of store supplies on December 1, but had only $350 worth on hand as of December 31. After both adjusting and closing entries have been posted as of December 31, the ledger accounts involved will appear as follows:

Assuming That the Accountant Initially Used

A Real Account   *A Nominal Account*

Store Supplies			
Dec. 1		Dec. 31	
Purchase	800	Adjusting	450

Store Supplies Expense			
Dec. 1		Dec. 31	
Purchase	800	Adjusting	350
		Dec. 31	
		Closing	450
	800		800

Store Supplies Expense			
Dec. 31		Dec. 31	
Adjusting	450	Closing	450

Store Supplies			
Dec. 31			
Adjusting	350		

Note that regardless of whether the accountant initially used a real or a nominal account, after the adjusting and closing entries are posted, the amount of supplies on hand is reflected in the real account (Store Supplies). If the real account ordinarily is used to record the purchase of store supplies, no readjusting entry is necessary. If, however, the nominal account is used, the following readjusting entry will be required:

Store Supplies Expense	350	
Store Supplies		350

After the readjusting entry has been posted, the ledger accounts involved will appear as follows:

Store Supplies Expense			
Dec. 1	Purchase	800	
		800	
Jan. 1	Readjusting	350	

Dec. 31	Adjusting	350
Dec. 31	Closing	450
		800

Store Supplies			
Dec. 31	Adjusting	350	

Jan. 1	Readjusting	350

CONTINUATION OF THE PENDERY ILLUSTRATION

At this time we shall briefly review the entire accounting process, with emphasis on the adjusting and closing phases. To do this we shall continue the Pendery illustration for the month of May. You will recall that this illustration was first introduced in Chapter 2 when we studied transaction analysis and the basic equation. It was continued in Chapter 3 when the role and function of the account were introduced. In Chapter 4, when we first examined the basic books of original entry, we took the illustration through the entire month of April. This included both the recording of Pendery's daily transactions and the adjusting and closing of his books as of April 30.

In Chapter 5, when subsidiary ledgers and controlling accounts were introduced, we continued the illustration by recording Pendery's May credit purchases in the purchases journal and his May credit sales in the sales journal. In Chapter 7, when columnar cash receipts and disbursements journals were introduced, we recorded his cash transactions for the month of May. Thus, as of now we have recorded all of Pendery's May transactions except those belonging in his general journal. Pendery had two such transactions during May. On May 13 he purchased $80 worth of office supplies on account from The Wyan Company, and on May 19 he purchased $400 worth of furniture and equipment on account from the Central Supply Company. When recorded in the general journal these transactions will result in an $80 increase in the Office Supplies account, a $400 increase in the Furniture and Equipment account, and a $480 increase in Pendery's Accounts Payable account.

Let us now complete the following steps in the order given:

1 **Examine** Pendery's general ledger as of May 31 before adjusting and closing entries have been made.
2 **Prepare** adjusting and closing entries using the work sheet approach.
3 **Record** the adjusting and closing entries in the general journal.
4 **Examine** the general ledger after adjusting and closing entries have been posted.
5 **Take** a postclosing trial balance.
6 **Prepare** any necessary readjusting entries.

Pendery's General Ledger before Adjusting
and Closing Entries Have Been Made for May

As you examine Pendery's general ledger as of May 31, before adjusting and closing entries have been made, note that the open accounts include real, nominal, and mixed accounts.

General Ledger

(Before adjusting and closing)

Cash   Account No. 101

Apr.	30		CR1	9,980	00	Apr.	30		CD1	5,583	00
							30	Balance	√	4,397	00
				9,980	00					9,980	00
May	1	Balance	√	4,397	00	May	31		CD4	2,434	00
	31		CR3	3,989	00						

Accounts Receivable   Account No. 110

May	1	Balance	√	225	00	May	31		CR3	800	00
	31		S2	1,475	00						

Merchandise Inventory   Account No. 131

Apr.	30	Adjusting	J1	3,700	00						

Store Supplies   Account No. 141

Apr.	10		CD1	40	00	Apr.	30	Adjusting	J1	10	00
May	4		CD4	30	00						

Office Supplies   Account No. 142

May	13		J2	80	00						

Prepaid Rent   Account No. 151

Apr.	1		CD1	600	00	Apr.	30	Adjusting	J1	100	00

Prepaid Insurance   Account No. 161

Apr.	10		CD1	108	00	Apr.	30	Adjusting	J1	6	00

Furniture and Equipment   Account No. 171

Apr.	2		CD1	500	00						
	2		J1	300	00						
May	19		J2	400	00						

Accounts Payable   Account No. 200

May	31		CD4	1,350	00	May	1	Balance	√	650	00
							13		J2	80	00
							19		J2	400	00
							31		P2	2,500	00

Notes Payable   *Account No. 211*

						Apr.	14		CR1	1,000	00

Ralph Pendery, Capital   *Account No. 301*

Apr.	30	Balance	√	8,104	00	Apr.	1		CR1	8,000	00
							30	Closing	J1	104	00
				8,104	00					8,104	00
						May	1	Balance	√	8,104	00
							1		CR3	3,000	00

Revenue and Expense Summary   *Account No. 310*

Apr.	30	Closing	J1	1,101	00	Apr.	30	Closing	J1	1,205	00
	30	Closing	J1	104	00						
				1,205	00					1,205	00

Sales   *Account No. 401*

Apr.	30	Closing	J1	1,205	00	Apr.	15		CR1	235	00
							30		CR1	700	00
							30		S1	270	00
				1,205	00					1,205	00
						May	5		CR3	200	00
							31		S2	1,475	00

Sales Discount   *Account No. 402*

May	31		CR3	11	00					

Advertising   *Account No. 501*

May	1		CD4	100	00					

Purchases   *Account No. 505*

Apr.	3		CD1	2,000	00	Apr.	30	Adjusting	J1	4,550	00
	4		CD1	1,000	00						
	15		CD1	1,000	00						
	30		P1	550	00						
				4,550	00					4,550	00
May	1		CD4	800	00						
	31		P2	2,500	00						

Sales Salary   *Account No. 507*

Apr.	30		CD1	60	00	Apr.	30	Closing	J1	60	00
May	31		CD4	60	00						

Miscellaneous Expense   *Account No. 508*

Apr.	30		CD1	75	00	Apr.	30	Closing	J1	75	00
May	31		CD4	40	00						

Store Supplies Expense*   *Account No. 509*

Apr.	30	Adjusting	J1	10	00	Apr.	30	Closing	J1	10	00

*In Chapter 4 this account was entitled Store Supplies Used.

Rent Expense   *Account No. 510*

Apr.	30	Adjusting	J1	100	00	Apr.	30	Closing	J1	100	00

Insurance Expense   *Account No. 511*

Apr.	30	Adjusting	J1	6	00	Apr.	30	Closing	J1	6	00

Purchase Discount   *Account No. 512*

						May	31		CD4	16	00

Transportation In   *Account No. 514*

May	31		CD4	70	00						

Adjusting and Closing the Books Using the Work Sheet Approach

Up to this time we have dealt with two trial balances, one taken before adjusting and closing entries are made and another taken after they have been made. As we learned in Chapter 4, the former is commonly referred to as an **unadjusted trial balance,** while the latter is known as a **postclosing trial balance.**

Some accountants take yet another trial balance during the adjusting and closing process. This one, known as the **adjusted trial balance,** is taken after the adjusting entries have been made but before the closing entries are made. When this procedure is followed, a 10-column work sheet is employed instead of the eight-column one we used in Chapter 4. The two additional columns, which contain the adjusted trial balance, fall between the adjustments columns and the income statement columns.

When using a 10-column work sheet, our first step is to take a trial balance from the ledger and enter it in the first two columns of the work sheet, just as we did for the eight-column work sheet in Chapter 4. Next, we enter the adjusting data in the adjustments columns. We then combine each account balance in the trial balance columns with the corresponding adjusting data, if any. The resulting adjusted account balances are entered in the adjusted trial balance columns along with those account balances which do not require adjusting. We then carry the nominal account balances to the income statement columns and the real account balances to the balance sheet columns. After these columns are totaled, the balancing amount in the income statement columns (the net income or loss for the period) is carried over as the balancing item in the balance sheet columns. Each of these steps can be followed on the work sheet shown below. The required information for adjustments appears at the top of page 223.

RALPH PENDERY
Work Sheet
May 31, 1972

	Trial Balance		Adjustments*		Adjusted Trial Balance		Income Statement		Balance Sheet	
	Debit	Credit	Debit	Credit	Debit	Credit	Debit	Credit	Debit	Credit
Cash	5,952				5,952				5,952	
Accounts receivable	900				900				900	
Merchandise inventory	3,700		(a) 5,650	(b) 3,700	5,650				5,650	
Store supplies	60			(c) 15	45				45	
Office supplies	80			(d) 28	52				52	
Prepaid rent	500			(e) 100	400				400	
Prepaid insurance	102			(f) 9	93				93	
Furniture and equipment	1,200				1,200				1,200	
Accounts payable		2,280				2,280				2,280
Notes payable		1,000				1,000				1,000
Ralph Pendery, capital		11,104				11,104				11,104
Sales		1,675				1,675		1,675		
Sales discount	11				11		11			
Advertising	100				100		100			
Purchases	3,300				3,300		3,300			
Sales salary	60				60		60			
Miscellaneous expense	40				40		40			
Purchase discount		16				16		16		
Transportation in	70				70		70			
	16,075	16,075								
Revenue & expense summary			(b) 3,700	(a) 5,650		1,950		1,950		
Store supplies expense			(c) 15		15		15			
Office supplies expense			(d) 28		28		28			
Rent expense			(e) 100		100		100			
Insurance expense			(f) 9		9		9			
Interest expense			(g) 5		5		5			
Accrued interest payable				(g) 5		5				5
Estimated loss on uncollectible accounts			(h) 36		36		36			
Allowance for uncollectible accounts				(h) 36		36				36
			9,543	9,543	18,066	18,066	3,774	3,641	14,292	14,425
Net loss								133	133	
							3,774	3,774	14,425	14,425

*Adjustments
(a) May 31 inventory.
(b) May 1 inventory.
(c) Store supplies used during May.
(d) Office supplies used during May.
(e) Rent expired during May.
(f) Insurance expired during May.
(g) Interest accrued as of May 31.
(h) Estimated loss on uncollectible accounts.

Information for adjustments, May 31, 1972:

Merchandise inventory on hand	$5,650
Store supplies on hand	45
Office supplies on hand	52
Prepaid rent	400
Prepaid insurance	93
Accrued interest on notes payable	5
Estimated loss on uncollectible accounts	36

Recording the Adjusting and Closing Entries in the General Journal

After the work sheet is completed, the adjusting entries are copied from the adjustments columns into the general journal, and the closing entries are copied from the income statement columns into the general journal. Remember that the income statement accounts are closed to the Revenue and Expense Summary account by "debiting the credits" and "crediting the debits." The Revenue and Expense Summary account is then closed to the Capital account.

General Journal   *Page 3*

Date		Account Titles and Explanation	PR	Debit		Credit	
		Adjusting Entries					
1972							
May	31	Merchandise Inventory	131	5,650	00		
		Revenue and Expense Summary	310			5,650	00
		To record the May 31 merchandise inventory.					
	31	Revenue and Expense Summary	310	3,700	00		
		Merchandise Inventory	131			3,700	00
		To close the May 1 merchandise inventory into the Revenue and Expense Summary account.					
	31	Store Supplies Expense	509	15	00		
		Store Supplies	141			15	00
		To adjust the Store Supplies account for supplies used.					
	31	Office Supplies Expense	516	28	00		
		Office Supplies	142			28	00
		To adjust the Office Supplies account for supplies used.					
	31	Rent Expense	510	100	00		
		Prepaid Rent	151			100	00
		To adjust the Prepaid Rent account for rent used.					

General Journal

Date		Account Titles and Explanation	PR	Debit		Credit	
1972 May	31	Insurance Expense _____	511	9	00		
		Prepaid Insurance _____	161			9	00
		To adjust the Prepaid Insurance account for insurance used.					
	31	Interest Expense _____	517	5	00		
		Accrued Interest Payable _____	212			5	00
		To adjust for accrued interest on notes payable.					
	31	Estimated Loss on Uncollectible					
		Accounts _____	518	36	00		
		Allowance for Uncollectible					
		Accounts _____	120			36	00
		To adjust for estimated loss on uncollectible accounts.					
		Closing Entries					
	31	Sales _____	401	1,675	00		
		Purchase Discount _____	512	16	00		
		Revenue and Expense Summary ____	310			1,691	00
		To close all income statement accounts with credit balances.					
	31	Revenue and Expense Summary _____	310	3,774	00		
		Sales Discount _____	402			11	00
		Advertising _____	501			100	00
		Purchases _____	505			3,300	00
		Sales Salary _____	507			60	00
		Miscellaneous Expense _____	508			40	00
		Transportation In _____	514			70	00
		Store Supplies Expense _____	509			15	00
		Office Supplies Expense _____	516			28	00
		Rent Expense _____	510			100	00
		Insurance Expense _____	511			9	00
		Interest Expense _____	517			5	00
		Estimated Loss on Uncollectible					
		Accounts _____	518			36	00
		To close all income statement accounts with debit balances.					
	31	Ralph Pendery, Capital _____	301	133	00		
		Revenue and Expense Summary ____	310			133	00
		To close the Revenue and Expense Summary account.					

Pendery's General Ledger after Adjusting and Closing Entries Have Been Posted

When you examine Pendery's general ledger after the adjusting and closing entries have been posted, note that only *real* accounts are open.

General Ledger

(After adjusting and closing)

Cash — *Account No. 101*

Apr.	30		CR1	9,980	00	Apr.	30		CD1	5,583	00
							30	Balance	√	4,397	00
				9,980	00					9,980	00
May	1	Balance	√	4,397	00	May	31		CD4	2,434	00
	31		CR3	3,989	00		31	Balance	√	5,952	00
				8,386	00					8,386	00
June	1	Balance	√	5,952	00						

Accounts Receivable — *Account No. 110*

May	1	Balance	√	225	00	May	31		CR3	800	00
	31		S2	1,475	00						

Allowance for Uncollectible Accounts — *Account No. 120*

						May	31	Adjusting	J4	36	00

Merchandise Inventory — *Account No. 131*

Apr.	30	Adjusting	J1	3,700	00	May	31	Adjusting	J3	3,700	00
May	31	Adjusting	J3	5,650	00						

Store Supplies — *Account No. 141*

Apr.	10		CD1	40	00	Apr.	30	Adjusting	J1	10	00
May	4		CD4	30	00	May	31	Adjusting	J3	15	00

Office Supplies — *Account No. 142*

May	13		J2	80	00	May	31	Adjusting	J3	28	00

Prepaid Rent — *Account No. 151*

Apr.	1		CD1	600	00	Apr.	30	Adjusting	J1	100	00
						May	31	Adjusting	J3	100	00

Prepaid Insurance — Account No. 161

Date			Ref	Amount		Date		Item	Ref	Amount	
Apr.	10		CD1	108	00	Apr.	30	Adjusting	J1	6	00
						May	31	Adjusting	J4	9	00

Furniture and Equipment — Account No. 171

Date			Ref	Amount	
Apr.	2		CD1	500	00
	2		J1	300	00
May	19		J2	400	00

Accounts Payable — Account No. 200

Date			Ref	Amount		Date		Item	Ref	Amount	
May	31		CD4	1,350	00	May	1	Balance	✓	650	00
							13		J2	80	00
							19		J2	400	00
							31		P2	2,500	00

Notes Payable — Account No. 211

						Date		Item	Ref	Amount	
						Apr.	14		CR1	1,000	00

Accrued Interest Payable — Account No. 212

						Date		Item	Ref	Amount	
						May	31	Adjusting	J4	5	00

Ralph Pendery, Capital — Account No. 301

Date		Item	Ref	Amount		Date		Item	Ref	Amount	
Apr.	30	Balance	✓	8,104	00	Apr.	1		CR1	8,000	00
							30	Closing	J1	104	00
				8,104	00					8,104	00
May	31	Closing	J4	133	00	May	1	Balance	✓	8,104	00
	31	Balance	✓	10,971	00		1		CR3	3,000	00
				11,104	00					11,104	00
						June	1	Balance	✓	10,971	00

Revenue and Expense Summary — Account No. 310

Date		Item	Ref	Amount		Date		Item	Ref	Amount	
Apr.	30	Closing	J1	1,101	00	Apr.	30	Closing	J1	1,205	00
	30	Closing	J1	104	00						
				1,205	00					1,205	00
May	31	Adjusting	J3	3,700	00	May	31	Adjusting	J3	5,650	00
	31	Closing	J4	3,774	00		31	Closing	J4	1,691	00
							31	Closing	J4	133	00
				7,474	00					7,474	00

Sales — Account No. 401

Apr.	30	Closing	J1	1,205 00	Apr.	15		CR1	235 00	
						30		CR1	700 00	
						30		S1	270 00	
				1,205 00					1,205 00	
May	31	Closing	J4	1,675 00	May	5		CR3	200 00	
						31		S2	1,475 00	
				1,675 00					1,675 00	

Sales Discount — Account No. 402

May	31		CR3	11 00	May	31	Closing	J4	11 00

Advertising — Account No. 501

May	1		CD4	100 00	May	31	Closing	J4	100 00

Purchases — Account No. 505

Apr.	3		CD1	2,000 00	Apr.	30	Adjusting	J1	4,550 00
	4		CD1	1,000 00					
	15		CD1	1,000 00					
	30		P1	550 00					
				4,550 00					4,550 00
May	1		CD4	800 00	May	31	Closing	J4	3,300 00
	31		P2	2,500 00					

Sales Salary — Account No. 507

Apr.	30		CD1	60 00	Apr.	30	Closing	J1	60 00
May	31		CD4	60 00	May	31	Closing	J4	60 00

Miscellaneous Expense — Account No. 508

Apr.	30		CD1	75 00	Apr.	30	Closing	J1	75 00
May	31		CD4	40 00	May	31	Closing	J4	40 00

Store Supplies Expense — Account No. 509

Apr.	30	Adjusting	J1	10 00	Apr.	30	Closing	J1	10 00
May	31	Adjusting	J3	15 00	May	31	Closing	J4	15 00

Rent Expense   *Account No. 510*

| Apr. | 30 | Adjusting | J1 | 100 | 00 | Apr. | 30 | Closing | J1 | 100 | 00 |
| May | 31 | Adjusting | J3 | 100 | 00 | May | 31 | Closing | J4 | 100 | 00 |

Insurance Expense   *Account No. 511*

| Apr. | 30 | Adjusting | J1 | 6 | 00 | Apr. | 30 | Closing | J1 | 6 | 00 |
| May | 31 | Adjusting | J4 | 9 | 00 | May | 31 | Closing | J4 | 9 | 00 |

Purchase Discount   *Account No. 512*

| May | 31 | Closing | J4 | 16 | 00 | May | 31 | | CD4 | 16 | 00 |

Transportation In   *Account No. 514*

| May | 31 | | CD4 | 70 | 00 | May | 31 | Closing | J4 | 70 | 00 |

Office Supplies Expense   *Account No. 516*

| May | 31 | Adjusting | J3 | 28 | 00 | May | 31 | Closing | J4 | 28 | 00 |

Interest Expense   *Account No. 517*

| May | 31 | Adjusting | J4 | 5 | 00 | May | 31 | Closing | J4 | 5 | 00 |

Estimated Loss on Uncollectible Accounts   *Account No. 518*

| May | 31 | Adjusting | J4 | 36 | 00 | May | 31 | Closing | J4 | 36 | 00 |

Pendery's Postclosing Trial Balance

Pendery's postclosing trial balance as of May 31, 1972, would appear as shown on page 229. Note that only balance sheet accounts (real accounts) are open.

Readjusting Pendery's Accounts

Let us assume that Pendery uses readjusting entries. An examination of his adjusting entries will reveal that only one readjusting entry is required for the month of May. Although eight adjusting entries were necessary, seven pertain either to estimated items or to deferrals originally entered in real accounts. Thus, only the accruals require readjusting; there was only one as of the end of May, accrued interest on notes payable. To readjust, we turn the adjusting entry around by debiting the Accrued Interest Payable account for $5 and by crediting the Interest Expense account for the same amount.

RALPH PENDERY
Postclosing Trial Balance
As of May 31, 1972

Cash	$5,952	
Accounts receivable	900	
Allowance for uncollectible accounts		$ 36
Merchandise inventory	5,650	
Store supplies	45	
Office supplies	52	
Prepaid rent	400	
Prepaid insurance	93	
Furniture and equipment	1,200	
Accounts payable		2,280
Notes payable		1,000
Accrued interest payable		5
Ralph Pendery, capital		10,971
	$14,292	$14,292

SUMMARY

Under the accrual basis of accounting, revenue is recognized in the period in which it is earned regardless of when it is collected, and expenses are recognized in the period in which they contribute to revenue regardless of when they are paid. Ordinarily, all the revenue earned by an organization in a period will not be collected in that period, and all the expenses incurred in earning the revenue will not be paid in the period. Thus, before sound financial statements can be prepared, it is usually necessary to adjust some of an organization's accounts. Items requiring adjustment may be categorized as accruals, deferrals, and estimated items. Accruals must be pulled into the accounting period, while deferrals must be pushed out.

After the adjusting and closing process has been completed, some accountants make readjusting, or reversing, entries so that future transactions can be handled in a routine manner. It is particularly important to remember that when readjusting entries are made:

1 Accrued items are **always** readjusted.

2 Estimated items are **never** readjusted.

3 Some deferred items are readjusted (those initially recorded in nominal accounts).

QUESTIONS AND PROBLEMS

9-1 Why are accountants inclined to recognize revenue as being earned only when a sale is made, although many of them recognize that revenue may be earned in the economic sense by production?

9-2 What are the essential differences between the **accrual basis** and the **cash basis** of accounting?

9-3 Distinguish between **accrued revenue** and **deferred revenue,** and between **an accrued expense** and **a deferred expense.**

9-4 Describe the what, why, and when of readjusting entries.

9-5 Publishers of magazines and periodicals conventionally solicit subscriptions for 2 to 5 years in advance. On their balance sheets portions of such subscriptions are commonly shown as deferred revenues (liabilities). How do you reconcile this practice with the fact that the balance sheet is almost universally understood to be a statement of assets, liabilities, and owner equity?

9-6 The D. Hylton Company regularly charges the cost of office supplies to an expense account. Office supplies on hand at the beginning of the month of June cost the company $382, whereas those on hand at the end of June cost the company $569. Supplies used during the month cost the company $465.

Instructions

(1) Determine the cost of office supplies purchased during the month of June.
(2) Prepare the necessary adjusting entry on June 30, assuming that the company adjusts and closes its books monthly.

9-7 Instructions From the following data, which pertain to the accounts of the W. Higley Company, reconstruct the adjusting entries that were made when the accounts were adjusted.

Account	Balance before Adjustment	Balance after Adjustment
(1) Prepaid Rent	$900	$ 600
(2) Prepaid Insurance	480	160
(3) Interest Collected in Advance	45	28
(4) Accrued Interest Receivable	—	42
(5) Accrued Interest Payable	—	12
(6) Accrued Wages Payable	—	2,500

9-8 Instructions The T. Hinderlang Company operates on a calendar-year basis and adjusts and closes its books annually. It uses readjusting entries. From the following information, which pertains to some of the current year's operations, prepare the entries necessary to adjust and readjust the accounts involved.

(1) On November 1, the company purchased a 3-year insurance policy which became effective on the date of purchase. The company recorded the $360 premium in a real account.

(2) On November 16, the company gave a creditor its $5,000, 90-day, 6 percent interest-bearing note to apply on account.

(3) On December 1, the company collected $1,800 for 3 months' rent beginning on that date. The company recorded the collection in a real account.

(4) On December 16, the company received a $2,000, 6 percent, 60-day, interest-bearing note from a customer to apply on account. The note was dated and received the same day.

(5) On December 19, the company borrowed money from the Midstate National Bank, giving the bank its $10,000, 60-day, non-interest-bearing note. The bank discounted the note at 6 percent. The company recorded the discount in a nominal account.

(6) On January 15, the company purchased $473 worth of store supplies, recording the purchase in a nominal account. As of December 31, the store supplies on hand amounted to $126.

9-9 The Skadden Company adjusts and closes its books annually on December 31. Before the books are adjusted on December 31, 19X4, the company has among its account balances the following:

	Debit	Credit
Office Supplies Expense	$296	
Interest Revenue		$70
Prepaid Insurance	800	
Interest Expense	30	
Advertising Expense	390	

Instructions Prepare the entries necessary to adjust the above accounts, taking into consideration the following information:

(1) A count of the office supplies on December 31, 19X4, shows $88 worth on hand.

(2) On December 11, 19X4, the company received a $4,000, 90-day, non-interest-bearing note from a customer. The company accepted the note at 7 percent discount.

(3) The company purchased a 2-year fire insurance policy on August 1, 19X4, paying the full 2-year premium of $800 in advance.

(4) On November 21, 19X4, the company issued a $1,500, 120-day, non-interest-bearing note to the Smith Company in settlement of an open account. The Smith Company accepted the note at 6 percent discount.

(5) On December 1, 19X4, the company purchased advertising space in the *Gazette* for 3 months for $390, paying for the space in advance.

(6) The company has a $3,000 weekly payroll. The employees work a 5-day week and are paid on Fridays. December 31, 19X4, is a Wednesday.

9-10 The Haseman Company adjusts and closes its books annually on June 30. Before the books are adjusted on June 30, 19X4, the company has among its account balances the following:

	Debit	Credit
Unconsumed Office Supplies _____	$ 430	
Rent Expense _____	1,200	
Unexpired Insurance_____	300	
Interest Revenue _____		$90

The following additional information is available:

(1) The company holds Smith's $2,100, 6 percent, 70-day note dated June 20, 19X4.

(2) Office supplies on hand on June 30, 19X4, amount to $140.

(3) The company paid 3 months' rent, at $400 per month, in advance on May 1, 19X4.

(4) The Silvoso Company holds the Haseman Company's $4,800, 6 percent, 90-day note dated May 26, 19X4.

(5) On January 1, 19X3, the company purchased a 3-year insurance policy for $360.

Instructions Prepare the entries necessary to adjust the company's books as of June 30, 19X4, considering only the above data. List the numbers of the adjusting entries which should be readjusted after the books are closed, assuming that the company uses readjusting entries.

9-11 Instructions If accruals of any one year are reflected in the cash transactions of the following year and prepayments of any year are reflected in the revenue or expense accounts of the following year, indicate the effect:

(1) On 19X1 net income of the omission of accrued expenses as of the end of 19X1

(2) On 19X2 net income of the omission of accrued expenses as of the end of 19X1

(3) On 19X3 net income of the omission of accrued expenses as of the end of 19X1

(4) On 19X1 net income of the omission of accrued income at the end of 19X1

(5) On 19X2 net income of the omission of accrued income at the end of 19X1

(6) On 19X1 net income of the omission of prepaid expenses at the end of 19X1

(7) On 19X2 net income of the omission of prepaid expenses at the end of 19X1

(8) On 19X2 net income of the omission of deferred income at the end of 19X2

(9) On 19X3 net income of the omission of deferred income at the end of 19X2

(10) On 19X3 net income of the omission of accrued expenses as of the end of 19X2 and accrued income at the end of 19X3

*9-12 On January 1, 19X3, the J. Weston Company paid $3,000 for a 3-year fire insurance policy. As of December 31, 19X4, a question has arisen as to the amount of prepaid insurance that should be shown on the company's balance sheet.

One proposal is to show prepaid insurance at $600, which is the short-rate cancellation value of the policy on December 31, 19X4.

A second proposal is to show prepaid insurance at $1,000, representing one-third of the original premium cost.

A third proposal is to show prepaid insurance at $1,200, which is the 1-year premium cost for a policy for the same amount as the policy in force.

Instructions Discuss each of the proposals with respect to the general principle underlying it, its acceptability, and its effect upon net income for the years involved.

9-13 An examination of the insurance policies carried by the J. Greene Company reveals the following:

*AICPA adapted.

Policy Number	Date Acquired	Term, Years	Premium	Unexpired Dec. 31, 19X1
1	Jan. 1, 19X1	3	$360	$240
2	June 1, 19X1	1	180	75
3	Apr. 1, 19X2	1	72	
4	June 1, 19X2	1	192	
			$804	$315

Instructions Prepare the entry or entries necessary to both adjust and readjust the company's insurance accounts as of December 31, 19X2, assuming that:

(1) The company initially records insurance premiums in a real account.

(2) The company initially records insurance premiums in a nominal account.

9-14 The H. Courtney Company reported a net income of $64,000 for the year ended December 31, 19X4. The company's computation, however, ignored the following items:

1 Accrued wages payable, $1,500

2 Accrued interest on notes receivable, $900

3 Prepaid rent of $3,500 initially charged to the Rent Expense account

4 Interest collected in advance of $300 initially entered in the Interest Revenue account

Instructions Compute the company's corrected net income for 19X4.

9-15 During the year 19X4, the D. Dupree Company collected interest amounting to $962 while paying $460 for interest. On December 31, 19X4, accrued interest on notes receivable amounted to $112. Included in the Interest Revenue account on December 31, 19X4, was an item of $34 representing interest collected in advance. Accrued interest on notes payable at the end of the year was $28, whereas interest paid in advance on notes payable to the bank amounted to $40.

Instructions Compute the:

(1) Amount of interest earned during the year

(2) Amount of interest expense for the year

9-16 The Unexpired Insurance account in the December 31, 19X5, unadjusted trial balance of the M. Onsi Company has a debit balance of $1,200.

An examination of the company's insurance policy shows that it is a 5-year policy taken out 2 years earlier.

Instructions Determine the:

(1) Amount initially paid for the policy

(2) Amount of insurance expense for the year 19X5

9-17 Keith Allen established a retail business in 19X1. Early in 19X4, he entered into negotiations with Tom Jones with a view to selling the business to Jones. You have been asked by the two men to examine Allen's records for the past 3 years.

The profits per Allen's income statements were as follows:

	Year Ending Dec. 31	
19X1	*19X2*	*19X3*
$9,023	$10,109	$10,340

During your examination, you find the following:

	Year Ending Dec. 31		
Omission from the records:	*19X1*	*19X2*	*19X3*
1 Accrued expenses at end of year	$2,160	$2,904	$4,624
2 Accrued income at end of year	200	—	—
3 Prepaid expenses at end of year	902	1,210	1,406
4 Deferred income at end of year	—	610	—

Instructions Considering only the above data and assuming that accruals as of the end of any year are reflected in the cash transactions of the next year, determine Allen's corrected profits for each of the years involved.

9-18 The K. Fox Company was established in 19X1. The company's records have not been kept on a strict accrual basis. As a result, the following items were omitted from the books as of the dates indicated:

Dec. 31	Prepaid Expense	Prepaid Income	Accrued Expense	Accrued Income
19X1	$900	—	$200	—
19X2	700	$400	75	$125
19X3	500	—	100	—
19X4	600	300	50	150

The profits per the books were: 19X1, $3,500; 19X2, $15,000; 19X3, $11,000; 19X4, $13,000.

Instructions Considering only the above data and assuming that accruals as of the end of any year are reflected in the cash transactions of the next year, determine the company's corrected profits for each of the years involved.

*9-19 On September 1, 19X1, the Eaton Company entered into an agreement with the Faulkner Company, whereby the Faulkner Company was to construct a building to be rented to the Eaton Company for a 10-year period. The rental agreement provided for annual payments in advance of $12,000 per year. The building was to be completed by March 1, 19X2, at which time the first annual payment would be due and the 10-year period started.

The building was not completed until March 15, 19X2, at which time the Eaton Company moved in. Because of the delay in completion and consequent additional expense and loss of revenue to the Eaton Company, the Faulkner Company agreed to reduce the first annual payment to $11,200. The Eaton Company paid the $11,200 on March 15, and recorded the payment with the following entry:

Prepaid Rent Expense	12,000	
Rental Revenue		800
Cash		11,200

Instructions Assuming that the Eaton Company's fiscal year ends on March 31, make any adjustments you consider necessary regarding the above transaction as of March 31, 19X2. State the reasons underlying your action and discuss any alternatives which may be acceptable.

*9-20 The State Gas Company follows the practice of cycle billing in order to minimize peak work loads for its clerical employees. All customers are billed monthly on various dates, except in those cases when the meter readers are unable to enter the premises to obtain a reading.

The following information for the year ended September 30, 19X5, is presented by the company:

Cycle	Billing Period, Inclusive	Number	Amount	Customers Not Billed
1	Aug. 7–Sept. 5	2,760	$13,800.00	324
2	Aug. 12–Sept. 10	3,426	13,704.00	411
3	Aug. 17–Sept. 15	3,265	14,692.50	335
4	Aug. 22–Sept. 20	2,630	12,492.50	370
5	Aug. 27–Sept. 25	3,132	13,311.00	468

*AICPA adapted.

We are further advised that all customers have been billed for prior periods and that the company's experience shows that charges for those customers whose meters were not read average the same amount as the charges for the customers billed in their cycle. In addition, the company assumes that each customer's usage will be uniform from month to month.

Instructions Using the above information, compute the unbilled revenues of the company as of September 30, 19X5, for cycles No. 1 and No. 3.

10
Accounting for Inventories

The expiration of certain assets such as prepaid insurance and prepaid interest can be specifically associated with a particular accounting period. Other asset expirations, however, cannot be so precisely assigned and estimates must be made if the accountant is to allocate costs and expenses among fiscal periods.

Assets presenting difficult allocation problems include inventories and long-lived assets. The former will be discussed in this chapter and the latter in Chapter 11. There is considerable similarity in the types of problems encountered in the two categories; in each instance the solution is essentially a matter of determining (1) the appropriate portion of the total cost to be allocated to the income statement as an expense and (2) the appropriate portion to be deferred to a future period as an asset on the balance sheet.

BASIC INVENTORY PROBLEMS

The AICPA, in its *Accounting Research Bulletin No. 43*,[1] defines **inventory** as the "aggregate of those items of tangible personal property which (1) are held for sale

---

[1] American Institute of Certified Public Accountants, *Accounting Research and Terminology Bulletins,* Final Edition (New York: 1961), p. 27.

in the ordinary course of business, (2) are in process of production for such sale, or (3) are to be currently consumed in the production of goods or services to be available for sale." Thus far we have dealt with inventories only as they related to the adjusting process and financial statement preparation. Now we shall examine them in more detail, considering some of the problems involved in their compilation and valuation. In addition we shall study some of the methods of handling them in the accounts.

TAKING A PHYSICAL INVENTORY

To take a physical inventory is to make a systematic physical count of all items belonging in the inventory. The determination of the items to be included, of course, implies the exclusion of those items which do not belong therein. Although some organizations take inventory more often than others, it is customarily considered necessary to take at least one a year. In many organizations "taking inventory" is an annual year-end event.

Contents of an Inventory

Questions frequently arise as to whether or not particular items should be included in an inventory. For example, an organization may have purchased merchandise which is in transit but which has not arrived at the time the physical inventory is being taken, or it may have sold merchandise that is still on hand at inventory time. The decision as to whether or not to include such items is usually based on the legal passage of title; that is, an organization should include in its inventory all goods to which it has title, regardless of where particular items are located.

Purchased Merchandise in Transit   From a legal standpoint, title to merchandise passes from seller to buyer when the merchandise is delivered. In the case of items in transit, *delivery* is dependent upon the terms of purchase. If goods are purchased f.o.b. shipping point, they belong to the buyer as soon as the seller delivers them to the transportation agency; therefore, the buyer should include them in his inventory. On the other hand, if goods are purchased f.o.b. destination, title does not pass to the buyer until the transportation agency delivers the goods to him; thus he should exclude them from his inventory.

Sold Merchandise on Hand   At the time a physical inventory is taken, an organization may have on hand some goods which have been segregated from the other inventoriable items in order to fill sales orders which were received prior to the date of the inventory. Title may already have passed (for example, when goods are being held for later delivery at the request of the buyer) but generally it has not; therefore, such merchandise should be included in the seller's inventory.

Counting an Inventory

Various methods are used to determine physical quantities of an inventory, many of which employ a team approach. In the simplest method one team member counts, weighs, measures, or estimates the quantity of each item and calls out the description and quantity to another team member, who records the data on an **inventory sheet.**

Another method is to record the description and quantity on an inventory tag and then transfer the count from the tag to the inventory sheet. The tag system is particularly useful in large organizations where several persons or groups of persons take the inventory. A tag is placed on each item or group of items counted; this tends to prevent errors resulting from double counting or the omission of items from the count. In some organizations inventory tags are replaced by punched cards which permit machine tabulation of the inventory quantities.

Regardless of the method used, it is extremely important that an accurate count and description of the items be made so that a sound valuation of the inventory may be determined.

VALUATION OF INVENTORIES

Because inventory valuations affect both the income statement and the balance sheet, they are of major significance in many organizations. This is particularly true when inventories are sizable in relation to other assets of the organization.

Since the ending inventory in one period becomes the beginning inventory in the following period, it is important to recognize that an error in valuation as of the end of a period will also, if not corrected, result in an error on the income statement in the following period; however, the effect of the error will be in the opposite sense. That is, if an error results in an *overstatement* of income in one period, it will result in an *understatement* of income in the following period. The effect of inventory errors on the determination of income may be summarized as follows:

1 **Overstatement** of the **ending inventory** understates the cost of goods sold, which in turn overstates net income.

2 **Understatement** of the **ending inventory** overstates the cost of goods sold, which in turn understates net income.

3 **Overstatement** of the **beginning inventory** overstates the cost of goods sold, which in turn understates net income.

4 **Understatement** of the **beginning inventory** understates the cost of goods sold, which in turn overstates net income.

To illustrate the effect of an error in inventory valuation, let us assume that the beginning inventory for a fiscal period was $20,000; that during the period

Accounting for Inventories
1

sales amounted to $100,000, purchases to $50,000, and operating expenses to $30,000; and that the ending inventory of $25,000 was erroneously determined to be $35,000. The effect of the error is shown as follows:

		Correct Data		Erroneous Data	
Sales		$100,000		$100,000	
Cost of goods sold:					
Beginning inventory	$20,000		$20,000		
Purchases	50,000		50,000		
Cost of goods available for sale	$70,000		$70,000		
Less: Ending inventory	25,000		35,000		
Cost of goods sold	$45,000	45,000	$35,000	35,000	
Gross margin		$ 55,000		$ 65,000	
Operating expenses		30,000		30,000	
Net income		$ 25,000		$ 35,000	

Inventory Valuation and Accounting Conventions

Accountants often use certain practices, or "conventions," which are of particular significance when valuing inventories. Among the more important of these are:

1 Objectivity
2 Consistency
3 Conservatism
4 Materiality

Objectivity In accounting the term **objectivity** refers to the lack of prejudice on the part of the accountant in relation to his expression of financial data. It is used in contrast to **subjectivity,** which suggests the possibility that personal opinion or judgment might have an effect on the data. In order to be objective, the accountant must be able to verify his data with sources outside the particular organization for which he is accounting. Authentic business documents such as purchase invoices, promissory notes, or freight bills are forms of verification that derive their validity principally from outside sources.

The accountant's idea of objectivity does not necessarily imply certainty. As has been pointed out previously, accountants have had to develop a philosophy regarding an acceptable degree of uncertainty in order to make their records and reports useful. For example, estimates made by the accountant, although not certain, may still be objective. However, they must be based on reliable evidence which is subject to verification by other competent investigators.

Consistency In accounting, **consistency** implies the application to an entity of the same accounting practices, procedures, and methods, unchanged from one period to the next. Many items of revenue and expense may be treated properly in the accounts and on financial statements in more than one way. Nevertheless, once a procedure has been chosen it should be followed consistently. Inventories, for example, can be valued in various ways, any one of which may be satisfactory. However, if inventories of several periods are valued on varying bases, the accounting results will be distorted.

Failure to maintain consistency from period to period in the procedures followed could damage, if not destroy, the comparability of the financial statements. It would be possible to affect reported income arbitrarily from one accounting period to the next merely by changing from one acceptable procedure to another. The result of consistency is that successive financial statements are comparable.

Conservatism This implies the accountant's use of caution or moderation in recording transactions and in preparing financial statements. Under conditions of uncertainty the accountant traditionally has taken a "safeside," or conservative, viewpoint. For example, if two or more equally acceptable alternatives were available, he would choose the one which would result in the lower asset valuation and net income. The tendency under the conservative approach is to understate rather than overstate.

Accountants are not in complete agreement regarding the extent to which conservatism should be followed; in fact, many are critical of the way it is used. When carried to the nth degree, conservatism means that the accountant "prepares for all losses and anticipates no profits."

In being conservative the accountant must be constantly aware of the interrelationship of the income statement and the balance sheet. For example, if the inventory is understated on the balance sheet, net income will be understated on the income statement.

It should be emphasized that conservatism is applicable only when there is a reasonable choice between appropriate alternatives, and it is, of course, secondary to the proper matching of cost and revenue.

Materiality The term **materiality** as used in accounting pertains to the relative value or inherent significance of an item. If the nature of any item, monetary or otherwise, is such that the method of treating it in the accounts or disclosing it on the financial statements is likely to influence users of the accounting information, the item is considered to be material.

Applied to the valuation of inventories, the idea of materiality means that the accountant attaches little importance to the precise valuation of insignificant or trivial items, but on the other hand he is especially concerned with the treatment of significant items. The decision as to whether or not an item is material is largely a matter of judgment based upon the attendant circumstances. An item that is material for one organization may be strictly immaterial for another. For example, for the corner grocery store a $100 item may be material, while for the multi-million-dollar organization a $10,000 item may be immaterial.

Inventory Valuation Bases

There are a number of acceptable methods of valuing inventories in the accounts and on financial statements. Most are based either directly or indirectly on **cost** or on the **lower of cost or market.**

Cost The primary basis of accounting for inventories is **cost.** This has been stressed repeatedly by the AICPA in its various publications. We have learned that cost is generally defined as the price paid or the consideration given to acquire an asset. This, of course, includes readying it for use. Therefore, applied to inventories, cost is the price paid or consideration given to acquire the inventory and put it into a salable condition and position. Inventoriable costs include:

1 Invoice price less cash discounts

2 Freight and cartage in, including insurance while in transit

3 Buying expenses

4 Receiving and storing expenses

5 Applicable taxes and tariffs

Market While cost ordinarily provides the most appropriate basis for the valuation of inventories, there are times when a departure from cost may be in order. If the residual usefulness (utility as measured by its market value) of an inventory falls below its cost because of physical deterioration, obsolescence, or a decline in the price level, a loss occurs. Such losses are normally recognized in the period in which they happen. This is ordinarily accomplished by valuing the inventory at its market value rather than its cost. As a general rule, the term **market** as used in the phrase **lower of cost or market** means the current replacement cost.

Valuation of Inventories at Cost

As used in inventory valuation, cost may be either the actual cost of a specific item, or a cost based upon an assumption of the order in which the inventory items are sold or used. (The assumed order in which the items are sold or used may or may not be identical to the order of their actual physical flow through an organization. When the two are not the same, the inventory valuation in reality is based upon an assumption of the flow of cost rather than the flow of inventory.)

The method chosen for assigning costs to inventories, and thus to the cost of goods sold, should be the one that best matches appropriate costs and revenues.

While several methods are available to the accountant, all are either closely related to or directly based upon one of the following:

1 Specific identification method

2 Average method

3 First-in, first-out method (FIFO)

4 Last-in, first-out method (LIFO)

When the **specific identification** method is used, the actual cost of a particular item is assigned to the item. Under the **average** method, the total cost of the goods available for sale is divided by the number of units to arrive at an average unit cost. Under the **FIFO** method it is assumed that the first items purchased are the first sold. As a consequence, items on hand when the inventory is taken are considered to be from the most recent purchases. The **LIFO** method assumes that the last items purchased are the first sold, hence the inventory on hand is composed of items from the oldest purchases.

To illustrate the four methods, let us assume the following basic data for the month of January:

		Inventory Data, January 31	
Jan. 1	On hand	100 units @ $2.00	$ 200
Jan. 5	Purchased	100 units @ 2.20	220
Jan. 10	Purchased	100 units @ 2.30	230
Jan. 15	Purchased	100 units @ 2.40	240
Jan. 20	Purchased	100 units @ 2.50	250
Totals		500 units	$1,140
Sales		200 units	
On hand, Jan. 31		300 units	

Note that 500 units were available for sale during January, 200 units were sold during January, 300 units were on hand at the end of January, and the 500 units available for sale were acquired at five different prices.

In the following illustrations observe that the inventory on hand plus the cost of goods sold is equal to the total cost of goods available for sale of $1,140 in each case, but that the mix is different.

Specific Identification Method When the specific identification method is used to value an inventory, each item is specifically identified and valued at its actual cost.

Assume that the January 31 inventory was composed of 20 units from the units on hand at the beginning of January, 50 units from the January 5 purchase, 60 units from the January 10 purchase, 80 units from the January 15 purchase, and 90 units from the January 20 purchase. The cost to be assigned to the inventory under the specific identification method would be $705, determined as follows:

Inventory, January 31—Specific Identification Method

20 units @ $2.00	$ 40
50 units @ 2.20	110
60 units @ 2.30	138
80 units @ 2.40	192
90 units @ 2.50	225
300 units at a value of	$705

The cost of goods sold during January is determined by subtracting the January 31 inventory from the cost of goods available for sale. Under the specific identification method this would be $435, determined as follows:

Cost of Goods Sold for January

Cost of goods available for sale	$1,140
Less: Jan. 31 inventory	705
Cost of goods sold	$ 435

It should be recognized that the specific identification method may not be practical when an inventory contains a large number of low-priced items purchased at various times and prices. The expense of specifically determining the cost of each item could be prohibitive.

Average Method When the average method is used to value an inventory, it is assumed that the cost of goods on hand at the end of an accounting period is the average of the cost of the inventory on hand at the beginning of the period and the cost of the goods purchased or produced during the period.

To continue our illustration, the January 31 inventory of 300 units, based on an average cost of $2.28 per unit, would be valued at $684, determined as follows:

Inventory, January 31—Average Method

Jan. 1	Inventory	100 units	$ 200
Jan. 5	Purchased	100 units	220
Jan. 10	Purchased	100 units	230
Jan. 15	Purchased	100 units	240
Jan. 20	Purchased	100 units	250
Totals		500 units	$1,140

Average unit cost: $1,140 ÷ 500 = $2.28

Ending inventory: 300 units @ $2.28 = $684.00

The cost of goods sold during January under the average method would be $456, determined as follows:

Cost of Goods Sold for January

Cost of goods available for sale	$1,140
Less: Jan. 31 inventory	684
Cost of goods sold	$ 456

The average method tends to "level out" the effects on net income of increases and decreases in costs. For this reason it is widely used by organizations which hold goods for long periods of time. It is also employed by organizations which handle large numbers of low-priced items purchased at various times and prices, since the expense of specifically identifying the costs of individual items is often prohibitive.

First-in, First-out Method When the FIFO method is used to value an inventory, the assumption is made that the items purchased first are the first to be used or sold. The goods on hand at the end of a period are assumed to be from the most recent purchases and those that have been sold are assumed to be from the earliest acquisitions.

Under the FIFO method, the January 31 inventory of 300 units in our illustration would be valued at $720, determined as follows:

Inventory, January 31—First-in, First-out Method	
100 units @ $2.50 from the Jan. 20 purchase	$250
100 units @ $2.40 from the Jan. 15 purchase	240
100 units @ $2.30 from the Jan. 10 purchase	230
300 units at a value of	$720

The cost of goods sold during January under the FIFO method would be $420, determined as follows:

Cost of Goods Sold for January

Cost of goods available for sale	$1,140
Less: Jan. 31 inventory	720
Cost of goods sold	$ 420

In practice the FIFO method, or some variation thereof, is used in the majority of inventory valuations. For example, mercantile businesses frequently employ FIFO because it tends to value an inventory at current prices, thus resulting in a valuation that is in conformity with price trends.

Last-in, First-out Method The LIFO method of valuing an inventory is based on the assumption that the last items purchased are the first to be used or sold. That is, the goods on hand at the end of a fiscal period are assumed to be part of the first acquisitions of that period and the items sold are assumed to be from the latest purchases.

Under the LIFO method, the January 31 inventory of 300 units in our illustration would be valued at $650, determined as follows:

Inventory, January 31—Last-in, First-out Method
100 units @ $2.00 from the beginning inventory ———————— $200
100 units @ $2.20 from the January 5 purchase ———————— 220
100 units @ $2.30 from the January 10 purchase ——————— 230
300 units at a value of ——————————————————————— $650

The cost of goods sold during January under the LIFO method would be $490, determined as follows:

Cost of Goods Sold for January

Cost of goods available for sale ———————————————	$1,140
Less: Jan. 31 inventory ————————————————————	650
Cost of goods sold ———————————————————————	$ 490

While LIFO is commonly referred to as an inventory method, it is in reality primarily a method of valuing the cost of goods sold. Under the LIFO method the costs of the last goods received will be the first costs to be charged against revenue, leaving the older costs for inventory valuation purposes. Hence, LIFO actually places primary emphasis upon the determination of the cost of sales and only secondary emphasis on inventory valuation. For this reason many accountants oppose its use. Some of the basic arguments on both sides of the issue are presented below.

LIFO—Pro and Con Advocates of LIFO claim that its use results in a better matching of costs and revenues because, when prices are moving either upward or downward, the method will result in charging to the Cost of Goods Sold account costs more nearly in line with the price level at which sales of the goods are made. They also point out that over the life of the business cycle the LIFO method tends to show a smaller net income during inflationary phases and a larger net income during deflationary phases than any of the other acceptable inventory valuation methods. This, they argue, tends to "smooth out" the peaks and valleys of the business cycle, thus in some measure promoting economic stability.

Opponents of LIFO maintain that its use results in an inventory valuation for the balance sheet typical of price levels at a much earlier date and having little relation to the present price level, thus reducing the significance of the balance sheet. They argue that although the use of LIFO may result in a better matching of costs and revenues insofar as the cost of goods sold and sales are concerned, this is only a piecemeal attack on the effects of changing price levels. According to them, if the problem of changing price levels is to be dealt with by the accountant, all phases of it should be considered, and both the income statement and the balance sheet should be adjusted to reflect such changes.

Comparison of Cost Methods Based on Assumptions as to the Flow of Cost

While the specific identification method is based on actual costs, the average method, FIFO, and LIFO are based on assumptions as to the flow of cost; as would be expected, each assumption gives a different result. If we use the foregoing illustrations and assume total sales of $1,000 and operating expenses of $100 for the month of January, the three methods based on assumptions as to the flow of cost may be illustrated for comparative purposes as follows:

	FIFO Method	Average Method	LIFO Method
Sales	$1,000	$1,000	$1,000
Cost of goods sold	420	456	490
Gross margin	$ 580	$ 544	$ 510
Operating expenses	100	100	100
Net income	$ 480	$ 444	$ 410

We can see from the illustration that during a period of rising prices, which was the case in January, the FIFO method results in the highest net income, and the LIFO method results in the lowest net income. The average method tends to level or "smooth out" the effect of changing prices. During a period of falling prices the average method will still tend to have a leveling effect, while LIFO and FIFO will each have exactly the opposite effect of that which they had during a period of rising prices; that is, use of FIFO will result in the lowest net income and use of LIFO will result in the highest net income.

Since FIFO assigns the earlier purchases to the cost of goods sold and thus to the income statement, the inventory valuation on the balance sheet is reflected in terms of more current costs, although they may not necessarily be current market prices. The LIFO method assigns the more current costs to the income statement; hence the inventory valuation on the balance sheet reflects costs in terms of earlier dates. The use of the average method results in current costs being assigned in part to the income statement and in part to the balance sheet.

In the following comparative summary, note that the inventory valuation plus the cost of goods sold is equal to the total cost to be accounted for regardless of the method being used, but that the mix is different in each instance.

	FIFO Method	Average Method	LIFO Method
Inventory valuation	$ 720	$ 684	$ 650
Cost of goods sold	420	456	490
Totals	$1,140	$1,140	$1,140

Valuation of Inventories at Lower of Cost or Market (LCM)

Although, as we learned earlier, cost ordinarily provides the most appropriate basis for the valuation of inventories, there are times when a departure from cost may be in order. In such cases the inventory is valued at cost or market, whichever is lower. Three basic methods for valuing inventories at the lower of cost or market are available to the accountant. They are:

1 Item-by-item method

2 Major category method

3 Total inventory method

To illustrate these methods we shall employ a different inventory than the one used to illustrate the methods of valuing an inventory at cost. You will see that the items have been segregated into categories, a procedure which is often followed in organizations with inventories made up of various types of similar items.

Item-by-item Method of LCM When the item-by-item method is used, cost and market are compared for each item in the inventory. The individual items are then valued at their lower valuations as follows:

Lower of Cost or Market—Item-by-item Method				
		Per Unit		Lower of
	Quantity	Cost	Market	Cost or Market
Category A				
Item 1	100	$16	$14	$ 1,400
Item 2	300	15	19	4,500
Item 3	150	30	27	4,050
Category B				
Item 1	200	25	18	3,600
Item 2	150	20	21	3,000
Item 3	100	18	20	1,800
Inventory at the lower of cost or market				$18,350

Major Category Method of LCM When the major category method is used, the total cost and the total market for each category of items are compared. Each category is then valued at the lower valuation as shown.

| | | Per Unit | | Total | | Lower of |
	Quantity	Cost	Market	Cost	Market	Cost or Market
Lower of Cost or Market—Major Category Method						
Category A						
Item 1	100	$16	$14	$ 1,600	$ 1,400	
Item 2	300	15	19	4,500	5,700	
Item 3	150	30	27	4,500	4,050	
Totals				$10,600	$11,150	$10,600
Category B						
Item 1	200	25	18	$ 5,000	$ 3,600	
Item 2	150	20	21	3,000	3,150	
Item 3	100	18	20	1,800	2,000	
Totals				$ 9,800	$ 8,750	8,750
Inventory at the lower of cost or market						$19,350

Total Inventory Method of LCM When the total inventory method is used, the total cost and the total market for the entire inventory are compared. The inventory is then valued at the lower valuation as shown.

| | | Per Unit | | Total | | Lower of |
	Quantity	Cost	Market	Cost	Market	Cost or Market
Lower of Cost or Market—Total Inventory Method						
Category A						
Item 1	100	$16	$14	$ 1,600	$ 1,400	
Item 2	300	15	19	4,500	5,700	
Item 3	150	30	27	4,500	4,050	
Category B						
Item 1	200	25	18	5,000	3,600	
Item 2	150	20	21	3,000	3,150	
Item 3	100	18	20	1,800	2,000	
Totals				$20,400	$19,900	$19,900
Inventory at the lower of cost or market						$19,900

Determination of Market When Using LCM In our illustrations both the cost and market values for each inventory item were supplied. The cost data could have been determined on any of the bases previously discussed. Market values are ordinarily determined in the replacement market. At times, however, they are limited by the selling market. For example, an inventory item which originally cost $22 at wholesale can now be replaced for $16 because of a decline in wholesale prices. If it can be sold at retail for $20, its replacement cost may not reflect its true market value. In cases such as this, market value, as used in the lower of cost or market computations, is ordinarily limited by both a ceiling and a floor as determined in the selling market.

The ceiling, generally known as an item's **net realizable value** (NRV), is the estimated selling price of the item in the ordinary course of business less reasonably predictable costs of disposal. If the inventoriable item in our illustration has an estimated selling expense of $1, its NRV will be $19 ($20 selling price minus $1 selling expense).

The floor is an item's **net realizable value minus a normal profit margin** [NRV($-$)]. If the above item normally yields a 10 percent profit based on its selling price, its NRV($-$) will be $17 ($20 selling price $-$ $1 selling expense $-$ $2 normal profit). Since the current replacement cost of $16 is less than the item's NRV($-$) of $17, we must use the $17 as the market value when determining the lower of cost or market.

In the illustration that follows, the correct market value for inventory valuation purposes is circled for each item. As you study the illustration, bear in mind that the market value used in LCM computations cannot be more than NRV or less than NRV($-$). Also note that the amount chosen from the three market alternatives is always the middle amount.

Determination of Market in LCM Computations

Item	Replacement Market	NRV	Selling Market NRV ($-$)
1	($8)	$9	$7
2	9	(8)	7
3	5	7	(6)

Federal Income Taxes and LCM Certain requirements regarding inventory valuation for federal income tax purposes have been established by the Internal Revenue Service. Valuation at either cost or the lower of cost or market is acceptable except for inventories valued under the LIFO method; for these only cost may be used. The regulations also prohibit the use of the total inventory method for income tax purposes when an inventory is valued at the lower of cost or market.

ESTIMATION OF INVENTORIES

Thus far in this chapter we have dealt with the problems of taking and valuing a physical inventory. Our work has been based on the assumption that it is both possible and practicable to take a physical inventory and arrive at its valuation on an acceptable cost basis or on the basis of cost or market, whichever is lower. There may be times, however, when it is not possible to take a physical inventory, and there may also be occasions when it is not practicable to determine cost for each item or group of items in an inventory. In such cases, the accountant usually estimates the value of the inventory. The methods most frequently employed for this purpose are the **gross margin method** and the **retail method.**

Gross Margin Method of Estimating Inventories

In organizations in which the relationship between the cost of goods sold and sales is relatively stable from period to period, it is possible to estimate the cost of the inventory on hand at a particular time without taking a physical inventory. First, the ratio of gross margin to sales is determined from historical data. For example, if the data indicate that $100,000 of sales normally cost $75,000, the rate of gross margin is 25 percent. This rate is then applied to the sales of the period in order to estimate the cost of goods sold. After the estimated cost of goods sold is determined, it is deducted from the cost of goods available for sale in order to determine the estimated cost of the inventory on hand. This method may be illustrated as follows:

Beginning inventory—at cost			$20,000
Purchases—at cost			70,000
Cost of goods available for sale			$90,000
Less: Cost of goods sold:			
Sales—at selling price		$100,000	
Less gross margin (25%)		25,000	75,000
Estimated valuation of ending inventory			$15,000

Although its reliability is dependent upon the validity of the ratio of cost of goods sold to selling prices, the gross margin method is nevertheless a rather simple and inexpensive means of approximating the value of an inventory for the following purposes:

1 Preparing interim financial statements (for example, monthly or quarterly statements)

2 Testing the validity of a reported inventory

3 Determining the amount of inventory lost either in a fire or from other causes when specific cost data are not available

Retail Method of Estimating Inventories

As the name implies, the retail method is used primarily by retail establishments such as department stores. Under this method, an approximate ratio which cost bears to the retail selling price is determined so that an inventory taken at retail can be converted to an estimate of the lower of cost or market. Thus, if the total of the retail sales for a period is deducted from the total of the goods available for sale (at retail), the resulting balance should represent the retail value of the inventory on hand. The ratio of cost to retail, often referred to as the **cost ratio,** is then applied to the retail inventory valuation to reduce it to an approximation of the lower of cost or market.

Although the application of the retail inventory method may vary as to format and procedure, the basic approach is as follows:

	Cost	Retail
Beginning inventory	$30,000	$ 50,000
Net purchases during the period	59,800	80,000
Transportation in	1,200	
Merchandise available for sale	$91,000	$130,000
Cost ratio (ratio of cost to retail) = 70%		
($91,000 ÷ $130,000 = 70%)		
Sales during the period		90,000
Ending inventory at retail		$ 40,000
Cost ratio		70%
Estimated valuation of ending inventory		$ 28,000

HANDLING INVENTORIES IN THE ACCOUNTS

There are two basic approaches to handling (recording and adjusting) inventories in the accounts: the **periodic inventory method** and the **perpetual inventory method.**

Periodic Inventory Method

Under the periodic inventory method, when merchandise is purchased it is recorded in the Purchases account, and the Inventory account is adjusted periodically. This is the method we have used in previous chapters.

While there is basically only one way to record the initial purchase of merchandise under this method, there are several ways in which the periodic adjustments may be made. Two of the more prominent methods are illustrated in the following paragraphs. One uses the Revenue and Expense Summary account to adjust the inventory, the other the Cost of Goods Sold account. In order to permit a more detailed comparison with the perpetual method, an illustration of which will follow the periodic illustration, the recording of the initial purchase is also illustrated.

Recording Purchases under the Periodic Inventory Method If we assume a cash purchase of $10,000 and a credit purchase from the ABC Company of $20,000, in general journal form they would be recorded as follows:

Purchases	30,000	
Cash		10,000
Accounts Payable (ABC Company)		20,000

Adjustments Using the Revenue and Expense Summary Account Under the periodic method inventories may be adjusted by transferring the items involved directly to the Revenue and Expense Summary account. If we assume a beginning inventory of $10,000, purchases of $30,000, and an ending inventory of $12,000, the adjusting entries would be:

Revenue and Expense Summary	10,000	
Merchandise Inventory		10,000

To transfer the beginning inventory to the Revenue and Expense Summary account.

Revenue and Expense Summary	30,000	
Purchases		30,000

To transfer the balance of the Purchases account to the Revenue and Expense Summary account.

Merchandise Inventory	12,000	
Revenue and Expense Summary		12,000

To record the ending inventory.

After these entries have been posted, the Merchandise Inventory account and the Revenue and Expense Summary account will appear as shown. Note that the cost of goods sold of $28,000 is left in the Revenue and Expense Summary account.

Merchandise Inventory

Beginning inventory	10,000	To R & E Summary	10,000
Ending inventory	12,000		

Revenue and Expense Summary

Old inventory	10,000	New inventory	12,000
Purchases	30,000		

Adjustments Using the Cost of Goods Sold Account Some accountants prefer to measure the cost of goods sold in the Cost of Goods Sold account rather than in the Revenue and Expense Summary account. When this method is used, the Cost of Goods Sold account is closed to the Revenue and Expense Summary account in the closing process. If we assume the same data as before, the adjusting and closing journal entries would be as follows:

Cost of Goods Sold	10,000	
Merchandise Inventory		10,000

To transfer the beginning inventory to the Cost of Goods Sold account

Cost of Goods Sold	30,000	
Purchases		30,000

To transfer the balance of the Purchases account to the Cost of Goods Sold account

Merchandise Inventory	12,000	
Cost of Goods Sold		12,000

To record the ending inventory.

Revenue and Expense Summary	28,000	
Cost of Goods Sold		28,000

To close the Cost of Goods Sold account to the Revenue and Expense Summary account

After these entries have been posted, the Merchandise Inventory account, the Cost of Goods Sold account, and the Revenue and Expense Summary account will appear as shown below. Note that the account balances are exactly the same as in the preceding illustration when the cost of goods sold was measured in the Revenue and Expense Summary account.

Merchandise Inventory

Beginning inventory	10,000	Cost of goods sold	10,000
Ending inventory	12,000		

Cost of Goods Sold

Old inventory	10,000	New inventory	12,000
Purchases	30,000	To R & E Summary	28,000
	40,000		40,000

Revenue and Expense Summary

Cost of goods sold	28,000	

It is important to note that when the Cost of Goods Sold account is used to measure the cost of sales, all items entering into the computation should be reflected therein. In our illustration we used only the beginning and ending inventories and purchases, but we could have included purchase returns and allowances, purchase discounts, and transportation charges. Thus, under the appropriate circumstances, the Cost of Goods Sold account could reflect any or all of the following debits and credits:

Cost of Goods Sold

Possible *Debits:*	Possible *Credits:*
Beginning inventory	Ending inventory
Purchases	Purchase returns
Transportation in	Purchase allowances
	Purchase discounts

Perpetual Inventory Method

In contrast to the periodic method, which only periodically reflects the amount of inventory on hand in the Merchandise Inventory account, the perpetual method provides a continuous "running" record of the inventory. Whenever a purchase of merchandise is made, its cost is "run" into the Merchandise Inventory account by debiting the account; whenever a sale is made, the cost of the item sold is "run" out of the account by crediting it.

Recording Purchases under the Perpetual Inventory Method If we assume a cash purchase of $10,000 and a credit purchase from the ABC Company of $20,000, in general journal form they would be recorded as follows. Note that under the perpetual method we charge purchases to the Merchandise Inventory account rather than to the Purchases account.

Merchandise Inventory	30,000	
Cash		10,000
Accounts Payable (ABC Company)		20,000

Recording Sales under the Perpetual Inventory Method Assuming that merchandise which cost $28,000 was sold for $40,000, the entries necessary to record the transaction would be as follows:

Cash	40,000	
Sales		40,000
Cost of Goods Sold	28,000	
Merchandise Inventory		28,000

After the entries have been posted, the Merchandise Inventory and Cost of Goods Sold accounts will appear as follows:

Merchandise Inventory

Purchases	30,000	Sales	28,000

Cost of Goods Sold

Cost of sales	28,000	

Physical Inventories Necessary under the Perpetual Method The use of the perpetual inventory method does not eliminate the need for taking periodic physical inventories.   In fact, if the perpetual and physical inventories do not agree (as may sometimes happen because of errors, pilferage, or other losses), the physical takes precedence.   The book (perpetual) inventory must then be adjusted to agree with the physical.   If the book inventory is greater than the physical inventory, the Cost of Goods Sold account is debited for the difference and the Merchandise Inventory account is credited.   If the physical inventory is greater than the book inventory, the Merchandise Inventory account is debited for the difference and the Cost of Goods Sold account is credited.

SUMMARY

From an accounting standpoint inventory problems include (1) taking a physical inventory, (2) valuing an inventory, and (3) handling an inventory in the accounts.

Taking an inventory is basically a matter of determining what should be inventoried and then physically counting it.

Valuation consists of determining (1) the cost to be assigned to the current period as cost of sales and (2) the cost to be deferred as an asset.   Inventory valuations are usually based on cost or the lower of cost or market.   Cost may be the actual cost of a purchased or manufactured item, or it may be a cost based upon some consistently applied basis such as FIFO, LIFO, or the average method. Market, as used in the lower of cost or market computations, ordinarily reflects an item's current replacement cost.

When it is impossible to take an inventory, its value may be estimated by either the gross margin method or the retail method.   Inventories may be handled in the accounts on either a periodic or a perpetual inventory basis.

QUESTIONS AND PROBLEMS

10-1 Why should inventories be included both on the balance sheet and in the computation of net income?

10-2 When a physical inventory is taken, how should the following items be handled?

(1) Merchandise ordered but not yet on hand

(2) Merchandise on hand but not yet entered in the accounts

(3) Merchandise on hand which has already been sold and is being held for delivery

10-3 The first-in, first-out, average, and last-in, first-out inventory methods are often employed in preference to the specific identification method. Compare each of these methods with the specific identification method. Include in your comparison an analysis of the theoretical soundness of each method in the determination of income and in asset valuation.

10-4 Jones owns a business enterprise in which inventories of merchandise represent his major investment. He has written you a letter stating that he has heard of an inventory valuation method called LIFO, and understands in part what is meant by it. He requests advice regarding the possible use of LIFO in his business. State the factors that you would include in your answer to him, bringing out the possibility of any advantages or disadvantages which might result from the use of LIFO.

10-5 List arguments for and against the following statement: "Specific identification is the ideal method for assigning cost to inventory and to cost of goods sold."

10-6 In your opinion, is an organization which regularly follows the practice of valuing its inventory at the lower of cost or market being consistent and conservative? Discuss critically and include an explanation of the meaning of the terms **consistent** and **conservative.**

10-7 Demonstrate by a summary statement how the gross margin test is applied. (Use assumed amounts.)

10-8 (1) Define **cost** and **market** as applied to the valuation of inventories.

(2) Why are inventories valued at the lower of cost or market? Discuss.

10-9 State and explain the effect upon both the balance sheet and the income statement of the use of the last-in, first-out method of determining inventory valuation by comparing it with the effect of the first-in, first-out method.

(1) Assume that prices have risen during the year.

(2) Assume that prices have fallen during the year.

10-10 (1) The acquisition cost of a certain inventoriable item changes frequently. The value assigned to the inventory of this item at year-end will be the same if perpetual records are kept as it would be under a periodic inventory method only if the value assigned is computed by the:

    (a) Average method

    (b) First-in, first-out method

    (c) Last-in, first-out method

    (d) Lower of cost or market method

(2) An item of inventory purchased this period for $15 has been written down to its current replacement cost of $10. It sells for $30 with disposal costs of $3 and normal profit of $12. Which of the following statements is *not* true?

    (a) The cost of sales of the following year will be understated.

    (b) The current year's income is understated.

    (c) The closing inventory of the current year is understated.

    (d) Income of the following year will be understated.

10-11 **Instructions** Using the following unit data and assuming that an inventory is being valued at the lower of cost or market, determine the proper unit valuation to be used in each case:

	Case 1	Case 2	Case 3	Case 4	Case 5
Cost	$2.00	$2.00	$2.00	$2.00	$2.00
Net realizable value	1.30	2.05	1.80	2.40	1.90
Net realizable value less normal profit	1.10	1.85	1.60	2.20	1.70
Market (replacement cost)	1.20	2.10	1.85	2.15	1.60

10-12 The Fairfield Company sells four major items, the inventories of which are priced at cost or market, whichever is lower. A normal profit margin rate of 30 percent is usually maintained on each of the four items.

    The following information was compiled as of December 31, 19X2:

Item	Cost	Cost to Replace	Estimated Cost to Dispose	Expected Selling Price
A	$35.00	$42.00	$15.00	$ 80.00
B	47.50	45.00	20.50	95.00
C	17.50	15.00	5.00	30.00
D	45.00	46.00	26.00	100.00

Instructions Prepare a schedule containing unit values (including "floor" and "ceiling") for determining the lower of cost or market on an individual item basis. (The last column should contain the LCM valuation for each item.)

10-13 Instructions Based on the following data, compute the ending inventory at both retail and cost by the retail method.

Opening inventory—cost	$14,250
Opening inventory—retail	19,105
Purchases—cost	33,771
Purchases—retail	46,295
Purchase allowances	1,093
Transportation in	814
Transportation out	925
Sales	37,300

10-14 Company B purchased 140 units of item C during the first year at $100 per unit, 100 units during the second year at $120 per unit, and 150 units during the third year at $160 per unit. Each year 100 units were sold at a 50 percent markup on the purchase price of that year.

Instructions Using the above information, prepare:

(1) A schedule comparing inventory and cost of goods sold valuations under both FIFO and LIFO for each of the 3 years.

(2) A schedule reflecting the gross margins under both FIFO and LIFO for each of the 3 years.

10-15 John Allen operates a retail store. He is concerned about the apparent discrepancy between the store's income and its volume of sales. He has asked you to examine his records to determine whether there is any indication of an inventory shortage. In the course of your investigation you obtain the following facts regarding the calendar year 19X2:

1 The physical inventory taken December 31, 19X2, amounted to $4,442 cost, $4,171 market. The inventory of December 31, 19X1, was $6,256 cost, $6,013 market. It has been the store's practice to value inventory at the lower of cost or market.

2 The average gross margin in recent years has been 35 percent of net sales. Allen informs you that this percentage seems reasonable and that he expected the same result for 19X2, since his markup percentage was approximately the same as in the past.

3 The December 31, 19X1, balance sheet shows accounts receivable of $2,057. Notes payable to banks and trade accounts payable, combined on the December 31, 19X1, balance sheet, totaled $9,622. The firm records accounts payable at the net figure, as cash discounts are seldom missed. Purchases have been shown net in past income statements. Sales discounts have been treated as deductions from sales in the past.

4 During 19X2, accounts were written off in the amount of $216, and an account for $148 written off in 19X1 was collected and recorded as a regular collection on account.

5 Unpaid sales slips show that customers owed $3,246 on December 31, 19X2.

6 Unpaid invoices indicate that the store owed trade creditors $5,027 at the end of 19X2. Record of notes outstanding indicates that $3,000 was owed to banks on December 31, 19X2.

7 Sales returns amounted to $95, and purchase returns amounted to $272.

8 Of the items in the cash records, the following are pertinent:

Receipts:
From customers (after $272 discounts) _____ $49,851
From bank loan (net of 60–day, 6% discount) _____ 2,970

Disbursements:
To trade creditors (after $916 cash discounts) _____ 38,970
To banks on loans _____ 4,000
To customers for returned goods _____ 72

Instructions Assuming that the gross margin rate of 35 percent is reasonable, compute the apparent inventory shortage.

10-16 Instructions Using the following data and assuming that the company values its inventory at the lower of cost or market, determine the value of its inventory in accordance with the:

(1) Item-by-item method

(2) Major category method

(3) Total inventory method

		Per Unit	
	Quantity	Cost	Market
Category A			
Item AA	100	$ 2.50	$ 2.30
Item AB	200	3.20	3.60
Item AC	300	4.00	4.50
Item AD	400	4.50	4.00
Category B			
Item BB	500	6.00	6.40
Item BC	400	6.50	6.60
Item BD	300	7.50	6.90
Item BE	150	9.00	8.50
Category C			
Item CC	100	10.00	9.00
Item CD	150	15.00	18.00
Item CE	170	17.00	13.00
Item CF	200	19.00	19.00

10-17 On January 1, 19X2, an organization had an inventory of merchandise valued at a cost price of $20,000. The merchandise was marked to sell at 125 percent of cost and all subsequent purchases during the six months ending June 20, 19X2, were marked up at the same rate. The inventory on hand as of June 30, 19X2, was marked to sell at $24,000. Purchases and sales per month were as follows:

	Purchases (Cost)	Sales (Selling Price)
January	$ 8,000	$ 9,000
February	9,000	9,500
March	14,000	12,000
April	16,000	18,000
May	13,000	22,000
June	10,000	18,000

Instructions Estimate the value of the inventory on hand as of the end of each of the 6 months.

*10-18 You are assisting in the taking of a physical inventory. All merchandise received up to and including October 30 has been included in the physical count. The company's fiscal year ends on October 31. The following transactions, all of which pertain to the purchase of merchandise, are entered in the voucher register for the months of October and November as indicated:

Amount	f.o.b.	Date of Invoice	Date Merchandise Received
October			
$3,600	Destination	Oct. 20	Oct. 22
2,200	Destination	Oct. 21	Oct. 23
925	Shipping point	Oct. 20	Oct. 30
3,975	Shipping point	Oct. 26	Nov. 5
2,500	Destination	Nov. 3	Oct. 29
1,025	Shipping point	Oct. 26	Oct. 30
8,600	Shipping point	Oct. 26	Oct. 30
10,251	Destination	Oct. 21	Oct. 30
3,457	Destination	Oct. 28	Oct. 30
November			
$1,000	Destination	Oct. 29	Nov. 5
3,120	Destination	Oct. 30	Oct. 31
5,350	Shipping point	Oct. 28	Oct. 30
4,500	Shipping point	Nov. 1	Oct. 30
6,040	Shipping point	Oct. 26	Nov. 5
7,530	Shipping point	Oct. 28	Nov. 4
5,000	Destination	Oct. 28	Nov. 4

*AICPA adapted.

Instructions No perpetual inventory records are kept and the physical inventory is to be used as a basis for the financial statements.

(1) What adjusting journal entries would you suggest in view of the facts adduced from the voucher register?

(2) What adjustments, if any, would you suggest be made to the physical inventory as originally taken?

*10-19 The Johnson Corporation began business on January 1, 19X1. Information about its inventories under different valuation methods is shown below.

	LIFO Cost	FIFO Cost	Market	Lower of Cost or Market
Dec. 31, 19X1	$10,200	$10,000	$ 9,600	$ 8,900
Dec. 31, 19X2	9,100	9,000	8,800	8,500
Dec. 31, 19X3	10,300	11,000	12,000	10,900

Instructions Choose the phrase which best answers each of the following questions.

(1) The inventory basis which would show the highest net income for 19X1 is:
  (a) LIFO cost   (c) Market
  (b) FIFO cost   (d) Lower of cost or market

(2) The inventory basis which would show the highest net income for 19X2 is:
  (a) LIFO cost   (c) Market
  (b) FIFO cost   (d) Lower of cost or market

(3) The inventory basis which would show the lowest net income for the three years combined is:
  (a) LIFO cost   (c) Market
  (b) FIFO cost   (d) Lower of cost or market

(4) For the year 19X2, how much higher or lower would profits be on the FIFO cost basis than on the lower of cost or market basis?
  (a) $400 higher   (e) $1,000 higher
  (b) $400 lower   (f) $1,000 lower
  (c) $600 higher   (g) $1,400 higher
  (d) $600 lower   (h) $1,400 lower

(5) On the basis of the information given, it appears that the movement of prices for the items in the inventory was:
  (a) Up in 19X1 and down in 19X3
  (b) Up in both 19X1 and 19X3
  (c) Down in 19X1 and up in 19X3
  (d) Down in both 19X1 and 19X3

*AICPA adapted.

*10-20 The Smith Company sells item A. Information as to balances on hand and purchases and sales of item A are given in the following table.

| Date | Quantities | | | Unit Price | Dollars | | |
	Received	Sold	Balance		Received	Sold	Balance
Jan. 1			100	$1.50			$150
Jan. 24	300		400	1.56	$468		
Feb. 8		80	320				
Mar. 16		140	180				
June 11	150		330	1.60	240		
Aug. 18		130	200				
Sept. 6		110	90				
Oct. 15	150		240	1.70	255		
Dec. 29		140	100				

Instructions Based on this information, choose the best answer to each question.

(1) If a perpetual inventory record of item A is operated on a FIFO basis, it will show a closing inventory of:
    (a) $150   (c) $159   (e) $170
    (b) $152   (d) $162   (f) Answer not given

(2) If a perpetual inventory record of item A is operated on a LIFO basis, it will show a closing inventory of:
    (a) $150   (c) $156   (e) $170
    (b) $152   (d) $160   (f) Answer not given

(3) Assume that no perpetual inventory is maintained for item A and that quantities are obtained by an annual physical count. The accounting records show information as to purchases but not as to sales. On this assumption the closing inventory on a FIFO basis will be:
    (a) $150   (c) $159   (e) $170
    (b) $156   (d) $160   (f) Answer not given

(4) Assume that no perpetual inventory is maintained for item A and that quantities are obtained by an annual physical count. The accounting records show information as to purchases but not as to sales. On this assumption the closing inventory on a LIFO basis will be:
    (a) $150   (c) $156   (e) $170
    (b) $152   (d) $160   (f) Answer not given

(5) If the inventory record of item A is operated on the average basis, it will show a closing inventory which is:
    (a) Lower than on the LIFO basis
    (b) Lower than on the FIFO basis
    (c) Higher than on the FIFO basis
    (d) Answer not given

*AICPA adapted.

11
Accounting for Long-lived Assets

In Chapter 3 we learned that noncurrent assets differ from current assets in that they are relatively long-lived.   Since they are necessary in the continued operation of an organization, they are neither acquired for resale nor, as a general rule, converted into cash during the next operating cycle as inventories are.   Because of their relative permanency, long-lived assets are often referred to as **fixed assets.** Another descriptive title frequently used is **plant and equipment.**

Long-lived assets can be classified in several ways.   For our purposes they perhaps can best be categorized as either tangible or intangible and then further classified as follows:

Tangible Long-lived Assets	Intangible Long-lived Assets
1 Property, plant, and equipment	**1** Intangibles with a limited life
2 Natural resources	**2** Intangibles with an unlimited life

In accounting, the term **tangible** is applied to assets which have actual physical existence (material objects), whereas **intangible** refers to assets which do not have physical properties.   Tangible assets include land, buildings, machinery, and equipment.   Goodwill, patents, and trademarks are examples of intangible assets.

BASIC LONG-LIVED ASSET PROBLEMS

As with inventories, the basic accounting problems associated with long-lived assets are the determination of (1) the appropriate portion of the total cost to be allocated to the income statement as an expense and (2) the appropriate portion of the total cost to be deferred to a future period as an asset on the balance sheet.

At least four questions pertinent to these problems must be answered if long-lived assets are to be accounted for correctly. They are:

1 How is the cost of a long-lived asset determined?

2 How is the periodic allocation of its cost accomplished?

3 How are expenditures incurred subsequent to the original acquisition of a long-lived asset treated?

4 How are long-lived asset transactions handled in the accounts?

COSTS OF LONG-LIVED ASSETS

The cost of a long-lived asset is measured in terms of the cash or cash equivalent needed to acquire the asset, plus all incidental expenditures required to put it into the proper condition and location for use.

Long-lived assets are ordinarily acquired by one of the following types of transactions:

1 Cash purchase

2 Noncash purchase

3 Lump-sum purchase

Determining Cost in a Cash Transaction

The cost of a long-lived asset purchased for cash includes the net price paid (the invoice price less cash discounts) plus all incidental cash outlays required to put it into an appropriate condition and location for use. For example, if a long-lived asset were purchased at a net price of $10,000, with transportation and installation expenditures amounting to $2,000, its cost would be $12,000.

Determining Cost in a Noncash Transaction

If property other than cash is used to acquire a long-lived asset, the cost of the asset is measured in terms of the fair market value (FMV) of the property given up; that is, we consider the transaction as if the property had first been converted into cash, and the cash in turn used to acquire the new asset. For example, if we assume that an asset with a fair market value of $10,000 was the consideration given in return for a new asset, the cost of the new asset would be $10,000 plus all incidental expenditures necessary to put it into an appropriate condition and location for use.

Determining Cost in a Lump-sum Purchase

Occasionally several different assets are acquired by an organization for one lump-sum price. In such cases the purchase price is usually apportioned among the assets on the basis of their relative values as determined in a competent appraisal. As an example, let us assume that a lump-sum purchase of property, plant, and equipment was made for $100,000 with appraisal valuations of $60,000, $40,000, and $20,000, respectively. The apportionment would be made as follows:

	Appraised Valuation	Apportionment			Cost
Property	$ 60,000	$\frac{60,000}{120,000} \times \$100,000$	=		$ 50,000
Plant	40,000	$\frac{40,000}{120,000} \times 100,000$	=		33,333
Equipment	20,000	$\frac{20,000}{120,000} \times 100,000$	=		16,667
	$120,000				$100,000

Determining Costs of Specific Assets

To illustrate some of the problems involved in determining the costs of long-lived assets, let us consider three typical assets: land, buildings, and machinery.

Land The cost of land includes the purchase price plus any incidental expenditures required to consummate the transaction and put the land into a usable condition. These expenditures may include commissions to real estate agents, legal fees, accrued taxes paid by the purchaser, cost of draining, clearing, and grading, and assessments for local improvements such as streets and sewage systems.

Let us assume that an organization buys a plant site for a net purchase price of $300,000, pays a brokerage fee of $9,000 and legal fees of $2,000, pays $8,000 to have an old building on the site razed, and receives $2,000 salvage from the old building. The cost of the land will be $317,000, determined as follows:

Net purchase price		$300,000
Brokerage fee		9,000
Legal fees		2,000
Razing old building	$8,000	
Less: Salvage	2,000	6,000
Cost of land		$317,000

Buildings The cost of a building is dependent upon whether an organization purchases an existing building or constructs a new one. If an existing building is purchased, its cost will include not only the net purchase price but also all repair and renovation expenses required to put it into a usable condition. When an organization constructs its own buildings, cost will include all pertinent expenditures such as those for labor, supervision, excavation, material, building permits, architects' and engineers' fees, legal fees, and insurance during the construction period. If an organization has someone else construct its buildings, cost will include the net contract price plus all incidental expenditures necessary to put the buildings into usable condition.

Machinery The cost of machinery includes all expenditures incurred in acquiring a machine and readying it for use. These include, but are not necessarily limited to, the following:

1 Invoice price less cash discounts

2 Freight and cartage in, including insurance

3 Installation costs

4 Test runs in readying the machine for operation

5 Buying expenses

6 Excise taxes and tariffs

Periodic Allocation of Costs of Long-lived Assets

After the cost of a long-lived asset has been determined and entered into the accounting system, the accountant periodically must allocate its expired portion to the income statement as an expense and defer its unexpired portion on the balance sheet as an asset.

The periodic allocation procedure is called **depreciation, depletion,** or **amortization,** depending on the nature of the particular asset. Although these procedures will be examined in more detail later in this chapter, we should have a general understanding of their meaning and use at this time.

Depreciation In accounting, depreciation refers to the periodic allocation of the cost of a tangible long-lived asset over its useful life. It is associated with man-made assets only. Thus, buildings, machinery, and equipment are subject to depreciation, whereas land is not, because it is neither man-made nor does it have a limited life.

Depletion This refers to the periodic allocation of the cost of a natural resource over its useful life. Timberlands, oil wells, and mineral deposits are subject to depletion.

Amortization When used in accounting in a precise fashion, amortization refers to the periodic allocation of an intangible long-lived asset over its useful life. Patents, copyrights, and goodwill are examples of intangible assets which may be subject to amortization.

Unfortunately for the accounting student, the term amortization is not always employed in the precise form mentioned in our definition. Rather it is often used in a general sense to describe any gradual extinguishment of the amount in an asset or liability account. Thus, in a broad view, amortization would include the depreciation of long-lived tangible assets and the depletion of natural resources, as well as the amortization of intangible long-lived assets. In addition it is sometimes applied to the gradual extinguishment of a liability such as a mortgage.

Capital versus Revenue Expenditures

When an expenditure is charged to an asset account, as is the case with the net purchase price when an asset is acquired initially, it is said to be **capitalized** and is termed a **capital expenditure.**

All expenditures pertinent to the acquisition of an asset properly are capitalized; however, this is not necessarily true of all asset-related expenditures incurred subsequent to the original acquisition of the asset. Some expenditures of this kind are chargeable to expense accounts and are known as **revenue expenditures.**

Examples of asset-related expenditures incurred subsequent to the original acquisition of the asset include:

1 Recurring expenditures for servicing necessary to maintain an asset in good operating condition

2 Cost of renewing structural parts of an asset

3 Cost of overhauling an asset (which may or may not extend its useful life beyond the original expectation)

Some of these expenditures will benefit future periods and thus should be treated as capital expenditures, whereas others will benefit only the period in which the expenditure is incurred and therefore properly should be charged to expense accounts.

Proper distinction between capital and revenue expenditures is essential to the matching of appropriate costs and revenues, which in turn is fundamental to the preparation of reliable financial statements. For example, if a capital expenditure is incorrectly charged to an expense account, an understatement of both current income in the income statement and the assets owned by the organization on the balance sheet will result. The error will also affect future financial statements: Net income will be overstated, and assets will be understated. Likewise, if a revenue expenditure is capitalized, the opposite effect will result: Net income will be overstated in the period in which the error is made and understated in future periods. The error will also result in assets being overstated both in the period in which the error is made and in future periods.

The effects of errors created by improperly distinguishing between capital and revenue expenditures may be summarized as follows:

Error	Resultant Effect			
	Current Period		Future Periods	
	Income	Assets	Income	Assets
Capital expenditure expensed _____	−	−	+	−
Revenue expenditure capitalized _____	+	+	−	+

It is important that an organization establish a reasonable policy for distinguishing between capital and revenue expenditures and follow it consistently if it is to avoid financial statement distortion. Among the factors which ordinarily should be taken into consideration when establishing such a policy are the following:

1 Length of probable life of the item purchased in relation to the usual accounting period. Items which will last beyond the current accounting period and thereby benefit future periods should be capitalized to avoid understating current income and overstating future income, as well as to avoid understating assets both presently and in the future.

2 Materiality of the expenditure involved, and frequency and regularity of purchase. Items costing relatively small amounts may be expensed without distorting net income; this is especially true if the organization purchases similar items regularly. However, if the aggregate cost of such items is material and purchases are not more or less uniform from period to period, the items, if of long life, should be capitalized.

3 Nature of the expenditure in relation to the asset's estimated useful life. If an expenditure prolongs the useful life beyond the original estimate, it should be capitalized; if not, it should be expensed. Therefore, as a general rule, expenditures for ordinary repairs and maintenance are expensed when incurred, whereas expenditures for major replacement of parts and major additions are capitalized, because they extend the asset's useful life beyond the original estimate.

ACCOUNTING FOR DEPRECIABLE ASSETS

Depreciation accounting is described by the AICPA in its *Accounting Research Bulletin No. 43* as follows:

The cost of a productive facility is one of the costs of the services it renders during its useful economic life. Generally accepted accounting principles require that this cost be spread over the expected useful life of the facility in such a way as to allocate it as equitably as possible to the periods during which services are obtained from the use of the facility. This procedure is known as depreciation accounting, a system of accounting which aims to distribute the cost or other basic value of tangible capital assets, less salvage (if any), over the estimated useful life of the unit . . . in a systematic and rational manner. It is a process of allocation, not of valuation.[1]

Inherent in the AICPA's description is the fact that all tangible assets except land eventually wear out or become obsolete. Wear and tear and the action of the elements cause physical deterioration, ultimately limiting an asset's useful life. Similarly, functional deterioration may result from obsolescence caused by such factors as changes in technology, inadequacy of an asset, the shifting of business centers, or the enactment of prohibitory laws. The classic description of the nature of depreciation was presented by Professor Henry Rand Hatfield,[2] an early leader in accounting education, when he said, "All machinery is on an irresistible march to the junk heap, and its progress, while it may be delayed, cannot be prevented by repairs."

Handling Depreciation in the Accounts

From the expense side, the handling of depreciation in the accounts is somewhat similar to our earlier treatment of expired insurance, whereas from the asset standpoint it is more like our treatment of estimated uncollectibles.

You will recall that when accounting for insurance, we debited the Insurance Expense account for the portion of insurance that expired during the period. We do basically the same thing for depreciation; that is, we debit a Depreciation Expense account for the portion that expired during the period.

When accounting for estimated uncollectibles, we credited the Allowance for Uncollectible Accounts account for the amount that we estimated had become uncollectible during the period. We then deducted the accumulated amount of estimated uncollectibles in the allowance account from the Accounts Receivables account in order to reflect the net receivables on the balance sheet. We do essentially the same thing for depreciation from the asset standpoint; that is, we credit an Accumulated Depreciation account for the periodic estimate of the amount of cost used up during the period. The balance in the account is then deducted from the cost of the asset on the balance sheet in order to reflect the unexpired portion.

To illustrate, let us assume that a delivery truck which cost $5,000 as of January 1 depreciated in the amount of $1,000 during its first year of use. The

---

[1] American Institute of Certified Public Accountants, *Accounting Research and Terminology Bulletins,* Final Edition (New York: 1961), p. 76.
[2] Henry Rand Hatfield, *Accounting: Its Principles and Problems* (New York: Appleton-Century-Crofts, 1927), p. 130.

following journal entries and T accounts reflect the handling of both the original transaction and the subsequent depreciation in the accounts:

January 1

Delivery Truck	5,000	
Cash		5,000

Purchased a delivery truck.

December 31

Depreciation Expense—Delivery Truck	1,000	
Accumulated Depreciation—Delivery Truck		1,000

To record periodic depreciation.

Delivery Truck

Jan. 1	5,000		

Accumulated Depreciation—Delivery Truck

		Dec. 31 Adjusting	1,000

Depreciation Expense—Delivery Truck

Dec. 31 Adjusting	1,000		

The Depreciation Expense—Delivery Truck account would appear in the income statement as a selling expense, and the Accumulated Depreciation—Delivery Truck account would be deducted from the asset account on the balance sheet as follows:

Delivery truck	$5,000	
Less: Accumulated depreciation	1,000	4,000

The unexpired portion of the cost of an asset (for example, the $4,000 in our illustration) is usually called its **book value** or **carrying value**. In this text we shall use the latter term.

Depreciation Factors

Several factors enter into the determination of the amount of depreciation to be allocated to a period. They are:

1 Cost

2 Residual value

3 Depreciable cost

4 Estimated useful life

Cost As defined previously, cost is the net purchase price plus all incidental expenditures necessary to prepare an asset for use.

Residual Value An asset's residual value is its estimated net scrap, salvage, or trade-in value as of the estimated date of disposal.

Depreciable Cost An asset's depreciable cost is its cost minus its residual value.

Estimated Useful Life The estimated useful life of an asset is the number of years it is expected to be used, the number of units expected to be produced by its use, the number of miles it is expected to be driven, or some similar measurement.

Reliable guides for determining the useful life of an asset include (1) past experience with similar assets, (2) informed opinion regarding the asset's present physical condition, and (3) a knowledge of current developments within both the industry and the organization itself. The determination should be based on all relevant information such as the purpose for which the asset is to be used, the conditions under which it is to be operated, the policy as to maintenance, repairs, renewals, and improvements, and the climatic and other local conditions. For example, the maintenance policy of an organization has a decided effect on the length of useful life of an asset. If the policy is poor, the useful life will be shorter than if it is good, all other factors being equal.

Methods of Computing Depreciation

Several methods are available for computing depreciation, each of which, under the appropriate circumstances, achieves a proper matching of the cost of service capacity used up in the period with the revenue earned in the period. The most common methods are:

1 Straight-line method

2 Production methods

    a Unit-of-output method

    b Working-hours method

3 Accelerated methods

    a Sum-of-years'-digits method

    b Fixed-percentage-on-declining-balance method

The **straight-line method** is based upon the assumption that depreciation is dependent only upon the passage of time. In direct contrast to the straight-line method are the **production methods** which are based upon the assumption that depreciation depends solely on how much an asset is used, with the passage of time having no bearing as such. Thus, the straight-line method allocates the depreciable cost of an asset over its useful life regardless of use, whereas the production methods allocate the depreciable cost strictly on use with no regard for time.

The **accelerated methods** are based upon the assumption that an asset depreciates more in its early life than in its later life. Thus, under these methods proportionately more of the depreciable cost of an asset is allocated to its earlier years of useful life than to its later years.

In the illustrations that follow, note that the depreciation schedules reflect not only the cost of the asset and the amount of periodic depreciation, but also the total amount of accumulated depreciation and the carrying value (cost minus accumulated depreciation) of the asset.

Straight-line Method Illustrated   Under the **straight-line method** the depreciable cost of an asset is allocated over its useful life on a straight-line or uniform basis. Stated another way, straight-line depreciation "spreads" the depreciable cost of an asset uniformly over its useful life.   Let us assume that office equipment with an estimated useful life of 4 years and a residual value of $1,000 cost $9,000. The yearly depreciation computed on a straight-line basis would be $2,000 [($9,000 − $1,000) ÷ 4].   The depreciation schedule for the entire 4 years would appear as follows:

Depreciation Schedule—Straight-line Method			
	Cost	Yearly Depreciation	Accumulated Depreciation	Carrying Value
Date of purchase	$9,000	—	—	$9,000
End of first year	9,000	$2,000	$2,000	7,000
End of second year	9,000	2,000	4,000	5,000
End of third year	9,000	2,000	6,000	3,000
End of fourth year	9,000	2,000	8,000	1,000

As you study the schedule, note that when the straight-line method of computing depreciation is used:

1 The yearly provision for depreciation remains the same.

2 The accumulated depreciation increases on a uniform basis.

3 The carrying value decreases on a uniform basis until it reaches the estimated residual value.

The relationships among the periodic depreciation, the accumulated depreciation, and the carrying value may be depicted graphically as shown.

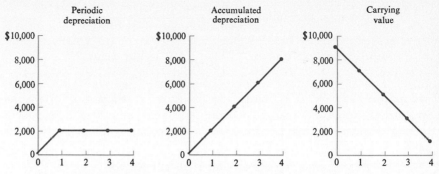

Straight-line depreciation relationships.

The following entry and T accounts show how the periodic adjusting entry would be made and how the related accounts would appear after the adjusting entry for the third year has been made and posted, but before closing entries for the third year have been made:

Depreciation Expense—Office Equipment ———————————————— 2,000
      Accumulated Depreciation—Office Equipment ———————————— 2,000
To adjust for annual depreciation.

Office Equipment		
Date of purchase	9,000	

Accumulated Depreciation—Office Equipment		
	End of first year	2,000
	End of second year	2,000
	End of third year	2,000

Depreciation Expense—Office Equipment		
End of first year	2,000	To R & E Summary	2,000
End of second year	2,000	To R & E Summary	2,000
End of third year	2,000		

Unit-of-output Method Illustrated   The unit-of-output method of depreciating an asset is based upon the assumption that depreciation is strictly a function of use, and that the passage of time in itself is not relevant to the depreciation process. If we assume the same data that were used when the straight-line method was illustrated, except that the asset's useful life is expressed in terms of estimated units of output—say 80,000 units, the depreciation per unit would be 10 cents, determined as follows:

$$\text{Depreciation per unit} = \frac{\text{depreciable cost}}{\text{estimated units of useful life}}$$

$$\text{Depreciation per unit} = \frac{\$9,000 - \$1,000}{80,000} = 10 \text{ cents}$$

If we assume that the 80,000 units were produced at the rate of 20,000 the first year, 30,000 the second year, 10,000 the third year, and 20,000 the fourth year, the depreciation schedule for the asset would appear as follows:

Depreciation Schedule—Unit-of-output Method			
	Cost	*Yearly Depreciation*	*Accumulated Depreciation*	*Carrying Value*
Date of purchase	$9,000	—	—	$9,000
End of first year	9,000	$2,000	$2,000	7,000
End of second year	9,000	3,000	5,000	4,000
End of third year	9,000	1,000	6,000	3,000
End of fourth year	9,000	2,000	8,000	1,000

As you study the schedule note that:

1 The yearly provision for depreciation is directly related to the number of units produced during a period.

2 The accumulated depreciation increases in direct proportion to the units produced during a period.

3 The carrying value decreases in direct proportion to the units produced during a period.

Again, the relationships among the periodic depreciation, the accumulated depreciation, and the carrying value may be depicted graphically as shown below.

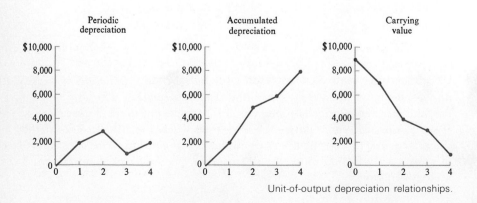

Unit-of-output depreciation relationships.

The following entry and T accounts show how the adjusting entry for the third year would be made and how the related accounts would appear after the adjusting entry has been made and posted, but before closing entries are made:

Depreciation Expense—Office Equipment _____ 1,000
    Accumulated Depreciation—Office Equipment _____ 1,000
To adjust for the third year's depreciation.

Office Equipment

Date of purchase	9,000		

Accumulated Depreciation—Office Equipment

		End of first year	2,000
		End of second year	3,000
		End of third year	1,000

Depreciation Expense—Office Equipment

End of first year	2,000	To R & E Summary	2,000
End of second year	3,000	To R & E Summary	3,000
End of third year	1,000		

Working-hours Method Illustrated This method of computing depreciation is another of the so-called production methods. However, in this method the depreciable cost of an asset is allocated over its estimated useful life on the basis of the hours the asset is used rather than on the number of units produced. Let us assume the same data used for the unit-of-output method except that the estimated useful life is expressed in terms of working hours—say 100,000. The amount of depreciation per hour worked would be 8 cents, determined as follows:

$$\text{Depreciation per hour} = \frac{\text{depreciable cost}}{\text{estimated working hours of useful life}}$$

$$\text{Depreciation per hour} = \frac{\$9,000 - \$1,000}{100,000} = 8 \text{ cents}$$

Since the basic procedures followed when applying the working-hours method to a particular situation are essentially the same as those for the unit-of-output method, the depreciation schedules, graphic presentations, adjusting entry, and related accounts will not be illustrated.

Sum-of-years'-digits Method Illustrated The accelerated methods of computing depreciation are based upon the assumption that an asset depreciates more in its early life than in its later years. Thus, their aim is to allocate more depreciation to the early years of an asset's life and less to the later. Their use results in a constantly decreasing charge for depreciation each year.

Under the **sum-of-years'-digits** method a series of fractions is applied against the asset's depreciable cost. The denominator of each fraction is the sum of the digits representing the asset's estimated years of useful life. The numerator is the estimated number of remaining years of useful life as of the beginning of the year under consideration. To illustrate, if the useful life of an asset is estimated to be 4 years, the denominators of all the fractions will be 10, the sum of $1 + 2 + 3 + 4$. The numerators, however, will vary: For the first year the numerator will be 4 (the number of years remaining as of the beginning of the year); for the second year, 3; for the third year, 2; and for the fourth year, 1. If we assume that an asset has a depreciable cost of $8,000 and an estimated useful life of 4 years, the depreciation computation for the first year will be $\frac{4}{10} \times \$8,000$, or $3,200; for the second year, $\frac{3}{10} \times \$8,000$, or $2,400; for the third year, $\frac{2}{10} \times \$8,000$, or $1,600; and for the fourth year, $\frac{1}{10} \times \$8000$, or $800.

In order to avoid the "pick-and-shovel" work involved in determining the denominator to be used in a sum-of-years'-digits computation, the following formula, in which S is equal to the sum of the digits and N is equal to the number of years of estimated useful life, may be employed:

$$S = \frac{N(N + 1)}{2}$$

For example, the denominator to be used when an asset's useful life is estimated at 10 years would be 55, determined as follows:

$$S = \frac{N(N + 1)}{2}$$

$$S = \frac{10(10 + 1)}{2}$$

$$S = 55$$

The formula is particularly helpful in computing depreciation on assets which have many years of estimated useful life.

If we assume the same data as were used in the preceding illustrations, the depreciation schedule under the sum-of-years'-digits method would appear as follows:

Depreciation Schedule—Sum-of-years'-digits Method				
	Cost	*Depreciation Computation*	*Yearly Depreciation*	*Accumulated Depreciation*	*Carrying Value*
Date of purchase	$9,000	—	—	—	$9,000
End of first year	9,000	($\frac{4}{10} \times \$8,000$)	$3,200	$3,200	5,800
End of second year	9,000	($\frac{3}{10} \times \$8,000$)	2,400	5,600	3,400
End of third year	9,000	($\frac{2}{10} \times \$8,000$)	1,600	7,200	1,800
End of fourth year	9,000	($\frac{1}{10} \times \$8,000$)	800	8,000	1,000

Again, the relationships among the periodic depreciation, the accumulated depreciation, and the carrying value may be depicted graphically.

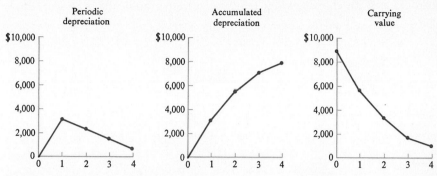

Sum-of-years'-digits depreciation relationships.

Fixed-percentage-on-declining-balance Method Illustrated Like the sum-of-years'-digits method, the fixed-percentage-on-declining-balance method results in a decreasing charge for depreciation each year. Any of a variety of rates may be used to determine depreciation charges under this method. One commonly used (because of income tax ramifications) is double the straight-line rate.

In our illustration of the straight-line basis, we automatically used a rate of 25 percent when we assumed an estimated life of 4 years; if doubled, this rate would be 50 percent. Thus, if we use the same data, under the fixed-percentage-on-declining-balance method we would apply a constant rate of 50 percent in succeeding years to the declining carrying value of the asset. When depreciation is computed at the end of the year, the rate is applied to the carrying value as of the beginning of the year. Observe that residual value is *not* taken into consideration in this computation. The depreciation schedule under this method would appear as follows:

Depreciation Schedule—Fixed-percentage-on-declining-balance Method					
	Cost	*Depreciation Computation*	*Yearly Depreciation*	*Accumulated Depreciation*	*Carrying Value*
Date of purchase	$9,000	—	—	—	$9,000.00
End of first year	9,000	(50% × $9,000)	$4,500.00	$4,500.00	4,500.00
End of second year	9,000	(50% × $4,500)	2,250.00	6,750.00	2,250.00
End of third year	9,000	(50% × $2,250)	1,125.00	7,875.00	1,125.00
End of fourth year	9,000	(50% × $1,125)	562.50	8,437.50	562.50

Although the residual value of an asset is not taken into consideration when computing depreciation under the fixed-percentage-of-declining-balance method, for federal income tax purposes depreciation is not allowable beyond the estimated residual value. If we assume a salvage value of $1,000 as of the end of the fourth year, the depreciation for the fourth year would be $125 ($1,125 − $1,000) rather than $562.50.

Again, the relationships among the periodic depreciation, the accumulated depreciation, and the carrying value may be depicted graphically as shown below.

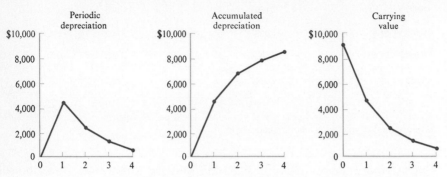

Fixed-percentage-on-declining-balance depreciation relationships.

Revision of Depreciation Rates

After an asset has been in use for some time, it is not uncommon for the periodic depreciation charge to prove to be either inadequate or excessive. The original estimate of its useful life may have been incorrect (either too long or too short), or perhaps the original estimate of the residual value was over- or understated. If the error in the periodic charge is material, the depreciation rate must be revised.

There are two basic approaches to handling the revision of depreciation rates in the accounts. One method allocates the remaining depreciable cost of the asset over its remaining useful life, while the other corrects prior years' profits and uses the rate that should have been used originally both for the correction and for future charges. Either approach is acceptable, but the first is more commonly employed because of its simplicity.

To illustrate, let us assume that office equipment which cost $21,000 and had an estimated residual value of $1,000 was depreciated on a straight-line basis for 6 years using an estimated useful life of 8 years. At the beginning of the seventh year it was estimated that the asset probably would be useful for another 4 years; that is, the estimated useful life was changed from 8 to 10 years. As of the beginning of the seventh year, the asset account and its related allowance account would appear as follows:

Office Equipment

Cost	21,000

Accumulated Depreciation—Office Equipment

Depreciation first year	2,500
Depreciation second year	2,500
Depreciation third year	2,500
Depreciation fourth year	2,500
Depreciation fifth year	2,500
Depreciation sixth year	2,500

Future Adjustment Only   Under the first method of handling the revision of depreciation rates in the accounts, the remaining depreciable cost (cost minus residual value minus depreciation already taken) is allocated over the remaining useful life.   Here the remaining depreciable cost would be $5,000 ($21,000 — $1,000 — $15,000), whereas the remaining useful life would be 4 years (10 — 6). Thus, the future periodic depreciation charge would be $1,250 ($5,000 ÷ 4), and the periodic adjusting entry would be:

Annual Adjusting Entry

Depreciation Expense—Office Equipment _____	1,250	
Accumulated Depreciation—Office Equipment _____		1,250

Past Correction and Future Adjustment   Under the second method, prior years' profits are corrected for the erroneous depreciation charges, and the rate that should have been employed originally is used for the remaining future adjustments.   If we assume the same data used in the preceding illustration, we can determine that the periodic charge in prior periods should have been $2,000 ($20,000 ÷ 10).   Since $2,500 ($20,000 ÷ 8) has been used in the past for the periodic charge, $3,000 ($500 × 6) more in depreciation has been taken than should have been.   This error has resulted in an understatement of profits of $3,000 and an overstatement of accumulated depreciation of $3,000.   The necessary correction would be made as shown.   For comparison purposes, the periodic adjusting entry is also given.

Correction Entry

Accumulated Depreciation—Office Equipment _____	3,000	
Correction of Prior Years' Profits_____		3,000

Annual Adjusting Entry

Depreciation Expense—Office Equipment _____	2,000	
Accumulated Depreciation—Office Equipment _____		2,000

Two Methods Reconciled   Although the two methods generally used for revising depreciation rates differ in approach, the ultimate effect of each is the same; both allocate the depreciable cost of the asset over its useful life.   This can be seen by comparing the respective Accumulated Depreciation accounts in the table which follows.

	Comparison of Methods for Revision of Depreciation Rates			

	Method Used			
Future Adjustment Only		*Past Correction and Future Adjustment*		
Accumulated Depreciation—Office Equipment		**Accumulated Depreciation—Office Equipment**		
Balance 20,000	Depreciation first year 2,500	Correction 3,000	Depreciation first year	2,500
	Depreciation second year 2,500		Depreciation second year	2,500
	Depreciation third year 2,500		Depreciation third year	2,500
	Depreciation fourth year 2,500		Depreciation fourth year	2,500
	Depreciation fifth year 2,500		Depreciation fifth year	2,500
	Depreciation sixth year 2,500		Depreciation sixth year	2,500
	Depreciation seventh year 1,250		Depreciation seventh year	2,000
	Depreciation eighth year 1,250		Depreciation eighth year	2,000
	Depreciation ninth year 1,250		Depreciation ninth year	2,000
20,000	Depreciation tenth year 1,250	Balance 20,000	Depreciation tenth year	2,000
	20,000	23,000		23,000
	Balance 20,000		Balance	20,000

Disposal of Depreciable Assets

When a depreciable asset is no longer as useful to an organization as is desired, it ordinarily is disposed of in one of three ways: discarded or "junked," sold, or traded in on another asset.

Regardless of the method of disposal, from an accounting standpoint, we must:

1 Record any asset received in the disposal.

2 Remove the carrying value of the asset being disposed of from the accounts.

3 Recognize any gain or loss involved in the disposal.

Discarding Depreciable Assets When a no longer useful, depreciable asset cannot be sold or traded in, it usually is junked. Since no new asset is received, we merely remove the carrying value of the asset from the accounts and recognize any loss involved. If the asset being discarded has been fully depreciated, no loss will be sustained. If it has not been fully depreciated, there will be a loss equal to the amount of the carrying value.

If a piece of office equipment which cost $5,000 and which has been fully depreciated is junked, the entry to record the disposal will be:

Accumulated Depreciation—Office Equipment	5,000	
Office Equipment		5,000

Accounting for Long-lived
Assets

283

If the equipment has not been fully depreciated at the date of disposal, it will be necessary to recognize a loss. If as of the date of disposal the equipment has been depreciated only to the extent of $4,000, the entry to record the disposal will be:

Accumulated Depreciation—Office Equipment	4,000	
Loss on Disposal of Office Equipment	1,000	
Office Equipment		5,000

Sale of Depreciable Assets The sale of a depreciable asset is handled in the accounts in essentially the same way as the discarding of an asset, except that the cash or other asset received in the sale must be recorded. While the discarding of a depreciable asset results either in no gain or loss or in a loss, the sale of a depreciable asset can result in one of three possibilities: no gain or loss, a gain, or a loss.

If the asset is disposed of at a price equal to its carrying value, no gain or loss is involved. If it is disposed of at a price greater than its carrying value, a gain results. If it is disposed of at a price less than its carrying value, a loss is sustained.

Let us assume that a piece of office equipment which cost $5,000 and which has been depreciated to the extent of $4,000 as of the date of sale is sold for $1,000. The disposal will be recorded as follows:

Cash	1,000	
Accumulated Depreciation—Office Equipment	4,000	
Office Equipment		5,000

With the same data, except that the asset is sold for $1,500 instead of $1,000, the disposal will be recorded as follows:

Cash	1,500	
Accumulated Depreciation—Office Equipment	4,000	
Gain on Disposal of Office Equipment		500
Office Equipment		5,000

If the asset is sold for $750, the disposal will be recorded as follows:

Cash	750	
Accumulated Depreciation—Office Equipment	4,000	
Loss on Disposal of Office Equipment	250	
Office Equipment		5,000

Trading in Depreciable Assets It is common practice for an organization to trade in a used asset when it acquires a new one. The trade-in allowance given by the seller is deducted from the selling price and the buyer either pays or agrees to pay the balance. As with the sale of a depreciable asset, a trade-in can result in no gain or loss, a gain, or a loss, dependent upon whether the asset traded in is accepted by the seller of the new asset at (1) an amount equal to its carrying value, (2) an amount greater than its carrying value, or (3) an amount less than its carrying value.

Let us assume that a new piece of office equipment with a net purchase price of $7,000 is acquired for $6,000 cash plus an old piece of office equipment which originally cost $5,000 and upon which depreciation has been taken in the amount of $4,000 as of the date of the trade. The trade will be recorded as follows:

Office Equipment (new)	7,000	
Accumulated Depreciation—Office Equipment	4,000	
Office Equipment (old)		5,000
Cash		6,000

If the trade-in allowance is $1,500 instead of $1,000, the trade will be recorded as follows:

Office Equipment (new)	7,000	
Accumulated Depreciation—Office Equipment	4,000	
Gain on Disposal of Office Equipment		500
Office Equipment (old)		5,000
Cash		5,500

If the trade-in allowance is only $750, the trade will be recorded as followed:

Office Equipment (new)	7,000	
Accumulated Depreciation—Office Equipment	4,000	
Loss on Disposal of Office Equipment	250	
Office Equipment (old)		5,000
Cash		6,250

Nonrecognition of Gains or Losses on Trade-ins Generally accepted accounting procedures with regard to trade-ins, as outlined above, do not always coincide exactly with the income tax treatment of trade-ins. In accordance with the Internal Revenue Code, gains and losses resulting from the exchange of similar types of depreciable assets are not recognized for income tax purposes. In a situation where the results obtained from following the income tax procedures do not differ *materially* from those obtained when generally accepted accounting procedures are followed, there frequently are practical advantages in maintaining the accounts in agreement with the income tax approach.

Under this procedure, the cost of an asset acquired in a trade-in is considered to be the sum of the carrying value of the asset traded in and the amount of cash the buyer pays or agrees to pay.

To illustrate, let us assume that a new piece of office equipment with a net purchase price of $7,000 is acquired for $6,000 cash plus an old asset which had originally cost $5,000 and upon which depreciation has been taken in the amount of $4,000 as of the date of the trade. The trade will be recorded as follows:

Office Equipment (new)	7,000	
Accumulated Depreciation—Office Equipment	4,000	
Office Equipment (old)		5,000
Cash		6,000

Note that the entry is exactly the same as the one made before when we handled the trade in accordance with generally accepted accounting procedures. This is as it should be, since there was no gain or loss involved in the trade. Such will not be the case in the following two situations, where we have a gain in one instance and a loss in the other.

If the trade-in allowance is $1,500 instead of $1,000, the trade will be recorded as follows:

Office Equipment (new)	6,500	
Accumulated Depreciation—Office Equipment	4,000	
Office Equipment (old)		5,000
Cash		5,500

If the trade-in allowance is only $750, the trade will be recorded under the income tax approach as follows:

Office Equipment (new)	7,250	
Accumulated Depreciation—Office Equipment	4,000	
Office Equipment (old)		5,000
Cash		6,250

ACCOUNTING FOR NATURAL RESOURCES

Like depreciable assets, natural resources such as timberlands, oil wells, and mineral deposits should be recorded initially in the accounts at cost. As is also true of depreciable assets, after the cost of a natural resource has been determined and entered into the accounts, most of the subsequent accounting problems pertain to (1) the periodic allocation of the expired portion of the cost to the income statement and (2) the periodic deferment of the unexpired portion of the cost on the balance sheet as an asset to be allocated to future periods.

Accounting for Depletion

As we learned earlier, the periodic allocation of the cost of a natural resource over its useful life is usually called **depletion**. (Remember—we **depreciate** man-made assets and **deplete** natural resources.)

Unit-of-output Method   Depletion is generally computed by the unit-of-output method.   The **depletable cost** (cost minus residual value) of a natural resource is divided by the estimated number of recoverable units to determine a per-unit depletion charge.   The per-unit charge is then multiplied by the number of units extracted or otherwise produced during the period to obtain the periodic depletion charge.   In a specific situation, the marketing unit is usually the preferred unit of output, for example, *board feet* of lumber, *barrels* of crude oil, or *tons* of ore. Stated as a general formula, we have:

$$\text{Depletion per unit} = \frac{\text{cost} - \text{residual value}}{\text{estimated recoverable units}}$$

Let us assume that a mine with a cost of $100,000 and an estimated residual value of $10,000 is estimated to contain 300,000 tons of ore.   The per-unit depletion charge of 30 cents is determined as follows:

$$\text{Depletion per unit} = \frac{\$100,000 - \$10,000}{300,000} = 30 \text{ cents}$$

If we assume that 10,000 tons of ore were mined during the first year of operation, the depletion charge of $3,000 (10,000 × 30 cents) will be recorded as follows:

Depletion Expense—Mine	3,000	
Accumulated Depletion—Mine		3,000

Revision of Depletion Rates   Per-unit depletion charges, like depreciation charges, may sometimes prove to be either inadequate or excessive as a result of an error in the original estimated data.   For example, the original estimate of the number of recoverable units may have been too high or too low.   When it becomes apparent that the number of recoverable units in a natural resource is *materially* more or less than the original estimate, the depletion rate must be revised.   The accounting treatment of the revision of depletion rates is not illustrated, as it is essentially the same as that for the revision of depreciation rates.

ACCOUNTING FOR INTANGIBLE ASSETS

Patents, copyrights, franchises, and goodwill are examples of intangible assets.

A **patent** is an exclusive right granted by the U.S. Patent Office for the production, use, or sale of an invention or process for a period of 17 years.   A **copyright** is an exclusive right granted by the federal government to publish and sell a literary or artistic work for a period of 28 years. **A franchise** is an exclusive right to render a service or sell a product; it may be granted by either a governmental body or a private business organization. For example, a franchise may be granted by a community to a public utility for the purpose of providing a specific service, or by a manufacturer to a distributor or retailer to sell a certain product.

Goodwill in accounting terminology refers to the ability of an organization to earn more than the normal rate on its tangible assets. For example, if the normal rate of earnings of an industry is 8 percent, an organization earning more than 8 percent is considered to have goodwill. In general, goodwill is the result of an established reputation based on such factors as the handling of quality merchandise, prompt and courteous service, convenient location, and fair and reliable dealings.

Amortization of Intangibles

The periodic allocation of an intangible asset over its useful life is called amortization. Intangible assets may be classified for amortization purposes into two broad categories: those having a limited life and those having an unlimited life.

The cost of an intangible asset with a limited life should be amortized in a systematic and rational manner over either its useful life or its limited life, whichever is shorter. A patent, for example, should be amortized over 17 years or its useful life, whichever is shorter, and a copyright should be amortized over 28 years or its useful life, whichever is shorter.

The cost of an intangible asset with an unlimited life is not amortized but instead is carried indefinitely in the asset account. However, if its life should become limited at some time in the future, it must be reclassified into the first category and amortized accordingly.

While the amortization of intangible assets is similar in nature to the depreciation of depreciable assets and the depletion of natural resources, the periodic adjustment is handled in a somewhat different manner in the accounts. Instead of setting up an allowance account such as an Accumulated Depreciation account, it is common practice to credit the asset account directly. Let us suppose that a patent which cost $51,000 is being amortized over its legal life. The adjusting entry and the subsequent postings at the end of the first year will be made as follows:

Adjusting Entry

Patent Expense		3,000
Patent		3,000

Patent

Cost	51,000	Adjusting entry	3,000

Patent Expense

Adjusting entry	3,000		

SUMMARY

Long-lived assets may be classified as tangible or intangible assets. The former include property, plant, and equipment, as well as natural resources such as timberlands, oil wells, and ore mines. Intangible assets include patents, copyrights, franchises, and goodwill.

An asset-related expenditure may be handled as a capital expenditure and charged to an asset account or as a revenue expenditure and charged to an expense account.

Some long-lived assets are depreciated, some are depleted, and others are amortized, depending on their natures. Property, plant, and equipment are depreciated if they have limited useful lives; natural resources are depleted; and intangible assets with limited useful lives are amortized.

Several methods are used for computing depreciation, each of which is acceptable under the proper circumstances. Under the straight-line method, depreciation is considered to be a function of time, whereas under the production methods it is recognized as a function of use. The accelerated methods result in higher charges for depreciation in the early life of an asset and decreasing charges in its later life.

When a periodic depreciation or depletion charge proves inadequate or excessive, the rate must be revised.

QUESTIONS AND PROBLEMS

11-1 Asset-related expenditures may be divided into two general categories: capital expenditures and revenue expenditures.

(1) Distinguish between these two categories of expenditures and between their treatment in the accounts.

(2) Discuss the effect on both present and future balance sheets and income statements of the improper distinction between capital and revenue expenditures.

(3) What criteria do business organizations generally use in establishing a policy for classifying expenditures under these two general categories? Discuss.

11-2 On the balance sheets of many companies the largest classification of assets in amount is that of long-lived assets. Name the items, in addition to the amount paid to the former owner or contractor, that may be properly included as part of the acquisition cost of the following long-lived assets:

(1) Land

(2) Buildings

(3) Machinery

11-3 What is **depreciation accounting,** and what is its objective?

11-4 A vacant piece of land is purchased for use as a parking lot. In addition to the cost of the unimproved land, expenditures are made for grading, drainage, paving, curbs and gutters, marking of parking spaces, and lighting installations. Which, if any, of these costs are subject to depreciation? Explain.

11-5 The invoice price of a new piece of equipment is $10,000. Various other costs relating to the acquisition and installation of the equipment amount to $2,000 and include such items as transportation, electrical wiring, etc. The equipment has an estimated useful life of 10 years, with no residual value at the end of that period.

   The owner of the business suggests that the incidental costs of $2,000 be charged against revenue immediately for the following reasons: (1) If the equipment should be sold, these costs cannot be recovered in the sales price, and (2) the inclusion of the $2,000 in the Equipment account on the books will not necessarily result in a closer approximation of the market price of this asset over the years, because of the possibility of changing price levels. Discuss *each* of the points raised by the owner.

11-6 It has been suggested by some that plant and equipment would be replaced more quickly if depreciation rates for both income tax and accounting purposes were substantially increased. As a result, business operations would receive the benefit of more modern and more efficient plant facilities. Discuss the merits of this proposition.

11-7 The organization for which you work as an accountant found three suitable sites, each having certain unique advantages, for a new plant facility. In order to investigate the advantages and disadvantages of each site, 1-year options were purchased by the organization for an amount equal to 5 percent of the contract price of each site. The costs of the options could not be applied against the contracts. Before the options expired, one of the sites was purchased at the contract price of $60,000. The option on this site had cost $3,000. The two options not exercised had cost $3,500 each. Present arguments in support of recording the cost of the site purchased at each of the following amounts: (1) $60,000, (2) $63,000, or (3) $70,000.

11-8 A building with a depreciable cost of $600,000, which was originally estimated to have a useful life of 40 years, has been in use for 30 years. At the end of the thirtieth year the building is estimated to be serviceable for another 20 years. Illustrate two ways of reflecting the above information in the accounts. Include in your illustration the depreciation entry for the thirty-first year.

11-9 A machine which cost $12,000 and which has been depreciated at 10 percent per year is traded in on the purchase of a new machine at the end of the sixth year.

Instructions

(1) Prepare the entry necessary to record the trade-in assuming that the new machine has a list price of $15,000, that an allowance of $4,000 is made on the old machine, and that the balance is paid in cash.

(2) Prepare the entry necessary to record the trade-in assuming that the new machine has a list price of $17,000, that an allowance of $7,000 is made on the old machine, and that the balance is paid in cash.

(3) Prepare the journal entries that would have been required in (1) and (2) above if the income tax approach to trade-ins had been followed.

11-10 The amortization of intangible assets involves basic accounting principles of income determination and balance sheet presentation.

(1) Give the two broad classifications of intangible assets and indicate the factors you would consider in classifying an intangible asset.

(2) State the generally accepted accounting procedures for the amortization of the two classifications of intangible assets.

***11-11** Webben & Sons, Inc., purchased land, together with a building standing on it, as the site for an additional plant which they planned to construct. The company obtained bids from several contractors for demolition of the old and the construction of the new building, but finally rejected all bids and undertook the construction using company labor, facilities, and equipment.

All transactions relating to these properties were charged or credited to an account titled Real Estate. The various items in that account are

*AICPA adapted.

summarized below. You decide that separate Land and Buildings accounts should be set up and that all the items in the Real Estate account should be reclassified.

Instructions On your answer sheet list the numbers 1 through 15. Indicate the disposition of each numbered item by printing beside the item number the capital letter which identifies your answer. If you recommend a reclassification involving two or more of the following accounts, list the appropriate letters.

A Transfer to Land account.

B Transfer to Buildings account.

C Transfer to a revenue (or gain) account.

D Transfer to an expense (or loss) account.

E Make some other disposition of the item.

Items Charged or Credited to "Real Estate"

1 Contract price of "package" purchase (land and old building)

2 Legal fees relating to conveyance of title

3 Invoice cost of materials and supplies used in construction

4 Costs arising from demolition of old building

5 Discounts earned for early payment of item 3

6 Total depreciation on equipment used during construction period partially for construction of building and the remainder of the time for regular operations

7 Total cost of excavation

8 Proceeds of sale of materials salvaged from razing of old building

9 Net cost of temporary structure (tool sheds, construction offices, etc.) erected for use in construction activity

10 Cost of building permits and licenses

11 Architects' fees

12 Allocated portion of certain corporation engineering executives' salaries (based upon time devoted to planning and supervision of construction)

13 Allocated portion of employees' wages for the period of excavation and of construction of the new building

14 Payment of property taxes on land and old building, owed by the former owner and assumed by the company

15 Premiums for insurance against natural hazards during construction

*11-12 You have been assigned to examine the vouchers of a lumber company which cuts approximately 40 million board feet of logs per year and has sales of approximately $2.8 million. You have been cautioned to be alert for errors in distribution caused by the inexperience of the bookkeeper in charge of recording company purchases. During the course of your examination, you find the following payments and distribution thereof:

(1) Purchase of new band-saw blades for the sawmill—$14,567. Charged to Sawmill Supplies Expense.

(2) Purchase of a 2-ton truck—$3,500. Charged to a long-lived asset account—Autos and Trucks.

(3) Travel expense for Mr. and Mrs. R. L. Jones, manager and his wife—$1,000 (no detail). Charged to Travel Expense.

(4) Purchase of an electric stove for the sales manager's personal residence—$350. Charged to Miscellaneous Sales Expense.

(5) Payment of an adjustment of a sales invoice as a result of using the wrong price—$110. Charged to Transportation In account.

(6) Purchase of a used crane to lift logs from the pond—$1,500. Charged to Pond Expense—Repairs.

(7) Purchase of new conveyor chain for a newly constructed dry kiln—$2,500. Charged to Dry Kiln Repairs.

(8) Purchase of a new conveyor chain to replace a worn-out chain on the log deck—$2,500. Charged to Sawmill Repairs.

Instructions Comment briefly on the correctness of each distribution (account to which charged), emphasizing the governing considerations involved.

11-13 Machine A, which cost $120,000, is estimated to have a useful life of 6 years and an estimated residual value of $15,000.

Instructions Prepare depreciation schedules showing yearly depreciation, accumulated depreciation, and the carrying value at the end of each year, assuming that depreciation is computed by:

(1) The straight-line method

(2) The sum-of-years'-digits method

(3) The fixed-percentage-on-declining-balance method (twice the straight-line rate in this case)

11-14 The Z Company computes depreciation on its plant and equipment on the basis of units of production. On January 1, 19X1, the balance in the

*AICPA adapted.

Plant and Equipment account was $2,500,000, and the balance in the Accumulated Depreciation—Plant and Equipment account was $790,000. It was then estimated that starting January 1, 19X1, 1,900,000 units would be produced over the remaining useful life of the plant and equipment. During 19X1, 250,000 units were produced.

No change occurred in the plant accounts, except for the 19X1 depreciation, until January 1, 19X2. On that date an item of equipment which cost $75,000 was retired and scrapped. The management's policy is to charge the cost of plant assets retired to the Accumulated Depreciation account. On the same date new equipment which cost $115,000 was placed in service and payment was made in cash for the equipment. It was then reestimated that, as a consequence, there would be produced 2,000,000 units over the remaining useful life of the plant and equipment from the beginning of business on January 1, 19X2. The production was 245,000 units in the year 19X2.

Instructions Prepare, in general journal form, all entries necessary to record the retirement of the old equipment, the addition of the new equipment, and the depreciation for the years 19X1 and 19X2.

11-15 The following information relates to the purchase of a new asset which was paid for by the trade-in of an old asset and the balance in cash:

List price of new asset	$10,000
Cash payment	5,800
Cost of old asset	8,000
Accumulated depreciation—old asset	5,000
Second-hand market value—old asset	3,600

Instructions Prepare journal entries showing three different ways of recording the above transaction. Explain the reasoning behind each entry and indicate the circumstances in which it might be appropriate.

11-16 A machine, which cost $100,000 four years ago when it was estimated to have a useful life of 5 years and a residual value of $10,000, is sold as of the end of the fourth year for $20,000.

Instructions Prepare entries to record the sale, assuming that depreciation has been computed by:

(1) The straight-line method

(2) The sum-of-years'-digits method

(3) The fixed-percentage-on-declining-balance method (double the straight-line rate in this case)

11-17 A new piece of office equipment with a net purchase price of $10,000 is acquired for $7,500 cash plus an old piece of office equipment which 3 years ago had cost $9,000, when it was estimated to have a useful life of 4 years and a residual value of $2,000.

Instructions Prepare the entries necessary to record the trade-in in accordance with generally accepted accounting procedures, assuming that depreciation has been computed by:

(1) The straight-line method

(2) The sum-of-years'-digits method

(3) The fixed-percentage-on-declining-balance method (40 percent in this case)

11-18 The Jackson Company purchased a machine on June 1, 19X1, for $5,000, f.o.b. shipping point. Freight to the point of installation was $200, and $125 was expended on the installation. The machine's useful life was estimated at 10 years and its salvage value at $50. On June 1, 19X3, an electronic accessory which had been developed to reduce the cost of operating such machines was obtained at a cost of $600. On June 1, 19X6, the company purchased another machine of greater capacity for $9,000, f.o.b. destination. A trade-in allowance of $2,000 was received for the old machine with the $7,000 balance being paid in cash. Installation expenditures on the new machine amounted to $300. Its useful life was estimated at 10 years and its salvage value at $100.

Instructions Use straight-line depreciation for both machines and compute the amount of depreciation that should be taken on the new machine for the year ending May 31, 19X7, in accordance with:

(1) Generally accepted accounting procedures

(2) Federal income tax regulations

11-19 The table below shows certain facts concerning selected assets of the ABC Company. For depreciation purposes, the company follows the policy of taking only one-half year's depreciation in the year of acquisition, but a full year in the year of disposal.

	Acquisitions		*Disposals*	
Year	Acquisition Cost	Estimated Useful Life, Years	Year of Acquisition	Acquisition Cost
19X2	$50,000	10		
19X3	20,000	10	19X2	$7,000

Instructions Using this information, and disregarding salvage values, prepare a summary of the asset and accumulated depreciation accounts, showing beginning balances, additions, disposals, and ending balances for the years 19X2 and 19X3, assuming that:

(1) The straight-line method of depreciation is in use.

(2) The sum-of-years'-digits method is used.

*11-20 The ABC Manufacturing Company started in business on January 1, 19X1, by acquiring three machines costing $5,240, $4,000, and $4,400, respectively. Since that date the company has computed depreciation at 20 percent on the balance of the asset account at the end of each year and has credited it directly to the asset account. All purchases since January 1, 19X1, have been debited to the Machinery account and the cash received from sales has been credited to the account.

The following transactions took place:

1 On September 30, 19X1, a machine was purchased on an installment basis. The list price was $6,000, but 12 payments of $600 each were made by the company. Only the monthly payments were recorded in the Machinery account starting with September 30, 19X1. Freight and installation charges of $200 were paid and entered in the Machinery account on October 10, 19X1.

2 On June 30, 19X2, a machine was purchased for $8,000, 2/10, n/30, and recorded at $8,000 when paid for on July 7, 19X2.

3 On June 30, 19X3, the machine acquired for $5,240 was traded for a larger one having a list price of $9,300. An allowance of $4,300 was received on the old machine, the balance of the list price being paid in cash and charged to the Machinery account.

4 On January 1, 19X4, the machine which cost $4,400 was sold for $2,500, but because the cost of removal and crating was $125, the Machinery account was credited with only $2,375.

5 On October 1, 19X5, the machine purchased for $4,000 was sold for cash and the cash received was credited to the Machinery account.

6 The balance of the Machinery account on January 1, 19X5, was $14,505.50; on December 31, 19X5, after adjustment for depreciation, it was $10,644.40.

The company has decided that its method of handling its Machinery account has not been satisfactory. Accordingly, after the books were closed in 19X5, the management decided to correct the account as of December 31, 19X5, in accordance with usual accounting practices, and to provide

*AICPA adapted.

depreciation on a straight-line basis with a separate accumulation account. Straight-line depreciation is estimated to be at the rate of 10 percent per annum computed on a monthly basis, over one-half of a month being considered as a full month for this purpose.

Instructions Prepare:

(1) A schedule showing the balance of the Machinery account and its related Accumulated Depreciation account as of December 31, 19X5, on the revised basis.

(2) A schedule of gain and loss on disposal of assets for the 5-year period.

(3) A computation of the corrected depreciation expense for the year 19X5 on the new basis. Do not consider income tax procedures in your solution.

EDP PROBLEMS

11-21 Building A, which cost $400,000, is estimated to have a useful life of 20 years and an estimated residual value of $35,000.

Instructions Using a computer, prepare a depreciation schedule showing yearly depreciation by the straight-line method, accumulated depreciation, and the carrying value at the end of each year.

11-22 Building B, which cost $700,000, is estimated to have a useful life of 25 years and an estimated residual value of $50,000.

Instructions Use a computer to prepare a depreciation schedule showing yearly depreciation by the sum-of-years'-digits method, accumulated depreciation, and the carrying value at the end of each year.

11-23 Building C, which cost $500,000, is estimated to have a useful life of 20 years and no residual value.

Instructions Use a computer to prepare a depreciation schedule showing yearly depreciation, accumulated depreciation, and the carrying value at the end of each year, assuming that the fixed-percentage-on-declining-balance method is followed. (Use twice the straight-line rate in this case.)

11-24 Building D, which cost $500,000, is estimated to have a useful life of 20 years and an estimated residual value of $65,000.

Instructions   Using a computer, prepare a depreciation schedule showing yearly depreciation, accumulated depreciation, and the carrying value at the end of each year, assuming that depreciation is computed by the fixed-percentage-on-declining-balance method.   (Use three times the straight-line rate in this case.)

11-25 Building E, which cost $500,000, is estimated to have a useful life of 20 years and no residual value.

Instructions   Use a computer to prepare a depreciation schedule showing yearly depreciation, accumulated depreciation, and the carrying value at the end of each year, assuming that depreciation is computed by the following procedure: The fixed-percentage-on-declining-balance method (twice the straight-line rate in this case) is used until such time as the year's depreciation charge is equal in amount to what the charge would be if the remaining undepreciated cost of the asset were to be allocated over the remaining life of the asset on a straight-line basis.   After this point is reached, depreciation is computed by the straight-line method.

12

Accounting for Current Liabilities

Up to this time we have discussed liabilities only in a general way. In order to crystallize our thinking on the subject and at the same time investigate some of the more difficult problems which may be encountered in accounting for specific kinds of liabilities, we shall examine them in greater detail in this chapter.

BASIC NATURE OF LIABILITIES

When the basic equation $A = L + OE$ was first introduced, liabilities were defined as things of value owed by an entity. This definition should be expanded before we continue our study. As the term is used in accounting, liabilities are debts of a business organization or other entity which must be met by:

1 Paying sums of money
2 Conveying (transferring title to) assets other than money
3 Rendering services

It is particularly important to note that the accountant does not look upon liabilities merely as monetary obligations.

The AICPA, in its *Accounting Research Study No. 7,*[1] states that liabilities result from past actions and transactions which require settlement in the future. To illustrate, when an organization purchases merchandise on credit or borrows money from a bank, a transaction takes place and a liability results. Similarly, when taxes are levied on a business concern, a liability is created by the action of a taxing authority. As a matter of fact, taxes comprise some of the accountant's most difficult problems in the liability area.

Recognition and Measurement of Liabilities

The major problems in accounting for liabilities relate to their recognition and measurement. Liability recognition consists of determining when a legal obligation has been incurred; it is primarily a matter of **timing.** Thus, a liability for the purchase of goods or services is created with the passage of title to the goods or the rendering of the services. Likewise, a legally enforceable claim against an organization is ordinarily established at the time a taxing agency levies a tax.

Before liabilities can enter the accounting system, they must be expressible in monetary terms; that is, like assets, they must be **quantifiable.** Liabilities are measured by:

1 The amount of cash received in a transaction (as when money is borrowed)
2 The fair market value of noncash assets or services rendered (as when merchandise or services are acquired on credit)
3 Estimates, when the amount owed cannot be measured precisely

All known liabilities should be reflected in the accounts as of the balance sheet date, whether or not the dollar amount is definitely determinable. If it is not possible to determine the amount, it should be estimated. For example, the exact dollar amount of a tax liability may not be precisely determinable as of the balance sheet date; thus it must be estimated.

Classification of Liabilities

Liabilities are classified on the balance sheet as either current or noncurrent. The current category is usually entitled "current liabilities," while the noncurrent category may be termed "long-term debt," "fixed liabilities," or some similar title. Current liabilities will be covered in this chapter, and long-term debt will be discussed in Chapter 13.

[1] Paul Grady, "Inventory of Generally Accepted Accounting Principles for Business Enterprises," *Accounting Research Study No. 7* (New York: AICPA, 1967), p. 276.

CURRENT LIABILITIES

Current liabilities were defined in Chapter 3 as those debts or obligations of an organization which must be satisfied within the current operating cycle or one year, whichever is longer. The AICPA, in its *Accounting Research Bulletin No. 43,* defines the term more specifically:

> The term *current liabilities* is used principally to designate obligations whose liquidation is reasonably expected to require the use of existing resources properly classifiable as current assets, or the creation of other current liabilities. As a balance sheet category, the classification is intended to include obligations for items which have entered into the operating cycle, such as payables incurred in the acquisition of materials and supplies to be used in the production of goods or in providing services to be offered for sale; collections received in advance of the delivery of goods or performance of services; and debts which arise from operations directly related to the operating cycle, such as accruals for wages, salaries, commissions, rentals, royalties, and income and other taxes.[1]

You will recall that the operating cycle in a trading concern is the time required to buy merchandise, sell it, convert the receivable into cash, and buy new merchandise; in a manufacturing concern it is the time required to acquire raw materials, produce the product, sell the product, collect the receivable, and purchase new material.

Typical Current Liabilities

Some of the more common current liability accounts found in published financial statements are:

1 Accounts Payable, or Accounts Payable—Trade
2 Notes Payable, or Notes Payable—Trade
3 Notes Payable to Bank
4 Accrued Interest Payable
5 Accrued Property Taxes Payable
6 Income Taxes Payable
7 Sales Taxes Payable
8 Employees' Income Taxes Withheld
9 F.I.C.A. Taxes Payable

[1] American Institute of Certified Public Accountants, *Accounting Research and Terminology Bulletins,* Final Edition (New York: 1961), pp. 21–22.

10 Federal Unemployment Taxes Payable

11 State Unemployment Taxes Payable

12 Accrued Payroll Payable

Accounts Payable or Accounts Payable—Trade and Notes Payable or Notes Payable—Trade are accounts with trade creditors. The former are generally created when an organization purchases goods or services on open account, and the latter when promissory notes are given. The Notes Payable to Bank account as a rule is established when an organization borrows money from a bank.

An accrued expense, as we learned in Chapter 9, is one for which a liability has been incurred as of a given date but which is payable at some future time. Thus, the Accrued Interest Payable account on a balance sheet represents the amount of interest which has been incurred on interest-bearing obligations as of the balance sheet date but which will not be paid until a future date. The Accrued Property Taxes Payable account will be discussed in the next section of this chapter.

The account Income Taxes Payable or, as it sometimes is called, Estimated Income Taxes Payable, reflects the estimated liability for income taxes as of the date of the balance sheet. The determination of the actual liability for income taxes of a complex organization is a difficult and often lengthy process; therefore, it is common practice to estimate the amount of the liability as of the end of the fiscal period, with the estimate being subject to later adjustments when the final return is filed. While an in-depth study of income taxes is generally a subject for advanced work in accounting, the basic computation of the estimated liability is covered in Chapter 18 of this text. At this time, however, we should recognize that the liability for the amount of income taxes payable as of the date of the balance sheet is a *current* liability.

The caption of the account Sales Taxes Payable is self-explanatory. If the balance in the account is correct, it reflects the amount payable to the political subdivision that has levied the tax. The handling of sales taxes in the accounts will be covered later in this chapter.

The last five accounts listed, namely, Employees' Income Taxes Withheld, F.I.C.A. Taxes Payable, Federal Unemployment Taxes Payable, State Unemployment Taxes Payable, and Accrued Payroll Payable, are all associated with the payroll (earnings of the employees) of an organization. Payroll accounting is the subject of a subsequent section of this chapter.

Accounting for Property Taxes

Property taxes are levied both on **real property,** which includes land and buildings, and **personal property,** which in a business organization includes such things as merchandise, machinery, and other equipment.

Real and personal property taxes are based upon an assessed valuation of the properties as of a certain date and are payable as of a specific date to the local tax collector. When accounting for property taxes, an entity is confronted with two basic questions:

1 When should the liability be reflected in the accounts?

2 How should the periodic expense be determined?

Methods of Accounting for Property Taxes Laws governing the dates of tax levies, the dates of collection, and the dates of fiscal years of political subdivisions levying and collecting property taxes vary from one jurisdiction to another. As a consequence, the methods followed by accountants when accounting for property taxes are not necessarily uniform. For example, property taxes have been charged to expense in each of the following periods:

1 Year in which paid

2 Year ending on the assessment date

3 Year beginning on the assessment date

4 Calendar or fiscal year of the taxpayer prior to the assessment date

5 Calendar or fiscal year of the taxpayer prior to the payment date

6 Fiscal year of the governing body levying the tax

Although various methods of accounting for property taxes may be acceptable under particular circumstances, the one recommended by the AICPA[1] provides for the systematic accrual of the taxes on the taxpayer's books over the fiscal year of the taxing authority. If the fiscal years of the taxing authority and the taxpayer are the same, no major accounting difficulties will be experienced. It is when their fiscal years do not coincide that the accountant may have a problem.

For illustrative purposes, let us assume that the taxpayer is on a calendar-year basis but that the fiscal year of the taxing authority extends from July 1 to June 30. If the taxing authority levies property taxes of $5,200, $5,400, and $5,500 for three successive fiscal years, the taxpayer's property tax expense for the two full calendar years which fall within the three fiscal years will be $5,300 and $5,450, respectively, determined as follows:

Taxing authority's fiscal year	6/30 $5,200	6/30 $5,400	6/30 $5,500 6/30
Taxpayer's fiscal year	12/31 $2,600 + $2,700	12/31 $2,700 + $2,750	12/31
Property tax expense	$5,300	$5,450	

[1] *Ibid.,* pp. 83–84.

The \$5,300 expense should be accrued by the taxpayer at the rate of \$433.33 per month (\$2,600 ÷ 6) for the first 6 months of the calendar year and at the rate of \$450 per month (\$2,700 ÷ 6) for the last 6 months. The \$5,450 expense should be accrued at the rate of \$450 per month (\$2,700 ÷ 6) for the first 6 months and at \$458.33 per month (\$2,750 ÷ 6) for the second 6 months. To illustrate, each of the \$450 monthly accruals would be recorded as follows:

Property Tax Expense	450	
Property Taxes Payable		450

Estimating Property Taxes It is common practice in many jurisdictions for taxing authorities to assess property a year in advance of the due date of the taxes. Often, however, the tax rate for the year being taxed will not yet have been established. Thus, the exact amount of the tax liability sometimes is not known until several months after the date of assessment. The liability for the taxes ordinarily is accrued by using an estimate based on the immediately preceding year's taxes plus any information available as to possible changes in assessed values or tax rates. As a rule the amount which actually has to be paid will vary only slightly from the estimate. Therefore, the difference is ordinarily handled as an adjustment of prior accruals.

Accounting for Sales Taxes

Many states, counties, and cities levy sales taxes on certain retail sales and services. As a rule these taxes are levied as a percentage of the selling price. They generally are paid by consumers and collected by sellers (business organizations); thus, the seller acts as a tax collector for the government. He must therefore maintain his records in such a way as to provide for adequate control over both the collection and the remittance of the taxes.

Collection of Sales Taxes Sales taxes may be collected when a cash sale is made or may be charged to the customer's account when a credit sale is transacted. In either case the amount of the taxes should be credited to the organization's Sales Taxes Payable account. If we assume a \$1,000 sale subject to a 5 percent sales tax, in general journal form the transaction would be recorded as follows:

Cash (or Accounts Receivable)	1,050	
Sales Taxes Payable		50
Sales		1,000

In an organization where the collection of sales taxes is a significant part of the operation of the business, the usual procedure is to design the accounting records in a way that will permit the taxes to be handled routinely. For example, a special column may be set up in the cash receipts journal to handle the taxes on cash sales. If we add a column for sales taxes payable in our columnar cash receipts journal, the transaction for a cash sale would be recorded as follows:

Columnar Cash Receipts Journal

| | | | | Debit | | Credit | | |
| | | | | Cash | Sales Discount | Accounts Receivable | Sales Taxes Payable | General Ledger |
Date	Account Credited	Explanation	PR					
	Sales	Cash sales		1,050			50	1,000

In order to handle the sales taxes associated with credit sales in a systematic and routine fashion, the columnar sales journal also could be expanded by the addition of a column for sales taxes payable. The credit transactions would then be handled as follows:

Columnar Sales Journal

| | | | | | Debits | Credits | |
| | | | | | Accounts Receivable | Sales Taxes Payable | Sales |
Date	Account Debited	Invoice No.	Terms	PR			
	John Jones	108	2/10, n/30		1,050	50	1,000

Remittance of Sales Taxes Sales taxes are remitted to the taxing authority periodically (monthly, quarterly, or semiannually) as prescribed by law. The amount to be remitted is computed on the taxable sales of the organization for the period regardless of the amount of taxes actually collected. Thus, at times the amount remitted may differ from the amount collected. Although the difference could be caused by error, it usually results either from rounding off mathematically when computing the tax—for example, $3\frac{1}{2}$ cents would be rounded to 4 cents—or from the fact that the tax rate changes at various levels. To illustrate the latter, let us assume that in a given jurisdiction no tax is collected on sales less than 10 cents, 1 cent is collected on sales of 10 to 29 cents, 2 cents on sales of 30 to 49 cents, and so on. Three separate sales of 10 cents each would result in 3 cents in taxes being collected, but only 2 cents would be required for remittance to the taxing authority.

The difference between the amount of taxes collected and the amount to be remitted is normally treated in the accounts as a miscellaneous item of expense or income, depending upon whether the amount remitted is more or less than the amount collected. For example, if an organization collected $174.67 in taxes but had to remit $176.22, the difference would be handled as follows:

Sales Taxes Payable	174.67	
Miscellaneous Expense	1.55	
Cash		176.22

PAYROLL ACCOUNTING

Payroll costs make up a large and steadily increasing component of the cost of operating most organizations. Accounting for payrolls is a major task in many business entities, and it is further complicated by the fact that various tax laws having direct bearing on payroll computations are almost constantly being enacted or revised by our federal, state, and local governments.

The term **payroll** is often employed in a somewhat narrow sense to mean the take-home pay of employees. For accounting purposes, however, it refers to the total earnings of employees for an accounting period. **Payroll accounting** consists of accumulating, summarizing, and reporting payroll costs. The basic problems involved relate primarily to the following activities:

1 Determination of employee earnings

2 Determination of payroll taxes

3 Maintenance of payroll records

Determination of Employee Earnings

Employee earnings fall into two major categories: (1) **wages,** which generally are paid for work or services on an hourly, daily, or weekly basis, or on unit of output, and (2) **salaries,** which are fixed amounts of compensation paid periodically to employees for regular work or services. The determination of a salaried employee's total (gross) earnings generally presents no difficulty. Therefore, in order to best illustrate some of the problems of computing employee earnings, we shall think in terms of wages based on "so much per hour."

In general, hourly rates are set by the employer and confirmed by either an oral or written agreement between the employer and employee. Organizations engaged in interstate commerce must conform to the regulations of the Federal Fair Labor Standards Act, commonly known as the Wage and Hour Law. This act places a ceiling on working hours and a floor on wage rates. For example, organizations covered by the act are required to pay overtime wages at the rate of $1\frac{1}{2}$ times the regular rate for all hours worked in excess of 40 hours per week.

To illustrate the determination of gross wages, let us assume that Clyde Clark, whose regular (base) rate is $3.20 per hour and whose overtime rate is $1\frac{1}{2}$ times the base rate, works 46 hours during a given week. His gross earnings will be $156.80, determined as follows:

Regular earnings (40 hours $\times$ $3.20)	$128.00
Overtime earnings [6 $\times$ ($3.20 $\times$ $1\frac{1}{2}$)]	28.80
Total (gross) earnings	$156.80

Payroll Taxes

The amount of an employee's take-home pay seldom equals the amount of his total wages or salary for a payroll period. Various deductions, both voluntary and involuntary in nature, may be made from his gross earnings before his pay-check is issued. Depending upon circumstances, sums may be deducted for any or all of the following purposes:

1 Payment of income taxes (federal, state, and local)

2 Payment of F.I.C.A. taxes

3 Payment of voluntary contributions (union dues, savings bonds, group life insurance, etc.)

Although accounting for voluntary payroll deductions may present problems on occasion, at this time we shall concentrate primarily on involuntary deductions imposed by law. However, it is important that we be aware of the existence and nature of deductions that are made at the instigation of an employee and thus are more or less voluntary.

The amounts withheld for both voluntary and involuntary deductions are considered liabilities of the withholding organization until they are paid, and must be accounted for accordingly.

Income Taxes Almost without exception the amount withheld for the payment of federal income taxes constitutes the largest single deduction from employee earnings. The federal income tax collection system in the United States is commonly known as a "pay-as-you-go" system. A major objective of a program of this kind is to place the payment of income taxes on a current basis, that is, to collect them in the year in which the income is received rather than in the year following. Thus employers are required by law to withhold funds for the payment of federal income taxes from the earnings of their employees. The amount to be withheld depends upon (1) the amount of the employee's earnings and (2) the number of exemptions he is permitted to claim. Each employee is entitled to one exemption for himself and an additional exemption for each of his dependents. Other exemptions are allowed if the employee or his spouse is 65 years of age or older or will become 65 on or before January 1 of the following year, or if either he or his spouse is blind. Each exemption lowers the amount of income taxes the employee is required to pay.

Every employee is required by law to file with his employer a Form W-4 (Employee's Withholding Exemption Certificate), on which he states the number of exemptions to which he is entitled. This form is illustrated below.

Form W-4. Employee's withholding exemption certificate.

To assist employers, tables showing amounts of income taxes to be withheld based on (1) a given amount of earnings and (2) a given number of dependents are furnished by the Internal Revenue Service. They are available for weekly, biweekly, monthly, and miscellaneous pay periods.

In addition to the federal government, some states and cities levy income taxes on employee earnings. We shall not attempt to cover state and city income tax legislation here as regulations vary widely. As a general rule, however, deductions for such taxes are determined (1) by applying a fixed percentage to the amount withheld for federal income tax purposes or (2) by applying a fixed percentage to the employee's earnings. Again, tax tables generally are made available by the taxing authorities.

To illustrate the recording of federal income tax withholdings, let us assume that $1,200 in federal income taxes is withheld from a monthly payroll of $10,000 and that there are no other deductions. The monthly accrual will be recorded as follows:

Payroll Expense		10,000
Employees' Income Taxes Withheld		1,200
Accrued Payroll Payable		8,800

F.I.C.A. Taxes The tendency of modern governments to assume greater responsibility for their citizens is illustrated by the development in the United States of the so-called social security system. Beginning with the passage of the Federal Social Security Act of 1935 benefits have been provided which currently include:

1 Retirement benefits

2 Disability benefits

3 Survivors' benefits

4 Unemployment benefits

5 Hospitalization insurance

6 Insurance against other medical expenses

In theory, the basic idea behind our social security system is a simple one. During working years, employees, their employers, and self-employed individuals pay social security taxes which go into trust funds. When earnings cease upon a worker's disability, retirement, or death, payments are made from the funds to the worker and his dependents, or to his survivors.

The Federal Insurance Contributions Act (F.I.C.A.) requires that both employees and employers in occupations covered by the act contribute to the social security program. Taxes for this purpose, generally referred to simply as F.I.C.A. taxes, are withheld from the earnings of the employees and are levied on employers at the same rate and on the same amount of earnings as on employees. For example, if an employee has earnings of $1,000 subject to F.I.C.A. taxes of 5 percent, his employer should withhold $50 ($1,000 $\times$ .05) from the earnings. The employer, however, must remit $100 [($1,000 $\times$ .05) + ($1,000 $\times$ .05)] to the Internal Revenue Service, which acts as a collection agency for the federal government.

You will note that two items enter into an F.I.C.A. computation: the **rate** and the taxable earnings, normally called the **base.** Established by congressional action, both the rate and the base have been changed several times in the past and no doubt will be changed many times in the future. Since such changes do not affect the accounting procedures involved, for illustrative purposes in this text we shall use a constant 5 percent rate and a $9,000 base.

A $9,000 base means that the tax is levied on the *first* $9,000 of an employee's annual earnings. Thus, if a 5 percent rate is in effect, the maximum amount of

F.I.C.A. taxes owed by any employee would be $450 ($9,000 × .05) per year. The employer's liability would be limited to the same amount. If an individual works for more than one employer during a year, each employer must withhold and pay taxes on the first $9,000 of the employee's earnings. An employee can obtain a refund from the government for F.I.C.A. taxes deducted from his annual earnings in excess of $9,000; however, the employers involved cannot.

If we assume that an organization has a monthly payroll of $10,000 subject to a 5 percent F.I.C.A. rate, and that $1,200 in federal income taxes is withheld, the monthly accrual will be recorded as follows:

Payroll Expense	10,000	
Payroll Tax Expense ($10,000 × .05)	500	
Employees' Income Taxes Withheld		1,200
F.I.C.A. Taxes Payable ($10,000 × .10)		1,000
Accrued Payroll Payable		8,300

Note that the employees' portion of the tax is considered part of the organization's payroll expense, while the employer's portion is considered a payroll tax expense.

Federal Unemployment Compensation Taxes Like the Federal Insurance Contributions Act, the Federal Unemployment Tax Act, commonly referred to as F.U.T.A., is part of our national social security program. As its title implies, the act was designed to provide temporary relief for unemployed workers. Unlike the F.I.C.A. tax, which is levied on both employees and employers, the F.U.T.A. tax, more commonly known as "federal U.C." (federal unemployment compensation), is levied only on employers. Because federal U.C., like the employer's portion of the F.I.C.A. tax, is considered a payroll tax expense, it will be discussed at this time even though it does not fall into the category of deductions from earnings.

Although tax rates and types of covered employment change from time to time, for illustrative purposes in this text we shall assume that every employer of four or more covered employees is subject to a federal unemployment tax of 3.5 percent on the first $3,000 of each employee's wages. An employer may, however, take credit against the tax (the amount taken not to exceed 90 percent of the first 3 percent of the federal tax) for amounts paid to state governments toward the cost of state-sponsored but federally approved unemployment compensation programs. In other words, the federal U.C. tax is split into two parts, with up to 2.7 percent (.90 × .03) being payable to the state and the remainder to the federal government. (State unemployment taxes will be discussed in greater detail in the next section of this chapter.)

To illustrate the interrelationship of federal and state U.C. taxes, let us assume that a covered employee earns wages of $3,000 subject to a state unemployment tax of 2.7 percent and a federal unemployment tax of 3.5 percent. The employer would be required to pay a total U.C. tax of $105 ($3,000 × .035), with $81 ($3,000 × .027) of the tax being payable to the state government and $24 ($3,000 × .008) to the federal government.

If we assume that a monthly payroll of $10,000 is subject to a 5 percent
F.I.C.A. rate and a federal U.C. rate of .8 percent, and that $1,200 in federal income
taxes is withheld, the monthly accrual will be recorded as follows:

Payroll Expense	10,000	
Payroll Tax Expense ($10,000 × .05) + ($10,000 × .008)	580	
Employees' Income Taxes Withheld		1,200
F.I.C.A. Taxes Payable ($10,000 × .10)		1,000
Federal U.C. Taxes Payable ($10,000 × .008)		80
Accrued Payroll Payable ($10,000 − $1,200 − $500)		8,300

If we were to assume that only $9,000 of the $10,000 payroll is subject to
the F.I.C.A. tax and only $5,000 to the federal U.C. tax during a particular month,
the accrual would be recorded as follows:

Payroll Expense	10,000	
Payroll Tax Expense ($9,000 × .05) + ($5,000 × .008)	490	
Employees' Income Taxes Withheld		1,200
F.I.C.A Taxes Payable ($9,000 × .10)		900
Federal U.C. Taxes Payable ($5,000 × .008)		40
Accrued Payroll Payable ($10,000 − $1,200 − $450)		8,350

State Unemployment Compensation Taxes All states, jurisdictions, and ter-
ritories of the United States maintain unemployment compensation insurance
programs of some kind. While a few levy taxes on both employers and employees,
most tax only the employer. The laws vary somewhat as to the types of employment to be covered and the number of persons an employer must employ before
he is subject to the tax. At the time of this writing, as a general rule the tax
is levied at a rate of 2.7 percent on the first $3,000 of a covered employee's earnings
during a calendar year.

Theoretically, the cost of any insurance program is related to the degree of
risk involved; for example, the greater the risk, the higher the cost, and vice versa.
Consistent with this theory, most states employ a merit-rating plan whereby an
employer may receive a reduced state unemployment compensation rate once he
has been established as a good risk. Thus, an employer whose employees collect
little or no unemployment compensation will have a lower rate than one whose
employees frequently draw compensation.

When paying federal U.C. taxes, as stated earlier, an employer may take credit
for state unemployment compensation taxes paid in an amount not to exceed 90
percent of the first 3 percent of the federal tax. In addition, any amount saved
as the result of a favorable merit rating may be credited against the federal tax.
Thus, the employer will receive credit for the total amount he would have been
required to pay in state U.C. taxes if he had not had a favorable merit rating.

To illustrate, let us assume that a covered employee earns wages of $3,000 subject to a federal U.C. tax of 3.5 percent and, because of the employer's favorable merit rating, a state U.C. tax of only 1.2 percent. The employer would be required to pay a total U.C. tax of $60 [$3,000 $\times$ (.012 + .008)] with $36 ($3,000 $\times$ .012) of the tax payable to the state and $24 ($3,000 $\times$ .008) to the federal government. Without a merit rating, the employer would have paid a total U.C. tax of $105 ($3,000 $\times$ .035).

The following comparison illustrates the effect of a favorable merit rating on the amount of taxes payable on $3,000:

	No Merit Rating	*Merit Rating of 1.2%*
State U.C. tax	$ 81	$36
Federal U.C. tax	24	24
Total U.C. tax	$105	$60

Since tax rates and merit systems vary considerably among states, for illustrative purposes we shall assume a 2.7 percent state tax without a merit rating, unless specifically stipulated otherwise.

If we assume that a monthly payroll of $10,000 is subject to a 5 percent F.I.C.A. rate, a federal U.C. rate of 3.5 percent, and a state U.C. rate of 2.7 percent, and that $1,200 in federal income taxes is withheld, the monthly accrual will be recorded as follows:

Payroll Expense	10,000	
Payroll Tax Expense [$10,000 $\times$ (.05 + .027 + .008)]	850	
Employees' Income Taxes Withheld		1,200
F.I.C.A. Taxes Payable ($10,000 $\times$ .10)		1,000
Federal U.C. Taxes Payable ($10,000 $\times$ .008)		80
State U.C. Taxes Payable ($10,000 $\times$ .027)		270
Accrued Payroll Payable ($10,000 − $1,200 − $500)		8,300

If we were to assume that only $9,000 of the $10,000 payroll is subject to the F.I.C.A. tax, and only $5,000 to federal and state U.C. taxes during a particular month, the payroll would be accrued as follows:

Payroll Expense	10,000	
Payroll Tax Expense ($9,000 $\times$ .05) + ($5,000 $\times$ .035)	625	
Employees' Income Taxes Withheld		1,200
F.I.C.A. Taxes Payable ($9,000 $\times$ .10)		900
Federal U.C. Taxes Payable ($5,000 $\times$ .008)		40
State U.C. Taxes Payable ($5,000 $\times$ .027)		135
Accrued Payroll Payable ($10,000 − $1,200 − $450)		8,350

Remittance of Payroll Taxes F.I.C.A. and federal income taxes withheld from employees, plus the employer's share of the F.I.C.A. tax, must be reported and paid to the Internal Revenue Service by the employer on or before the last day of the month following the ending of the calendar quarter. Taxes for the first quarter of the year, for example, must be reported and paid on or before April 30. The necessary information is reported on Form 941 (Employer's Federal Tax Return) and payment generally is included when the form is filed.

However, if the above amount exceeds $100 in any month other than the last month of the quarter, instead of being retained for payment at a later date, it must be deposited to the credit of the Internal Revenue Service in an authorized local bank or a Federal Reserve Bank prior to the fifteenth of the following month. For example, if F.I.C.A. and federal income taxes withheld from employees in January, plus the employer's share of the F.I.C.A. tax, add up to a combined total of more than $100, the entire amount must be deposited in an authorized bank before February 15. In return, the bank will provide the depositor with a validated depository receipt known as Form 450 (Federal Depository Receipt) which must be filed with the quarterly return to show that the amount has been paid.

On or before January 31 of each year, every employer is required to supply his present employees, as well as any others who have been employed by him at any time during the past calendar year, with two copies of Form W-2 (Wage and Tax Statement) showing the amounts of federal income taxes withheld from the employee's earnings during the previous year, wages paid to him that were subject to withholding, F.I.C.A. employee taxes withheld, and wages paid that were subject to F.I.C.A. tax. This form is illustrated below.

The employee is required to file one copy of the W-2 with his personal income tax return; he retains the other copy for his personal file. The employer also is

Form W-2. Wage and tax statement.

required to provide the Internal Revenue Service with a copy of the form, so that the employee's individual income tax return may be reconciled.

Federal U.C. taxes are reported on Form 940 (Employer's Federal Unemployment Tax Return), which must be filed and the taxes paid on or before January 31 of the year following the taxable calendar year. State U.C. tax returns must be filed and the taxes paid on or before the last day of the month following the end of the calendar quarter.

Some of the major factors to be considered when accounting for payroll taxes are summarized in "Payroll Taxes: A Summarized Schedule," shown below.

Payroll Taxes—A Summarized Schedule					
	Imposed by			*Imposed on*		*When*
Tax	*Federal*	*State*	*Local*	*Employer*	*Employee*	*Paid*
Income tax	Yes	Sometimes		No	Yes	Quarterly or monthly*
F.I.C.A.	Yes	No	No	Yes	Yes	Quarterly or monthly*
Federal U.C.	Yes	No	No	Yes	No	Yearly
State U.C.	No	Yes	No	Yes	Sometimes	Quarterly

*Paid monthly if the total amount of federal income taxes and employee F.I.C.A. taxes withheld and the employer's share of the F.I.C.A. taxes is in excess of $100 for the first or second month of a quarter.

Payroll Records

As a rule, payroll accounting involves the preparation of three basic records: a payroll register, payroll checks or envelopes, and an employee earnings record.

Payroll Register An organization's **payroll register,** also termed **payroll journal** or **payroll summary,** is a form or record in which the gross earnings, deductions, and net earnings of all employees are accumulated. The data assembled therein are used primarily in the preparation of individual employees' paychecks or pay envelopes and as the bases for journal entries. The payroll register itself may be used as a book of original entry, or the data contained therein may be summarized and recorded in the general journal. Although payroll registers will vary among organizations, the sample on page 314 is illustrative of their form and content.

Payroll Checks and Payroll Envelopes Payroll checks and payroll envelopes (used when payment is made in cash) are prepared from the payroll register. While they are primarily employed as means of payment rather than as records, they may also be used for the latter purpose. The checks generally are prenumbered

Payroll register.

for control purposes. Frequently a stub will be attached to the check, providing the employee with a statement of his earnings and deductions. Many such statements not only provide data for the particular pay period but also year-to-date data. When employees are paid in cash, the information provided on the check stub is normally included on the pay envelope. The check and stub shown on page 315 are typical.

Employee Earnings Record In order to expedite the filing of the various periodic payroll reports to governmental bodies and to furnish individual employees with cumulative payroll data at the time of employment termination or at the end of the calendar year, employers must maintain some kind of individual employee earnings record. The form in use may vary among organizations, but the one illustrated on page 315 is typical. Needless to say, the individual earnings record for a period must agree with the payroll register data for the same period.

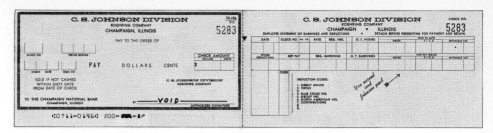

Payroll check and stub.

EMPLOYEE EARNINGS RECORD

THE C. S. JOHNSON CO.
FORM NO. 57 2-1-57

| | SOCIAL SECURITY NO. | | | | EMPLOYEE NAME | | | | QUARTER | PAYROLL | | EMPL. NO. |

RATE	WK. NO.	HOURS		EARNINGS					DEDUCTIONS			EMPLOYEE NO.
		REGULAR	OVERTIME	REGULAR	OVERTIME	GROSS	NET		F.I.C.A.	INCOME TAX	OTHER	

DEDUCTION CODES:
1. CREDIT UNION
2. TOOLS
3. BLUE CROSS INS.
4. GROUP INS.
5. NORTH AMERICAN INS.
6. CONTRIBUTIONS
7.

Individual employee earnings record.

Payroll Accounting and EDP   Because many payroll operations are more or less mechanical in nature, as well as largely repetitious, electronic data processing equipment has proved to be particularly valuable in the preparation of payroll records.   Its use for this purpose is becoming fairly commonplace in accounting systems of any size.

SUMMARY

Liabilities are obligations of an organization which must be met by paying sums of money, conveying other assets, or rendering services.   The major problems in accounting for liabilities relate to their recognition and measurement.   A liability is recognized when a legal obligation is incurred and is measured by the amount of cash or cash equivalent involved.

Liabilities are broadly classified as current or noncurrent.   Current liabilities are obligations of an organization which must be met within the current operating cycle or one year, whichever is longer.   Some of the most difficult problems in accounting for current liabilities are created by the actions of taxing authorities, particularly in the area of payroll taxes.

QUESTIONS AND PROBLEMS

12-1   How does the accountant usually distinguish between **current** and **non-current** liabilities?

12-2   One of the major problems in accounting for liabilities is that of measurement.   How are liabilities ordinarily measured?

12-3   The fiscal year of Brenner City ends on June 30, whereas the fiscal year of the Bondar Company of Brenner City ends on December 31.   Assuming that Brenner City levies property taxes of $10,800, $11,600, and $12,200 in three successive years on the Bondar Company, what amounts of property taxes would Bondar report on its income statements for the two intervening calendar years?

12-4   The fiscal year of Central City ends on June 30, whereas the fiscal year of the D. French Company of Central City ends on March 31.   Assuming that Central City levies property taxes of $21,600, $23,200, and $24,400 in three successive years on the D. French Company, what amounts of property taxes would the company report in its income statements for the two intervening years?

12-5 According to the laws of a certain state, property taxes for 19X4 are due on April 1, 19X4. The taxes are based on assessed valuations as of April 1, 19X3, and are intended to pay the expense of government for the fiscal year ending June 30, 19X4. As an accountant, how would you treat a 19X4 property tax of $6,000, due and payable on April 1, 19X4, in the accounts of the ABC Company as of March 31, 19X4, the end of its fiscal year?

12-6 The state in which the Casler Company operates levies a 5 percent sales tax on all items sold by the company. Journalize both the collection and remittance of the tax for a year in which the company collects taxes of $4,500 on cash sales of $92,480 and charges customers $5,010 in taxes on credit sales of $100,200.

12-7 You have been called upon by L. Biagioni, the president and owner of a large independent construction company, to examine his company's system of internal control over unclaimed wages.

During your examination you find that all employees are paid in cash because Biagioni believes this arrangement reduces clerical expenses and is preferred by his employees. Unclaimed wages are kept in the petty cash fund. When the claimant to the wages appears, he is paid from the petty cash fund. Biagioni contends that this procedure reduces the number of checks drawn to replenish the petty cash fund and centers the responsibility for all cash on hand in one person, inasmuch as the petty cash custodian distributes the pay envelopes. At the time of your examination the petty cash fund contains $400, $375 of which, according to the petty cash custodian, is unclaimed wages.

Does Biagioni's system provide proper internal control of unclaimed wages? Explain fully.

12-8 You have been engaged by T. Secoy, president of the Generous Loan Company, which has 100 branch loan offices, to examine his company's system of internal control over its payroll.

During your examination you find that each branch office has a manager and four or five subordinates who are employed by the manager. Branch managers prepare the weekly payroll, including their own salaries, and pay employees from cash on hand. The employees sign the payroll sheet signifying receipt of their salaries. Hours worked by hourly personnel are inserted in the payroll sheet from time cards prepared by the employees and approved by the manager.

The weekly payroll sheets are sent to the home office along with other accounting statements and reports. The home office compiles employee earnings records and prepares all federal and state payroll tax returns from the weekly payroll sheets.

Salaries are established by home office job evaluation schedules. Salary adjustments, promotions, and transfers of full-time employees are approved by a home office salary committee based upon the recommendations of branch managers and area supervisors. Branch managers advise the salary committee of new full-time employees and terminations. Part-time and temporary employees are hired without referral to the salary committee.

Based upon your examination and review of the company's payroll system, state at least five ways in which payroll funds might be diverted.

12-9 You have been asked by G. Brieske, president and general manager of the G. Brieske Company, a nationwide organization, to examine the company's financial statements as of the end of its fiscal year.

Briefly outline the procedure you would follow in order to satisfy yourself that the company is handling state and federal social security and unemployment taxes correctly.

12-10 K. Yauch works for an organization which is covered by the Federal Fair Labor Standards Act. Yauch's base rate is $3.80 per hour. Determine the amount of his gross earnings for a week in which he works 9 hours on Monday, 7 hours on Tuesday, 11 hours on Wednesday, 10 hours on Thursday, $11\frac{1}{2}$ hours on Friday, and $4\frac{1}{2}$ hours on Saturday.

12-11 The Ohm Manufacturing Company sells Zohms, its major product, at $1,000 each under an agreement which provides for free maintenance for one year from date of sale. The customer is also given the option of buying maintenance services for succeeding years for an additional $100 per year. The company operates and accounts for a service department separate and distinct from its sales department.

Instructions Assuming that the company sells a Zohm on January 2, 19X3, along with a service contract covering 19X4, for $1,100 cash,

(1) Journalize the transaction.

(2) Briefly justify your treatment of the transaction.

12-12 **Instructions** Assuming that all 50 employees of the E. Mulgrew Company earned over $3,000 during the current year, compute the:

(1) State U.C. tax for the year, assuming that the company is subject to a state tax rate of 2.7 percent.

(2) State U.C. tax for the year, assuming that the company is subject to a state tax rate of 1.4 percent.

(3) Federal U.C. tax for the year, assuming the same facts as in (1) above.

(4) Federal U.C. tax for the year, assuming the same facts as in (2) above.

(5) Total U.C. tax for the year, assuming the same facts as in (1) above.

(6) Total U.C. tax for the year assuming the same facts as in (2) above.

12-13 The following payroll data pertain to the current year's operations of the Welch Company:

Gross employee earnings	$80,000
Employee earnings not subject to F.I.C.A. tax	12,000
Employee earnings not subject to U.C. tax	20,000

Instructions Compute the amount of the company's payroll tax expense for the year, assuming that the payroll is subject to:

(1) A 5 percent F.I.C.A. rate, a 2.7 percent state U.C. rate, and a federal U.C. rate of .8 percent.

(2) A 5 percent F.I.C.A. rate, a 1.6 percent state U.C. rate, and a federal U.C. rate of .8 percent.

12-14 R. Hartley is one of 20 full-time employees of the J. Wheeler Company. Hartley's gross earnings for the year 19X2 amounted to $9,800.

Instructions Assuming that his earnings are subject to an F.I.C.A. rate of 5 percent, a state U.C. rate of 1.8 percent, a federal U.C. rate of .8 percent, and a federal income tax withholding of $1,820, determine:

(1) The total amount of Hartley's take-home pay for 19X2.

(2) The total payroll cost to the Wheeler Company of Hartley's services for the year.

12-15 R. Brown is one of 30 full-time employees of the C. Smith Company. Brown's take-home pay for the year 19X4 amounted to $8,570.

Instructions Assuming that his earnings are subject to an F.I.C.A. rate of 5 percent, a state U.C. rate of 2.7 percent, a federal U.C. rate of .8 percent, and a federal income tax withholding rate of 20 percent, determine:

(1) Brown's gross earnings for 19X4.

(2) The total payroll cost to the C. Smith Company of Brown's services for the year.

320

PART THREE:
CHAPTER TWELVE

12-16 Baer, Baker, Basi, and Beard are four of 40 full-time employees of the R. Fitzpatrick Company. Baer and Baker's take-home pay for the year 19X5 amounted to $5,400 and $7,170, respectively, whereas Basi and Beard's gross earnings amounted to $7,700 and $9,100, respectively.

Instructions Assuming that the company's payroll is subject to an F.I.C.A. rate of 5 percent, a state U.C. rate of 1 percent, a federal U.C. rate of .8 percent, and a federal income tax rate of 20 percent, determine:

(1) Baer's gross earnings for 19X5

(2) The total payroll cost of Baer's services for the year

(3) Baker's gross earnings for 19X5

(4) The total payroll cost of Baker's services for the year

(5) Basi's take-home pay for 19X5

(6) The total payroll cost of Basi's services for the year

(7) Beard's take-home pay for 19X5

(8) The total payroll cost of Beard's services for the year

12-17 The following payroll data pertain to the current year's operations of the A. Johnson Company:

Gross employee earnings	$400,000
Employee earnings not subject to F.I.C.A. tax	88,000
Employee earnings not subject to U.C. tax	280,000
Federal income taxes withheld	84,000

Instructions Assuming that the company's payroll is subject to an F.I.C.A. rate of 5 percent, a state U.C. rate of 1.5 percent, and a federal U.C. rate of .8 percent, determine:

(1) Total employee take-home pay for the year

(2) Total payroll cost for the year

12-18 The B. Aschbacker Company's August payroll of $120,000 is subject to (a) a 5 percent F.I.C.A. rate to the extent of $80,000 of the payroll, (b) a 2.7 percent state U.C. tax and an .8 percent federal U.C. tax on $55,000 of the payroll, and (c) a federal income tax withholding of $24,400.

Instructions Journalize the:

(1) Accrual of the August payroll

(2) Payment of the August payroll

(3) Deposit, if any, required on or before September 15

*12-19 W. Barrett, president of the W. Barrett Company, has reason to believe that the company's payroll records are not being handled correctly. He has asked you to examine them for the year 19X4. The following T accounts are summarized transcripts of the company's general ledger payroll accounts as of December 31, 19X4:

Payroll Expense

19X4 (Wages paid)	43,660		

Payroll Tax Expense

19X4			
Jan. 10 (Quarterly remittance)	4,100		
Apr. 10 (Quarterly remittance)	4,311		
July 10 (Quarterly remittance)	3,777		
Oct. 10 (Quarterly remittance)	3,710		

Payroll Taxes Withheld

		19X4	
		Jan. 1 Balance	3,200

Employer Payroll Taxes Payable

		19X4	
		Jan. 1 Balance	900

The following additional information is available:

1 Copies of the quarterly tax returns are not available because the typist did not understand that the returns were to be typed in duplicate. The pencil drafts of the tax returns were discarded.

2 Your examination of the payroll records revealed that the payroll clerk properly computed the payroll tax deductions. You are able to develop the following summary:

Quarter	Gross Earnings	Payroll Taxes Withheld F.I.C.A.	Income	Net Earnings
First	$13,600	$ 680	$ 2,600	$10,320
Second	12,000	600	2,280	9,120
Third	12,800	520	2,400	9,880
Fourth	18,700	360	4,000	14,340
	$57,100	$2,160	$11,280	$43,660

*AICPA adapted.

3 The company did not make monthly deposits of taxes withheld, but your examination of the records revealed that the payroll clerk properly computed the quarterly remittances. You are able to develop the following information regarding the remittances for 19X4:

	Apr. 10	July 10	Oct. 10	Jan. 10
F.I.C.A. (10%)	$1,360	$1,200	$1,040	$ 720
Income tax	2,600	2,280	2,400	4,000
State unemployment insurance (2.7%)	351	297	270	162
Total	$4,311	$3,777	$3,710	$4,882

Instructions Assuming that the company's payroll is subject to a federal U.C. rate of .8 percent, prepare a journal entry to correct the above payroll accounts as of December 31, 19X4.

12-20 The R. Ashamy Manufacturing Company employs six men in its machine shop. The regular wage rate is $3 per hour for a 40-hour week plus time and a half for overtime. The foreman's rate is $4 per hour plus time and a half for overtime. The men do not work on Sunday. The payroll records for the week ending Thursday, December 7, show that all employees of the shop except Wilson worked 10 hours per day every day except Saturday. On Saturday each worked a half day (4 hours). Wilson, who was absent on Monday, Tuesday, Wednesday, and Thursday, worked 10 hours on Friday and 4 hours on Saturday.

Employee withholding exemption certificates (Form W-4) indicate the following weekly exemptions:

Berger	$35
Broom (foreman)	58
Devos	35
Graham	93
Prosen	70
Wilson	12

As of November 30, the earnings record shows the following accumulated earnings for the year:

Berger	$6,900
Broom	9,080
Devos	7,650
Graham	5,600
Prosen	2,900
Wilson	2,400

Instructions Assuming that the company's payroll is subject to an F.I.C.A. rate of 5 percent, a state U.C. rate of 2.7 percent, a federal U.C. rate of .8 percent, and a federal income tax withholding rate of 20 percent:

(1) Prepare a schedule showing the number of hours worked by each employee during the week ending Thursday, December 7.

(2) Prepare a schedule showing gross earnings per employee for the week.

(3) Compute the amount of F.I.C.A. taxes withheld during the week.

(4) Compute the amount of federal U.C. taxes payable for the week.

(5) Compute the amount of state U.C. taxes payable for the week.

(6) Compute the amount of federal income taxes withheld during the week.

(7) Journalize the payroll for the week.

(8) Prepare a schedule showing the total amount of F.I.C.A. taxes withheld during the period January 1–December 7.

(9) Prepare a schedule showing the total cost of the state U.C. tax for the period January 1–December 7.

(10) Prepare a schedule showing the total cost of the federal U.C. tax for the period January 1–December 7.

(11) Prepare a schedule showing each employee's take-home pay for the week ending December 7.

(12) Prepare a schedule showing total payroll cost per employee for the period January 1–December 7.

EDP PROBLEMS

12-21 Instructions Each of the following statements is either true or false. Identify those that are true.

(1) Debugging is the process of locating and correcting errors in a computer program.

(2) An error listing will not be produced as a by-product of processing by a computer unless provision was made for such a listing in the program.

(3) The term "grandfather-father-son" refers to a method of computer record security rather than to generations in the evolution of computer hardware.

(4) A control total is an example of a self-checking number within a batch control.

(5) A test deck can be contained on magnetic or paper tape as well as on punched cards.

12-22 Instructions The items which follow contain examples of internal control deficiencies in the computer operations of the M Company. For each of these conditions or situations, select from a list of control features or procedures giving the one which, if properly utilized, would have been most useful either in preventing the error or in ensuring its immediate detection and prompt correction.

(1) The master payroll file on magnetic tape was inadvertently written on by another processing run. The best control procedure would be a:
 (a) File protection ring
 (b) File destruction date on header label
 (c) Control figure
 (d) Trailer label check

(2) A weekly payroll check was issued to an hourly employee based on 98 hours worked instead of 38 hours. The time card was slightly illegible and the number looked somewhat like 98. The best control procedure would be:
 (a) A hash total
 (b) A code check
 (c) Desk checking
 (d) A limit test

(3) In preparing payroll checks, the computer omitted 24 of a total of 2,408 checks which should have been processed. The error was not detected until the foremen distributed the checks. The best control procedure would be:
 (a) A parity check
 (b) A module N check
 (c) Control totals
 (d) Desk checking

(4) The magnetic tape containing payroll transactions could not be located. A data-processing supervisor said that it could have been put among the scratch tapes available for use in processing. The best control procedure would be a:
 (a) Header label
 (b) Trailer label
 (c) External label
 (d) File protection ring

(5) A payroll transaction was coded with an invalid employee account code (7 digits rather than 8). The error was not detected until the updating

run when it was found that there was no such account to which the
transaction could be posted. The best control procedure would be:

(a) Parity checks

(b) Keypunch verification

(c) A hash total check

(d) A check digit

12-23 Instructions Assuming that the payroll is subject to an F.I.C.A. rate of
5 percent, prepare:

(1) A subroutine to test whether F.I.C.A. taxes should be withheld from
an employee's earnings

(2) A flow chart for the subroutine

12-24 Instructions Assuming that the payroll is subject to a state U.C. rate of
1.8 percent, prepare:

(1) A subroutine to test whether state U.C. taxes should be paid on an
employee's earnings

(2) A flow chart for the subroutine

13

Accounting for Long-term Debt

Long-term debt, the caption commonly employed to designate noncurrent liabilities on the balance sheet, refers to obligations of an organization which do not have to be satisfied until after the current operating cycle or one year, whichever is longer. It usually is incurred to finance the acquisition of relatively long-lived assets. Thus, long-term debt is the opposite of current liabilities, which more often relate to day-to-day operations. Mortgages and bonds are typical examples of long-term debt.

Since the basic problems related to the issuance of mortgages and bonds, the payment of periodic interest, and their ultimate retirement were covered in Chapter 6, we shall not reexamine them at this time. Instead, we shall move on to some of the more difficult accounting problems in this area, specifically those related to the retirement of mortgages on an installment basis and the retirement of bonds on a serial basis. In addition, we shall examine the amortization of bond premium and discount by the effective-rate-of-interest method, a more scientific method than the straight-line one discussed in Chapter 6. Finally, to round out our thinking on the subject of bonds, we shall look at them as a form of investment from the buyer's point of view.

MATHEMATICS OF COMPOUND INTEREST

Both the retirement of a mortgage on an installment basis and the amortization of bond premium and discount by the effective-rate-of-interest method are predicated upon the theory of compound interest. Therefore, a brief review of the mathematics of compound interest should prove helpful at this time.

Interest—the payment for the use of money or credit—is classified as either simple or compound. **Simple interest** is interest computed on the principal only, whereas **compound interest** is interest computed not only on the principal but also on any interest that has been earned but not paid. For example, simple interest on $1,000 for 2 years at 6 percent would be $120, while compound interest on the same amount for two years at 6 percent compounded annually would be $123.60, determined as follows:

		Simple Interest	*Compound Interest*
First year	($1,000 × .06)	$ 60.00	$ 60.00
Second year	($1,000 × .06)	60.00	60.00
	($60 × .06)		3.60
Total interest		$120.00	$123.60

As can readily be observed, the $3.60 difference between the simple interest of $120 and the compound interest of $123.60 results from the calculation of interest on interest ($60 × .06). It is perhaps needless to point out that as a rule investors are partial to compound interest.

Computations Based on Compound Interest

It is important that the accounting student be familiar with four computations involving compound interest which are widely used in various phases of modern business. They are:

1 Amount of 1 computation

2 Present value of 1 computation

3 Amount of an annuity computation

4 Present value of an annuity computation

Amount of 1 Computation By employing an **amount of 1** computation, we can determine the total amount to which a given principal will accumulate if invested at compound interest for a stated period of time. For example, $1 invested for 5 years at 6 percent interest compounded annually will amount to $1.3383, determined as follows:

	Amount at Beginning of Year	Computation	Amount at End of Year
First year	$1.00	× 1.06 =	$1.06
Second year	1.06	× 1.06 =	1.1236
Third year	1.1236	× 1.06 =	1.1910
Fourth year	1.1910	× 1.06 =	1.2625
Fifth year	1.2625	× 1.06 =	$1.3383

Note that when we multiply the balance as of the beginning of the year by the factor 1.06, which is 1 plus the rate of interest expressed decimally, we are (1) computing the interest for the period on the beginning balance, and at the same time (2) adding it to the beginning balance.

If $1 of principal invested at 6 percent and compounded annually for 5 years will grow to $1.3383, a principal of $100 invested under the same terms will grow to $133.83. Other principal amounts invested under similar terms will grow in the same way. For example, $210 invested at 6 percent and compounded annually will grow to $281.04 ($210 × 1.3383). Note that the factor 1.3383 is nothing more than $1.06 \times 1.06 \times 1.06 \times 1.06 \times 1.06$; that is, 1.06 raised to the fifth power, or $(1.06)^5$.

Present Value of 1 Computation By employing a **present value of 1** computation, it is possible to determine the amount of money that would have to be invested at compound interest in order to accumulate to a given sum at some definite future time. For example, if $1 invested for 5 years at 6 percent and compounded annually will amount to $1.3383 in 5 years, it follows that $1.3383, 5 years from now, is worth $1 now. In contrast to an amount of 1 computation, where we must determine the future value of a known present value, in a present value of 1 computation we know the future amount and must determine what it is worth now, the present.

To determine the $1.3383 in the amount of 1 computation, we multiplied $1 \times 1.06 \times 1.06 \times 1.06 \times 1.06 \times 1.06$. Therefore, to determine the present value we simply reverse the process. Since the opposite of multiplication is division, we divide the known future amount, in this case $1.3383, by $(1.06)^5$ as follows:

	Amount at End of Year	Computation	Present Value at Beginning of Year
Fifth year	$1.3383	÷ 1.06 =	$1.2625
Fourth year	1.2625	÷ 1.06 =	1.1910
Third year	1.1910	÷ 1.06 =	1.1236
Second year	1.1236	÷ 1.06 =	1.0600
First year	1.0600	÷ 1.06 =	$1.0000

Amount of an Annuity Computation   By definition, an **annuity** is a series of equal payments made at equal intervals of time.   By using an **amount of an annuity** computation, we can determine the total amount to which such a series of payments will accumulate if invested at compound interest for a given number of periods.   (Although to some the term *annuity* carries a yearly connotation, in finance it refers to payments made on a weekly, monthly, quarterly, or some other predetermined periodic basis, as well as to yearly ones.)

Since the amount of an annuity is based on equal periodic investments, its computation consists of nothing more than adding up the amounts to which each of the individual investments will accumulate at the end of a specified time.   For example, if $1 is invested at the beginning of each year for 5 years and each investment earns 6 percent interest compounded annually, in total the investments will amount to $5.9754 at the end of the 5 years, determined as follows:

	Periodic Investment		Computation		Amount at End of Fifth Year
First year	$1	×	1.3383	=	$1.3383
Second year	1	×	1.2625	=	1.2625
Third year	1	×	1.1910	=	1.1910
Fourth year	1	×	1.1236	=	1.1236
Fifth year	1	×	1.0600	=	1.0600
Amount of the annuity					$5.9754

Note the relationship of the factors in the above computation to those in the amount of 1 computation.   For example, the factor 1.3383 is simply $(1.06)^5$, 1.2625 is $(1.06)^4$, and so on.

If $1 invested at the beginning of each year for 5 years will grow to $5.9754 at the end of the fifth year when compounded annually at 6 percent, a periodic investment of $100 invested under the same terms will grow to $597.54 ($100 × 5.9754).   Other periodic investments invested under similar conditions will produce like results.   For example, $210 invested at the beginning of each year for 5 years and compounded annually at 6 percent will amount to $1,254.83 ($210 × 5.9754) at the end of 5 years.   By studying the illustration we can see that the factor 5.9754 results from adding $1.06 + (1.06)^2 + (1.06)^3 + (1.06)^4 + (1.06)^5$.

Present Value of an Annuity Computation   There are times when an investor may wish to know what lump-sum amount should be invested *now* in order to produce an annuity of so much a period for so many periods.   Stated more formally, the **present value of an annuity** is the sum which, if invested at compound interest, will provide a given series of equal periodic withdrawals.   In contrast to an amount of an annuity computation, where the future value of known present values must be determined, in a present value of an annuity computation we know the future amounts to be withdrawn and must determine what those amounts are worth now, the present.

When we determined the $1.3383 amount for the first investment in our amount of an annuity computation, we in reality multiplied $1 × 1.06 × 1.06 × 1.06 × 1.06 × 1.06. Likewise, the $1.2625 for the second investment was determined by multiplying $1 × 1.06 × 1.06 × 1.06 × 1.06. Since we multiplied to obtain these amounts, we must reverse the procedure and divide to get the present values. Thus, the present value of an annuity of $1 for five periods at compound interest of 6 percent would be $4.2124, determined by adding $1 ÷ 1.06 + $1 ÷ (1.06)^2 + $1 ÷ (1.06)^3 + $1 ÷ (1.06)^4 + $1 ÷ (1.06)^5. In tabular form the computation would appear as follows:

	Periodic Withdrawal		*Computation*		*Present Value at Beginning of First Year*
First year	$1	÷	1.0600	=	$0.9434
Second year	1	÷	1.1236	=	0.8900
Third year	1	÷	1.1910	=	0.8396
Fourth year	1	÷	1.2625	=	0.7921
Fifth year	1	÷	1.3383	=	0.7473
Present value of the annuity					$4.2124

If $4.21 invested now at 6 percent compounded annually will permit us to withdraw $1 a year for 5 years, $421.24 ($100 × 4.2124) invested under similar conditions would permit us to withdraw $100 a period for five periods. Likewise, an investment of $884.60 ($210 × 4.2124) under similar conditions would provide five periodic withdrawals of $210 each.

Tables of Amounts and Present Values

Since there is frequent need in business for quick computations of the compound amount of 1, the present value of 1, the amount of an annuity, and the present value of an annuity, printed tables have been made available for ready reference. Although the tables on page 331 are incomplete, they are indicative of the arrangement of such tables.

ACCOUNTING FOR MORTGAGES

Entries to record the issuance of a mortgage, the payment of periodic interest, and the retirement of the mortgage were illustrated in Chapter 6. For simplicity the mortgage was retired by a lump-sum payment. Most mortgages, however, are

		Tables of Amounts and Present Values		

	Amount of 1		Present Value of 1	
Periods	5%	6%	5%	6%
1	1.0500	1.0600	0.9524	0.9434
2	1.1025	1.1236	0.9070	0.8900
3	1.1576	1.1910	0.8638	0.8396
4	1.2155	1.2625	0.8227	0.7921
5	1.2763	1.3383	0.7835	0.7473

	Amount of an Annuity of 1		Present Value of an Annuity of 1	
Periods	5%	6%	5%	6%
1	1.0500	1.0600	0.9524	0.9434
2	2.1525	2.1836	1.8594	1.8334
3	3.3101	3.3746	2.7232	2.6730
4	4.5256	4.6371	3.5460	3.4651
5	5.8019	5.9753	4.3295	4.2124

retired in installments rather than on a lump-sum basis; that is, they are paid off by periodic payments over their lives. Some of the accountant's most difficult problems in accounting for mortgages are associated with these payments.

Recording the Issuance of a Mortgage

As an illustration, let us assume that an organization purchases a $70,000 building by paying $20,000 cash and giving a mortgage for the balance; that the mortgage is to be paid off in five yearly installments of equal amounts; that the payments are to be secured by notes; and that interest at 6 percent is to be included in each payment. The issuance of the mortgage would be recorded as follows:

Building	70,000	
Cash		20,000
Mortgage Notes Payable		50,000

Recording the Periodic Payments

Most of us are familiar with home mortgages where each monthly payment consists of part interest and part principal. The same thing is true of business mortgages that are paid off on an installment basis. Part of each payment is made up of interest and part of principal.

Since the $50,000 mortgage in our illustration is the present value of the mortgage and since the yearly installments of equal amounts create an annuity, we are actually dealing with the present value of an annuity. When computing the present value of an annuity in our earlier illustrations, we multiplied the known periodic payment by the factor, which can either be computed or taken from a precomputed table. Thus, since we know the present value of the annuity, in order to determine the periodic payments we would reverse the process and divide the known present value by the factor. In our illustration, therefore, the periodic payments would be $11,869.80 ($50,000 ÷ 4.2124).

Amortization Schedule In order to expedite the recording of the periodic payments, it is usually desirable to prepare an amortization schedule similar to the one that follows. While there is no set form for such a schedule, note that:

1 The amount in column (a) when multiplied by 6 percent gives us the amount in column (b).

2 The amount in column (c) minus the amount in column (b) gives us the amount in column (d).

3 The amount in column (a) minus the amount in column (d) gives us the amount in column (e).

4 The amount shown in column (e) as of the end of one year becomes the amount in column (a) as of the beginning of the next year.

Amortization Schedule
Mortgage Notes Payable

		Yearly Payments		
	Balance Beginning of Year (a)	Applicable to Interest (b)	Total (c)	Applicable to Principal (d)	Balance End of Year (e)
First year	$50,000.00	$3,000.00	$11,869.80	$ 8,869.80	$41,130.20
Second year	41,130.20	2,467.80	11,869.80	9,402.00	31,728.20
Third year	31,728.20	1,903.70	11,869.80	9,966.10	21,762.10
Fourth year	21,762.10	1,305.70	11,869.80	10,564.10	11,198.00
Fifth year	11,198.00	671.80	11,869.80	11,198.00	–0–
		$9,349.00	$59,349.00	$50,000.00	

Illustration of the Periodic Entry The following journal entry and T accounts show how the periodic payments would be handled in the accounts. The entry illustrates the first payment. Similar entries would be made each year with the credit to the Cash account remaining the same but the debit to the Interest Expense account decreasing, while the debit to the Mortgage Notes Payable account would increase. In order to show the full picture, the Interest Expense and Mortgage Notes Payable accounts reflect the entries for all five years.

Interest Expense	3,000.00	
Mortgage Notes Payable	8,869.80	
Cash		11,869.80

Interest Expense				Mortgage Notes Payable		
First year	3,000.00	To R&E Sum	3,000.00	First year	8,869.80	50,000.00
Second year	2,467.80	To R&E Sum	2,467.80	Second year	9,402.00	
Third year	1,903.70	To R&E Sum	1,903.70	Third year	9,966.10	
Fourth year	1,305.70	To R&E Sum	1,305.70	Fourth year	10,564.10	
Fifth year	671.80	To R&E Sum	671.80	Fifth year	11,198.00	
					50,000.00	50,000.00

ACCOUNTING FOR BONDS

When we first studied bonds in Chapter 6, we looked at them primarily as credit instruments. Although we covered their issuance, the periodic interest calculations, and their ultimate retirement, we concentrated chiefly on routine problems. At this time we shall consider some of the more complicated problems in accounting for bonds, namely, those related to the amortization of bond premium and bond discount by the effective-rate-of-interest method and those involved when bonds are retired on an installment or serial basis instead of in a lump sum.

Recording the Issuance of Bonds

To illustrate, let us assume that on January 1, 1972, an organization sells for $104,327 a $100,000, 5-year bond issue bearing interest at 6 percent, the interest payable annually on December 31. The entry to record the sale of the bonds would be made as follows:

Cash	104,327	
Premium on Bonds Payable		4,327
Bonds Payable		100,000

Effective Rate of Interest

We learned in Chapter 6 that when an investor buys bonds at a premium, he is willing to earn less than the rate of interest stipulated on the bonds. The stipulated rate is known as the **nominal rate,** whereas the rate the investor is willing to "settle for" is referred to as the **effective rate.**

Although it is not readily apparent from the above entry, the 6 percent bonds were sold at a price which would permit investors to earn 5 percent on their money; that is, the bonds would yield 5 percent. Therefore, the effective rate of interest in the illustration is 5 percent, and obviously it is less than the nominal rate. If the bonds had sold at a discount, the opposite would be true; the effective rate would be more than the nominal rate.

Determining the Price of a Bond

Precomputed tables are available for determining the price to pay for a given bond in order to secure a desired yield. However, we should be familiar with the mathematics of the computations in order to have a better understanding of the scientific method of amortization.

When an investor buys a bond, he acquires two rights: (1) the right to receive at a designated future date a stated sum of money, synonymously referred to as the **par value, maturity value,** or **face value** of the bonds, and (2) the right to receive cash interest at a specific percentage of the face value at regular intervals. Thus, the price of a bond is composed of two elements, the amount paid for par and the amount paid for the periodic interest payments. Since the par value of the bond is paid to the investor only once, we are here dealing with the present value of 1. Bond interest, however, is composed of a series of periodic payments, so here we are dealing with the present value of an annuity. Using the abbreviated tables illustrated on page 331, we can determine the $104,327 price paid for the bond in our illustration as follows:

Amount paid for par ($100,000 × .7835*)	$ 78,350
Amount paid for interest ($6,000 × 4.3295†)	25,977
Total price of bond	$104,327

*The present value of 1 at 5% for five periods.
†The present value of an annuity of 1 at 5% for five periods.

Straight-line Amortization

If we were to amortize the $4,327 premium in our illustration on the straight-line basis, we would allocate $865.40 ($4,327 ÷ 5) to each year. Since the yearly interest payments are $6,000 ($100,000 × .06), our periodic entry for interest and amortization would appear as shown. To present the full picture, the entries for all 5 years are reflected in the Interest Expense and Premium on Bonds Payable accounts.

Interest Expense	5,134.60	
Premium on Bonds Payable	865.40	
Cash		6,000.00

Interest Expense				Premium on Bonds Payable			
First year	5,134.60	To R&E Sum	5,134.60	Dec. 31, 1972	865.40	Jan. 1, 1972	4,327.00
Second year	5,134.60	To R&E Sum	5,134.60	Dec. 31, 1973	865.40		
Third year	5,134.60	To R&E Sum	5,134.60	Dec. 31, 1974	865.40		
Fourth year	5,134.60	To R&E Sum	5,134.60	Dec. 31, 1975	865.40		
Fifth year	5,134.60	To R&E Sum	5,134.60	Dec. 31, 1976	865.40		
					4,327.00		4,327.00

Scientific, or Effective-rate, Amortization

Although the straight-line method of amortization is widely used in practice, a more scientific procedure is one based on the effective rate of interest. The effective-rate method is founded on the premise that bond interest (either income or expense) should be computed at the effective rate at which the bonds were bought or sold. Under this method, when either discount or premium is involved, the periodic interest expense will vary in amount, whereas under the straight-line method it will be the same for all periods.

Amortization Schedule When the effective-rate method of amortization is employed, a schedule is usually prepared to expedite the recording process. As you examine the illustrated schedule, note that:

1 The amount in column (a) is 5 percent of the carrying value of the bonds as of the beginning of the year. For example, the $5,216.35 is 5 percent of $104,327.

2 The amount in column (b) is determined by deducting the amount in column (a) from the amount in column (c).

3 The balance in column (d) as of the end of any given year is determined by deducting the amount in column (b) for that year from the amount in column (d) for the preceding year.

<table>
<tr><th colspan="5">Amortization Schedule
6% Bonds Sold to Yield 5%</th></tr>
<tr><th>Date</th><th>Debit
Interest Expense
(a)</th><th>Debit
Premium on
Bonds Payable
(b)</th><th>Credit
Cash
(c)</th><th>Carrying Value
of the Bonds*
(d)</th></tr>
<tr><td>Sale date</td><td>—</td><td>—</td><td>—</td><td>$104,327.00</td></tr>
<tr><td>End of first year</td><td>$ 5,216.35</td><td>$ 783.65</td><td>$ 6,000.00</td><td>103,543.35</td></tr>
<tr><td>End of second year</td><td>5,177.17</td><td>822.83</td><td>6,000.00</td><td>102,720.52</td></tr>
<tr><td>End of third year</td><td>5,136.03</td><td>863.97</td><td>6,000.00</td><td>101,856.55</td></tr>
<tr><td>End of fourth year</td><td>5,092.83</td><td>907.17</td><td>6,000.00</td><td>100,949.38</td></tr>
<tr><td>End of fifth year</td><td>5,047.47</td><td>952.53</td><td>6,000.00</td><td>$ 99,996.85†</td></tr>
<tr><td></td><td>$25,669.85</td><td>$4,330.15†</td><td>$30,000.00</td><td></td></tr>
</table>

*The balance in the Bonds Payable account plus the balance in the Premium on Bonds Payable account.
†A result of using four-place tables. If we had used eight-place tables, the carrying value would exactly equal $100,000 as of the end of the fifth year, and the amount of the premium amortized during the 5-year period would have been $4,327.

Recording the Periodic Payments Once the amortization schedule has been prepared, recording the periodic entries is just a matter of taking them from the schedule. Entries for the first and fifth years are illustrated, the entry for the fifth year showing how the error due to "rounding" is handled. (We merely adjust the Interest Expense account accordingly.) In order to complete the illustration, the Interest Expense and the Premium on Bonds Payable accounts are also shown.

December 31, 1972

Interest Expense	5,216.35	
Premium on Bonds Payable	783.65	
Cash		6,000.00

December 31, 1976

Interest Expense	5,050.62	
Premium on Bonds Payable	949.38	
Cash		6,000.00

Interest Expense				Premium on Bonds Payable			
First year	5,216.35	To R&E Sum	5,216.35	Dec. 31, 1972	783.65	Jan. 1, 1972	4,327.00
Second year	5,177.17	To R&E Sum	5,177.17	Dec. 31, 1973	822.83		
Third year	5,136.03	To R&E Sum	5,136.03	Dec. 31, 1974	863.97		
Fourth year	5,092.83	To R&E Sum	5,092.83	Dec. 31, 1975	907.17		
Fifth year	5,050.62	To R&E Sum	5,050.62	Dec. 31, 1976	949.38		
					4,327.00		4,327.00

Accounting for Serial Bonds

A bond issue may be due in one lump sum at one maturity date, or it may mature serially; that is, some of the bonds may mature each year over a period of years. When the individual bonds of a serial issue do not mature in equal periodic amounts, it may be difficult to develop a scientific plan by which amortization computations can be shortened or systematized. As a consequence, a combination of the straight-line and scientific methods known as the **bonds outstanding method** is often employed.

Bonds Outstanding Method of Amortization The bonds outstanding method is based upon the assumption that the discount or premium applicable to each bond in the issue is the same in amount *per dollar per year*. When this method is used, the amount of premium or discount to be amortized for a period is determined by multiplying the total premium or discount by a fraction, the numerator of which is the par value of the bonds outstanding during the period and the denominator the sum total of the par value of the bonds outstanding over the life of the issue.

Let us assume that an organization sells a $100,000, 5-year bond issue at 97 (that is, $97,000) and that one-fifth of the bonds mature at the end of each year. Under the bonds outstanding method, the $3,000 discount would be amortized as follows:

	Amortization Schedule **Bonds Outstanding Method**		
	Bonds Outstanding	*Computation*	*Discount Amortization*
First year	$100,000	$\left(\dfrac{100,000}{300,000} \times \$3,000\right) =$	$1,000
Second year	80,000	$\left(\dfrac{80,000}{300,000} \times \$3,000\right) =$	800
Third year	60,000	$\left(\dfrac{60,000}{300,000} \times \$3,000\right) =$	600
Fourth year	40,000	$\left(\dfrac{40,000}{300,000} \times \$3,000\right) =$	400
Fifth year	20,000	$\left(\dfrac{20,000}{300,000} \times \$3,000\right) =$	200
	$300,000		$3,000

If the bond issue carries a 5 percent rate of interest, a schedule for recording the periodic interest payments and the amortization of discount could be prepared as shown below. Note that the amount in column (a) is equal to the amount in column (b) plus the amount in column (c).

	Interest Schedule **Bonds Outstanding Method**		
	Debit Interest Expense (a)	Credit *Discount on Bonds Payable* (b)	*Cash* (c)
End of first year	$ 6,000	$1,000	$ 5,000
End of second year	4,800	800	4,000
End of third year	3,600	600	3,000
End of fourth year	2,400	400	2,000
End of fifth year	1,200	200	1,000
	$18,000	$3,000	$15,000

The interest payments and related amortizations of discount for the first and fifth years would be journalized as shown. Again, in order to complete the illustration, the T accounts for Interest Expense and Discount on Bonds Payable are included.

End of First Year

Interest Expense	6,000	
Discount on Bonds Payable		1,000
Cash		5,000

End of Fifth Year

Interest Expense	1,200	
Discount on Bonds Payable		200
Cash		1,000

Interest Expense				Discount on Bonds Payable			
First year	6,000	To R&E Sum	6,000	Issue date	3,000	First year	1,000
Second year	4,800	To R&E Sum	4,800			Second year	800
Third year	3,600	To R&E Sum	3,600			Third year	600
Fourth year	2,400	To R&E Sum	2,400			Fourth year	400
Fifth year	1,200	To R&E Sum	1,200			Fifth year	200
					3,000		3,000

Balance Sheet Presentation of Unamortized Bond Discount and Premium

As we shall see when we study the basic financial statements in detail in Chapter 19, on occasion the unamortized balance in the Discount on Bonds Payable account is classified as a "deferred charge" on the balance sheet and the unamortized balance in the Premium on Bonds Payable account is classified as a "deferred credit." As the captions imply, the deferred charge category contains items which will be charged (debited) against income in the future, while the deferred credit category contains items which will be credited to future income.

Another method preferred by many accountants is to deduct unamortized bond discounts from and add unamortized premiums to the related Bonds Payable account. This method of balance sheet presentation is illustrated as follows:

Long-term debt:		
Bonds payable (4%)	$100,000	
Discount on bonds payable	5,000	$ 95,000
Bonds payable (6%)	$100,000	
Premium on bonds payable	4,000	104,000

BOND SINKING FUND

To make a bond issue more attractive to investors, the issuing organization may agree to set aside stipulated sums of money periodically to be used to retire, or pay off, the bonds at maturity. Such funds are called **sinking funds,** the name indicating that the resources therein are tied up, or "sunk," and as a consequence are not available for use by the organization for other purposes. Physical control over a sinking fund may be exercised by the organization or it may be placed in the hands of a trustee, usually a bank or trust company. Cash deposited in a sinking fund ordinarily is invested in revenue-producing securities, dependent upon the terms (usually referred to as indentures) of the bond issue.

Recording Sinking Fund Transactions

The major problems in accounting for sinking funds pertain to (1) the periodic contributions, (2) the earnings of the fund, and (3) the use of the fund to retire the bonds. To illustrate these problems, let us assume that an organization issues a 5-year, $100,000, 6 percent bond issue with the proviso that equal annual deposits will be made to a sinking fund at the beginning of each of the 5 years and that the fund is to be invested at 5 percent compounded annually.

Since the annual deposits are of equal amount, we are dealing with an annuity, and since we know the amount to which the deposits are to accumulate, we are dealing with the amount of an annuity. Reference to our abbreviated tables on page 331 shows that the amount of an annuity of 1 compounded at 5 percent for five periods is 5.8019. If the factor taken from the table, when multiplied by the periodic deposit, is equal to $100,000, it follows that the periodic deposit must be $17,235.38 ($100,000 ÷ 5.8019).

The following accumulation schedule, journal entries, and T accounts illustrate the workings of a sinking fund. When studying the accumulation schedule, note that the amount in column (b) is 5 percent of the combined amount of the balance in the fund at the beginning of the year and the annual deposit, and that the amount in column (a) plus the amount in column (b) equals the amount in column (c). The balance at the beginning of the year is the same as the balance at the end of the preceding year appearing in column (d), except for the balance at the beginning of the first year, which is simply the first deposit. To obtain the balance in column (d) as of the end of a given year, we merely add the annual increase in column (c) to the balance in column (d) as of the end of the preceding year.

Accumulation Schedule Bond Sinking Fund			
Annual Deposit (a)	Interest Revenue (b)	Annual Increase (c)	Balance in the Fund (d)
First year $17,235.38	$ 861.77	$18,097.15	$18,097.15
Second year 17,235.38	1,766.63	19,002.01	37,099.16
Third year 17,235.38	2,716.73	19,952.11	57,051.27
Fourth year 17,235.38	3,714.33	20,949.71	78,000.98
Fifth year 17,235.38	4,761.82	21,997.20	$99,998.18*
$86,176.90	$13,821.28	$99,998.18	

*As a result of using four-place tables.

First Year

Bond Sinking Fund	17,235.38	
Cash		17,235.38

First deposit—as of the beginning of the first year.

Bond Sinking Fund	861.77	
Interest Revenue		861.77

First year's interest.

Fifth Year

Bond Sinking Fund	17,237.20	
Cash		17,237.20

Fifth deposit (including $1.82 due to rounding).

Bond Sinking Fund	4,761.82	
Interest Revenue		4,761.82

Fifth year's interest.

End of Fifth Year

Bonds Payable	100,000.00	
Bond Sinking Fund		100,000.00

To retire the bonds at maturity.

Bond Sinking Fund				**Interest Revenue**			
First year	17,235.38			To R&E Sum	861.77	First year	861.77
	861.77			To R&E Sum	1,766.63	Second year	1,766.63
Second year	17,235.38			To R&E Sum	2,716.73	Third year	2,716.73
	1,766.63			To R&E Sum	3,714.33	Fourth year	3,714.33
Third year	17,235.38			To R&E Sum	4,761.82	Fifth year	4,761.82
	2,716.73						
Fourth year	17,235.38						
	3,714.33						
Fifth year	17,237.20						
	4,761.82	Payment	100,000.00				
	100,000.00		100,000.00				

Financial Statement Presentation of Sinking Fund Accounts

The cash or securities which comprise a sinking fund are classified as "investments" on the balance sheet. The investment section normally appears between the current asset and long-lived asset sections on the statement. Interest revenue associated with a sinking fund ordinarily appears in the income statement as "other revenue."

BONDS AS AN INVESTMENT

In addition to issuing bonds as a form of long-term debt, an organization also may acquire bonds as a form of long-term investment. Although the accounting problems are similar in both cases, there are some basic differences. For example:

1 The Bonds Payable account is *credited* for *par* when bonds are issued, whereas the Bond Investment account is *debited* for *cost* when bonds are acquired as an investment.

2 Premium or discount is recorded in a separate account when bonds are issued, but not when they are acquired as an investment.

Recording the Acquisition of a Bond

When bonds are purchased as an investment, they are recorded like any asset, at cost. For example, let us assume that as of January 1, 1972, a 5-year, $1,000, 5 percent bond with interest payable annually is purchased at a price of $957.92. The transaction would be recorded as follows:

Investment in Bonds	957.92	
Cash		957.92

Straight-line Amortization of Bond Investments

We can see from the preceding entry that the premium (or discount) associated with the purchase of a bond is *not* recorded in a separate account, as is done when bonds are issued. Instead, it is reflected directly in the asset account. As a consequence, when amortizing a premium or discount associated with the purchase of a bond, we must reflect the amortization in the asset account. That is, over the life of the bond, we must write the investment account *up* to par for a discount and *down* to par for a premium. For example, in our illustration we would write the $957.92 up to $1,000 over the 5-year life of the bond. On a straight-line basis this would mean writing the investment account up $8.42 [($1,000 − $957.92) ÷ 5] each year. The periodic interest payment and amortization would be recorded as follows. Again, for illustrative purposes, the appropriate T accounts are included.

Cash ($1,000 × .05)	50.00	
Investment in Bonds	8.42	
Interest Revenue		58.42

Investment in Bonds				Interest Revenue			
Purchase date	957.92			To R&E Sum	58.42	First year	58.42
First year	8.42			To R&E Sum	58.42	Second year	58.42
Second year	8.42			To R&E Sum	58.42	Third year	58.42
Third year	8.42			To R&E Sum	58.42	Fourth year	58.42
Fourth year	8.42			To R&E Sum	58.40	Fifth year	58.40*
Fifth year	8.40*						
Balance	1,000.00						

*Due to rounding.

Scientific, or Effective-rate, Amortization of Bond Investments

Premium and discount on bonds purchased, like that on bonds issued, may also be amortized by using the scientific, or effective-rate, method. To do this, we need to know the yield, or effective rate of the investment. In our illustration, the 5 percent bond was purchased at a price to yield 6 percent. While the price to be paid for a bond so that it will yield a given return can be taken from a bond table, it can also be computed from our abbreviated compound interest tables on page 331 as follows:

Price paid for par ($1,000 × .7473*)	$747.30
Price paid for interest ($50 × 4.2124†)	210.62
Total price of bond	$957.92

*The present value of 1 at 6% for five periods.
† The present value of an annuity of 1 at 6% for five periods.

The following amortization schedule, journal entries, and T accounts illustrate the use of the effective-rate method in amortizing a bond investment. In the schedule, the amount in column (a) is 5 percent of the par value of the bond, the amount in column (c) is 6 percent of the carrying value of the bond as of the beginning of the year, the amount in column (b) is the difference between the amounts in columns (c) and (a), and the balance in column (d) as of the end of a given year is determined by adding the amount in column (b) for that year to the balance in column (d) as of the beginning of the year. While the schedule does not round out to exactly $1,000 (par value), note that in the entry for the fifth year we amortize just enough to bring the investment account up to $1,000. As pointed out in the footnote to the table, if we had used eight-place tables rather than our abbreviated four-place tables, the "math" would have come out even.

Amortization Schedule
5% Bond Bought to Yield 6%

Date	Debit Cash (a)	Debit Bond Investment (b)	Credit Interest Revenue (c)	Carrying Value of the Bond (d)
Purchase date	—	—	—	$ 957.92
End of first year	$ 50.00	$ 7.48	$ 57.48	965.40
End of second year	50.00	7.92	57.92	973.32
End of third year	50.00	8.40	58.40	981.72
End of fourth year	50.00	8.90	58.90	990.62
End of fifth year	50.00	9.44	59.44	$1,000.06*
	$250.00	$42.14	$292.14	

*Because of using four-place tables.

End of First Year

Cash ($1,000 × .05)	50.00	
Investment in Bonds	7.48	
Interest Revenue		57.48

End of Fifth Year

Cash	50.00	
Investment in Bonds	9.38	
Interest Revenue		59.38

Investment in Bonds

Purchase date	957.92
First year	7.48
Second year	7.92
Third year	8.40
Fourth year	8.90
Fifth year	9.38*
Balance	1,000.00

Interest Revenue

To R&E Sum	57.48	First year	57.48
To R&E Sum	57.92	Second year	57.92
To R&E Sum	58.40	Third year	58.40
To R&E Sum	58.90	Fourth year	58.90
To R&E Sum	59.38	Fifth year	59.38*

*Due to rounding.

Disposal of an Investment in Bonds

From an accounting standpoint, the disposal of an investment in bonds is similar to the disposal of any asset. You will recall from Chapter 11 that when we dispose of an asset, we must:

1 Record any asset received in the disposal.

2 Remove the carrying value of the asset being disposed of from the accounts.

3 Recognize any gain or loss involved in the disposal.

To illustrate, assume that the bond in our illustration is sold at the end of the fourth year for $995. Since the carrying value (and therefore the gain or loss on disposal) is dependent upon the method of amortization employed, entries for both the straight-line and effective-rate methods are given below. While we can determine the carrying value of the investment directly from the amortization schedule for the effective-rate entry, we must compute it for the straight-line entry by adding 4 years' amortization to the original cost ($957.92 + $8.42 + $8.42 + $8.42 + $8.42 = $991.60).

Assuming Straight-line Amortization

Cash	995.00	
Gain on Sale of Investment in Bonds		3.40
Investment in Bonds		991.60

Assuming Effective-rate Amortization

Cash _____ 995.00
    Gain on Sale of Investment in Bonds _____ 4.38
    Investment in Bonds _____ 990.62

Financial Statement Presentation of Bond Investment Accounts

Bond investment accounts, like sinking fund accounts, are classified on the balance sheet as "investments," and interest revenue earned on the investment in bonds normally appears in the income statement as "other revenue."

SUMMARY

Long-term debt is the term applied to obligations of an organization which do not have to be satisfied until after the current operating cycle or one year, whichever is longer. Mortgages and bonds are typical examples of long-term debt.

    In addition to sharing the accounting problems peculiar to liabilities in general—particularly those of recognition and measurement—long-term debt also creates special problems in the area of amortization.

    Bond premium and discount may be amortized either on a straight-line basis or more scientifically by the effective-rate-of-interest method. In order to understand clearly the scientific basis of amortization, we must be familiar with the theory of compound interest.

QUESTIONS AND PROBLEMS

13-1 Distinguish between **nominal** and **effective** interest rates.

13-2 On January 1, 19X1, the Plywood Homes Company issued 20-year, 4 percent bonds having a par value of $1,000,000. The interest on the bonds is payable semiannually on June 30 and December 31. The proceeds to the company were $975,000; that is, on the day they were issued the bonds had a market value of $975,000.

    Explain the nature of the $25,000 difference between the par value and the market value of the bonds on January 1, 19X1.

13-3 (1) A company administers the sinking fund applicable to its own outstanding long-term bonds. Which of the following proposals relative to the treatment of sinking fund cash and securities would you recommend? State the reasons for your selection.

(a) Mingle sinking fund cash with general cash and sinking fund securities with other securities, and show both as current assets on the balance sheet.

(b) Keep sinking fund cash in a separate bank account and sinking fund securities separate from other securities, but on the balance sheet treat sinking fund cash as a part of the general cash and the securities as a part of general investments, showing both as current assets.

(c) Keep sinking fund cash in a separate bank account and sinking fund securities separate from other securities, but combine the two amounts on the balance sheet under one caption, such as "Sinking Fund Cash and Investments," listing it as a noncurrent asset.

(d) Keep sinking fund cash in a separate bank account and sinking fund securities separate from other securities, and identify each separately on the balance sheet among the current assets.

(e) None of the above.

(2) If bonds are initially sold at a discount and the straight-line method of amortization is used, interest expense in the earlier years:

(a) Will exceed what it would have been had the scientific (compound interest) method of amortization been used.

(b) Will be less than what it would have been had the scientific method of amortization been used.

(c) Will be the same as what it would have been had the scientific method of amortization been used.

(d) Will be less than the nominal rate of interest.

(e) None of the above.

13-4 Using the appropriate table on page 331, compute the amount to which the following sums would accumulate at compound interest by the end of the designated periods:

(1) $1,000 for 4 years at 5% per year

(2) $1,000 for 5 years at 5% per year

(3) $1,000 for 4 years at 6% per year

(4) $1,000 for 5 years at 6% per year

(5) $1,000 for 5 years at 5% per year, and at 6% per year for another 5 years

(6) $1,000 for 5 years at 6% per year, and at 5% per year for another 5 years

13-5 Using the appropriate table on page 331, compute the amounts to be invested now at compound interest in order to provide the following sums at the end of the designated periods:

(1) Invested for 4 years at 5% per year to amount to $1,000

(2) Invested for 5 years at 5% per year to amount to $1,000

(3) Invested for 4 years at 6% per year to amount to $1,000

(4) Invested for 5 years at 6% per year to amount to $1,000

(5) Invested for 5 years at 5% per year, then at 6% per year for another 5 years to amount to $1,000

(6) Invested for 4 years at 6% per year, then at 5% per year for another 4 years to amount to $1,000

13-6 Using the appropriate table on page 331, compute the amounts to which the following periodic investments would accumulate at compound interest by the end of the last year in which an investment is made (unless stipulated otherwise):

(1) $1,000 each year for 4 years at 5% per year

(2) $1,000 each year for 5 years at 5% per year

(3) $1,000 each year for 4 years at 6% per year

(4) $1,000 each year for 5 years at 6% per year

(5) $1,000 each year for 3 years at 5% per year, with the amount accumulated at the end of the third year being invested at 6% per year for another 5 years

(6) $1,000 each year for 3 years at 6% per year, with the amount accumulated at the end of the third year being invested at 5% per year for another 5 years

13-7 Using the appropriate table on page 331, compute the amounts which, if invested now at compound interest, will provide the following periodic withdrawals:

(1) $1,000 at the end of each year for 4 years; compound interest computed at 5% per year

(2) $1,000 at the end of each year for 5 years; compound interest computed at 5% per year

(3) $1,000 at the end of each year for 4 years; compound interest computed at 6% per year

(4) $1,000 at the end of each year for 5 years; compound interest computed at 6% per year

(5) $1,000 at the end of the sixth, seventh, eighth, ninth, and tenth years; compound interest computed at 5% per year

(6) $1,000 at the end of the sixth, seventh, eighth, ninth, and tenth years; compound interest computed at 5% per year during the first 5 years and at 6% per year during the second 5 years

13-8 Using the appropriate table on page 331 and assuming that interest is payable annually in all cases, compute the price of each of the following bonds:

(1) A 5-year, $2,000 par value, 5% bond bought to yield 6%

(2) A 5-year, $2,000 par value, 6% bond bought to yield 5%

(3) A 4-year, $2,000 par value, 6% bond bought to yield 5%

(4) A 4-year, $2,000 par value, 5% bond bought to yield 6%

(5) A 3-year, $3,000 par value, 6% bond bought to yield 5%

(6) A 3-year, $3,000 par value, 5% bond bought to yield 6%

13-9 The Gaffney Company purchases a $200,000 building, paying $50,000 cash and giving a mortgage for the balance. The mortgage is to be paid off in four yearly installments of equal amounts. The yearly installments are secured by notes which include interest at 6 percent compounded annually.

Instructions Using the appropriate table on page 331, prepare:

(1) An amortization schedule for the 4-year period

(2) An entry to record the issuance of the mortgage

(3) An entry to record the payment of the second installment

(4) An entry to record the payment of the fourth installment

13-10 The B. Forbes Company purchases a building site for $500,000, paying $100,000 cash and giving a mortgage for the balance. The mortgage is to be paid off in four yearly installments of equal amounts. The yearly installments are secured by notes which include interest at 5 percent compounded annually.

Instructions Using the appropriate table on page 331, prepare:

(1) An amortization schedule for the 5-year period

(2) An entry to record the issuance of the mortgage

(3) An entry to record the payment of the third installment

(4) An entry to record the payment of the fourth installment

13-11 The Worrells Company purchases a $300,000 building, paying $60,000 cash and giving a mortgage for the balance. The mortgage is to be paid off in five yearly installments of equal amounts. The yearly installments are secured by notes which include interest at 5 percent compounded annually. The mortgage notes contain the proviso that the balance due on the mortgage notes can be paid off at any time by the payment of a penalty of 1 percent on the amount retired before its due date.

Instructions Using the appropriate table on page 331, prepare:

(1) An amortization schedule for the 5-year period

(2) An entry to record the issuance of the mortgage

(3) An entry to record the payment of the first installment

(4) An entry to record the early retirement of the mortgage at the end of the third year

13-12 The ABC Company is considering the following plans for the issuance of bonds as of January 1, 19X1:

PLAN 1 $1,000,000 par value, 5 percent, 5-year bonds, at 94 (that is, 94 percent of par)

PLAN 2 $1,000,000 par value, 5 percent, 5-year bonds, with provision for payment of a 6 percent premium upon maturity

Instructions Assuming that straight-line amortization is to be used, prepare a set of journal entries for each of the plans showing the accounting treatment which the proposed plan would necessitate:

(1) At the time of issue

(2) When the yearly interest is paid

(3) When the yearly amortization entry is made

(4) When the bonds are retired at maturity

13-13 On January 1, 19X1, Company Z issues a 5-year, $300,000 par value, 5 percent bond issue.

Instructions Assuming that the bonds are sold at a price to yield 6 percent prepare:

(1) An entry to record the issuance of the bonds

(2) An amortization schedule for the 5-year period, assuming that straight-line amortization is used

(3) An amortization schedule for the 5-year period, assuming that scientific amortization is used

(4) An entry to record the amortization and interest payment for the second year, assuming straight-line amortization

(5) An entry to record the amortization and interest payment for the second year, assuming scientific amortization

13-14 On January 1, 19X1, Company A issues a 5-year, $200,000 par value, 3 percent bond issue at 90. One-fifth of the bonds mature at the end of each of the 5 years. Interest is payable annually.

Instructions Assuming that the company uses the bonds outstanding method of amortization, prepare:

(1) An amortization schedule for the 5-year period

(2) An interest schedule for the 5-year period

(3) An entry to record the issuance of the bonds

(4) An entry to record the amortization and interest payment for the third year

(5) An entry to record the retirement of the bonds retired at the end of the third year

13-15 On January 1, 19X1, Company B issues a 5-year, $300,000 par value, 4 percent bond issue at 105. One-third of the bonds mature at the end of the second year, one-sixth at the end of the third year, one-third at the end of the fourth year, and the balance at the end of the fifth year. Interest is payable annually.

Instructions Assuming that the company uses the bonds outstanding method of amortization, prepare:

(1) An amortization schedule for the 5-year period

(2) An interest schedule for the 5-year period

(3) An entry to record the issuance of the bonds

(4) An entry to record the amortization and interest payment for the fourth year

(5) An entry to record the retirement of the bonds retired at the end of the third year

13-16 The Johnson-Hartley Company issues a 4-year, $200,000, 5 percent bond issue, with the provision that equal annual deposits will be made to a sinking fund at the beginning of each of the 4 years.

Instructions Using the appropriate table on page 331 and assuming that the fund can be invested at 6 percent compounded annually, prepare:

(1) An accumulation schedule for the 4-year period

(2) An entry to record the first deposit

(3) An entry to record the third year's interest

(4) An entry to record the fourth deposit

(5) An entry to record the retirement of the bonds

13-17 The I. Gleim Company issues a 4-year, $400,000, 6 percent bond issue, with the provision that equal annual deposits will be made to a sinking fund at the beginning of each of the 4 years.

Instructions Using the appropriate table on page 331 and assuming that the fund can be invested at 5 percent compounded annually, prepare:

(1) An accumulation schedule for the 4-year period

(2) An entry to record the first deposit

(3) An entry to record the second year's interest

(4) An entry to record the fourth deposit

(5) An entry to record the retirement of the bonds

13-18 The Friedrich Company paid $31,900 for a 4-year, $30,000 par value, 6 percent bond on the date it was issued.

Instructions Prepare:

(1) An amortization schedule, assuming that straight-line amortization is used

(2) An entry to record the purchase of the bond

(3) An entry to record the receipt of interest at the end of the first year

(4) An entry to record the sale of the bond by the Friedrich Company at the end of the second year for $31,200

13-19 The G. Fish Company purchased a 4-year, $20,000, 6 percent bond on the date it was issued at a price which yielded 5 percent on an annual basis.

Instructions Using the appropriate table on page 331, prepare:

(1) An amortization schedule, assuming that scientific amortization is used

(2) An entry to record the purchase of the bond

(3) An entry to record the receipt of interest at the end of the second year

(4) An entry to record the sale of the bond by the Fish Company at the end of the third year for $20,100

13-20 The Rexroad Company purchased a 4-year, $10,000 bond on the date it was issued at a price to yield 5 percent on an annual basis. The following entry was made at the end of the second year to record the receipt of the year's interest:

Cash	600.00	
Investment in Bonds		86.38
Interest Revenue		513.62

Instructions Using the appropriate table on page 331:

(1) Determine the price the company paid for the bond.

(2) Prepare the entry or entries necessary when the Rexroad Company sells the bond at the beginning of the fourth year for $9,900.

EDP PROBLEMS

13-21 The Graves Brummet Company purchases a building site for $1,000,000, paying $100,000 cash and giving a mortgage for the balance. The mortgage is to be paid off in 40 yearly installments of equal amounts. The yearly installments are secured by notes which include interest at 6 percent compounded annually.

Instructions Using a computer, prepare an amortization schedule for the 40-year period.

13-22 The Brummet Graves Company purchases a building site for $1,000,000, paying $200,000 cash and giving a mortgage for the balance. The mortgage is to be paid off in 80 semiannual installments of equal amounts. The installments are secured by notes which include interest compounded semiannually at 3 percent.

Instructions Using a computer, prepare an amortization schedule for the 40-year period.

13-23 On January 1, 1971, Company A issues a 20-year, $1,000,000 par value, 6 percent bond issue at a $21,000 discount. One-twentieth of the bonds mature at the end of each year.

Instructions Using a computer and the bonds outstanding method of amortization, prepare an amortization schedule for the 20-year period

13-24 On January 1, 1971, Company B issues a 20-year, $2,000,000 par value, 5 percent bond issue. Interest is payable on June 30 and December 31 each year. The bonds are sold for $1,768,852.28 (a price to yield 3 percent on a semiannual basis).

Instructions Using a computer, and assuming scientific amortization, prepare an amortization schedule for the 20-year period.

13-25 On January 1, 1971, Company C purchases a 20-year, $1,000,000, 6 percent bond on the date it is issued for $1,125,513.87 (a price to yield $2\frac{1}{2}$ percent on a semiannual basis). Interest is payable semiannually on June 30 and December 31.

Instructions Using a computer and assuming that scientific amortization is used, prepare an amortization schedule for the 20-year period.

Part Four
Accounting for Partnerships and Corporations

14
Partnerships

Up to this point we have concentrated primarily on assets and liabilities. We have not been concerned with particular forms of business organization, because the concepts and principles underlying asset and liability accounts with few exceptions apply equally well in all of them. However, this is not true of owner equity accounts. Their nature and operation are dependent upon the form of business organization in existence in a particular situation.

The three major forms of business organization in the United States are the proprietorship, partnership, and corporation. Accounting problems peculiar to the owner equity accounts of proprietorships and partnerships will be discussed in this chapter with primary emphasis on those of partnerships, since as a rule the difference between the two is chiefly one of size. In Chapters 15 through 17 we shall concentrate on problems related to the owner equity accounts of corporations.

PARTNERSHIPS VERSUS PROPRIETORSHIPS

Generally speaking, a **proprietorship** is a business enterprise owned by one individual, who is usually both the manager and pivot of the business as well as its owner. A **partnership,** on the other hand, is a form of joint proprietorship, a combination of the skills and resources of two or more individuals who jointly own and manage a business.

Capital Accounts

Ordinarily, the owner equity sections in the books of proprietorships and partnerships are subdivided into capital accounts and drawing accounts. The term **capital,** as used in accounting, is defined broadly as the amount invested in a business organization. Thus, **capital accounts** are used to reflect the amount of capital invested on a more or less permanent basis. In a proprietorship there is only one Capital account, whereas in a partnership each partner has a Capital account.

Drawing Accounts

In addition to capital accounts, many proprietorships and partnerships employ **drawing accounts** to reflect temporary changes in owner equity. Items recorded in these accounts include withdrawals of cash or other assets by the owner or owners, and losses from operations. Profits also are recorded in drawing accounts, where they remain until a decision is made either to leave them in the business as permanent capital or to withdraw them. Withdrawals and losses are charged (debited) to the accounts, whereas profits are credited. As with capital accounts, there is one Drawing account in a proprietorship and one for each partner in a partnership. When dealing with proprietorships and partnerships in our future work, we shall close Revenue and Expense Summary accounts into drawing accounts at the end of a period rather than into capital accounts as we have done in the past.

To illustrate the operation of a drawing account, let us assume that the Revenue and Expense Summary account of the John Jones Proprietorship reflects a profit of $1,000 for the period. In T-account form the profit would be closed to the Drawing account as follows:

Revenue and Expense Summary

Expenses	9,000	Revenues	10,000
To Drawing	1,000		
	10,000		10,000

John Jones, Drawing

From R & E Summary	1,000

If Jones decides to leave the $1,000 in the business permanently, at the end of the period it should be transferred to the Capital account as follows:

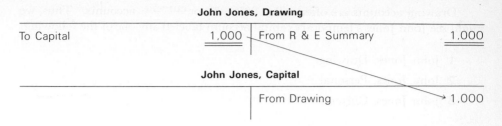

John Jones, Drawing

To Capital	1,000	From R & E Summary	1,000

John Jones, Capital

	From Drawing	1,000

To illustrate the same situation in a partnership, let us assume that the Revenue and Expense Summary account of the A & B Partnership reflects a profit of $1,000 for the period and that the partners share profits and losses equally. The profit would be closed to the drawing accounts as follows:

Revenue and Expense Summary

Expenses	9,000	Revenues	10,000
To Drawing	1,000		
	10,000		10,000

James Able, Drawing

	From R & E Summary	500

Fred Baker, Drawing

	From R & E Summary	500

However, if Able and Baker decide to leave their respective shares of the profits for the period in the business on a more or less permanent basis, their decision would be reflected in the accounts as follows:

James Able, Drawing

To Capital	500	From R & E Summary	500

James Able, Capital

	From Drawing	500

Fred Baker, Drawing

To Capital	500	From R & E Summary	500

Fred Baker, Capital

	From Drawing	500

Drawing accounts are often called **personal,** or **current,** accounts. Thus, we might see John Jones's temporary capital account labeled any one of the following:

1 John Jones, Drawing

2 John Jones, Personal

3 John Jones, Current

LEGAL ASPECTS OF PARTNERSHIPS

The Uniform Partnership Act, which has been adopted by most of the states in this country, defines a partnership as "an association of two or more persons to carry on as coowners of a business for profit." A **person,** as defined by the act, includes other partnerships and corporations as well as individuals. Thus, from a legal standpoint, a partnership is based on the right of individuals or "persons" to contract with one another.

Because of the nature of its legal creation, the partnership form of business organization contains some peculiar characteristics. Among the more noteworthy are:

1 Mutual agency

2 Unlimited liability

3 Coownership of property

4 Cosharing of profits and losses

5 Limited life

Mutual Agency

According to law, each partner in a partnership is an agent for all the other partners. Therefore, all the partners are bound by any act of any other partner which falls within the normal operating scope of the business in which the partnership is engaged. In a trading concern, for example, a purchase of merchandise on credit by one partner automatically binds the other partners.

Unlimited Liability

Each partner is personally liable for all debts of the partnership. This is true even if one partner creates a partnership debt without the consent of the other partners; as far as outsiders are concerned, each partner has the right to act for the partnership. Thus, if a partnership cannot meet its obligations, a partnership creditor may seek recovery from any of the partners, regardless of the amount of capital a particular partner has invested in the business. The unlimited liability feature of partnerships is considered by many investors to be one of the most serious drawbacks to this form of business organization. For example, a "person" with substantial personal resources may be hesitant to invest in a partnership when it means that his personal assets could be used to satisfy partnership debts.

Coownership of Property

All resources invested in a partnership by the partners, along with partnership assets purchased with partnership funds, become property jointly owned by all the partners. Thus, each partner has an undivided interest in all the partnership property rather than a claim against specific partnership assets. (As we shall see in the last section of this chapter, upon the dissolution of a partnership, each partner's undivided interest in the assets is measured by the balance in his capital account.)

Cosharing of Profits and Losses

Profits and losses of a partnership may be shared in any way agreed upon by the partners. However, if no agreement has been made, according to law each partner must receive an equal share of the profits and bear an equal share of the losses. This applies regardless of the amount of capital a partner has invested in the partnership. The method by which partnership profits and losses are shared is ordinarily referred to as the **profit and loss sharing ratio.**

Limited Life

Another major objection to the partnership form of business organization concerns the constant danger of untimely dissolution. Since a partnership is formed for the purpose of operating, as coowners, a business for profit, when a partner ceases to be associated with the operation of the business, the life of that partnership is ended. A partnership is automatically dissolved upon the death or withdrawal of a partner, by the bankruptcy of a partner or the partnership, and as a result of the incapacity (legal insanity) of a partner. The admission of a new partner also terminates an existing partnership and requires that a new one be formed.

Articles of Partnership

A partnership is based upon an agreement which, in order to prevent future misunderstandings, preferably should be in the form of a written document, although this is not a legal requirement. An agreement of this kind, generally known as the **articles of partnership,** contains all the terms pertinent to the formation, operation, and dissolution of the partnership, including:

1 Names of the partners
2 Name of the partnership

3 Nature of the business to be conducted by the partnership

4 Effective date of the agreement

5 Expiration date, if any, of the agreement

6 Location of the place of business

7 Amount of capital to be contributed by each partner

8 Nature and division of work, and authority of the partners

9 Amounts of drawings or salaries to partners, including a statement to the effect that they are, or are not, to be deducted from profits before such profits are allocated to the partners

10 Procedure to be followed in allocating partnership profits and losses

11 Procedure to be followed in arbitrating disputes among partners

12 Procedure to be followed in liquidating the partnership in the event that it is discontinued

OPENING PARTNERSHIP BOOKS

In most respects the routine accounting problems associated with the asset, liability, revenue, and expense accounts of a partnership are the same as those we have encountered throughout the preceding chapters, and they are handled in the same way. The basic books of original entry employed in the Pendery illustration could be used without major modification in many partnerships. Likewise, the same chart of accounts could be utilized simply by including some additional owner equity accounts.

The major accounting problems associated with the partnership form of business organization pertain to the owner equity accounts at the time of (1) the initial formation of the enterprise, (2) the admission of a new partner, (3) the sharing of profits and losses, and (4) the liquidation of the business. The remainder of this chapter will be devoted to problems relating to these areas.

Opening the books of a partnership differs little from opening the books of a proprietorship. In the Pendery illustration, when Pendery initially invested $8,000 cash in the clothing business, we opened his books by debiting his Cash account for $8,000 and crediting his capital account for the same amount. Partnership books are opened in a similar manner, that is:

1 The proper asset accounts are debited for the appropriate amounts.

2 Any liabilities assumed by the partnership are credited to the appropriate accounts.

3 The capital accounts are credited for the net amount (assets minus liabilities).

To avoid future disputes regarding the investments initially made by the various partners, each partner's original investment is generally recorded in a separate entry. Let us assume that James Able contributes $8,000 cash and $2,000 worth of inventory to the A & B Partnership; that Fred Baker contributes a building worth $30,000; and that the partnership assumes a $5,000 mortgage on the building. The partnership books will be opened as follows:

Cash	8,000	
Inventory	2,000	
James Able, Capital		10,000
To record the original investment of James Able in the A & B Partnership.		
Building	30,000	
Mortgage Payable		5,000
Fred Baker, Capital		25,000
To record the original investment of Fred Baker in the A & B Partnership.		

When a partnership is initially formed, one of the more difficult problems to be dealt with is the proper valuation of noncash assets contributed by a partner. Since the partners become coowners of all partnership assets, any gain or loss on subsequent disposal will be shared by all the partners. Thus, if the building contributed by Baker which was valued at $30,000 turns out to be worth only $26,000, the $4,000 difference will be charged to the partners in accordance with their procedure for sharing profits and losses. Assuming that profits and losses are shared equally, Able's capital account will eventually absorb $2,000 of the difference, as will Baker's capital account. However, when the asset was initially valued at $30,000, Baker's capital account received all the credit. As can readily be seen, the ultimate effect of the error in the initial valuation of the building is to increase Baker's capital account by $2,000 more than he actually contributed and to reduce Able's capital account by $2,000.

Obviously, if a partnership is to be successful, equity among the partners is essential. Thus, valuations assigned to noncash assets must be carefully set. Being only human, a partner who contributes noncash assets to a partnership may tend to place a higher value on them than is warranted. To avoid this problem, general agreement as to appropriate valuation bases for such assets should be reached by all the partners at the time the partnership is formed. Generally, noncash assets are valued at their fair market values, determined by a disinterested appraiser, as of the date of transfer to the partnership.

ADMISSION OF A NEW PARTNER

With the consent of the other partners, a new partner may be admitted to an existing partnership in one of two ways:

1 By **purchasing** an interest from one or more of the old partners
2 By **investing** additional assets in the partnership

Admission by Purchase

When an incoming partner purchases his interest in the partnership directly from one or more of the old partners, no changes are made in the asset or liability accounts of the partnership; all accounting changes take place in the owner equity accounts. A capital account is opened for the incoming partner and credited for the agreed-upon amount. This amount in turn is deducted from the capital accounts of the old partners from whom the purchase was made.

To illustrate the purchase approach, let us assume that after the A & B Partnership has been operating for some time, the owner equity accounts of the partners, Able and Baker, contain credit balances of $15,000 and $30,000, respectively. If we assume that Tom Cain is admitted to the partnership by purchasing one-half of Baker's interest for $20,000 cash, the transaction will be recorded on the partnership books as follows:

Fred Baker, Capital ————————————————————— 15,000
    Tom Cain, Capital ———————————————————— 15,000
To record Tom Cain's admission into the partnership.

In T-account form, the effect of Cain's admission on the owner equity accounts of the partnership will be as follows:

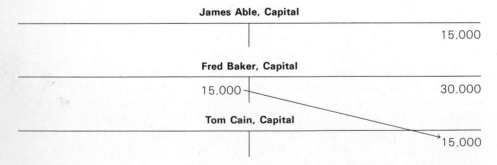

Note that the cash that actually changed hands between Cain and Baker is not reflected on the partnership books. This is as it should be, because the transfer of cash is a personal transaction between Cain and Baker, not a partnership transaction.

To further illustrate the procedure involved in recording the admission of a new partner under the purchase approach, let us assume that Cain is admitted to the partnership by paying Able $7,500 for one-third of his interest and by paying Baker $15,000 for one-third of his interest. The entry to record Cain's admission and the ledger accounts reflecting the admission would appear as follows:

James Able, Capital _____ 5,000
Fred Baker, Capital _____ 10,000
    Tom Cain, Capital _____   15,000
To record Tom Cain's admission into the partnership.

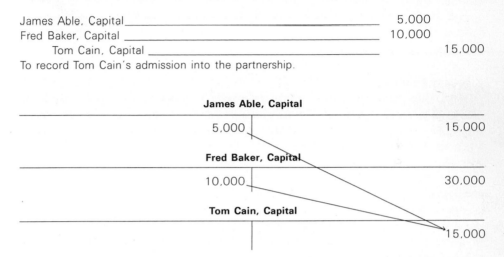

Although in both of the foregoing illustrations Cain was admitted into the partnership with one-third interest in its total capital ($15,000 out of $45,000), he did not automatically gain the right to receive one-third of the profits and bear one-third of the losses. As we learned earlier, the extent to which Cain will participate in profits and losses must be agreed upon by all the partners. The sharing of profits and losses will be discussed in greater detail in a later section of this chapter.

Admission by Investment

Under the investment approach, an incoming partner acquires his interest by contributing assets (cash or other) to the partnership. As a result, both the assets and the capital of the partnership are increased.

Recording the admission of a partner by investment is not always as simple as recording the admission of a partner by purchase. If the partnership asset accounts are to be increased by the exact amount contributed by the incoming partner, and if he in turn is to receive credit in his capital account for the exact amount contributed, the entry to record his admission is routine. We merely debit the proper asset accounts for the appropriate amounts and credit the new partner's capital account for the total amount of his contribution.

On occasion, however, when a new partner is admitted, the partnership asset accounts are not increased by the exact amount he contributes nor is the new partner's capital account credited for this amount. In such cases either goodwill or a bonus may be involved.

Goodwill and Bonus   Goodwill in business, as was pointed out in Chapter 11, refers to the ability of an organization to earn more than the normal rate on its tangible assets because of its established reputation. When a new partner is admitted into partnership in a business with an established reputation, the old partners frequently will charge him for the goodwill they have built up. On the other hand, the incoming partner may possess the established reputation. If this is the case, he ordinarily will expect to receive credit for the goodwill which he is bringing into the partnership.

Although many business organizations possess goodwill, accountants are often reluctant to record it in the accounts because of its subjective nature. However, they are in general agreement that once the value of goodwill has been objectively determined by a purchase or sale, it may be recorded. Thus, when a monetary valuation has been set on goodwill as the result of bargaining between the old partners and the incoming partner, it may be recorded in the accounts of the new partnership. If the goodwill has been established by the old partners, the Goodwill account is debited and the old partners' capital accounts are credited in accordance with the old profit and loss sharing ratio. If the goodwill has been created by the incoming partner, the Goodwill account is debited and the new partner's capital account is credited.

Occasionally, the price paid for an interest in a partnership by an incoming partner or the amount of capital given to an incoming partner by the old partners will indicate that goodwill is involved; however, because goodwill is an intangible asset, the partners may prefer not to recognize it in the accounts. In such cases accountants employ a bonus method to record the admission of a partner. The word bonus is used here in the sense of giving "something extra," in this case, capital. The old partners may give the incoming partner some of their capital as a bonus for joining the partnership, or the new partner may give the old partners some of his capital as a bonus for their permission to join the partnership.

When a bonus is given to the incoming partner, his capital account is credited for the total amount of the bonus, and the old partners' capital accounts are debited for the amounts of their pro rata shares of the contribution, based on the old profit and loss sharing ratio. When the bonus is given to the old partners, the incoming partner's capital account is debited for the total amount of the bonus, and the old partners' capital accounts are credited for the amounts of their pro rata shares, based on the old profit and loss sharing ratio.

From the foregoing discussion, it should be recognized that there are at least five major ways by which the admission of a new partner under the investment approach may be effected. He may be admitted with:

1 No goodwill or bonus involved
2 Credit for goodwill given to new partner
3 Credit for goodwill given to old partners
4 Bonus given to new partner
5 Bonus given to old partners

To illustrate the ways in which a new partner may be admitted under the investment approach, let us assume that in the A & B Partnership, James Able, who receives 40 percent of the profits, has a $15,000 credit balance in his capital account, and Fred Baker, who receives 60 percent of the profits, has a $30,000 credit balance in his capital account. Let us also assume that Tom Cain is admitted to partnership under the various assumptions which follow. In each case he is to receive a 25 percent interest in the capital of the new partnership.

1 Cain invests $15,000; total capital to be $60,000
2 Cain invests $12,000; total capital to be $60,000
3 Cain invests $18,000; total capital to be $72,000
4 Cain invests $12,000; total capital to be $57,000
5 Cain invests $18,000; total capital to be $63,000

Regardless of the method used to record the admission of a new partner by investment, certain procedural steps should be followed. In summary form, they are:

1 Determine the **total amount of capital** to be **recognized** by the new partnership. (This should be either expressed or implied in the partnership agreement.)
2 Determine the **total amount of capital** to be **contributed** by all the partners. (This should be either expressed or implied in the partnership agreement.)
3 Determine the **amount of capital** that the incoming partner is to **receive.** (This should be either expressed or implied in the partnership agreement.)
4 Determine whether either **goodwill** or **bonus** is involved.
5 Record cash and other tangible assets contributed by the new partner.
6 Record goodwill, if any.
7 Record incoming partner's capital.
8 Adjust the other partners' capital accounts, if necessary.

Admission of Partner: No Goodwill or Bonus Involved If Cain is admitted to the partnership by investing $15,000 for a one-fourth interest in a total capital of $60,000, his admission would be recorded as follows:

Cash	15,000	
Tom Cain, Capital		15,000

Since both the total amount of capital contributed by the partners ($15,000 + $30,000 + $15,000) and the total amount to be recognized by the new partnership is $60,000, goodwill is not involved. Likewise, since Cain contributed $15,000 and is to receive credit for capital of $15,000 ($\frac{1}{4} \times$ $60,000), no bonus is involved. Thus, all that is necessary to record his admission into the partnership is to debit the Cash account for the amount of cash contributed and credit Cain's capital account for his share of the capital.

Admission of Partner: Goodwill to New Partner If Cain is admitted to the partnership by investing only $12,000 for a one-fourth interest in a total capital of $60,000, his admission will be recorded as follows:

Cash	12,000	
Goodwill	3,000	
Tom Cain, Capital		15,000

Note that the total amount of capital to be recognized by the new partnership is $60,000, but only $57,000 ($15,000 + $30,000 + $12,000) of capital is being contributed. Hence, goodwill is involved in the amount of $3,000 ($60,000 − $57,000). Since Cain is contributing only $12,000 in tangible assets but is receiving credit for $15,000 ($\frac{1}{4} \times$ $60,000), it follows that he must be contributing goodwill. Thus, when Cain's admission into the partnership is recorded, he receives credit not only for his cash contribution but also for the goodwill he brings to the business.

Admission of Partner: Goodwill to Old Partners If Cain is admitted to the partnership by investing $18,000 for a one-fourth interest in a total capital of $72,000, his admission will be recorded as follows:

Cash	18,000	
Goodwill	9,000	
James Able, Capital (40% $\times$ $9,000)		3,600
Fred Baker, Capital (60% $\times$ $9,000)		5,400
Tom Cain, Capital		18,000

In this case, the total amount of capital to be recognized by the new partnership is $72,000, and since only $63,000 ($15,000 + $30,000 + $18,000) of capital is being contributed, goodwill is involved in the amount of $9,000 ($72,000 −

$63,000). Cain is contributing $18,000 in tangible assets and receiving credit for $18,000 ($\frac{1}{4}$ × $72,000), so the goodwill is apparently being contributed by the old partners. Goodwill created by an old partnership is recorded on the books of the new partnership by debiting the Goodwill account and crediting the capital accounts of the old partners in their old profit and loss sharing ratio. The $9,000 of goodwill created by Able and Baker is allocated to them in the old 40 : 60 ratio.

Admission of Partner: Bonus to New Partner If Cain is admitted to the partnership by investing $12,000 for a one-fourth interest in a total capital of $57,000, his admission will be recorded as follows:

Cash	12,000	
James Able, Capital (40% × $2,250)	900	
Fred Baker, Capital (60% × $2,250)	1,350	
Tom Cain, Capital ($\frac{1}{4}$ × $57,000)		14,250

Since the total amount of capital to be recognized by the new partnership is $57,000 and the total amount contributed by the partners is $57,000 ($15,000 + $30,000 + $12,000), goodwill is not involved. However, since Cain is contributing $12,000 and is to receive capital of $14,250 ($\frac{1}{4}$ × $57,000), he is receiving a bonus. When a bonus is given to an incoming partner, his admission into the partnership is recorded by (1) debiting the appropriate asset accounts for his investment, (2) debiting the old partners' capital accounts in the old profit and loss sharing ratio for the bonus, and (3) crediting the new partner's capital account for the total.

Admission of Partner: Bonus to Old Partners If Cain is admitted to the partnership by investing $18,000 for a one-fourth interest in a total capital of $63,000, his admission will be recorded as follows:

Cash	18,000	
James Able, Capital (40% × $2,250)		900
Fred Baker, Capital (60% × $2,250)		1,350
Tom Cain, Capital ($\frac{1}{4}$ × $63,000)		15,750

Since the total amount of capital to be recognized by the new partnership is $63,000 and the total amount contributed by the partners is $63,000 ($15,000 + $30,000 + $18,000), goodwill is not involved. However, since Cain is investing $18,000 but only receives credit for capital of $15,750 ($\frac{1}{4}$ × $63,000), it follows that he must be giving a bonus to the old partners. In this case, the admission of a new partner is recorded by (1) debiting the appropriate asset accounts for his investment, (2) crediting the new partner's capital account for the agreed-upon capital, and (3) crediting the old partners' capital accounts in the old profit and loss sharing ratio for the bonus.

SHARING OF PROFITS AND LOSSES

Partnership profits and losses may be shared in any way agreed upon by the partners. However, if they are not to be shared equally, it is highly important that the procedure for allocation be clearly outlined in the articles of partnership.

If equity in the sharing of profits and losses is to be achieved, consideration must be given to at least two factors: capital investments and services rendered. When the partners contribute both in equal amounts, profits and losses should be shared equally. Otherwise, each factor must be considered separately. Generally, a partner who contributes more capital or services than other partners should receive a larger share of the profits, and vice versa.

Profit and Loss Sharing Bases

Some of the more commonly employed profit and loss sharing bases are:

1 Fixed ratio

2 Capital ratio

3 Interest on capital plus fixed ratio

4 Salary plus fixed ratio

5 Salary plus interest on capital plus fixed ratio

To illustrate the accounting procedures involved in allocating the periodic profits and losses of a partnership, let us assume in each of the following cases that Able, Baker, and Cain, partners in the A & B Partnership, have credit balances in their capital accounts of $15,000, $30,000, and $15,000, respectively, and that the profit for the period is $21,000, unless stipulated otherwise.

Fixed Ratio The fixed ratio method of profit and loss sharing may be employed (1) to allocate profits and losses equally or (2) to allocate them on the basis of the amounts of capital and services contributed by the partners. If the partners are to share on an equal basis, the journal entry for the allocation will appear as follows:

Revenue and Expense Summary	21,000	
James Able, Drawing ($\frac{1}{3}$ × $21,000)		7,000
Fred Baker, Drawing ($\frac{1}{3}$ × $21,000)		7,000
Tom Cain, Drawing ($\frac{1}{3}$ × $21,000)		7,000

Let us assume, on the other hand, that the partners contributed unequal amounts of both capital and services, and as a result the profits and losses are to be allocated in the following ratio (expressed in percentages for convenience):

30 percent to Able, 45 percent to Baker, and 25 percent to Cain. In journal entry form the allocation will appear as follows:

Revenue and Expense Summary	21,000	
James Able, Drawing (30% × $21,000)		6,300
Fred Baker, Drawing (45% × $21,000)		9,450
Tom Cain, Drawing (25% × $21,000)		5,250

Capital Ratio On occasion, partners may agree to share profits and losses in a ratio based upon the balances in their capital accounts; this is known as a **capital ratio.** Since capital balances are subject to change, the partnership agreement should indicate the capital ratio to be used. For example, the agreement might specify (1) the capital ratio as of the beginning of the period, (2) the capital ratio as of the end of the period, or (3) an average ratio throughout the period. For illustration, we shall use the $15,000, $30,000, and $15,000 balances given above. In journal entry form the allocation will be:

Revenue and Expense Summary	21,000	
James Able, Drawing ($\frac{15}{60}$ × $21,000)		5,250
Fred Baker, Drawing ($\frac{30}{60}$ × $21,000)		10,500
Tom Cain, Drawing ($\frac{15}{60}$ × $21,000)		5,250

Interest on Capital plus Fixed Ratio To compensate a partner for providing more capital to a partnership than is provided by other partners, partnership agreements often stipulate that an allowance shall first be made for interest on the invested capital and the balance of the profits or losses allocated according to some fixed ratio. Assuming in our illustration that the partners are to be allowed 5 percent interest on their capital accounts and that the balance is to be allocated equally, $3,000 (5% × $60,000) of the $21,000 net income will be allocated as interest, and $18,000 ($21,000 − $3,000) will be allocated equally. In journal entry form the allocation will be:

Revenue and Expense Summary	21,000	
James Able, Drawing		
[(5% × $15,000) + ($\frac{1}{3}$ × $18,000)]		6,750
Fred Baker, Drawing		
[(5% × $30,000) + ($\frac{1}{3}$ × $18,000)]		7,500
Tom Cain, Drawing		
[(5% × $15,000) + ($\frac{1}{3}$ × $18,000)]		6,750

Salary plus Fixed Ratio In cases where one of the partners assumes operational control of the partnership, it is common practice for the partnership agreement to allow him a salary in addition to his participation in the profits. Let us assume that Cain is to receive a salary of $12,000, and that the balance of the profits or losses is to be shared by Able, Baker, and Cain in a 30 percent, 45 percent, and 25 percent ratio. The $21,000 net income in our illustration will be allocated as follows: (1) $12,000 as salary, and (2) $9,000 ($21,000 − $12,000) in accordance with the profit and loss ratio. The journal entry to record the allocation will be:

Revenue and Expense Summary	21,000	
James Able, Drawing (30% × $9,000)		2,700
Fred Baker, Drawing (45% × $9,000)		4,050
Tom Cain, Drawing [$12,000 + (25% × $9,000)]		14,250

If a partnership agreement provides for a salary for one or more of the partners, the salary portion of the allocation must be made even if the net income to be allocated is less than the salary allowance. The debit balance in the Revenue and Expense Summary account after such a salary allowance has been made is then allocated as a loss to the partners in the appropriate profit and loss ratio. For example, in our immediately preceding illustration, if the partnership's net income before Cain's salary allowance was made had been $10,000 rather than $21,000, his salary allowance would have created a $2,000 debit balance in the Revenue and Expense Summary account. This balance would then have been allocated as a loss in a 30 percent, 45 percent, and 25 percent ratio to Able, Baker, and Cain, as follows:

Revenue and Expense Summary	10,000	
James Able, Drawing (30% × $2,000)	600	
Fred Baker, Drawing (45% × $2,000)	900	
Tom Cain, Drawing [$12,000 − (25% × $2,000)]		11,500

For illustrative purposes the T accounts are also shown:

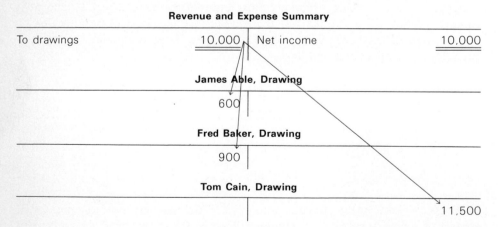

Salary plus Interest on Capital plus Fixed Ratio Occasionally an attempt is made in a partnership agreement to compensate the partners on some kind of pro rata basis for their time, capital, and "know-how." In this case, the partnership profits and losses may be shared on a combination of bases such as (1) salary, (2) interest on investment, and (3) a fixed ratio. If we assume that (1) Cain is to receive a salary of $12,000, (2) all partners are to receive 5 percent interest on their capital, and (3) the balance is to be allocated equally, the $21,000 net income will be allocated by giving $2,750 to Able, $3,500 to Baker, and $14,750 to Cain, computed as follows:

Computation of Income Allocation				
	Net Income	*Able*	*Baker*	*Cain*
Total to be allocated	$21,000			
Salary (to Cain)	(12,000)			$12,000
Interest (5% on capital)	(3,000)	$ 750	$1,500	750
Balance (equally)	(6,000)	2,000	2,000	2,000
Totals		$2,750	$3,500	$14,750

As was the case in the salary plus fixed ratio illustration, if a partnership agreement provides that a salary or interest on investment is to be allowed one or more partners, the salary and interest portions of the allocation must be made even if the net income to be allocated is less than the salary and interest allowance. Again, the resulting debit balance in the Revenue and Expense Summary account is allocated to the partners as a loss on the basis of the fixed ratio. For example, if the net income in our immediately preceding illustration had been $9,000 rather than $21,000, Cain's salary allowance of $12,000 and the $3,000 of interest would have created a debit balance in the Revenue and Expense Summary account of $6,000. This debit balance would have been allocated as a loss on an equal basis to Able, Baker, and Cain. As a consequence, Able's drawing account would ultimately receive a net debit of $1,250 and Baker's drawing account a net debit of $500, while Cain's drawing account would receive a net credit of $10,750. The computation would be made as follows:

Computation of Income Allocation				
	Net Income	*Able*	*Baker*	*Cain*
Total to be allocated	$ 9,000			
Salary (to Cain)	(12,000)			$12,000
Interest (5% on capital)	(3,000)	$ 750	$ 1,500	750
Balance (equally)	6,000	(2,000)	(2,000)	(2,000)
Totals		$(1,250)	$ (500)	$10,750

In journal entry form the allocation would be recorded as shown. Note that the $10,750 credit increase in Cain's drawing account is the result of the $9,000 net income plus the decreases in Able's and Baker's drawing accounts of $1,250 and $500, respectively. For illustrative purposes, the T accounts are also included.

Revenue and Expense Summary	12,000	
Tom Cain, Drawing		12,000
To record Cain's salary.		
Revenue and Expense Summary	3,000	
James Able, Drawing (5% × $15,000)		750
Fred Baker, Drawing (5% × $30,000)		1,500
Tom Cain, Drawing (5% × $15,000)		750
To record interest on capital investment.		
James Able, Drawing ($\frac{1}{3}$ × $6,000)	2,000	
Fred Baker, Drawing ($\frac{1}{3}$ × $6,000)	2,000	
Tom Cain, Drawing ($\frac{1}{3}$ × $6,000)	2,000	
Revenue and Expense Summary		6,000
To allocate the debit balance in the R & E Summary account.		

Revenue and Expense Summary

Cain's salary	12,000		Net income	9,000
Interest on capital	3,000		To drawing accounts	6,000
	15,000			15,000

James Able, Drawing

From R & E Sum	2,000		Interest on capital	750

Fred Baker, Drawing

From R & E Sum	2,000		Interest on capital	1,500

Tom Cain, Drawing

From R & E Sum	2,000		Salary	12,000
			Interest on capital	750

PARTNERSHIP LIQUIDATION

The decision to liquidate a partnership may result from one or more of several causes:

1 Accomplishment of the purpose for which the partnership was formed

2 Inability of the partnership to make a profit

3 Internal dissension among the partners

4 Bankruptcy of the partnership or of a partner

Regardless of the reasons for dissolving a partnership, the liquidation procedure requires that:

1 All assets be converted into cash

2 All partnership creditors be paid in full

3 The remaining cash be distributed to the partners

The illustrations which follow, while not exhaustive, are indicative of the kinds of problems that may arise in partnership liquidations. To conserve space, we shall use the term **noncash assets** in lieu of the individual asset accounts other than cash, the term **liabilities** in lieu of the individual liability accounts, and the term **realization** for the conversion of noncash assets into cash. The illustrations are based on the following data taken from the books of the A & B Partnership just prior to liquidation, and at a time when the partners Able, Baker, and Cain were sharing profits and losses in a 30 percent, 30 percent, 40 percent ratio.

Cash	$ 15,000	
Noncash assets	90,000	
Liabilities		$ 5,000
James Able, Capital		40,000
Fred Baker, Capital		30,000
Tom Cain, Capital		30,000
	$105,000	$105,000

As you study the illustrations, note that all gains and losses are allocated to the partners' capital accounts before any cash is distributed to the partners. It is especially important to note also, *and to remember,* that gains and losses are allocated in the profit and loss ratio, whereas cash is distributed to the partners *not* in the profit and loss ratio but rather in accordance with the balances in their capital accounts after all gains and losses are allocated.

Gain on Realization

Let us assume that the noncash assets are sold for $100,000, resulting in a $10,000 gain on realization. The ultimate cash distribution to the partners will result in

Able receiving $43,000, Baker receiving $33,000, and Cain receiving $34,000, determined as follows:

		Noncash			Capital	
Liquidation Schedule						
	Cash	Assets	Liabilities	Able	Baker	Cain
P & L ratio _____				30%	30%	40%
Balances per books _____	$ 15,000	$90,000	$5,000	$40,000	$30,000	$30,000
Realization of assets and allocation of gain _____	+100,000	−90,000		+3,000	+3,000	+4,000
Balances _____	$115,000		$5,000	$43,000	$33,000	$34,000
Payment of liabilities _____	−5,000		−5,000			
Balances _____	$110,000			$43,000	$33,000	$34,000
Payment to partners _____	−110,000			−43,000	−33,000	−34,000

The transactions involved in the liquidation process will be recorded as shown in the following entries, taken directly from the liquidation schedule. For example, entries (1) and (2) are taken from the line entitled "Realization of assets and allocation of gain."

(1)

Cash _____	100,000	
Noncash Assets _____		90,000
Gain on Realization _____		10,000
To record sale of the assets.		

(2)

Gain on Realization _____	10,000	
James Able, Capital_____		3,000
Fred Baker, Capital _____		3,000
Tom Cain, Capital _____		4,000
To allocate gain on sale of assets.		

(3)

Liabilities_____	5,000	
Cash _____		5,000
To record payment of liabilities.		

(4)

James Able, Capital_____	43,000	
Fred Baker, Capital _____	33,000	
Tom Cain, Capital _____	34,000	
Cash _____		110,000
To record final distribution of cash to partners.		

Loss on Realization

If the noncash assets are sold for only $70,000, resulting in a $20,000 loss on realization, in the ultimate cash distribution to the partners Able will receive $34,000, Baker $24,000, and Cain $22,000, determined as follows:

	Cash	Noncash Assets	Liabilities	Able	Capital Baker	Cain
Liquidation Schedule						
P & L ratio				30%	30%	40%
Balances per books	$15,000	$90,000	$5,000	$40,000	$30,000	$30,000
Realization of assets and allocation of loss	+70,000	−90,000		−6,000	−6,000	−8,000
Balances	$85,000		$5,000	$34,000	$24,000	$22,000
Payment of liabilities	−5,000		−5,000			
Balances	$80,000			$34,000	$24,000	$22,000
Payment to partners	−80,000			−34,000	−24,000	−22,000

In journal entry form the liquidation transactions will be recorded as follows:

(1)

Cash	70,000	
Loss on Realization	20,000	
Noncash Assets		90,000

To record sale of the assets.

(2)

James Able, Capital	6,000	
Fred Baker, Capital	6,000	
Tom Cain, Capital	8,000	
Loss on Realization		20,000

To allocate loss on sale of assets.

(3)

Liabilities	5,000	
Cash		5,000

To record payment of liabilities.

(4)

James Able, Capital	34,000	
Fred Baker, Capital	24,000	
Tom Cain, Capital	22,000	
Cash		80,000

To record final distribution of cash to partners.

Loss on Realization with a Capital Deficiency

In the preceding illustration, where we had a loss on realization of the noncash assets, all partners had sufficient capital in their capital accounts to withstand their shares of the loss, and each one shared in the final cash payment to the extent of his capital balance. There may be times, however, when a partner's share of the loss on realization exceeds his equity in the partnership. As a consequence, he ends up with a capital **deficiency,** represented by a debit balance in his capital account. When this happens, the partnership has a claim against him in the amount of the deficiency.

Capital Deficiency: Partner Has Sufficient Personal Assets If a partner with a capital deficiency has personal assets available to meet the claim, he should, of course, contribute them to the partnership; however, if he fails to do so, the other partners must absorb his deficiency.

Let us assume that the noncash assets in our illustration are sold for only $10,000, resulting in an $80,000 loss on realization. By studying the following liquidation schedule, we can see that Cain will have a capital deficiency of $2,000. If he has personal assets available to meet this deficiency, he should pay $2,000 into the partnership. This will permit Able to receive $16,000 and Baker to receive $6,000 in the final cash distribution.

Liquidation Schedule*						
		Noncash			Capital	
	Cash	Assets	Liabilities	Able	Baker	Cain
P & L ratio				30%	30%	40%
Balances per books	$15,000	$90,000	$5,000	$40,000	$30,000	$30,000
Realization of assets and allocation of loss	+10,000	−90,000		−24,000	−24,000	−32,000
Balances	$25,000		$5,000	$16,000	$ 6,000	$−2,000
Cain's payment	+2,000					+2,000
Balances	$27,000		$5,000	$16,000	$ 6,000	
Payment of liabilities	−5,000		−5,000			
Balances	$22,000			$16,000	$ 6,000	
Payment to partners	−22,000			−16,000	−6,000	

*Assuming that Cain has enough in personal assets to meet his capital deficiency.

The liquidation entries will be journalized as in the preceding illustrations with the exception of Cain's cash payment to the partnership. It will be recorded by debiting the Cash account and crediting his capital account, as follows:

Cash	2,000	
Tom Cain, Capital		2,000

To record Cain's cash contribution to the partnership to meet his capital deficiency.

Capital Deficiency: Partner Has No Personal Assets If Cain has no personal assets to contribute to the partnership, Able will receive $15,000 and Baker $5,000 in final payment from the partnership. The liquidation schedule follows:

Liquidation Schedule*

	Cash	Noncash Assets	Liabilities	Able	Capital Baker	Cain
P & L ratio				30%	30%	40%
Balances per books	$15,000	$90,000	$5,000	$40,000	$30,000	$30,000
Realization of assets and allocation of loss	+10,000	−90,000		−24,000	−24,000	−32,000
Balances	$25,000		$5,000	$16,000	$ 6,000	$−2,000
Allocation of Cain's deficiency				−1,000	−1,000	+2,000
Balances	$25,000		$5,000	$15,000	$ 5,000	
Payment of liabilities	−5,000		−5,000			
Balances	$20,000			$15,000	$ 5,000	
Payment to partners	−20,000			−15,000	−5,000	

*Assuming that Cain has no personal assets available to contribute to the partnership.

Again, the liquidation would be journalized as in the preceding illustrations, with the exception of Cain's capital deficiency. Since he has no personal assets with which to meet the deficiency, it becomes a loss to be borne by the other partners in the profit and loss sharing ratio that exists between them. In this case, since both Able and Baker were receiving 30 percent of the profits, they would bear Cain's $2,000 deficiency 30:30, or equally. It should be emphasized that if they had been sharing profits and losses in some other ratio, they would have absorbed the deficiency according to that ratio. For example, if their profit and loss sharing ratio had been 45:15 instead of 30:30, Able would have absorbed $1,500 (45/60 × $2,000) and Baker would have absorbed $500 (15/60 × $2,000).

The absorption of Cain's deficiency, assuming that Able and Baker share profits and losses in a 30:30 ratio, would be journalized as follows:

James Able, Capital	1,000	
Fred Baker, Capital	1,000	
Tom Cain, Capital		2,000

Capital Deficiency: Partner Has Some Personal Assets In the two immediately preceding illustrations, we assumed that Cain could make good on either all or none of his deficiency. There is, of course, also the possibility that a partner can partially cover the deficiency in his capital account. If we assume that Cain is able to contribute $500 toward his deficiency, Able and Baker will have to absorb only $1,500. As a consequence, in the ultimate cash distribution Able will receive $15,250 and Baker will receive $5,250, as shown in the following schedule.

Liquidation Schedule*						
		Noncash			Capital	
	Cash	Assets	Liabilities	Able	Baker	Cain
P & L ratio				30%	30%	40%
Balances per books	$15,000	$90,000	$5,000	$40,000	$30,000	$30,000
Realization of assets and allocation of loss	+10,000	−90,000		−24,000	24,000	−32,000
Balances	$25,000		$5,000	$16,000	$ 6,000	$−2,000
Cain's payment	+500					+500
Balances	$25,500		$5,000	$16,000	$6,000	$−1,500
Allocation of Cain's deficiency				−750	−750	+1,500
Balances	$25,500		$5,000	$15,250	$5,250	
Payment of liabilities	−5,000		−5,000			
Balances	$20,500			$15,250	$5,250	
Payment to partners	−20.500			−15,250	−5,250	

*Assuming that Cain can contribute $500 to the partnership toward meeting his capital deficiency.

Cain's $500 payment into the partnership and Able's and Baker's absorption of Cain's remaining deficiency would be journalized as follows:

(1)

Cash	500	
Tom Cain, Capital		500

(2)

James Able, Capital	750	
Fred Baker, Capital	750	
Tom Cain, Capital		1,500

SUMMARY

Partnership relations are contractual in nature; preferably, the contract should be in writing. It is important that the partnership agreement state clearly the rights and duties of the partners at the time of formation, during the existence, and at the time of the liquidation of the partnership.

The routine accounting entries do not differ materially from those of an individual proprietorship. The opening entries record the assets contributed, the liabilities assumed, and the partners' beginning capitals. Profits and losses may be shared in any way the partners desire. In the absence of an agreement, the law holds that they are to be shared equally.

A new partner may be admitted to a partnership by purchasing an interest from one or more of the old partners in a personal transaction, or by contributing assets directly to the partnership.

When a partnership is liquidated, all assets are converted into cash, partnership liabilities are paid, and the remaining cash is distributed to the partners. When accounting for a partnership liquidation, we must remember to allocate gains and losses in the profit and loss ratio, but to distribute cash in accordance with the balances in the partners' capital accounts, after first providing for all known and possible losses.

QUESTIONS AND PROBLEMS

14-1 You are engaged to draw up a partnership agreement for a firm about to be organized. State at least ten important points to be covered in such an agreement.

14-2 (1) Name at least four important items relating to the **accounts** of a partnership for which information should be obtainable by reference to the partnership agreement.

(2) In the absence of specific directions in the partnership agreement, how would you treat withdrawals by a partner during a fiscal year which exceeded his share of profits for the year?

14-3 Partnership agreements ordinarily specify a profit and loss ratio. They may also provide for such additional profit and loss sharing features as salaries, bonuses, and interest allowances on invested capital. What is the objective of a profit and loss sharing arrangement, and why may there be a need for profit and loss sharing features in addition to the profit and loss ratio? Discuss.

14-4 A and B are partners and have agreed to share profits and losses equally. State your reasons in support of one of the following methods of dividing losses incurred in liquidation of the partnership.

(1) Profit and loss ratio

(2) Ratio of capital balances

14-5 Show by illustrative entries how the transfer of a one-third interest in a partnership would be recorded, when:

(1) The interest is acquired by cash being paid into the partnership.

(2) The interest is acquired from a retiring partner.

14-6 A and B are in partnership, with balances in their capital accounts of $24,000 and $30,000, respectively. The partners share profits and losses equally. For each case described below, prepare the entry or entries necessary to record the described change in the partnership.

CASE 1   A sells his interest in the partnership to C for $25,000.

CASE 2   B sells one-half of his interest in the partnership to C for $20,000.

CASE 3   A and B each sell one-third of their interests in the partnership to C for $20,000. In the settlement, A receives $12,000 and B receives $8,000.

CASE 4   B sells one-third of his share in the profits of the partnership to A for $7,000.

14-7 (1) The total of the partners' capital accounts was $110,000 before recognition of partnership goodwill in preparation for the withdrawal of a partner whose profit and loss sharing ratio was 2:8. The partner was paid $28,000 by the firm in final settlement for his interest. The remaining partners' capital accounts, excluding their shares of the goodwill, totaled $90,000 after his withdrawal. The total goodwill of the firm agreed upon was:
   (a) $40,000
   (b) $28,000
   (c) $20,000
   (d) $ 8,000
   (e) None of the above

   (2) In a partnership liquidation, the final cash distribution to the partners should be made in accordance with the:
   (a) Partners' profit and loss sharing ratio
   (b) Balances of the partners' capital accounts
   (c) Ratio of the capital contributions by the partners
   (d) Ratio of capital contributions less withdrawals by the partners
   (e) None of the above

14-8 You are to direct the liquidation of the partnership of A and B. Based on the following balance sheet, how would you distribute the $15,000 cash?

A AND B

Balance Sheet

As of December 31, 19X2

Cash	$ 15,000	Liabilities	$ 5,000
Other assets	100,000	A, capital	40,000
		B, capital	70,000
	$115,000		$115,000

14-9 A, B, and C are in partnership. Their capital account balances were as follows: A, $11,000; B, $5,700; and C, $1,300. The partnership agreement provides that profits and losses shall be divided $\frac{4}{9}$, $\frac{3}{9}$, and $\frac{2}{9}$, respectively. The partnership has become insolvent and is therefore to be dissolved. The liabilities have been paid and $9,000 of cash on hand is the only asset. How should the $9,000 be distributed?

14-10 E and F are partners sharing profits and losses 2:1, respectively. Their capital account balances are as follows: E, $15,000, and F, $5,000. When the partnership is dissolved, all the assets are sold and cash sufficient to pay all the firm's liabilities but one is realized. The amount of the liability is $4,000. Each partner is personally solvent. How much should each partner contribute from his personal assets in satisfying this claim?

14-11 In the A and B Partnership, A has $30,000 capital and receives two-thirds of the profits and B has $20,000 capital and receives one-third of the profits. C is admitted to partnership under the various assumptions shown below, but in every case he is to receive a one-fifth interest in both profits and capital of the new partnership.

(1) C invests $15,000; total capital to be $65,000

(2) C invests $12,000; total capital to be $62,000

(3) C invests $12,500; total capital to be $62,500

(4) C invests $12,000; total capital to be $62,500

(5) C invests $15,000; total capital to be $75,000

Instructions Prepare the necessary entry or entries to record C's admittance in each case.

14-12 Austin and Bradford are partners. They share profits and losses equally and have equal capital investments of $10,000 each. Crane is admitted to the partnership with a one-third interest in both profits and capital. Crane pays $9,000 into the partnership for his interest.

Instructions Prepare journal entries showing at least two possible methods of recording Crane's admission on the books of the partnership and state the conditions under which each method would be appropriate.

14-13 A and B are equal partners. Their balance sheet as of a certain date is as follows:

Cash	$ 4,000	Accounts payable	$20,000
Accounts receivable	23,000	A, capital	30,000
Merchandise inventory	36,500	B, capital	30,000
Plant and machinery	12,500		
Auto trucks	2,500		
Furniture and fixtures	1,500		
Total	$80,000	Total	$80,000

A and B agree to admit C and D into the partnership as partners. C is to provide $30,000 cash as his capital. D, in consideration of his many business connections, is to provide $20,000 cash, but his capital account is to be credited with the same amount as C's.

C and D agree to accept the balance sheet of A and B subject to the following changes, the changes being agreed upon by all:

Accounts receivable to be subject to a 5 percent discount

Merchandise inventory to be valued at $33,000

Plant and machinery to be valued at $11,000

Auto trucks to be valued at $2,000

Accounts payable to be subject to a 3 percent discount

Instructions

(1) Prepare the entry or entries necessary to adjust the accounts of the A and B partnership prior to the admission of C and D.

(2) Prepare the entry or entries necessary to record C and D's admission into the partnership.

14-14 Instructions A, B, and C are partners. For each of the following cases, which deal with profit and loss sharing ratios, indicate how a net income of $24,000 would be allocated among the partners.

CASE 1   The partnership is silent as to how profits and losses are to be shared.

CASE 2   Partner A is to be allowed a salary of $15,000 per year with any balance being shared equally by all three partners.

CASE 3   Partner A is to be allowed a salary of $15,000 per year with any balance being shared in accordance with the capital ratio existing as of the beginning of the year. As of the beginning of the year, A's capital account showed a balance of $30,000, B's a balance of $40,000, and C's one of $50,000.

CASE 4   Partner A is to be allowed a salary of $15,000 and each partner is to be allowed an 8 percent return on his capital as of the beginning of the year (see Case 3 above). Any balance is to be shared in the ratio of 2:3:5 to A, B, and C, respectively.

14-15 The partnership agreement between A, B, and C (all the partners of The ABC Company) provides for 6 percent interest on each partner's capital balance at the beginning of the fiscal year and for salaries of $10,000 for A and $5,000 for B before the profits or losses are divided $33\frac{1}{3}$ percent to each partner.

    The opening capital balances are A, $20,000; B, $30,000; and C, $40,000; the net profit, before partners' salaries and interest are deducted, is $13,800.

Instructions

(1) Prepare a schedule showing how the $13,800 net profit should be allocated to the three partners.

(2) Prepare the entry, in general journal form, necessary to close the Revenue and Expense Summary account into the partners' drawing accounts.

14-16 Adams, Baker, Charles, and Day are partners. Their interests in the capital and their profit and loss ratios are as follows: Adams, 40 percent; Baker, 30 percent; Charles, 20 percent; and Day, 10 percent.

    To provide a means whereby the remaining partners might purchase a deceased partner's interest from his estate, a life insurance program was inaugurated whereby life insurance proceeds would be paid to the remaining partners in proportion to their percentage ownership in the partnership. Since each partner was in effect insuring the life of each of the other partners, it was agreed that no partner would pay any part of the premiums on policies covering his own life.

In 19X6 the premium on all policies amounted to $9,000, which was charged as an expense on the books and thereby deducted from the year's profit. The profit was then credited to the partners' capital accounts in accordance with the profit and loss sharing ratio.

Investigation of the insurance premiums revealed the following:

Premium on life of Adams	$3,500
Premium on life of Baker	1,400
Premium on life of Charles	2,300
Premium on life of Day	1,800

Instructions Prepare the correcting entry that should be made to the partners' capital accounts in order to reflect properly the agreement as to the insurance. Present your supporting computations in good form.

14-17 The ABCD Partnership was formed on January 1, 19X2, with four partners, A, B, C, and D. Capital contributions were:

A	$100,000
B	50,000
C	50,000
D	40,000

The partnership agreement provides that each partner shall receive 5 percent interest on the amount of his capital contribution. In addition, A is to receive an annual salary of $10,000 and B one of $6,000.

The agreement further provides that C shall receive from the partnership a minimum of $5,000 per year and D a minimum of $12,000 per year, both including amounts allowed as interest on capital and their respective shares of profits. The balance of the profits is to be shared in the following proportions:

A	30%
B	30%
C	20%
D	20%

Instructions Prepare a schedule showing the amount of income which must be earned by the partnership during 19X2 in order that A may receive an aggregate of $25,000 including his share of the interest, salaries, and profits.

14-18 A and B formed a partnership on January 1, 19X1. The partnership reported a profit of $40,000 for 19X1, a $20,000 loss for 19X2, and a $30,000 profit for 19X3. Their profit and loss sharing ratios for the three years were as follows:

		A	B
19X1		50%	50%
19X2		60%	40%
19X3		70%	30%

On January 1, 19X4, it was discovered that:

(1) The ending inventory on December 31, 19X1, was $11,000 and not $1,000 as reported.

(2) The ending inventory on December 31, 19X2, was $12,000 and not $15,000 as reported.

(3) Excessive depreciation of $5,000 a year was charged on equipment for the years 19X1 and 19X3.

Instructions Prepare the entry or entries necessary to correct the books as of January 1, 19X4.

14-19 Partners A, B, and C have $8,800, $4,700, and $5,500 capitals, respectively. They share profits and losses in the ratio of 40 percent, 30 percent, and 30 percent, respectively. They now have $500 in cash and $20,500 in other assets and owe $2,000 to outside creditors. They decide to liquidate the business. They sell $5,500 worth of assets for $2,500 and want to distribute immediately the proper amount of cash to each partner.

Instructions Prepare a liquidation schedule showing how the distribution should be made.

*14-20 Flint, Durant, and Nash are partners in a wholesale business. On January 1, 19X2, their total capital was $48,000, divided as follows: Flint, $10,000; Durant, $8,000; Nash, $30,000. Their 19X2 withdrawals were $6,000, $4,000, and $2,000, respectively. Through the failure of debtors to pay their obligations, the partnership is compelled to liquidate. After exhausting the partnership assets, including those arising from an operating profit of $7,200 in 19X2, the partnership still owes $8,400 to creditors on December 31, 19X2. Flint has no personal assets but the other partners are personally financially well off.

Instructions

(1) Compute the partnership liquidating loss.

(2) Prepare a schedule of the liquidation.

(3) Based upon your liquidation schedule, prepare the entry or entries necessary to carry out the liquidation.

*AICPA adapted.

15
Corporations: Nature and Terminology

Generally speaking, a business corporation is a unit formed and controlled by an association of private individuals for the purpose of making a profit. Although individual proprietorships and partnerships are far more numerous than corporations, the corporate form of business organization is responsible for the major volume of goods and services produced in the United States today. As was true with partnerships, in order to appreciate some of the major problems involved in accounting for corporations, we should first become familiar with the more pertinent legal aspects.

LEGAL ASPECTS OF CORPORATIONS

As defined by Chief Justice Marshall in the famous, and now classic, Dartmouth College case, a corporation is "an artificial being, invisible, intangible, and existing only in contemplation of the law." Defined more fully, a **corporation** is a legal entity in itself, created by law or under authority of the law, having a continuous existence independent of the existences of its members, and powers and liabilities distinct from those of its members.

All the states in the United States have passed statutes governing the formation, operation, and liquidation of corporations, many adopting the Model Business Corporation Act of the American Bar Association. Although there is not complete uniformity in the various state laws regarding corporations at the present time, a trend appears in that direction.

Legal Formation of Corporations

In order to form a legally valid corporation, the incorporators must meet the requirements of the applicable state statutes. While legal procedures vary from one state to another, the following routine is typical:

1 An application for a charter, generally referred to as **articles of incorporation,** is drawn up, usually by an attorney, for those persons involved in forming the corporation (the **incorporators**).

2 The articles are signed by at least three of the incorporators.

3 The articles, together with the necessary incorporation fees, are submitted to the secretary of state or other state official charged with administering the corporation laws of the state.

4 If the articles and fees are found to be in order, a certificate of incorporation is issued by the state and corporate existence begins.

5 The certificate and a copy of the articles are filed for record within a specified time (usually 15 days) in the office of the recorder of the county in which the registered office of the corporation will be located.

Articles of Incorporation

The articles of incorporation set forth the essential information required under the statutes of the state in which the business is incorporated. They generally include:

1 Name of the corporation

2 Date of incorporation

3 Name of the state where incorporated

4 Purpose of the corporation

5 Expected duration of the corporation (perpetuity in most states)

6 Location of its main office

7 Amount and kinds of capital stock to be issued, including any preferences or limitations applicable to the stock

8 Number of directors

9 Qualifications of directors

10 Names and addresses of incorporators and number of shares of capital stock subscribed to by them

11 Names and addresses of members of the first board of directors

12 Any special powers of the corporation or its board of directors

Corporate Ownership

In order to secure capital, corporations issue shares of stock which they sell to investors. Corporate ownership rests in the hands of these investors, who are known as **stockholders** or **shareholders.** A corporation may have as few as one or two stockholders or as many as several million. (While most states require a minimum of three stockholders, a few require only one.) Stockholders' ownership interests are represented by shares of stock, and their rights of ownership are exercised through a board of directors.

Rights of the Stockholder

As a rule, unless specifically stipulated otherwise, the ownership of a share of stock in a corporation gives the stockholder the following rights:

1 **Right to transfer his ownership interest.** One of the chief advantages of the corporate form of business organization is the relative ease with which shares of stock may be transferred from one person to another. Ordinarily, this may be done merely by delivering the stock certificate, properly endorsed.

2 **Right to vote.** Corporate directors are elected by a vote of the stockholders. Stockholders also vote on various matters pertaining to corporate policy.

3 **Right to share in profits.** Unless specified otherwise, the owner of a share of stock has the right to share proportionately in all corporate earnings when they are distributed to the stockholders in the form of dividends.

4 **Right to share in the distribution of assets** in case of dissolution. Unless stipulated otherwise, in the event of the dissolution of the corporation, after all creditors have been paid, the owner of a share of stock has the right to share proportionately in the distribution of assets.

5 **Right to subscribe to a new issue of the corporation's stock** in proportion to his existing holdings before the shares are offered to the general public. This is generally referred to as a **preemptive right.**

Board of Directors

The management and operation of the corporation reside in the board of directors, elected by the stockholders in accordance with the articles of incorporation. The duties of the board include electing or appointing the corporate officers, determining their compensation, determining policies regarding pricing, expansion, the development of new products, and the like, and deciding upon the distribution of profits. The directors do not themselves attend to the day-to-day operation of the business but delegate this responsibility, under their supervision, to the officers—usually a president, vice president, secretary, treasurer, and others. The power of the board, while considerable, is of course subject to any restrictions which may be imposed either by law or by the corporation charter.

The separation of corporate ownership and control, frequently referred to as **absentee ownership,** and often considered to be one of the chief advantages of the corporate form of business organization, is illustrated in the following organization chart.

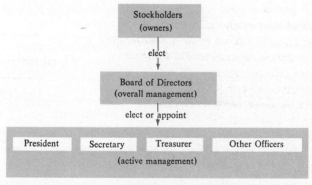

Corporate organization chart.

CORPORATIONS VERSUS PARTNERSHIPS

Historical studies dealing with the development of the various forms of business organization generally point out that the corporate form came into being as a result of the need for:

1 A means of obtaining larger amounts of capital than was ordinarily possible in a proprietorship or partnership
2 A way of ensuring continuity and permanency in the life of a business organization

3 An easy way of transferring the rights of ownership in a business

4 A procedure for limiting the financial liability of the owners of a business

Although this is not the place for a detailed analysis of the history of business organization, it is important that we, as students of accounting, understand how the major forms differ from one another. We have already compared the proprietorship and the partnership. Perhaps the best way to compare the partnership and the corporation is to spotlight their legal differences and their accounting differences.

Legal Comparison

The major legal differences between a corporation and a partnership may be summarized as follows:

1 A corporation is a legal entity and may come into existence only by the sanction of a state. A partnership is not a legal entity and may be formed simply by an agreement among the partners.

2 A partnership has a limited life, but a corporation's existence is continuous and is independent of its stockholders. It cannot be terminated except by law or the expiration of its charter.

3 A partner is personally liable for the debts of a partnership, but a corporate stockholder's liability is limited to the amount of his investment.

4 A partner is an agent of a partnership, but a corporate stockholder is not an agent of a corporation, and he cannot act for the other owners or commit them financially.

5 A partner must have the consent of the other partners before selling part or all of his interest in a partnership, but shares of stock may be transferred at will by corporate stockholders.

You will note in the above comparison that the corporate form of business organization tends to eliminate most of the major legal disadvantages of the partnership.

Accounting Comparison

In most respects the routine accounting problems associated with the asset, liability, revenue, and expense accounts of a corporation are the same as those of a partnership, except that there are usually more of them. Again, we could employ the same basic books of original entry that we used in the Pendery illustration, unless the volume of transactions is so great that mechanical or electronic equipment is necessary to process the data. Thus, the major difference between partnerships and corporations from an accounting standpoint is to be found in the composition of the owner equity accounts.

A simple comparative illustration at this time should help in our subsequent study of problems related to the owner equity accounts of corporations. You will recall that when we were accounting for partnerships we used a capital account for each partner. When accounting for a corporation, we usually employ one capital account, which is generally entitled Capital Stock. Occasionally, however, more than one class of stock may be involved. In such cases we use a separate capital stock account for each class.

To illustrate the difference between the capital accounts of a partnership and the Capital Stock account of a corporation, let us assume that Able, Baker, and Cain have $30,000, $30,000, and $40,000, respectively, to invest in a business enterprise. If they form a partnership, their initial investments will appear as shown on the left below; if they form a corporation, their combined initial investment will appear as shown on the right.

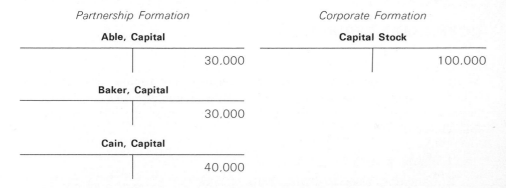

Another difference between the corporation and the partnership from an accounting standpoint is to be found in the treatment of profits and losses. In a partnership, as you will recall, we have a drawing account for each partner into which we close his share of the profits or losses until a decision is made as to what is to be done with them. In a corporation we have only one account, generally entitled Retained Earnings, into which all profits and losses are closed.

To illustrate the difference between the drawing accounts of a partnership and the Retained Earnings account of a corporation, let us assume that the firm formed by Able, Baker, and Cain earns a net income of $10,000 during its first year of operation. Under a partnership formation, if Able, Baker, and Cain shared profits in a 3:3:4 ratio, the Revenue and Expense Summary account would be closed as shown on the left in the following illustration. If the organization were set up as a corporation, it would be closed as shown on the right.

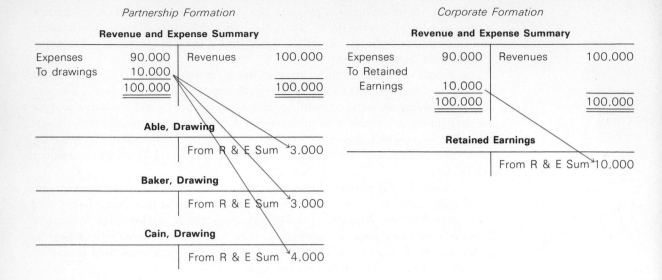

Partnership Formation

Revenue and Expense Summary

Expenses	90,000	Revenues	100,000
To drawings	10,000		
	100,000		100,000

Able, Drawing

| | | From R & E Sum | 3,000 |

Baker, Drawing

| | | From R & E Sum | 3,000 |

Cain, Drawing

| | | From R & E Sum | 4,000 |

Corporate Formation

Revenue and Expense Summary

Expenses	90,000	Revenues	100,000
To Retained Earnings	10,000		
	100,000		100,000

Retained Earnings

| | | From R & E Sum | 10,000 |

CORPORATE TERMINOLOGY

Many of the accountant's terminology problems center around corporate owner equity accounts. It will be our purpose in this section to explain some of the more important terms commonly employed in this area, most of which relate to the following topics:

1 Shares of stock
2 Valuations associated with shares of stock
3 Classes of stock
4 Types of owner equity accounts

Shares of Stock

A share of stock represents the shareholder's undivided interest in the net assets (assets minus liabilities) of the corporation. For example, if a corporation has 1,000 shares of stock in the hands of its stockholders and you own 100 of them, you have a one-tenth ownership in the organization; in other words, you have a 10 percent claim against the net assets and the earnings of the corporation.

Corporations issue **stock certificates** as evidence of the ownership interests of their stockholders. These certificates are simply pieces of paper certifying that the holder owns a certain number of shares of stock. The Model Business Corporation Act requires that the certificate include:

1 Name of the state where the organization is incorporated

2 Name of the person to whom the stock is issued

3 Number and class of shares represented

4 Par value of each share, or a statement that the stock has no par value

5 If more than one class of stock is involved, a summary of the rights and restrictions of each class

A few of the terms associated with the authorization and issuance of shares of stock should be explained at this time. They include:

1 Authorized shares

2 Unissued shares

3 Subscribed shares

4 Treasury shares

5 Outstanding shares

Authorized Shares Those shares of stock which a corporation is permitted to issue under its articles of incorporation are called **authorized shares.** Although the total number of authorized shares is fixed by the articles, as a general rule it may be changed by a vote of the stockholders.

Unissued Shares It is common practice for a corporation to obtain authorization for more shares of stock than it intends to issue initially. Shares which have been authorized but not yet issued to the stockholders are called **unissued shares.**

Subscribed Shares When a corporation puts shares of its unissued stock up for sale, it normally uses a subscription procedure whereby the buyer agrees to purchase a certain number of shares at a specified price and date. **Subscribed shares** are those shares of authorized stock for which subscription agreements have been made, but which will not be issued until full payment is received.

Treasury Shares Shares of a corporation's authorized stock which have been issued and later reacquired by the corporation are known as **treasury shares.** The difference between treasury shares and unissued shares should be noted. Ownership of the former has at some time been in the hands of the stockholders, whereas ownership of the latter has never rested in the hands of the stockholders.

Outstanding Shares Shares of authorized, issued stock which are in the hands of the stockholders are **outstanding.** (It is important to note that treasury shares are not considered outstanding, because although they once were owned by the stockholders, they now belong to the corporation.)

If we assume that a corporation has 1,000 shares of authorized stock, 200 unissued shares, and 100 shares in the treasury, the number of shares outstanding will be determined as follows:

Authorized shares	1,000
Less: Unissued shares	200
Issued shares	800
Less: Treasury shares	100
Shares outstanding	700

Share Values

The most important terms of a profession are sometimes the most difficult to define. Often they are words used, with a different meaning, by the layman in everyday conversation. The word **value** is such a term. In accounting terminology it ordinarily indicates the amount at which an item is stated in the accounts, in accordance with the accounting principles related to that item. For example, as you will recall, assets are normally carried at cost; in this case, value is cost. It is important to recognize that in accounting the term value does not necessarily assume the idea of "worth," but rather refers to a particular method of quantitative determination. It is normally preceded by a qualifying adjective and used in a precise fashion. Therefore, whenever we meet the term in our study, we must be sure that we understand its meaning. When we associate it with shares of stock, we may encounter:

1 Par value

2 No-par value

3 Stated value

4 Market value

5 Book value

Par Value The par value of a share of stock is a nominal, fixed, dollar amount assigned to it by a corporation's charter. A stock's par value has no relationship to its market value. Its only significance in accounting, as we shall see in more detail in Chapter 16, is that the Capital Stock account must be credited for the par value of each share issued. For example, if a corporation issues 10,000 shares of $10 par value stock, the corporation's Capital Stock account must be credited for $100,000 (10,000 $\times$ $10).

No-par Value The term **no-par value** means that no fixed dollar amount is assigned to the stock by the corporation's charter. When a corporation issues no-par stock, any amount decided upon by the board of directors may be credited to the Capital Stock account. However, unless specifically directed otherwise by the board, the accountant should credit the entire proceeds of the issue to the Capital Stock account. For example, if a corporation sells 10,000 shares of no-par value stock for $15 per share and the board of directors does not stipulate otherwise, the corporation's Capital Stock account should be credited for $150,000 (10,000 × $15).

Stated Value Because most state statutes require that at least part of the price received by a corporation for a share of its stock be allocated (credited) to the Capital Stock account, incorporators normally stipulate a nominal, fixed dollar amount known as the stated value to be assigned to each share of no-par stock, thus making it essentially par value stock. If not stipulated by the incorporators in the articles of incorporation, stated value is assigned by the stockholders, operating through the board of directors.

Market Value The market value of a share of stock is the price per share at which the stock is currently being traded (purchased and sold) on the market.

Book Value The term book value, as used in accounting, refers to the amount at which an item is reflected in the "books of account." Since a share of stock represents an undivided interest in the ownership of a corporation, its book value is determined by dividing the owner equity by the number of shares outstanding. For example, let us assume that a corporation with an owner equity of $100,000 has 1,000 shares of stock outstanding; the book value per share will be $100 ($100,000 ÷ 1,000). When a corporation issues more than one class of stock, the owner equity must be allocated to the various classes in order to determine the book value per share. After we examine classes of stock in the next section of this chapter, we shall study in greater detail the computation of the book value of a share of stock.

Comments on Share Valuations Before we leave our discussion of share values, it should again be emphasized that the term value is not used in accounting in the same way that it is used by the layman. Accountants use it in several rather precise ways, and when used correctly, it is always accompanied by a qualifying adjective. This adjective is often more indicative of the meaning than is the word value itself. It is also important to recognize that there is not necessarily any relationship among the various share valuations.

Common and Preferred Stock

When a number of persons contribute some or all of their resources to an organization as capital, it is perhaps only logical that they have divergent investment objectives. Some investors may be so confident of the organization's ultimate success that they are willing to wait for their shares of the profits until others who are less optimistic have received theirs. Needless to say, the former will expect something in return for the risk they run. This may be the possibility of receiving a larger share of the corporation's earnings or perhaps the right to exert a dominating influence in the control of the organization. The cautious investor, on the other hand, usually prefers to be more certain of his return, even though it means that he must be content with a smaller share of the profits and little or no influence in the control of the corporation.

In order to appeal to as wide a range of investors as possible, many corporations issue more than one type, or class, of stock. The two major classes are common stock and preferred stock, the latter often being further categorized as to type of preferred stock.

Common stock, as the name implies, is the "ordinary" stock. Generally, ownership of a share of common stock carries the customary rights of a stockholder such as the right to vote and the right to participate both in the corporation's profits and in its assets in case of dissolution. If a corporation has only one class of stock, it is common stock.

Preferred stock carries certain preferential rights which common stock does not have, chiefly (1) the right to share in earnings ahead of the common stock and (2) the right to a priority claim against the assets in the event of dissolution. In addition to these rights which, along with any particular limitations or preferences, must be specifically provided for in the articles of incorporation, the owner of a share of preferred stock has essentially the same rights as an owner of a share of common stock. However, as a general rule, preferred stock does not carry voting rights; thus, a preferred stockholder ordinarily does not have a voice in the control of the organization. The common stockholder, on the other hand, depending upon the number of shares of stock he owns, may be able to exercise considerable control in the operation of the business.

From an accounting standpoint, one of the most important attributes of preferred stock is its priority claim against earnings. A corporation's earnings are distributed in the form of **dividends,** which generally are declared and paid on the basis of a certain dollar amount per share or a percentage of the stock's par value. For example, a $7 per share yearly dividend on preferred stock with a par value of $100 per share would have its dividend preference stipulated as "$7 preferred" or "7 percent preferred." (Although dividends are often paid quarterly, they are usually stated on a yearly basis.)

As a general rule, preferred stockholders have more assurance of receiving their dividends than common stockholders, since preferred stock shares in earnings ahead of common stock. However, because there ordinarily is a limit on preferred stock earnings, an owner of common stock usually has the potential for receiving larger dividends.

Preferred stock may be categorized as cumulative or noncumulative and participating or nonparticipating, depending upon the preferences and limitations ascribed to it.

Cumulative and Noncumulative Preferred Stock If for some reason, financial or otherwise, part or all of a stipulated preferred dividend is passed over (not declared) for a particular period, it generally accumulates and is payable out of subsequent earnings. Stock carrying this kind of provision is called **cumulative stock.** Passed-over cumulative preferred dividends must be paid in full before any dividends can be paid on the common stock. For example, if a corporation decides not to declare any dividends for a given year, resulting in a $7 cumulative preferred dividend being passed over, the preferred stock must receive $14 per share the next year before the common stock can receive any dividend. Likewise, if a $7 cumulative dividend is passed over two years in a row, in the third year the preferred stock must receive $21 per share before the common stock can receive a dividend.

Obviously, if dividend rights on preferred stock did not accumulate, it would be possible for the directors of a corporation to circumvent the rights of the preferred stockholders in favor of the common stockholders. Let us assume that the payment of a $7 preferred dividend is passed over in each of 5 years. If dividends are declared at the end of the sixth year, and the stock is noncumulative, it will receive only $7 before the common stock receives a dividend. However, if the stock is cumulative, it will be entitled to $42 (6 × $7) per share before the common stock is entitled to anything. To protect against the former situation, the law usually holds that unless stipulated otherwise, preferred stock is cumulative.

To illustrate further the cumulative feature, let us assume that an organization has 1,000 shares of $7 cumulative preferred stock and 2,000 shares of common stock outstanding and that it has $50,000 earnings to be distributed as dividends. In addition, let us assume that:

CASE 1   Preferred dividends have not been paid for the current year but have not been passed over in previous years.

CASE 2   Preferred dividends are 2 years in arrears. (That is, they were passed over last year and have not as yet been paid for the current year.)

CASE 3   Preferred dividends are 6 years in arrears.

CASE 4   Preferred dividends are 8 years in arrears.

The distributions would be determined as follows:

	Preferred Stock	*Common Stock*	*Total*
Case 1	$ 7,000 ($7 × 1,000)	$43,000 ($50,000 − $7,000)	$50,000
Case 2	14,000 ($7 × 2 × 1,000)	36,000 ($50,000 − $14,000)	50,000
Case 3	42,000 ($7 × 6 × 1,000)	8,000 ($50,000 − $42,000)	50,000
Case 4	50,000*	—	50,000

*The preferred stock receives the entire $50,000 since its claim of $56,000 ($7 × 8 × 1,000) exceeds the total amount to be distributed.

Participating and Nonparticipating Preferred Stock   Most preferred stock is **nonparticipating;** that is, the amount or percentage of earnings it can receive as dividends is limited according to prior legal agreement. However, there are times when provision is made for it to participate in a corporation's earnings in excess of its stipulated dividend. Such stock is known as **participating** stock. The procedure is this: The stipulated dividend is first paid on the preferred stock; then a dividend of the same amount, or one based on the same percentage rate, is paid on the common stock. After this is done, any additional earnings are divided between the preferred and common stockholders, either on a ratable basis if the stock is fully participating or according to any stipulated limitations if it has limited participation.

To illustrate both the cumulative and participating features at the same time, let us assume that a corporation has 1,000 shares of $7 preferred stock (par value $100) and 2,000 shares of common stock (par value $100) outstanding. Let us also assume that the corporation has $50,000 to be distributed as dividends, that preferred dividends have not been paid for 3 years including the current year, and that:

CASE 1 The preferred stock is noncumulative and nonparticipating.

CASE 2 The preferred stock is noncumulative but fully participating.

CASE 3 The preferred stock is cumulative but nonparticipating.

CASE 4 The preferred stock is cumulative and fully participating.

The distributions would be determined as follows:

	Preferred Stock	Common Stock	Total
Case 1	$ 7,000	$43,000	$50,000
Case 2	$16,667[1]	33,333[2]	50,000
Case 3	21,000[3]	29,000[4]	50,000
Case 4	26,000[5]	24,000[6]	50,000

[1] $\frac{1}{3} \times \$50,000 = \$16,667$
[2] $\frac{2}{3} \times \$50,000 = \$33,333$
[3] $\$7 \times 3 \times 1,000 = \$21,000$
[4] $\$50,000 - \$21,000 = \$29,000$
[5] $[(\$7 \times 3 \times 1,000) + (\frac{1}{3} \times \$15,000)] = \$26,000$
[6] $[(\$7 \times 2,000) + (\frac{2}{3} \times \$15,000)] = \$24,000$

Callable Preferred Stock A preferred stock issue will often contain what is known as a **callable** feature. This gives the issuing organization the right to redeem, or "call," the stock at a later date at a predetermined price. The "call price" is ordinarily an amount in excess of the original issue price, and is frequently stated in terms related to the par value. For example, a callable feature may give the issuing organization the right to redeem the preferred stock at 110 percent of par.

Convertible Preferred Stock   Preferred stock may be made additionally attractive to investors by the inclusion of a **convertible** feature which provides the stockholder with an option to convert it into common stock if he wishes.   Thus, if the corporation's common stock should become more desirable than its preferred stock as a result of unexpectedly large earnings or the prospect thereof, the preferred stockholder could exercise his option and become a common stockholder.

Corporate Owner Equity Accounts

As you have observed throughout the preceding chapters, the outlining of proper accounting procedures and the preparation of proper accounting entries for the operation of any account become matters of comparative simplicity once there is a clear understanding of the account's role and function.   Therefore, before we study corporate accounting in greater detail, it is important that we familiarize ourselves with the basic accounts peculiar to the corporation.

As we learned earlier, the composition and operation of asset, liability, revenue, and expense accounts are essentially the same in proprietorships, partnerships, and corporations.   The composition and operation of owner equity accounts, however, are somewhat dependent upon the existing form of business organization.   While account titles may vary from one organization to another, typical corporate owner equity accounts include:

1 Capital Stock
2 Capital in Excess of Par Value
3 Capital in Excess of Stated Value
4 Discount on Capital Stock
5 Retained Earnings
6 Treasury Stock

Capital Stock Account   The Capital Stock account reflects the par or stated value of the corporation's issued shares.   For example, if a corporation issues 1,000 shares of $10 par value stock, the Capital Stock account must be credited for $10,000. Likewise, the issuance by a corporation of 1,000 shares of no-par stock with a stated value of $1 per share would result in a credit of $1,000 to the Capital Stock account.   In T-account form, the issuance of the no-par stock would be reflected in the ledger as follows:

Capital Stock

	1,000

If a corporation issues more than one class of stock, a separate account, appropriately entitled, should be used for each class.   For example, if a corporation issues 2,000 shares of $100 par value common stock and 1,000 shares of $100 par value preferred stock, the capital stock accounts will appear as follows:

Common Stock

	200,000

Preferred Stock

	100,000

Capital in Excess of Par Value When a corporation sells par value stock at an amount in excess of its par value, the excess is credited to an appropriately labeled account, such as Capital in Excess of Par Value or Premium on Capital Stock. For example, if a corporation sells 1,000 shares of $10 par value stock at $15 a share, the Capital Stock account will be credited for $10 a share, and the Capital in Excess of Par Value account will be credited for $5 a share, as follows:

Capital Stock

	10,000

Capital in Excess of Par Value

	5,000

Capital in Excess of Stated Value When a corporation sells no-par stock with a stated value at an amount in excess of its stated value, the excess is credited to an appropriately labeled account, for example, Capital in Excess of Stated Value. Thus, if a corporation sells 1,000 shares of no-par stock with a stated value of $1 per share for $15 per share, the Capital Stock account will be credited for $1,000 (1,000 × $1) and the Capital in Excess of Stated Value account will be credited for $14,000 (10,000 × $14), as follows:

Capital Stock

	1,000

Capital in Excess of Stated Value

	14,000

Discount on Capital Stock When a corporation sells par value stock for an amount less than its par value, the deficiency (difference between par and the issue price) is debited to an appropriately labeled account, for example, Discount on Capital Stock. Let us assume that a corporation sells 1,000 shares of $10 par value stock for $8 a share; the Capital Stock account will be credited for $10,000

$(1,000 \times \$10)$ and the Discount on Capital Stock account will be debited for $2,000
$(1,000 \times \$2)$, as follows:

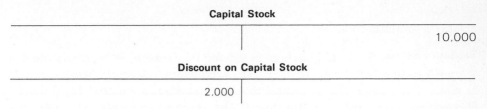

Capital Stock

	10,000

Discount on Capital Stock

2,000	

When the balance sheet is prepared, the Discount on Capital Stock account
is handled as a **contra** account; that is, its debit balance is offset against (deducted
from) the credit balance in the Capital Stock account in order to show the amount
of capital actually contributed by the stockholders.

It is important to note that we do not amortize the Discount on Capital Stock
account as we do the Discount on Bonds Payable account. You will recall that
the issuance of bonds at a discount is in reality an adjustment of the rate of interest,
and as a consequence should be amortized against income. Such is not the case
with the issuance of stock at a discount. This is a capital transaction and should
not be allowed to enter into the determination of net income.

Retained Earnings At the inception of a business organization, the balances in
the owner equity accounts are composed of the resources invested in the organization by the owners. As the business grows and prospers, however, its owner
equity increases as a result of profitable operations. The owner equity of a going
concern is then normally composed of two increments, one of which we might
think of as "invested capital" and the other as "earned capital."

In an individual proprietorship there is ordinarily no need to account for these
increments separately. This is also true in a partnership, unless the partnership
agreement restricts the capital to the original investment and provides for the
immediate distribution of all earnings to the partners. Under the corporate form
of business organization, however, generally it is legally required that invested
capital be segregated from earned capital both in the accounts and on the financial
statements. As the title implies, the Retained Earnings account is the account
used to reflect the earned capital.

We learned earlier in this chapter that the Revenue and Expense Summary
account is closed into the Retained Earnings account in the closing process. As
we shall see in Chapter 17, dividend distributions are charged to the Retained
Earnings account. Thus, the balance in the Retained Earnings account as of the
balance sheet date is composed of the accumulated earnings of the organization
minus any losses and minus all dividends which have been distributed to the
stockholders since inception. The basic operation of the Retained Earnings account may be summarized in T-account form as follows:

Retained Earnings

Debited for:	Credited for:
1 Losses	1 Profits
2 Dividend distributions	

Treasury Stock Stock that has been issued and later reacquired by a corporation is known as **treasury stock.** It is normally reflected in a Treasury Stock account at cost. For example, let us assume that a corporation reacquired 1,000 shares of its outstanding stock at $10 a share. The Treasury Stock account would be debited for $10,000, as follows:

Treasury Stock

10,000	

Although the Treasury Stock account has a debit balance, treasury stock is not an asset. Rather it is a negative owner equity account. That is, it is deducted from the total of all the other owner equity accounts when the balance sheet is prepared.

COMPUTING BOOK VALUE PER SHARE

As we noted earlier in this chapter, when there is only one class of stock outstanding, the book value per share is determined simply by dividing the dollar amount of the owner equity by the number of shares outstanding. Thus, the basic formula for computing book value per share is:

$$\frac{\text{Owner equity}}{\text{Number of shares outstanding}}$$

Book value computations become more involved when there is more than one class of stock outstanding, as the respective rights of each class must be taken into consideration. For example, the rights of preferred stockholders may involve a consideration of callable, participating, and cumulative features. In such cases we must first determine the preferred stock's claim against the total dollar amount of the owner equity and then allocate the remainder of the owner equity to the common shares. Using the abbreviation BV for book value and OE for owner equity, we now have the following basic formula:

$$\text{Preferred BV per share} = \frac{\text{preferred claim against OE}}{\text{preferred shares outstanding}}$$

$$\text{Common BV per share} = \frac{\text{common claim against OE}}{\text{common shares outstanding}}$$

To illustrate book value per share computations when more than one class of stock is outstanding, let us assume the following account balances:

Common stock ($10 par value)	$200,000
Preferred stock ($100 par value)	100,000
Capital in excess of par value	50,000
Retained earnings	150,000
Total owner equity	$500,000

Let us also assume that the organization has 20,000 shares of common and 1,000 shares of $7 cumulative preferred stock outstanding and that:

CASE 1 Preferred dividends have been paid to date.

CASE 2 Preferred dividends are 2 years in arrears.

CASE 3 Preferred dividends have been paid to date, but the preferred stock is callable at 110 percent of par.

CASE 4 Preferred dividends are 2 years in arrears, and the preferred stock is callable at 110 percent of par.

The computations would be as follows:

	Case 1	Case 2	Case 3	Case 4
Total OE	$500,000	$500,000	$500,000	$500,000
Preferred Stock:				
Claim	$100,000[1]	$114,000[2]	$110,000[3]	$124,000[4]
Shares outstanding	1,000	1,000	1,000	1,000
BV per share	$100	$114	$110	$124
Common Stock:				
Claim	$400,000	$386,000	$390,000	$376,000
Shares outstanding	20,000	20,000	20,000	20,000
BV per share	$20.00	$19.30	$19.50	$18.80

[1]$100,000 par
[2][$100,000 par + ($7 × 1,000 × 2)]
[3](110% × $100,000 par)
[4][(110% × $100,000 par) + ($7 × 1,000 × 2)]

SPECIAL CORPORATE RECORDS AND PROCEDURES

Since many corporations have large numbers of stockholders, it would not be feasible for their general ledgers to contain accounts with each of the various owners. In addition, the composition of the stockholder group may constantly change as the result of transfers of stock. Therefore, in addition to the usual ledgers and books of original entry, most corporations employ certain special books and records and also require that a few procedures be followed which differ from those in a proprietorship or partnership.

Corporate Books and Records

Some of the more important books and records peculiar to the corporate form of business organization are:

1 Minute book
2 Stock certificate book
3 Stockholders' ledger

Minute Book The minute book is used to record the official proceedings of the meetings of the stockholders and the board of directors. It is kept by the secretary of the corporation, and all resolutions offered and actions taken thereon are recorded in it. From an accounting standpoint, the minute book frequently serves as a basis for journal entries. For example, the declaration of a dividend by the board of directors is first reflected in the minute book and then in the appropriate book of original entry.

Stock Certificate Book A stock certificate book contains blank prenumbered stock certificates and stubs, somewhat like a checkbook. When stock is sold, both the certificate and the stub are filled out with (1) the name of the stockholder, (2) the number of shares, and (3) the date issued. The certificate is sent to the stockholder, and the stub is retained by the corporation as a record of stock outstanding. When a stockholder sells his shares, his certificate is returned to the corporation, canceled, and as a general rule, attached to the corresponding stub in the stock certificate book. A new certificate is issued to the new stockholder, and a new stub is filled out to correspond.

Stockholders' Ledger A stockholders' ledger is a subsidiary ledger which contains a separate account for each stockholder of the corporation. It supports a controlling account such as Capital Stock, Common Stock, or Preferred Stock. The individual stockholders' accounts in the stockholders' ledger do not reflect dollar amounts; instead the number of shares owned, certificate numbers, and various purchase and sale dates are recorded therein.

Transfer Agent and Registrar

Most large corporations, as well as many smaller ones, turn the issuance and transfer of their stock over to an independent outside agency. In fact, if a corporation's stock is traded on a stock exchange, the appointment of such an agency is usually mandatory. The New York Stock Exchange, for example, requires corporations whose stock is traded thereon to maintain facilities close to the Exchange for both the transfer and registration of the stock. In addition, it requires that the transfer agent and the registrar shall not be identical, and that both be acceptable to the Exchange. As a general rule, transfer agents and registrars are banks or trust companies.

When the ownership of stock is transferred from one person to another through a transfer agent and a registrar, the stock certificates are sent to the transfer agent. He cancels the old certificates and forwards new ones to the registrar for registration. Registration of stock certificates is essential to prevent their improper issuance. With millions of shares of stock being traded on the various stock exchanges daily, the need for a fast, reliable transfer service becomes obvious.

SUMMARY

A business corporation is a unit formed and controlled by an association of private individuals for the purpose of making a profit. It must be authorized by a charter from the state or federal government.

The owners of a corporation are known as stockholders, or shareholders. Their ownership interests are evidenced by shares of stock. Authorized shares are those shares of stock which a corporation is permitted to issue under its charter. Until shares have been issued to a stockholder, they are known as unissued shares. Once issued, they are called issued shares. Issued shares in the hands of stockholders are referred to as outstanding shares. Issued shares reacquired by a corporation are known as treasury shares.

Many corporations issue both common and preferred stock in order to appeal to a wide range of investors. Preferred stock may be cumulative or noncumulative, and participating or nonparticipating.

Overall corporate plans and policies are determined by a board of directors elected by the stockholders and are implemented by corporate officers elected or appointed by the board of directors.

Corporate owner equity accounts differ from those in proprietorships and partnerships, as do certain corporate records and procedures. Most of the problems in accounting for corporations relate to the owner equity accounts.

The corporate form of business organization tends to eliminate most of the major legal disadvantages of the partnership.

QUESTIONS AND PROBLEMS

15-1 What are the basic legal requirements for the formation of a corporation?

15-2 In general, what are the basic rights of a stockholder?

15-3 Define the following terms as they are used in reference to a share of stock: (1) authorized shares, (2) unissued shares, (3) subscribed shares, (4) treasury shares, and (5) outstanding shares.

15-4 Define the following terms as they are used in reference to a share of stock: (1) par value, (2) no-par value, (3) stated value, (4) market value, and (5) book value.

*15-5 The owners of the P. K. Leash Company, a closely held corporation, have offered to sell their 100 percent interest in the company's common stock at an amount equal to the book value of the common stock. They will retain their interest in the company's preferred stock.

(1) Explain the significance of "book value" in establishing a value for a business which is expected to continue in operations indefinitely.

(2) Describe the procedure for computing book values of corporate ownership equities.

15-6 Define the terms cumulative and participating as they apply to preferred stock.

15-7 Indicate briefly the major legal differences between a corporation and a partnership.

15-8 What is meant by the preemptive right of a stockholder?

15-9 Describe briefly the purpose of the following corporate records: (1) minute book, (2) stock certificate book, and (3) stockholders' ledger.

15-10 As of January 1, Corporation Z was granted a charter which authorized it to issue 10,000 shares of common stock, par value $10 per share. On February 1, the corporation sold 4,000 shares of the stock at $15 per share and on March 1, it sold an additional 3,000 shares at $18 per share. On April 1, the corporation purchased 1,000 shares of the stock in the market at $13 per share.

*AICPA adapted.

Instructions Prepare a schedule showing the number of shares outstanding as of January 1, February 1, March 1, and April 1.

15-11 Instructions Corporation B has 3,000 shares of $5 preferred stock and 6,000 shares of common stock outstanding. The preferred stock is cumulative but nonparticipating. The company has $70,000 available for the payment of dividends. Show how the dividends would be distributed assuming that:

CASE 1 Preferred dividends have not been paid during the current year but have not been passed over in previous years.

CASE 2 Preferred dividends are 2 years in arrears including the current year.

CASE 3 Preferred dividends are 4 years in arrears including the current year.

CASE 4 Preferred dividends are 5 years in arrears including the current year.

15-12 Instructions Corporation A has 2,000 shares of $8 preferred stock and 8,000 shares of common stock outstanding. Preferred dividends have not been paid for 2 years including the current year. The company has $100,000 available for the payment of dividends. Show how the distribution would be made assuming that:

CASE 1 The preferred stock is noncumulative and nonparticipating.

CASE 2 The preferred stock is cumulative but nonparticipating.

CASE 3 The preferred stock is noncumulative but fully participating.

CASE 4 The preferred stock is cumulative and fully participating.

15-13 You have been retained by the preferred stockholders of Corporation M to determine whether the amount of dividends paid to them during the last 3 years was correct. The corporation received its charter on January 1, 19X1, and since that time has had $100,000 of 6 percent preferred and $200,000 of common stock outstanding. Both the common and the preferred stock have a par value of $10 per share. The preferred stock is cumulative and fully participating.

Instructions If the following schedule of payments is incorrect, prepare a correct one.

	Net Income	Dividends Paid Preferred	Common
19X1	$ 5,000	—	$ 5,000
19X2	12,000	$ 6,000	6,000
19X3	24,000	9,000	15,000
	$41,000	$15,000	$26,000

15-14 The following data were taken from the accounts of the R & J Corporation:

Common stock	$ 500,000
Preferred stock	300,000
Capital in excess of par value	400,000
Retained earnings	200,000
	$1,400,000

Instructions The company has 20,000 shares of common and 12,000 shares of $4 cumulative preferred stock outstanding. Compute the book value per share of stock (both common and preferred), assuming that:

CASE 1 Preferred dividends have been paid to date.

CASE 2 Preferred dividends are 3 years in arrears.

CASE 3 Preferred dividends have been paid to date, but the preferred stock is callable at 105 percent of par.

CASE 4 Preferred dividends are 4 years in arrears and the preferred stock is callable at 110 percent of par.

15-15 Company C has the same number of shares of both preferred and common stock outstanding. The preferred stock has a par value of $100 per share and the common stock has a stated value of $10 per share. The preferred stock was issued at its par value and the common was issued at its stated value. The preferred stock is 6 percent cumulative and is callable at 105 percent of its par value.

Instructions Determine the book value per share of both the common and the preferred stock, assuming that the balance in the Retained Earnings account is equal to $275 per combined par and stated value of one share each of the common and preferred (that is, $110), and that:

CASE 1 Preferred dividends have been paid to date.

CASE 2 Preferred dividends are 2 years in arrears.

CASE 3 Preferred dividends are 5 years in arrears.

15-16 The following information was taken from the owner equity section of a corporate balance sheet:

7% preferred stock ($5 par value)	$150,000
Common stock ($5 par value)	500,000
Capital in excess of par value	90,000
Retained earnings	40,000
Total owner equity	$780,000

Instructions In each of the following cases, determine the book value per share of each class of stock, assuming that the:

CASE 1 Preferred stock is cumulative with dividends paid to date.

CASE 2 Preferred stock is cumulative and is callable at 110 percent of par. Dividends are paid to date.

CASE 3 Preferred stock is cumulative with dividends 6 years in arrears.

CASE 4 Preferred stock is cumulative and is callable at 110 percent of par. Dividends are 12 years in arrears.

15-17 The following data were taken from the owner equity section of a corporate balance sheet:

8% preferred stock (10,000 shares issued)	$125,000
Common stock (40,000 shares issued)	500,000
Capital in excess of par value	20,000
Retained earnings	25,000
Treasury stock (10,000 shares of common)	80,000

Instructions For each of the following cases, determine the book value per share of each class of stock, assuming that the:

CASE 1 Preferred stock is cumulative with dividends 2 years in arrears.

CASE 2 Preferred stock is cumulative and is callable at 108 percent of par. Dividends are 2 years in arrears.

CASE 3 Preferred stock is cumulative with dividends 5 years in arrears.

CASE 4 Preferred stock is cumulative and is callable at 115 percent of par. Dividends are 6 years in arrears.

15-18 The following items appear on the liability and owner equity side of the balance sheet of the R. S. Corporation on September 30, 19X4:

Current liabilities	$103,732
Bonds payable	300,000
Reserve for bond retirement	160,000
6% cumulative preferred stock, $100 par value (callable at 110% of par); authorized—3,000 shares, issued and outstanding—1,850 shares	185,000
Common stock, $100 par value; authorized—10,000 shares, issued and outstanding—4,000 shares	400,000
Capital in excess of par value	77,300
Retained earnings	131,260

Instructions Compute the book value per share of common stock as of September 30, 19X4. (Preferred dividends have been paid or set up as payable through September 30, 19X4.)

15-19 The Fisher Corporation has $100,000 of 6 percent preferred stock and $200,000 of common stock outstanding. Both the preferred and common have a $5 par value per share. All the stock was issued at par when the corporation was formed in 19X1. Earnings for 19X1 were $60,000; for 19X2, $80,000; and for 19X3, $100,000. No dividends have been paid since the corporation was formed.

Instructions Determine the book value per share of each class of stock, assuming a contemplated distribution of a dividend of $72,000 under each of the following conditions:

CASE 1 Preferred stock is noncumulative and nonparticipating.

CASE 2 Preferred stock is cumulative but nonparticipating.

CASE 3 Preferred stock is cumulative and fully participating.

15-20 A corporation presents the following condensed balance sheet as of the close of the current year:

Condensed Balance Sheet

Assets ————————	$1,602,000	Liabilities ———————	$ 500,000
		6% preferred stock ——	300,000
		8% preferred stock ——	200,000
		Common stock ————	500,000
		Retained earnings ——	102,000
	$1,602,000		$1,602,000

The 6 percent stock is cumulative but nonparticipating. The 8 percent stock is cumulative and fully participating. Both the common stock and the preferred stock have a par value of $10 per share.

Instructions Compute the book value per share of stock for each class of stock, assuming that:

CASE 1 Dividends have not been paid for the current year.

CASE 2 Dividends have not been paid for 2 years.

CASE 3 Dividends have not been paid for 3 years.

16

Corporations: Capital Stock Transactions

Now that we have become familiar with the more important legal ramifications of the formation of a corporation, the fundamental differences between the partnership and the corporation, and terminology and procedures peculiar to the corporation, we shall concentrate in this chapter on some of the accounting problems involved. These problems will generally be found, as we have already noted, in the owner equity area. In corporate terminology the terms **shareholder equity** and **stockholder equity** are often used in lieu of owner equity, and in this text we shall use the former.

INVESTED CAPITAL VERSUS EARNED CAPITAL

In the corporate form of business organization, a clear distinction between invested and earned capital must be maintained at all times; this is essential from the standpoint of both the stockholder and the creditor. For example, when a stockholder receives a distribution of assets in the form of a dividend, he is entitled to know whether these assets have resulted from operations or whether they are in reality a return of a portion of his invested capital. (Unless notified otherwise, the stockholder generally assumes that dividends result from earnings.)

Corporate creditors also have an interest in the proper distinction between invested and earned capital. The invested capital is generally considered to be a sort of minimum buffer, or margin of safety, for the creditors; hence, any reduction of this capital through its distribution to stockholders throws additional risks on the creditors. The importance of the buffer becomes apparent when we contrast the limited liability feature of the corporation with the unlimited liability aspect of the proprietorship and the partnership. Under the latter forms of business organization, as you recall, if a creditor's claim cannot be satisfied from the assets of the business, it attaches to the personal assets of the proprietor or partners. Thus, the distinction between invested and earned capital in proprietorships and partnerships is of little importance to the creditor. In corporations, however, since only corporate assets are available for use in satisfying creditor claims, it is essential that there be some limitation on dividend distribution.

A distinction between invested and earned capital is generally accomplished in a corporation by:

1 Maintaining separate accounts in which to reflect invested capital transactions
2 Maintaining separate accounts in which to reflect the results of operations
3 Distinguishing between invested capital and earned capital on the financial statements

Since the transactions involved are associated primarily with the Capital Stock and Retained Earnings accounts, for discussion purposes we shall refer to invested capital transactions as **capital stock transactions** and to earned capital transactions as **retained earnings transactions.** We shall concentrate on the former in this chapter and on the latter in Chapter 17.

From an accounting standpoint, the problems associated with the capital stock transactions of a corporation normally pertain to:

1 Authorization of capital stock
2 Issuance of capital stock
3 Reacquisition of capital stock
4 Financial statement presentation of capital stock

AUTHORIZATION OF CAPITAL STOCK

Authorization for a corporation to issue capital stock does not, in itself, fit into our concept of a transaction; that is, no exchange of value takes place. Thus, as a general rule, the first record made on the books of a corporation is not in the form of our usual journal entry but is, instead, a statement in narrative form made in the general journal regarding the opening of the organization. In accounting terminology, such a statement is usually called a **memorandum entry.**

To illustrate the use of the memorandum entry to record the authorization of capital stock, let us assume that the ABC Corporation was authorized by the State of Delaware as of January 1, 19X2, to issue 1 million shares of common stock with a $5 par value and 25,000 shares of $100 par value, 6 percent cumulative preferred stock. In addition to the memorandum entry in the general journal, ledger T accounts are also included.

General Journal

19X2		Memorandum					
Jan.	1	The ABC Corporation has this day (January 1, 19X2) been authorized by the State of Delaware to issue 1,000,000 shares of $5 par value common stock and 25,000 shares of $100 par value, 6% cumulative preferred stock.					

Common Stock

(1,000,000 shares authorized with a $5 par value)

Preferred Stock

(25,000 shares authorized with a $100 par value)

ISSUANCE OF CAPITAL STOCK

When the issuance of capital stock is recorded, it makes little difference whether the stock is common or preferred. Therefore, we shall not concern ourselves now with the various classes of capital stock. Just remember that when we record the issuance of *both* common and preferred stock, we identify the respective capital stock accounts by including the terms "common" and "preferred."

Although the class of stock is not important to us at this time, it is necessary that we know whether the stock being issued is par value or no-par stock, whether it is being issued for cash or for property other than cash, and whether it is being sold outright or on a subscription basis. Each case presents a different problem.

We ordinarily think of capital stock as being issued when a new business is formed or when an existing corporation issues additional stock. Sometimes, however, a proprietorship or partnership will incorporate and thereby require the issuance of capital stock. Certain incidental costs incurred in the issuance of capital stock also must be accounted for. Consequently, this section will be devoted to problems in accounting for:

1 Issuance of par value stock

2 Issuance of no-par stock

3 Issuance of stock for property other than cash

4 Issuance of stock on a subscription basis

5 Incorporation of an existing proprietorship or partnership

6 Stock issue costs

Issuance of Par Value Stock

Capital stock with a par value may be issued at par, above par, or below par. In all cases, the Capital Stock account must be credited for the par value of the stock, with any difference between par and the issue price being credited to the Capital in Excess of Par Value account or debited to the Discount on Capital Stock account, depending upon whether the stock is issued at a premium (above par) or at a discount (below par).

To illustrate the procedure for recording the issuance of par value stock, let us assume that a corporation sells 1,000 shares of $100 par value stock:

CASE 1 At $100 per share

CASE 2 At $120 per share

CASE 3 At $90 per share

The entries would appear in general journal form as follows:

Case 1

Cash	100,000	
Capital Stock		100,000
To record the issuance of par value stock at par.		

Case 2

Cash	120,000	
Capital Stock		100,000
Capital in Excess of Par Value		20,000
To record the issuance of par value stock at a premium.		

Case 3

Cash	90,000	
Discount on Capital Stock	10,000	
Capital Stock		100,000
To record the issuance of par value stock at a discount.		

Issuance of No-par Stock

You will recall from Chapter 15 that there is no relationship between the par value of a share of stock and what it is actually worth as determined by its market value. For example, a share of stock may have a par value of $100 but be worth little or nothing on the market. When the corporate form of business was first established and only par value stock was used, unscrupulous corporate promoters often misled investors into believing that a stock's par value was its true worth. Similarly, when capital stock was issued for property other than cash, as is sometimes done, if the par value of the stock was greater than the actual value of the property, corporate directors had a tendency to value the property in the accounts at the stock's par value rather than to record the issuance of the stock at a discount. This was done because in certain states both the directors and stockholders could be held liable by creditors for the amount of the discount. Needless to say, this practice often gave rise to gross overvaluations of assets. For example, intangible assets such as goodwill, patents, copyrights, and franchises frequently appeared in financial statements at absurdly high amounts.

In order to protect the unsophisticated investor from being misled by the implied representation that a share of stock is worth its par value, and to prevent corporate directors from being more or less forced into overvaluing assets, the State of New York in 1912 enacted legislation permitting the issuance of no-par stock. Today, practically all states permit its use.

The theory underlying no-par stock is based upon the fact that in the final analysis a share of stock represents nothing more or less than a proportionate interest in the ownership of a corporation. However, in order to provide creditors with some assurance that their claims against a corporation will be protected at least to a certain extent, most state statutes require that a stated value be assigned to no-par shares. Like the amount of par, this amount must be permanently dedicated to the business for the protection of the creditors. Stated value may be:

1 A legal minimum established by statute

2 An amount in excess of the legal minimum, such amount being established by the corporate directors

3 The total amount received for no-par stock

To illustrate the procedure for recording the issuance of no-par stock, let us assume that a corporation sells 1,000 shares of no-par stock for a total amount of $15,000 and that:

CASE 1 Stated value is considered to be the legally established minimum of $1 per share.

CASE 2 Stated value as established by the board of directors is $5 per share.

CASE 3 Stated value is considered to be the total amount received for the stock.

We learned in Chapter 15 that when recording the issuance of no-par stock, we must credit the Capital Stock account for the stated value and credit the difference between the stated value and the value of the assets received to the Capital in Excess of Stated Value account. Thus, in our current illustration we would (1) debit the Cash account for $15,000, (2) credit the Capital Stock account for the stated value in each instance, and (3) credit the Capital in Excess of Stated Value account for the difference between (1) and (2)—that is, the difference between the amount of cash received and the stated value. In abbreviated journal form, the entries would be:

	Debit	Credits		
		Case 1	*Case 2*	*Case 3*
Cash _____	15,000			
Capital Stock _____		1,000	5,000	15,000
Capital in Excess of Stated Value _____		14,000	10,000	—

Issuance of Stock for Property Other Than Cash

Thus far, all of our illustrations pertaining to the issuance of capital stock have been based on the assumption that the stock was being issued for cash. This may not always be the case. Some of the invested capital of a corporation may result from contributions of property other than cash. For example, capital stock may be issued for fixed tangible property such as land, buildings, and equipment, or for intangible property such as goodwill, patents, copyrights, and franchises.

When capital stock is issued for property other than cash, the property received should be recorded at either its fair market value (FMV) or the fair market value of the stock issued, whichever is more clearly evident. For example, if the FMV of the stock is readily determinable, we use it as a basis for recording the transaction. If it is not readily determinable but that of the property being received is, we use the FMV of the property as the basis for recording the transaction. If neither the FMV of the stock being issued nor the property being received is readily determinable, the value to be assigned is determined by an appraisal of the property, and the transaction is recorded on the basis of the appraised valuation. Appraisals of this nature are made by or under the direction of the board of directors. In order to be as objective as possible, independent third parties are frequently brought in to make such appraisals.

To illustrate the procedure for recording the issuance of stock for property other than cash, let us assume that a corporation issues 1,000 shares of $10 par value stock for a building and that:

CASE 1 The FMV of the stock is determined to be $110 per share.

CASE 2 The FMV of the stock is not readily determinable, but the FMV of the building is determined to be $108,000.

CASE 3 Neither the FMV of the stock nor the FMV of the property is readily determinable. An appraisal company appraises the building as being worth $105,000.

To record the various cases, all we have to do is (1) debit the value of the asset received to the appropriate asset account (the Building account in this instance), (2) credit the Capital Stock account for the par value of the stock issued, and (3) credit the Capital in Excess of Par Value account for the difference between (1) and (2)—that is, the difference between the value of the asset received and the par value of the stock issued. In journal form the entries would be:

Case 1

Building (FMV of the stock)	110,000	
Capital Stock (1,000 × $10)		10,000
Capital in Excess of Par Value		100,000

Case 2

Building (FMV of the building)	108,000	
Capital Stock (1,000 × $10)		10,000
Capital in Excess of Par Value		98,000

Case 3

Building (Appraised value of the building)	105,000	
Capital Stock (1,000 × $10)		10,000
Capital in Excess of Par Value		95,000

Issuance of Stock on a Subscription Basis

In all our preceding illustrations dealing with the issuance of capital stock, we have assumed that the consideration to be received by the corporation in exchange for the stock was receivable in full at the time the stock was issued. However, this may not always be the case. On occasion, when stock is purchased on a subscription basis, a stockholder may agree to pay for the stock over a period of time rather than in one lump sum.

From the corporation's point of view, the claim against the subscriber is a receivable. It is accounted for in the same way as any other receivable in an account ordinarily called Stock Subscriptions Receivable. This account is debited for the amount of the claim and credited when payments are received. If the account has a balance at the time the balance sheet is prepared and payment is expected within the current operating cycle or one year, it is classified on the statement as a current asset.

Since the subscription to capital stock is a capital transaction, the increase in the corporate asset accounts must be matched by an increase in the shareholder equity accounts. As the stock will not be issued until final payment is received, the accountant ordinarily uses a temporary capital account called Capital Stock Subscribed to account for the par or stated value of the subscribed stock. This account is credited at the time the subscription is received, and debited when the final payment is received and the stock is issued. If the account has a balance at the time the balance sheet is prepared, it is included in the shareholder equity section of the statement.

To illustrate the accounting procedures involved in the issuance of capital stock on a subscription basis, let us assume that a corporation is authorized to issue 10,000 shares of $5 par value stock and that:

1 As of January 1, 19X2, the corporation received subscriptions for 4,000 shares at $18 per share, with a down payment of 50 percent of the subscription price.

2 On April 1, 19X2, the corporation received 50 percent of the balance due from all subscribers.

3 On July 1, 19X2, the corporation received the balance due from all subscribers, and the stock was issued.

The entries and T accounts to record the transactions follow:

(1)

Stock Subscriptions Receivable	72,000	
Capital Stock Subscribed		20,000
Capital in Excess of Par Value		52,000
Cash ($\frac{1}{2} \times$ $72,000)	36,000	
Stock Subscriptions Receivable		36,000

(2)

Cash ($\frac{1}{2} \times$ $36,000)	18,000	
Stock Subscriptions Receivable		18,000

(3)

Cash ($72,000 − $36,000 − $18,000)	18,000	
Stock Subscriptions Receivable		18,000
Capital Stock Subscribed	20,000	
Capital Stock		20,000

Stock Subscriptions Receivable

(1)	72,000	(1)	36,000
		(2)	18,000
		(3)	18,000
	72,000		72,000

Capital Stock Subscribed

(3)	20,000	(1)	20,000

Capital Stock		**Capital in Excess of Par Value**	
(3)	20,000	(1)	52,000

When studying the entries and T accounts, note that the ultimate effect is the same as it would have been if the stock had initially been issued for cash. That is, the Cash account has been increased $72,000 (the subscription price), the Capital Stock account has been increased $20,000 (the par value of the stock issued), and the Capital in Excess of Par Value account has been increased $52,000 (the difference between the subscription price and par).

When a corporation sells capital stock on a subscription basis, there is always the possibility that a subscriber may pay a portion of the subscription price and fail to pay the balance. In such cases the corporation must act in accordance with the laws of the state of incorporation. In some states the defaulting subscriber must forfeit the amount he has paid in; in others he may have the right to a refund, or he may be entitled to the number of shares for which he has, in effect, paid in full. If a defaulting subscriber forfeits any of the amount he has paid in, it becomes part of the invested capital of the corporation and should be reflected in an appropriately labeled account, such as Capital from Forfeited Subscriptions.

Incorporation of an Existing Proprietorship or Partnership

Whereas the process of forming and incorporating an entirely new business requires (1) state authorization, (2) issuance of capital stock, and (3) the acquisition of assets, the incorporation of an existing business usually requires only (1) state authorization and (2) the issuance of capital stock. The acquisition of the charter is essentially a legal matter; thus, the primary accounting problems are associated with the issuance of stock. It is important to recognize, however, that the assets acquired and liabilities assumed by the newly created organization must be correctly reflected in its accounts. This not only means that all existing assets and liabilities of the old business must be reflected in the accounts of the newly created organization, but also that they must be valued appropriately therein. Since liabilities are contractual in nature, their existence and amounts are usually easily determined; however, this may not be true of assets. The existence of an asset can ordinarily be rather readily determined, but its value may not be so easy to ascertain. Thus, when accounting for the incorporation of an existing proprietorship or partnership, the accountant may have to handle problems associated with the valuation of the assets as well as with the issuance of capital stock. In reality, however, as we saw earlier when dealing with the issuance of stock for property other than cash, these two areas are interrelated and as a consequence the solutions are interdependent.

As you will recall from the earlier section on the issuance of stock for property other than cash, we record the transaction at the stock's fair market value or the fair market value of the assets received, whichever is more clearly evident. If neither is readily determinable, the transaction is recorded on the basis of the appraised value of the property being received. In the illustration that follows, since the stock has never been issued and as a consequence no "market" for it exists, we shall use the fair market value of the property received as the basis for recording the transaction.

To illustrate the incorporation of a partnership, let us assume that Able, Baker, and Cain, owners of the A & B Partnership, are granted a corporate charter authorizing them to incorporate the partnership under the name ABC, Inc., and to issue 10,000 shares of $5 par value stock. In addition, let us assume that Able, Baker, and Cain shared partnership profits and losses equally, and that they are to receive 6,000 shares of the authorized stock on a basis proportionate to the balances in their capital accounts, after any adjustments which may be deemed necessary as a result of incorporating are provided for.

A trial balance of the partnership as of the date of incorporation follows. Note that all nominal accounts have been closed. This is as it should be, since only the assets and liabilities will be recorded on the books of the corporation, with the partners' capital accounts being replaced by the corporate capital accounts.

A & B PARTNERSHIP
Trial Balance
As of Date of Incorporation

Cash	$ 10,000	
Accounts receivable	20,000	
Allowance for uncollectible accounts		$ 2,000
Merchandise inventory	40,000	
Equipment	30,000	
Accumulated depreciation—equipment		6,000
Accounts payable		32,000
James Able, capital		25,000
Fred Baker, capital		20,000
Tom Cain, capital		15,000
	$100,000	$100,000

The fair market value of the partnership property as of the date of incorporation is determined to be the same as the book value of the assets as shown on the partnership books, except for the fair market value of the inventory, which is determined to be $55,000 rather than $40,000. Since Able, Baker, and Cain will not necessarily be sharing profits and losses in the corporation on the same basis as they did in the partnership, the following entry should be made before incorporating:

Merchandise Inventory	15,000	
James Able, Capital		5,000
Fred Baker, Capital		5,000
Tom Cain, Capital		5,000

After the above adjustment is made, our next entries depend upon whether the old books are to be retained or new books are to be opened. If the old books are to be retained, all we have to do is substitute corporate capital accounts for the partnership capital accounts. This is accomplished, of course, by debiting the capital accounts of the partnership and crediting the capital accounts of the corporation as follows:

James Able, Capital	30,000	
Fred Baker, Capital	25,000	
Tom Cain, Capital	20,000	
Capital Stock (6,000 × $5)		30,000
Capital in Excess of Par Value		45,000

To record the incorporation of the A & B Partnership into ABC, Inc.

If new books are to be opened, we must close out all the accounts on the partnership books and open new corporate books. The partnership accounts are closed out by merely "debiting the credits" and "crediting the debits." The corporate books are opened by (1) recording the assets acquired at their cost to the corporation, (2) recording the liabilities assumed, and (3) crediting the difference between (1) and (2) to the appropriate corporate capital accounts. In the illustration that follows, note that whereas we record the equipment net of the accumulated depreciation, we do not record the accounts receivable net of the allowance for uncollectibles. Since we do not as yet know which receivables will not be collected, it is best to record them at the gross amount. The closing of the partnership books and the opening of corporate books, as well as the computation involved in the allocation of the 6,000 shares of ABC, Inc., stock to Able, Baker, and Cain, are shown.

Partnership Books

Allowance for Uncollectible Accounts	2,000	
Accumulated Depreciation—Equipment	6,000	
Accounts Payable	32,000	
James Able, Capital	30,000	
Fred Baker, Capital	25,000	
Tom Cain, Capital	20,000	
Cash		10,000
Accounts Receivable		20,000
Merchandise Inventory		55,000
Equipment		30,000

To close out the books of the A & B Partnership

Corporate Books

Cash	10,000	
Accounts Receivable	20,000	
Merchandise Inventory	55,000	
Equipment ($30,000 − $6,000)	24,000	
Allowance for Uncollectible Accounts		2,000
Accounts Payable		32,000
Capital Stock (6,000 × $5)		30,000
Capital in Excess of Par Value		45,000

To open the books of ABC, Inc.

When the 6,000 shares of ABC, Inc., stock are issued to Able, Baker, and Cain on a basis proportionate to the balances in their capital accounts after any necessary adjustments are provided for, Able will receive 2,400 shares, Baker 2,000 shares, and Cain 1,600 shares, determined as follows:

	Capital Balances	Computation		Distribution of Shares
Able ————	$30,000	30,000/75,000 × 6,000	=	2,400
Baker ————	25,000	25,000/75,000 × 6,000	=	2,000
Cain ————	20,000	20,000/75,000 × 6,000	=	1,600
	$75,000			6,000

Accounting for Stock Issue Costs

The cost of issuing capital stock is charged to an intangible asset account called Organization Costs. This is done whether the cost is associated with the original issue at the time the corporation is formed or with a subsequent issue. Such costs include professional fees paid to accountants and lawyers whose services are directly related to the issue of the stock, as well as printing costs, clerical costs, and taxes and fees paid to the appropriate governmental agencies.

In addition to the cost of issuing stock, the cost of formally organizing the corporation is also charged to this account. This includes legal fees, taxes and fees paid to state agencies, and promotional costs incurred in founding the organization.

Like other intangible assets, organization costs theoretically should be amortized over their useful lifes. In practice, however, they ordinarily are amortized over the early years of the corporation's life, with the usual amortization period being 5 years.

To illustrate the procedures involved in recording and amortizing organization costs, let us assume that in the formation of a corporation and the issuance of its capital stock, $5,000 of organization costs are incurred. In addition, let us assume that the corporation decides to amortize such costs on a straight-line basis over a 5-year period. In general journal and T-account form, the organization costs would be capitalized and amortized as follows:

Organization Costs ———————————————————	5,000	
Cash ———————————————————————		5,000
To record organization costs.		
Organization Expense———————————————————	1,000	
Organization Costs ———————————————————		1,000
To record periodic amortization of organization costs.		
Revenue and Expense Summary———————————————	1,000	
Organization Expense———————————————————		1,000
To close the periodic amortization of organization costs to R & E Summary.		

Organization Costs

Date of formation	5,000	End of 1st year	1,000
		End of 2nd year	1,000
		End of 3rd year	1,000
		End of 4th year	1,000
		End of 5th year	1,000
	5,000		5,000

REACQUISITION OF CAPITAL STOCK

Corporations for various reasons frequently find it desirable to reacquire some of their previously issued capital stock. A corporation may, for example, reacquire some of its own stock in order to sustain the market for it, or to have shares available for resale to its employees in accordance with an employee stock option or stock purchase plan.[1] Corporations also frequently reacquire shares of their own stock in order to have them available for use in the acquisition of other companies. For example, the ABC Company might purchase the XYZ Company by exchanging ABC stock for XYZ stock, rather than using cash.

Reacquired shares of a corporation's capital stock may be (1) formally retired (canceled), (2) held in the corporate treasury, or (3) reissued. The laws of most states permit corporations to retire some of their once-issued and outstanding stock under certain conditions. When reacquired stock is formally retired and the stock certificates legally canceled, the corporation's accountability for the stock is ended. Since the formality of retirement and cancellation is essentially a legal matter, we shall concern ourselves primarily with the accounting problems associated with reacquired shares held in the corporate treasury and the reissuance of such shares. As you will recall from Chapter 15, shares of its own stock reacquired by a corporation are called **treasury shares,** or more commonly, **treasury stock.**

Nature of Treasury Stock

A corporation may either purchase its treasury stock or receive it as a donation. It is not an asset; obviously a corporation cannot own part of itself. Likewise, we must not confuse treasury stock with unissued stock, the difference being that the latter has never been in the hands of the stockholders while the former has

---

[1]Employee stock option and stock purchase plans are essentially incentive plans whereby corporations hope to increase employee performance. The option plan gives the employee the option to buy stock from the corporation at a stated price, either at a specified time or during a determinable period of time. Although there are many variations in practice, purchase plans ordinarily permit the employee to purchase stock from the company on a more or less continuing basis by having a certain amount withheld periodically from his paycheck. In most purchase plans the corporation contributes toward the purchase in some manner along with the employee. As a consequence, the employee, in essence, gets a favored price compared to the market price.

at one time been owned by stockholders. There are, however, certain similarities between the two. Neither carries the right to vote or to receive dividends, and neither is considered to be outstanding when book value per share or earnings per share are computed. (We shall study earnings per share computations in Chapter 21.)

Purchased Treasury Stock

The reacquisition of a corporation's own capital stock by purchase is permitted under the laws of some states only under specified conditions, chief of which is the requirement that the retained earnings of the corporation exceed the purchase price of the treasury stock. In addition, in order to maintain at least a minimum buffer for creditors, the statutes of many states restrict the corporation's use of retained earnings by an amount equal to the cost of any treasury stock the corporation might own. For example, if a corporation operating in a state which has such a law has retained earnings of $100,000 and treasury stock costing $20,000, the retained earnings will have a restriction of $20,000. Thus, only $80,000 will be legally available for the payment of dividends.

Treasury Stock Transactions and the Cost Basis Although there are various ways in which the purchase and reissuance of treasury stock may be handled in the accounts, since "cost" is more or less inherent in the legal restrictions associated with treasury stock, the so-called **cost basis** is normally used. Thus, the acquisition of treasury stock is recorded by debiting the Treasury Stock account for cost; when the stock is reissued, the account is credited for cost.

Gains on Treasury Stock Transactions If treasury stock is purchased and then resold at a price above its cost, the difference becomes an addition to invested capital and is generally reflected in an account typically entitled Capital from Treasury Stock Transactions. Let us assume (1) that a corporation purchases 200 shares of its own stock at $120 per share, and (2) that it resells 100 of these shares at $125 per share. In chronological order the entries would be:

(1)

Treasury Stock (200 × $120)	24,000	
Cash		24,000

(2)

Cash (100 × $125)	12,500	
Treasury Stock [cost (100 × $120)]		12,000
Capital from Treasury Stock Transactions		500

Losses on Treasury Stock Transactions If treasury stock is purchased and then resold at a price less than its cost, the difference is reflected as a reduction, or loss, in invested capital. To the extent possible, such losses are charged to the Capital from Treasury Stock Transactions account. If this account cannot absorb all the loss, however, the excess is then charged against any invested capital other than the Capital Stock accounts. If the loss exceeds not only the balance in the Capital from Treasury Stock Transactions account but also the balances in all the invested capital accounts other than the Capital Stock accounts, any excess is charged against the Retained Earnings account.

To illustrate the procedures involved in accounting for losses on treasury stock transactions, we shall continue our preceding illustration, in which we assumed (1) that a corporation purchased 200 shares of its own stock at $120 per share and (2) that it resold 100 of these shares at $125. In addition, let us assume that:

CASE 1 The corporation resells the remaining 100 shares of treasury stock at $116 per share.

CASE 2 The corporation resells the remaining 100 shares of treasury stock at $112 per share, and that the corporation has a credit balance in its Capital in Excess of Stated Value account of $10,000.

CASE 3 The corporation resells the remaining 100 shares of treasury stock at $108 per share, and that the corporation has no invested capital other than that resulting from treasury stock transactions and that reflected in the Capital Stock accounts.

The entries to record these transactions would appear as follows:

Case 1

Cash (100 × $116)	11,600	
Capital from Treasury Stock Transactions	400	
Treasury Stock (cost)		12,000

Case 2

Cash (100 × $112)	11,200	
Capital from Treasury Stock Transactions	500	
Capital in Excess of Stated Value	300	
Treasury Stock (cost)		12,000

Case 3

Cash (100 × $108)	10,800	
Capital from Treasury Stock Transactions	500	
Retained Earnings	700	
Treasury Stock (cost)		12,000

If we were to assume the same basic data as in Case 3, except that the corporation had no invested capital whatsoever other than that reflected in the Capital Stock accounts, the entire loss in Case 3 would be charged to the Retained Earnings account as follows:

Cash (100 × $108)	10,800	
Retained Earnings	1,200	
Treasury Stock (cost)		12,000

Donated Treasury Stock

When a corporation is in urgent need of cash, it is not uncommon for stockholders to donate some of their shares so that the corporation may resell them to raise the necessary money. Since there is no cost involved when treasury stock is acquired by donation, no entry is necessary to record the acquisition other than a memorandum entry indicating the number of shares acquired. Thus, the resale of treasury stock obtained by donation always results in a gain, and as a consequence, an increase in invested capital. To illustrate the resale of treasury stock obtained by donation, let us assume (1) that a corporation receives 200 shares of its own stock by donation, and (2) that it resells 100 of the shares at $125 per share. The entry to record the resale would be:

Cash (100 × $125) ———————————————————————— 12,500
         Capital from Treasury Stock Transactions ————————— 12,500*

*Note that the entire proceeds become invested capital.

BALANCE SHEET PRESENTATION OF CAPITAL STOCK

As a general rule, full disclosure requires that the various sources of capital be presented separately on the balance sheet; that is, invested capital should be shown separately from earned capital. In addition, the different types of capital stock should be shown separately. The description of each class of capital stock should include not only its par or stated value, but also the number of shares authorized, issued, and outstanding. If preferred stock is cumulative, convertible, or callable, it should be so described. Dividend arrearage, conversion rights, and call price should also be indicated.

Common Stock on the Balance Sheet

To illustrate the balance sheet presentation of common stock, let us assume that a corporation is authorized to issue 6 million shares of $5 par value common stock, and that as of the balance sheet date it has issued 4 million shares at $25 per share. If, as of the balance sheet date, the corporation has $110 million in retained earnings, its shareholder equity section will appear as follows:

Shareholder Equity

Capital stock:
  Common, $5 par value, authorized 6,000,000 shares;
    issued 4,000,000 shares————————————————————— $ 20,000,000
Capital in excess of par value ————————————————————— 80,000,000*
Retained earnings ———————————————————————————— 110,000,000
  Total shareholder equity———————————————————————— $210,000,000

*4,000,000 × $20 = $80,000,000

Both Common and Preferred Stock on the Balance Sheet

To illustrate the balance sheet presentation of both common and preferred stock, let us assume the same basic data as were used in the foregoing illustration except that the corporation is also authorized to issue 250,000 shares of $100 par value preferred stock, and that as of the balance sheet date it has issued 180,000 of the shares at $110 per share. If we also assume that the preferred stock is 6 percent cumulative, the shareholder equity section will appear as follows:

Shareholder Equity

Capital stock:
Preferred, $100 par value, 6% cumulative, authorized 250,000 shares;
  issued 180,000 shares _____ $ 18,000,000
Common, $5 par value, authorized 6,000,000 shares;
  issued 4,000,000 shares_____ 20,000,000
Capital in excess of par value _____ 81,800,000*
Retained earnings _____ 110,000,000
  Total shareholder equity_____ $229,800,000

$$*4,000,000 \times \$20 = \$80,000,000$$
$$180,000 \times \$10 = \underline{1,800,000}$$
$$\underline{\$81,800,000}$$

Although they were not used in the preceding illustration, footnotes are often employed on the balance sheet as a means of disclosing important aspects of preferred stock issues such as callable and convertible features. They are also used to disclose the amount of dividends in arrears, since such dividends cannot be listed as liabilities until they are declared by the board of directors.

Treasury Stock on the Balance Sheet

Although legal considerations have substantial effect upon the financial statement presentation of treasury stock, as a general rule it is deducted from the total of the shareholder equity at cost. To illustrate, let us assume the same data as were used in the foregoing illustration except that the corporation has 10,000 shares of the common stock in its treasury. Let us also assume that the treasury stock is carried in the accounts at its cost of $175,000. The shareholder equity section of the balance sheet would appear as follows:

Shareholder Equity

Capital stock:
Preferred, $100 par value, 6% cumulative, authorized 250,000 shares;
  issued 180,000 shares _____ $ 18,000,000
Common, $5 par value, authorized 6,000,000 shares;
  issued 4,000,000 shares_____ 20,000,000
Capital in excess of par value _____ 81,800,000
Retained earnings _____ 110,000,000*
Less: Treasury stock (10,000 shares of common at cost)_____ (175,000)
  Total shareholder equity_____ $229,625,000

*Retained earnings is restricted to the extent of $175,000, the cost of the treasury stock.

SUMMARY

The corporate form of business organization requires that a clear distinction between invested capital and earned capital be maintained at all times, because claims against such capital may not be proportionate. In order to fulfill this requirement, the corporation must distinguish between invested and earned capital both in the accounts and on the financial statements.

The accounting problems associated with capital stock transactions pertain to the authorization and issuance of capital stock, the reacquisition of capital stock, and the financial statement presentation of capital stock. When capital stock is issued, the method of recording it depends on whether it is par value or no-par stock, whether it was issued for cash or property other than cash, and whether or not it was issued on a subscription basis. Problems related to the issuance of stock also are encountered when a proprietorship or partnership incorporates.

If a corporation reacquires some of its previously issued stock and holds it in the corporate treasury, such stock must be accounted for separately in the accounts and on the financial statements. This stock, commonly known as treasury stock, has no voting or dividend rights.

QUESTIONS AND PROBLEMS

16-1 In the shareholder equity section of the balance sheet, a distinction is made between invested capital and earned capital. Why is this distinction made? Discuss.

16-2 When a corporation issues preferred stock for land, the land should be recorded at the:

(1) Total par value of the stock issued

(2) Total book value of the stock issued

(3) Appraised value of the land

(4) Total liquidating value of the stock issued

16-3 How should capital stock be described on the balance sheet?

16-4 May the excess of resale prices over the purchase prices of a corporation's own common stock be reflected in retained earnings, or should the difference be reflected in an invested capital account? Give your reasons for the conclusion you draw.

16-5 How would you describe (from an accounting point of view) the capital of a corporation which has an issue of 100,000 shares of common stock of no-par value, but a stated value fixed by the board of directors of $5 per share and an excess of assets over liabilities of $1,500,000?

16-6 There is frequently a difference between the purchase price and the sale price of treasury stock, but accounting authorities agree that the purchase or sale of its own stock by a corporation cannot result in a profit or loss to the corporation. Why isn't the difference recognized as a profit or loss to the corporation? Discuss.

16-7 James & Jones, a partnership operating a retail store, transferred its assets and business to James & Jones, Inc., a newly formed corporation, as of the close of business December 31, 19X5, in consideration for issuance of all the authorized stock of the new corporation to the two partners in proportion to their interests in the partnership's net assets and business, and assumption of the partnership's liabilities.

Instructions Assume a simple set of facts and, in accordance with your assumption, prepare the opening journal entry for James & Jones, Inc. Specify the source from which each item of information required for your journal entry would be obtained.

16-8 The LMN Corporation was authorized under its charter to issue 10,000 shares of 7 percent cumulative preferred stock, par value $100 per share, and 100,000 shares of common stock, par value $10 per share.

Instructions Journalize the sale and issuance of the stock, assuming that:

(1) The entire issue of preferred stock was sold for cash at $110 per share.
(2) 50 percent of the common stock was sold for cash at a discount of 20 percent.
(3) 25 percent of the common stock was sold for cash at par.
(4) 20 percent of the common stock was sold for cash at a 10 percent premium.

16-9 Instructions Assume a simple set of facts and illustrate by the use of journal entries three ways of valuing an asset acquired in exchange for capital stock.

16-10 The M Company, organized with an authorized capital of 50,000 shares of $100 par value each, of which 30,000 are outstanding, offers 15,000 shares for subscription at $160 per share under the following terms: 50 percent of the subscription price with the subscription, 25 percent 10 days after the subscription is accepted, and the balance 30 days later.

Under these terms, subscriptions were received for the entire 15,000 shares during the month of August 19X3. Notices of acceptance were dated September 12, 19X3. All amounts payable by subscribers were paid promptly.

Instructions Prepare all journal entries necessary to record the sale and issuance of the 15,000 shares.

16-11 Instructions Journalize the following transactions:

On April 1, 19X4, the MN Company was organized with an authorized capitalization of $150,000, divided into 500 shares of common stock and 1,000 shares of preferred stock, all of a par value of $100 per share.

On the same day, 300 shares of the common stock were subscribed for at par, to be paid, without interest, in four equal calls due May 1, June 1, July 1, and August 1. The first call was paid on May 1.

On June 1 the second call on the common stock was paid, and 200 shares of the preferred stock were subscribed and paid for at $90 per share.

On July 1 the third call on the common stock was paid, and 300 shares of the preferred stock were subscribed and paid for at par.

On July 15 subscriptions were taken and payments received for 70 shares of the common stock at $105 per share.

On August 1 the fourth call on the common stock was paid, and the stock was issued.

16-12 Instructions

(1) Journalize the following transactions:
   (a) A corporation receives subscriptions for $100,000 of par value stock. The subscription price is 120 percent of par.
   (b) Another $100,000 of par value stock is subscribed for at the same price but is to be paid in three installments of $48,000, $48,000, and $24,000.
   (c) The first subscription is paid in cash, and the stock is issued.
   (d) The first two installments are paid on the second subscription.

(2) Prepare a trial balance to prove your work.

16-13 John Doe and Richard Roe, copartners in the Doe and Roe Partnership, decided to incorporate their business and to that end took the usual preliminary steps. They obtained a corporate charter authorizing them to issue 10,000 shares of $10 par value stock. The balance sheet of the partnership as of the date of incorporation contained the following accounts and amounts:

Cash	$ 9,000	Notes payable	$ 8,000
Receivables	20,598	Accounts payable	5,598
Inventories	14,000	Doe, capital	25,000
Buildings and equipment	10,000	Roe, capital	15,000
	$53,598		$53,598

Doe and Roe shared partnership profits equally, but agreed to share 4,800 shares of the authorized stock on a basis proportionate to their capital account balances after taking into consideration the following adjustments:

1 An allowance of $2,000 is to be set up for uncollectible accounts.

2 Inventory values are to be increased by 50 percent.

3 Buildings and equipment are to be valued at $25,000.

Instructions

(1) Assuming that the partnership books are to be retained, make all journal entries necessary to:
   (a) Adjust the books of the partnership.
   (b) Record the incorporation of the partnership.

(2) Assuming that new books are to be opened, make all journal entries necessary to:
   (a) Adjust the books of the partnership.
   (b) Close the books of the partnership.
   (c) Open the books of the corporation.

(3) Indicate how the 4,800 shares would be distributed in both (1) and (2) above.

16-14 The net assets of the XYZ Partnership as of January 1, 19X4, were valued at $90,000. The three partners shared profits and losses equally and they had equal capital investments as of that date.

The partnership was incorporated as of March 1, 19X4, with the issuance of $75,000 of par value stock. The change in organization, however, was not reflected on the books at that time. The business sustained a $9,000 loss from operations for the year 19X4.

Instructions Assuming that the operating loss was incurred uniformly throughout the year, that the books were closed as of December 31, 19X4, and that no drawings were made during the year, prepare the journal entry or entries necessary to adjust the books as of January 1, 19X5. (The company plans to use the old books.)

16-15 The shareholder equity section of the Smith Company's balance sheet at December 31, 19X3, was as follows:

Common stock—$100 par (authorized, 50,000 shares;
   issued and outstanding, 10,000 shares) _____ $1,000,000
Capital in excess of par value _____ 200,000
Retained earnings _____ 100,000
                                                           $1,300,000

Because it had idle cash, on January 3, 19X4, the company re-purchased 400 shares of its stock for $50,000. During the year it sold 100 of the reacquired shares at $135 per share and 100 at $122.50 per share.

Instructions Prepare journal entries for each transaction in accordance with the principles which you believe should be applied.

16-16 The shareholder equity section of the Gordon Company's balance sheet at December 31, 19X4, was as follows:

Preferred stock, $10 par value, 7% cumulative, authorized 1,000,000 shares; issued 600,000 shares	$ 6,000,000
Common stock, $5 par value, authorized 10,000,000 shares; issued 7,000,000 shares	35,000,000
Capital in excess of par value	60,000
Retained earnings	10,000,000
Total shareholder equity	$51,060,000

Instructions

(1) Prepare journal entries for each of the following transactions in accordance with the principles which you believe should be applied.
  (a) January 1, 19X5, the company reacquired 100,000 shares of its common stock at $10 per share.
  (b) February 1, 19X5, the company sold 10,000 of the shares reacquired on January 1, at $13 per share.
  (c) March 1, 19X5, the company sold another 10,000 of the shares reacquired on January 1, 19X5, at $9 per share.
  (d) April 1, 19X5, the company sold 30,000 of the shares reacquired on January 1, 19X5, at $7 per share.

(2) Prepare the shareholder equity section of the balance sheet as it would appear after all the transactions have been recorded and posted.

16-17 Instructions

(1) Journalize the following transactions which pertain to the incorporation of the AB Company.
  (a) The AB Company is authorized to issue $500,000 of preferred stock of $100 par value, and 5,000 shares of no-par common stock.
  (b) Subscriptions are received for $200,000 of the preferred stock at par, payment to be made in two installments, 60 percent and 40 percent, respectively. Subscriptions are also received for 3,000 shares of the no-par common stock at $35 a share.
  (c) The first installment on the preferred stock subscriptions is received in cash. The subscriptions for the no-par common stock are paid and the stock is issued.

(d) A donation of 3,000 shares of the company's no-par common stock is made to the company. These shares are offered to the public at $10 a share on condition that a share of preferred stock be bought at par with each no-par common share. Subscriptions are received for 3,000 shares of each class of stock. These subscriptions are paid and the stock is issued.

(2) Prepare a trial balance to prove your work.

16-18 Instructions From the following information, prepare the shareholder equity section of the Thurman Corporation's balance sheet as of December 31, 19X2:

Preferred stock issued	$ 375,000
Common stock issued	4,000,000
Preferred stock authorized ($7.50 par value)*	750,000
Common stock authorized ($5 stated value)	10,000,000
Capital in excess of par value	250,000
Retained earnings	965,000

*The preferred stock is 5% cumulative.

16-19 Instructions From the following information, prepare the shareholder equity section of the Darling Corporation's balance sheet as of December 31, 19X3:

Capital stock issued	$ 300,000
Capital stock subscribed	150,000
Capital stock authorized ($20 par value)	1,000,000
Discount on capital stock	12,000
Subscriptions to capital stock	41,400
Retained earnings	89,000
Dividends payable	2,300
Treasury stock (500 shares at cost)	8,000

16-20 Instructions From the following information prepare the shareholder equity section of the Combs Corporation's balance sheet as of December 31, 19X5:

Preferred stock issued (100,000 shares)	$ 160,000
Common stock issued (2,000,000 shares)	3,000,000
Preferred stock authorized ($1 par value)*	1,000,000
Common stock authorized ($1 stated value)	6,000,000
Preferred stock subscribed (10,000 shares)	16,000
Common stock subscribed (30,000 shares)	45,000
Stock subscriptions receivable	40,000
Retained earnings	310,000
Treasury stock (15,000 common shares at cost)	18,000

*The preferred is 5% noncumulative.

17

Corporations: Retained Earnings Transactions

In our study of capital stock transactions, we examined the workings of the Capital Stock account in some detail. Our study of retained earnings transactions in this chapter can perhaps best be approached by a similar examination of the Retained Earnings account. This will include a detailed investigation of each debit and credit typically reflected in the account.

RETAINED EARNINGS ACCOUNT

In Chapter 15 the Retained Earnings account was described as the account in which the earned capital of a corporation is reflected. Other account titles commonly used in lieu of Retained Earnings include Retained Income, Earnings Reinvested in the Business, and Income Reinvested in the Business. Earned Surplus is an older caption occasionally found on corporate financial statements. However, because the term **surplus** has different meanings for different people, the accounting profession has discouraged its use. Although to many the word connotes an excess, or "something not needed," the resources represented by the balance in the Retained Earnings account seldom fit into this category. In accordance with the profession's recommendation, the use of Earned Surplus as an account title is gradually diminishing.

The Retained Earnings account will normally have a credit balance; however, there is always the possibility that accumulated losses will exceed accumulated profits, in which case the account will have a debit balance. Such a balance, known as a **deficit,** is deducted from the total of the other shareholder equity accounts when the balance sheet is prepared.

When accounting for a corporation, as we learned in Chapter 15, we close the Revenue and Expense Summary account into the Retained Earnings account at the end of the fiscal period. If a profit has been earned, the Retained Earnings account is credited; if a loss has been sustained, it is debited. As we shall see in greater detail in the next section of this chapter, the Retained Earnings account is also debited for distributions to stockholders. For example, a cash dividend is recorded by debiting the Retained Earnings account and crediting the Cash account.

Frequently a part of the retained earnings of an organization may be "reserved" in special accounts for some future use such as the financing of plant expansion. When reserve accounts are used, the Retained Earnings account is subdivided into two broad categories in which the retained earnings are ordinarily described as **appropriated** and **unappropriated.** The Retained Earnings account is debited when the appropriations are made to the reserve accounts and credited when the reserve accounts are reduced or closed out.

If we assume that all gains and losses resulting from operations are run through the Revenue and Expense Summary account, the Retained Earnings account may be summarized as follows:

Retained Earnings

Debited for:	Credited for:
1 Net losses resulting from operations	1 Net income resulting from operations
2 Distributions to stockholders	2 Appropriations no longer needed in reserve accounts
3 Appropriations to reserve accounts	

Since the determination of net income or net loss resulting from operations has been covered to some extent in previous chapters and is also part of the subject matter of Chapter 19, we shall not discuss it at any length in this chapter. At this time we shall concern ourselves primarily with (1) distributions to stockholders, and (2) appropriations of retained earnings.

DISTRIBUTIONS TO STOCKHOLDERS

As we learned in Chapter 15, corporate earnings are distributed to stockholders in the form of dividends. Used in this sense, the term **dividend** means a pro rata distribution by a corporation to its stockholders. If a corporation has more than one class of stock outstanding, the distribution must be on a pro rata basis within each class.

Types of Distributions

Although the great majority of corporate dividends are paid in cash, they may also be paid in property other than cash, or in stock of the corporation if unissued or treasury stock is available. Because the term dividend, when used alone, may carry the connotation to some persons that it is always payable in cash, it usually is preceded by a qualifying adjective. Thus, dividends are described as (1) cash dividends, (2) property dividends, or (3) stock dividends.

Legal Aspects of Dividends

The accounting treatment accorded a given transaction, to be acceptable, must reflect the financial facts relating to the transaction, and in addition, must be consistent with any statutory requirement which bears on the category into which the transaction falls. Since the corporation is a creation of the law, if the accountant is to be of most service when accounting for distributions to stockholders, he must be familiar with the legal as well as the financial aspects of the transactions. Therefore, before studying the accounting problems associated with the different types of distributions to stockholders, we shall first examine the legal and financial aspects of dividends.

Legally, all retained earnings are available for dividends unless specifically restricted by a statutory or contractual requirement. As we saw in Chapter 16, for example, the purchase of treasury stock by a corporation automatically places a statutory restriction on the corporation's retained earnings in an amount equal to the cost of the treasury stock. Similarly, contracts with bondholders or stockholders often require that a portion of the accumulated earnings be retained in the business. A contract with bondholders may place a restriction on the use of retained earnings during the life of the bond issue; in like manner, preferred stock subject to redemption may be issued with the provision that retained earnings will be restricted during the time the stock is outstanding.

From the legal standpoint, unless there are statutory or contractual requirements to the contrary, it is generally agreed that decisions on dividends rest with the corporate directors. Stated in legal terms, "Dividends are declared only within the discretion of the board of directors."

Financial Aspects of Dividends

When declaring a dividend, the board of directors is responsible for ascertaining that its payment is (1) legal, (2) financially sound, and (3) consistent with the corporation's financial policy.

Even when retained earnings are legally available in substantial amounts, there may be, and often are, financial considerations which make it undesirable or even impossible to declare a dividend. A corporation, for example, may have ample retained earnings legally available for a cash dividend, but at the same time its cash position may be very weak. Likewise, corporate management may follow a policy of financing expansion through the retention and investment of retained earnings, rather than through the issuance of additional stock or bonds.

Ordinarily, dividends may not be legally declared or paid (1) when a corporation is insolvent, or (2) when the payment of the dividend would render the corporation insolvent or impair its invested capital. There are times, however, when dividends are declared out of invested capital. These are known as **liquidating dividends.** They are usually declared and paid only (1) when a corporation is going out of business, or (2) when it is permanently curtailing some of its operations. Since stockholders normally view a dividend as being a distribution of earnings, whenever a liquidating dividend is declared and paid, the recipient stockholders must be notified accordingly.

As a general rule, then, there are three prerequisites to the payment of a dividend:

1 Retained earnings must be legally available.

2 The proposed distribution must be financially sound.

3 The dividend must be formally approved by an action of the board of directors.

Declaration of Dividends

Dividends are declared by a formal action of the board of directors, with the action being recorded in the minute book. The board's resolution authorizing the dividend designates a rate or an amount to be paid on each share of stock and the date on which it is to be paid. Since it takes a certain amount of time for the ownership of a share of stock which is being traded on an exchange to be transferred from one person to another and since there is always "paper work" involved in the actual payment of a dividend, dividends are normally declared as of one date and payable at another date to stockholders of record as of still another date. From the standpoint of the distributing corporation, these dates are known, respectively, as the (1) date of declaration, (2) date of payment, and (3) date of record. For example, a dividend declared on January 1 might be payable on February 15 to stockholders of record as of February 1.

The period between the date of declaration and the date of record is provided to permit time for any stock transfers then in process to be completed and registered with the transfer agent. The period between the record date and the payment date is provided to permit time for the preparation of a list of the stockholders as of the record date, and for the preparation of checks or stock certificates, depending on whether the dividends are cash dividends or stock dividends.

From the accounting point of view, a dividend distribution requires formal entries only on the (1) date of declaration, and (2) date of payment. The liability for the dividend is recorded as of the declaration date, and the payment of the liability is recorded as of the payment date. As the date of record merely fixes the identity of the dividend recipients, no transaction takes place and as a consequence no entry is necessary.

Closely related to our study of dividends, although it creates no accounting problem, is what is known as the **ex-dividend date.** When a share of stock is said to be ex-dividend, this means that it is selling without, or not including, a previously declared dividend, and the seller rather than the buyer will receive the dividend. From an accounting standpoint the ex-dividend date is important only because it facilitates the preparation of the list of stockholders of record. Since it generally takes about three business days for a share of stock to be transferred from one owner to another, stock customarily "goes ex-dividend" three business days before the record date. Thus, assuming that no holidays intervene, if a dividend is to be paid to stockholders of record on a given Thursday, the stock will start selling ex-dividend on the preceding Monday.

Accounting for Cash Dividends

The majority of dividends are paid in cash. When a cash dividend is declared, the amount to be paid is expressed in terms of either (1) a certain dollars and cents amount per share, or (2) a certain percentage of par value per share. Dividends on common stock are usually stated in terms of dollars and cents, whereas dividends on preferred stock are frequently stated in terms of a percentage of par value. Under the dollars and cents approach, the designated amount per share is multiplied by the number of shares outstanding to determine the total amount of the dividend. Under the percentage of par value approach, the designated rate is multiplied by the par value of the shares outstanding to determine the total amount of the dividend.

Once a cash dividend has been declared, the stockholders become creditors of the corporation to the extent of the dividend. Thus, the declaration of a cash dividend by the board of directors constitutes all the authority necessary to transfer the amount of the dividend from the Retained Earnings account to a Dividends Payable account. Since cash dividends are ordinarily paid within a reasonably short time after their declaration, the Dividends Payable account is classified as a current liability on the balance sheet.

To illustrate the entries required to record the declaration and payment of a cash dividend, let us assume that on January 1 the board of directors of the ABC Company declares a cash dividend of $1.20 per share on the 10,000 shares of its common stock outstanding, and a 5 percent dividend on its $100 par value preferred stock, of which 5,000 shares are outstanding. Assuming that both dividends are payable as of February 15 to stockholders of record as of February 1, the entries would be:

January 1

Retained Earnings	37,000*	
Cash Dividends Payable		37,000

February 15

Cash Dividends Payable	37,000	
Cash		37,000

*Common dividend: $1.20 × 10,000   = $12,000
Preferred dividend: $100 × 5,000 × .05 = 25,000
                               $37,000

Cash dividends are frequently declared and paid on a quarterly basis. When this is the case, it is not uncommon for a corporation to debit a temporary retained earnings account when declaring the quarterly dividend and then to close the temporary account to the permanent retained earnings account at the end of the year. Temporary accounts of this kind are typically entitled Dividends Declared or Dividends Paid. To illustrate this procedure, let us assume the same basic data as were used in the preceding illustration, except that everything is reduced to one-fourth in order to put our illustration on a quarterly basis. To round out the illustration, the ledger account for the temporary account is also included.

Declaration Date

Dividends Declared ($\frac{1}{4}$ × $37,000)	9,250	
Cash Dividends Payable		9,250

Payment Date

Cash Dividends Payable	9,250	
Cash		9,250

End of Year

Retained Earnings	37,000	
Dividends Declared		37,000

Dividends Declared

End of 1st quarter	9,250			
End of 2nd quarter	9,250			
End of 3rd quarter	9,250			
End of 4th quarter	9,250	End of year	37,000
	37,000		37,000

Accounting for Property Dividends

On occasion, corporations declare dividends payable in assets of the corporation other than cash. Dividends of this type are called **property dividends** or **dividends in kind.** As is the case with a cash dividend, once a property dividend is declared, the stockholders become creditors of the corporation to the extent of the dividend, and the Dividends Payable account becomes a current liability on the balance sheet.

To illustrate the entries required for the declaration and payment of a property dividend, let us assume that the board of directors of the ABC Company, desiring to distribute a dividend to the stockholders at a time when the corporation is in a tight cash position, declares a dividend to be paid by the distribution of $20,000 in merchandise and $10,000 in bonds of the XYZ Company which had been purchased earlier as an investment.

Declaration Date

Retained Earnings	30,000	
Property Dividends Payable		30,000

Payment Date

Property Dividends Payable	30,000	
Merchandise Inventory		20,000
Investment in Bonds of XYZ Company		10,000

Accounting for Stock Dividends

A dividend payable in the stock of the declaring corporation is a **stock dividend.** Although this term is used with varying degrees of preciseness in financial circles, when used in accounting it ordinarily refers to the distribution by a corporation of its common stock to its common stockholders, with the corporation receiving no consideration of any kind from the stockholders. In addition, to qualify as a stock dividend from an accounting standpoint, the number of shares to be distributed by the corporation must be less than 20 to 25 percent of the number of shares outstanding before the distribution; distributions greater than 20 to 25 percent are accounted for as **stock splits,** which we shall study in the next section of this chapter.

In the illustrations that follow, it is important to note that stock dividends are unlike cash dividends and property dividends in that no assets of the corporation are distributed to the stockholders. Whereas cash dividends and property dividends reduce both the assets and the shareholder equity of a corporation, stock dividends reduce neither; they merely convert a portion of a corporation's earned capital, as reflected in its Retained Earnings account, into invested capital, as reflected in its Capital Stock and Capital in Excess of Par or Stated Value accounts.

Capitalization of Retained Earnings As was pointed out earlier in this chapter, there may be financial considerations which make it undesirable or impossible for a corporation to declare cash or property dividends, even though retained earnings are legally available in substantial amounts. For example, many corporations follow a practice of regularly "plowing back" into the business a portion of the assets generated by operations, thus financing expansion out of earnings rather than through the issuance of bonds or by the sale of capital stock. Hence, when a corporation declares a stock dividend, it is in essence telling the stockholder that assets generated by past operations are to be retained in the business as part of the permanent capital of the organization and will not be available for subsequent distribution as cash or property dividends. The transfer of retained earnings to permanent capital is known as the **capitalization of retained earnings.**

There is more or less unanimity among accountants that when a stock dividend is declared, retained earnings should be capitalized, but there is not complete agreement as to the amount. Some accountants believe that retained earnings should be capitalized only to the extent necessary to meet the legal requirement that par or stated value must be reflected in the Capital Stock account. Others argue that they should be capitalized in an amount equal to the fair market value of the shares distributed. For discussion purposes, we shall refer to the former as the legal requirement approach and the latter as the FMV approach.

Accountants supporting the legal requirement approach maintain that since the corporation distributes nothing but additional stock certificates, which simply divide the ownership of the corporation into more but proportionately smaller pieces, and since the stockholder is merely the recipient of a certificate to the effect that he has received a pro rata distribution of the additional shares, from a technical standpoint a stock dividend in reality is not a dividend. They would argue, for example, that a stockholder who owns 120 of 1,200 shares after a 20 percent stock dividend has been declared and paid, rather than 100 shares out of 1,000 prior to the dividend, is, relatively speaking, in exactly the same position as he was before the dividend; that is, he has nothing after the dividend that he didn't have before.

Accountants who support the FMV approach maintain that many recipients of stock dividends tend to regard the dividends as distributions of corporate earnings, usually in an amount equal to the fair market value of the additional shares received. They argue that under the legal requirement approach, except for those earnings used to satisfy legal requirements, the earnings which the stockholders think have been distributed to them will be left in the Retained Earnings account subject to the possibility of being used in additional dividend distributions. This procedure, they contend, is apt to mislead the stockholder, especially if a corporation repeatedly distributes stock dividends while at the same time it distributes few or no cash dividends. Thus, to avoid the possibility of misleading the stockholder, the FMV proponents would limit the number of shares which could be distributed as stock dividends out of a given amount of retained earnings by capitalizing the FMV of the shares distributed. Their reasoning may be illustrated by assuming that a corporation with 10,000 shares of $1 par value common stock outstanding and retained earnings of $100,000 declares a 10 percent stock dividend at a time when the stock is selling on the market at $100 a share. Under the legal requirement approach, the corporation would have to capitalize only $1,000 of the retained earnings (10,000 $\times$ 10% $\times$ $1). Under the FMV approach, however, the corporation would have to capitalize the entire $100,000 of retained earnings (10,000 $\times$ 10% $\times$ $100). Based on our assumptions regarding the illustration, under the FMV approach the corporation would be permitted to issue only one 10 percent stock dividend, whereas under the legal requirement approach it could issue as many as 25.[1]

While both groups have sound arguments, the American Institute of Certified Public Accountants in its various pronouncements tends to support the FMV approach, and that approach is followed in this text. Thus, if we assume the same basic data as were used in the preceding illustration except that the corporation distributes a 5 percent rather than a 10 percent stock dividend, the journal entries required to record the declaration and payment of the stock dividend would be as follows:

Declaration Date

Retained Earnings (10,000 × 5% × $100)	50,000	
Stock Dividend Payable		50,000

Payment Date

Stock Dividend Payable	50,000	
Capital in Excess of Par Value		49,500
Capital Stock (500 × $1)		500

If financial statements are prepared between the date of declaration and the date of payment of a stock dividend, the Stock Dividend Payable account should be presented in the shareholder equity section of the balance sheet as an addition to the invested capital section. The amount is not shown on the balance sheet as a liability, because no legally binding corporate obligation is created by the declaration of a stock dividend.

Stock Dividends and Treasury Stock Corporations frequently use treasury stock to the extent available for the payment of stock dividends. In this event the accountant merely debits the Stock Dividend Payable account for the FMV of the dividend, credits the Treasury Stock account for the carrying value of the treasury stock used, credits the Capital Stock account for the par or stated value of the new stock issued, and credits the Capital in Excess of Par or Stated Value account for the balance. To illustrate the entry required to record the payment of a stock dividend when treasury stock is used as a portion of the payment, let us assume the same basic facts as were used in the preceding illustration except that the dividend is paid by using 100 shares of treasury stock, which are carried in the accounts at a cost of $9,000, and 400 shares of previously unissued stock.

[1]Since only $1 per share would be capitalized under the legal requirement approach, a quick glance might lead one to assume that a hundred 10 percent stock dividends could be distributed out of the $100,000 of retained earnings in our illustration. This is not the case, however, because the dividend base would be constantly increasing; as a consequence, the amount capitalized in each succeeding dividend would be larger than the amount capitalized in the preceding dividend. For example, $1,000 as was noted above, would be capitalized on the first dividend, $1,100 on the second (10,000 shares + 1,000 shares × 10% × $1), and $1,210 on the third (10,000 shares + 1,000 shares + 1,100 shares × 10% × $1). Mathematically, a small amount of the $100,000 of retained earnings would be left after the twenty-fifth dividend.

The entry would be:

Stock Dividend Payable	50,000	
Capital in Excess of Par Value (balance)		40,600
Treasury Stock (carrying value)		9,000
Capital Stock (400 × $1)		400

Our use of treasury stock in the payment of the dividend logically presents us with another rather important question. Are dividends paid on treasury shares? As far as cash and property dividends are concerned, the answer is no. Cash and property dividends are paid only on outstanding shares, and treasury shares are not considered to be outstanding. It would be superfluous, if not fictitious, for a corporation to pay a cash or property dividend to itself. Stock dividends, however, are different. Some states permit the payment of stock dividends on treasury stock, whereas others do not. In either case, the accounts affected by the declaration and payment are the same; only the amounts differ. For example, in our previous illustration where the corporation had 10,000 shares outstanding and 100 shares in the treasury, a 10 percent stock dividend issued only on the outstanding shares would result in a distribution of 1,000 shares (10,000 × 10%), whereas a 10 percent stock dividend issued on both the outstanding shares and the treasury shares would result in a distribution of 1,010 shares [(10,000 + 100) × 10%].

Accounting for Stock Splits

Closely related to the stock dividend is the **stock split.** This is a procedure whereby a corporation increases the number of its outstanding shares in order to reduce the selling price per share. Like the stock dividend, the stock split is a distribution by a corporation of its stock to its stockholders, with the corporation receiving no consideration as such from the stockholders. Unlike the stock dividend, however, which is ordinarily declared in lieu of a cash or property dividend, the stock split is employed primarily as a means of obtaining wider distribution, the intent being to increase the marketability of the stock.

American corporations have found the stock split approach to marketability particularly useful when the market prices of their stocks have reached exceptionally high levels. In fact, most major American corporations have split their stock at least once, and many have split theirs several times.

For a stock distribution to qualify as a stock split from an accounting standpoint, the distribution must be greater than 20 to 25 percent of the number of shares outstanding before the distribution. Experience has shown that in order to increase the marketability of stock by the use of a stock distribution, the distribution must be substantial; as a general rule, a distribution of less than 20 to 25 percent will not appreciably affect the marketability of stock. Since it is difficult to draw a fine line between distributions that will and will not increase stock marketability, accountants use the 20 to 25 percent dividing line as a guideline only.

When accounting for a stock split, all we have to do is meet the legal requirement; that is, par or stated value must be reflected in the Capital Stock account. Since a stock split technically is not a dividend, although there are times when it may be referred to as one, it is unnecessary to capitalize retained earnings other than to the extent of meeting the legal requirement. Thus, in the final analysis, accounting for a stock split is dependent upon the way in which the split is effected. Ordinarily, it is carried out in one of three ways:

1 Par or stated value is reduced in proportion to the distribution.

2 Par or stated value is not changed.

3 Par or stated value is reduced on a basis not in proportion to the distribution.

When par or stated value is reduced in proportion to the split, no formal journal entry is necessary, because the legal requirement will already have been met. For example, if we assume that a corporation with 10,000 shares of $10 par value stock outstanding splits its stock on a 4 for 1 basis and at the same time changes the par value per share to $2.50, we can see that the legal requirement will already be reflected in the Capital Stock account, because 10,000 × $10 is equal to 40,000 × $2.50. When par or stated value is reduced in proportion to the split, the split is commonly referred to as a **pure split.**

If par or stated value is not changed at all in a stock split, retained earnings are capitalized to the extent of the par or stated value of the distribution.

When par or stated value is reduced, but not in proportion to the distribution, retained earnings are capitalized in an amount large enough to bring the Capital Stock account up to the legal requirement.

To illustrate the journal entries required to record a stock split, let us assume that a corporation with 10,000 shares of $10 par value common stock outstanding splits its stock on a 2 for 1 basis, and that it:

CASE 1 Reduces the par value per share to $5.

CASE 2 Does not change the par value per share.

CASE 3 Reduces the par value per share to $7.50.

Case 1
(No entry required)

Case 2

Retained Earnings	100,000	
Capital Stock (10,000 × $10)		100,000

Case 3

Retained Earnings	50,000	
Capital Stock		50,000*

*Legal requirement (20,000 × $7.50)	$150,000
Already in the account (10,000 × $10.00)	100,000
Amount needed	$ 50,000

Stock Dividend versus Stock Split

Although stock dividends and stock splits appear to be very similar in nature and at times it is difficult to distinguish between them, they are, as a general rule, substantially different, and, as we have seen, they receive different accounting treatment. Accountants distinguish between the two based on the size of the distribution as a clue to the intent of the board of directors when authorizing the distribution. If the aim of the board is to give the stockholder some evidence of his interest in the accumulated earnings of the corporation without giving him cash or other property, the distribution is considered to be a dividend. If, however, the intent of the board is to increase the marketability of the stock, the distribution is considered to be a split. In summary form, the effect of stock dividends and stock splits on both the corporate accounts and the individual stockholder's holdings may be contrasted as follows:

Corporate Accounts	Stock Dividend	Stock Split
Shares outstanding	Increased	Increased
Capital Stock account	Increased	May increase
Retained Earnings account	Decreased	May decrease
Total shareholder equity	No change	No change
Book value per share	Decreased	Decreased
Individual Stockholder		
Shares owned	Increased	Increased
Book value per share	Decreased	Decreased
Book value of total equity	No change	No change
Percentage of ownership	No change	No change

APPROPRIATION OF RETAINED EARNINGS

As was pointed out earlier in this chapter, there may be times when part of a corporation's retained earnings are restricted because of contractual or legal requirements, or because they have been earmarked by the board of directors for some future purpose. Although restrictions of this kind may be handled in the records by memorandum entries and on the financial statements by parenthetical or footnote disclosure, many accountants believe that a certain amount of benefit is derived from transferring the appropriated amounts to specific accounts.

Mandatory Appropriations

Provisions of bond, preferred stock, or other contractual agreements often impose mandatory restrictions on a corporation's retained earnings. For example, bond agreements frequently contain a requirement that a specified amount of retained earnings be appropriated each year during the life of the bonds. Preferred stock subject to redemption is frequently issued under a similar provision.

To illustrate the journal entries required to handle a bond issue which contains a mandatory appropriation requirement, let us assume that a corporation sells a $100,000, 10-year bond issue with the provision that, as added protection for the bondholder, it will transfer $10,000 per year from the Retained Earnings account to a reserve account. The entries to record (1) the periodic appropriation, (2) the retirement of the bonds, and (3) the return of the appropriations to the Retained Earnings account would be:

Periodic Appropriation

Retained Earnings	10,000	
Reserve for Bond Redemption		10,000

Retirement of Bonds

Bonds Payable	100,000	
Cash		100,000

Return of Reserve to Retained Earnings

Reserve for Bond Redemption	100,000	
Retained Earnings		100,000

Discretionary Appropriations

On occasion, the board of directors may conclude that it is financially unsound to make all of a corporation's retained earnings available for dividends. For example, the board may desire to finance expansion through the retention and investment of part of the corporation's accumulated earnings, or it may anticipate the possibility of the organization sustaining unusual losses which could impair its financial position, if not its legal capital, unless retained earnings are withheld to meet such contingencies. As a result, the board may decide to restrict a portion of the retained earnings by making a discretionary appropriation.

To illustrate the journal entries involved in the handling of a discretionary appropriation, let us assume that a corporation operates in an area that is occasionally subject to flooding, and that flood insurance is either unavailable or its cost is prohibitive. Let us further assume that (1) in order to provide for possible flood losses as well as other unpredictable losses, the board of directors authorized the establishment of a Reserve for Contingencies account and appropriated $100,000 of retained earnings thereto; that (2) the corporation subsequently sustained a $30,000 flood loss; and that (3) after the loss was sustained, the board decided to reduce the reserve account to $60,000. The entries necessary to reflect these events would be:

Establishment of the Reserve Account

Retained Earnings	100,000	
Reserve for Contingencies		100,000

Recording a Loss

Flood Loss	30,000	
Cash		30,000

Reduction of the Reserve Account

Reserve for Contingencies	40,000	
Retained Earnings		40,000

Special attention should be given to our entry recording the flood loss. Note that the debit is not made to the reserve account but instead is made to a loss account which, as we shall see illustrated in Chapter 19, is closed to the Revenue and Expense Summary account in the closing process. Although we credited the Cash account, the credit could just as easily have been made to a liability account or some other asset account under appropriate circumstances. We merely assumed that cash was paid out for the repair of the damage caused by the flood.

Funds and Reserves

Before concluding our discussion on the appropriation of retained earnings, we must be certain that we have our thinking straight as far as funds and reserves are concerned. All too often readers of financial statements confuse the two. A **reserve** is simply an appropriation of retained earnings, whereas, as you will recall from our study of the petty cash fund in Chapter 7 and the bond sinking fund in Chapter 13, a **fund** is an accumulation of cash or other assets. Since a fund is an asset, it has a debit balance, whereas a reserve, which is a shareholder equity account, has a credit balance. Even though a reserve contains no assets as such, we must nevertheless realize that because of the restriction placed on the Retained Earnings account, a reserve indirectly retains assets in the business by not permitting them to be distributed in the form of dividends.

Although a fund and a reserve are separate and distinct, it is possible that both may be associated with a given situation. Thus, we could have (1) a reserve and no fund, (2) a fund and no reserve, or (3) both a fund and a reserve.

When we studied the sinking fund associated with a bond issue in Chapter 13, we did not use a reserve. Likewise, when we studied the reserve for bond redemption earlier in this chapter, we did not use a fund. To illustrate the use of both simultaneously, let us assume that a corporation sells a $100,000, 10-year bond issue with the provision that it will transfer $10,000 per year from the Retained Earnings account to a reserve account and at the same time transfer $10,000 per year from the Cash account to a sinking fund account. The entries to record (1) the periodic appropriations, (2) the retirement of the bonds, and (3) the return of the reserve to the Retained Earnings account would be:

Entries for the Fund			Entries for the Reserve	

Periodic Appropriation

Bond Sinking Fund _____	10,000		Retained Earnings _____	10,000
Cash _____		10,000	Reserve for Bond Sinking	
			Fund _____	10,000

Retirement of Bonds

Bonds Payable _____	100,000		
Bond Sinking Fund _____		100,000	No entry

Return of Reserve to Retained Earnings

		Reserve for Bond Sinking Fund _	100,000
No entry		Retained Earnings _____	100,000

Reserve Terminology and Classification

The accountant's use of the word **reserve** unfortunately has not always been restricted to appropriations of retained earnings. It was widely used in the past as a descriptive term in the titles of valuation and liability accounts as well as shareholder equity accounts. Although the accounting profession has made a concentrated effort to limit its use to appropriations of retained earnings, misuse of the term is still found in accounting records and on published financial statements; needless to say, it takes time to phase out old usage completely. When it is used in a valuation account title, we may find an account entitled Reserve for Bad Debts instead of our familiar Allowance for Uncollectible Accounts, or Reserve for Depreciation instead of Accumulated Depreciation. When it is used in a liability account title, we may encounter Reserve for Federal Income Taxes instead of Federal Income Taxes Payable.

As we shall see in more detail in Chapter 19, the Retained Earnings account on the balance sheet is frequently supported by a separate retained earnings statement. However, the details of the account may be presented on the balance sheet, as shown. The unappropriated portion in the illustration is the balance of the Retained Earnings account.

Retained earnings:		
Unappropriated _____		$120,000
Appropriated:		
Reserve for plant expansion _____	$30,000	
Reserve for contingencies _____	20,000	
Reserve for bond sinking fund _____	60,000	110,000
Total retained earnings _____		$230,000

SUMMARY

Under the corporate form of business organization, it is essential that earned capital be clearly distinguished from invested capital in the accounts and on the financial statements. Proper maintenance of this distinction is important both to stockholders and creditors, because they are likely to be misled, if not financially injured, by the payment of a dividend out of invested capital.

The dividend policy of a corporation is principally governed by two factors: (1) the legal availability of retained earnings, and (2) the financial position of the organization. When retained earnings are legally available for distribution, the board of directors may declare a dividend payable in cash, property, or stock.

The administration of a corporation's earned capital frequently requires the use of reserve accounts to reflect appropriations of retained earnings. Retained earnings appropriations are simply segregations of the Retained Earnings account, and unless specifically restricted to the contrary, they are still legally available for dividend purposes.

QUESTIONS AND PROBLEMS

17-1 (1) What is a **stock dividend?**

(2) What is the accounting distinction between a **stock dividend** and a **stock split?**

17-2 Retained earnings are often appropriated as a means of:
(a) Setting aside cash for a specific purpose
(b) Disclosing managerial policy
(c) Preventing unusual losses
(d) Improving stockholder morale
(e) None of the above

17-3 List the principal transactions or items that reduce the amount of retained earnings. (Do not include appropriations of retained earnings.)

17-4 Why does the accounting profession discourage the accountant's use of the term **surplus** and attempt to restrict his use of the term **reserve?**

17-5 Why is a distinction made between invested capital and earned capital in the shareholder equity section of the balance sheet? Discuss.

17-6 A corporation has noncumulative preferred stock outstanding. One of the directors maintains that no dividend on the preferred stock may be paid this year because the operations of the corporation for the current year have resulted in a loss although there were accumulated earnings at the beginning of the year in excess of the amount of the loss.

Instructions

(1) Give reasons why you agree or disagree that the accumulated earnings may, in the light of accepted accounting principles, be used for the payment of a dividend on the preferred stock.

(2) Would your arguments differ if the corporation had only common stock outstanding and the proposal was to pay a dividend on common stock?

17-7 Differentiate between a **fund** and a **reserve,** as these terms are used in accounting.

17-8 For what reasons does a corporation usually declare a stock dividend? A stock split?

17-9 The STU Company issued 10-year bonds of a par value of $500,000 to finance plant expansion. Pursuant to the terms of the bond agreement, a sinking fund was created for the eventual retirement of the bonds, and also a sinking fund reserve was established. At the maturity date of the bonds, the sinking fund was utilized to retire the bonds.

(1) What purposes are served by having both a sinking fund and a sinking fund reserve?

(2) Assuming that the bond agreement required the company to transfer $50,000 per year from the Retained Earnings account to a reserve account and $50,000 per year from the Cash account to a sinking fund account, prepare the entries necessary to record (a) the periodic appropriations, (b) the retirement of the bonds, and (c) the return of the reserve to the Retained Earnings account.

17-10 As of January 1, 19X5, the ABC Company had outstanding 1 million shares of common stock of a par value of $10 each. The balance in its Retained Earnings account as of that date was $12 million and it had a balance of $2.5 million in its Capital in Excess of Par Value account. The company's net income for 19X5 was 4.6 million. A cash dividend of 50 cents a share was declared and paid on June 30, 19X5, and a 10 percent stock dividend was distributed to stockholders of record at the close of business on December 31, 19X5. The market price of ABC's stock just prior to the declaration of the stock dividend was $25 per share, and it remained at substantially that price for more than a month after the issuance of the dividend shares.

Instructions

(1) Journalize the declaration and payment of the cash dividend.

(2) Journalize the declaration and payment of the stock dividend.

(3) Compute the book value per share as of January 1, 19X5.

(4) Compute the book value per share as of January 1, 19X6.

17-11 On June 1, 19X6, the board of directors of the BA Corporation declared a stock dividend equal to 8 percent of the corporation's outstanding common stock, to be issued to common stockholders of record as of September 15, 19X6. The market value of the common stock just prior to the declaration was $45 per share; it remained at that level for several months after the issuance of the additional shares.

The company's shareholder equity accounts at both the declaration date and record date contained the following balances:

Preferred stock,* 1,000 shares issued	$100,000
Common stock, 100,000 shares issued	500,000
Capital in excess of par value	60,000
Retained earnings	340,000
Treasury stock (10,000 shares of common at cost)	(80,000)
Total shareholder equity	$920,000

*Callable at 110% of par value.

Instructions

(1) Determine the book value per share of common stock just prior to the declaration of the stock dividend.

(2) Prepare the journal entry necessary to record the declaration of the dividend.

(3) Prepare the journal entry necessary to pay the dividend.

(4) Determine the book value per share of common stock immediately after the dividend is paid.

17-12 The following information was taken from the owner equity section of a corporate balance sheet.

8% preferred stock ($10 par value)	$ 300,000
Common stock ($5 par value)	750,000
Capital in excess of par value	110,000
Retained earnings	2,300,000
Total owner equity	$3,460,000

Instructions Assuming that the common stock is split on a 4 for 1 basis at a time when the stock is selling on the market at $25 a share, prepare the journal entry or entries necessary to record the split if the:

(1) Par value per share of common stock is not changed.

(2) Par value per share of common stock is reduced to $1.25 per share.

(3) Par value per share of common stock is reduced to $2.50 per share.

(4) Par value per share of common stock is reduced to $3 per share.

17-13 The board of directors of the Tabac Corporation declared a stock dividend equal to 5 percent of the corporation's outstanding common stock, to be issued to common stockholders of record as of April 15, 19X4. The board directed that the corporation's treasury stock was to be used for this purpose to the extent available. The market value of the common stock just prior to the declaration was $64 per share, and it remained at substantially that figure for more than a month after the issuance of the dividend shares.

　　The corporation's shareholder equity accounts at the dates of declaration and record included the following balances:

Preferred stock, $5 cumulative (no par), authorized 25,000 shares, in treasury 130 shares, outstanding 10,402 shares	$1,053,200
Common stock (par $50), authorized 50,000 shares; in treasury 880 shares, outstanding 27,780 shares	1,433,000
Capital contributed in excess of par value of common shares	251,464
Retained earnings	963.425
Treasury stock, $5 cumulative preferred (at cost)	14,922
Treasury stock, common (at cost)	40,920

Instructions

(1) Prepare an entry to record the net effect of the board's action.

(2) Prepare an entry to record the net effect of the board's action assuming the same facts as set forth above, except that the distribution equaled 10 percent (instead of 5 percent) of the outstanding common shares.

*17-14 The Arcain Corporation was formed in July, 19X1. At date of incorporation, it issued $1 million of $100 par value common stock at par for cash.

*AICPA adapted.

Operations during the remainder of 19X1 resulted in $60,000 net income. As a result of its operating experience, it was decided that $800,000 of invested capital would be adequate to meet forseeable operating needs and provide for reasonable expansion. At a director's meeting in January, 19X2, the following independent suggestions were made to take care of the excess capitalization:

(1) Reduce shares from $100 to $80 par value.

(2) Invest $200,000 of excess cash in the firm's own shares.

(3) Distribute a cash dividend of $20 per share.

Instructions Briefly discuss each suggestion with regard to its soundness in light of the corporation's objective.

17-15 You have been asked by the chief accountant of the Chenault Corporation to assist in the preparation of a balance sheet. The classifications suggested by the chief accountant are as follows:

Assets	*Liabilities and Owner Equity*
A Current	**F** Current
B Investments	**G** Long-term
C Plant and equipment	**H** Deferred credits
D Intangibles	**I** Preferred stock
E Deferred charges	**J** Common stock
	K Retained earnings
	L Capital in excess of par or stated value

Instructions Using the above classifications, classify the following accounts according to the preferred balance sheet presentation. (Do not concern yourself with terminology as such.)

(1) Dividend Payable (on Chenault's preferred stock)

(2) Reserve for Higher Replacement Costs

(3) Reserve for Bad Debts

(4) Sinking Fund Cash (First National Bank, Trustee)

(5) Reserve for Retirement of Preferred Stock

(6) Reserve for Possible Decline in Inventory Value

(7) Reserve for Self-insurance

(8) Reserve to Reduce Inventory to Market

(9) Matured Capital Stock Subscriptions (called by the board of directors and considered collectible)

(10) Common Stock Subscribed (Chenault Corporation's stock)

*17-16 At December 31, 19X6, the balance sheet of the Petroleum Corporation contained the following item and accompanying explanation:

Reserve for Contingencies (see Schedule A) —————————— $7,396,604

Schedule A
Reserve for Contingencies

Balance, Jan. 1, 19X6	$8,399,886
Charged against current income	466,400
	$8,866,286
Credited to current income	(1,424,619)
Payment for which the reserve was established	(45,063)
Balance, Dec. 31, 19X6	$7,396,604

Instructions

(1) Give your opinion of the accounting practices which are indicated by the Petroleum Corporation's balance sheet item and accompanying schedule.

(2) Indicate the effect of these accounting practices upon the Petroleum Corporation's 19X6 income statement.

17-17 Instructions Journalize the following capital transactions engaged in by the Mystic Company during the first 3 years of its existence:

1 Mystic Company's charter became effective on January 1, 19X1, when 1,000 shares of no-par common and 1,000 shares of 6 percent cumulative, nonparticipating, preferred stock were issued. The no-par common stock was sold at its stated value of $150 per share, and the preferred stock was sold at its par value of $100 per share.

2 Mystic was unable to pay preferred dividends at the end of its first year. The owners of the preferred stock agreed to accept 1 share of common stock for every 20 shares of preferred stock owned in discharge of the preferred dividends due on December 31, 19X1. The shares were issued on January 2, 19X2, which was also the declaration date. The fair market value was $120 per share for common on the date of issue.

3 On April 30, 19X3, Mystic paid a 10 percent stock dividend in preferred

*AICPA adapted.

stock (1 share for every 10 shares held) to all common stockholders. The fair market value of preferred stock was $85 per share on that date.

4 Mystic split its common stock 10 for 3 on January 1, 19X4. At the time of the split, Mystic changed the stated value of its common stock from $150 to $50 per share.

17-18 The board of directors of the ABC Corporation on December 1, 19X6, declared a 2 percent stock dividend on the common stock of the corporation, payable on December 28, 19X6, to the holders of record at the close of business December 15, 19X6. They stipulated that cash dividends were to be paid in lieu of issuing any fractional shares. They also directed that the amount to be charged against the Retained Earnings account should be an amount equal to the market value of the stock on the record date multiplied by the total of (a) the number of shares issued as a stock dividend and (b) the number of shares upon which cash is paid in lieu of the issuance of fractional shares.

The following facts are given:

1 At the dividend record date:
 a Shares of ABC common issued _____ 2,771,600
 b Shares of ABC common held in treasury _____ 1,000
 c Shares of ABC common included in (a) held by persons who will receive cash in lieu of fractional shares _____ 202,500

2 Values of ABC common were:
 Par value _____ $ 5
 Market value at Dec. 1 and 15 _____ 22
 Book value at Dec. 1 and 15 _____ 16

Instructions Prepare the entries necessary to record the:

(1) Declaration of the stock dividend

(2) Declaration of the cash dividend

(3) Payment of the stock dividend

(4) Payment of the cash dividend

17-19 The shareholder equity section of the Bar Corporation's December 31, 19X7, balance sheet appeared as follows:

Shareholder Equity

Common stock, $10 par value; authorized, 500,000 shares, issued,
 75,000 shares _____ $ 750,000
Capital in excess of par value _____ 375,000
Retained earnings _____ 725,000
 Total _____ $1,850,000
Less: Cost of 4,700 shares of common stock in treasury ____ 11,500
 Total shareholder equity _____ $1,838,500

During the year ended December 31, 19X8, the following events occurred:

Date	Transaction
Jan. 16	A cash dividend of 20 cents per share was declared, payable February 15 to stockholders of record on February 5.
Mar. 1	A 2 for 1 stock split was declared. The additional stock was issued March 15 to stockholders of record on March 5. The par value of the stock was reduced to $6.
Oct. 1	A 10 percent stock dividend was declared, payable November 1 to stockholders of record on October 15.
Dec. 31	Net income for Bar Corporation for the year ended December 31, 19X8, amounted to $850,000 before provision for income taxes of $450,000.

Instructions Assuming that the market price of the Bar Corporation's stock remained around $25 a share throughout the year and that the corporation does not pay stock dividends on treasury stock:

(1) Prepare the entries necessary to record the above transactions.

(2) Prepare the shareholder equity section as it would appear on the Bar Corporation's December 31, 19X8, balance sheet.

*17-20 The following were some of the account balances of the Victoria Products Company on January 1, 19X4:

Reserve for contingencies	$ 45,000
Accumulated depreciation	280,000
Reserve for fire insurance	21,000
Reserve for future inventory loss	40,000
6% preferred stock ($100 par)	100,000
Common stock ($10 par)	560,000
Capital in excess of par value	84,000
Retained earnings	88,684
Treasury stock—preferred (50 shares at cost)	5,300
Treasury stock—common (1,000 shares at cost)	10,000

The price of the company's common stock has been advancing steadily on the market; it was $25 on January 1, $25 on July 1, and $30 at the end of 19X4. The preferred stock is callable at $105 per share.

During the year the regular dividends on the preferred stock were paid. A 25 cents per share cash dividend was paid on the common stock on April 1; in addition, 4 percent dividends on shares of common stock were

*AICPA adapted.

paid on the common on June 30 and December 31. Treasury shares, to the extent available, were used to pay the stock dividends. The balance came from authorized but unissued shares. (The company does not pay stock dividends on treasury stock.)

Instructions

(1) Prepare the entries necessary to record the declaration and payment of all dividends declared and paid during the year.

(2) Assuming that the company's net income for the year was $266,600, determine the book value per share of common stock as of December 31, 19X4.

Part Five

Accounting for
Federal Income Taxes

18
Federal Income Taxes

"In this world nothing is sure but death and taxes," Benjamin Franklin reputedly wrote to a friend in 1789. Since that time, taxes levied in the United States have increased considerably both in kinds and amounts. You will recall that we examined the accounting aspects of payroll taxes, property taxes, and sales taxes in Chapter 12 when we studied current liabilities.

Another major form of taxation important to us as students of accountancy is the income tax. Although of comparatively recent origin, coming into prominence since the ratification of the Sixteenth Amendment to the Constitution in 1913, the income tax is the main source of revenue of the federal government. The laws governing the tax are contained in the Internal Revenue Code, which is administered by the Internal Revenue Service, a division of the Treasury Department.

A number of cities and states also derive revenue from income taxes; however, because the laws pertaining to each jurisdiction have their own peculiarities and because city and state income taxes are ordinarily predicated upon the federal tax, only the latter will be considered here.

Federal income taxes are imposed upon taxable entities, namely, individuals, corporations, estates, and trusts. Ordinarily, businesses organized as sole proprietorships or partnerships are not taxable entities in the eyes of the law. Instead their owners are taxed as individuals, with proprietorship and partnership earnings being included along with income from other sources on their individual tax returns. In this chapter we shall concern ourselves primarily with individual and corporate federal income taxes.

The amount of federal income taxes payable in a given situation is frequently based upon income as determined by the accountant, and for a corporation it is considered as an expense of the business. Therefore, although an in-depth study of the federal income tax is too vast and complex to be covered adequately in a basic text, it is important that we be familiar with:

1 What is and what is not taxable income

2 How taxes are computed

3 The difference between accounting income and taxable income

4 The effect of income taxes upon the accounting process

INDIVIDUAL TAXPAYERS

To expedite the collection of income taxes, the Internal Revenue Service supplies standard income tax forms with instructions thereon for computing both taxable income and the amount of the tax. Individuals are required to report their tax information on Form 1040, the U.S. Individual Income Tax Return. The illustration on page 463 depicts diagrammatically both the general content of Form 1040 and the formula for computing the tax.

The procedure for determining an individual taxpayer's federal income tax liability can perhaps best be understood if we discuss each step in the diagram in turn. As we proceed, bear in mind that while the tax forms, tax rates, amounts and kinds of deductions and exemptions, and similar factors discussed in this chapter are applicable as of the time of this writing, all are subject to legislative change and quite probably will not remain constant.[1]

Gross Income

From the standpoint of the individual taxpayer, **gross income** for federal income tax purposes includes all income not specifically excluded by law. This must be included in the tax return even though some of the income may be offset by subsequent adjustments or deductions. The tabulation on page 464, which is not intended to be exhaustive, illustrates both includable and excludable items.

---

[1] The rates and schedules used in this chapter are based on the Tax Reform Act of 1969 and are scheduled to take effect on or before January 1, 1973.

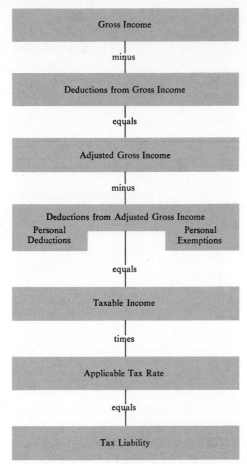

Basic tax formula for individual taxpayers.

Deductions from Gross Income

In working toward taxable income, the individual taxpayer is allowed to take certain deductions from gross income and others from adjusted gross income. Deductions from gross income include:

1 **Business expenses** As defined by the Internal Revenue Service, business expenses include all ordinary and necessary expenses incurred (other than as an employee) by a taxpayer in the carrying on of a trade or business or the practice of a profession.

2 Certain **expenses incurred as an employee:**
   a **Travel expenses** If a taxpayer is away from home overnight in the

Includable and Excludable Items of Gross Income	
Includable in Gross Income	*Excludable from Gross Income*
Taxpayer's share of earnings from a business or profession conducted as a sole proprietorship or partnership	Interest on obligations of states and municipalities
Taxpayer's share of the income from an estate or trust	Life insurance proceeds received because of the death of the insured
Wages, salaries, bonuses, commissions, fees, tips, and gratuities	Disability retirement payments and other benefits paid by the Veterans Administration
Dividends, rents, and royalties	Dividends on life insurance policies
Interest on commercial bank deposits, bonds, and notes	Workmen's compensation for injury or sickness
Interest on obligations of the federal government, including U.S. Savings Bonds and tax refunds	State unemployment benefits
Gains from the sale or exchange of real estate, securities, or other property	Federal social security benefits
Alimony	Gifts, inheritances, and bequests
Income from illegal activities	Undergraduate and graduate scholarships (provided no services are required)
Prizes won in contests	Up to $20,000 per year of income earned by a United States citizen in a foreign country (provided the taxpayer resides in the foreign country for at least 18 months)

performance of his duties as an employee, all ordinary and necessary expenses incurred are deductible. If the required travel permits the employee to return home at night, only transportation expenses are deductible. (Commuting expenses are *not* deductible.)

b **Moving expenses** In general, expenses incurred by a taxpayer when changing his place of residence from one location to another because of a change in his principal place of employment are deductible.

c **Expenses of an "outside salesman"** Expenses incurred by an outside salesman (an employee who solicits business for his employer principally while away from his employer's place of business) are deductible from gross income.

d **Reimbursed expenses** Expenses incurred by an employee for which he is reimbursed by his employer are deductible. Since the reimbursement is included in the employee's gross income, the inclusion of the expenses as a deduction from gross income has an offsetting effect.

Note: Items (a) through (c) are deductible from gross income whether or not they are reimbursed. Item (d) includes *all* expenses for which the taxpayer was reimbursed. Employee expenses not included in (a) through (d) are deductible from adjusted gross income if the taxpayer elects to itemize his deductions. (Itemized deductions are discussed in the next section of this chapter.)

Adjusted Gross Income

Gross income less the applicable deductions is **adjusted gross income.** The amount of an individual taxpayer's adjusted gross income is of particular importance in the determination of his taxable income because certain major deductions are directly related to it. These include charitable and medical deductions as well as the so-called percentage standard deduction.

Deductions from Adjusted Gross Income

Deductions from adjusted gross income may be divided into two broad categories: personal deductions and personal exemptions.

Personal Deductions Personal deductions include expenses, contributions, and losses that are of a personal rather than a business nature. The taxpayer has an option regarding this category. He may either take a lump-sum percentage standard deduction or itemize his deductions. If the latter option is chosen, only items specifically identified in the law may be deducted. The taxpayer, of course, should take care to elect the option that will benefit him most.

1 Percentage standard deduction Certain of the federal income tax laws recently were changed as the result of congressional action. The 10 percent standard deduction which applied for many years has been replaced by the **percentage standard deduction.** This change, which is being implemented on a graduated scale, will result in 1973 in the deduction being 15 percent of adjusted gross income, with the actual amount deductible being subject to both maximum and minimum limitations. The maximum amount deductible for all taxpayers other than married persons filing separate returns[1] is $2,000; for the latter it is $1,000. The minimum deduction for all taxpayers other than married persons filing separate returns is $1,000; for the latter it is $500. This so-called low-income allowance provision was written into the law to provide relief for low-income taxpayers with large families.

To illustrate the operation of both the maximum and minimum provisions, let us assume that in each of the following cases the taxpayer is a married person filing a joint return.

[1]Married persons may file separate returns or they may combine their incomes and deductions in a joint return. Since certain restrictions are placed on married persons filing separate returns, it is usually advantageous for them to file jointly.

	Case 1	Case 2	Case 3
Adjusted gross income	$24,000	$12,000	$6,000
Standard 15% deduction	3,600	1,800	900
Maximum deductible	2,000	2,000	2,000
Minimum deductible	1,000	1,000	1,000
Allowable deduction	2,000	1,800	1,000

2 Itemized deductions If a taxpayer elects to itemize his personal deductions rather than take the standard deduction, he may deduct, among others, the following personal expenditures, some of which are subject to limitations:

a Interest on any indebtedness incurred strictly for personal use, such as a bank loan or home mortgage.

b Taxes imposed by state and local taxing authorities directly upon the individual taxpayer in the form of sales taxes, gasoline taxes, income taxes, and real estate and personal property taxes. (Fees and licenses such as auto inspection fees, drivers' licenses, and hunting and fishing licenses are *not* deductible. If part or all of the cost of an automobile license is based upon the value of the automobile, such amount is deductible as personal property tax; otherwise, the licensing fee is not deductible.)

c Contributions of a charitable nature to recognized religious, charitable, educational, scientific, and literary organizations, and to organizations for the prevention of cruelty to children or animals, provided the organization is not profit-oriented and does not devote a major portion of its time to attempting to influence legislation. In general, the contributions may not exceed 50 percent of the taxpayer's adjusted gross income.

d Medical and dental expenses of the taxpayer and his dependents which were paid by the taxpayer and were not compensated for by insurance or otherwise, subject to limitations, most of which are related to the taxpayer's adjusted gross income. In general, medical and dental expenses are deductible only to the extent that the amount paid exceeds 3 percent of the taxpayer's adjusted gross income. In addition, the deductibility of amounts paid for medicine and drugs must be reduced by an amount equal to 1 percent of the adjusted gross income. An amount equal to one-half of the insurance premium paid for medical care for the taxpayer and his dependents is deductible up to a maximum of $150. The other one-half, plus any excess over the $150 limit, is deductible subject to the overall 3 percent limitation. Within these limitations, the taxpayer may deduct amounts paid to or for physicians, dentists, nurses, drugs, medicines, hospitals, transportation necessary to obtain medical care, eyeglasses, artificial teeth, medical or surgical appliances, x-ray examination or treatments, and premiums on hospital or medical insurance. (He *cannot* deduct payments for funeral expenses, illegal operations or drugs, travel ordered or suggested by his doctor for rest or change, cosmetics, or premiums on life insurance.)

To illustrate the medical deduction computation, let us assume that during a taxable year in which a taxpayer had an adjusted gross income of $20,000, he paid $450 for medicines and drugs, $425 for medical care insurance, and $800 for other medical and dental expenses. Letting the letters AGI stand for adjusted gross income, we can determine his medical deduction of $875 as follows:

Medicines and drugs (amount paid)		$ 450
Less: 1% of AGI (.01 × $20,000)		(200)
Allowable medicines and drugs		$ 250
Medical care insurance (amount paid)	$425	
Less: Special deduction	(150)*	275
Other medical and dental expenses paid		800
		$1,325
Less: 3% of AGI (.03 × $20,000)		600
		$ 725
Plus: Special deduction		150*
Medical deduction		$ 875

*One-half of the medical care insurance premiums paid with a maximum deductible amount of $150. Since one-half of $425 is more than $150, the limitation applies.

Unlike the standard deduction, which is limited to a maximum of $2,000, there is no limitation on the total amount for itemized deductions.

Personal Exemptions In moving from adjusted gross income to taxable income, the individual taxpayer is entitled to deduct, in addition to either the allowable standard deduction or the itemized deductions, a specified amount (in 1973 and thereafter, $750) for each of the following exemptions:

1 One exemption as the taxpayer.
2 If married, one exemption for his spouse if a joint return is filed. If a separate return is filed but the spouse has no taxable income and is not taken as a dependent by another taxpayer, this exemption is also allowable.
3 An additional exemption for the taxpayer who is 65 years of age or older.
4 An additional exemption for a spouse who is 65 or older, provided the regular exemption for the spouse outlined in (2) above is taken.
5 An additional exemption if the taxpayer is blind.
6 An additional exemption for a spouse who is blind, provided that the regular exemption for the spouse as outlined in (2) above is taken.
7 One exemption for each dependent other than spouse.

A dependent is defined as a person who meets the following requirements:

1 He is either closely related to the taxpayer or resides in the taxpayer's home.

2 He receives more than one-half of his support from the taxpayer.

3 If married, he does not file a joint return with his spouse.

4 He has gross income of less than $750 during the taxable year. (There are two exceptions to this requirement. If the dependent is a child under 19 years of age, or if he is a full-time student during each of five calendar months of the taxable year, the $750 limitation on income does not apply.)

Since each exemption is worth a specified amount, the computation involved is simply a matter of determining the total number of exemptions to which the taxpayer is entitled and multiplying that number by the amount allowable per exemption. A taxpayer with six exemptions, for example, would be entitled to deduct $4,500 (6 × $750) from his adjusted gross income for his personal exemptions, whereas a taxpayer with four exemptions would be entitled to deduct $3,000 (4 × $750).

Taxable Income

The base against which tax rates are applied when tax liabilities are computed is known as **taxable income.** In the case of the individual taxpayer, it consists of his gross income less deductions from gross income, less either the standard deduction or the itemized deductions, less the deduction for personal exemptions.

Individual Tax Rates

Because of a more or less general acceptance by the tax-paying public of the theory that every member of a society should contribute to its support in proportion to his ability, individual income tax rates in the United States are, as a rule, **progressive** in nature; that is, the more income a taxpayer receives, the more taxes he must pay. A former version of the tax law, for example, imposed a tax of 20 percent on the first $2,000 of a single person's taxable income, 22 percent on the next $2,000, and so on up to 91 percent on his taxable income in excess of $200,000. In contrast, the present rates progress from 14 percent on the first $500 of a single person's taxable income up to 70 percent on his taxable income in excess of $100,000.

Once taxable income has been properly determined, the computation of the tax is simply a matter of multiplying the appropriate portions of the taxable income by the applicable rates, which are obtained from tax tables or tax rate schedules, and then summing up the tax.

Tax Tables and Tax Rate Schedules Simplified tax tables are available for the taxpayer whose adjusted gross income is less than $10,000 and who wishes to choose the standard deduction. (Itemized deductions cannot be taken in conjunction with these tables because the standard deduction is built into the tables.) A taxpayer who itemizes his deductions or who has an adjusted gross income of $10,000 or more must use the appropriate tax rate schedule. Because the construction of the tables and the schedules is somewhat similar, only the schedules are illustrated here; as you use them, bear in mind that they, like the exemptions, are subject to change from time to time.

In general, the rates that apply depend upon whether the taxpayer is (1) a single person, (2) a married person, or (3) a taxpayer who qualifies as a head of a household. Tables and schedules are available for each of these classifications.

Single Taxpayers   Schedule I which follows contains the tax rates applicable to single persons.

Schedule I Income Tax Rates for Single Taxpayers	
Taxable Income	*Tax*
Not over $500	14% of the taxable income.
$ 500 to $ 1,000	$ 70 plus 15% of excess over $ 500
1,000 to 1,500	145 plus 16% of excess over 1,000
1,500 to 2,000	225 plus 17% of excess over 1,500
2,000 to 4,000	310 plus 19% of excess over 2,000
4,000 to 6,000	690 plus 21% of excess over 4,000
6,000 to 8,000	1,110 plus 24% of excess over 6,000
8,000 to 10,000	1,590 plus 25% of excess over 8,000
10,000 to 12,000	2,090 plus 27% of excess over 10,000
12,000 to 14,000	2,630 plus 29% of excess over 12,000
14,000 to 16,000	3,210 plus 31% of excess over 14,000
16,000 to 18,000	3,830 plus 34% of excess over 16,000
18,000 to 20,000	4,510 plus 36% of excess over 18,000
20,000 to 22,000	5,230 plus 38% of excess over 20,000
22,000 to 26,000	5,990 plus 40% of excess over 22,000
26,000 to 32,000	7,590 plus 45% of excess over 26,000
32,000 to 38,000	10,290 plus 50% of excess over 32,000
38,000 to 44,000	13,290 plus 55% of excess over 38,000
44,000 to 50,000	16,590 plus 60% of excess over 44,000
50,000 to 60,000	20,190 plus 62% of excess over 50,000
60,000 to 70,000	26,390 plus 64% of excess over 60,000
70,000 to 80,000	32,790 plus 66% of excess over 70,000
80,000 to 90,000	39,390 plus 68% of excess over 80,000
90,000 to 100,000	46,190 plus 69% of excess over 90,000
Over $100,000	53,090 plus 70% of excess over 100,000

In accordance with the rates contained in this schedule, a single taxpayer with a taxable income of $14,600 would incur a tax liability of $3,396, computed as follows:

Tax on the first $14,000 ⸺ $3,210
Tax on the next $600 @ 31% ⸺ 186
    Total tax ⸺ $3,396

Married Taxpayers Married couples, if they so desire, may legally file separate tax returns; however, it is generally to their financial advantage to file jointly. Schedule II which follows contains the tax rates applicable to taxpayers filing joint returns; Schedule III contains the tax rates applicable to married taxpayers filing separate returns.

Schedule II
Income Tax Rates for Married Taxpayers Filing Joint Returns

Taxable Income	Tax
Not over $1,000	14% of the taxable income.
$ 1,000 to $ 2,000	$ 140 plus 15% of excess over $ 1,000
2,000 to 3,000	290 plus 16% of excess over 2,000
3,000 to 4,000	450 plus 17% of excess over 3,000
4,000 to 8,000	620 plus 19% of excess over 4,000
8,000 to 12,000	1,380 plus 22% of excess over 8,000
12,000 to 16,000	2,260 plus 25% of excess over 12,000
16,000 to 20,000	3,260 plus 28% of excess over 16,000
20,000 to 24,000	4,380 plus 32% of excess over 20,000
24,000 to 28,000	5,660 plus 36% of excess over 24,000
28,000 to 32,000	7,100 plus 39% of excess over 28,000
32,000 to 36,000	8,660 plus 42% of excess over 32,000
36,000 to 40,000	10,340 plus 45% of excess over 36,000
40,000 to 44,000	12,140 plus 48% of excess over 40,000
44,000 to 52,000	14,060 plus 50% of excess over 44,000
52,000 to 64,000	18,060 plus 53% of excess over 52,000
64,000 to 76,000	24,420 plus 55% of excess over 64,000
76,000 to 88,000	31,020 plus 58% of excess over 76,000
88,000 to 100,000	37,980 plus 60% of excess over 88,000
100,000 to 120,000	45,180 plus 62% of excess over 100,000
120,000 to 140,000	57,580 plus 64% of excess over 120,000
140,000 to 160,000	70,380 plus 66% of excess over 140,000
160,000 to 180,000	83,580 plus 68% of excess over 160,000
180,000 to 200,000	97,180 plus 69% of excess over 180,000
Over $200,000	110,980 plus 70% of excess over 200,000

Schedule III
Income Tax Rates for Married Taxpayers Filing Separate Returns

Taxable Income	Tax
Not over $500	14% of the taxable income.
$ 500 to $ 1,000	$ 70 plus 15% of excess over $ 500
1,000 to 1,500	145 plus 16% of excess over 1,000
1,500 to 2,000	225 plus 17% of excess over 1,500
2,000 to 4,000	310 plus 19% of excess over 2,000
4,000 to 6,000	690 plus 22% of excess over 4,000
6,000 to 8,000	1,130 plus 25% of excess over 6,000
8,000 to 10,000	1,630 plus 28% of excess over 8,000
10,000 to 12,000	2,190 plus 32% of excess over 10,000
12,000 to 14,000	2,830 plus 36% of excess over 12,000
14,000 to 16,000	3,550 plus 39% of excess over 14,000
16,000 to 18,000	4,330 plus 42% of excess over 16,000
18,000 to 20,000	5,170 plus 45% of excess over 18,000
20,000 to 22,000	6,070 plus 48% of excess over 20,000
22,000 to 26,000	7,030 plus 50% of excess over 22,000
26,000 to 32,000	9,030 plus 53% of excess over 26,000
32,000 to 38,000	12,210 plus 55% of excess over 32,000
38,000 to 44,000	15,510 plus 58% of excess over 38,000
44,000 to 50,000	18,990 plus 60% of excess over 44,000
50,000 to 60,000	22,590 plus 62% of excess over 50,000
60,000 to 70,000	28,790 plus 64% of excess over 60,000
70,000 to 80,000	35,190 plus 66% of excess over 70,000
80,000 to 90,000	41,790 plus 68% of excess over 80,000
90,000 to 100,000	48,590 plus 69% of excess over 90,000
Over $100,000	55,490 plus 70% of excess over 100,000

The joint return is designed to eliminate tax inequities between married couples living in states which have community property laws and those who reside in states which do not. Under a community property law, income earned by a husband, his wife, or both together is considered to be jointly earned and equally shared, and thus is divided equally for tax purposes.

The effect of the joint return is to divide, or "split," a couple's combined taxable income equally between the two spouses, with the result that their income normally will be subject to a lower tax rate than if they filed separate returns. We can see this more clearly if we compare Schedules II and III. Note that the percentages are the same in both schedules, but that the income bracket on each line of the joint return (Schedule II) is double the amount on the same line in the separate return (Schedule III). For example, the percentage on line 4 is 17 percent on both schedules, but the income bracket is $1,500 to $2,000 on Schedule III, and $3,000 to $4,000 on Schedule II.

To illustrate the benefit to be derived from filing a joint return, let us assume that a married couple has a taxable income of $14,600. In accordance with the rates contained in Schedule II, if they file a joint return they will incur a tax liability of $2,910, computed as follows:

Tax on the first $12,000	$2,260
Tax on the next $2,600 @ 25%	650
Total tax	$2,910

If the husband earned the entire $14,600 and were to file a separate return, his tax liability would be $3,784, computed as follows using Schedule III:

Tax on the first $14,000	$3,550
Tax on the next $600 @ 39%	234
Total tax	$3,784

Thus, if the couple file a joint return, they will save $874 ($3,784 − $2,910).

If, on the other hand, the husband earned only $9,500 of the taxable $14,600 and his wife earned the remainder ($5,100), their combined tax liability, if they were to file separate returns, would be $2,982 [$1,630 + ($1,500 × 28%)] + [$690 + ($1,100 × 22%)]. In this case, by filing jointly they would save $72 ($2,982 − $2,910).

Heads of Households Recognizing that an unmarried person who maintains a household for dependents incurs many of the same expenses as a married couple, the law gives some tax relief (roughly one-half of the benefit granted a married couple filing a joint return) to taxpayers who qualify as heads of households. To meet this qualification, a taxpayer must be either unmarried or married and living apart from his spouse and filing a separate return and must furnish over one-half of the cost of maintaining a household in which he and at least one of the following persons resides:

1 An unmarried child, stepchild, or descendant of a child of the taxpayer

2 Any dependent of the taxpayer

Dependent parents are an exception to the residency requirement. They may live apart from the taxpayer without affecting his head of household status as long as the taxpayer maintains their household.

Schedule IV, which follows, contains the tax rates applicable to heads of households. In accordance with the rates contained therein, a taxpayer qualifying

---

Schedule IV
Income Tax Rates for Heads of Households

Taxable Income	Tax
Not over $1,000	14% of the taxable income.
$ 1,000 to $ 2,000	$ 140 plus 16% of excess over $ 1,000
2,000 to 4,000	300 plus 18% of excess over 2,000
4,000 to 6,000	660 plus 19% of excess over 4,000
6,000 to 8,000	1,040 plus 22% of excess over 6,000
8,000 to 10,000	1,480 plus 23% of excess over 8,000
10,000 to 12,000	1,940 plus 25% of excess over 10,000
12,000 to 14,000	2,440 plus 27% of excess over 12,000
14,000 to 16,000	2,980 plus 28% of excess over 14,000
16,000 to 18,000	3,540 plus 31% of excess over 16,000
18,000 to 20,000	4,160 plus 32% of excess over 18,000
20,000 to 22,000	4,800 plus 35% of excess over 20,000
22,000 to 24,000	5,500 plus 36% of excess over 22,000
24,000 to 26,000	6,220 plus 38% of excess over 24,000
26,000 to 28,000	6,980 plus 41% of excess over 26,000
28,000 to 32,000	7,800 plus 42% of excess over 28,000
32,000 to 36,000	9,480 plus 45% of excess over 32,000
36,000 to 38,000	11,280 plus 48% of excess over 36,000
38,000 to 40,000	12,240 plus 51% of excess over 38,000
40,000 to 44,000	13,260 plus 52% of excess over 40,000
44,000 to 50,000	15,340 plus 55% of excess over 44,000
50,000 to 52,000	18,640 plus 56% of excess over 50,000
52,000 to 64,000	19,760 plus 58% of excess over 52,000
64,000 to 70,000	26,720 plus 59% of excess over 64,000
70,000 to 76,000	30,260 plus 61% of excess over 70,000
76,000 to 80,000	33,920 plus 62% of excess over 76,000
80,000 to 88,000	36,400 plus 63% of excess over 80,000
88,000 to 100,000	41,440 plus 64% of excess over 88,000
100,000 to 120,000	49,120 plus 66% of excess over 100,000
120,000 to 140,000	62,320 plus 67% of excess over 120,000
140,000 to 160,000	75,720 plus 68% of excess over 140,000
160,000 to 180,000	89,320 plus 69% of excess over 160,000
Over $180,000	103,120 plus 70% of excess over 180,000

as a head of a household and having a taxable income of $14,600 would incur a tax liability of $3,148, computed as follows:

Tax on the first $14,000	$2,980
Tax on the next $600 @ 28%	168
Total tax	$3,148

The benefit to be derived from filing a joint return or a head of household return in preference to a single taxpayer's return may be seen in the following comparison. Note that the tax differential between the single taxpayer and the head of household taxpayer is roughly one-half of that between the single taxpayer and the joint return taxpayer. (Again, taxable incomes of $14,600 are assumed.)

Single taxpayer	$3,396
Joint return taxpayer	2,910
Head of household taxpayer	3,148

Capital Gains and Losses

One area of an individual taxpayer's taxable income, commonly known as capital gains and losses, falls into a category by itself and is subject to special treatment with respect to income tax rates. For this reason, a discussion of it has been postponed until this time.

Capital gains and losses result from the sale or exchange of capital assets and as a rule are treated as additions to or deductions from gross income. In general, capital assets are assets which are not held primarily for sale or use in the taxpayer's business or profession. Typical examples are stocks and bonds. A personal residence is also considered to be a capital asset, subject to the above limitation.

If an asset was held by the taxpayer for six months or less before its sale or exchange, the resulting gain or loss is referred to as **short-term;** if it was held longer than six months, the gain or loss is said to be **long-term.** All short-term gains (or losses) pertaining to a taxable year are combined in order to determine the **net short-term gain** (or **loss**) for the year; the same procedure is followed with regard to long-term gains or losses. The results are then added algebraically to obtain a **net capital gain** or **net capital loss.**

Subject to certain limitations, net capital gains are included in gross income, whereas net capital losses are deducted therefrom. If a net capital gain is composed entirely of net short-term gains, the total is included in taxable income; if it is made up entirely of net long-term gains, only 50 percent of the total is included therein. If the net capital gain is composed of both a net short-term and a net long-term gain, the gains are handled separately; that is, the entire net short-term gain is included in taxable income, but only one-half of the net long-term gain is included.

If, on the other hand, a net capital gain is composed of both a net gain and a net loss, one of which is short-term and the other long-term, the net capital gain is handled in accordance with the net gain. Thus, if the net gain is short-term, the entire net capital gain is included in taxable income, whereas if the net gain is long-term, only one-half of the net capital gain is included. Net capital losses are deductible from gross income to the extent of $1,000, with any excess being carried forward for use as a deduction in future years.

If we let STCG (or L) equal short-term capital gain or loss, LTCG (or L) equal long-term capital gain or loss, and CG (or L) equal capital gain or loss, the provisions applicable to capital gains and losses may be illustrated as follows:

	Case 1	Case 2	Case 3	Case 4
Net STCG (or L)	$4,000	$6,000	($4,000)	$4,000
Net LTCG (or L)	5,000	(4,000)	7,000	(9,000)
Net CG (or L)	$9,000	$2,000	$3,000	($5,000)
Includable in taxable income	$6,500*	$2,000	$1,500†	—
Deductible from gross income				($1,000)
Carry-over				($3,000)‡

*$4,000 + (50% of $5,000)
†50% of $3,000
‡It takes $2 of long-term capital loss to offset $1 of ordinary income.

Proprietorships and Schedule C

Any individual who engages in a business or practices a profession as a sole proprietor and who earns $400 or more from the proprietorship during a taxable year must file an income tax return on which the details of his business earnings are disclosed. Schedule C (Form 1040) entitled "Profit (or Loss) from Business or Profession" is employed for this purpose and is filed along with the individual's personal income tax return. It is illustrated on page 476 in abbreviated form.

Partnerships and Form 1065

Although partners, like sole proprietors, are ordinarily taxed as individuals, every partnership doing business in or receiving income from sources within the United States is required to file an informational return each year. Form 1065 entitled "U.S. Partnership Return of Income" is employed for this purpose. It includes an income statement form similar to Schedule C (Form 1040), a balance sheet to be filled out both as of the beginning and the end of the taxable year, a form for reconciliation of the partners' capital accounts as of the beginning and the end of the taxable year, and a schedule showing each partner's share of the partnership's earnings. Being informational in nature, Form 1065 does not require any tax payment as such. Each partner, however, must include his share of partnership income on his personal income tax return.

CORPORATIONS AS TAXPAYERS

Unlike proprietorships and partnerships, corporations are taxable entities, and income taxes play a major role in their operation. Many management decisions regarding expansion or cutbacks, product changes, and similar factors are based at least partially on the probable tax effect of the transaction.

Profit (or Loss) from Business or Profession
(Sole Proprietorship)

1	Gross receipts or gross sales $_____ Less: Returns and allowances $_____		$	
2	Inventory at beginning of year (if different from last year's closing inventory attach explanation)			
3	Merchandise purchased $_____ , less cost of any items withdrawn from business for personal use $_____			
4	Cost of labor (do not include salary paid to yourself) . .			
5	Material and supplies			
6	Other costs (explain in Schedule C-1)			
7	Total of lines 2 through 6			
8	Inventory at end of this year			
9	Cost of goods sold and/or operations (subtract line 8 from line 7)			
10	Gross profit (subtract line 9 from line 1)			

OTHER BUSINESS DEDUCTIONS

11	Depreciation (explain in Schedule C-2)			
12	Taxes on business and business property (explain in Schedule C-1)			
13	Rent on business property			
14	Repairs (explain in Schedule C-1)			
15	Salaries and wages not included on line 4 (exclude any paid to yourself)			
16	Insurance			
17	Legal and professional fees			
18	Commissions			
19	Amortization (attach statement)			
20	Retirement plans			
21	Interest on business indebtedness			
22	Bad debts arising from sales or services			
23	Depletion			
24	Other business expenses (explain in Schedule C-1) . . .			
25	Total of lines 11 through 24			
26	Net profit (or loss) (subtract line 25 from line 10)			

SCHEDULE C (Form 1040)

Corporate taxpayers file their returns on Form 1120 entitled "U.S. Corporation Income Tax Return." The form includes an income statement, the format of which is essentially the same as that of Schedule C (Form 1040), a balance sheet to be filled out both as of the beginning and the end of the taxable year, a schedule for the reconciliation of any difference between net income as computed per the corporation's books and taxable income as reported on the return, and a schedule for the reconciliation of retained earnings.

The basic tax formula for computing the corporate taxpayer's tax liability is depicted in the following diagram. As you study it, compare it with the tax formula for individual taxpayers on page 463 and note that the concept of adjusted gross income does not apply to corporations.

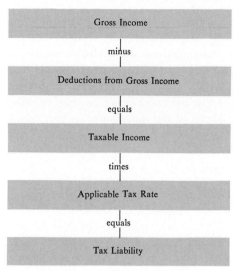

Basic tax formula for corporate taxpayers.

Corporate Taxable Income

Generally, corporate gross income and the deductions therefrom are determined in essentially the same way as those of the individual taxpayer. Adjusted gross income, however, is not pertinent to the determination of corporate taxable income because the optional standard deduction, the itemized deductions, and the deduction for personal exemptions do not apply. Thus, the taxable income of an incorporated business tends to approximate the adjusted gross income of an individual taxpayer who operates a similar but unincorporated business.

Corporate Tax Rates

Unlike tax rates applicable to the individual taxpayer's income, corporate rates are not graduated. Instead, the corporate income tax is composed of two separate elements, a **normal tax** and a **surtax,** both of which are computed at flat rates. The normal tax is a fixed percentage of the corporation's taxable income, whereas the surtax is a fixed percentage of the taxable income in excess of a certain amount. As of this writing, the normal tax is 22 percent, and the surtax is 26 percent of taxable income in excess of $25,000. Employing these rates, a corporation with $100,000 of taxable income would incur a tax liability of $41,500, computed as follows:

Normal tax ($100,000 × .22)	$22,000
Surtax ($75,000 × .26)	19,500
Total tax	$41,500

Corporate Capital Gains and Losses A corporation's capital gains and losses are determined in the same manner as those of an individual taxpayer but are taxed somewhat differently. For example, corporations are not allowed the 50 percent long-term capital gains deduction, and they may deduct capital losses only to the extent of capital gains. If, however, capital losses exceed capital gains, any capital loss which is not allowed because of this limitation may be used to offset capital gains of the 3 previous years and those of the subsequent 5 years until used up.

Accounting Income versus Taxable Income

Form 1120 requires the corporate taxpayer to reconcile any difference between net income as computed in accordance with the corporation's books and taxable income as reported on the tax return. This may have raised a question in your mind as to why such a difference should exist. Simply stated, the answer is this: Taxable income must be determined according to statutory rules and regulations, whereas accounting, or book, income is determined according to generally accepted accounting principles. Obviously, whenever the tax treatment and the accounting treatment of items of revenue and expense differ, the resulting incomes will also differ.

When a major difference exists between accounting income and taxable income, it is usually the result of one or more of the following conditions:

1 Certain revenue items are included in accounting income but not in taxable income. For example, interest earned on state or municipal obligations is included in accounting income but not in taxable income.

2 Some revenue items are included in taxable income in one period but in accounting income in another. For example, interest collected in advance is considered as taxable income in the period collected but as accounting income in the year earned. The reverse, of course, is also true: In the subsequent year in which the interest is earned, the item is included in accounting income but not in taxable income.

3 Some revenue items are included in both taxable and accounting income but in different amounts. For example, subject to certain limitations, only 15 percent of the dividend income received by a corporation is ordinarily included in taxable income, whereas 100 percent is included in accounting income.

4 Certain expense items are deducted for accounting purposes but not for tax purposes. For example, goodwill is frequently amortized for accounting purposes, but it is not deductible for tax purposes. Likewise, federal income taxes themselves are deducted as expenses in the determination of accounting income but are not deductible for tax purposes.

5 Some expense items are deducted for accounting purposes in one period and for tax purposes in another. For example, estimated expenses such as product warranties and service agreements are deductible for accounting purposes in the year in which the sale is made, but they are not deductible for tax purposes until the actual liability is incurred. Again, the reverse is true: In the year in which the liability is incurred, the item is deductible for tax purposes but not for accounting purposes.

6 Some expense items are deducted from both taxable and accounting income, but in different amounts. For example, the charitable contributions of a corporation are deductible in their entirety for accounting purposes, but on the tax return they are limited to a maximum of 5 percent of taxable income computed before either the contributions or the special deduction for dividends received is subtracted. Likewise, a depreciable asset may be depreciated at one rate for tax purposes and at another for accounting purposes. Thus, accelerated depreciation may be taken for tax purposes and straight-line depreciation for accounting purposes. To illustrate, let us assume that an asset with a depreciable cost of $300,000 and an estimated useful life of 5 years is depreciated by the sum-of-years'-digits method for tax purposes and by the straight-line method for accounting purposes. As you can see in the following tabulation, the amount deductible for depreciation would be the same for both tax and accounting purposes in only 1 of the 5 years (the third year).

Depreciation Schedule

	Computations	Annual Depreciation Tax Purposes	Annual Depreciation Accounting Purposes
First year	($\frac{5}{15}$ and $\frac{1}{5}$ of $300,000)	$100,000	$ 60,000
Second year	($\frac{4}{15}$ and $\frac{1}{5}$ of $300,000)	80,000	60,000
Third year	($\frac{3}{15}$ and $\frac{1}{5}$ of $300,000)	60,000	60,000
Fourth year	($\frac{2}{15}$ and $\frac{1}{5}$ of $300,000)	40,000	60,000
Fifth year	($\frac{1}{15}$ and $\frac{1}{5}$ of $300,000)	20,000	60,000
		$300,000	$300,000

Allocation of Income Taxes

Since some revenue and expense items may affect the determination of accounting income in one period and the computation of taxable income in another, the question often arises as to the proper amount of tax expense to be shown in the income statement and the appropriate treatment of the tax liability on the balance sheet.

The Accounting Principles Board takes the position that taxes levied on business organizations are expenses which should be accrued, deferred, and estimated in the same manner as other expenses.[1] Accordingly, the Income Taxes account in the income statement should reflect the amount of taxes properly allocable to the income reported therein, and the tax liability should be shown on the balance sheet in accordance with the usual classifications. The allocation of income taxes, as is the case with any expense, is particularly important when the tax effect of an item is material.

Tax Effect of an Item   The tax effect of an item is computed by multiplying the difference between the amounts at which the item is reported in the tax return and in the books by the applicable tax rate.

The following schedules, based upon the data in the preceding depreciation schedule, illustrate the tax effect of accelerated depreciation. Assume that income, before depreciation and income taxes are taken into consideration, is $160,000 for each of the 5 years; also, for simplicity, assume a 40 percent tax rate.

Schedule A—Tax Computation per Tax Returns
Depreciation Computed by Sum-of-years'-digits Method

	First Year	Second Year	Third Year	Fourth Year	Fifth Year
Income before taxes and depreciation	$160,000	$160,000	$160,000	$160,000	$160,000
Depreciation	100,000	80,000	60,000	40,000	20,000
Taxable income per tax returns	$ 60,000	$ 80,000	$100,000	$120,000	$140,000
Taxes per tax returns	$ 24,000	$ 32,000	$ 40,000	$ 48,000	$ 56,000

Schedule B—Tax Computation per Books
Depreciation Computed by the Straight-line Method

	First Year	Second Year	Third Year	Fourth Year	Fifth Year
Income before taxes and depreciation	$160,000	$160,000	$160,000	$160,000	$160,000
Depreciation	60,000	60,000	60,000	60,000	60,000
Taxable income per books	$100,000	$100,000	$100,000	$100,000	$100,000
Taxes per books	$ 40,000	$ 40,000	$ 40,000	$ 40,000	$ 40,000

[1] AICPA, "Accounting for Income Taxes," *Opinion No. 11 of the Accounting Principles Board* (New York: 1967), p. 160.

	Schedule C—Tax Effect of Accelerated Depreciation				
	Depreciation		Difference	Tax Rate, %	Tax Effect
	Per Tax Return	Per Books			
First year	$100,000	$60,000	$40,000	40	$−16,000
Second year	80,000	60,000	20,000	40	− 8,000
Third year	60,000	60,000	—	40	—
Fourth year	40,000	60,000	20,000	40	+ 8,000
Fifth year	20,000	60,000	40,000	40	+16,000

Tax Allocation Illustrated Continuing our accelerated depreciation example, the following journal entries and T account illustrate the accounting procedures involved in the allocation of income taxes.

First Year

Income Taxes	40,000	
Deferred Income Tax Liability		16,000
Income Taxes Payable		24,000

Second Year

Income Taxes	40,000	
Deferred Income Tax Liability		8,000
Income Taxes Payable		32,000

Third Year

Income Taxes	40,000	
Income Taxes Payable		40,000

Fourth Year

Income Taxes	40,000	
Deferred Income Tax Liability	8,000	
Income Taxes Payable		48,000

Fifth Year

Income Taxes	40,000	
Deferred Income Tax Liability	16,000	
Income Taxes Payable		56,000

Deferred Income Tax Liability

Fourth year	8,000	First year		16,000
Fifth year	16,000	Second year		8,000

The Deferred Income Tax Liability account is classified on the balance sheet in accordance with the usual classifications. Thus, the accruals set up during the first two years would be classified as noncurrent items at the end of the first and second years, with $8,000 of the $24,000 being reclassified as a current item as of the end of the third year and the remaining $16,000 being reclassified as of the end of the fourth year.

Tax Allocation within a Period Thus far we have considered tax allocation only as it relates to different fiscal periods. At times, however, taxes are also allocated *within* a given fiscal period. Intraperiod allocation is employed when an item included in the determination of taxable income is treated for accounting purposes either as (1) an extraordinary item in the income statement or (2) a direct adjustment to the Retained Earnings account, in which case the item bypasses the Revenue and Expense Summary account and consequently does not appear in the income statement.[1]

To illustrate the application of tax allocation to an extraordinary item, let us assume that the ABC Company, which has an income of $100,000 from operations and a tax rate of 40 percent, sustains an uninsured flood loss of $60,000. We can readily see that without the flood loss income taxes would be $40,000 (40 percent of $100,000). If we take the flood loss into consideration, however, the income tax will be only $16,000 [40 percent of ($100,000 − $60,000)]. The following entry and T account illustrate the allocation:

Income Taxes	40,000	
Flood Loss		24,000
Income Taxes Payable		16,000

Flood Loss

Uninsured loss	60,000	Tax effect of loss	24,000

SUMMARY

Federal income taxes are imposed upon taxable entities, namely, individuals, corporations, estates, and trusts. The owners of sole proprietorships and partnerships are taxed as individuals.

An individual's taxable income consists of his gross income less deductions from gross income, less either the standard deduction or itemized deductions, less the deduction for personal exemptions.

Tax tables and tax rate schedules are employed to determine the amount of tax an individual must pay. Tax rates vary depending on whether the taxpayer is a single taxpayer, a married taxpayer who files a joint return, a married taxpayer who files a separate return, or a head of a household.

Capital gains and losses resulting from the sale or exchange of capital assets are treated as additions to or deductions from gross income. They are subject to special tax rules.

[1]Extraordinary items and items entered directly in the Retained Earnings account are covered in some detail in Chapter 19.

The taxable income of corporations is determined in much the same manner as that of individuals, with certain differences. The tax itself is composed of two separate elements, a normal tax and a surtax.

Differences frequently exist between accounting income and taxable income because of variations between accounting procedures and statutory regulations.

Income taxes are considered as business expenses by the corporate taxpayer; they should be allocated both between and within periods in the same way as other expenses.

QUESTIONS AND PROBLEMS

18-1 (1) Assume that a married couple has a combined taxable income of $16,000, $12,000 of which was earned by the husband and $4,000 by the wife. How much income tax will they be required to pay (a) if they file a joint return, and (b) if they file separate returns?

(2) Assume that a married couple has a combined taxable income of $16,000, $12,600 of which was earned by the husband and $3,400 by the wife. How much income tax will they be required to pay (a) if they file a joint return, and (b) if they file separate returns?

(3) Assume that a married couple has a combined taxable income of $18,900, $17,800 of which was earned by the husband and $1,100 by the wife. How much income tax will they be required to pay (a) if they file a joint return, and (b) if they file separate returns?

18-2 In each of the following cases, a married couple with three teen-age dependents is filing a joint return.

	Gross Income	Adjusted Gross Income	Itemized Deduction
Case 1	$ 6,500	$ 6,500	$ 300
Case 2	7,000	6,800	1,250
Case 3	8,000	7,500	700
Case 4	10,000	9,600	1,300
Case 5	22,000	21,000	2,900

(1) Compute the standard deduction in each case.

(2) Indicate whether or not you would recommend that it be claimed.

18-3 Determine the number of exemptions to which each of the following taxpayers is entitled:

(1) A single taxpayer who is over 65 years of age

(2) A married couple, both of whom are over 65, filing a joint return

(3) A single taxpayer who is over 65 and also is blind

(4) A single taxpayer with two dependent parents, both of whom are over 65

(5) A married couple, both of whom are over 65 and blind, filing a joint return

18-4 John Jones, age 29, is married and the sole support of his wife, age 27, and their four small children. During the taxable year his income consisted of $9,000 in salary and $200 interest on municipal bonds. Jones and his wife file a joint return.

(1) How many personal exemptions may Jones claim?

(2) What is his adjusted gross income?

(3) How much income tax will Jones have to pay?

18-5 It is not uncommon to find that the net income reported in an organization's income statement varies from the taxable net income reported to the Internal Revenue Service. While the difference between taxable income and accounting income is directly attributable to the use of different accounting procedures, it indirectly results from a variance between the objectives of income tax laws and those of generally accepted accounting principles. What, in your opinion, are the basic objectives of (1) generally accepted accounting principles as applied to the income statement, and (2) income tax laws?

18-6 Many business organizations report taxable incomes which are materially different from their accounting incomes. When such differences occur, the question arises as to whether the amount of income taxes shown in the income statement should be the amount of taxes actually payable for the period or the amount allocable to the income reported in the statement. Briefly discuss income tax allocation, including in your discussion (1) a general idea as to what is meant by the term, and (2) any arguments that you consider valid either for or against allocation.

18-7 Instructions Using the tax rate schedules in this chapter, determine the tax liability in each of the cases below for (1) a single person, (2) a head of a household, and (3) a married person filing a joint return.

Taxable Income

Case 1	$ 8,000
Case 2	$ 16,000
Case 3	$ 32,000
Case 4	$ 64,000
Case 5	$128,000

18-8 Six married couples' taxable incomes for the current year are shown below:

	Husband's Income	Wife's Income	Combined Incomes
Case 1	$ 12,000	—	$ 12,000
Case 2	8,000	$ 4,000	12,000
Case 3	6,000	6,000	12,000
Case 4	20,000	20,000	40,000
Case 5	40,000	—	40,000
Case 6	200,000	—	200,000

Instructions Employing the tax rate schedules in this chapter, determine the amount of tax that will be saved in each case if the couple files a joint return instead of separate returns.

18-9 Instructions Select the correct answer to each of the following problems. Unless stipulated otherwise, you are to assume that all events took place during the taxpayer's taxable year.

1 Medical expenses paid by the Browns included the following: Dr. Hawkins, $350; hospitalization insurance, $100; use of personal car for weekly trips to doctor's office for therapeutic treatments, $50; hospital fees and services, $170 ($90 of which was reimbursed under hospitalization insurance coverage); and $60 for laboratory x-rays which disclosed no evidence of disease. In itemizing their deductions and before application of any limitations, the Browns should list medical expenses totaling:
a $730
b $670
c $640
d $530
e None of the above

2 In general, medical and dental expenses are deductible only to the extent that the amount paid exceeds a certain percentage of the taxpayer's adjusted gross income, whereas the amount paid for medicine and drugs must be reduced by an amount equal to a certain percentage of the taxpayer's adjusted gross income. With the medical and dental limitation stated first, the applicable percentages are:
a 1% and 5%
b 5% and 1%
c 1% and 3%
d 3% and 1%
e None of the above

3 Assuming that the Browns' adjusted gross income is $8,000, you will find by applying the appropriate limitations to their medical expenses that they are entitled to a medical deduction of:

a $430

b $400

c $350

d $290

e None of the above

4 Jones was hospitalized during the year. He paid a $780 hospital bill and a $100 drug bill. His doctor bill amounted to $500, $300 of which he paid during the year. He paid $120 for hospitalization insurance and collected $505 therefrom. Jones, who is 40 years of age, has an adjusted gross income of $6,500 and his taxable income before any deduction is taken for medical expenses is $5,300. His medical expense deduction for the year will be:

a $583

b $535

c $326

d $295

e None of the above

5 Medical expenses paid by Smith during the year included: hospital bill, $600; doctor bill, $400; dental bill, $300; and medicine and drugs, $700. If Smith's adjusted gross income for the year is $12,000, he is entitled to a medical deduction of:

a $1,640

b $1,620

c $1,520

d $1,440

e None of the above

6 At the beginning of the taxable year, Al Brinskle, a South Carolina resident, accepted a position in Oregon with a new employer by whom he is still employed. His new employer paid him a $1,500 moving expense allowance, which Mr. Brinskle applied to the following expenses incurred in moving to Oregon:

$200—Plane fare for himself

$400—Bus fare for Mrs. Brinskle and children

$1,100—Cost of moving household effects

$150—Meals and miscellaneous expenses for Mrs. Brinskle and children during trip

Brinskle included the $1,500 moving expense allowance in his gross income. In computing his adjusted gross income he is permitted to deduct:

a $1,850
b $1,700
c $1,300
d $600
e None of the above

18-10 Instructions Mr. and Mrs. T. E. Edison, both 50 years of age, file a joint federal income tax return. Their adjusted gross income for the taxable year is $40,000. Indicate the extent to which each of the following items, all of which were paid during the current taxable year, is deductible.

Contributions:

Church	$ 200
State University	100
Union official to prevail on him to settle a wage dispute	1,000
United Fund	200
Republican Party	25
City of Chicago for parking violations	50

Taxes:

Real estate	600
Special assessment for street improvement	150
Deficiency in prior year's federal income tax	2,000
State sales tax	300

Medical:

Doctors	2,000
Hospital	1,500
Nurses	500
Dentist	200
Premium on hospitalization insurance	120
Life insurance premiums	1,000
Medicines and drugs	200
Check received from insurance company on hospitalization policy	1,000

18-11 Instructions Each of the following cases pertains to an individual tax-payer. Determine the amount of net capital gain that is includable in taxable income or net capital loss that is deductible therefrom in each case.

	STCG	STCL	LTCG	LTCL
Case 1	$6,000	$ 5,000	$5,000	$3,000
Case 2	5,000	6,000	7,000	1,000
Case 3	3,000	2,000	2,000	6,000
Case 4	3,000	10,000	5,000	2,000
Case 5	6,000	3,000	3,000	5,000

18-12 The Dane Davis Partnership was formed to conduct an architectural practice. The firm's bookkeeper prepared the following tabulation of income and deductions for the taxable year from the accounting records:

Income

Billings for services		$64,720
Rental income from property owned at 210 Main Street		2,700
Total		$67,420

Deductions

Salaries:		
Draftsmen	$10,000	
Bookkeeper	4,400	
Rent	1,800	
Depreciation:		
Furniture and equipment	180	
210 Main Street	900	
Taxes:		
Based on payroll	450	
Property at 210 Main Street	400	
Federal income—Dane	600	
Federal income—Davis	500	
Other	100	
Maintenance at 210 Main Street	700	
Contributions:		
Village community center	100	
United Fund	100	
Miscellaneous business expenses	1,880	
Loss on sale of:		
Property at 210 Main Street	1,500	
Indor Corporation stock	3,000	26,610
Net profit		$40,810

Instructions Assuming that both the property at 210 Main Street and the Indor Corporation stock have been held for over a year and that Davis's share of the partnership profits is 40 percent, determine how he should handle his share of the partnership income and deductions in his individual income tax computation. Show both major categories and amounts.

18-13 The ABC Corporation has taxable income comprised of $60,000 derived from operations and $30,000 from long-term capital gains.

Instructions Using the tax rates presented in this chapter, and assuming a maximum tax rate of 25 percent on long-term capital gains, determine the ABC Corporation's tax liability.

18-14 Instructions In the problems which follow, unless instructed otherwise, you are to assume that book income has been determined in accordance with generally accepted accounting principles and is to be interpreted as income before federal income taxes. Select the correct answer in each.

1 The A Corporation's book income for the taxable year is $100,000. The corporation received interest of $5,000 on State of Florida bonds and made a $1,000 contribution to the United Fund. Its taxable income is:

a $105,000
b $100,000
c $95,000
d $94,000
e None of the above

2 The B Corporation's book income for the taxable year is $40,000. The corporation sustained a $10,000 short-term capital loss and received $20,000 in dividends from a nonaffiliated corporation. Its taxable income is:

a $50,000
b $33,000
c $10,000
d $7,500
e None of the above

3 The C Corporation's book income for the taxable year is $95,000. The corporation received $20,000 in dividends from a nonaffiliated corporation, paid $2,000 in real estate taxes on corporate property, and paid interest of $1,000 on a bank loan. Its taxable income is:

a $95,000
b $92,000
c $89,000
d $78,000
e None of the above

4 The D Corporation's book income for the taxable year is $200,000. The corporation computes depreciation by the straight-line method for accounting purposes but by the sum-of-years'-digits method for tax purposes. Straight-line depreciation amounts to $25,000 for the year, whereas depreciation computed by the sum-of-years'-digits method amounts to $37,000. D Corporation's taxable income is:

a $225,000
b $212,000
c $188,000
d $175,000
e None of the above

5 The E Corporation's book income for the taxable year is $92,000. The

corporation sustained a net long-term capital loss of $2,000 during the
year. Its taxable income is:

a $94,000
b $92,000
c $91,000
d $90,000
e None of the above

18-15 Instructions Employing the following corporate taxpayer data, determine
the amount of net capital gain includable in taxable income or net capital
loss deductible therefrom in each of the 5 years.

	STCG	STCL	LTCG	LTCL
19X1	$8,000	$6,000	$4,000	$2,000
19X2	4,000	8,000	6,000	1,000
19X3	3,000	9,000	3,000	2,000
19X4	3,000	2,000	4,000	3,000
19X5	5,000	2,000	6,000	4,000

18-16 An asset with a depreciable cost of $1.1 million and an estimated useful
life of 10 years is being depreciated on the sum-of-years'-digits basis for
tax purposes and on the straight-line basis for accounting purposes.

Instructions Assuming a tax rate of 48 percent, prepare a schedule showing
the tax effect of the accelerated depreciation for the 10-year period.

18-17 The ABC Company is contemplating changing its method of computing
depreciation for federal income tax purposes from a straight-line method
to a sum-of-years'-digits method. The company has not yet decided
whether it will continue to compute depreciation by the straight-line
method for book purposes or whether it will use the sum-of-years'-digits
method for both book and tax purposes. The following data pertain to
the current year:

Taxable income before depreciation	$500,000
Depreciation: Straight-line	100,000
Sum-of-years'-digits	150,000
Income taxes: Based on $400,000	192,000
Based on $350,000	168,000

Instructions Prepare the entry or entries necessary to record the income
tax expense for the year, assuming that:

(1) Depreciation for tax purposes is to be computed by the sum-of-years'-

digits method, but straight-line depreciation is to be recorded in the accounts.

(2) Depreciation for both tax and book purposes is to be computed by the sum-of-years'-digits method.

18-18 The Ace Manufacturing Company presents you with the following information regarding its taxable year:

Sales	$2,000,000
Cost of goods sold	1,100,000*
Operating expenses	400,000

*This figure includes straight-line depreciation on an asset with a depreciable cost of $300,000 and an estimated useful life of 20 years. The asset has been in use 3 years. For tax purposes, it is being depreciated on a straight-line basis over a 60-month period.

Instructions Using only the data given and assuming a normal tax rate of 22 percent and a surtax of 26 percent on taxable income in excess of $25,000:

(1) Determine book income before the provision for federal income taxes is made.

(2) Determine taxable income.

(3) Prepare the entry to record the income tax expense for the year.

(4) Prepare the entry which will be necessary to record the income tax expense for the sixth year that the asset is used. (Assume that all other data in the problem remain constant.)

18-19 The Brace Manufacturing Company presents you with the following information regarding its taxable year:

Sales	$3,000,000
Cost of goods sold	1,600,000
Operating expenses	700,000
Uninsured flood loss	120,000

Instructions Using only the data given and assuming a normal tax rate of 22 percent and a surtax of 26 percent on taxable income in excess of $25,000:

(1) Determine book income before either the provision for federal income taxes is made or recognition is given to the flood loss.

(2) Determine taxable income.

(3) Prepare the entry to record the income tax expense for the year.

18-20 The Chase Manufacturing Company presents you with the following information regarding its taxable year:

Sales	$4,000,000
Cost of goods sold	2,000,000
Operating expenses	1,200,000
Long-term capital gain (bonds held as an investment)	200,000

Instructions Using only the data given and assuming a normal tax rate of 22 percent, a surtax of 26 percent on taxable income in excess of $25,000, and a maximum tax rate of 25 percent on corporate long-term capital gains:

(1) Determine book income before either the provision for federal income taxes is made or recognition is given to the long-term capital gain.

(2) Determine taxable income.

(3) Prepare the entry to record the income tax expense for the year.

Part Six
Dissemination and Interpretation of Accounting Data

19

Basic Financial Statements

The collecting and processing of accounting data, which we have been studying up to this time, comprise a major part of the accounting function. Necessary companion aspects, however, are the presentation of the information derived from the data in an appropriate and understandable form and the dissemination of this information to interested groups and individuals. These steps make up what is known in accounting jargon as the reporting process. It follows that once the information has been reported, it must be interpreted. Therefore, we shall cover reporting in this and the following chapter and cover interpretation in Chapters 21 and 22.

Because the flow of business activity normally is continuous, the ultimate outcome of many transactions lies in the future. However, many business decisions must be made immediately. Therefore, management, investors, governmental agencies, and others frequently require some kind of "test reading" which will enable them to gauge an organization's progress as well as its present financial position. Management, for example, must know what the organization has done in the past and where it stands today before a decision can be made as to what actions may be sound and profitable for tomorrow. Information of this nature is taken from the accounting records by the accountant and presented to the user in the form of financial statements.

Broadly stated, any formal tabulation of the financial facts of an organization is a financial statement. However, when we refer to the basic financial statements, we usually mean (1) the balance sheet, (2) the income statement, and (3) in the case of a corporation, the retained earnings statement. Although a comprehensive understanding of the financial position and operating activities of an organization may be derived only in part from a study of these statements, it nevertheless is possible for a person moderately experienced in business and finance to obtain basic information from them on which he may rely with confidence.

REPORTING STANDARDS

If the user of a financial statement is to base a decision on data contained therein, obviously he must be confident that the statement is reliable. In an attempt to assure this reliability, the accounting profession has adopted certain standards of reporting. Unless stipulated otherwise, the user of a financial statement is justified in assuming that:

1 The statement is presented in accordance with generally accepted principles of accounting.

2 Such principles have been observed consistently in the current period in relation to the preceding period.

3 Information disclosed in the statement is reasonably adequate.

Stated another way, the basic financial statements of an organization purport to present fairly the financial position and results of operations for the period in accordance with generally accepted accounting principles applied consistently with those of the preceding period.

As you have seen throughout this text, there often are several equally acceptable ways of handling certain transactions. Thus, if it were not for the consistency standard, an accountant could arbitrarily affect the financial statements from one period to another merely by changing from one acceptable accounting procedure to another. Inventories, for example, may be valued in various ways, any one of which may be in accordance with generally accepted accounting principles. However, if inventories of successive periods are valued on varying bases, the accounting results may be materially distorted.

It is also important to bear in mind that the basic financial statements are essentially historical in nature; that is, they reflect past events. Therefore, although they are frequently used as bases for predicting future earnings or values, this is not their primary purpose. As we shall see in Chapters 21 and 22, in any decision-making situation there probably will be a number of factors apart from the information appearing in the financial statements that should be considered by the statement user. In many cases, for example, the trends in both the industry and the organization under consideration are important considerations and merit attention.

Statement Form

The accounting profession has not dealt officially with financial statement form. However, since the statements often convey extremely technical information to a wide variety of users, care must be exercised in their construction to make them as useful as possible and at the same time to reduce to a minimum the possibility of their being misinterpreted. Generally this is accomplished by:

1 Grouping the reported items into a few major categories
2 Arranging the items in the categories and the categories in the statements in a logical and consistent order
3 Using proper headings and indentions to emphasize the relationships of items and categories to one another

Statement Content

Much that has been said about financial statement form may also be said about content. Again, the profession has not dealt officially with content, but a number of powerful legal and financial influences have helped to define desirable practice. The following rules, generally referred to as disclosure standards, are customarily observed:

1 Any impression clearly conveyed by a financial statement should be a true one. (It is possible for a statement to be technically correct and yet to create a wrong impression in the mind of the statement user, perhaps by the way that it is presented. This is, of course, to be avoided.)
2 No information should be omitted from a statement which, if included, would materially alter the impressions given by the statement.

In sum, acccounting reports should disclose all information necessary to prevent them from being misleading; at the same time the disclosed information should be presented in such a way that it will not give a false impression.

Variations in Statement Form and Terminology

Technical form and terminology in statement presentation are helpful in achieving precision, but they should be departed from freely whenever they obstruct understandability and usefulness. For example, precise account titles are intended for use by experienced personnel who are familiar with the transactions to be included under a specific title. However, it is unlikely that a statement reader with little experience in a particular industry will understand the full significance of extremely technical account titles; therefore, descriptive captions which can be readily understood by the statement user should be substituted.

Parenthetical or footnote disclosure should also be employed whenever it will aid understandability and usefulness. For example, in cases when inventory is valued at the lower of cost or market, if it is valued at cost, market may be disclosed parenthetically; if it is valued at market, cost may be disclosed parenthetically. Footnotes are used to explain any data pertinent to an organization's financial position and the results of its operations which cannot be explained fully in the body of the statement. Typical footnote disclosure includes information relative to (1) changes in accounting procedures, such as a change from LIFO to FIFO, (2) the existence of long-term leases, and (3) the existence of contingent liabilities (possible liabilities arising from past circumstances or actions).

BALANCE SHEET

To fulfill its primary function of providing information about the financial condition of an organization as of a particular moment of time, the balance sheet must reflect all facts pertinent to the nature and amount of the organization's assets, liabilities, and owner equity.

The term **balance sheet** is widely used in business organizations. However, other titles such as **statement of financial position, position statement, statement of financial condition,** and **statement of condition** are often encountered.

Balance Sheet Format

Although balance sheet format will vary, the statement is customarily presented in one of two forms: the account form or the report form. The **account form** presents the assets on the left side of the statement with the liabilities and owner equity claims appearing on the right side. The **report form** presents the same data, but in a vertical fashion, with the assets being listed first and the liability and owner equity items following. In skeletal form the two types would appear as follows:

Balance Sheet Formats

Account Form		Report Form	
Assets _____ $xxx	Liabilities____ $xxx	Assets _____	$xxx
	Owner equity xxx		
$xxx	$xxx		$xxx
		Liabilities_____	$xxx
		Owner equity _____	xxx
			$xxx

Balance Sheet Classification

As we shall see in Chapter 21 when we study the analysis of financial statements, balance sheet usage ordinarily involves two primary types of analysis: One is based upon a comparison of like items on consecutive balance sheets, whereas the other is based upon a comparison of items within a given statement. Obviously, if a balance sheet is to furnish a sound basis for such comparisons, the data appearing in the statement must be properly classified. This requires not only that the individual items appearing in the statement be properly categorized, but also that grouping of items be clearly indicated, accurately described, and consistently maintained from period to period. The following format is representative both of balance sheet classification and arrangement; we should bear in mind, however, that some of the classifications may not be pertinent to a given organization and in some cases other classifications might be more appropriate.

Balance Sheet Classification and Arrangement	
Assets	**Liabilities**
1 Current assets	**1** Current liabilities
2 Investments	**2** Long-term debt
3 Plant and equipment (tangible fixed assets)	**3** Deferred credits
	Owner Equity
4 Intangible assets	**1** Invested capital
5 Deferred charges	**2** Earned capital

Balance Sheet Valuation

The usefulness of the balance sheet is sometimes limited because statement users misunderstand the nature of the valuations appearing on it. The balance sheet does not necessarily reflect present or future values. Although some items, of course, are expressed on the statement in terms of their current market values, others are not. For example, the balance sheet does not purport to reflect the current value of a long-lived asset if this value is understood to be its current sales price or replacement cost. You will recall from Chapter 11 that long-lived assets generally are acquired by an organization for long-term use and that their costs are allocated to the benefited periods by either the depreciation, depletion, or amortization process. Thus, at any balance sheet date, long-lived assets are reflected on the statement at their original costs minus the accumulated depreciation, depletion, or amortization. Stated another way, the carrying value of a long-lived asset, as expressed on a balance sheet which has been prepared in the customary fashion, merely reflects the amount of the original cost of the asset remaining to be allocated to future periods.

Other assets may be reflected on the balance sheet in terms of different values. Receivables, for example, are generally stated in terms of their estimated realizable values, which are determined by deducting the estimated amount of uncollectible receivables from the total amount of receivables. Other items such as inventories and marketable securities are often stated in terms of cost or market, whichever is lower.

Classified Balance Sheet Illustrated

The balance sheets which follow illustrate typical presentation. The account form is presented in fairly complete detail; the report form, on the other hand, is somewhat abbreviated since the data on both statements are the same. When studying the account form, note particularly the order of the groups within the

Balance Sheet—Account Form

COMPANY A

Balance Sheet

As of December 31, 19___

Assets

Current Assets:		
Cash		$ 44,000
Marketable securities (at cost, market value $22,500)		20,000
Accounts receivable (net of $3,000 estimated uncollectible)		60,000
Notes receivable		10,000
Inventories (lower of FIFO cost or market)		135,000
Prepaid insurance		1,000
Total current assets		$ 270,000
Investments:		
Investment in bonds of XYZ Company (at cost)	$ 40,000	
Investment in common stock of LMNO Company (at cost)	20,000	
Total investments		60,000
Plant and equipment:		
Land	$ 80,000	
Buildings (cost less $50,000 accumulated depreciation)	200,000	
Machinery (cost less $20,000 accumulated depreciation)	220,000	
Equipment (cost less $40,000 accumulated depreciation)	110,000	
Total plant and equipment		610,000
Intangible assets:		
Goodwill	$ 20,000	
Patents (less amortization of $10,000)	30,000	
Total intangible assets		50,000
Deferred charges:		
Organization costs	$ 6,000	
Unamortized bond discount	4,000	
Total deferred charges		10,000
Total assets		$1,000,000

statement and also the order of the items within the groups. For instance, current assets are listed in the order of their liquidity, with the most liquid asset (cash) being listed first; current liabilities are listed in the order of their due dates, with the most current obligation (usually accounts payable) being listed first; and long-lived assets are listed in the inverse order of their liquidity, with the least liquid asset (land) being listed first.[1]

[1]You will recall that accountants use the term *current assets* to designate cash and other resources which are reasonably expected to be converted into cash or consumed during the current operating cycle or one year, whichever is longer, and the term *current liabilities* to designate those obligations which will require the use of current assets or the creation of other current liabilities for liquidation.

Liabilities and Owner Equity

Current liabilities:

Accrued payroll payable		$ 2,500
Accounts payable		132,000
Notes payable		50,000
Estimated income taxes payable		60,000
Dividends payable		7,500
Total current liabilities		$ 252,000
Long-term debt:		
Mortgage payable	$ 20,000	
Bonds payable	80,000	
Total long-term debt		100,000
Deferred credits:		
Rent collected in advance	$ 2,000	
Interest collected in advance	1,000	
Total deferred credits		3,000
Total liabilities		$ 355,000
Shareholder equity:		
Capital stock, $5 par value, 100,000 shares		
issued and outstanding	$500,000	
Capital in excess of par value	20,000	
Retained earnings	125,000	
Total shareholder equity		645,000
Total liabilities and owner equity		$1,000,000

Balance Sheet—Report Form

COMPANY A
Balance Sheet
As of December 31, 19___

Assets

Current assets	$ 270,000
Investments	60,000
Plant and equipment (net)	610,000
Intangible assets	50,000
Deferred charges	10,000
Total assets	$1,000,000

Liabilities and Owner Equity

Current liabilities	$ 252,000
Long-term debt	100,000
Deferred credits	3,000
Invested capital	520,000
Earned capital	125,000
Total liabilities and owner equity	$1,000,000

INCOME STATEMENT

For the typical businessman of 100 years ago income determination was a simple matter. Generally, he took his unpaid bills from the nail on the wall or bushel basket under the counter and added them up; that much he owed, and the balance was his. If the balance at the end of the year was more than the balance at the beginning of the year, he ordinarily assumed he had made a profit; if it was less, he considered that he had sustained a loss.

With the passage of time, however, things changed. The businessman of today is not satisfied merely with the knowledge that his business has made a profit or suffered a loss; he wants to know where the profit came from or why the loss was incurred, as well as what his sales were, what his costs were, and a multitude of similar facts. As was emphasized in Chapter 1, it is imperative that he have information of this nature if he is to compete effectively in the business arena. Thus, over the years income as determined by the accountant has assumed a major role in the decision-making process.

Although the form and content of the basic financial statements are of major concern to us in this chapter, in order to understand the format of the income statement clearly, we must be sure that we have an appreciation for (1) the uses made of the accountant's computation of net income, (2) the nature of income determination, and (3) the concepts which underlie income statement presentation.

Uses of the Accountant's Income Computation

The accountant's income calculation is, or should be, employed primarily as a guide to the management of an organization in the conduct of its affairs. However, it also has other important uses. We have already learned, for example, that it is the basis of one of the principal forms of taxation and that it is employed as a criterion for the determination of the availability of dividends. In addition, it is used in reports to stockholders and the investing public as a measure of the success of an organization, and by rate-regulating authorities as an indicator as to whether particular rates are fair and reasonable.

Nature of Income Determination

As a general rule, the accountant measures income in accordance with the accrual basis of accounting, utilizing both the realization principle and the matching concept.

Accrual Basis Under the accrual basis, revenues are recognized in the period in which they are realized regardless of when the cash is received, and expenses are recognized in the period in which they contribute to revenue regardless of when they are paid. Thus, the essence of accrual accounting, as it relates to income determination, is the matching of an organization's efforts and accomplishments for the period in order to determine the progress made during the period.

Realization Principle Although accountants recognize that in an economic sense income is earned by the totality of an organization's operations, they are more or less in agreement that revenue generally becomes real, or is realized, at the time goods are delivered or services are rendered, that is, when a legitimate sale, either of goods or services, has been consummated.

Accountants ordinarily object to the recognition of revenue prior to sale consummation because (1) there is usually no objective evidence as to the amount that should be recognized, and (2) no transaction has taken place whereby the original asset or service is converted into a different kind of asset. On the other hand, upon consummation of a sale, objective evidence generally is available as to the amount of revenue that has been realized. Such evidence normally consists of a new and relatively liquid asset such as cash, accounts receivable, or notes receivable.

Although we shall continue to employ the sales basis for the recognition of revenue, it should be pointed out that there are at least two theoretically sound objections to its use as a basis of measuring income:

1 The sale is usually only one of many functions performed in the earning of income, and in some instances it may be a relatively minor one. Logically, we may conclude that each function contributes to the final net income and that such income is earned as the function is performed.

2 In some situations the actual sale may be routine, the market being so broad as to ensure its completion at any time. Thus, in such cases income could easily be recognized as being earned at some time other than when the sale is made.

When these objections appear to be material, accountants do not always adhere to the sales basis. As you will see in your intermediate and advanced accounting courses, the use of the **percentage of completion** as a basis for revenue realization in long-term construction contracts, and the pricing of inventories of precious metals such as gold and silver at market value, are examples of deviations from the sales basis.

Matching Concept Once an amount of revenue is recognized as being realized, the problem then arises of determining the appropriate deductions to be made in order to arrive at the net revenue, or net income. As you will recall from previous chapters, the offsetting of an organization's efforts (costs and expenses) against its accomplishments (revenues) is referred to in modern accounting as the **matching process.**

Matching is primarily a matter of finding satisfactory bases of association, with the essential test being economic reasonableness in view of all pertinent conditions. While there are numerous ways of determining the periodic efforts to associate with (or deduct from) periodic accomplishments in order to arrive at net income, the principal criteria are association with revenue and association with the accounting period.

If an effort is directly associated with the revenue of the period, there is usually no problem other than an appropriate calculation. For instance, the cost of goods sold during a period is obviously one of the important deductions to be made from sales revenue. Other items, however, such as salaries and commissions paid to salesmen, are often less directly connected to the revenue transaction but are, nevertheless, still clearly necessary deductions. When the causal relationship is obvious, the association is obvious, and vice versa.

When the accountant cannot properly establish the causal relationship, he falls back on timing. That is, he associates particular costs and expenses with the accounting period itself rather than with specific revenue. For example, supplies are ordinarily expensed as they are used, and insurance is usually expensed as the premium expires. Likewise, the cost of a long-lived asset such as a truck or building is ordinarily amortized as depreciation over the periods of its useful life.

Basic Income Statement Concepts

In general, most accountants agree on the importance of attempting to attain the matching goal when determining net income. There is no unanimity, however, as to exactly what should be included in the income calculation. Two major concepts are available. One, which is often called the historical or all-inclusive concept, is based on the premise that net income for a period should be measured by deducting the amount of net income accumulated as of the beginning of the period from the amount accumulated as of the end of the period. The other, which is ordinarily known as the earning power or current operating performance concept, emphasizes the relationship of revenue and expense items to operations and to the period, excluding from the income calculation any material items which are not so related.

The essential difference between the two concepts is the way in which extraordinary items of an unusual and nonrecurring nature are handled. Examples of extraordinary items include:

1 Material losses of a type not usually insured against
2 Material gains and losses from the sale of assets not acquired for resale and not of the type in which the organization generally deals
3 Write-off of a material amount of intangibles because of unusual developments during the period

All-inclusive Concept Advocates of the all-inclusive income statement approach maintain that all items of a profit and loss nature recognized during a given period should be included in the determination of net income for that period. Under this concept income determination is predicated upon the basis that a cumulative income statement based on past reports should show the total profit (or loss) for the organization from its inception to the current date.

The principal arguments ordinarily advanced in support of the all-inclusive income statement approach may be summarized as follows:

1 The sum of the net incomes as shown on a series of income statements should represent total net income for the periods covered.
2 If items are allowed to bypass the income statement, manipulation of net income is possible.
3 There is no clear-cut procedure for distinguishing between an ordinary item and an extraordinary item; it is usually a matter of opinion.
4 Inconsistency in recognizing extraordinary items affects the comparability of an organization's earnings with prior periods and with earnings of other organizations.

Current Operating Performance Concept Advocates of the current operating performance income statement maintain that the only relevant items of a profit and loss nature are those which have been associated with the normal recurring operations of the organization during the period being reported upon, and that these items alone should be used to ascertain net income for the period. They believe that only net income determined in this fashion is indicative of the long-run earning power of the organization. Under this approach, extraordinary items of a profit and loss nature are closed directly to the Retained Earnings account and do not pass through the Revenue and Expense Summary account.

The principal arguments ordinarily advanced in support of the current operating performance income statement may be summarized as follows:

1 Net income for a period should reflect an organization's earnings under the conditions existing during the period.

2 The inclusion of material extraordinary items in the determination of income may impair the significance of the reported net income to the extent that misleading inferences might be drawn therefrom.

3 The inclusion of material extraordinary items in income statements weakens the comparability of a series of income statements.

Concepts Illustrated Although the statements included in the following illustration are greatly condensed, they are nevertheless indicative of statement presentation based on the all-inclusive and current operating performance concepts. Obviously, an organization would not use both concepts, and they are included under the same heading for comparative purposes only. For simplicity, a 50 percent tax rate is assumed.

COMPANY A
Income Statement

	All-inclusive Concept	Current Operating Performance Concept
Sales revenue	$1,000,000	$1,000,000
Cost of goods sold	600,000	600,000
Gross margin	$ 400,000	$ 400,000
Operating expenses	100,000	100,000
Flood loss	60,000	
Income taxes	120,000*	150,000†
Net income	$ 120,000	$ 150,000

*50% of ($400,000 − $100,000 − $60,000)
†50% of ($400,000 − $100,000)

Although the reported net income differs by $30,000 (the net effect of the flood loss), the ultimate effect upon retained earnings is the same regardless of the concept used.

Since the tax effect of an item should follow the item, under the current operating performance concept the tax effect of the flood loss would be allocated directly to the Retained Earnings account along with the flood loss. If we assume a balance in the Retained Earnings account of $100,000 as of the beginning of the period and there are no other retained earnings transactions except those in our illustration, the ending balance in the Retained Earnings account will be $220,000, regardless of which concept is used. This is evidenced in the following illustration:

COMPANY A
Retained Earnings
As of End of Period

	All-inclusive Concept	Current Operating Performance Concept
Beginning balance	$100,000	$100,000
Add: Net income	120,000	150,000
Deduct: Flood loss less applicable tax effect		(30,000)*
Ending balance	$220,000	$220,000

*$60,000 flood loss less $30,000 (50% of $60,000) reduction in income taxes.

AICPA's Position The Accounting Principles Board of the AICPA has taken the position that the net income reported for a given period should reflect all items of profit and loss recognized during the period, with the sole exception of prior period adjustments. By stressing the fact that prior period adjustments are rare, the Board in essence supports the all-inclusive concept. It specifically defines prior period adjustments[1] as:

> . . . those material adjustments which (a) can be specifically identified with and directly related to the business activities of particular prior periods, and (b) are not attributable to economic events occurring subsequent to the date of the financial statements for the prior period, and (c) depend primarily on determinations by persons other than management and (d) were not susceptible of reasonable estimation prior to such determination.

Examples of prior period adjustments are (1) material, nonrecurring adjustments or settlements of income taxes, and (2) settlements of significant amounts

[1] AICPA, "Reporting the Results of Operations," *Opinion No. 9 of the Accounting Principles Board* (New York: 1966), p. 115.

resulting from litigation. Normal recurring adjustments and corrections resulting from the use of estimates are not to be treated as prior period adjustments. For instance, an adjustment resulting from a change in the estimated useful life of a depreciable asset does not qualify as a prior period adjustment, even though it may be material. Likewise, relatively immaterial adjustments of estimated liabilities (including income taxes) should be considered as normal recurring items and thus be reflected in operations of the current period.

In single-period statements, as indicated by the Accounting Principles Board, prior period adjustments should be reflected as adjustments (net of the income tax effect) of the opening balance of retained earnings. When multiperiod statements are presented, prior period adjustments should be retroactively reflected in all pertinent accounts reported therein.[1]

Although the Board, in *Opinion No. 9*, essentially supports the all-inclusive statement, the opinion does state that extraordinary items should be segregated from the results of ordinary operations and shown separately in the income statement, along with an adequate disclosure of the nature and amounts of such items.[2] Under this approach, the income statement would contain, among others, the following elements:

Income before extraordinary items		$xxx
Extraordinary items	$xxx	
Less: applicable income tax	xxx	xxx
Net income		$xxx

Recasting our previous illustration in light of *Opinion No. 9*, we would have:

COMPANY A
Income Statement
Current Period

Sales revenue		$1,000,000
Cost of goods sold		600,000
Gross margin		$ 400,000
Operating expenses		100,000
Income taxes		150,000
Income before extraordinary items		$ 150,000
Flood loss	$(60,000)	
(less applicable tax effect)	30,000	(30,000)
Net income		$ 120,000

The Accounting Principles Board defines extraordinary items as items resulting from events and transactions significantly different from an organization's custom-

[1] *Ibid.*, p. 113.
[2] *Loc. cit.*

ary business activities but having a material effect on operating results, and not considered to be recurring factors in the ordinary operating processes of the organization. The Board lists the following examples of extraordinary items. (In each case a material gain or loss is assumed.)[1]

1 Sale or abandonment of a plant or a significant segment of a business

2 Sale of an investment not acquired for resale

3 Write-off of goodwill due to unusual developments during the period

4 Condemnation or expropriation of property

5 Major devaluation of a foreign currency

To clarify further its position on prior period adjustments and extraordinary items, the Board emphasizes that certain gains or losses, regardless of size, do not constitute extraordinary items or prior period adjustments because they are the result of normal business activities. These activities include the write-downs of receivables, inventories, and research and development costs. According to the Board, the effects of such write-downs should be reflected in the income statement before extraordinary items are considered.[2]

Income Statement Format

Like the balance sheet, the income statement has no mandatory format. Although consistency and uniformity are desirable in the reporting of income, flexibility is also important. Because the statement is directed toward a wide variety of readers, the best format in a particular situation is one which serves the user's needs in the most reliable and understandable manner.

Regardless of the format used, the income statement should be arranged in such a way that it will report consistently and in reasonable detail the (1) particulars of revenue and expense items pertaining to operations of the current period, and (2) extraordinary gains and losses recognized during the period. Although numerous variations exist in practice both as to arrangement and terminology, two general formats predominate. They are commonly known as **single-step** and **multistep** income statements.

Single-step Format In its simplest form the single-step statement presents (1) revenue of the period, (2) applicable expenses, and (3) net income or loss. Thus, the single-step format might be expressed mathematically as $(R - E = NI)$. When an extraordinary item is involved, the single-step statement, as a result of the APB's issuance of *Opinion No. 9,* actually becomes a two-step statement. The following illustration, in outline form, is typical of the single-step format:

[1] *Ibid.,* p. 115.
[2] *Loc. cit.*

Single-step Income Statement

Revenues:
    Sales (less returns, allowances, and discounts) ———————————— $xxx
    Other revenue (interest, dividends, etc.) ————————————— xxx
        Total revenue ————————————————————————— $xxx

Costs and expenses:
    Cost of goods sold ——————————————————————— $xxx
    Selling expenses ————————————————————————— xxx
    General and administrative expenses ———————————————— xxx
    Other expenses ——————————————————————————— xxx
    Income taxes ———————————————————————————— xxx
        Total expenses ———————————————————————— xxx
Income before extraordinary items ———————————————————— $xxx
    Add or deduct extraordinary items (net of applicable tax effect) ——————— xxx
Net income for the period ———————————————————————— $xxx

Multistep Format Many income statement users maintain that there are a number of significant relationships between total revenue and net income which are not brought out by the single-step statement. They contend, for example, that in some cases intermediate subtotals for such items as the gross margin on sales, operating income, and net income before taxes are just as important as total revenue, total costs and expenses, and net income. Thus, they prefer a statement which presents several intermediate steps. Again in outline form, the following illustration is typical of the multistep format:

Multistep Income Statement

Gross sales ——————————————————————————————— $xxx
Less: Sales returns, allowances, and discounts ——————————————— xxx
Net sales ————————————————————————————————— $xxx
Less: Cost of goods sold —————————————————————————— xxx
Gross margin ————————————————————————————————— $xxx
Less: Operating expenses —————————————————————————— xxx
Operating income ——————————————————————————————— $xxx
Add or deduct other revenue and expense ———————————————— xxx
Income before income taxes ———————————————————————— $xxx
Less: Income taxes ————————————————————————————— xxx
Income before extraordinary items ———————————————————— $xxx
Add or deduct extraordinary items (net of applicable tax effect) ——————— xxx
Net income for the period ———————————————————————— $xxx

Revenue and Expense Classifications Income statement classification was introduced in Chapter 3, but we should perhaps review and enlarge on it briefly here before illustrating the income statement in detail. Although classification is a relative matter depending upon the particular circumstances in a given situation, the following classifications are typical:

Revenue	Selling Expenses
Sales	Advertising
Service	Delivery expense
Rental	Transportation on outgoing sales
Interest	Salesmen's salaries
Dividends	Salesmen's commissions
	Depreciation on store equipment
	Insurance expense—selling
	Miscellaneous selling expense
	Depreciation on delivery equipment

General and Administrative Expenses	Other Expenses
Office salaries	Interest expense
Rent	
Insurance expense—general	
Property taxes	
Heat, light, and power	
Depreciation of office equipment	
Estimated loss on uncollectible accounts	

Classification is a relative matter. For example, we classified the provision for estimated losses on uncollectible accounts as a general and administrative expense, but other classifications may be justified. When the granting of credit is a function of the administrative staff—that is, when the credit department is a unit of the general and administrative offices—this item is normally classified as a general and administrative expense. However, in cases where the sales department is responsible for granting credit or where a liberal credit policy has been adopted for the purpose of "pushing" sales, the provision for losses on uncollectible accounts may be classified as a selling expense. In addition, at times it may be deducted directly from gross sales, on the theory that the amount of revenue which should be recognized on a sale is the cash or cash equivalent received. Under this theory, the actual amount of revenue to be reported is arrived at by deducting from the total gross sales all allowances, discounts, and uncollectible amounts reflected in gross sales.

A similar problem arises with the classification of cash discounts. As you will recall from Chapter 5, we consider purchase discounts taken as reductions of cost, and deduct them from gross purchases when determining the cost of goods sold; on the other hand, we consider sales discounts granted as reductions in revenue, and deduct them from gross sales when arriving at net sales in the income statement. Some authorities, however, consider purchase discounts taken as a form of financial income, and sales discounts granted as a form of financial expense. Under the latter approach, purchase discounts are classified as other revenue, and sales discounts are classified as other expense.

Classified Income Statements Illustrated The following statements are indicative of the basic classifications and subclassifications of the data presented. For comparative purposes, both single-step and multistep statements are included.

Single-step Format

COMPANY A

Income Statement

For the Year Ended December 31, 19___

Revenues:		
Net sales		$ 970,000
Interest		10,000
Dividends		25,000
Total revenue		$1,005,000
Costs and expenses:		
Cost of goods sold	$600,000	
Salaries and commissions	55,200	
Advertising	30,000	
Delivery expense	5,800	
Depreciation	2,700	
Rent	3,000	
Interest	5,000	
Heat, light, and power	1,200	
Estimated loss on uncollectible accounts	1,000	
Insurance expense	700	
Miscellaneous expense	400	
Income taxes	150,000	
Total expenses		855,000
Income before extraordinary items		$ 150,000
Flood loss (less applicable tax effect)		(30,000)
Net income for the year		$ 120,000

Multistep Format

COMPANY A
Income Statement
For the Year Ended December 31, 19___

Sales revenue			$1,000,000
Less: Sales returns and allowances		$ 13,000	
Sales discounts		17,000	30,000
Net sales revenue			$ 970,000
Cost of goods sold:			
Beginning inventory		$100,000	
Purchases		650,000	
Transportation in		18,000	
Purchase returns and allowances		(19,000)	
Purchase discounts		(14,000)	
Cost of goods available for sale		$735,000	
Ending inventory		(135,000)	
Cost of goods sold			600,000
Gross margin			$ 370,000
Operating expenses:			
Selling expenses:			
Sales salaries	$40,000		
Sales commissions	5,200		
Advertising	30,000		
Delivery expense	5,000		
Transportation-out	800		
Depreciation of delivery equipment	1,200		
Depreciation of store equipment	1,000		
Insurance expense—selling	500		
Miscellaneous selling expense	300	$84,000	
General and administrative expenses:			
Office salaries	$10,000		
Rent	3,000		
Heat, light, and power	1,200		
Estimated loss on uncollectible accounts	1,000		
Depreciation of office equipment	500		
Insurance expense—office	200		
Miscellaneous office expense	100	16,000	
Total operating expenses			100,000
Operating income			$ 270,000
Other revenue:			
Interest	$10,000		
Dividends	25,000	$35,000	
Other expense:			
Interest		(5,000)	30,000
Income before income taxes			$ 300,000
Income taxes			150,000
Income before extraordinary items			$ 150,000
Flood loss (less applicable tax effect)			(30,000)
Net income for the year			$ 120,000

STATEMENT OF RETAINED EARNINGS

When accounting for a corporation, the accountant closes the Revenue and Expense Summary account into the Retained Earnings account as of the end of the fiscal period, and also charges distributions to stockholders against the account. In addition, items which qualify as prior period adjustments are debited or credited to the Retained Earnings account. A statement of retained earnings for a given period merely presents such changes in statement form. Two examples follow. The first is a simple statement prepared on the assumption that no prior period adjustments were involved, whereas the second assumes the existence of prior period adjustments.

COMPANY A
Statement of Retained Earnings
For the Year Ended December 31, 19___

Retained earnings at beginning of year		$100,000
Net income		120,000
		$220,000
Dividends declared:		
On preferred stock	$ 5,000	
On common stock	10,000	(15,000)
Retained earnings at end of year		$205,000

COMPANY A
Statement of Retained Earnings
For the Year Ended December 31, 19___

Retained earnings at beginning of year:		
As previously reported		$100,000
Prior period adjustments:		
Additional income taxes	$50,000	
Loss on patent infringement suit	30,000	(80,000)
As restated		$ 20,000
Net income		120,000
		$140,000
Dividends declared:		
On preferred stock	$ 5,000	
On common stock	10,000	(15,000)
Retained earnings at end of year		$125,000

Combined Statement of Income and Retained Earnings

Because of the close relationship between the income statement and the retained earnings statement, the two are frequently combined into one. The principal advantage of the combined statement is that all items affecting an organization's earnings, whether they are current ordinary items, extraordinary items, or prior period adjustments, are included in one statement. In the combined statement, the income statement is presented first in its usual format, with the retained earnings statement following immediately after the net income figure. The following condensed statement is illustrative:

COMPANY A

Statement of Income and Retained Earnings

For the Year Ended December 31, 19__

Sales revenue		$ 1,000,000
Cost of goods sold		600,000
Gross margin		$ 400,000
Operating expenses		100,000
Income taxes		150,000
Income before extraordinary items		$ 150,000
Flood loss	$(60,000)	
(less applicable tax effect)	30,000	(30,000)
Net income		$ 120,000
Retained earnings at beginning of year:		
As previously reported		$ 100,000
Prior period adjustments:		
Additional income taxes	$ 50,000	
Loss on patent infringement suit	30,000	(80,000)
As restated		$ 20,000
		$ 140,000
Dividends declared:		
On preferred stock	$ 5,000	
On common stock	10,000	(15,000)
Retained earnings at end of year		$ 125,000

SUMMARY

The purpose of the balance sheet is to provide information regarding the financial position of an organization as of a particular point in time. Although it is generally considered to be essentially a historical statement and one which does not purport to reflect current values, in reality it reflects a conglomeration of values, and a user of the statement must be aware of this feature. For example, long-lived assets are reflected at acquisition costs less accumulated amortization, whereas receivables are ordinarily reflected at their estimated realizable values, and inventories and marketable securities may be reflected at cost or market, whichever is lower.

The purpose of the income statement is to show the results of operations for a period of time in the past. It, too, is essentially historical and of itself does not attempt to predict future earning power. It merely reflects the amount of revenue recognized as having been realized during the period, less that portion of all costs and expenses incurred in the past which do not appear to be fairly deferrable to future periods. The statement is, however, frequently prepared in a way which permits the results of ordinary recurring operations to be segregated from the results of extraordinary nonrecurring operations.

The retained earnings statement presents changes in the Retained Earnings account in statement form. The income statement and retained earnings statement are often combined in order to present all the items affecting an organization's earnings in one statement.

QUESTIONS AND PROBLEMS

19-1 Discuss briefly the primary objective of the consistency standard of reporting as applied to the basic financial statements.

19-2 Explain briefly the use of footnotes in the preparation of financial statements and indicate the type of information one might find therein.

19-3 Select the answer choice which *best* completes each of the following statements:

1 The term **matching costs and revenues** means:
  a That all expenses should be allocated to accounting periods on the basis of the effect on net income
  b That costs should be carried forward to future accounting periods if they have not resulted in revenue during the current accounting period
  c That if costs are charged off as expenses in the accounting period when they are actually incurred, they will be matched properly with the revenues actually earned during that accounting period
  d That costs which can be associated directly with specific revenue should be carried forward in the balance sheet until the associated revenue is recognized
  e None of the above

2 Income tax allocation consists of procedures intended to cause:
   a Tax expense shown in the income statement to bear a normal relation to the net income before tax reported in the income statement
   b Tax expense shown in the income statement to bear a normal relation to the tax liability for the current year
   c Tax liability shown in the balance sheet to bear a normal relation to the net income before tax reported in the income statement
   d Actual tax payments to be evenly distributed over a period of time
   e None of the above

3 The consistency standard of reporting requires that:
   a Expenses be reported as charges against the period in which they are incurred
   b The effect of changes in accounting procedure upon income be properly disclosed
   c Extraordinary gains and losses should not appear in the income statement
   d Accounting procedures be adopted which give a consistent rate of net income
   e None of the above

19-4 (1) Describe briefly the form and content of the single-step income statement.

(2) Present arguments both for and against this form of statement.

19-5 State the generally accepted accounting principle applicable to the valuation on the balance sheet of each of the following assets:

(1) Accounts receivable

(2) Long-lived assets

(3) Inventories

(4) Marketable securities

(5) Prepaid expenses

19-6 Some items in the basic financial statements are ordinarily expressed in current dollars, while others are normally expressed in dollars of a prior year or years.

Instructions

(1) Name the principal balance sheet items which might not be expressed in current dollars. (If any part of your answer depends on the accounting procedures employed, explain briefly.)

(2) Name the principal items in the income statement which might not be expressed in current dollars. (If any part of your answer depends on the accounting procedures employed, explain briefly.)

19-7 The basic financial statements are often criticized because the income statement does not give a clear picture of an organization's earning power and the balance sheet does not disclose the true value of the assets. Considering the criticism, discuss briefly the nature and purpose of each of the statements, including an explanation of their limitations.

19-8 Information concerning the operations of a corporation may be presented in an income statement or in a combined statement of income and retained earnings. Income statements may be prepared on a current operating performance basis or an all-inclusive basis. Proponents of the two types of income statements do not agree upon the proper treatment of material extraordinary charges and credits.

(1) Define "current operating performance" and "all-inclusive" as used above.

(2) Explain the differences in content and organization of a "current operating performance" income statement and an "all-inclusive" income statement. Include a discussion of the proper treatment of extraordinary charges and credits.

19-9 It is often maintained that much of accounting is concerned with the determination of income and the valuation of assets through the application of accounting principles. For example, the realization principle is said to pervade both the income statement and the balance sheet.

(1) Explain briefly the significance of the realization principle as it is related to the process of periodic income determination.

(2) Discuss the effect of the realization principle on the valuation of assets for balance sheet purposes.

19-10 Write a short paragraph (not over 150 words) presenting your views on the advantages and disadvantages of the single-step income statement.

19-11 The following data pertain to the operations of the VKZ Company for the year 19X4:

Sales revenue	$700,000
Beginning inventory	100,000
Ending inventory	140,000
Purchases	400,000

Operating expenses	$60,000
Flood loss	80,000
Assume an income tax rate of	50%

Instructions Prepare an income statement assuming that the company uses the:

(1) All-inclusive concept

(2) Current operating performance concept

19-12 Instructions From the following data, which pertain to the operations of the CAM Company for the year ended December 31, 19X6, prepare a statement of retained earnings assuming that the company uses the:

(1) All-inclusive concept

(2) Current operating concept

Sales revenue	$600,000
Retained earnings as of beginning of year	100,000
Beginning inventory	60,000
Purchases	200,000
Ending inventory	70,000
Flood loss	50,000
Operating expenses	240,000
Assume an income tax rate of	50%

19-13 Instructions From the following data, which pertain to the operations of the ARW Company for the year 19X5, prepare a combined statement of income and retained earnings assuming that the company uses the:

(1) All-inclusive concept

(2) Current operating performance concept

Sales revenue	$900,000
Retained earnings as of beginning of year	190,000
Beginning inventory	80,000
Ending inventory	60,000
Purchases	400,000
Operating expenses	110,000
Flood loss	90,000
Additional income taxes for the year 19X2	70,000
Dividends declared on preferred stock	6,000
Dividends declared on common stock	8,000
Assume an income tax rate of	50%

19-14 Instructions Comment critically on the following data, which represent the concluding section of a corporation's 19X6 income statement. (As part of your answer, comment on the general acceptability of the treatment accorded each item. If an item has not been handled correctly, indicate the correct treatment.)

Extraordinary items:

Loss on sale of land and buildings	$70,000	
Provision for future declines in market value of inventories	10,000	
Additional assessment for 19X1 income tax	22,000	
Elimination of entire reserve created in 19X5 for possible award under a damage suit	(20,000)	$82,000
Net income		$50,888

*19-15 Instructions The transactions listed below relate to Jekyll Chemicals, Inc. You are to assume that on the date on which each of the transactions occurred the corporation's accounts showed a substantial net income for the year to date (before giving effect to the transaction concerned).

Each numbered transaction is to be considered as completely independent of the others, and its related answer should be based on the effect of that transaction alone. Assume that all numbered transactions occurred during 19X3 and that the amount involved in each case is sufficiently material to distort reported net income if improperly included in the determination of net income. Assume further that each transaction was recorded in accordance with generally accepted accounting principles and, where applicable, in conformity with the all-inclusive concept of the income statement.

For each of the numbered transactions you are to decide whether it:

A Increased the corporation's 19X3 net income

B Decreased the corporation's 19X3 net income

C Increased the corporation's total retained earnings directly (that is, not via net income)

D Decreased the corporation's total retained earnings directly

E Had none of the above effects

Transactions

1 Treasury stock, which had been repurchased at and carried at $102 per share, was issued as a stock dividend. In connection with this distribution the board of directors of Jekyll Chemicals, Inc., had authorized a

*AICPA adapted.

transfer from retained earnings to permanent capital of an amount equal to the aggregate market value ($104 per share) of the shares issued. No entries relating to this dividend had been made previously.

2 In January the board directed the write-off of certain patent rights which had suddenly and unexpectedly become worthless.

3 Treasury stock originally repurchased and carried at $101 per share was sold for cash at $103.50 per share.

4 The corporation sold at a profit land and a building which had been idle for some time. Under the terms of the sale, the corporation received a portion of the sales price in cash immediately, with the balance maturing at 6-month intervals.

5 The corporation called in all its outstanding shares of stock and exchanged them for new shares on a 2 for 1 basis, reducing the par value at the same time from $100 to $50 per share.

6 The corporation paid a cash dividend, the declaration of which had been recorded in the accounts at the time of declaration.

7 Litigation involving Jekyll Chemicals, Inc., as defendant was settled in the corporation's favor, with the plaintiff paying all court costs and legal fees. The corporation had appropriated retained earnings in 19X1 as a special contingency reserve for this court action, and the board directed abolition of the reserve.

8 The corporation received a check for the proceeds of an insurance policy from the company with which it is insured against theft of trucks. No entries concerning the theft had been made previously, and the proceeds reduce but do not cover completely the loss.

*19-16 Instructions State briefly what changes in classification and terminology you would advocate in the XYZ Company's balance sheet in order to make it conform with generally accepted accounting principles and with present-day terminology. (Note: Additional data continued on page 523.)

Additional Data

1 Reserve for damages was set up by a charge against the current fiscal year's income to cover damages possibly payable by the company as a defendant in a lawsuit in progress at the balance sheet date. The suit was subsequently compromised for $50,000 prior to issuance of the statement.

2 Reserve for possible future inventory losses was set up in prior years, by action of the board of directors, by charges against earned surplus. No change occurred in the account during the current fiscal year.

*AICPA adapted.

XYZ COMPANY
Balance Sheet
December 31, 19X2

Assets

Current Assets:

Cash		$1,900,000
Accounts receivable customers	$3,900,000	
Less reserve for bad debts	50,000	3,850,000
Inventories—at the lower of cost (determined by the first-in, first-out method) or market		3,500,000
Total current assets		$9,250,000

Long-lived Assets:

Land—at cost		$ 200,000	
Buildings, machinery and equipment, furniture and fixtures—at cost	$4,200,000		
Less reserves for depreciation	1,490,000	2,710,000	2,910,000

Deferred Charges and Other Assets:

Cash surrender value of life insurance	$ 15,000	
Unamortized discount on first mortgage note	42,000	
Prepaid expenses	40,000	97,000
		$12,257,000

Liabilities

Current Liabilities:

Notes payable to bank—unsecured		$ 750,000
Current maturities of first mortgage note		600,000
Accounts payable—trade		1,900,000
Reserve for income taxes for the year ended Dec. 31, 19X2		700,000
Accrued expenses		550,000
		$ 4,500,000

Funded Debt:

4% first mortgage note payable in quarterly installments of $150,000	$4,200,000	
Less current maturities	600,000	3,600,000

Reserves:

Reserve for damages	$ 50,000	
Reserve for possible future inventory losses	300,000	
Reserve for contingencies	500,000	
Reserve for additional federal income taxes	100,000	950,000

Capital:

Capital stock—authorized, issued and outstanding 100,000 shares of $10 par value	$1,000,000	
Capital surplus	300,000	
Earned surplus	1,907,000	3,207,000
		$12,257,000

3 Reserve for contingencies was set up by charges against earned surplus over a period of several years by the board of directors to provide for a possible future recession in general business conditions.

4 Reserve for additional federal income taxes was set up in a prior year and relates to additional taxes which the Internal Revenue Service contends the company owes. The company believes that the amount of $100,000 set up on the balance sheet will cover this assessment.

5 Capital surplus consists of the difference between the par value of $10 per share of stock and the price at which the stock was actually issued.

*19-17 The financial statement on page 524 was prepared by employees of the Melhus Corporation.

Instructions Identify and discuss the weaknesses in classification and disclosure in Melhus's single-step statement of income and retained earnings. Your discussion should explain why you consider these treatments to be weaknesses and what you consider to be the proper treatment of the items. (Do *not* discuss form and terminology or prepare a revised statement.)

19-18 **Instructions** Assuming that accruals of any one year are reflected in the cash transactions of the following year and that prepayments of any one year are reflected in the revenue or expense accounts of the following year, place an X in each correct column on page 525.

19-19 On July 1, 19X1, Ace Jones began business with a cash investment of $58,500.

On June 30, 19X2, his ledger showed the following balances:

Accounts payable	$20,962.50
Accounts receivable	17,144.40
Expenses	3,185.00
Merchandise inventory	19,743.10

53890.60

All sales and purchases during the year were made on account. During the year, cash paid to creditors amounted to $63,780.60. Jones's loss for the year was $10,496.85.

3.15

Instructions Prepare in simple form:

(1) A balance sheet as of June 30, 19X2

(2) An income statement for the year ended June 30, 19X2

*AICPA adapted.

MELHUS CORPORATION

Statement of Income and Retained Earnings

Years Ended December 31, 19X3, and December 31, 19X2

	19X3	19X2
Revenues:		
Gross sales, including sales taxes	$876,900	$782,500
Less returns, allowances, and cash discounts	18,800	16,200
Net sales	$858,100	$766,300
Dividends, interest, and purchase discounts	30,250	18,300
Recoveries of accounts written off in prior years	11,800	3,000
Gains on sale of treasury stock	2,050	
Total revenues	$902,200	$787,600
Costs and expenses:		
Cost of goods sold, including sales taxes	$415,900	$332,200
Salaries and related payroll expenses	60,500	62,100
Rent	19,100	19,100
Freight-in and freight-out	3,400	2,900
Bad debt expense	24,000	26,000
Addition to reserve for possible inventory losses	3,800	2,000
Total costs and expenses	$526,700	$444,300
Income before extraordinary items	$375,500	$343,300
Extraordinary items:		
Loss on discontinued styles (note 1)	$ 24,000	$ 4,800
Loss on sale of marketable securities (note 2)	52,050	
Loss on sale of warehouse (note 3)	86,350	
Retroactive settlement of federal income taxes for		
19X2 and 19X1 (note 4)	31,600	
Total extraordinary items	$194,000	$ 4,800
Net income	$181,500	$338,500
Retained earnings at beginning of year	310,700	163,100
Total	$492,200	$501,600
Less: Federal income taxes	$120,000	$170,000
Cash dividends on common stock	21,900	20,900
Total	$141,900	$190,900
Retained earnings at end of year	$350,300	$310,700

Notes to the Statement of Income and Retained Earnings:

1 New styles and rapidly changing consumer preferences resulted in a $24,000 loss on the disposal of discontinued styles and related accessories.

2 The corporation sold an investment in marketable securities at a loss of $52,050 with no income tax effect.

3 The corporation sold one of its warehouses at an $86,350 loss.

4 The corporation was charged $31,600 retroactively for additional income taxes resulting from a settlement in 19X3. Of this amount $14,000 was applicable to 19X2 and the balance was applicable to 19X1.

**19-18
(cont'd.)**

	Effect on Income		
	Overstated	*Understated*	*No Effect*
1 On 19X1 income of the omission of accrued expenses as of the end of 19X1			
2 On 19X2 income of the omission of accrued expenses as of the end of 19X1			
3 On 19X3 income of the omission of accrued expenses as of the end of 19X1			
4 On 19X2 income of the omission of deferred income at the end of 19X2			
5 On 19X1 income of the omission of accrued income at the end of 19X1			
6 On 19X2 income of the omission of accrued income at the end of 19X1			
7 On 19X3 income of the omission of accrued income at the end of 19X1			
8 On 19X1 income of the omission of prepaid expenses at the end of 19X1			
9 On 19X2 income of the omission of prepaid expenses at the end of 19X1			
10 On 19X1 income of the omission of prepaid expenses at the end of 19X2			

*19-20 You have been engaged to review the records and prepare corrected financial statements for the Graber Corporation. The accounting records are in agreement with the following balance sheet:

GRABER CORPORATION
Balance Sheet
As of December 31, 19X4

Assets

Cash	$ 5,000
Accounts receivable	10,000
Notes receivable	3,000
Inventory	25,000
	$43,000

Liabilities and Owner Equity

Accounts payable	$ 2,000
Notes payable	4,000
Capital stock	10,000
Retained earnings	27,000
	$43,000

A review of the accounting records indicates that the following errors and omissions had not been corrected during the applicable years:

December 31	Inventory Overvalued	Inventory Undervalued	Prepaid Expense	Prepaid Income	Accrued Expense	Accrued Income
19X1	—	$6,000	$900	—	$200	—
19X2	$7,000	—	700	$400	75	$125
19X3	8,000	—	500	—	100	—
19X4	—	9,000	600	300	50	150

Profits as reported per the books were: 19X2, $7,500; 19X3, $6,500; and 19X4, $5,500. No dividends were declared during these years and no adjustments were made to retained earnings.

Instructions Ignoring possible income tax effects:

(1) Determine the corrected profit or loss for each of the years 19X2, 19X3, and 19X4.

(2) Prepare a corrected balance sheet as of December 31, 19X4.

*AICPA adapted.

20
Special Financial Statements

Although the basic statements discussed in the preceding chapter present important and useful financial data, in the opinion of many accountants and financial analysts they do not, as ordinarily prepared, present all the valuable information included in the accounts.

The balance sheet reflects the financial condition of an organization as of a moment of time, and the income statement summarizes the results of operations for a period of time. Neither, however, adequately discloses the sources and disposition of the resources which financed the organization's activities for the period. Little useful information, for example, is included in either statement with respect to (1) how much cash was generated by operations, (2) how the acquisition of new assets was financed, or (3) how the retirement of a bond issue was accomplished.

The reporting of the important sources of an organization's financial resources and the ways in which these resources are used enables statement readers to more readily evaluate the organization's financial policies. In addition, it provides answers to such questions as: Why weren't dividends increased? Why was additional debt incurred? Why is the cash balance so low?

For this reason, many business organizations prepare various special statements designed to disclose this information. We shall study some of the more important ones in this chapter.

FINANCIAL POSITION FORM OF BALANCE SHEET

From a financial viewpoint, the assets and liabilities of an organization naturally fall into two broad categories: current and noncurrent.   The current category consists of assets and liabilities which are constantly changing form, or "working," whereas the noncurrent category contains those which are more or less permanent. In the working category, the excess of current assets over current liabilities is known as **working capital** or, as it is sometimes called, **net working capital**.

Inadequate working capital in an organization is often the forerunner, if not the actual cause, of financial disaster; therefore, there is a certain demand by financial statement users that working capital be spotlighted on the balance sheet. Such disclosure is often accomplished by the use of the **financial position form** of balance sheet, which is in reality merely one type of the report form.   Its usual format is as follows:

> Current assets
> —Current liabilities
> _____
> Working capital
> +Noncurrent assets
> —Noncurrent liabilities
> _____
> Net assets (owner equity)

The following condensed statement is indicative of the form and content of the financial position form of balance sheet.   The basic data are the same as those used in the balance sheet illustrations in Chapter 19.

Financial Position Form of Balance Sheet

COMPANY A
Balance Sheet
As of December 31, 19___

Current assets	$270,000
Less: Current liabilities	252,000
Working capital	$ 18,000
Plus: Noncurrent assets	730,000
Less: Noncurrent liabilities	(103,000)
Net assets (excess of assets over liabilities)	$645,000
Shareholder equity:	
Invested capital	$520,000
Earned capital	125,000
Shareholder equity (excess of assets over liabilities)	$645,000

SOURCE AND DISPOSITION OF WORKING CAPITAL

Although the financial position form of balance sheet emphasizes the amount of an organization's working capital, it generally does not report either the changes that took place in the working capital during the period being reported upon or why the changes came about. In order to provide this information, the basic financial statements are frequently supplemented by (1) a schedule reflecting the net changes in the various working capital elements, and (2) a statement summarizing how these changes came about.

Schedule of Working Capital Changes

The following illustration is indicative of the form and content of the schedule of changes in working capital.

COMPANY A
Schedule of Net Changes in Working Capital
For the Year Ended December 31, 19X2

	December 31 19X2	December 31 19X1	Changes in Working Capital Increase	Changes in Working Capital Decrease
Current Assets:				
Cash	$ 44,000	$ 30,000	$14,000	
Marketable securities	20,000	25,000		$ 5,000
Accounts receivable (net)	60,000	39,500	20,500	
Notes receivable	10,000	10,500		500
Inventories	135,000	100,000	35,000	
Prepaid insurance	1,000	1,000		
Total current assets	$270,000	$206,000		
Current Liabilities:				
Accrued payroll payable	$ 2,500	$ 2,500		
Accounts payable	132,000	80,000		52,000
Notes payable	50,000	50,500	500	
Income taxes payable	60,000	53,000		7,000
Dividends payable	7,500	10,000	2,500	
Total current liabilities	$252,000	$196,000		
Working capital (CA − CL)	$ 18,000	$ 10,000		
Net increase in working capital				8,000
			$72,500	$72,500

As can be observed in the schedule, as of December 31, 19X2, Company A's current assets of $270,000 exceeded its current liabilities of $252,000 by $18,000, whereas as of December 31, 19X1, its current assets of $206,000 exceeded its current liabilities of $196,000 by $10,000, thus indicating a net increase in working capital of $8,000 ($18,000 − $10,000). Although the formal schedule of net changes in working capital, as presented in our illustration, is frequently employed, the data included in it are often summarized somewhat as follows:

COMPANY A
Summary of Working Capital Changes
For the Year Ended December 31, 19X2

	December 31		Working Capital Increase (Decrease)
	19X2	19X1	
Cash	$ 44,000	$ 30,000	$14,000
Marketable securities	20,000	25,000	(5,000)
Accounts receivable (net)	60,000	39,500	20,500
Notes receivable	10,000	10,500	(500)
Inventories	135,000	100,000	35,000
Prepaid insurance	1,000	1,000	
Accrued payroll payable	2,500	2,500	
Accounts payable	132,000	80,000	(52,000)
Notes payable	50,000	50,500	500
Income taxes payable	60,000	53,000	(7,000)
Dividends payable	7,500	10,000	2,500
Net increase in working capital			$ 8,000

It is apparent in both the schedule and the summary that the net increase of $8,000 in Company A's working capital is the result of net changes in all the current asset and current liability accounts except two, the Prepaid Insurance and the Accrued Payroll Payable accounts. However, the fact that these accounts have exactly the same balances at the end of the period that they had at the beginning does not necessarily mean that no change has taken place in them during the period. Both asset and liability accounts properly classified in the current category are, as a general rule, constantly changing. Thus, a net change of zero in an account in itself means nothing. Further analysis may indicate that actually many changes took place during the period, even though the net effect upon the balance in the account was zero.

When studying the schedule and the summary, note that an increase in a current asset increases working capital, whereas a decrease in a current asset decreases working capital, and that the opposite is true for a change in a current liability. We can summarize current asset and current liability changes and their resultant effects on working capital as follows:

	Change	Resultant Effect on Working Capital
Current asset	+	+
Current asset	−	−
Current liability	+	−
Current liability	−	+

Statement of Source and Disposition of Working Capital

Although both the schedule and the summary of working capital changes reflect the net change in working capital and the net changes that took place in the various elements of working capital during the period, neither reflects the source and disposition of all the working capital that management had at its disposal during the period. Stated another way, they reflect the changes that took place during the period but they give no indication as to the underlying causes of these changes. In order to spotlight the causes, organizations frequently prepare a **statement of source and disposition of working capital.** The usual procedure is to present the statement and support it with either the schedule or a summary of working capital changes. In this text we shall support it in our illustrations with the latter.

In order to understand better the method of preparation of the statement of source and disposition of working capital, it is important that we bear in mind that some transactions merely result in a change in the composition of the various elements of working capital, while others have no effect whatsoever on working capital, and still other transactions affect both the composition of the working capital elements and the total amount of working capital. Thus, when we are preparing the statement, it is often helpful if we think in terms of the following categories:

1 Transactions that affect only working capital accounts
2 Transactions that affect only nonworking capital accounts
3 Transactions that affect both working capital and nonworking capital accounts

Transactions Affecting Only Working Capital Accounts Transactions that take place wholly within the working capital accounts do not affect the amount of working capital and, as a consequence, they are not reflected as individual transactions in the statement of source and disposition of working capital. For example, the collection of a customer's account causes an increase in one working capital account (Cash) and a decrease in another (Accounts Receivable). Since these accounts normally have like balances, an increase in one with an equal decrease in the other has the net result of no change in the amount of working capital. Likewise, the payment of a creditor's account results in decreases in two working capital accounts (Accounts Payable and Cash). These accounts normally have opposite balances; therefore, an equal decrease in each results in no change in the amount of working capital. Although transactions which affect only working capital accounts are not reflected as individual transactions in the statement of source and disposition of working capital, they are, of course, summarized in the schedule or the summary of working capital changes.

Transactions Affecting Only Nonworking Capital Accounts Transactions which take place entirely outside the working capital accounts do not affect the amount of working capital and, as a consequence, they are not reflected as individual transactions in the statement of source and disposition of working capital. For example, the acquisition of a plant site or the retirement of a bond issue by the issuance of some of a corporation's previously unissued stock would have no effect on working capital. Other transactions in this category include the appropriation of retained earnings, the issuance of stock dividends, and the acquisition of long-lived assets by the use of long-term debt.

Transactions Affecting Both Working Capital and Nonworking Capital Accounts Because only those transactions which affect both working capital and nonworking capital accounts result in changes in the amount of working capital, they are the relevant ones so far as the statement of source and disposition of working capital is concerned. For example, the acquisition of a plant site or the retirement of a bond issue for cash change working capital and are, therefore, pertinent to the statement. Similarly, an increase or decrease in working capital as the result of operations is pertinent, since working capital accounts such as Cash, Accounts Receivable, and Accounts Payable are affected in addition to the non-working capital account, Retained Earnings.

Typical Sources and Uses of Working Capital

During any given period, an organization's working capital may be increased from a number of sources, while at the same time it may be decreased by various uses.

Typical Sources	Typical Uses
1 Income from operations	1 Loss from operations
2 Sale of noncurrent assets	2 Purchase of noncurrent assets
3 Increase in long-term debt	3 Decrease in long-term debt
4 Sale of additional stock	4 Dividends on capital stock

Working Capital and the Results of Operations An organization's working capital is ordinarily affected by its income-producing activities in one of two ways: Either it is increased as the result of net income or it is reduced in the event of a net loss. The amount of the effect, however, is usually not the same as the amount of reported net income or net loss.

Certain charges to revenue and expense accounts reduce the reported net income or increase the reported net loss without having any effect on working capital. In like manner, some credits to revenue and expense accounts increase the reported net income or decrease the reported net loss but have no effect on working capital.

For example, the amount of depreciation taken on a long-lived asset in a period will be charged against the revenue of the period, but the depreciation entry will have no effect on working capital because neither the Depreciation Expense account, which is debited, nor the Accumulated Depreciation account, which is credited, is a working capital account.

Similarly, the amortization of an Unamortized Bond Premium account results in an increase in reported net income or a decrease in a reported net loss, but does not affect working capital because neither the Unamortized Bond Premium account, which is debited, nor the Interest Expense account, which is credited, is a working capital account. Therefore, in order to determine the actual amount of working capital provided by operations, the accountant must adjust the reported net income or loss for such items. That is, he must add back charges and deduct credits which were made to revenue and expense accounts but which did not affect working capital. Typical items of this nature are:

1 Depreciation of long-lived assets

2 Depletion of wasting assets

3 Amortization of intangibles

4 Amortization of unamortized bond premium or discount

Working Capital and Gains and Losses on the Disposal of Noncurrent Assets
Similar to the problem created by nonworking capital charges and credits being reflected in an organization's ordinary revenue and expense accounts, and thus in its reported net income or loss, is the problem of gains and losses associated with the disposal of noncurrent assets.

You will recall from Chapter 19 that under the all-inclusive income statement approach such gains and losses are reported in the income statement and as a consequence are reflected in the reported net income or loss. The impact on working capital of the disposal of a noncurrent asset is limited to the amount of cash or its equivalent associated with the disposal. This means, therefore, that when a gain is involved and the amount of the gain is included in the reported net income, the gain element must be deducted either from the amount of working capital shown as provided by operations or from the amount shown as provided by the disposal. Otherwise it will be reflected twice.

For example, if a noncurrent asset with a net book, or carrying, value of $40,000 is sold for $50,000, the gain is $10,000. If the $10,000 gain is reflected as part of the amount of working capital provided by operations, while at the same time the $50,000 is shown as being provided by the disposal, we have a total of $60,000 being provided. Since only $50,000 was actually provided, we have a problem. We could, of course, leave the $10,000 gain in the reported net income or loss and thus reflect it as part of the working capital provided by operations, and reflect only $40,000 as being provided by the disposal. This, however, does not present the true picture. Therefore, the usual procedure is to show the $50,000 as being provided by the disposal and the $10,000 gain as an adjustment of the reported net income or loss (a deduction in the case of reported net income and an addition in the case of a reported net loss) when the amount of working capital provided by operations is determined.

Whereas gains on the disposal of noncurrent assets are deducted from reported net income and added to reported net losses when the amount of working capital provided by operations is determined, the opposite is true regarding losses on the disposal of noncurrent assets. For example, if a noncurrent asset with a net book value of $40,000 is sold for $35,000, when the amount of working capital provided by operations is determined, the loss of $5,000 would have to be added back to a reported net income and deducted from a reported net loss. The entire $35,000 would be reflected as being provided by the disposal.

Typical Nonworking Capital Adjustments Summarized The following summary is not intended to be exhaustive, but it is indicative of the types of adjustments that must be made when the amount of working capital provided by operations is being determined. As you study the summary, the important thing to remember is that the reported net income or loss must be adjusted for all transactions reflected therein which did not affect working capital. This includes so-called "paper" or "book" gains and losses related to the disposal of noncurrent assets.

Summary		
	Reported Net Income	*Reported Net Loss*
Depreciation	Add back	Deduct
Depletion	Add back	Deduct
Amortization of intangible assets	Add back	Deduct
Amortization of unamortized bond discount	Add back	Deduct
Amortization of unamortized bond premium	Deduct	Add back
Gains on the disposal of noncurrent assets	Deduct	Add back
Losses on the disposal of noncurrent assets	Add back	Deduct

Statement Format

Although there are variations in practice, the following format is typical of the statement of source and disposition of working capital:

COMPANY A

Statement of Source and Disposition of Working Capital

For the Year Ended December 31, 19___

Working capital was provided by:

Operations: Reported net income _____	$xxx*	
Add: Nonworking capital charges closed to R & E Summary account _____	xxx	
Deduct: Nonworking capital credits closed to R & E Summary account _____	(xxx)	$xxx
Sale of noncurrent assets _____		xxx
Increase in long-term debt _____		xxx
Sale of capital stock _____		xxx
		$xxx

Working capital was used for:

Purchase of noncurrent assets _____	$xxx	
Decrease in long-term debt _____	xxx	
Dividend on capital stock _____	xxx	xxx
Increase in working capital (per schedule) _____		$xxx†

*A reported net loss would be shown as the first item under the disposition section.
†In the case of a decrease in working capital, uses are listed first and the provisions are deducted therefrom.

Statement Preparation

Because the statement centers on working capital and the changes therein for a particular period of time and because working capital is the excess of current assets over current liabilities, the statement is logically prepared from data derived from a comparison of balance sheets as of the beginning and end of a period.

If we are to interpret correctly some of the changes which occur in balance sheet accounts during a period, additional information taken from analyses of specific accounts is often necessary. For example, a net increase in the Retained Earnings account may be the result of:

1 Net income only

2 Net income minus dividends

3 Net income minus dividends plus or minus corrections of prior years' earnings

4 Some similar combination

Similarly, the net increase in a noncurrent asset may be the result of one or more acquisitions or a combination of acquisitions and disposals. Thus, the basic information for the statement of source and disposition of working capital is provided by (1) data taken from comparative balance sheets, and (2) data relevant to the analyses of specific balance sheet accounts.

When carried out in sequential order, these steps usually prove helpful in the preparation of the statement:

Step 1 Prepare a schedule or summary of working capital changes.

Step 2 Analyze the net change in each noncurrent account to determine the individual elements of the change and their effects on working capital.

Step 3 Prepare the statement by filling in the format with the changes determined in step 2.

Step 4 Prove the statement: Working capital provided minus working capital used equals the increase in working capital; and vice versa, working capital used minus working capital provided equals the decrease in working capital.

Statement Preparation Illustrated To illustrate the recommended procedure for preparing the statement of source and disposition of working capital, we shall begin with a very simple situation and move to the more complex. The comparative balance sheets and changes in accounts which follow appear in a highly condensed form. They will be expanded as the need arises as we progress through the illustrations.

COMPANY B
Condensed Balance Sheets and
Changes in Balance Sheet Accounts

| | December 31 | | Differences | |
Accounts	19X2	19X1	Dr	Cr
Current assets	$100,000	$ 90,000	$10,000	
Noncurrent assets	300,000	300,000		
	$400,000	$390,000		
Current liabilities	$ 60,000	$ 65,000	5,000	
Noncurrent liabilities	100,000	100,000		
Capital stock	100,000	100,000		
Retained earnings	140,000	125,000		$15,000
	$400,000	$390,000	$15,000	$15,000

If we assume that there were no changes in the noncurrent asset and liability accounts and that the only change in the Retained Earnings account, except for the declaration of a $5,000 cash dividend, resulted from operations, the statement of source and disposition of working capital, supported by the summary of working capital changes, would appear as follows:

COMPANY B
Statement of Source and Disposition of Working Capital
For the Year Ended December 31, 19X2

Working capital was provided by:

Operations _____	$20,000*
Working capital was used for:	
Declaration of cash dividend _____	5,000
Increase in working capital (see Schedule A) _____	$15,000

*$15,000 change in retained earnings plus $5,000 dividend.

Schedule A
Summary of Working Capital Changes

	December 31 19X2	19X1	Working Capital Increase (Decrease)
Current assets _____	$100,000	$90,000	$10,000
Current liabilities_____	60,000	65,000	5,000
Net increase in working capital _____			$15,000

To illustrate next the effect of depreciation on the statement of source and disposition of working capital, let us assume that the comparative balance sheets and differences in the accounts appear as follows:

	December 31		Differences	
Accounts	19X2	19X1	Dr	Cr
Current assets _____	$102,000	$ 90,000	$12,000	
Noncurrent assets (net) _____	298,000	300,000		$ 2,000
	$400,000	$390,000		
Current liabilities_____	$ 60,000	$ 65,000	5,000	
Noncurrent liabilities _____	100,000	100,000		
Capital stock _____	100,000	100,000		
Retained earnings _____	140,000	125,000		15,000
	$400,000	$390,000	$17,000	$17,000

If we assume that there were no changes in the noncurrent liability accounts, that the only change in the noncurrent asset accounts was for the amount of depreciation taken during the period, and that the only change in the Retained Earnings account, except for the declaration of a $5,000 cash dividend, resulted from operations, the statement of source and disposition of working capital would appear as follows:

COMPANY B

Statement of Source and Disposition of Working Capital
For the Year Ended December 31, 19X2

Working capital was provided by:		
Operations:		
Reported net income	$20,000*	
Add: Depreciation	2,000†	$22,000
Working capital was used for:		
Declaration of cash dividend		5,000
Increase in working capital (see Schedule A)		$17,000

*$15,000 change in retained earnings plus $5,000 dividend.
†Decrease in net noncurrent assets.

Schedule A
Summary of Working Capital Changes

	December 31 19X2	December 31 19X1	Working Capital Increase (Decrease)
Current assets	$102,000	$90,000	$12,000
Current liabilities	60,000	65,000	5,000
Net increase in working capital			$17,000

To illustrate the effect of the purchase of a noncurrent asset on the source and disposition of working capital, let us assume that the comparative balance sheets and account differences appear as follows:

	December 31 19X2	December 31 19X1	Differences Dr	Cr
Accounts				
Current assets	$ 92,000	$ 90,000	$ 2,000	
Noncurrent assets (net)	308,000	300,000	8,000	
	$400,000	$390,000		
Current liabilities	$ 60,000	$ 65,000	5,000	
Noncurrent liabilities	100,000	100,000		
Capital stock	100,000	100,000		
Retained earnings	140,000	125,000		$15,000
	$400,000	$390,000	$15,000	$15,000

Let us assume that there were no changes in the noncurrent liability accounts, that the change in the noncurrent asset accounts was the result of (1) the periodic depreciation entry and (2) the purchase of machinery for $10,000 cash, and that the only change in the Retained Earnings account, except for the declaration of a $5,000 cash dividend, resulted from operations. Then the statement of source and disposition of working capital would appear as follows:

COMPANY B
Statement of Source and Disposition of Working Capital
For the Year Ended December 31, 19X2

Working capital was provided by:
Operations:

Reported net income	$20,000	
Add: Depreciation	2,000	$22,000

Working capital was used for:

Purchase of machinery	$10,000	
Declaration of cash dividend	5,000	15,000
Increase in working capital (see Schedule A)		$ 7,000

Schedule A
Summary of Working Capital Changes

	December 31 19X2	19X1	Working Capital Increase (Decrease)
Current assets	$92,000	$90,000	$2,000
Current liabilities	60,000	65,000	5,000
Net increase in working capital			$7,000

To illustrate the effect of the disposal of a noncurrent asset on the statement of source and disposition of working capital, let us assume that the comparative balance sheets and account differences appear as follows:

Accounts	December 31 19X2	19X1	Differences Dr	Cr
Current assets	$122,000	$ 90,000	$32,000	
Noncurrent assets (net)	278,000	300,000		$22,000
	$400,000	$390,000		
Current liabilities	$ 60,000	$ 65,000	5,000	
Noncurrent liabilities	100,000	100,000		
Capital stock	100,000	100,000		
Retained earnings	140,000	125,000		15,000
	$400,000	$390,000	$37,000	$37,000

If we assume that there were no changes in the noncurrent liability accounts, that the change in the noncurrent asset accounts was the result of (1) the periodic depreciation entry, and (2) the sale of machinery with a book value of $20,000 for $12,000 cash, and that the only change in the Retained Earnings account, except for the declaration of a $5,000 cash dividend, resulted from operations, the statement of source and disposition of working capital would appear as follows:

COMPANY B
Statement of Source and Disposition of Working Capital
For the Year Ended December 31, 19X2

Working capital was provided by:
  Operations:

Reported net income	$20,000	
Add: Depreciation	2,000	
Loss on sale of machinery	8,000*	$30,000
Sale of machinery		12,000
		$42,000

Working capital was used for:

Declaration of cash dividend		5,000
Increase in working capital (see Schedule A)		$37,000

*$20,000 carrying, or book, value minus proceeds of $12,000.

Schedule A
Summary of Working Capital Changes

	December 31		Working Capital Increase (Decrease)
	19X2	*19X1*	
Current assets	$122,000	$90,000	$32,000
Current liabilities	60,000	65,000	5,000
Net increase in working capital			$37,000

The preceding illustrations have purposely been relatively simple in order to illustrate specific points. Now we shall study a more comprehensive example, using the step-by-step procedure outlined earlier. The comparative balance sheets and differences in the account balances appear as follows:

Assets	December 31 19X2	19X1	Differences Dr	Cr
Cash	$ 65,000	$ 39,000	$26,000	
Accounts receivable (net)	25,000	30,000		$ 5,000
Inventories	21,300	20,000	1,300	
Prepaid expenses	700	1,000		300
Plant and equipment (net)	288,000	300,000		12,000
Total assets	$400,000	$390,000		

Liabilities and Owner Equity				
Accounts payable	$ 55,000	$ 63,000	8,000	
Income taxes payable	3,750	2,000		1,750
Dividends payable	1,250			1,250
Bonds payable	80,000	100,000	20,000	
Capital stock	120,000	100,000		20,000
Retained earnings	140,000	125,000		15,000
Total liabilities and owner equity	$400,000	$390,000	$55,300	$55,300

Step 1 Our suggested procedure for the preparation of the statement of source and disposition of working capital requires the preparation of a schedule or summary of working capital changes. Thus, we first categorize the working capital items and prepare a summary as follows:

Schedule A
Summary of Working Capital Changes

	December 31 19X2	19X1	Working Capital Increase (Decrease)
Cash	$65,000	$39,000	$26,000
Accounts receivable (net)	25,000	30,000	(5,000)
Inventories	21,300	20,000	1,300
Prepaid expenses	700	1,000	(300)
Accounts payable	55,000	63,000	8,000
Income taxes payable	3,750	2,000	(1,750)
Dividends payable	1,250		(1,250)
Net increase in working capital			$27,000

Step 2 This requires that we analyze the net change in each of the noncurrent accounts in order to determine the effect on working capital of each individual element of the change.

The comparative account balances on page 541 indicate that the carrying value of plant and equipment decreased $12,000 during the year. An analysis of the asset account and its related accumulated depreciation account reveals, as we can see in the T accounts which follow, that (1) depreciation of $10,000 was taken during the period, (2) an asset with a carrying value of $30,000 (a cost of $45,000 and accumulated depreciation of $15,000) was sold during the period, and

Plant and Equipment

Beginning balance	350,000	Sold during year	45,000
Purchased during year	28,000		

Accumulated Depreciation—Plant and Equipment

Sale	15,000	Beginning balance	50,000
		Depreciation for year	10,000

(3) an asset costing $28,000 was purchased during the period. Additional analysis of related accounts reveals that cash of $22,000 was received for the asset sold and that the new asset was acquired by the issuance of $5,000 of par value stock, $10,000 of par value bonds, and the payment of the remaining $13,000 in cash. On the assumption that both the asset sold and the asset purchased were machinery, data for the statement preparation and the classification within the format for the changes in the Plant and Equipment account and the Accumulated Depreciation—Plant and Equipment account would be:

1 Working capital provided by operations: Add $10,000 depreciation to the reported net income.

2 Working capital provided by sale of machinery: $22,000.

3 Working capital provided by operations: Add $8,000 loss on disposal of machinery to the reported net income.

4 Working capital used for the purchase of machinery: $13,000. Note that only the effect on working capital is reported in the statement. Since the use of capital stock and bonds payable did not involve working capital items, these are not included in the statement.

The comparative account balances on page 541 show that the Bonds Payable account decreased $20,000. An analysis of the account reveals, as we can see in the T account which follows, that additional bonds with a par value of $20,000 were issued during the period. Entries to record the issuance indicate that one-half of the bonds were sold at par for cash, and the other half, as we saw earlier, were issued as partial payment for the machinery purchased. The analysis also reveals that bonds with a par value of $40,000 were retired. The entry to record the transaction indicates that this was accomplished by the issuance of $5,000 of par value stock and the payment of $35,000 in cash.

Bonds Payable

Retired during year	40,000	Beginning balance	100,000
		Issued during year	20,000

Data for the statement preparation and the classification within the format would be:

1 Working capital provided by the issuance of bonds: $10,000. As pointed out earlier, the issuance of bonds when the machinery was purchased did not involve working capital.

2 Working capital used for the retirement of bonds: $35,000. Since the use of capital stock to retire part of the bonds did not involve working capital, it is not reflected in the statement.

An analysis of the Capital Stock account, which is illustrated below, reveals that additional stock with a par value of $20,000 was issued during the year. The entries to record the issuance indicate that (1) one-fourth of the stock was used to purchase machinery, (2) one-fourth was used in the retirement of bonds, and (3) the remaining one-half was issued at par value for cash. Because the issuance of capital stock to retire bonds or to purchase a noncurrent asset does not involve the use of working capital, the only item needed for the preparation of the statement of source and disposition of working capital would be: Working capital provided by the issuance of capital stock, $10,000.

Capital Stock

	Beginning balance	100,000
	Issued during year	20,000

An analysis of the Retained Earnings account which follows reveals that (1) cash dividends of $5,000 were declared during the year, and (2) a net income of $20,000 was reported.

Retained Earnings

Declaration of dividends	5,000	Beginning balance	125,000
		Net income	20,000

The statement data would be:

1 Working capital used for the declaration of cash dividends: $5,000

2 Working capital provided by operations: $20,000

Step 3 The preparation of the statement simply entails filling in the format with the data obtained in step 2. In fact, steps 2 and 3 may be completed more or less simultaneously. The data obtained in step 2 would be displayed in the format as follows:

COMPANY B
Statement of Source and Disposition of Working Capital
For the Year Ended December 31, 19X2

Working capital was provided by:
  Operations:

Reported net income	$20,000	
Add: Depreciation	10,000	
Loss on sale of machinery	8,000	$38,000
Sale of machinery		22,000
Issuance of bonds		10,000
Issuance of capital stock		10,000
		$80,000

Working capital was used for:

Purchase of machinery	$13,000	
Retirement of bonds	35,000	
Declaration of cash dividends	5,000	53,000
Increase in working capital (see Schedule A)		$27,000

Step 4 This requires that we prove the statement. This is done by reconciling the increase or decrease in working capital as determined in the statement of source and disposition of working capital with the amount of increase or decrease as determined in the schedule or summary of working capital changes. In this case both reconcile to $27,000.

FUND FLOW ANALYSIS

In financial circles increased emphasis is being placed on what has generally come to be known as **fund flow analysis,** that is, the process of determining where an organization's funds came from and what was done with them. Consequently, it is becoming fairly commonplace to find a so-called **funds statement** included in many corporate annual reports along with the usual balance sheet, income statement, and retained earnings statement.

Funds Defined

The plural term **funds,** like the singular **fund,** is used in a variety of ways in accounting and financial jargon. You will recall, for example, that we used the term fund when working with both the petty cash fund and the bond sinking fund. In the case of the petty cash fund the term refers to cash, but when used in reference to a bond sinking fund it includes both cash and other assets. Similarly, the term funds, as related to a funds statement, carries various connotations, depending upon the way it is used. Obviously, the connotation adopted when we are preparing the statement will govern its scope and content.

From the standpoint of the funds statement, funds is generally defined in one of three ways:

1 In terms of cash

2 In terms of working capital

3 In terms of all financial resources resulting from transactions with parties external to the organization

When the term funds is defined strictly as cash, the funds statement is simply a statement of cash receipts and disbursements; this approach will be illustrated in the next section of this chapter. When the term is defined as working capital, the funds statement is synonymous with the statement of source and disposition of working capital studied in the preceding section of this chapter. When funds is defined as all financial resources, the concept of the statement is similar to, but broader than, that of working capital. The working capital definition restricts the content of the statement to transactions which affect current assets and current liabilities; however, the definition of funds as all financial resources considers all financial transactions between the organization and its debtors, creditors, and owners to be fund transactions.

To illustrate the basic differences in the concepts, let us assume that an organization purchases a noncurrent asset for $100,000, paying for it by giving (1) $30,000 in cash, (2) a $20,000 short-term note, and (3) a long-term mortgage for the balance. Under the cash approach, only the $30,000 cash payment would be considered as funds. Under the working capital approach, both the cash payment of $30,000 and the short-term note of $20,000 would be considered as funds. If all financial resources are included in the concept, the entire $100,000— that is, $30,000 in cash, $20,000 short-term note, and $50,000 mortgage—would be considered as funds.

Each concept has its usefulness under the appropriate circumstances. However, the Accounting Principles Board of the AICPA recommends that the all financial resources approach be used in preparing statements for presentation in annual reports.[1] Under this approach, the concept of funds includes not only working capital items, but also such nonworking capital transactions as:

1 Acquisition of noncurrent assets by exchange

2 Acquisition of noncurrent assets by the incurrence of long-term debt

---

[1] AICPA, "The Statement of Source and Application of Funds," *Opinion No. 3 of the Accounting Principles Board* (New York: 1963), p. 16.

3 Acquisition of noncurrent assets by the issuance of capital stock

4 Payment of long-term debt by the issuance of capital stock

Funds Statement

The funds statement is prepared in essentially the same way as the statement of source and disposition of working capital, except that it is expanded to include not only the results of working capital transactions but the results of all other transactions as well. The statement format is likewise essentially the same, except that a decrease in working capital is classified as a **provision of funds** and an increase in working capital is classified as an **application of funds.** Thus, the steps we followed when preparing the statement of source and disposition of working capital still obtain, except that they are expanded to include all financial resources rather than only those that flow through working capital.

In practice, the terminology of the statement varies considerably, all the way from the heading to the subdivisions of the statement. Typical headings include:

1 Statement of funds, or funds statement

2 Statement of source and application of funds

3 Statement of resources provided and applied

4 Where-got, where-gone statement

The last title, although somewhat unsophisticated, pinpoints very succinctly the purpose of the statement.

Funds Statement Illustrated The illustration which follows should be contrasted with the statement of source and disposition of working capital on page 544, as both are based on the same data.

COMPANY B
Statement of Source and Application of Funds
For the Year Ended December 31, 19X2

Funds were provided by:

Operations:		
Reported net income	$20,000	
Add: Depreciation	10,000	
Loss on sale of machinery	8,000	$ 38,000
Sale of machinery		22,000
Issuance of bonds		20,000*
Issuance of capital stock		20,000†
Total funds provided		$100,000

Funds were applied to:

Purchase of machinery	$ 28,000‡
Retirement of bonds	40,000§
Declaration of cash dividends	5,000
Increase in working capital (see Schedule A)	27,000
Total funds applied	$100,000

* $10,000 issued for cash plus $10,000 for machinery.

† $10,000 issued for cash plus $5,000 issued for machinery plus $5,000 issued to retire bonds payable.

‡ $13,000 paid in cash plus $10,000 paid in bonds plus $5,000 paid in capital stock.

§ $35,000 paid in cash plus $5,000 paid in capital stock.

Schedule A*
Summary of Working Capital Changes

	December 31 19X2	December 31 19X1	Working Capital Increase (Decrease)
Cash	$65,000	$39,000	$26,000
Accounts receivable (net)	25,000	30,000	(5,000)
Inventories	21,300	20,000	1,300
Prepaid expenses	700	1,000	(300)
Accounts payable	55,000	63,000	8,000
Income taxes payable	3,750	2,000	(1,750)
Dividends payable	1,250		(1,250)
Net increase in working capital			$27,000

*Note that the schedule is exactly the same for both the statement of source and disposition of working capital and the statement of source and application of funds.

CASH FLOW ANALYSIS

The final special statement to be discussed in this chapter is the **statement of source and disposition of cash,** also known as the **cash flow statement.**

The statement of source and disposition of cash is based on essentially the same logic as that underlying the statement of source and disposition of working capital: Whereas the latter accounts for the increase or decrease in working capital, the statement of source and disposition of cash for a particular period spotlights those factors which caused the net change in the Cash account during the period. This statement is often of interest to financial analysts, long-term investors, and short-term credit grantors; it is of particular significance to management, because a knowledge of "cash flow" is fundamental to the solution of the important problem of effective utilization of cash.

Statement of Source and Disposition of Cash

As to format, the statement of source and disposition of cash presents the flow of cash in the same way that the statement of source and disposition of working capital presents the flow of working capital. The procedure for analyzing transactions pertinent to the two statements is also fundamentally the same, except that changes in current asset and current liability accounts are handled separately under the cash flow approach rather than netted as is done under the working capital approach. The major difference in the preparation of the two statements is related to the determination of the amount of resources provided by operations.

In the statement of source and disposition of working capital, the amount of working capital provided by operations is based upon income determined on the accrual basis, whereas in the statement of source and disposition of cash, the amount of cash provided by operations must, of course, be based upon income determined on the cash basis. Thus, in order to prepare the statement of source and disposition of cash, we must be able to convert accrual basis income to cash basis income.

Converting Accrual Basis Income to Cash Basis Income Accrual accounting, whereby revenue is recognized in the period in which the sale is made or the service is rendered, and costs and expenses are recognized in the period in which they contribute to revenue, has been discussed throughout the preceding chapters. Cash basis accounting, which was first defined in Chapter 9, is a method of accounting whereby revenue is recognized only when cash is received, and costs and expenses are recognized only when cash is paid out. Therefore, to convert accrual basis income to cash basis income, we must adjust reported net income for all noncash charges and credits reflected therein. An adjustment may be necessary because:

1 A noncash gain or loss on the disposal of a noncurrent asset is included in reported net income.

2 A noncash charge, such as depreciation taken on a long-lived tangible asset or amortization taken on an intangible asset, is included in reported net income.

3 A noncash charge or credit resulting from an accrual, deferral, sale, purchase, or change in an inventory account is included in reported net income.

Items falling into the first two categories are handled in exactly the same way as in the statement of source and disposition of working capital and the statement of source and application of funds. That is, we add back losses, deduct gains, and add back depreciation. However, whereas the first two categories deal with nonworking capital items, the third is a different story; all items included in this category affect working capital. Thus, when converting accrual basis income to cash basis income, we must consider not only the effect of nonworking capital transactions on reported net income, but also the effect of working capital items.

The accounts ordinarily involved include receivables, payables, inventories, prepaid expense, and prepaid income.

To illustrate the effect of a change in a receivable account on reported net income, let us assume for a period:

Cash sales	$100,000
Credit sales	50,000
Accounts receivable at beginning of period	10,000
Accounts receivable at end of period	15,000

Under the accrual basis, revenue of $150,000 (cash sales of $100,000 plus credit sales of $50,000) would be recognized, whereas under the cash basis only $145,000 [cash sales of $100,000 plus collections from customers of $45,000 ($10,000 + $50,000 − $15,000)] would be recognized. Note that the $5,000 difference between the two sales computations is equal to the net change in the receivable account. Thus, to convert accrual income to cash income, we must **deduct** an **increase** in a receivable account from reported net income and **add** a **decrease.**

Since the purchase of merchandise may cause a change in both the Accounts Payable and Inventory accounts, we perhaps should examine both at the same time. Let us assume for a period:

Cash purchases	$200,000
Credit purchases	100,000
Beginning inventory	50,000
Ending inventory	60,000
Accounts payable at beginning of period	20,000
Accounts payable at end of period	15,000

The cost of goods sold under the accrual basis would be computed as $290,000 (beginning inventory of $50,000 plus purchases of $300,000 less ending inventory of $60,000), whereas under the cash basis it would be computed as $305,000 [cash purchases of $200,000 plus payments to creditors of $105,000 ($20,000 + $100,000 − $15,000)]. Note that the $15,000 difference between the results of the two cost of goods sold computations is equal to the sum of the differences between the beginning and ending balances of the payable account ($5,000) and the beginning and ending balances of the inventory account ($10,000). Thus, when converting accrual basis income to cash basis income, we must deduct *increases* in inventory accounts and *decreases* in payable accounts from reported net income. The opposite, of course, is also true: *Decreases* in inventory accounts are added, whereas *increases* in payable accounts are added.

To illustrate the effect of a change in a prepaid account on reported net income, let us assume:

Prepaid insurance at beginning of period	$1,000
Cash premium paid during period	200
Prepaid insurance at end of period	900

Under the accrual basis, insurance expense for the period would be $300 ($1,000 + $200 − $900), whereas under the cash basis it would be $200, the amount of cash paid out during the period. To convert, we would add $100, the amount of the change in the account, to the reported net income. Thus, when we convert accrual basis income to cash basis income, the amount of a *decrease* in a prepaid expense account should be added to reported net income, whereas an *increase* should be deducted. In contrast, a change in a prepaid income account such as Rent Collected in Advance would be corrected in the opposite sense. That is, an *increase* in a prepaid income account should be added to reported net income, whereas a *decrease* should be deducted.

The following summary illustrates the corrections required for a change in a working capital account when accrual basis income is converted to cash basis income.

Converting Accrual Basis Income to Cash Basis Income

Account	Change in Account	Correction Required
Receivables	+	−
	−	+
Payables	+	+
	−	−
Inventories	+	−
	−	+
Prepaid Expense	+	−
	−	+
Prepaid Income	+	+
	−	−

Cash Flow Statement Illustrated As was pointed out earlier, the cash flow statement is prepared essentially in the same manner, and with the same format, as the statement of source and disposition of working capital, except that cash provided by operations is predicated upon cash basis income, whereas working capital provided by operations is based upon accrual basis income. The following illustration utilizes the same data as were used in the comprehensive examples of both the statement of source and disposition of working capital and the statement of source and application of funds:

COMPANY B
Statement of Source and Disposition of Cash
For the Year Ended December 31, 19X2

Cash was provided by:

Operations (see Schedule A)	$35,750
Sale of machinery	22,000*
Issuance of bonds	10,000*
Issuance of capital stock	10,000*
	$77,750

Cash was used for:

Purchase of machinery	$13,000*	
Retirement of bonds	35,000*	
Payment of dividends	3,750†	51,750
Increase in cash		$26,000

*The same analysis, and thus the same computation, as was used in the comprehensive source and disposition of working capital example.
†Although dividends of $5,000 were declared, the balance sheet shows that only $3,750 of them were paid.

Schedule A
Conversion of Reported Net Income from Accrual to Cash Basis

Reported net income (accrual basis)		$20,000
Add: Depreciation		10,000
Loss on sale of machinery		8,000
Decrease in accounts receivable		5,000
Decrease in prepaid expenses		300
Increase in income taxes payable		1,750
		$45,050
Deduct: Increase in inventories	$1,300	
Decrease in accounts payable	8,000	9,300
Net income on the cash basis		$35,750

SUMMARY

To be able to evaluate properly an organization's financial policies and decisions, the financial statement reader often requires information which may not be readily obtainable from the basic financial statements. Special statements, such as the statement of source and disposition of working capital, the statement of source and application of funds, and the statement of source and disposition of cash, have been designed in an attempt to meet this need.

The statement of source and disposition of working capital accounts for changes that occur in the organization's working capital position, and reflects only transactions that have had an effect on its working capital. The statement of source and application of funds accounts for all the organization's financial changes, and reflects the results of all its financial transactions. The statement of source and disposition of cash accounts only for changes that occur in the cash position of an organization, and thus reflects only transactions that have had an effect on the Cash account.

QUESTIONS AND PROBLEMS

20-1 What is the major advantage of the financial position form of balance sheet over the typical form of balance sheet?

20-2 What is the basic format of the financial position form of balance sheet?

20-3 The amount of net income reported in the income statement and the amount of funds provided by operations on a statement of source and disposition of working capital, or on a statement of source and application of funds, are not ordinarily the same. Why?

20-4 Name the principal items in the statement of source and application of funds which might not be expressed in current dollars. (If any part of your answer depends on the accounting procedures employed, explain.)

20-5 From the standpoint of fund flow analysis, the term **funds** may be defined in three different ways. What are they?

20-6 To convert accrual basis income to cash basis income, we must adjust reported net income for all noncash charges and credits reported therein. Indicate the nature of such adjustments.

20-7 Indicate whether each of the following transactions was (a) a source of funds, (b) an application of funds, or (c) neither.

(1) Declared a cash dividend.

(2) Paid a cash dividend which had been declared in the preceding period.

(3) Issued a stock dividend to common stockholders.

(4) Issued common stock in exchange for a building site.

(5) Purchased machinery, paying $10,000 in cash and giving a long-term note for the balance.

20-8 When accrual basis income is being converted to cash basis income, what adjustment would be necessary if a company started the period with $2,000 of prepaid insurance, ended the period with $1,800 of prepaid insurance, and paid a cash premium of $800 during the period?

20-9 Instructions From the following information taken from the records of the M & N Company for the calendar year ended December 31, 19X4, determine the amount of increase or decrease in the company's working capital for the year, assuming that the all-inclusive income statement concept is in use.

Reported net income	$16,000
Cash loan obtained by the issuance of a 10-year mortgage	30,000
Cash loan obtained by the issuance of a 1-year note	10,000
Cash dividend declared and paid	46,000
Purchase of treasury stock	44,000
Amortization of bond discount	6,000
Gain on sale of marketable securities	18,000

20-10 Instructions Using the following information taken from the records of the O and P Company for the calendar year ended December 31, 19X5, and assuming that the all-inclusive income statement is in use, determine the amount of increase or decrease in the company's working capital for the year.

Reported net loss	$24,000
Cash loan obtained by the issuance of a 6-month note	10,000
Cash dividend paid (the dividend was declared during December, 19X4)	8,000
Amortization of bond premium	2,000
Loss on discard of machinery and equipment	5,000

20-11 Instructions For each of the following unrelated cases, determine the amount of revenue which would be recognized for the period:

(1) Under the accrual basis

(2) Under the cash basis

	Case 1	Case 2	Case 3	Case 4
Cash sales	$150,000	$100,000	$200,000	$275,000
Credit sales	100,000	150,000	300,000	250,000
Accounts receivable at beginning of period	20,000	30,000	90,000	40,000
Accounts receivable at end of period	30,000	20,000	40,000	90,000

20-12 Instructions For each of the following unrelated cases, determine the cost of goods sold for the period:

(1) Under the accrual basis
(2) Under the cash basis

	Case 1	Case 2	Case 3	Case 4
Cash purchases	$90,000	$80,000	$70,000	$50,000
Credit purchases	80,000	90,000	60,000	60,000
Beginning inventory	30,000	40,000	20,000	15,000
Ending inventory	40,000	30,000	15,000	20,000
Accounts payable at beginning of period	25,000	15,000	20,000	10,000
Accounts payable at end of period	15,000	25,000	10,000	20,000

20-13 Instructions Using the information in the following condensed balance sheets of Company C and assuming that there were no changes in the noncurrent asset and liability accounts and that the only change in the Retained Earnings account, except for the declaration and payment of a $10,000 cash dividend, resulted from operations:

(1) Prepare a statement of source and disposition of working capital.

(2) Support it by a summary of working capital changes.

COMPANY C
Condensed Balance Sheets

	December 31	
Accounts	19X2	19X1
Current assets	$150,000	$130,000
Noncurrent assets	400,000	400,000
	$550,000	$530,000

Current liabilities	$ 90,000	$100,000
Noncurrent liabilities	150,000	150,000
Capital stock	200,000	200,000
Retained earnings	110,000	80,000
	$550,000	$530,000

20-14 Instructions Using the information in the following condensed balance sheets of Company D and assuming that there were no changes in the noncurrent liability accounts, that the only change in the noncurrent asset accounts was for the amount of depreciation taken during the period, and that the only change in the Retained Earnings account, except for the declaration and payment of a $20,000 cash dividend, resulted from operations:

(1) Prepare a statement of source and disposition of working capital.

(2) Support it by a summary of working capital changes.

COMPANY D
Condensed Balance Sheets

	December 31	
Accounts	*19X4*	*19X3*
Current assets	$180,000	$300,000
Noncurrent assets	470,000	500,000
	$650,000	$800,000
Current liabilities	$150,000	$140,000
Noncurrent liabilities	160,000	160,000
Capital stock	200,000	200,000
Retained earnings	140,000	300,000
	$650,000	$800,000

20-15 Instructions Using the information in the following condensed balance sheets of Company E and assuming that there were no changes in the noncurrent liability accounts, that the only changes in the noncurrent asset accounts were the result of (1) the periodic depreciation entry and (2) the purchase of machinery for $25,000 cash, and that the only change in the Retained Earnings account, except for the declaration of a $15,000 cash dividend, resulted from operations, prepare a statement of source and disposition of working capital.

COMPANY E
Condensed Balance Sheets

Accounts	December 31 19X5	December 31 19X4
Current assets	$120,000	$100,000
Noncurrent assets	200,000	200,000
	$320,000	$300,000
Current liabilities	$130,000	$ 90,000
Noncurrent liabilities	50,000	50,000
Capital stock	100,000	100,000
Retained earnings	40,000	60,000
	$320,000	$300,000

20-16 Instructions   From the following information, prepare a statement showing the sources and applications of funds for the year 19X6.   (Make all reasonable assumptions necessary.)

COMPANY G
Condensed Balance Sheets

Accounts	December 31 19X6	December 31 19X5
Current assets	$100,000	$116,000
Long-lived assets	360,000	340,000
Patents	20,000	22,000
Unamortized bond discount	10,000	11,000
	$490,000	$489,000
Current liabilities	$160,000	$150,000
Bonds payable	35,000	50,000
Accumulated depreciation	50,000	30,000
Capital stock	100,000	100,000
Retained earnings	145,000	159,000
	$490,000	$489,000

*20-17 **Instructions** From the following information, prepare a statement showing the sources and applications of funds for the year 19X7. (Make all reasonable assumptions necessary.)

COMPANY H
Condensed Balance Sheets

	December 31	
Accounts	*19X7*	*19X6*
Current assets	$200,000	$150,000
Long-lived assets	370,000	380,000
Patents	30,000	34,000
Unamortized bond discount	9,000	
	$609,000	$564,000
Current liabilities	$ 80,000	$175,000
Bonds payable	100,000	
Accumulated depreciation	110,000	120,000
Capital stock	150,000	100,000
Capital in excess of par value	12,000	
Retained earnings	157,000	169,000
	$609,000	$564,000

1 Long-lived assets which cost $40,000 and which were 75 percent depreciated were sold during the year for $6,000.

2 The amortization of bond discount for the year amounted to $2,000.

3 Depreciation taken for the year amounted to $20,000.

4 Cash dividends amounting to $50,000 were declared and paid during the year.

*20-18 **Instructions** Criticize the following statement, considering mainly its *function* and *content*.

*AICPA adapted.

ENAK MANUFACTURING CO., INC.

Statement Showing Causes of Net Change in Working Capital

Funds Were Obtained from:

Operations (net income transferred to retained earnings)		$179,001.12
Current assets used up in year's operations:		
Cash on hand and in banks	$ 33,427.73	
Postal stamps	20.00	33,447.73
Issuance of common stock		30,000.00
		$242,448.85

Funds Were Applied to:

Payments of cash dividends		$ 35,442.00
Declaration of stock dividends (not yet issued)		27,400.00
Investment in additions to:		
Accounts receivable—trade	$ 10,004.43	
Notes receivable—trade	2,500.00	
Inventories	101,442.21	
Marketable securities	10,440.00	
Cash surrender value of life insurance	1,141.25	
Long-lived assets (net increase)	15,142.50	
Patents	20,000.00	
Prepaid expense	2,452.03	163,122.42
Payments of serial bond maturities		10,000.00
Reduction in current liabilities		6,484.43
		$242,448.85

*20-19 Instructions From the following information taken from the records of the IJK Company, prepare a statement showing the sources and applications of funds for the year 19X4.

*AICPA adapted.

Balance Sheet Accounts

	December 31	
Debits	*19X4*	*19X3*
Cash	$ 30,337	$ 40,409
Accounts receivable	65,638	67,186
Temporary investments	85,000	112,500
Prepaid insurance	755	710
Inventories	94,438	82,164
Cash surrender value of life insurance policies	9,061	8,315
Unamortized bond discount	2,867	4,305
Land, buildings, machinery and equipment	207,782	172,778
	$495,878	$488,367

Credits

Accounts payable	$ 38,814	$ 35,081
Notes payable to banks	45,000	40,000
Accrued interest, taxes, etc.	7,763	12,307
First-mortgage 4% bonds	82,000	82,000
Allowance for loss on accounts	3,815	4,630
Accumulated depreciation	81,633	96,618
Reserve for contingencies	63,600	37,500
Common stock, $100 par value	92,500	100,000
Capital in excess of par	10,175	11,000
Retained earnings	70,578	69,231
	$495,878	$488,367

The following information concerning the year's transactions is available:

1 Net income for 19X4 was reported in the income statement as $48,097.

2 During the year 75 shares of the capital stock were repurchased at $111 and were being held in the treasury. Subsequent to the stock reacquisition, a 10 percent cash dividend was declared and paid.

3 The 19X4 premium on life insurance policies was $1,673. Expense was charged with $927 of this payment.

4 Machinery was purchased for $31,365 and machinery costing $32,625 was retired. The retired machinery had accumulated depreciation of $29,105 at date of retirement. It was sold as scrap for $1,000 which was credited against the Gain and Loss on Retirement of Assets account. The remaining increase in long-lived assets resulted from construction of a building.

5 The reserve for contingencies was provided by charges against retained earnings. A debit to the reserve of $11,400 was made during the year. This represented the final settlement of a part of 19X1 income tax liability which had been the subject of controversy.

*20-20 Instructions From the following data, which pertain to the Thomas Manufacturing Company, prepare a statement of source and disposition of cash for the year ended December 31, 19X3:

*AICPA adapted.

	December 31, 19X3	December 31, 19X2	Increase (Decrease)
Buildings	$ 810,000	$ 560,000	$250,000
Land	140,000	150,000	(10,000)
Machinery	330,000	200,000	130,000
Tools	40,000	70,000	(30,000)
Bond investment	18,000	15,000	3,000
Inventories	210,000	218,000	(8,000)
Accounts receivable	180,000	92,000	88,000
Notes receivable—trade	21,000	27,000	(6,000)
Cash in bank	—	8,000	(8,000)
Cash on hand	2,000	1,000	1,000
Unexpired insurance— machinery	1,200	1,400	(200)
Unamortized bond discount	2,100	2,500	(400)
	$1,754,300	$1,344,900	$409,400
Capital stock	$ 700,000	$ 400,000	$300,000
Bonds payable	150,000	100,000	50,000
Accounts payable	62,000	52,000	10,000
Notes payable—trade	9,000	10,000	(1,000)
Bank loans—long term	5,500	6,800	(1,300)
Accrued interest	10,000	6,000	4,000
Accrued taxes	5,000	3,000	2,000
Allowance for bad debts	4,500	2,300	2,200
Accumulated depreciation	271,200	181,000	90,200
Retained earnings	537,100	583,800	(46,700)
	$1,754,300	$1,344,900	$409,400

You are advised that the following transactions took place during the year:

1 A 2 percent dividend was declared and paid on the outstanding capital stock at the first of the year.

2 There were no purchases or sales of tools.

3 Stock was sold during the year at 90; the discount was charged to the Retained Earnings account.

4 Old machinery which cost $4,500 was scrapped and written off the books. Accumulated depreciation on such equipment was $3,300. The loss was charged to the Retained Earnings account.

5 The income statement for the year showed a net profit of $2,500, computed as follows:

Sales (net)		$1,250,000
Operating charges:		
Cost of goods sold	$641.500	
Depreciation	123,500	
Selling expenses	245,000	
General expenses	230,000	
Interest expense	7,500	1,247,500
Net income		$ 2,500

6 The $10,000 decrease in the Land account was the result of the following entry:

Retained Earnings	10,000	
Land		10,000

21
Basic Tools of
Financial Statement Analysis

Interpretation, or the drawing of valid conclusions from reported data, is the final formal step in the accounting process. To be of value, accounting data, regardless of how well presented, must be interpreted by or for the user. Sound interpretation consists of:

1 **Analysis,** or the taking apart of reported data in order to examine critically each element with regard to its effect on a given problem

2 **Integration,** or the combining of selected elements of data, frequently in combination with other known elements of information, to form a logical pattern upon which to base deductions

3 **Deduction,** or the formulation of conclusions regarding the effects of the data being presented

These factors, when combined and applied to financial statements, make up what is generally known as **financial statement analysis.**

It is the task of the analyst to interpret the statements in a way which will enable owners, management, employers, creditors, and other users of the data to make decisions regarding an organization and its activities. As a general rule, financial statement users are particularly interested, although to varying degrees, in an organization's:

1 Solvency (its ability to meet its financial obligations as they come due)

2 Profitability (its ability to earn a return on its assets)

3 Stability (its ability both to meet its financial obligations as they come due and to earn a return on its assets over the long term)

Sound conclusions regarding an organization's solvency, profitability, and stability may often be reached solely from an analysis of the accounting data appearing in financial statements. However, it is important to recognize that there are likely to be a number of factors quite apart from the statements which must also be taken into consideration in the typical decision-making process. For example, the ability, experience, and continuity of management generally will have a definite bearing on the organization's well-being. Similarly, such important factors as the diversification of products and the competitive position of the organization may not be fully reflected in the financial statements. Therefore, as we study the basic analytical techniques, we must bear in mind that the statement user cannot always rely completely upon their results, but must instead use them principally as guideposts in his investigations.

The accounting data appearing in financial statements may be analyzed in different ways with varying degrees of sophistication, depending upon the situation; however, the discussion in this chapter will be limited to the basic analytical techniques in general use. They are (1) percentage analysis, (2) ratio analysis, and (3) turnover analysis.

PERCENTAGE ANALYSIS

In financial statement analysis, **percentage analysis** consists of converting dollar amounts into percentages.

When items or groups of items in financial statements are expressed in relative terms (percentages), they often are of greater significance to the analyst in making comparisons and disclosing trends than when they are expressed in absolute terms (dollars). Percentages are especially useful for (1) comparing successive statements of an individual organization, (2) comparing the statements of two or more organizations, and (3) comparing an organization's percentages with industry percentages.

Percentages may be presented along with regular statement data or in separate statements which do not include the regular dollar data. All percentages appearing in the statements are based on a common denominator of 100 percent. The separate statements are frequently referred to as **common size statements.**

Common Size Balance Sheet

When percentage analysis is applied to the balance sheet, total assets is ordinarily used as a base, or 100 percent, and all other items appearing on the statement are stated in relation to the base.

To expedite comparison and evaluation, common size balance sheets are usually presented in tabular form. The condensed statements which follow are illustrative of common size balance sheets prepared for (1) successive periods of an individual organization, and (2) two different organizations on a comparative basis for the same period.

COMPANY A
Common Size Balance Sheet

Assets	Current Year	Previous Year
Current assets	38%	48%
Plant and equipment (net)	49%	45%
Other assets	13%	7%
Total assets	100%	100%

Liabilities and Owner Equity		
Current liabilities	17%	28%
Long-term debt	28%	15%
Total liabilities	45%	43%
Capital stock	40%	35%
Retained earnings	15%	22%
Total shareholder equity	55%	57%
Total liabilities and shareholder equity	100%	100%

COMPANIES A AND B
Common Size Balance Sheets

Assets	Company A	Company B
Current assets	38%	55%
Plant and equipment (net)	49%	37%
Other assets	13%	8%
Total assets	100%	100%

Liabilities and Owner Equity

Current liabilities	17%	32%
Long-term debt	28%	16%
Total liabilities	45%	48%
Capital stock	40%	45%
Retained earnings	15%	7%
Total shareholder equity	55%	52%
Total liabilities and shareholder equity	100%	100%

Common Size Income Statement

When percentage analysis is applied to the income statement, net sales is ordinarily used as the base. Common size income statements for (1) Company A on an individual basis for the current and previous year, and (2) Companies A and B on a comparative basis for the current year could be presented as shown. Again, it should be noted that the statements as presented in the illustrations are greatly condensed.

COMPANY A
Common Size Income Statement

	Current Year	Previous Year
Net sales	100%	100%
Cost of goods sold	58%	60%
Gross margin	42%	40%
Operating expenses	29%	25%
Operating income	13%	15%
Income taxes	5%	6%
Net income	8%	9%

COMPANIES A AND B
Common Size Income Statements

	Company A	Company B
Net sales	100%	100%
Cost of goods sold	58%	62%
Gross margin	42%	38%
Operating expenses	29%	28%
Operating income	13%	10%
Income taxes	5%	4%
Net income	8%	6%

Limitations of Common Size Statements

Although common size statements are important in financial statement analysis, they have certain limitations. When successive periods of an organization are compared, the fact that the statements do not disclose the reasons behind changes which have taken place is one of their more obvious weaknesses. In addition, since an organization's percentages are generally computed on a different absolute (dollar) basis for each period although the relative (100 percent) basis remains the same, the statements may not reflect actual growth or shrinkage. If each item in a statement changes proportionately, for example, the change will not be reflected in the percentage.

The use of common size statements to compare different organizations also may be limited because of lack of uniformity in the reported data. Account classifications, for instance, may differ in the organizations being compared. Similarly, business policies, as well as the accounting treatment of certain items, may vary from one company to another. One organization may value its inventory on the LIFO basis and another on FIFO; or one may compute depreciation on a straight-line basis, while another uses the sum-of-years'-digits method.

RATIO ANALYSIS

In financial statement analysis the term **ratio** means a numerical relationship between items or groups of items. Ratios are determined simply by dividing one item in a relationship by the other. Financial statement ratios are usually stated in relation to **1.** Thus, when comparing current assets of $400,000 to current liabilities of $100,000, we would say that the ratio of current assets to current liabilities is 4 to 1, or, as it is ordinarily written, 4:1.

Ratios expressing relationships between items or groups of items on financial statements can be devised in almost unlimited numbers, but to be relevant the items must have meaningful relationships with one another. The ratios presented in the following pages have been selected on the basis of their general recognition and acceptance as tools in financial statement analysis.

When studying the ratios, bear in mind that although they are mathematical derivatives, they are not infallible. They do not carry the gift of prophecy or the mathematical means of making exact measurements of financial solvency, stability, or profitability; they can only indicate probabilities and suggest financial strengths or weaknesses.

Financial ratios may be classified in various ways, depending upon the use that is to be made of them. For study purposes we shall classify them as (1) balance sheet ratios, (2) income statement ratios, and (3) interstatement ratios.

Balance Sheet Ratios

Balance sheet ratios are indicators of an organization's financial strength. Those of greatest significance in the typical organization include:

1 Current ratio

2 Acid-test ratio

3 Debt ratio

4 Equity ratio

5 Debt-equity ratio

Current Ratio The current ratio expresses the relationship between current assets and current liabilities. Because the excess of current assets over current liabilities is often defined as working capital, the current ratio is sometimes called the **working capital ratio.** When it is stated as a formula, we have:

$$\frac{\text{Current assets}}{\text{Current liabilities}}$$

The following data indicate both the working capital positions and the current ratios of Companies A and B:

	Company A	Company B
Current assets	$400,000	$800,000
Current liabilities	100,000	500,000
Working capital	$300,000	$300,000
Current ratio	4:1	1.6:1

Both working capital and the current ratio are rough indicators of an organization's ability to meet its current obligations as they come due, and thus are of primary interest to its short-term creditors. The current ratio, however, as can readily be observed in the illustration, is more reliable as an indicator of solvency. For example, both Company A and Company B have working capitals of $300,000 but Company A has $4 in current assets for every $1 of current liabilities, whereas Company B has only $1.60 in current assets for every $1 in current liabilities.

Acid-test Ratio The acid-test ratio is used to provide an indication of an organization's "instant solvency" or its immediate ability to meet its current obligations. To obtain this ratio, we must first segregate the current assets into "quick" and "nonquick" categories. The term **quick assets** describes cash, receivables, and marketable securities. The acid-test ratio expresses the relationship between quick assets and current liabilities. When it is stated as a formula, we have:

$$\frac{\text{Quick assets}}{\text{Current liabilities}}$$

The acid-test ratio is sometimes used merely as a supplement to the current ratio. A complete analysis of an organization's current position would include the determination of (1) working capital, (2) the current ratio, and (3) the acid-test ratio. Continuing our earlier illustration, we would determine acid-test ratios for

Companies A and B as follows.   For comparative purposes the amounts of working capital and the current ratios are also included.

	Company A	Company B
Current assets:		
Cash	$ 60,000	$100,000
Marketable securities	12,000	40,000
Receivables (net)	68,000	200,000
Inventories	258,000	450,000
Prepaid expenses	2,000	10,000
Total current assets	$400,000	$800,000
Current liabilities	100,000	500,000
Working capital	$300,000	$300,000
Current ratio*	4 : 1	1.6 : 1
Acid-test ratio†	1.4 : 1	.68 : 1

*$400,000 ÷ $100,000 = 4
$800,000 ÷ $500,000 = 1.6
†($60,000 + $12,000 + $68,000) ÷ $100,000 = 1.4
 ($100,000 + $40,000 + $200,000) ÷ $500,000 = 0.68

Debt Ratio   This ratio expresses the relationship between the total debt and the total assets of an organization.   It is computed by dividing the sum of all liabilities by the total amount of assets.   The formula is:

$$\frac{\text{Total debt (current and long-term)}}{\text{Total assets}}$$

This ratio is of particular interest to an organization's creditors, because it is indicative of the degree of protection accorded their claims.   As a general rule, the higher the ratio—that is, the larger the debt in proportion to the total assets—the greater the risk to the creditors, and vice versa.

Equity Ratio   The equity ratio expresses the relationship between the total amount of owner equity and the total amount of assets of an organization.   It is the complement of the debt ratio; that is, the sum of the two ratios is always equal to 100 percent.   The equity ratio is an indicator of an organization's long-range stability.   Its formula is:

$$\frac{\text{Owner equity}}{\text{Total assets}}$$

The current and equity ratios are generally considered to be the two most important ratios in financial statement analysis, because taken together they are indicative of both the short-term and long-term solvency of an organization.

Debt-Equity Ratio This ratio expresses the relationship between an organization's debt and its owner equity. It is computed by dividing the sum of all liabilities by the total amount of owner equity. The formula is:

$$\frac{\text{Total debt (current and long-term)}}{\text{Owner equity}}$$

Essentially a combination of the debt and equity ratios, the debt-equity ratio is an indicator both of creditors' risk and of long-run solvency.

Trading on the Equity Not a ratio as such, but closely related to the balance sheet ratios (particularly the debt and equity ratios) is what is known as **trading on the equity.**

When, in preference to issuing additional stock, an organization borrows money for long-term purposes with the expectation of increasing its earnings, it is said to be trading on the equity. If the amount earned on the borrowed money is greater than the cost of borrowing the money, trading on the equity is advantageous, whereas the opposite is true if the cost of borrowing is greater than the return on the borrowed funds.

To illustrate trading on the equity, let us assume that an organization acquires assets of $200,000 by borrowing $100,000 from bondholders at 5 percent per annum, and by issuing $100,000 worth of capital stock. Also assume the following:

CASE 1 Annual earnings before interest are $5,000.

CASE 2 Annual earnings before interest are $10,000.

CASE 3 Annual earnings before interest are $15,000.

Trading on the Equity								
Allocation of Earnings								
	Annual Earnings	*ROI**	*Case 1*		*Case 2*		*Case 3*	
			Bonds	*Stock*	*Bonds*	*Stock*	*Bonds*	*Stock*
Case 1	$ 5,000	$2\frac{1}{2}\%^1$	$5,000	—				
Case 2	10,000	$5\%^2$			$5,000	$5,000		
Case 3	15,000	$7\frac{1}{2}\%^3$					$5,000	$10,000
ROI†				—		$5\%^4$		$10\%^5$

*Return on investment based on total assets.
†Return on investment based on owner equity.
[1]$5,000 ÷ $200,000
[2]$10,000 ÷ $200,000
[3]$15,000 ÷ $200,000
[4]$5,000 ÷ $100,000
[5]$10,000 ÷ $100,000

An analysis of the three cases indicates that in Case 1 trading on the equity is disadvantageous, since the cost of borrowing is 5 percent and the rate of return on the total investment is only $2\frac{1}{2}$ percent ($5,000 on $200,000). In Case 2, trading on the equity is neither advantageous nor disadvantageous, since the cost of borrowing is 5 percent and the return is 5 percent ($10,000 on $200,000). In Case 3, trading on the equity is advantageous since the cost of borrowing is only 5 percent, whereas the return is $7\frac{1}{2}$ percent ($15,000 on $200,000).

Income Statement Ratios

While balance sheet ratios are used primarily as aids in measuring financial solvency and stability, income statement ratios are employed as indexes of operating efficiency. Some of the more important income statement ratios are:

1 Operating ratio

2 Ratio of net income to net sales

3 Gross margin ratio

Operating Ratio This ratio expresses the relationship between an organization's total operating expenses and its net sales. The term **operating expenses,** as used in the ratio, includes the cost of goods sold as well as selling and administrative expenses. When the ratio is stated as a formula, we have:

$$\frac{\text{Total operating expenses}}{\text{Net sales}}$$

As a general rule, the lower the operating ratio the better; however, a high operating ratio in itself does not necessarily indicate a weakness. This is particularly true if it is accompanied by a sufficiently large volume of business. For example, a retail store might reduce its profit margin by lowering prices, but at the same time increase its volume to such as extent that its total net income is increased. Conversely, the apparent strength of a low operating ratio may be offset by a relatively small volume of business.

Ratio of Net Income to Net Sales This ratio expresses the relationship between profits and sales. Simply stated, it reflects the rate of return on the sales dollar. It is the complement of the operating ratio. Like the operating ratio, the ratio of net income to net sales may itself be meaningless. In order that it may be evaluated properly, consideration ordinarily must be given to such factors as the volume of sales and the rapidity of the turnover of inventory. (Turnover analysis will be covered in the next section of this chapter.) For instance, a low rate of return accompanied by a rapid turnover of inventory and a large sales volume may be more profitable than a high rate of return combined with a slow turnover and low sales volume. The formula is expressed as follows:

$$\frac{\text{Net income}}{\text{Net sales}}$$

Gross Margin Ratio The gross margin ratio expresses the relationship between the gross margin on sales and net sales. Its complement, which expresses the relationship between the cost of goods sold and net sales, is commonly known as the **cost of goods sold ratio.** When the gross margin ratio is stated as a formula, we have:

$$\frac{\text{Gross margin}}{\text{Net sales}}$$

This ratio indicates the spread, or difference, between the cost of goods sold and the sales price. A change in the ratio may be the result of a change in either cost or sales or both, and a change in cost or sales may be the result of a change in either price or volume or both. We shall study the procedures involved in analyzing the changes in Chapter 22.

Interstatement Ratios

Some of the more important analytical relationships are based upon data from both the balance sheet and the income statement. They are expressed in what are known as the ROI (return on investment) ratios and the earnings per share ratio. ROI ratios, which as a general rule are stated on a percentage basis, usually include:

1 ROI ratio based on total assets

2 ROI ratio based on total owner equity

3 ROI ratio based on common stockholders' equity

Ratio of Rate of Return on Total Assets The rate of return on total assets ratio expresses the relationship between the operating income and the total resources employed in an organization. It is an indicator of the earning power of the organization as a business entity. As we are interested in the earnings from all resources (both borrowed and invested), interest charges must be included as part of operating income. Because an organization's assets are constantly changing, the assets employed during a specific period should be averaged whenever possible. Thus, our formula is:

$$\frac{\text{Net income} + \text{interest charges}}{\text{Average assets employed in the business}}$$

Ratio of Rate of Return on Owner Equity   The rate of return on owner equity
ratio expresses the relationship between the income applicable to the owners of
an organization and the amount of their equity in the organization.   It is an
indicator of the organization's earning power based on that portion of assets
contributed by the owners.   The amount of owner equity, like the assets, changes
throughout the year, and as a consequence, we should use an average in our
computation.   As a formula, the rate of return on owner equity may be expressed
as:

$$\frac{\text{Net income}}{\text{Average owner equity}}$$

Ratio of Rate of Return on Common Stockholders' Equity   This ratio expresses
the relationship between the income applicable to the common stockholders of
an organization and the amount of their equity in the organization.   If there is
only one class of stock outstanding, the rate of return on common stockholders'
equity, of course, would be the same as the rate of return on the total owner equity.
However, if an organization has preferred stock outstanding, preferred dividends
must first be deducted from net income when the income applicable to the common
stockholders is determined.   The formula is:

$$\frac{\text{Net income} - \text{preferred dividends}}{\text{Average common stockholders' equity}}$$

This ratio is an indicator of an organization's earning power based on that portion
of assets contributed by the common stockholders.

ROI Computations Illustrated   To illustrate ROI computations, let us assume
that an organization finances its $300,000 worth of assets by borrowing $100,000
from bondholders at 5 percent per annum and issuing $100,000 of 6 percent
preferred stock and $100,000 worth of common stock.   Let us also assume that
the net income for the year in Case 1 is $25,000, in Case 2, $31,000, and in Case
3, $40,000.   As you study the illustration at the top of page 573, you may wish
to refer back to the pertinent formulas.

Earnings per Share Ratio   The **earnings per share ratio** expresses the relationship
between the net income earned by the common stockholders and the number of
shares of common stock outstanding.   The relationship is usually expressed in terms
of dollars and cents per share.   Since preferred dividend requirements must be
met before the common stockholders have a claim, preferred dividends for the
period are deducted from net income before it is divided by the number of shares
outstanding.   The formula is:

$$\frac{\text{Net income} - \text{preferred dividends}}{\text{Number of common shares outstanding}}$$

Return on Investment Computations				
	Net Income	ROI Total Assets	ROI Owner Equity	ROI Common Stockholders' Equity
Case 1	$25,000	10%[1]	$12\frac{1}{2}\%$[2]	19%[3]
Case 2	31,000	12%[4]	$15\frac{1}{2}\%$[5]	25%[6]
Case 3	40,000	15%[7]	20 %[8]	34%[9]

[1] $25,000 + $5,000 ÷ $300,000 = 10%
[2] $25,000 ÷ $200,000 = $12\frac{1}{2}\%$
[3] $25,000 − $6,000 ÷ $100,000 = 19%
[4] $31,000 + $5,000 ÷ $300,000 = 12%
[5] $31,000 ÷ $200,000 = $15\frac{1}{2}\%$
[6] $31,000 − $6,000 ÷ $100,000 = 25%
[7] $40,000 + $5,000 ÷ $300,000 = 15%
[8] $40,000 ÷ $200,000 = 20%
[9] $40,000 − $6,000 ÷ $100,000 = 34%

To illustrate the computation of earnings per share, let us assume that an organization has 10,000 shares of $10 par value common stock and 10,000 shares of $10 par value, 6 percent, preferred stock outstanding. Let us also assume that the net income for the year in Case 1 is $25,000, in Case 2, $31,000, and in Case 3, $40,000.

Earnings per Share Computations			
	Case 1	Case 2	Case 3
Net income _____	$25,000	$31,000	$40,000
Preferred dividends _____	6,000	6,000	6,000
Earnings associated with the common stock _____	$19,000	$25,000	$34,000
Shares of common stock outstanding _____	10,000	10,000	10,000
Earnings per share of common stock _____	$1.90	$2.50	$3.40

TURNOVER ANALYSIS

As used in the analysis of financial statements, **turnover** may be defined as (1) the number of times an asset or group of assets is converted, or "turned," into other assets during a period, or (2) the number of days required to "turn" an asset or group of assets. Thus, turnover may be stated as so many times per period, or as so many days. For example, an asset that turns over five times a year, turns over, on the average, once every 73 days (365 ÷ 5). Turnover computations are of particular value in the analysis of inventories and receivables.

Inventory Turnover

Inventory turnover may be computed either (1) by dividing the cost of goods sold by the average inventory at cost, or (2) by dividing sales by the average inventory valued at the selling price. The formulas are:

$$\frac{\text{Cost of goods sold}}{\text{Average inventory at cost}}$$

$$\frac{\text{Sales}}{\text{Average inventory at retail}}$$

The determination of the cost of goods sold and the sales in the formulas is generally fairly simple, but the determination of a sound average inventory may be somewhat more difficult. Although it would be best to base our average on inventory valuations determined at various intervals throughout the period, expediency frequently dictates the use of only the beginning and ending inventories. Obviously, such an average may not be representative, as the usual procedure in a business is to allow the inventory to "run down" as of the end of the period prior to the taking of a physical count. Thus, an average based strictly on the beginning and ending inventories may tend to overstate the turnover, because it probably will be abnormally small.

Inventory Turnover Illustrated Assuming for illustrative purposes that we have only the beginning and ending inventories upon which to base our average, we can determine inventory turnover using the first formula as illustrated at the top of page 575.

Significance of Inventory Turnover The rate at which an inventory turns over is an indicator of the liquidity of the investment in the inventory, and, to a considerable extent, of the efficiency of the organization. In a trading concern, for example, the rapidity of merchandise inventory turnover reflects the degree of efficiency in purchasing and inventory management as well as sales.

Inventory turnover is ordinarily an important factor in the control of inventory losses due to obsolescence and deterioration; generally, the faster the turnover the less the likelihood of their occurrence. In addition, an organization with a high inventory turnover in relation to previous turnovers, or compared to norms for similar organizations, frequently has relatively lower expenses for insurance, taxes, interest, storage, and other inventory-related expenses.

Inventory Turnover		
	First Year	*Second Year*
Cost of goods sold	$300,000	$450,000
Beginning inventory	$ 75,000	$125,000
Ending inventory	125,000	55,000
Total	$200,000	$180,000
Average inventory	$100,000[1]	$ 90,000[2]
Number of times inventory turned over during year	3[3]	5[4]
Number of days required to turn the inventory over	122[5]	73[6]

[1]$200,000 ÷ 2 = $100,000
[2]$180,000 ÷ 2 = $90,000
[3]$300,000 ÷ $100,000 = 3
[4]$450,000 ÷ $90,000 = 5
[5]365 ÷ 3 = 121.67, rounded to 122
[6]365 ÷ 5 = 73

To illustrate the use of the rate of inventory turnover as an indicator of efficiency, let us assume the following data for Companies A and B:

Significance of Rate of Inventory Turnover		
	Company A	*Company B*
Sales	$600,000	$600,000
Cost of goods sold	450,000	450,000
Gross margin	$150,000	$150,000
Average inventory at cost	$ 90,000	$ 45,000
Inventory turnover	5*	10†

*$450,000 ÷ $90,000 = 5
†$450,000 ÷ $45,000 = 10

Assuming that the two companies are comparable in all other respects, the lower turnover in Company A would tend to indicate one or more of the following probabilities:

1 An excessive amount of funds is tied up in inventories.
2 Excessive quantities of merchandise are being purchased.

3 Slow-moving merchandise is being carried.

4 The risk of obsolescence and deterioration has been increased.

5 Excessive facilities are being used for storage.

6 The risk of loss by fire, flood, and similar disasters has been increased, or excessive insurance premiums are being paid.

Accounts Receivable Turnover

When accounts receivable turnover is expressed as so many times per period, it is computed by dividing net credit sales by the average accounts receivable outstanding during the period. The formula is:

$$\frac{\text{Net credit sales}}{\text{Average accounts receivable}}$$

Just as it is necessary to determine an average for use in inventory turnover computations, we must also determine one for use in receivable turnover computations. For best results we should use an average that is representative of the balance of the receivables throughout the period. Thus, an average based on monthly balances would, as a general rule, be much better than one based only on the beginning and ending yearly balances. If, however, the latter are the only balances available, they are ordinarily used.

Accounts Receivable Turnover Illustrated Assuming that we have only the beginning and ending balances of accounts receivable available for our computations, the determination of the turnover may be illustrated as follows:

Accounts Receivable Turnover		
	First Year	*Second Year*
Net credit sales	$630,000	$720,000
Beginning accounts receivable	$ 75,000	$ 65,000
Ending accounts receivable	65,000	55,000
Total	$140,000	$120,000
Average accounts receivable	$ 70,000[1]	$ 60,000[2]
Accounts receivable turnover	9[3]	12[4]
Average number of days per turnover	41[5]	30[6]

[1]$140,000 ÷ 2 = $70,000
[2]$120,000 ÷ 2 = $60,000
[3]$630,000 ÷ $70,000 = 9
[4]$720,000 ÷ $60,000 = 12
[5]365 ÷ 9 = 40.56, rounded to 41
[6]365 ÷ 12 = 30.4, rounded to 30

Significance of Accounts Receivable Turnover The rapidity with which the accounts receivable of an organization turn over is an indication of the liquidity of the accounts, whereas the average number of days per turn, when considered in relation to the usual credit terms, is indicative of the effectiveness of the organization's credit and collection procedures. If, for example, the usual terms are 30 days net and sales are made uniformly throughout the month and year, a turnover of 12 would indicate that collections are being made, on the average, within the specified period of 30 days.

Number of Days' Sales in Receivables The effectiveness of an organization's credit and collection efforts may also be measured in terms of the daily credit sales as reflected in the accounts receivable. The **number of days' sales in receivables** is determined by dividing the accounts receivable as of the end of the period by the net credit sales for the period and then multiplying by the number of business days in the period. If we assume that the period is a year and that there are 300 business days in the year, the formula would be:

$$\frac{\text{Accounts receivable at end of period}}{\text{Net credit sales for the period}} \times 300$$

Assuming the same basic data as were used in the preceding illustration, we can compute the number of days' sales in receivables as follows:

Number of Days' Sales in Receivables		
	First Year	*Second Year*
Net credit sales	$630,000	$720,000
Receivables as of end of period	$ 65,000	$ 55,000
Number of days' sales in receivables	31*	23†

*$\frac{65,000}{630,000} \times 300 = 30.95$, rounded to 31

†$\frac{55,000}{720,000} \times 300 = 22.92$, rounded to 23

The computation may also be made by dividing the net credit sales for the period by the number of business days in the period to obtain the amount of credit sales per day, and then dividing the accounts receivable as of the end of the period by the amount of credit sales per day. The computation would be

1 [$65,000 ÷ ($630,000 ÷ 300)] = 30.95, rounded to 31

2 [$55,000 ÷ ($720,000 ÷ 300)] = 22.92, rounded to 23

Like accounts receivable turnover, the number of days' sales in receivables, when considered in relation to the usual credit terms of an organization, is an indication of its efficiency in carrying out its credit and collection policies. For example, when the 23 days' sales in receivables for the second year in our illustration are compared with the 31 days for the first year, it is apparent that the organization is doing a more effective job in the area of granting credit and collecting its receivables.

Aging Accounts Receivable Although the turnover of accounts receivable and the number of days' sales in receivables are useful tools in financial statement analysis, they are based on averages and therefore may not reflect the true composition of the receivables as of the balance sheet date; as is true with any average, extreme situations may distort the picture.

To gain a better overall view of the composition of the accounts receivable, we may find it of value to prepare a schedule or summary of the due dates of the receivables. This procedure, known as **aging the receivables,** may be illustrated as follows:

Aging Schedule

Customer	Balance	Under 30 Days Old	31–60 Days Old	61–90 Days Old	Over 90 Days Old
Adams	$ 400		$ 400		
Baker	200	$ 200			
Cain	300			$ 100	$ 200
Davis	50	50			
Evans	150	150			
Others	53,900	30,000	18,000	4,000	1,900
Total	$55,000	$30,400	$18,400	$4,100	$2,100

Aging Summary

Age	Amount	Percentage
Under 30 days	$30,400	55.27
31–60 days	18,400	33.46
61–90 days	4,100	7.45
Over 90 days	2,100	3.82
	$55,000	100.00

Estimated Uncollectibles Based on Aging Schedule In addition to aiding the credit and collection effort, the aging schedule is often used as a basis for estimating the periodic provision for uncollectible accounts. Average percentage rates for each of the age categories established in the analysis may be developed on the basis of past experience and applied to the accounts in the respective categories to determine the amount that should be in the allowance account as of the balance sheet date.

To illustrate the use of the aging process as a basis for determining the periodic provision for uncollectible accounts, let us assume that, in addition to the basic data appearing in the aging schedule, past experience indicates that 1 percent of the receivables under 30 days of age will not be collected, and 3 percent between 31–60 days, 8 percent between 61–90 days, and 15 percent of those over 90 days will not be collected. The amount needed in the allowance account would be determined as follows:

Estimated Uncollectible Accounts			
Age	*Amount*	*Percentage*	*Estimated Uncollectible*
Under 30 days	$30,400	1	$ 304
31–60 days	18,400	3	552
61–90 days	4,100	8	328
Over 90 days	2,100	15	315
Total	$55,000		$1,499

Assuming that the Allowance for Uncollectible Accounts has a credit balance of $600, the adjusting entry for the periodic provision will be:

Estimated Loss on Uncollectible Accounts	899	
Allowance for Uncollectible Accounts		899

SUMMARY

Sound financial statement analysis consists of three factors: analysis, integration, and deduction. Its chief purpose is to determine an organization's solvency, profitability, and stability.

The basic analytical techniques of financial statement analysis are percentage analysis, ratio analysis, and turnover analysis, all of which are closely related.

QUESTIONS AND PROBLEMS

21-1 (1) Give the formula for each of the following:
    (a) Current ratio
    (b) Inventory turnover
    (c) Accounts receivable turnover

(2) State briefly the significance of each to an analyst.

(3) Assuming that the current ratio of the Zeno Company is 2 to 1, would it be the same, more, or less, after cash is used to pay a current liability?

21-2 Which of the following types of businesses would you expect to have a high inventory turnover?   A high rate of gross margin?

(1) A gasoline service station

(2) An automobile dealer

(3) A department store

(4) A bakery

(5) A supermarket

(6) A manufacturer of earth-moving equipment

(7) An exclusive art gallery

(8) A drugstore

21-3 Define the term **working capital,** as used by accountants, and briefly state what is meant by **working capital ratio.**   Show how such a ratio is computed and how it is ordinarily expressed.

21-4 Define the term **turnover** as it is used in accounting, and illustrate its computation in connection with inventories and accounts receivable.

21-5 Comment briefly on the significance of inventory turnover in the administration and control of a merchandising operation.

21-6 (1) "Trading on the equity" refers to the practice of:
   (a) Purchasing and selling treasury stock
   (b) Trading in the stock of other companies
   (c) Retiring bonds before maturity
   (d) Using funds provided by creditors
   (e) None of the above

(2) Assuming that stable business conditions exist, a decline in the number of days' sales outstanding in a company's accounts receivable at year-end from one year to the next might indicate that:
   (a) The company's credit policies had been stiffened.
   (b) The second year's sales were made at lower prices than the first year's sales.
   (c) A longer discount period and a more distant due date were extended to customers in the second year.

(d) The volume of sales in the second year had significantly decreased.

(e) None of the above.

21-7 Instructions Based on the data included in the condensed financial statements which follow, prepare:

(1) A common size balance sheet

(2) A common size income statement

COMPANY A
Balance Sheet

Assets	19X2	19X1
Current assets	$150,000	$ 80,000
Plant and equipment (net)	270,000	300,000
Other assets	180,000	120,000
Total	$600,000	$500,000

Liabilities and Owner Equity		
Current liabilities	$ 60,000	$ 70,000
Long-term debt	180,000	150,000
Capital stock	270,000	200,000
Retained earnings	90,000	80,000
Total	$600,000	$500,000

COMPANY A
Income Statement

	19X2	19X1
Net sales	$600,000	$400,000
Cost of goods sold	252,000	180,000
Gross margin	$348,000	$220,000
Operating expenses	180,000	80,000
Operating income	$168,000	$140,000
Income taxes	78,540	60,700
Net income	$ 89,460	$ 79,300

21-8 Instructions From the balance sheet data which follow, determine the:

(1) Current ratio

(2) Acid-test ratio

(3) Debt ratio

(4) Equity ratio

(5) Debt-equity ratio

Cash	$ 60,000
Marketable securities	15,000
Accounts receivable (net)	90,000
Inventories	80,000
Prepaid expenses	7,000
Unamortized bond discount	10,000
Plant and equipment	300,000
Current liabilities	120,000
Long-term debt	200,000
Owner equity	242,000

21-9 Instructions From the income statement data which follow, determine the:

(1) Operating ratio

(2) Gross margin ratio

(3) Cost of goods sold ratio

(4) Ratio of net income to net sales

Sales (net)	$800,000
Cost of goods sold	300,000
Selling expenses	80,000
General and administrative expenses	100,000
Income taxes	140,000

21-10 Instructions From the following data, which were abstracted from the financial statements of the Zim Company, determine the:

(1) Rate of return on total assets

(2) Rate of return on owner equity

(3) Rate of return on common stockholders' equity

Average assets employed in the business	$800,000
Average owner equity	400,000
Average common stockholders' equity	300,000
Interest charges	12,000
Preferred dividends	6,000
Net income	90,000

21-11 Instructions Assume that an organization acquires assets of $100,000 by borrowing $80,000 from bondholders at 7 percent per annum, and by issuing $20,000 worth of capital stock. In each of the following cases, determine whether or not trading on the equity was advantageous.

CASE 1 Annual earnings before interest, $7,500

CASE 2 Annual earnings before interest, $7,000

CASE 3 Annual earnings before interest, $6,500

21-12 Instructions Assume that an organization finances its $500,000 worth of assets by borrowing $200,000 from bondholders at 6 percent per annum and issuing $200,000 of 5 percent preferred stock and $100,000 worth of common stock. Compute rates of returns based on (1) total assets, (2) owner equity, and (3) common stockholders' equity, assuming that the net income in Case 1 is $40,000, in Case 2, $50,000, and in Case 3, $60,000.

*21-13 Instructions From the following data, which pertain to the operations of the Sundex Corporation, prepare:

(1) A schedule showing the number of shares of both preferred and common stock outstanding as of the end of each of the 5 years.

(2) A schedule showing the earnings per share of common stock for each of the 5 years. (Use the number of shares outstanding as of the end of the year in your computation.)

   (a) Income statements show net income amounts as follows:

19X1	$20,000
19X2	(17,000) (loss)
19X3	30,000
19X4	38,000
19X5	42,000

   (b) On January 1, 19X1, there were outstanding 1,000 shares of common stock, par value $100, and 500 shares of 6 percent cumulative preferred stock, par value $50.

   (c) A 5 percent dividend was paid in common stock to common stockholders on December 31, 19X2. The fair market value of the stock was $150 per share at the time.

*AICPA adapted.

(d) On January 1, 19X3, 400 shares of common stock were issued to purchase another company.

(e) A dividend of cumulative preferred stock was distributed to common stockholders on January 2, 19X3. One share of preferred stock was distributed for every five shares of common stock held. The fair market value of the preferred stock was $55 per share before the distribution and $53 per share immediately after the distribution.

(f) The common stock was split 2 for 1 on December 31, 19X4, and December 31, 19X5.

21-14 The following data concerning the current year's sales and receivables of Companies A and B were compiled from their accounting records:

	Company A	Company B
Net credit sales	$490,000	$180,000
Accounts receivable, Jan. 1	40,000	8,000
Accounts receivable, Dec. 31	30,000	16,000

Instructions Determine:

(1) The number of times both Company A's and Company B's receivables turned over during the year

(2) The number of days required to turn them

21-15 Instructions From the following data, which pertain to the current year's operations, determine:

(1) The number of times both Company A's and Company B's inventory turned over during the year

(2) The number of days required to turn them

	Company A	Company B
Sales	$100,000	$400,000
Gross margin percentage:		
Based on cost price	25%	
Based on selling price		30%
Initial inventory	30,000	160,000
Ending inventory	34,000	90,000

21-16 The A Company and the B Company are engaged in the same kind of business with essentially the same dollar amounts of sales, cost of sales, and gross margins. The A Company, however, reports an inventory turnover of 4.5 whereas the B Company reports one of 10.

Instructions Explain, by the use of an illustration, how such a difference might occur.

21-17 A new buyer for the M & M Department Store is convinced that the selling prices of several items in his department should be revised. It has been the policy to apply a flat rate to total invoice cost for all items sold by the department, without giving any consideration to the factor of turnover. The buyer contends that this policy is inequitable and that quick-selling items should bear a smaller percentage of indirect selling expense per unit than the slow-moving articles.

Instructions After careful study, the controller's office presents the following data from which you are to determine new selling prices for items A and B. (Indirect selling expenses are to be allocated so as to give recognition to the rate of turnover.)

Total invoice cost:
    Item A ———————————————————— $9.12
    Item B ———————————————————— $6.00
Direct selling expense ——————————————— 12% of selling price
Desired net profit ————————————————— 6% of selling price
Average indirect selling expense ——————————— 8% of sales
Average stock turn —————————————————— 4 months
  (Once every 4 months)
Stock turn—item A ———————————————— 3 months
Stock turn—item B ———————————————— 1 month

21-18 **Instructions** From the information contained in the following customers' accounts as of December 31, prepare:

(1) An aging schedule

(2) An aging summary, classifying the account balances as under 30 days old, 31–60 days old, 61–90 days old, and over 90 days old.

Abbot

June 15	(a)	1,000	Aug. 25	(b)	600
Aug. 20	(b)	700	Sept. 1	(a)	1,000
Oct. 10	(c)	1,300			

Johnson

Aug. 10	(a)	900	Oct. 15	(a)	600
Oct. 15	(b)	800	Nov. 8	(a)	100
Nov. 8	(c)	600	Dec. 10	(b)	600

Lemna

Oct.	5	(a)	900	Oct.	30	(a) 800
Nov.	10	(b)	700	Nov.	15	(b) 400
Dec.	15	(c)	600	Dec.	5	(b) 200

Walker

Sept.	28	(a)	400	Nov.	1	(a) 300
Nov.	4	(b)	600	Dec.	4	(b) 300
Dec.	10	(c)	900	Dec.	20	(b) 100
				Dec.	24	(c) 200

*21-19 The following partially condensed financial statements and other data were taken from the records of the X Corporation as of December 31, 19X3:

*AICPA adapted.

X CORPORATION

Balance Sheet

As of December 31, 19X3

Cash	$ 63,000
Trade receivables, less estimated uncollectibles of $12,000	238,000
Merchandise inventory	100,000
Prepaid expenses	7,000
Property and equipment, cost less $182,000 charged to operations to date	460,000
Other assets	13,000
	$881,000

Accounts and notes payable—trade	$ 98,000
Accrued liabilities	17,000
Estimated federal income tax liability	18,000
First mortgage, 4% bonds, due in 19X8	150,000
$7 preferred stock—no par value (entitled to $110 per share in liquidation); authorized, 1,000 shares, in treasury, 400 shares; outstanding, 600 shares	108,000
Common stock—no par; authorized, 100,000 shares; issued and outstanding, 10,000 shares stated at a nominal value of $10 per share	100,000
Excess of amounts paid in for common stock over stated values	242,000
Reserve for plant expansion	50,000
Reserve for cost of treasury stock	47,000
Retained earnings	98,000
Cost of 400 shares of treasury stock	(47,000)
	$881,000

Notes:

1 Working capital on December 31, 19X2, was $205,000.

2 Trade receivables on December 31, 19X2, were $220,000 gross, $206,000 net.

3 Dividends for 19X3 have been declared and paid.

4 There has been no change in amount of bonds outstanding during 19X3.

X CORPORATION
Income Statement
For the Year Ended December 31, 19X3

	Cash	Charge	Total
Gross sales	$116,000	$876,000	$992,000
Less: Discounts	$ 3,000	$ 12,000	$ 15,000
Returns and allowances	1,000	6,000	7,000
	$ 4,000	$ 18,000	$ 22,000
Net sales	$112,000	$858,000	$970,000
Cost of sales:			
Inventory, Jan. 1		$ 92,000	
Purchases		680,000	
Inventory, Dec. 31		(100,000)	672,000
Gross margin on sales			$298,000
Selling expenses		$173,000	
General expenses		70,000	243,000
Net income from operations			$ 55,000
Other additions and deductions (net)			3,000
Net income before federal income tax			$ 58,000
Federal income tax (estimated)			18,000
Net income			$ 40,000

Instructions Determine the value of each of the following ratios, turnovers, and other measures:

(1) Acid-test ratio

(2) Average number of days' charge sales uncollected

(3) Average inventory turnover

(4) Number of times bond interest earned (before taxes)

(5) Number of times preferred dividend earned

(6) Earnings per share of common stock

(7) Book value per share of common stock

(8) Current ratio

*21-20 Argo Sales Corporation has in recent prior years maintained the following relationships among the data on its financial statements:

1 Rate of gross margin to net sales ⸺⸺⸺⸺⸺⸺ 40%

2 Rate of net income to net sales ⸺⸺⸺⸺⸺⸺ 10%

*AICPA adapted.

3 Rate of selling expenses to net sales _____ 20%

4 Accounts receivable turnover _____ 8 per year

5 Inventory turnover _____ 6 per year

6 Acid-test ratio _____ 2 to 1

7 Current ratio _____ 3 to 1

8 Quick-asset composition: 8% cash, 32% marketable securities, 60% accounts receivable

9 Total asset turnover _____ 2 per year

10 Ratio of total assets to intangible assets _____ 20 to 1

11 Ratio of accumulated depreciation to cost of long-lived assets _____ 1 to 3

12 Ratio of accounts receivable to accounts payable _____ 1.5 to 1

13 Ratio of working capital to shareholder equity _____ 1 to 1.6

14 Ratio of total debt to shareholder equity _____ 1 to 2

The corporation had a net income of $120,000 for 19X8 which resulted in earnings of $5.20 per share of common stock. Additional information includes the following:

1 Capital stock authorized, issued (all in 19X1), and outstanding: Common, $10 per share par value, issued at 10 percent premium Preferred, 6 percent nonparticipating, $100 per share par value, issued at a 10 percent premium

2 Market value per share of common at December 31, 19X8: $78

3 Preferred dividends paid in 19X8: $3,000

4 Times interest earned in 19X8: 33

5 The amounts of the following were the same at December 31, 19X8, as at January 1, 19X8: inventory, accounts receivable, 5 percent bonds payable—long-term, and total shareholder equity

6 All purchases and sales were on account.

Instructions Prepare (1) a balance sheet, and (2) an income statement for the year ending December 31, 19X8, presenting the amounts you would expect to appear on Argo's financial statements (ignoring income taxes). Major captions appearing on Argo's balance sheet are; Current Assets, Long-lived Assets, Intangible Assets, Current Liabilities, Long-term Debt, and Shareholder Equity. In addition to the accounts divulged in the problem, you should include accounts for Prepaid Expenses, Accrued Expenses, and Administrative Expenses.

22
Special Tools of Financial Analysis

In our discussion of the basic tools of financial statement analysis, emphasis was placed primarily on their application to single-period statements. Such statements are essentially interim reports on a going concern's continuing activities, and therefore may not be fully representative of its long-run solvency, stability, or profitability. This is particularly true if abnormally favorable or unfavorable economic conditions prevailed during the period under study.

Since single-period statements analyzed by the use of the basic tools seldom provide information regarding business trends and the changing relationships which occur within an organization with the passage of time, they may be of somewhat limited value to the analyst. For this reason, certain special methods of financial analysis, most of which are based on statements for a number of periods, have been developed; the more important of these are trend analysis and various special purpose analyses.

TREND ANALYSIS

A **trend** may be defined as the underlying tendency for something to take a particular direction. This definition, as far as the financial analyst is concerned, explains trend analysis exactly. He believes that if financial statements for a number of periods are properly analyzed, it is possible to obtain information which will indicate the direction in which an organization is heading. Information concerning financial trends and changes in an organization can best be presented by the use of the following tools:

1 Comparative statements

2 Financial summaries

3 Graphic presentations

Comparative Statements

Comparative financial statements present like data for two or more dates or periods so that similar items may be compared and deductions drawn accordingly. The practice of presenting statements for two or more consecutive years in comparative form is quite common. A few years ago, to encourage this practice, the AICPA's Committee on Accounting Procedure pointed out that:[1]

> The presentation of comparative financial statements in annual and other reports enhances the usefulness of such reports and brings out more clearly the nature and trends of current changes affecting the enterprise. Such presentation emphasizes the fact that statements for a series of periods are far more significant than those for a single period and that the accounts for one period are but an installment of what is essentially a continuous history.

The formats of comparative statements, like those of other financial statements, vary among organizations. The condensed statements which follow should be viewed merely as illustrations of methods of presenting comparative data.

The first two columns of data in the illustrations are usually presented in published financial statements, whereas the third and fourth columns are added for analytical purposes only, either by the organization presenting the data or by the analyst. The data appearing in the last two columns are especially important for analytical purposes because they are indicative of the financial direction in which a business is moving. The dollar changes are computed simply by subtracting one period's data from those of the other, and the percentage changes are computed by dividing the net dollar change by the dollar amount of the item for the preceding period.

While variations do occur, usually the current period's data are presented in the first column and the preceding period's data in the second column.

---

[1] P. Grady, *Inventory of Generally Accepted Accounting Principles for Business Enterprises,* American Institute of Certified Public Accountants, New York, 1965, p. 303.

COMPANY A
Comparative Balance Sheet

Assets	Current Year	Previous Year	Change Amount	Change Percentage
Current assets	$ 456,000	$ 480,000	$ − 24,000	− 5.0
Plant and equipment (net)	588,000	450,000	+138,000	+ 30.7
Other assets	156,000	70,000	+ 86,000	+122.9
Total assets	$1,200,000	$1,000,000	$ +200,000	+ 20.0*

Liabilities and Owner Equity	Current Year	Previous Year	Change Amount	Change Percentage
Current liabilities	$ 204,000	$ 280,000	$ − 76,000	− 27.1
Long-term debt	336,000	150,000	+186,000	+124.0
Total liabilities	$ 540,000	$ 430,000	$ +110,000	+ 25.6
Capital stock	$ 480,000	$ 350,000	$ +130,000	+ 37.1
Retained earnings	180,000	220,000	− 40,000	− 18.2
Total shareholder equity	$ 660,000	$ 570,000	$ + 90,000	+ 15.8
Total liabilities and owner equity	$1,200,000	$1,000,000	$ +200,000	+ 20.0*

*The individual percentage changes will not total to these amounts because, unlike the totals, the individual percentages are not weighted.

COMPANY A
Comparative Income Statement

	Current Year	Previous Year	Change Amount	Change Percentage
Net sales	$2,000,000	$1,500,000	$ +500,000	+33.3
Cost of goods sold	1,160,000	900,000	+260,000	+28.9
Gross margin	$ 840,000	$ 600,000	$ +240,000	+40.0
Operating expenses	580,000	375,000	+205,000	+54.7
Operating income	$ 260,000	$ 225,000	$ + 35,000	+15.6
Income taxes	100,000	90,000	+ 10,000	+11.1
Net income	$ 160,000	$ 135,000	$ + 25,000	+18.5

COMPANY A
Comparative Retained Earnings Statement

	Current Year	Previous Year	Change Amount	Change Percentage
Retained earnings, beginning of year	$220,000	$165,000	$ + 55,000	+ 33.3
Net income for the year	160,000	135,000	+ 25,000	+ 18.5
Totals	$380,000	$300,000	$ + 80,000	+ 26.7*
Dividends declared during the year	200,000	80,000	+120,000	+150.0
Retained earnings, end of year	$180,000	$220,000	$ − 40,000	− 18.2*

*Again the totals will not reconcile, because the individual changes are not weighted.

Financial Summaries

As a rule, financial analysis based upon comparative statements affords the analyst several advantages over that based on single-period statements. This is especially true with respect to trend analysis. However, certain analytical weaknesses are inherent in comparative statements. Changes or inconsistencies in accounting methods or policies during the periods covered by the statements can result in the misinterpretation of reported trends and changing relationships. A change in an organization's inventory valuation method or its depreciation policy, for example, even though the alternative procedures are acceptable, can easily destroy the comparability of corresponding items in successive periods. Similarly, material

COMPANY A
Five-year Financial Summary

Income Data	19X5	19X4	19X3	19X2	19X1
Net sales	$2,000,000	$1,500,000	$1,200,000	$1,300,000	$1,000,000
Net income	160,000	135,000	84,000	104,000	50,000
Net income percentage of net sales	8.0%	9.0%	7.0%	8.0%	5.0%
Financial Position Data					
Working capital	$252,000	$200,000	$130,000	$ 60,000	$ 50,000
Long-term debt	336,000	150,000	150,000	100,000	100,000
Shareholder equity	660,000	570,000	495,000	471,000	417,000
Per Share Data*					
Earnings per share	$1.33	$1.35	$0.84	$1.04	$0.50
Dividends per share	1.67	0.80	0.60	0.50	0.40
Book value per share	5.50	5.70	4.95	4.71	4.17

*Based on 100,000 shares of no-par common stock outstanding during the years 19X1 to 19X4, and 120,000 shares during 19X5.

errors and their correction in subsequent periods, and material nonrecurring gains or losses can contribute to the misinterpretation of dollar percentage changes in corresponding items on comparative statements.

Many organizations, in an attempt to counteract the analytical weaknesses of both single-period and comparative statements, present financial summaries covering 5- or 10-year periods in their published annual reports. The illustration at the bottom of page 592 is typical of such summaries.

Graphic Presentation

In most instances it is easier to interpret the rise and fall of a line on a graph than a series of figures that tell the same story; for this reason, accounting data are often presented in graphic form. The graph is a particularly useful device for depicting trends and relationships. When used to present accounting data, it supplements, rather than replaces, the conventional statements. The following illustration is indicative of the use of graphic presentation.

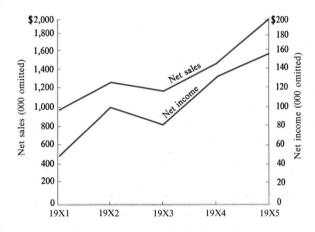

SPECIAL PURPOSE ANALYSES

On occasion more specialized information than that which is readily obtainable from an analysis of the basic financial statements may be necessary if sound conclusions are to be drawn regarding specific facets of an organization's liquidity, stability, and profitability. The following are representative of special purpose analyses:

1 Gross margin analysis

2 Break-even analysis

3 Marginal analysis

4 Segmental analysis

5 Capital expenditure analysis

Gross Margin Analysis

Although comparative income statements reflect net changes in gross margin (gross profit) from one period to another, they do not reveal the underlying reasons for the changes. For decision-making purposes, the causes of changes may be more significant than the net amounts; therefore, it is often desirable to break net changes down into their basic components.

Because gross margin is determined by deducting the cost of goods sold from net sales, a change in the amount of gross margin may result from:

1 An increase or decrease in sales

2 An increase or decrease in the cost of goods sold

3 A combination of the two

An increase or decrease in sales may be the result of:

1 A change in the per-unit selling price

2 A change in the number of units sold

3 A combination of the two

An increase or decrease in the cost of goods sold may be the result of:

1 A change in the per-unit cost price

2 A change in the number of units sold

3 A combination of the two

If we let NCGM equal the net change in gross margin, the breakdown may be depicted in tree form as follows:

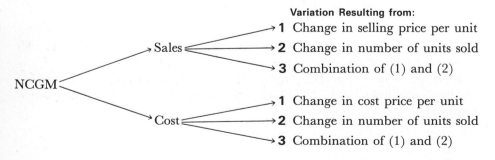

Although six possible variations are shown in the tree diagram, all result from changes either in (1) price, (2) volume, or (3) a combination of the two. The variances may be summarized as follows:

1 A **price variance** results from a change in either the unit selling price or the unit cost price. When computing it, we assume no change in the number of units sold. Thus, we simply multiply the price change per unit by the number of units sold in the preceding period. It is possible to have a price variance for both sales and cost of goods sold.

2 A **volume variance** results from a change in the number of units sold. When computing it, we assume no change in price. Thus, we simply multiply the change in the number of units sold by the unit price for the preceding period. If there is a volume variance, we will, of course, have one for both sales and cost of goods sold.

3 A **price-volume variance** results from a change in both a unit price and the number of units sold. It is computed by multiplying the change in price per unit by the change in the number of units sold. As is the case with a price variance, we may have a price-volume variance for both sales and cost of goods sold.

To illustrate the computations involved in gross margin analysis, let us assume the following data and also, for purposes of simplicity, assume that the organization sells only one type of item.

	Current Period	Preceding Period	Change
Sales	$245,000	$180,000	$65,000
Cost of goods sold	182,000	135,000	47,000
Gross margin	$ 63,000	$ 45,000	$18,000
Units sold	70,000	45,000	25,000
Unit selling price	$3.50	$4.00	$(.50)
Unit cost price	$2.60	$3.00	$(.40)

In the analysis that follows, note that the net increase in gross margin of $18,000 was the result of an increase in sales of $65,000 and an increase in the cost of goods sold of $47,000. The $65,000 increase in sales was the result of an unfavorable price variance of $22,500, a favorable volume variance of $100,000, and an unfavorable price-volume variance of $12,500. The $47,000 increase in the cost of goods sold resulted from a favorable price variance of $18,000, an unfavorable volume variance of $75,000, and a favorable price-volume variance of $10,000.

Gross Margin Analysis
For the Current Year

Increase in sales resulting from:
Price variance [($4.00 − $3.50) × 45,000] ———————————————— $ (22,500)
Volume variance [(70,000 − 45,000) × $4.00] ————————————— 100,000
Price-volume variance [($4.00 − $3.50) × (70,000 − 45,000)] —————— (12,500)
  Increase in sales ————————————————————————————— $65,000

Increase in cost of goods sold resulting from:
Price variance [($3.00 − $2.60) × 45,000] ———————————————— $ (18,000)*
Volume variance [(70,000 − 45,000) × $3.00] ————————————— 75,000*
Price-volume variance [($3.00 − $2.60) × (70,000 − 45,000)] —————— (10,000)*
  Increase in cost of goods sold ——————————————————— 47,000
Increase in gross margin ——————————————————————— $18,000

*If we were looking at the effect upon gross margin in each of these computations instead of the effect upon the cost of goods sold, each of the variances, of course, would have the opposite effect.

The foregoing data may be presented graphically as follows:

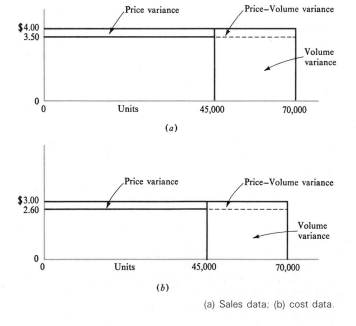

(a) Sales data; (b) cost data.

Break-even Analysis

That point at which the total of all revenues is exactly equal to the total of all expenses is the **break-even point.** Thus, at the break-even point an organization neither makes a profit nor sustains a loss. Although break-even analysis can be applied to past operations, it is particularly useful as a means of analyzing projected activities. For example, management may wish to know what effect an increase or decrease in selling prices or sales volume will have on its break-even point.

Break-even analysis is based upon certain assumptions as to the behavior of revenues and expenses. In the computation of the break-even point, a fixed sales price is assumed, whereas expenses are considered to be either "fixed" or "variable."

A **fixed expense** is one which is constant in amount within a particular range of activity (normally referred to as the **relevant range**). For our purposes in this text we shall assume that a fixed expense is one which is constant in amount at all volume levels. Depreciation, property taxes, and rent are examples of fixed expenses.

A **variable expense** is one which fluctuates in total amount with changes in volume, increasing with increases in volume and decreasing with decreases in volume. The cost of goods sold, sales commissions, and supplies used are examples of variable expenses.

Break-even Computations The basic formula for break-even analysis is the one used to compute the break-even point. If we let S equal sales at the break-even point, FE equal fixed expenses, and VE equal variable expenses, the formula may be written as:

$$S = FE + VE$$

To illustrate the computation, let us assume that, at a projected level of activity, fixed expenses are expected to be \$90,000 and variable expenses are expected to be equal to 40 percent of sales. To break even, the organization must generate sales of \$150,000, determined as follows:

$$S = FE + VE$$
$$S = \$90,000 + 40\%(S)$$
$$S = \$90,000 + .40S$$
$$S - .40S = \$90,000$$
$$.60S = \$90,000$$
$$S = \$150,000$$

In addition to determining break-even points, break-even analysis may be used to estimate the sales volume required to provide a specified net income, or rate of return, under given conditions. Let us assume the same data that were used in the preceding illustration, and also assume that the organization wants to earn a net income of 15 percent on its sales. If we let RS equal the required sales and NI equal the desired net income, we can determine, as shown below, that the organization must generate sales of $200,000.

$$RS = FE + VE + NI$$
$$RS = \$90{,}000 + 40\%(RS) + 15\%(RS)$$
$$RS = \$90{,}000 + .40RS + .15RS$$
$$RS - .40RS - .15RS = \$90{,}000$$
$$.45RS = \$90{,}000$$
$$RS = \$200{,}000$$

Break-even Chart The relationship of fixed and variable expenses to revenue at different volume levels is often portrayed graphically by what is ordinarily known as a **break-even chart.** Revenue points are plotted on the graph at various levels and the "revenue curve" is sketched in by joining the various points with a line. Expense points are plotted on the graph at various levels and the "cost curve" is sketched in by connecting the total expense points at the various levels. The point at which the revenue curve and the cost curve intersect is the break-even point. In the illustration that follows, note that the revenue curve starts at zero, whereas the cost curve starts at an amount equal to the fixed expenses. The chart is based on the same data we used in our preceding break-even illustrations.

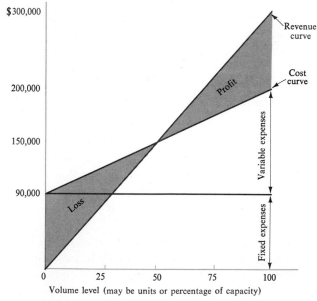

Break-even chart.

Marginal Analysis

In most business organizations, all except the most routine managerial decisions involve a choice of alternatives. For example, management may have to decide at one time or another whether to raise or lower prices, accept or reject sales orders, hire or fire employees, expand or contract operations, and so on.

When choosing among alternative courses of action, a profit-oriented management usually will give considerable weight to two factors commonly known as marginal revenue and marginal expense. **Marginal revenue** is the difference between the amount of revenue expected to be realized under one alternative and that expected to be realized under another; **marginal expense** is the difference between the total expenses expected to be incurred under one alternative and those expected to be incurred under another.

Two of the more useful analytical techniques based on the concept of the margin are the contribution margin ratio and the margin of safety. When studying the techniques, note their close relationship to break-even analysis.

Contribution Margin Ratio   In financial analysis the excess of sales over variable expenses is known as the **contribution margin.** The **contribution margin ratio,** sometimes referred to as the **profit-volume ratio,** expresses the relationship between the contribution margin and sales. The ratio is normally stated as a percentage of sales. It is the complement of the **variable expense ratio,** which expresses the relationship between variable expenses and sales. If we let CMR stand for the contribution margin ratio, S for sales, and VE for variable expenses, the formula for determining the contribution margin ratio will appear as follows:

$$CMR = \frac{S - VE}{S}$$

Like break-even analysis, the contribution margin ratio may be used to determine the break-even point or to estimate the sales volume required to provide a specified income under given conditions. To illustrate its use, let us assume the same data as were used in our break-even illustrations on pages 597 and 598; that is, fixed expenses are expected to be $90,000 and variable expenses are expected to equal 40 percent of sales for a projected level of activity. Since the contribution margin ratio is the complement of the variable expense ratio, it will be 60 percent of sales. In our earlier computation we determined that to break even the organization must generate sales of $150,000. If we let S equal the sales at the break-even point, we can determine the $150,000 using the contribution margin ratio as follows:

$$S = \frac{FE}{CMR}$$

$$S = \frac{\$90,000}{60\%(S)}$$

$$S = \frac{\$90,000}{.60S}$$

$$.60S = \$90,000$$
$$S = \$150,000$$

If the organization wishes to earn a net income of 15 percent on its sales, it must, as you will recall, generate sales of $200,000. If we let RS equal the required sales and NI the desired net income, using the contribution margin ratio we can determine the $200,000 as follows:

$$RS = \frac{FE + NI}{CMR}$$

$$RS = \frac{\$90,000 + 15\%(RS)}{60\%(RS)}$$

$$RS = \frac{\$90,000 + .15RS}{.60RS}$$

$$.60RS - .15RS = \$90,000$$
$$.45RS = \$90,000$$
$$RS = \$200,000$$

Margin of Safety The excess of projected or actual revenue over the amount of revenue required for the organization to break even is known as the **margin of safety.** It indicates the amount by which revenue may decrease without the organization sustaining a loss; it may be stated in dollar terms or expressed as a percentage. If we continue our preceding illustration and assume that the projected sales for the next period are $200,000, the margin of safety may be stated as either $50,000 or 25 percent. The $50,000 is determined simply by subtracting sales at the break-even point of $150,000 from the projected sales of $200,000. If we let MS equal the margin of safety, PS the projected sales, and S sales at the break-even point, a margin of safety of 25 percent may be determined as follows:

$$MS = \frac{PS - S}{PS}$$

$$MS = \frac{\$200,000 - \$150,000}{\$200,000}$$

$$MS = \frac{\$\ 50,000}{\$200,000}$$

$$MS = 25\%$$

Marginal Analysis and Break-even Chart   The contribution margin and the margin of safety may be depicted graphically on a break-even chart.   While it is possible to portray them on the same kind of chart we used on page 598, they are more easily seen on one which plots fixed expenses on top of variable expenses, rather than vice versa.   When studying the chart which follows, note that other than for this inverted feature, the two charts are sketched identically.

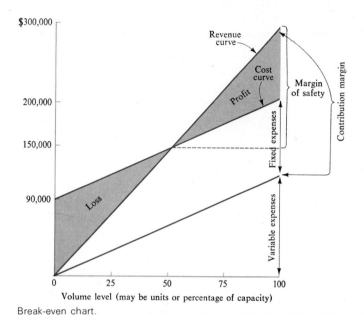

Break-even chart.

Segmental Analysis

In today's business environment, the successful organization must rely on sound planning and control to achieve maximum profits and realize minimum losses. This is especially important in the large, highly diversified concern that sells more than one kind of product or service.

  The overall operation of a business of this kind is ordinarily broken down into divisions, departments, or product lines.   A good example is the large supermarket in which we find a meat department, produce department, grocery department, and perhaps others, all operating as segments of the total operation.   Similar organizational breakdowns can be found in most large businesses, whether they are trading concerns, manufacturing concerns, or combinations of the two.   The analysis of the operations of such business subdivisions is commonly known as **segmental analysis.**   It is primarily useful for evaluating the profitability of the division, department, or product under study.

  Many organizations prefer to set up separate accounts in which to record the transactions of the various segments, and also to prepare separate financial reports.

As you will recall from our study of credit transactions, departmental data can easily be reflected in the accounting records simply by expanding the basic books of original entry. In Chapter 5, for example, we expanded our sales and purchases journals to include departmental credit sales and purchases. Other books of original entry may be expanded in similar fashion. Thus, as far as accounting is concerned, departmentalization of an organization creates no problem. This is also true with regard to divisions and product lines.

Segmental Analysis and Product Planning Segmental analysis is particularly valuable to management in making decisions in such areas as product planning, pricing, and advertising. To illustrate its usefulness in product planning, let us assume that the ABC Company has been producing and selling three products, A, B, and C. Management is confronted with the current year's data, as shown below, at a time when it is considering what products to produce and sell during the next year.

	Products			
	A	*B*	*C*	*Total*
Sales	$900,000	$800,000	$400,000	$2,100,000
Fixed expenses	$400,000	$200,000	$300,000	$ 900,000
Variable expenses	100,000	400,000	200,000	700,000
Total expenses	$500,000	$600,000	$500,000	$1,600,000
Net income (loss)	$400,000	$200,000	($100,000)	$ 500,000

A casual glance at the data might lead one to presume that Product C should be discontinued since it appears to be unprofitable. On closer analysis, however, as indicated in the following data, we can see that Product C is actually contributing $200,000 (which in reality is the excess of $400,000 sales over $200,000 of variable expenses) to the overall net income, assuming that the fixed expenses are rigidly fixed and the variable expenses are strictly variable.

	Totals	
	Including Product C	*Excluding Product C*
Sales	$2,100,000	$1,700,000
Fixed expenses	$ 900,000	$ 900,000
Variable expenses	700,000	500,000
Total expenses	$1,600,000	$1,400,000
Net income (loss)	$ 500,000	$ 300,000

Segmental Analysis and Product Pricing To illustrate the use of segmental analysis in the area of product pricing, let us assume in addition to the basic data used in the preceding illustration that the company produced 10,000 units of

Product C during the current year (full capacity being 15,000 units per year) and that the total expense at full capacity is $600,000 per year, with the fixed and variable elements being equal. While planning for next year's production, a year in which the domestic sales of Product C are expected to remain at last year's level (10,000 units), management is faced with the problem of making a decision regarding an offer from an exporter for the excess capacity. Sales management is confident that acceptance of the exporter's offer will not affect the present domestic market. Whereas the domestic price is $40 per unit, the exporter offers only $30 per unit for the excess capacity of 5,000 units. Since actual cost during the current year was $50 per unit [($300,000 *FE* + $200,000 *VE*) ÷ 10,000], at first glance it would appear that the answer to a $30 per unit offer should be negative. However, after the situation is analyzed somewhat as follows, the answer might be different:

	Product C	
	Domestic Sales Only	*Both Foreign and Domestic Sales*
Sales	$400,000	$550,000
Fixed expenses	$300,000	$300,000
Variable expenses	200,000	300,000
Total expenses	$500,000	$600,000
Net income (loss)	($100,000)	($ 50,000)

Although Product C still appears to be unprofitable in spite of the potential foreign sales, it should be recognized that acceptance of the offer will result in a $50,000 addition to the company's overall net income. This can be seen in the following data:

	Including Only Domestic Sales of Product C	*Including Both Foreign and Domestic Sales of Product C*
Sales	$2,100,000	$2,250,000
Fixed expenses	$ 900,000	$ 900,000
Variable expenses	700,000	800,000
Total expenses	$1,600,000	$1,700,000
Net income (loss)	$ 500,000	$ 550,000

Segmental Analysis and Advertising To illustrate the use of segmental analysis in the area of advertising, let us assume the same data as were used in the preceding illustration except that the exporter offers only $25 per unit for the excess capacity, and that management also wants to consider the possibility of employing additional advertising in order to sell the excess capacity in the domestic market rather than a foreign market. Sales management is confident that an additional advertising expenditure of $40,000 will do the job. As is indicated in the following data, the use of the advertising alternative would be more profitable than selling to the exporter, but selling to the exporter would be more profitable than producing and selling only 10,000 units in the domestic market as was done during the current year.

	Product C		
	Using Current Year Approach	Using Foreign Sales Approach	Using Advertising Approach
Sales	$400,000	$525,000	$600,000
Fixed expenses	$300,000	$300,000	$300,000
Variable expenses	200,000	300,000	340,000
Total expenses	$500,000	$600,000	$640,000
Net income (loss)	($100,000)	($ 75,000)	($ 40,000)

Capital Expenditure Analysis

Making capital expenditure decisions (decisions regarding the acquisition of long-lived assets) is one of the most important of all management activities in the area of long-range planning. Typical capital expenditures extend all the way from the replacement of individual items of machinery and equipment to complex projects such as plant expansion and the development of new products.

In today's large business organization, the competition among various departments and divisions for funds and other concessions is usually intense, and for this reason management must thoroughly examine all possibilities before making capital expenditure decisions. The estimated amount of investment required for a proposed project, its estimated economic life, estimated earnings, and the degree of risk involved must all be given serious consideration, and all possible alternatives must likewise be studied. In many instances the very future of the organization may depend on whether the right decision is reached.

Sound capital expenditure decisions are based upon a combination of engineering, marketing, and financial analysis plus a high degree of management judgment. The profitability of a proposal is of particular importance. Three basic types of analysis, or some variation thereof, are used to evaluate the profitability of capital expenditure proposals. They are:

1 Average investment method

2 Payback method

3 Discounted cash flow method

Average Investment Method This method, or as it is sometimes called, the **average rate of return method,** merely relates the average earnings of a project or an asset to the average investment over its lifetime. The amount of average earnings is estimated, whereas the average investment is commonly considered to be equal to one-half of the original investment. (One-half of the original investment is used as the average investment because it is equal to the average carrying value of an asset as determined by straight-line depreciation, assuming that the asset has no salvage value.) When the method is stated as a formula, we have:

$$\text{Average rate of return} = \frac{\text{average earnings}}{\text{average investment}}$$

To illustrate the average investment method, let us assume that management is considering the acquisition of an asset costing \$100,000 with an estimated useful life of 10 years, and that estimated earnings from the asset after all expenses including depreciation are deducted are \$50,000 for the 10-year period. If we let ARR equal the average rate of return, AE equal average earnings, and AI equal the average investment, a rate of return of 10 percent would be determined as follows:

$$ARR = \frac{AE}{AI}$$

$$ARR = \frac{(\$50,000 \div 10)}{(\$100,000 \div 2)}$$

$$ARR = \frac{\$\ 5,000}{\$50,000}$$

$$ARR = 10\%$$

Although the average investment method is easy to apply and can be used as a simple screening device to eliminate unprofitable proposals from consideration early in capital expenditure deliberations, it does have limitations. A serious weakness of the method is that it fails to take into consideration the timing of the earnings; it makes no distinction between investments which return capital outlays at an early date and those which return them sometime in the future. Obviously, the sooner capital outlays can be recovered, the sooner they can be reinvested in something else.

Payback Method This method, sometimes called the **payout method,** is a procedure for determining the **payback period,** which is the amount of time it will take for a project or an asset to earn enough to return the original outlay. Stated another way, it is the number of years required for the accumulated cash earnings from a project or asset to equal the original cash outlay. The formula is:

$$\text{Payback period} = \frac{\text{investment}}{\text{annual net cash flow}}$$

Technically, **net cash flow** is the excess of cash flowing into an organization from revenue over cash flowing out for expenses. For purposes of simplicity, however, in payback computations the term is used in much the same way the term "funds provided by operations" was used in Chapter 20; that is, net cash flow is considered to be equal to reported earnings plus depreciation. Letting *PBP* equal the payback period, *I* equal the investment, or original outlay, and *NCF* equal annual net cash flow, and assuming the same data that were used in the preceding illustration, we can determine a payback period of $6\frac{2}{3}$ years as follows:

$$PBP = \frac{I}{NCF} \text{ (annual earnings plus depreciation)}$$

$$PBP = \frac{\$100,000}{\$5,000 + \$10,000}$$

$$PBP = 6\frac{2}{3} \text{ years}$$

The payback method of analysis is very popular. Like the average investment method, it is easily applied and can be used to eliminate unprofitable proposals from consideration early in deliberations. For instance, a proposed project with a payback period of $6\frac{2}{3}$ years would be automatically screened out if an organization demanded a payback period of 5 years or less, whereas it would be retained for further consideration if the payback criterion were 10 years. Also, like the average investment method, the payback method does have weaknesses. It does not, for example, take into account the time value of money,[1] nor does it reflect the overall profitability of one project as compared to that of another. To illustrate the latter, assume:

Proposed Projects	Investment	Annual Net Cash Flow
A	$100,000	$15,000
B	120,000	18,000

Both projects have payback periods of $6\frac{2}{3}$ years ($I \div NCF$). Thus, if evaluated strictly on payback periods, they would appear to be equally desirable. Further analysis, however, indicates that Project A has an estimated useful life of 10 years, and Project B an estimated useful life of 20 years. Therefore the projects really are not equally desirable. Project B has the greater potential because it is capable of generating $18,000 a year for $13\frac{1}{3}$ years (20 years $- 6\frac{2}{3}$ years) after the initial investment is recovered. Project A, on the other hand, is capable of generating only $15,000 a year for $3\frac{1}{3}$ years (10 years $- 6\frac{2}{3}$ years) after its initial investment has been recouped.

Discounted Cash Flow Method Both the average rate of return and payback methods provide rather simple approaches to the evaluation of capital expenditure proposals. In order to include a consideration of the time value of money, many organizations use the more sophisticated **discounted cash flow method** of analysis.

---

[1] The term *time value of money* means that time is worth money. As you will recall from Chapter 13 in our study of long-term debt, it means that a dollar today is worth more than the promise of a dollar at some time in the future.

Under this method a capital expenditure is viewed as the acquisition of a series of future net cash flows composed of two elements: (1) the return of the original outlay, and (2) net income from the project. When an organization uses this method, it will not invest more in a given project than the sum of the net cash flows discounted back to the present at the desired rate of return.

The idea of discounting future amounts was first discussed in Chapter 13. You will recall that if we invest $1 for one year at 6 percent interest, the $1 will grow to be $1.06 at the end of the year. To determine the amount we simply multiply $1 by 1.06. If we were to work backward to the present, we would merely divide $1.06 by 1.06 and determine the present value to be $1. Thus, if we wanted to know the present value of a net cash flow of $1,000 for the first year, we would divide $1,000 by 1.06 (assuming the desired rate of return is 6 percent) and obtain a present value of approximately $943. The present value of a net cash flow of $1,000 for the second year would be determined by dividing $1,000 by 1.06, obtaining $943, and then by dividing $943 by 1.06 and obtaining roughly $890. (Of course, as you remember, the detailed computations can be eliminated if we take the correct factor from predetermined annuity tables and multiply it by the future amount in order to convert the future amount into the present value.)

To illustrate the discounted cash flow method, we shall assume the same data used in the preceding illustrations; that is, a proposed capital expenditure requires a $100,000 outlay; the estimated useful life of the asset under consideration is 10 years; and a net cash flow of $15,000 ($5,000 income plus $10,000 depreciation) per year is expected. In addition, we shall assume that the organization requires that at least 6 percent be made on all capital expenditures. Since, as is indicated in Schedule A, the amount to be invested ($100,000) is less than the present value ($110,385) of the expected cash flows, the proposal meets the discounted cash flow requirement.

Schedule A
Net Cash Flow Discounted at 6%

Year	Net Cash Flow		Present Value of 1 @ 6%		Present Value of Net Cash Flow
1	$15,000	×	.943	=	$ 14,145
2	15,000	×	.890	=	13,350
3	15,000	×	.840	=	12,600
4	15,000	×	.792	=	11,880
5	15,000	×	.747	=	11,205
6	15,000	×	.705	=	10,575
7	15,000	×	.665	=	9,975
8	15,000	×	.627	=	9,405
9	15,000	×	.592	=	8,880
10	15,000	×	.558	=	8,370

Present value of net cash flow_____ $110,385

Amount to be invested_____ 100,000

Excess of present value of net cash flow over amount to be invested $ 10,385

If the requirement were 10 percent rather than 6 percent, the proposal would not meet it. As you can see in Schedule B, the present value of the net cash flow when discounted at 10 percent is $7,840 less than the amount to be invested.

Schedule B
Net Cash Flow Discounted at 10%

Year	Net Cash Flow		Present Value of 1 @ 10%		Present Value of Net Cash Flow
1	$15,000	×	.909	=	$ 13,635
2	15,000	×	.826	=	12,390
3	15,000	×	.751	=	11,265
4	15,000	×	.683	=	10,245
5	15,000	×	.621	=	9,315
6	15,000	×	.564	=	8,460
7	15,000	×	.513	=	7,695
8	15,000	×	.467	=	7,005
9	15,000	×	.424	=	6,360
10	15,000	×	.386	=	5,790
Present value of net cash flow					$ 92,160
Amount to be invested					100,000
Excess of amount to be invested over the present value of net cash flow					$ (7,840)

Capital Expenditure Analysis Illustrated   To illustrate the simultaneous use of all three of the methods of analyzing capital expenditure proposals, let us assume that an organization has the following proposals under consideration:

Proposal	Estimated Cost	Estimated Useful Life, Years	Estimated Annual Earnings
A	$100,000	5	$20,000
B	120,000	5	26,000
C	160,000	8	16,000

Let us also assume that all capital expenditure proposals are initially evaluated against the following criteria:

1 Average rate of return must be equal to or greater than 10 percent.

2 Payback period is not to exceed 50 percent of the estimated useful life of the project or asset.

3 Discounted net cash flow must be equal to or greater than 30 percent.

We can see in Schedules 1, 2, and 3 which follow that all three proposals meet the average rate of return requirement, but that Proposal C is removed from consideration when it cannot meet the payback period requirement, and Proposal A is dropped when it fails to meet the discounted cash flow requirement.

Schedule 1
Average Rate of Return

Proposal	Estimated Annual Earnings		Average Investment*		Average Rate of Return, %
A	$20,000	÷	$50,000	=	40
B	26,000	÷	60,000	=	43.3
C	16,000	÷	80,000	=	20

*Estimated cost ÷ 2

Schedule 2
Payback Period

Proposal	Cost		Annual Net Cash Flow		Payback Period, Years
A	$100,000	÷	$40,000*	=	2.5
B	120,000	÷	50,000*	=	2.4
C	160,000	÷	36,000*	=	4.4†

*Estimated annual earnings plus depreciation.
† Does not meet the requirement.

Schedule 3
Net Cash Flow Discounted at 30%

			Proposal A	Proposal B	
Year	Present Value of 1 @ 30%	Net Cash Flow	Present Value of Net Cash Flow	Net Cash Flow	Present Value of Net Cash Flow
1	.769	$40,000	$ 30,760	$50,000	$ 38,450
2	.592	40,000	23,680	50,000	29,600
3	.455	40,000	18,200	50,000	22,750
4	.350	40,000	14,000	50,000	17,500
5	.269	40,000	10,760	50,000	13,450
Present value of net cash flow			$ 97,400		$121,750
Amount to be invested			100,000		120,000
Excess			$ (2,600)*		$ 1,750

*Does not meet the requirement.

SUMMARY

Trend analysis and a variety of special purpose analyses are analytical methods that provide information concerning business trends and changing relationships within organizations. Comparative statements, financial summaries, and graphic presentations are examples of tools used in trend analysis.

Special purpose analyses include (1) gross margin analysis, (2) break-even analysis, (3) marginal analysis, (4) segmental analysis, and (5) capital expenditure analysis.

QUESTIONS AND PROBLEMS

22-1 Discuss briefly the inherent limitations of single-period financial statements.

*22-2 The president of a small factory has come to you for advice. He says that his bookkeeper tells him each year that the business has been just about breaking even. He also says that the inventories, receivables, and payables have not varied much since the corporation was organized 10 years ago but that cash has been constantly increasing. He thinks that the business has been making money and that there is an error. The president states that there has been no sale of assets, refinancing of indebtedness, or change in corporate structure such as sale of stock. Present briefly the explanation that you would offer the president, giving examples of transactions to illustrate your explanation, and indicating any financial statements that you might prepare for the president's use.

22-3 (1) Define the following terms as they are used in capital budgeting:
  (a) Payback period
  (b) Discounted cash flow
  (c) Time value of money

(2) The method of project selection which considers the time value of money in a capital budgeting decision is known as:
  (a) Discounted cash flow
  (b) Payback period
  (c) Rate of return on original investment
  (d) Rate of return on average investment
  (e) All of the above
  (f) None of the above

(3) In 19X1 the marginal contribution rate of Lamesa Company was 30 percent. In 19X2 fixed costs are expected to be $120,000, the same as in 19X1, and sales are forecasted at $550,000, which is a 10 percent

*AICPA adapted.

increase over 19X1. For the company to increase its income by $15,000 in 19X2, the marginal contribution rate must be:
(a) 20 percent
(b) 30 percent
(c) 40 percent
(d) 70 percent
(e) None of the above

22-4 Assuming that the Atlas Sales Company has yearly fixed expenses of $1,600,000 and that its variable expenses ordinarily run about 60 percent of sales, determine:

(1) The amount of Atlas's net income or loss at a sales volume of (a) $6,000,000 and (b) $3,000,000

(2) Atlas's break-even point

(3) The amount of sales needed by Atlas in order to generate a net income of $200,000

(4) Atlas's margin of safety at a sales volume of $7,500,000

22-5 Assuming that the Apex Sales Company has yearly fixed expenses of $120,000 and a CMR (contribution margin ratio) equal to 20 percent of sales, determine:

(1) Apex's break-even point

(2) The amount of sales needed by Apex in order to generate a net income of $300,000

(3) Apex's margin of safety at a sales volume of $660,000

22-6 Based on the following data, which pertain to the current year's operations of the Ajax Sales Company, determine the extent to which sales can decrease before the company begins to lose money:

Sales		$2,000,000
Less: Fixed expenses	$600,000	
Variable expenses	750,000	1,350,000
Net income		$ 650,000

22-7 Instructions Determine the missing amount in each of the following unrelated cases:

	Case 1	Case 2	Case 3
Sales	$1,000,000	$ (2)?	$900,000
Variable expenses	640,000	640,000	(3)?
Fixed expenses	100,000	100,000	100,000
Contribution margin ratio	(1)?	20%	30%

*22-8 **Instructions** Identify the numbered components in the following break-even chart:

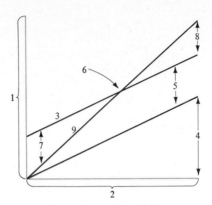

22-9 Engineering estimates indicate that the variable cost of manufacturing a new product will be $30,000 per unit. The sales department estimates that the variable cost of selling a unit will be $10,000 if the sales price is set at $90,000 per unit.

Instructions Assuming that fixed costs totaling $2 million per year will be incurred in the production of the new product, determine the number of units which must be sold annually at $90,000 per unit in order to cover all costs.

*22-10 The vertical axes of the following graphs represent total dollars of expense and the horizontal axes represent volume or activity:

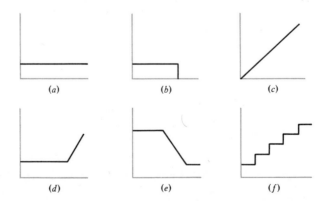

Instructions Select the graph which best illustrates each of the following expenses:

*AICPA adapted.

(1) The depreciation of equipment, when the amount of depreciation taken is computed by the machine-hours method

(2) The depreciation of equipment, when the amount of depreciation taken is computed by the straight-line method

(3) An electricity bill, when the amount charged is computed based on a flat fixed amount plus a variable amount after a certain number of kilowatt-hours are used

(4) Rent on a factory building donated by the city, when the agreement calls for a fixed fee payment unless 200,000 man-hours are worked, in which case no rent need be paid

(5) Salaries of repairmen, when one repairman is needed for every 1,000 hours of machine-hours or less; that is, zero to 1,000 hours requires one repairman, 1,001 to 2,000 hours requires two repairmen, and so forth

(6) Rent on a factory building donated by the county, when the agreement calls for a rent of $100,000 less $1 for each direct labor hour worked in excess of 200,000 hours, but a minimum rental payment of $20,000 must be paid

22-11 Instructions From the following data, which pertain to the E.Z. Cum Company, prepare a detailed analysis of the causes of the $105,000 change in gross margin:

	19X2	19X1
Sales	$750,000	$600,000
Cost of sales	675,000	420,000
Gross margin	$ 75,000	$180,000
Units sold	15,000	10,000
Unit selling price	$50	$60
Unit cost price	$45	$42

*22-12 Instructions Assuming that the Farmbrook Manufacturing Company makes and sells only one product, prepare from the following data a detailed analysis of the causes of the $7,960 change in gross margin:

	19X2		19X1	
	Amount	Per Unit	Amount	Per Unit
Sales	$112,200	$10.20	$100,000	$10.00
Cost of sales	64,240	5.84	60,000	6.00
Gross margin	$ 47,960	$ 4.36	$ 40,000	$ 4.00

*AICPA adapted.

22-13 The TBZ Company produces a single product. The company has a maximum productive capacity of 100,000 units a year. According to TBZ's marketing department, the market for its product varies with the price at which it is offered for sale, as follows:

Sales Price	Predicted Market, Units
$15	70,000
14	80,000
12	90,000
10	100,000

Instructions Assuming that the company's fixed expenses are $300,000 a year and that its variable expenses average 40 percent of gross sales, determine the price at which you would recommend that the company sell its product.

22-14 Instructions For each of the following proposals, determine the:

(1) Average rate of return

(2) Payback period

Proposed Project	Cost	Estimated Useful Life, Years*	Estimated Annual Earnings
A	$ 60,000	4	$10,000
B	80,000	5	12,000
C	120,000	6	16,000
D	150,000	8	15,000
E	200,000	10	18,000

*Assume no salvage value.

22-15 Instructions From the data which follow, determine for each proposal (1) the discounted net cash flow, and (2) whether or not it meets the company's cash flow criterion:

Proposed Project	Cost	Estimated Useful Life, Years*	Estimated Annual Earnings	Discounted NCF Criterion, %
AA	$30,000	3	$ 1,000	$\geq$† 6
BB	40,000	4	3,000	$\geq$ 10
CC	50,000	5	10,000	$\geq$ 30

*Assume no salvage value.
†Equal to or greater than.

	Present Values		
Periods	Present Value of 1 @ 6%	Present Value of 1 @ 10%	Present Value of 1 @ 30%
1	.943	.909	.769
2	.890	.826	.592
3	.840	.751	.455
4	.792	.683	.350
5	.747	.621	.269

22-16 Instructions From the following data, determine which, if any, of the Corley Corporation's capital expenditure proposals meet the initial criteria against which they are evaluated.

Proposed Project	Cost	Estimated Useful Life, Years*	Estimated Annual Earnings
A	$ 60,000	3	$ 6,000
B	80,000	3	5,600
C	90,000	4	13,500
D	100,000	4	20,000
E	120,000	5	30,000

*Assume no salvage value.

All capital expenditure proposals of the Corley Corporation are initially evaluated against the following criteria:

1 Average rate of return must be equal to or greater than 15 percent.

2 Payback period is not to exceed 60 percent of the estimated useful life of the project or asset.

3 Discounted net cash flow must be equal to or greater than 20 percent.

	Present Values
Periods	Present Value of 1 @ 20%
1	.833
2	.694
3	.579
4	.482
5	.402

*22-17 The following information was taken from the records of the State Gas Company as of December 31, 19X2:

	19X1	19X2
Average number of customers	27,000	26,000
MCF* sales	486,000	520,000
Revenue	$1,215,000	$1,274,000

*MCF = 1,000 cubic feet.

Instructions To assist in explaining the 19X2 increase in operating revenues of $59,000 ($1,274,000 − $1,215,000), prepare an analysis showing the effect of the change in:

(1) Average number of customers

(2) Average consumption per customer

(3) Average rate per MCF sold

*22-18 The M Company, which owns and operates an office building, is considering putting certain concessions in the main lobby. The investment in equipment, which would last 10 years, would be $2,000. An accounting study produces the following estimates on an average annual basis:

Salaries		$ 7,000
Licenses and payroll taxes		200
Cost of merchandise sold:		
Beginning inventory	$ 2,000	
Purchases	40,000	
Available	$42,000	
Ending inventory	2,000	40,000
Share of heat, light, etc.		500
Pro rata building depreciation		1,000
Concession advertising		100
Share of company administrative expense		400
Sales of merchandise		49,000

Instructions Assume that as an alternative a catering company has offered to rent the space for $750 per year for 10 years, and to put in and operate the same concessions at no cost to the M Company. Heat and light are to be furnished by the office building at no cost to the catering company. What would be your advice to M Company? Explain fully.

*22-19 The Johnson Meat Packing Company desires to study its distribution costs (selling, general, and administrative expenses) which in the aggregate constitute approximately 65 percent of the total cost of doing business.

*AICPA adapted.

An analysis made to determine the causes of cost variation in selling, general, and administrative expense items discloses that each element of expense varies according to one of the following three bases: (1) number of orders, (2) number of items per order, and (3) weight of order expressed in hundred weights. The analysis of each class of distribution expense discloses that these expenses are attributable to each of these three factors as follows:

	Expenses Based on			
Distribution Costs	Number of Orders	Number of Items	Number of Cwt	Total
Selling expenses _____	$2,310	$1,080	$ 210	$3,600
General expenses_____	260	320	620	1,200
Administrative expenses_____	1,170	580	340	2,090
Total distribution cost _____	$3,740	$1,980	$1,170	$6,890

Data by order-size classes follow:

Order-size Class	Number of Orders	Total Number of Items	Total Cwt
Under 50 pounds _____	2,800	4,090	700
50–199 pounds _____	2,900	8,410	2,610
200–499 pounds _____	600	2,280	1,860
500–999 pounds _____	400	2,400	2,800
1,000 pounds and over _____	100	820	1,030
All orders _____	6,800	18,000	9,000

Instructions From the data presented, prepare a schedule (or schedules) showing the allocation of total distribution cost per hundredweight of meat products for each size class of order (expressed in pounds per order).

*22-20 The management of the Southern Cottonseed Company has engaged you to assist in the development of information to be used for managerial decisions. The company has the capacity to process 20,000 tons of cottonseed per year. The yield of a ton of cottonseed is as follows:

Product	Average Yield per Ton of Cottonseed, Pounds	Average Selling Price per Trade Unit
Oil	300	$ .15 per pound
Meal	600	50.00 per ton
Hulls	800	20.00 per ton
Lint	100	3.00 per hundredweight
Waste	200	

*AICPA adapted.

A special marketing study revealed that the company can expect to sell its entire output for the coming year at the listed average selling prices.

You have determined the company's costs to be as follows:

Processing costs:
  Variable: $9 per ton of cottonseed put into process
  Fixed: $108,000 per year

Marketing costs:
  All variable: $20 per ton sold

Administrative costs:
  All fixed: $90,000 per year

Instructions From the above information you prepared and submitted to management a detailed report on the company's break-even point. In view of conditions in the cottonseed market, management told you that they would also like to know the average maximum amount that the company can afford to pay for a ton of cottonseed.

Management has defined this amount as that which would result in the company's having losses no greater when operating than when closed down under the existing cost and revenue structure. Management states that you are to assume that the fixed costs shown in your break-even point report will continue unchanged even when operations are shut down. Determine the average maximum amount that the company can pay per ton.

Part Seven

Planning and Controlling
Manufacturing Operations

23
Accounting for Manufacturing Operations

Up to this point we have been chiefly concerned with accounting as it relates to nonmanufacturing operations. Primary emphasis has been on merchandising concerns, although accounting for service organizations has also been discussed.

Manufacturing is another important area of business operations, and the remainder of this text will be devoted, for the most part, to a study of accounting for manufacturing concerns.

MANUFACTURING VERSUS NONMANUFACTURING OPERATIONS

A merchandising concern purchases finished merchandise and offers it for resale in essentially the same form. A manufacturing concern, on the other hand, purchases raw materials, converts them into finished products, and then sells the products. To illustrate, an automobile manufacturer converts raw materials such as steel, rubber, plastic, and aluminum into automobiles, which he then sells to dealers, who in turn sell them to consumers. (The dealers in this case are representative of merchandising concerns.)

From an accounting standpoint, most of the activities of manufacturing concerns are similar to those of merchandising organizations; many of the selling, administrative, and financing activities are the same. The major differences between the two, as far as accounting is concerned, are found in their methods of cost accumulation for (1) the valuation of inventories and (2) the determination of the cost of goods sold.

Elements of Manufacturing Cost

Three major elements enter into the cost of a manufactured product: direct material, direct labor, and factory overhead (occasionally called manufacturing overhead, manufacturing expenses, factory burden, or simply, indirect costs). In cost terminology the sum of the first two—direct material and direct labor—is called **prime cost,** whereas the sum of the latter two—direct labor and factory overhead—is known as **conversion cost.**

Direct Material That portion of raw material utilized in the manufacturing process which is readily identifiable and measurable as an integral part of the finished product is **direct material.** In contrast, **indirect material** is defined as that portion of raw material which either cannot be readily identified as a basic component of the finished product or which is used in such small quantities that the cost of accounting for it would be prohibitive. In the manufacture of a television set, for example, the picture tube, transistors, and controls are commonly considered to be direct materials, while glue, paint, and varnish are usually categorized as indirect materials. Direct material is treated as a separate element of manufacturing cost, whereas indirect material is included as part of factory overhead.

Direct labor **Direct labor** is that portion of work performed by factory employees which is directly associated with the finished product. Conversely, **indirect labor** is employee labor that does not have immediate bearing upon the production of the finished product. In the manufacture of a television set, the labor expended by both skilled and unskilled factory employees working directly upon the set is direct labor, while the efforts of such employees as foremen, shop clerks, and maintenance workers constitute indirect labor. Like indirect material, indirect labor employed in the manufacturing process is considered as part of factory overhead.

Factory Overhead That portion of costs associated with the manufacturing process which cannot be immediately identified as part of the cost of the finished product is known as **factory overhead.** In addition to indirect material and labor, it includes such items as factory rent, heat, light, power, insurance, and depreciation.

Product Costs versus Period Costs

Two kinds of costs are involved in accounting for manufacturing concerns.[1] Costs associated with the units of output are generally known as **product costs.** Costs that are charged off as expenses (charged to the Revenue and Expense Summary account) in the period in which they are incurred are known as **period costs.** Stated another way, product costs are inventoriable costs, while period costs are not. Thus, material, labor, and factory overhead are ordinarily considered as product costs, whereas selling and administrative expenses are generally treated as period costs.

Full Costing versus Variable Costing

Accountants have long recognized the importance of the product as an appropriate vehicle for matching manufacturing costs and revenues when determining periodic income. They are not, however, in complete agreement as to exactly what should be included in the cost of a product. Two schools of thought prevail: Full, or absorption, costing is favored by many "traditional" accountants, while others prefer what is known as variable, or direct, costing.

Full and Variable Costing Defined Under the **full costing** concept, both fixed and variable costs are considered as integral parts of the total cost of manufacturing a product. In contrast, under the **variable costing** concept, the cost of manufacturing a product is considered to be composed only of those costs that vary with production. Thus, in the valuation of inventories and the determination of cost of goods sold, under variable costing only direct material, direct labor, and variable factory overhead costs are taken into consideration. Fixed factory overhead costs are charged against revenue as period costs in the period of their incurrence.

In sum, accounting for direct material and direct labor is the same under both concepts; however, only variable factory overhead is charged to the product under variable costing, whereas both fixed and variable factory overhead are charged to the product under full costing.

Full and Variable Costing Illustrated The basic differences between full and variable costing can perhaps be best illustrated by contrasting income statements prepared under the respective approaches. Let VC equal variable costs, FC equal fixed costs, and assume the following data:

Sales for the period	$90,000
Beginning finished goods inventory ($\frac{3}{4}VC + \frac{1}{4}FC$)	20,000
Cost of goods manufactured ($\frac{3}{4}VC + \frac{1}{4}FC$)	40,000
Ending finished goods inventory ($\frac{3}{4}VC + \frac{1}{4}FC$)	15,000
Selling expenses	8,000
Administrative expenses	12,000

---

[1] As you recall from our previous study, the terms *cost* and *expense* in accounting are not mutually exclusive. The AICPA, however, has repeatedly emphasized in its terminology bulletins that items entering into the computation of the cost of manufacturing, such as material, labor, and overhead, should be described as costs rather than as expenses.

Income Statement

(Full Costing)

Sales		$90,000
Cost of sales:		
Beginning finished goods inventory (VC + FC)	$20,000	
Cost of goods manufactured (VC + FC)	40,000	
Cost of goods available for sale (VC + FC)	$60,000	
Ending finished goods inventory (VC + FC)	15,000	
Cost of goods sold (VC + FC)		45,000
Gross margin		$45,000
Period costs:		
Selling expenses	$ 8,000	
Administrative expenses	12,000	
Total period costs		20,000
Net income		$25,000

Income Statement

(Variable Costing)

Sales		$90,000
Cost of sales:		
Beginning finished goods inventory (VC only)	$15,000	
Cost of goods manufactured (VC only)	30,000	
Cost of goods available for sale (VC only)	$45,000	
Ending finished goods inventory (VC only)	11,250	
Cost of goods sold (VC only)		33,750
Gross margin		$56,250
Period costs:		
Fixed cost of production ($\frac{1}{4} \times$ $40,000)	$10,000	
Selling expenses	8,000	
Administrative expenses	12,000	
Total period costs		30,000
Net income		$26,250

As you study the composition of the income statements, note that the difference between the amounts of net income computed under the two concepts is simply the difference between the amounts of fixed cost associated with the beginning and ending finished goods inventories under full costing. That is, the $1,250 difference in net income ($26,250 − $25,000) is the difference between the $5,000 of fixed cost ($20,000 − $15,000) associated with the beginning inventory and the $3,750 of fixed cost ($15,000 − $11,250) associated with the ending inventory. Under variable costing the $5,000 would have been charged as a period cost during the previous period and the $3,750 during the current period; under full costing the $5,000 would have been charged to the current period and the $3,750 would be deferred to a future period as product costs.

Manufacturing Accounts

In addition to the usual accounts found in a merchandising concern, the typical manufacturing organization generally has some accounts that are peculiar to its particular type of activity. Many variations exist among manufacturing organizations, especially in relation to manufacturing costs, but their accounts differ from those of the typical merchandising concern chiefly in the inventory area. The Merchandise Inventory account of the merchandising concern is ordinarily replaced in the manufacturing organization by at least three inventory accounts both in the ledger and on the financial statements. Since a manufacturing organization may have on hand at any one time a certain amount of raw material, partially completed products, and fully completed products, these items are ordinarily accounted for in separate inventory accounts, typically entitled:

1 Raw Materials Inventory

2 Work in Process Inventory

3 Finished Goods Inventory

When the balance sheet of a manufacturing concern is prepared, the inventory accounts are listed among the current assets in the order of their expected liquidity, somewhat as follows:

Inventories:		
Finished goods	400,000	
Work in process	50,000	
Raw materials	150,000	600,000

As we learned in Chapter 10, there are two basic approaches to the handling of inventories in the accounts: the periodic method and the perpetual method. Either can be employed in accounting for manufacturing operations, but control is ordinarily best achieved by the use of a perpetual method.

When perpetual inventories are employed in a manufacturing concern, the Raw Materials Inventory account is debited for the cost of materials purchased and is credited for the cost of materials put into production. Likewise, the Work in Process Inventory account is debited for all costs (material, labor, and overhead) put into production and is credited for the cost associated with completed production, this cost being transferred to the Finished Goods Inventory account. The Finished Goods Inventory account in turn is debited for all costs transferred to it from the Work in Process Inventory account and is credited for all costs associated with the goods sold. The flow of costs through the inventory accounts may be illustrated in abbreviated form as follows:

Flow of Costs through Inventory Accounts

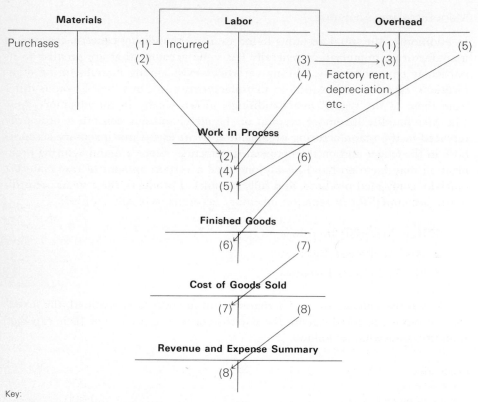

Key:
(1) Indirect materials used in production.
(2) Direct materials used in production.
(3) Indirect labor used in production.
(4) Direct labor used in production.
(5) Overhead charged to production.
(6) Cost of completed production transferred to the Finished Goods Inventory account.
(7) To relieve the Finished Goods Inventory account of the cost of goods sold.
(8) To close the Cost of Goods Sold account into the Revenue and Expense Summary account.

Determining the Cost of Goods Sold

Because the merchandising concern buys its merchandise for resale while the manufacturing organization makes its own, their methods for determining the cost of goods sold differ somewhat. As the following comparison shows, in the determination the finished goods inventory of the manufacturing concern is substituted for the merchandise inventory of the merchandising concern, and the cost of goods manufactured by the manufacturing organization is substituted for the purchases of the merchandising concern.

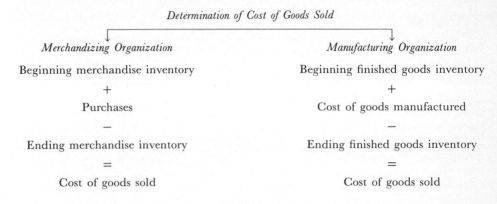

Determination of Cost of Goods Sold

Merchandizing Organization	*Manufacturing Organization*
Beginning merchandise inventory	Beginning finished goods inventory
+	+
Purchases	Cost of goods manufactured
−	−
Ending merchandise inventory	Ending finished goods inventory
=	=
Cost of goods sold	Cost of goods sold

To illustrate the cost of goods sold section of an income statement prepared for a manufacturing concern, let us assume a beginning finished goods inventory of $100,000 and an ending one of $60,000, with the cost of goods manufactured during the period amounting to $200,000.

Cost of goods sold:

Beginning inventory of finished goods	$100,000
Plus: Cost of goods manufactured	200,000
Goods available for sale	$300,000
Less: Ending inventory of finished goods	60,000
Cost of goods sold	240,000

Statement of Cost of Goods Manufactured

The principal new ingredient introduced in the transition from the cost of goods sold section of the income statement of a merchandising concern to that of a manufacturing organization is the item entitled "cost of goods manufactured." This is essentially the equivalent of "purchases" in the cost of goods sold section of a merchandising concern's income statement, the significant difference being that the item entitled "cost of goods manufactured" is ordinarily supported by a schedule or statement, typically called the **statement of cost of goods manufactured.** As may be seen in the following illustration, the statement details the composition of the three basic elements of manufacturing costs, considers the beginning and ending amounts of work in progress, and concludes with the cost of goods manufactured.

ABC MANUFACTURING COMPANY
Statement of Cost of Goods Manufactured
For the Current Period

Raw materials:

Beginning inventory	$ 20,000	
Add: Raw materials purchases	70,000	
Raw materials available for use	$ 90,000	
Deduct: Ending inventory	40,000	
Cost of raw material used		$ 50,000
Direct labor		80,000
Factory overhead:		
Indirect labor	$ 10,000	
Heat, light, and power	15,000	
Insurance	2,000	
Depreciation of factory building	5,000	
Depreciation of factory machinery and equipment	9,000	
Factory supervision	14,000	
Factory supplies used	2,000	
Miscellaneous factory expense	3,000	
Total factory overhead		60,000
Total manufacturing costs added to production during the period		$190,000
Add: Work in process at beginning of period		40,000
Total		$230,000
Deduct: Work in process at end of period		30,000
Cost of goods manufactured		$200,000

Manufacturing Work Sheet

As is the case in the merchandising concern, the work-sheet approach is used extensively in the preparation of financial statements for a manufacturing organization. In general, the work sheets differ only slightly from one another, the main difference being that the work sheet of the manufacturing organization ordinarily contains an extra pair of columns for the cost of goods manufactured. This, of course, entails no fundamental change in the basic principles and procedures developed back in Chapter 9. It does, however, pinpoint the data needed for the preparation of the statement of cost of goods manufactured.

The work sheet of the ABC Manufacturing Company (on pages 630 and 631) illustrates the work-sheet approach as used in a manufacturing concern. It is somewhat oversimplified in that only a limited number of accounts are used and the only adjustments involved are associated with the inventory accounts, indicated by the figures (1), (2), and (3) in the adjustments columns.

Preparing Financial Statements for a Manufacturing Concern   The formal basic financial statements of a manufacturing organization, like those of a merchandising concern, can be prepared directly from the work sheet.   For example, in our illustration all data necessary for the preparation of the income statement can be obtained from the income statement columns, and all data for the balance sheet are available in the balance sheet columns; in addition, the cost of goods sold section of the income statement can be supported by the statement of the cost of goods manufactured, which can be prepared directly from the manufacturing columns.   While the formal income statement and balance sheet are not presented here, the statement of the cost of goods manufactured would be the same as the one previously presented on page 628.

Closing the Books of a Manufacturing Concern   Entries to close the books of a manufacturing concern can, like those of a merchandising organization, be taken directly from the work sheet.   Unlike those of the merchandising organization, however, they include not only the entries from the income statement columns but also those from the manufacturing columns.   The accounts in the manufacturing columns could be closed in one entry merely by debiting the credits and crediting the debits and closing the balancing amount into the Revenue and Expense Summary account.   However, the usual procedure is to open a Manufacturing Summary account, close all the items in the manufacturing columns into it, and then close the Manufacturing Summary account into the Revenue and Expense Summary account.   Closing entries based on our work-sheet illustration would appear as shown below and on page 632.

Manufacturing Summary	270,000	
Work in Process (beginning inventory)		40,000
Raw Materials (beginning inventory)		20,000
Raw Materials Purchases		70,000
Direct Labor		80,000
Indirect Labor		10,000
Heat, Light, and Power		15,000
Insurance Expense		2,000
Depreciation of Buildings		5,000
Depreciation of Machinery and Equipment		9,000
Factory Supervision		14,000
Factory Supplies Used		2,000
Miscellaneous Expense		3,000

To close the beginning inventories and factory costs into the Manufacturing Summary account.

Work in Process (ending inventory)	30,000	
Raw Materials (ending inventory)	40,000	
Manufacturing Summary		70,000

To close the ending inventories into the Manufacturing Summary account.

ABC MANUFACTURING COMPANY
Manufacturing Work Sheet
For the Year Ended December 31, 19——

Account	Trial Balance Debits	Trial Balance Credits	Adjustments Debits	Adjustments Credits	Manufacturing Debits	Manufacturing Credits	Income Statement Debits	Income Statement Credits	Balance Sheet Debits	Balance Sheet Credits
Cash	20,000								20,000	
Accounts receivable (net)	60,000								60,000	
Inventories (beginning):										
Finished goods	100,000		60,000(1)				100,000		60,000	
Work in process	40,000		30,000(2)		40,000				30,000	
Raw materials	20,000		40,000(3)		20,000				40,000	
Prepaid insurance	1,000								1,000	
Factory supplies	2,000								2,000	
Land	8,000								8,000	
Buildings (net)	50,000								50,000	
Machinery and equipment (net)	60,000								60,000	
Furniture and fixtures (net)	10,000								10,000	
Accounts payable		30,000								30,000
Federal income taxes payable		12,000								12,000
Capital stock		200,000								200,000
Retained earnings (beginning)		66,000								66,000
Sales		350,000						350,000		
Raw materials purchases	70,000				70,000					

Direct labor	80.000			80.000		
Indirect labor	10.000			10.000		
Heat, light, and power	18.000			15.000	3.000	
Insurance expense	2.500			2.000	500	
Depreciation of buildings	6.000			5.000	1.000	
Depreciation of M & E	11.000			9.000	2.000	
Depreciation of F & F	1.000				1.000	
Factory supervision	14.000			14.000		
Factory supplies used	2.000			2.000		
Miscellaneous expense	4.500			3.000	1.500	
Advertising expense	10.000				10.000	
Sales salaries	28.000				28.000	
Office salaries	18.000				18.000	
Federal income taxes	12.000				12.000	
	658.000	658.000		270.000	200.000	
Inventories (ending):						
Finished goods			60.000(1)			60.000
Work in process			30.000(2)	30.000		
Raw materials			40.000(3)	40.000		
		130.000	130.000	70.000		
Cost of goods manufactured				200.000	377.000	410.000
				270.000	410.000	410.000
				270.000		341.000
Net income					33.000	33.000
					410.000	341.000

Revenue and Expense Summary_____	200,000	
Manufacturing Summary_____		200,000

To close the Manufacturing Summary account into the Revenue and
Expense Summary account.

Revenue and Expense Summary_____	177,000	
Finished Goods (beginning inventory) _____		100,000
Heat, Light, and Power _____		3,000
Insurance Expense _____		500
Depreciation of Buildings _____		1,000
Depreciation of Machinery and Equipment _____		2,000
Depreciation of Furniture and Fixtures_____		1,000
Miscellaneous Expense_____		1,500
Advertising Expense_____		10,000
Sales Salaries _____		28,000
Office Salaries _____		18,000
Federal Income Taxes _____		12,000

To close the beginning inventory and operating expenses into the
Revenue and Expense Summary account.

Sales _____	350,000	
Finished Goods (ending inventory) _____	60,000	
Revenue and Expense Summary_____		410,000

To close sales and the ending inventory into the Revenue and
Expense Summary account.

Revenue and Expense Summary_____	33,000	
Retained Earnings_____		33,000

To close net income into the Retained Earnings account.

ACCOUNTING FOR MANUFACTURING COSTS

Manufacturing costs are generally accounted for by cost systems. Although
numerous variations can be found in practice, only two types are in wide use:
the job order cost system and the process cost system. We shall cover both in
detail in the following chapter. First, however, it is important that we become
familiar with the basic procedures involved in accounting for the various elements
of manufacturing costs (material, labor, and overhead).

Accounting for Raw Materials

An important feature of a good accounting system in a manufacturing organization is the adequate control of raw materials from the time production is
planned until the materials become a component part of the finished product.
This includes the controlling of both quantity and cost, not only during the
planning stage but also during purchasing, receiving, storing, handling, and
utilization. Materials control is particularly important in those organizations
having large investments in raw materials. In these concerns the same care should
be exercised in safeguarding and accounting for materials as for cash.

In order to control both quantity and cost, the accounting system generally utilizes controlling accounts and subsidiary ledgers capable of reflecting both quantities and costs of materials received, issued, and on hand as of any moment of time. The subsidiary ledger that supports the Raw Materials Inventory controlling account is ordinarily known as the **stores ledger,** with the detailed information that makes up the ledger being reflected on **stores ledger cards.** The following illustration is indicative of a typical stores ledger card.

Stores Ledger Card											
Material _____ Reorder point* _____ Reorder quantity* _____											
Received				**Issued**				**Balance**			
Date	Quantity	Unit Cost	Total	Date	Quantity	Unit Cost	Total	Date	Quantity	Unit Cost	Total

*Whenever the quantity of an item on hand reaches its "reorder point," a requisition for the purchase of an amount equal to its "reorder quantity" is initiated. The determination of the reorder point and quantity will be discussed in greater detail in Chapter 26.

As you will recall from Chapter 10, cost as applied to an inventoriable item in a merchandising concern is the price paid or consideration given to put the item into a *salable* condition and position. As applied to raw materials in a manufacturing organization, cost is the price paid or consideration given to put the materials into a *usable* condition and position. In addition to the invoice price, this includes all reasonable and necessary costs involved in the purchasing, receiving, and storing of the materials.

Recording the Acquisition of Materials Once the cost of an inventoriable item is determined, it is recorded in much the same way as in a merchandising concern; that is, the appropriate inventory account is charged with the cost. In addition, however, in the case of raw materials, the appropriate stores ledger card in the subsidiary ledger must also be charged with the cost. To illustrate both the journalizing and posting processes, let us assume that materials A, B, and C are purchased on account in quantities of 1,000, 2,000, and 3,000 and for costs of $1,500, $4,000, and $7,500, respectively. In journal entry and T-account form the data would be recorded as follows:

Raw Materials Inventory_____ 13,000
　　　Accounts Payable (Vouchers Payable) _____ 　　　　13,000

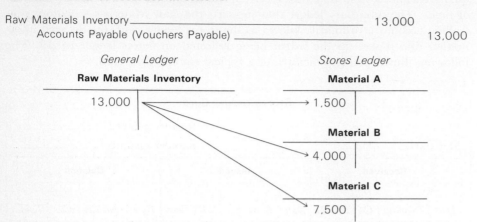

Recording the Issuance of Materials　As a rule materials are issued from factory storerooms only on the basis of properly authorized materials requisitions. The formal requisition has several functions: It serves as a means of establishing responsibility and accountability for the usage of materials; it is the source document for recording the issuance of materials in the books of original entry; and, in addition, it is the basis for posting in both the controlling account in the general ledger and the subsidiary account in the stores ledger.

　　　To illustrate both the journalizing and posting processes, let us assume that of the materials purchased in our illustration, 50 percent of A, 40 percent of B, and 30 percent of C were used directly in production (that is, direct material) and that 10 percent of each was used indirectly (as overhead). In journal entry and T-account form the data would appear as follows:

Work in Process (direct material) _____ 4,600
Factory Overhead (indirect material) _____ 1,300
　　　Raw Materials Inventory_____ 　　　5,900

General Ledger　　　　　　　　　　　　　　　Stores Ledger

Raw Materials Inventory　　　　　　　　　　**Material A**

13,000 | 5,900　　　　　　　　1,500 | 900

Work in Process　　　　(750)　　(150)**Material B**

4,600 |　　　　(1,600)　　　4,000 | 2,000

　　　　　　　　(2,250) (400)

Factory Overhead　　　　　　　　　　**Material C**

1,300 |　　　　(750)　　7,500 | 3,000

Costing Materials Requisitions Inventoriable items in a manufacturing organization, like those in a merchandising concern, may be costed out of the inventory on any of several bases, for example: specific identification; first-in, first-out; last-in, first-out; and weighted average. You will recall that these were first discussed in Chapter 10.

Accounting for Factory Labor

Since a large portion of Chapter 12 was devoted to payroll accounting, we shall deal with it only briefly here. It should suffice at this time to point out that data for the computation of factory payrolls are commonly gathered on **clock cards** or similar devices which employees punch or sign upon entering and leaving a plant, in order to provide a record of hours worked. In addition, time expenditure records, which record the amount of time employees spend on specific jobs, are also maintained. At the time the payroll is prepared, these two records are coordinated so that proper payroll distribution may be made.

Based upon the data taken from the clock cards and time expenditure records, the factory payroll is broken down into categories of direct and indirect labor, and appropriate entries are made to the accounts. To illustrate, let us assume that a factory payroll of $10,000 consists of $8,000 of direct labor and $2,000 of indirect labor. (For purposes of simplicity, payroll deductions are omitted here; they would, of course, be handled as in Chapter 12.) In general journal form the entry would be:

```
Work in Process (direct labor) _____  8,000
Factory Overhead (indirect labor) _____  2,000
     Accrued Payroll Payable _____          10,000
```

Accounting for Factory Overhead

Since factory overhead, unlike direct labor and material, cannot be readily identified as part of the cost of a specific job or product, it must be allocated to production by some method of approximation. This is ordinarily accomplished by the use of predetermined overhead rates.

Predetermined Overhead Rates Ideally, the method employed in allocating factory overhead to specific jobs or products should be based upon a factor which is common to all jobs or products and which measures precisely the extent to which the overhead was utilized in their production. In practice, however, conditions are seldom such that the selection of an ideal base is possible. This is particularly true in organizations that make a variety of products, the manufacture of which utilizes overhead in varying degrees and causes its incurrence in different ways. Such organizations must choose between (1) the use of several bases, each of which is appropriate for a single overhead item or group of items, and (2) the use of a single base that results in a reasonable although not precise allocation of the overhead. The bases most frequently used, regardless of approach, include:

1 Direct labor costs
2 Direct labor hours
3 Machine hours
4 Units of production

Computing Overhead Rates The procedure for computing overhead rates is as follows:

1 Estimate the amount of overhead expected to be incurred at the planned level of activity.
2 Estimate production in terms of the basis selected. (For example, if overhead is to be allocated on a machine-hour basis, production should be estimated in terms of machine hours.)
3 Divide the estimated overhead costs determined in step 1 by the estimated production determined in step 2.

To illustrate, let us assume that Company A estimates overhead expenses for the upcoming year to be $300,000. The company allocates overhead on a machine-hour basis and estimates that it will use 120,000 machine hours during the year. Overhead should be allocated at the rate of $2.50 per machine hour, determined as follows:

$$\text{Overhead rate} = \frac{\text{estimated overhead}}{\text{estimated machine hours}}$$

$$\text{Overhead rate} = \frac{\$300,000}{120,000} \text{ machine hours}$$

$$\text{Overhead rate} = \$2.50 \text{ per machine hour}$$

Advantages and Disadvantages of Overhead Bases One of the major advantages of an overhead rate based on **direct labor costs** is its simplicity of operation. Because all requisite data are readily available from the payroll summary, no additional record keeping is necessary. The primary drawback to the method is that it tends to ignore contributions to a specific job or product by factors of production other than direct labor. For example, in some manufacturing operations machinery is the prime production factor and direct labor is only incidental. When machine operators are paid at different rates, the use of an overhead rate based on direct labor costs could result in a misleading allocation, because production of highly paid employees would be charged with proportionately more overhead than that of lower-paid workers.

An overhead rate based on *direct labor hours* overcomes the objection to the direct labor costs method arising from differences in labor rates, but its use necessitates the collection of additional data, namely, direct labor hours per job or product.

In organizations in which machinery is the chief factor in production, a rate based on *machine hours* usually constitutes the best method of allocating overhead. However, an important drawback to this method is that additional data not otherwise needed must be provided in detail. For example, records of the amount of machine time spent on various operations must be maintained. Because this increases accounting costs, some organizations do not find it practical to use a machine-hour rate.

An overhead rate per *unit of production* is the simplest and most direct method of allocating overhead. Its usefulness, however, is limited to those situations in which one or a few closely related products possessing a common denominator (for example, weight or volume) are produced.

Overhead Application Illustrated[1] To illustrate overhead application using direct labor costs as a basis, let us assume that factory overhead is estimated to be $60,000 for a year and that direct labor costs will total $100,000. In a month in which $8,000 of direct labor costs are incurred, $4,800 ($60,000/$100,000, or 60 percent, of $8,000) of overhead will be applied as follows:

Work in Process		4,800
Factory Overhead		4,800

Factory Overhead

Indirect materials	1,300	Applied	4,800
Indirect labor	2,000		
Other overhead	1,800		

Work in Process

Direct materials	4,600
Direct labor	8,000
Applied overhead	4,800

Rather than credit the Factory Overhead account when overhead is applied to production, some accountants prefer to use an additional account typically entitled Factory Overhead Applied. This account is credited when overhead is applied to production during the period, and at the end of the period it is closed to the Factory Overhead account. Since the end result is the same, we shall use the simpler approach and merely credit the Factory Overhead account when applying overhead to production.

---

[1] The terms overhead allocation and overhead application are frequently used interchangeably. In this text, *overhead allocation* pertains to the assignment of overhead costs to a department or other subdivision of an organization, whereas the term *overhead application* pertains to the assignment of overhead to the product or job.

Underapplied and Overapplied Overhead As a general rule, debits to factory overhead accounts for a period seldom, if ever, equal the credits. If the account has a debit balance, as is the case in our illustration, the amount of overhead applied to production is less than the amount actually incurred. Conversely, a credit balance in the account means that more overhead has been charged to production than has actually been incurred. When the amount of overhead actually incurred (as reflected on the debit side of the account) is more than the amount applied (as reflected on the credit side of the account), the difference is commonly called **underapplied,** or **underabsorbed, overhead.** When the amount of overhead applied exceeds the amount incurred, the difference is called **over-applied,** or **overabsorbed, overhead.**

When the amount of actual overhead incurred differs from that applied to production, there are both control and financial statement implications. For control purposes, the deviation must be analyzed in terms of its causes. Since the overhead rate is computed by dividing estimated overhead by estimated production stated in terms of the basis selected, underapplied or overapplied overhead may result from (1) a difference between the estimated and actual overhead, (2) a difference between the estimated and actual production, or (3) a combination of (1) and (2). We shall treat the topic of overhead variances more fully in Chapter 25.

With regard to the financial statements, we have the problem of handling both monthly and year-end overhead balances. Monthly balances are normally carried forward on the balance sheet. An underapplied balance is classified as a deferred charge, and an overapplied balance as a deferred credit.

Year-end balances, on the other hand, should be closed out. Theoretically, they should be closed proportionately to (1) the Cost of Goods Sold account, (2) the Finished Goods Inventory account, and (3) the Work in Process Inventory account. Practically, however, they are frequently closed in their entirety to the Cost of Goods Sold account. This approach is particularly useful when the balances are not material.

To illustrate both the theoretical and practical treatment of a year-end overhead balance, let us assume that we have a Factory Overhead account with a year-end debit balance of $300. Let us also assume that of the $4,800 of overhead applied to production during the year, 50 percent was associated with the goods sold, 30 percent with the finished goods still on hand, and 20 percent with the production still in process. The first entry illustrates the theoretical treatment, and the second, the practical treatment.

(1)

Cost of Goods Sold (50% × $300)	150	
Finished Goods Inventory (30% × $300)	90	
Work in Process Inventory (20% × $300)	60	
Factory Overhead		300

(2)

Cost of Goods Sold	300	
Factory Overhead		300

Departmentalization of Factory Overhead   To enhance operational efficiency, most large business organizations, as well as many medium and smaller-sized ones, are divided into departments, each of which is responsible for one or more of the organization's operations.   For accounting purposes, factories are often further divided into **cost centers.**   These are the smallest units of activity or areas of responsibility for which manufacturing costs are accumulated; a department may itself be a cost center or it may contain several cost centers.

A major advantage of both departmentalization and the utilization of cost centers, as far as accounting is concerned, is that they are means of maintaining closer control over manufacturing costs and greater accuracy in the costing of jobs and products.   For example, the responsibility for costs incurred in a department or cost center falls directly upon its manager or foreman and he must answer to management if costs for his department are out of line.   Greater accuracy in costing jobs and products is possible because departmentalization generally results in the use of different overhead rates for individual departments and cost centers.   If a factory-wide overhead rate is used, the result may be an incorrect application of overhead to jobs or products that require processing only in specific departments or cost centers.

Production Departments and Service Departments   Departmentalized factories are generally divided into production departments and service departments.   As the terms imply **production departments** are directly involved in converting raw materials into finished products, whereas **service departments** render auxiliary services to the production departments.   Examples of service departments are production planning, maintenance, and power.

A predetermined departmental overhead rate is based on two factors: the producing department's overhead and its portion of the cost of operating the service departments.   Therefore, this cost must be allocated to the producing departments on some equitable basis.   For example, the cost of operating the power department in a factory may be allocated to the producing departments on the basis of power consumed.   To illustrate, let us assume that the cost of operating the Power Department of the Ace Manufacturing Company was \$9,000 during a month in which it produced 600,000 kilowatt-hours.   If producing departments A, B, and C used 100,000, 200,000, and 300,000 hours, respectively, the \$9,000 cost would be allocated as follows:

Factory Overhead—Department A ($\frac{1}{6} \times$ \$9,000) _____ 1,500
Factory Overhead—Department B ($\frac{2}{6} \times$ \$9,000) _____ 3,000
Factory Overhead—Department C ($\frac{3}{6} \times$ \$9,000) _____ 4,500
          Power Department _____ 9,000

There are times when the use of a single basis for the allocation of service department costs may not result in the most equitable distribution.   This is particularly true when a significant part of the cost of operating a service department is a function of time (fixed costs) and a significant part a function of activity (variable costs). If a service department's costs can be segregated into fixed and variable elements, a dual-basis approach may be the most appropriate for the allocation of its costs. For example, in a power department the fixed costs (depreciation, insurance, taxes, etc.) are primarily associated with the department's physical capacity to produce power, whereas the variable costs (wages, maintenance, fuel, etc.) are primarily associated with the actual power output. Thus, in the allocation of power department costs, the fixed elements may be allocated to the producing departments in the ratio of these departments' capacities to consume power, and the variable elements may be allocated to them in the ratio of their actual consumption of power. The former ratio is frequently referred to as the **capacity ratio,** and the latter as the **consumption ratio.**

To illustrate the use of a dual basis, let us assume the same data used in our preceding illustration; in addition, let us assume that the power department's $9,000 cost was composed of fixed costs of $6,000 and variable costs of $3,000, and that the capacities of producing departments A, B, and C to consume power were 300,000, 300,000, and 400,000 kilowatt-hours per month, respectively. Under the dual-basis approach, the $9,000 cost of operating the power department would be allocated as follows:

Factory Overhead—Department A	2,300*
Factory Overhead—Department B	2,800*
Factory Overhead—Department C	3,900*
Power Department	9,000

*Departments:	A	B	C	Total
Fixed costs (3:3:4)	$1,800	$1,800	$2,400	$6,000
Variable costs (1:2:3)	500	1,000	1,500	3,000
	$2,300	$2,800	$3,900	$9,000

SUMMARY

The major differences between merchandising and manufacturing organizations from an accounting viewpoint are in their methods of accumulating costs for the valuation of inventories and the determination of the cost of goods sold.

Two kinds of costs are involved in accounting for manufacturing concerns: product costs and period costs. Product costs are inventoriable costs and are charged against revenue in the period in which the product is sold, whereas period costs are charged against revenue in the period of their incurrence. The three major elements of the cost of a manufactured product are direct material, direct labor, and factory overhead. Although numerous variations and combinations exist in practice, manufacturing costs are generally accounted for either by a job order or a process cost system. Whereas direct material and direct labor costs are normally charged directly to the product in most systems, overhead costs are ordinarily applied to production by the use of a predetermined rate.

Two concepts of costing have gained acceptance by accountants: full costing, under which both fixed and variable costs are considered to be integral parts of the total cost of manufacturing a product, and variable costing, under which the cost of manufacturing a product is considered to be composed only of those costs that vary with production.

QUESTIONS AND PROBLEMS

23-1 (1) Distinguish between **direct** and **indirect** labor.

(2) Explain what is meant by the term **factory overhead.**

23-2 Select the *best* answer from the following statements, assuming that Companies A and B manufacture similar products that require negligible distribution costs, and that their assets, operations, and accounting are similar in all respects except that A uses variable costing and B uses full costing.

(1) A would report a higher inventory value than B for the years in which production exceeds sales.

(2) A would report a higher inventory value than B for the years in which production exceeds the normal capacity.

(3) B would report a higher inventory value than A for the years in which production exceeds sales.

(4) B would report a higher net income than A for the years in which production equals sales.

(5) None of the above.

23-3 Supporters of variable costing often contend that it provides management with more useful information than does full costing.

(1) Describe the concept of variable costing.

(2) Contrast it with full costing from the standpoint of product costing.

23-4 A manufacturing concern follows the practice of charging the cost of direct materials and direct labor to work in process but charges off all indirect costs (factory overhead) directly to the Revenue and Expense Summary account. State the effects of this procedure on the concern's financial statements.

*23-5 Discuss briefly the advantages and disadvantages of basing an overhead rate on each of the following: (1) direct labor costs, (2) direct labor hours, (3) machine hours, and (4) units of production.

23-6 (1) What is meant by overapplied overhead?

(2) What are likely to be its major causes?

(3) Does a credit balance in an overhead account represent an over- or an underapplication?

23-7 **Instructions** From the following data which pertain to the current year's operations of the Mace Manufacturing Company, determine the amount of cost to be assigned to the ending finished goods inventory (1) under full costing, and (2) under variable costing.

Units produced	13,000
Units sold	10,000
Beginning inventories	—
Direct materials used	$58,500
Direct labor incurred	26,000
Fixed factory overhead	29,250
Variable factory overhead	42,250

23-8 The data which follow pertain to the August operations of the Delta Manufacturing Company, whose product is sold under the brand name of Big Z:

Sales for the month	$117,000
Finished goods inventory, Aug. 1	16,000*
Cost of goods manufactured	60,000*
Finished goods inventory, Aug. 31	25,000*
Selling expenses	6,000
Administrative expenses	14,000

*Contains both fixed and variable costs.

Instructions Assuming that direct material, direct labor, and variable factory overhead account for 60 percent of the cost of manufacturing a Big Z:

(1) Prepare an income statement for the month under full costing.

(2) Prepare an income statement under variable costing.

(3) Account for the difference between the amounts of net income determined in (1) and (2).

*AICPA adapted.

23-9 Instructions Journalize the following transactions:

(1) Raw materials purchased on open account, $5,000

(2) Materials returned to vendor, $600

(3) Direct materials issued from storeroom, $1,260

(4) Indirect materials issued from storeroom, $140

(5) Direct materials returned to storeroom from factory, $80

(6) Indirect materials returned to storeroom from factory, $12

(7) Accrual of factory payroll consisting of $2,000 of direct labor and $1,000 of indirect labor

(8) Factory overhead applied to production, $1,800

23-10 Instructions From the following abbreviated trial balance of the LMNO Company, prepare a 10-column manufacturing work sheet for the year ended December 31, 19X2.

LMNO COMPANY

Trial Balance

As of December 31, 19X2

Inventories (beginning):

Finished goods	$200,000	
Work in process	80,000	
Raw materials	40,000	
Other assets	400,000	
Liabilities		$ 90,000
Capital stock		100,000
Retained earnings		60,000
Sales		700,000
Raw materials purchases	120,000	
Other manufacturing expenses	50,000	
Other expenses	60,000	
	$950,000	$950,000

Ending inventories:

Finished goods	$ 60,000
Work in process	90,000
Raw materials	50,000
	$200,000

23-11 Instructions The following data pertain to the ZBT Manufacturing Company. To the extent possible, prepare closing entries, assuming that the company uses a Manufacturing Summary account.

Beginning inventory of work in process	$ 10,000
Ending inventory of work in process	30,000
Beginning inventory of raw material	40,000
Ending inventory of raw material	50,000
Raw materials purchased	100,000
Direct labor	60,000
Factory overhead	75,000
Beginning inventory of finished goods	55,000
Ending inventory of finished goods	45,000

23-12 The AA Manufacturing Company, which applies factory overhead to production on a machine-hour basis, has the following account balances on its books at the end of its fiscal year:

Factory overhead (debit)	$ 6,000
Work in process inventory (debit)	80,000
Finished goods inventory (debit)	120,000
Cost of goods sold (debit)	400,000

Instructions Present two acceptable methods of disposing of the $6,000 debit balance in the Factory Overhead account.

23-13 Instructions Determine the missing amount in each of the following cases:

	Case 1	Case 2	Case 3	Case 4
Beginning inventory of finished goods	$ 10,000	$ (2)?	$ 20,000	$ 30,000
Cost of goods manufactured	100,000	120,000	(3)?	120,000
Ending inventory of finished goods	20,000	10,000	30,000	(4)?
Cost of goods sold	(1)?	150,000	110,000	100,000

23-14 Instructions Determine the missing amount in each of the following cases:

	Case 1	Case 2	Case 3	Case 4
Raw materials:				
Beginning inventory	$ 5,000	$ 4,000	$ 6,000	$ (4)?
Purchases	20,000	18,000	(3)?	26,000
Ending inventory	10,000	8,000	12,000	15,000
Direct labor	30,000	20,000	24,000	32,000
Factory overhead	45,000	30,000	36,000	48,000

	Case 1	Case 2	Case 3	Case 4
Beginning inventory of work in process	$20,000	$ (2)?	$10,000	$14,000
Ending inventory of work in process	30,000	20,000	15,000	16,000
Cost of goods manufactured	(1)?	90,000	70,000	98,000

23-15 The following data pertain to the operations of the Best Manufacturing Company for the month of March:

Inventory of raw material—Mar. 1	$ 7,000
Inventory of raw material—Mar. 31	8,000
Raw materials purchased	16,000
Inventory of work in process—Mar. 1	6,000
Inventory of work in process—Mar. 31	5,000
Direct labor costs	14,000
Variable factory overhead costs	6,400
Fixed factory overhead costs	5,600
Inventory of finished goods—Mar. 1	9,000
Inventory of finished goods—Mar. 31	10,000

Instructions For the month of March, determine the:

(1) Cost of raw materials used

(2) Cost of goods manufactured (completed), assuming that full costing was used

(3) Cost of goods manufactured (completed), assuming that variable costing was used

(4) Cost of goods sold, assuming that full costing was used

(5) Cost of goods sold, assuming that variable costing was used

23-16 Four men perform direct labor in Department A. In accordance with the labor agreement, the men work 40 hours per week and 50 weeks per year. Overhead is applied by the use of the direct labor-hours basis in Department A, and overhead expenses for the current year were estimated at $57,600.

Instructions Assuming that the men worked 500 hours during January and that the overhead incurred amounted to $4,200:

(1) Compute the overhead rate.

(2) Prepare the end-of-the-month overhead application entry.

(3) Determine the amount of under- or overapplied overhead.

23-17 The following data pertain to the Power Department of the Ace Manufacturing Company:

Schedule of Kilowatt-hours

	Producing Departments			
	A	B	C	D
Capacity to consume power_____	100,000	200,000	120,000	80,000
Used during the month_____	80,000	130,000	70,000	60,000

Instructions Prepare schedules showing how the cost of operating the Power Department should be allocated to the producing departments:

(1) Assuming that the cost amounted to $9,300 and was composed of fixed costs totaling $2,500 and variable costs totaling $6,800

(2) Assuming that the cost amounted to $11,000 and was composed of fixed costs totaling $2,500 and variable costs totaling $8,500

(3) Assuming that the cost amounted to $14,200 and was composed of fixed costs totaling $4,000 and variable costs totaling $10,200

23-18 Departments A and B are the only power-consuming departments in the XYZ Manufacturing Company. Normally Department B consumes twice as much power as Department A, but during the current month Department A consumed only 60 percent and Department B only 30 percent of their normal amounts of power.

Instructions Assuming that power expenses for the month amounted to $7,200 and that they were composed of $3,000 of fixed expense and $4,200 of variable expense, how much should be charged to (1) Department A, and (2) Department B?

23-19 The K. Smith Manufacturing Company is in the process of submitting a bid on the production of 100,000 units of Product X. If the company's bid is accepted, Departments A and B will be utilized to produce the product. It is estimated that the production will require 200,000 units of material at a total cost of $8,200 and 4,000 hours of direct labor at a cost of $3 per hour. Factory overhead is applied on the basis of 120 percent of direct labor costs in Department A and at the rate of $1 per direct labor hour in Department B. It is estimated that 1,500 hours of the direct labor will be required in Department B.

Instructions Assuming that the company's bid is accepted, determine:

(1) The amount of overhead that will be applied in Department A

(2) The amount of overhead that will be applied in Department B

(3) The estimated cost of producing the 100,000 units of Product X

(4) The company's bid, if a 25 percent profit based on sales is desired

(5) The company's bid, if a 25 percent profit based on cost is desired

*23-20 During the month of June the Hot and Cold Company produced and sold 50 air conditioning units at a sales price of $400 each. Production costs included direct material costs of $100 per unit and direct labor costs of $60 per unit. Factory overhead was incurred at a rate equal to 100 percent of direct labor cost. Effective July 1, direct material costs decreased 5 percent, whereas direct labor costs increased 20 percent.

Instructions For July:

(1) Assuming no change in the rate of factory overhead as related to the cost of direct labor, determine the sales price per unit necessary to produce the same rate of gross margin as was produced during June.

(2) Assuming that the fixed element of the factory overhead amounts to $20 per unit, determine the sales price per unit necessary to produce the same rate of gross margin as was produced during June.

*AICPA adapted.

24
Basic Cost Systems

It was pointed out in Chapter 23 that two major cost systems prevail in accounting practice: the job order cost system and the process cost system. Either or both may be employed in a given manufacturing organization. In this chapter we shall study the more important features of each.

JOB ORDER COST SYSTEMS

A **job order cost system** is one in which manufacturing costs are accumulated for each separate job, or lot, of production. For such a system to be feasible, the different jobs must be readily identifiable. Job order cost systems are especially applicable in manufacturing organizations where customers' orders are manufactured to their specifications, for example, orders for 200 orange and blue band uniforms in a garment factory or for 100 specially designed planes in an aircraft company. In the construction industry, orders for one or more houses, apartment buildings, or garages would be examples. Other users of job order cost systems include the motion picture, machine tool, and job printing industries.

Under a job order cost system the costs of direct materials and direct labor employed on a specific job and the applicable factory overhead must be accumulated and accounted for as the job is being worked upon. Generally, this is accomplished on **job cost sheets,** or **job order sheets.** The following is typical of their format:

Job Cost Sheet							

Job order no. _____   Date order received _____
Item _____   Date delivery promised _____
For _____   Date job completed _____

Direct Material			Direct Labor			Factory Overhead	
Date	*Reference*	*Amount*	*Date*	*Reference*	*Amount*	*Date*	*Amount*
	(Materials requisition number)			(Time expenditure record)			(Based on predetermined rate)

Summary

Direct material _____
Direct labor _____
Factory overhead _____
  Total cost _____
Number of units _____
Unit cost _____

Job Cost Sheets as Subsidiary Records

In a job order cost system, the Work in Process account, which is primarily a controlling account, is supported by the job cost sheets of the unfinished jobs. The file composed of these cost sheets is commonly known as the **cost ledger.** When a job is finished, the completed cost sheet becomes the basis for the entry that transfers the cost of the job from the Work in Process account to the Finished Goods Inventory account.

To illustrate the role of the cost sheet as a subsidiary record, let us assume that during the first month of its operations Company A, which employs a job cost system, began Jobs No. 101, 102, and 103, and that Jobs No. 101 and 102 were completed during the month, leaving only Job No. 103 in process as of the end of the month. In addition, let us assume that direct materials costing $4,600 and direct labor amounting to $8,000 were charged to the month's production, and that $4,800 of factory overhead was applied during the month. The entries in the Work in Process account and the cost ledger would appear as shown below. (The costs accumulated for the jobs are assumed, and to simplify the illustration only summaries from the cost sheets are used.)

General Ledger

Work in Process

Direct materials	4,600	Job No. 101	8,200
Direct labor	8,000	Job No. 102	5,340
Factory overhead	4,800	Balance (Job No. 103)	3,860
	17,400		17,400
Balance (Job No. 103)	3,860		

Cost Ledger (Cost Sheet Summaries)		
Job No. 101	**Job No. 102**	**Job No. 103**
Direct materials 1,800	Direct materials 1,500	Direct materials 1,300
Direct labor 4,000	Direct labor 2,400	Direct labor 1,600
Factory overhead 2,400	Factory overhead 1,440	Factory overhead 960
Total cost 8,200	Total cost 5,340	Cost to date 3,860
(Finished)	(Finished)	(Unfinished)

The relationship between the data appearing in the Work in Process account and the job cost sheets may be summarized as follows:

Work in Process*		Job Cost Sheets†	
Beginning balance	—		—
Direct materials	$ 4,600	Job No. 101	$ 1,800
		Job No. 102	1,500
		Job No. 103	1,300
Direct labor	8,000	Job No. 101	4,000
		Job No. 102	2,400
		Job No. 103	1,600
Factory overhead	4,800	Job No. 101	2,400
		Job No. 102	1,440
		Job No. 103	960
Total cost	$17,400		$17,400
Cost of jobs finished	(13,540)	Job No. 101	(8,200)
		Job No. 102	(5,340)
Balance (cost of jobs unfinished)	$ 3,860	Job No. 103	$ 3,860

*Controlling account in the general ledger.
† Subsidiary records in the cost ledger.

Job Cost System Illustrated

In order to illustrate more fully the job cost system, let us continue our illustration for the following month. Assume that Job No. 103 was completed and Jobs No. 104, 105, and 106 were begun during this month. At the end of the month Job No. 106 is still in process, but Jobs No. 104 and 105 have been completed. In summary form, the transactions related to the manufacturing operations for the month are as follows:

1 Raw materials purchased: Material A, $5,000; Material B, $6,000; Material C, $9,000. All raw materials are purchased on open account.

2 Raw materials requisitioned and used:

	Material A	Material B	Material C	Total
Job No. 103	$ 100	—	$ 150	$ 250
Job No. 104	1,000	$1,200	2,800	5,000
Job No. 105	1,500	1,300	4,000	6,800
Job No. 106	1,800	2,000	—	3,800
Factory overhead	—	1,000	1,600	2,600
Totals	$4,400	$5,500	$8,550	$18,450

3 Factory labor incurred:

Job No. 103	$ 800
Job No. 104	3,200
Job No. 105	4,400
Job No. 106	2,000
Factory overhead	2,100
Total	$12,500

4 Factory overhead, other than indirect labor and materials, incurred:

Accrued expenses	$ 500
Expiration of prepaid expenses	400
Depreciation of plant and equipment	1,000
Total	$1,900

5 Factory overhead applied to production at the rate of 60 percent of direct labor cost. See item (3) above.

Job No. 103	$ 480
Job No. 104	1,920
Job No. 105	2,640
Job No. 106	1,200
Total	$6,240

6 Jobs completed and transferred to the Finished Goods Inventory account:

Job No. 103	$ 5,390
Job No. 104	10,120
Job No. 105	13,840
Total	$29,350

7 Jobs No. 103 and 104 were sold on account at 25 percent above cost:

Job No. 103: $ 5,390 × 1.25	$ 6,737.50
Job No. 104: $10,120 × 1.25	12,650.00
Total	$19,387.50

The manufacturing operations for the month would be recorded as shown. (Journal entries are made in general journal form, and postings are shown only for the Work in Process account and the appropriate cost sheets.)

(1)

Raw Materials Inventory	20,000	
Accounts Payable (Vouchers Payable)		20,000
To record the purchase of raw materials.		

(2)

Work in Process	15,850	
Factory Overhead	2,600	
Raw Materials Inventory		18,450
To record raw materials used in production.		

(3)

Work in Process	10,400	
Factory Overhead	2,100	
Accrued Payroll Payable		12,500
To record labor incurred in production.		

(4)

Factory Overhead	1,900	
Accrued Expenses		500
Prepaid Expenses		400
Accumulated Depreciation—Plant and Equipment		1,000
To record factory overhead, other than indirect labor and materials, incurred.		

(5)

Work in Process	6,240	
Factory Overhead		6,240
To record the application of overhead to production.		

(6)

Finished Goods Inventory	29,350	
Work in Process		29,350

To transfer the cost of finished jobs from the Work in Process account to the Finished Goods Inventory account.

(7)

Accounts Receivable	19,387.50	
Sales		19,387.50

To record the sale of Jobs No. 103 and 104.

Cost of Goods Sold	15,510	
Finished Goods Inventory		15,510

To transfer the cost of Jobs No. 103 and 104 from the Finished Goods Inventory account to the Cost of Goods Sold account.

General Ledger

Work in Process

Beginning balance (Job No. 103)	3,860	Jobs No. 103, 104, 105	29,350
Direct materials	15,850		
Direct labor	10,400		
Factory overhead	6,240	Balance (Job No. 106)	7,000
	36,350		36,350
Balance (Job No. 106)	7,000		

**Cost Ledger
(Cost Sheet Summaries)**

Job No. 103

Beginning balance	3,860
Direct materials	250
Direct labor	800
Factory overhead	480
Total cost	5,390

(Finished)

Job No. 104

Direct materials	5,000
Direct labor	3,200
Factory overhead	1,920
Total cost	10,120

(Finished)

Job No. 105

Direct materials	6,800
Direct labor	4,400
Factory overhead	2,640
Total cost	13,840

(Finished)

Job No. 106

Direct materials	3,800
Direct labor	2,000
Factory overhead	1,200
Cost to date	7,000

(Unfinished)

The relationship between the data in the Work in Process account and the job cost sheets may be summarized as follows:

Work in Process		*Job Cost Sheets*	
Beginning balance	$ 3,860 ⟶	Job No. 103	$ 3,860
		Job No. 103	250
Direct materials	15,850	Job No. 104	5,000
		Job No. 105	6,800
		Job No. 106	3,800
		Job No. 103	800
Direct labor	10,400	Job No. 104	3,200
		Job No. 105	4,400
		Job No. 106	2,000
		Job No. 103	480
Factory overhead	6,240	Job No. 104	1,920
		Job No. 105	2,640
		Job No. 106	1,200
Total cost	$36,350		$36,350
		Job No. 103	(5,390)
Cost of jobs finished	(29,350)	Job No. 104	(10,120)
		Job No. 105	(13,840)
Balance (cost of jobs unfinished)	$ 7,000 ⟶	Job No. 106	$ 7,000

To round out our illustration of the job cost system, the Raw Materials and Finished Goods Inventory accounts along with their supporting records are presented in abbreviated form as follows:

General Ledger

Raw Materials Inventory

1st purchase*	13,000	Req. 1st month	5,900
2nd purchase	20,000	Req. 2nd month	18,450
Balance	8,650		

Stores Ledger

Material A

1st purchase	1,500	Req. 1st month	900
2nd purchase	5,000	Req. 2nd month	4,400
Balance	1,200		

Material B

1st purchase	4,000	Req. 1st month	2,000
2nd purchase	6,000	Req. 2nd month	5,500
Balance	2,500		

Material C

1st purchase	7,500	Req. 1st month	3,000
2nd purchase	9,000	Req. 2nd month	8,550
Balance	4,950		

*See pages 633 and 634 for detail.

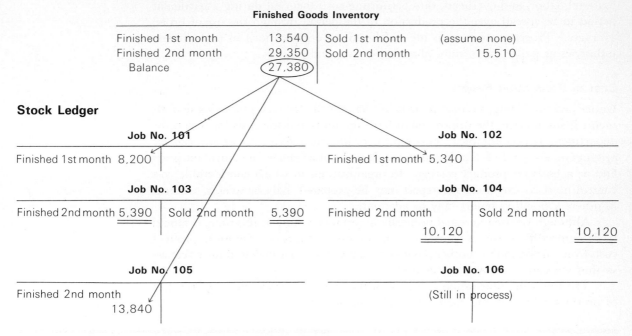

General Ledger

Finished Goods Inventory

Finished 1st month	13,540	Sold 1st month	(assume none)
Finished 2nd month	29,350	Sold 2nd month	15,510
Balance	(27,380)		

Stock Ledger

Job No. 101

Finished 1st month 8,200

Job No. 102

Finished 1st month 5,340

Job No. 103

| Finished 2nd month 5,390 | Sold 2nd month | 5,390 |

Job No. 104

| Finished 2nd month | Sold 2nd month |
| 10,120 | 10,120 |

Job No. 105

Finished 2nd month
13,840

Job No. 106

(Still in process)

Unit Costs and Job Costing

You perhaps noted on the job cost sheet illustrated on page 649 that a section was included for the computation of a cost per unit. To compute unit costs under a job order cost system, we simply divide the total cost of the lot by the number of units in the lot. For example, if we assume that Job No. 101 is composed of 1,000 units, the unit cost would be $8.20 ($8,200 ÷ 1,000). Likewise, if we assume that Job No. 105 consists of two units, the unit cost would be $6,920 ($13,840 ÷ 2). Unit cost computations are relatively simple under a job order cost system; however, this is not always true under a process cost system, as we shall see in the next section of this chapter.

PROCESS COST SYSTEMS

A process cost system is one in which both manufacturing costs and quantities of production are accumulated and reduced to a cost per unit of production; from this cost the cost of any quantity of production can be determined. Unlike a job order cost system in which costs are accumulated by the specific job, a process cost system accumulates costs by **processes** or **departments.**

The process cost system is particularly useful for product costing in mass-production operations where the product is more or less standardized and production more or less continuous. Process costing is feasible in operations of this nature because each unit of finished product requires essentially the same amount of material, labor, and overhead, thus permitting costs incurred during a particular period to be spread over the production of the period through the use of broad averages. Process cost systems are employed by organizations in such diverse industries as paper, petroleum, pharmaceuticals, and plastics.

Cost of Production Report

Under process costing, a report is prepared periodically for each processing department; it summarizes the disposition of both the units and the costs for which the department is accountable. This report, ordinarily referred to as the **cost of production report**, fulfills a dual purpose: It serves as a vehicle for control purposes and as a basis for product costing. In organizations in which considerable cost control must be exercised, the report may be prepared daily or weekly, whereas in others a monthly report may be adequate.

Although we are interested primarily in product costing at this time, it should be recognized that from a control standpoint any significant variation in product costs from one period to another should be analyzed in order to determine its causes so that corrective action may be taken.

The following illustration is typical of the form and arrangement of the cost of production report and the data usually included:

DEPARTMENT B
Cost of Production Report
For the Month Ended June 30, 19___

Part A

Units to be accounted for:

Units in process at beginning of period	1,200
Units started (or transferred in) during period	2,800
Total units to be accounted for	4,000

Disposition of units:

Units completed	3,000
Units in process at end of period	1,000
Total units accounted for	4,000

Costs to be accounted for:

Costs in process at beginning of period	$ 5,200
Costs transferred in from previous process or department (2,800 units @ $2 per unit)	5,600
Costs added during period:	
Material (2,800 units @ $1 per unit)	2,800
Labor (3,000 units @ $2 per unit)	6,000
Overhead (3,000 units @ $3 per unit)	9,000
Total cost to be accounted for	$28,600

Disposition of costs:

Transferred out (to finished goods or next process or department)		$24,100*
Work in process at end of period:		
Cost from previous process or department (1,000 units @ $2 per unit)	$2,000	
Material added this period (1,000 units @ $1 per unit)	1,000	
Labor added this period (1,000 units × 30% × $2)	600	
Overhead added this period (1,000 units × 30% × $3)	900	4,500
Total cost accounted for		$28,600

*See notes and computations.

Part B

Notes:

Material is added at the beginning of processing in Department B.

Work in process at the beginning of the period: approximately 25% complete.

Work in process at the end of the period: approximately 30% complete.

Equivalent units of production:	
Work done on beginning inventory (1,200 units × 75%)	900
Work done on units started and finished (2,800 units − 1,000 units)	1,800
Work done on ending inventory (1,000 units × 30%)	300
Equivalent units of production	3,000

Cost added per unit in department or process:	
Material ($2,800 ÷ 2,800 units)	$1.00
Labor ($6,000 ÷ 3,000 units)	2.00
Overhead ($9,000 ÷ 3,000 units)	3.00
Total cost added per unit	$6.00

Cost of units transferred out of department or process:	
Units in process at beginning of period:	
Costs in process at beginning of period	$ 5,200
Costs added this period:	
Material (none added)	—
Labor (1,200 × ¾ × $2)	1,800
Overhead (1,200 × ¾ × $3)	2,700
Units started and finished:	
Costs transferred in (1,800 × $2)	3,600
Costs added this period:	
Material (1,800 × $1)	1,800
Labor (1,800 × $2)	3,600
Overhead (1,800 × $3)	5,400
Cost of 3,000 units transferred out	$24,100

As you examined the production report, you perhaps noted that it encompasses five rather distinct phases of activity. The study of process costing can best be approached by examining these phases in their logical sequence. As evidenced in the report, process costing requires that we:

1 Determine the physical flow of production.

2 Express production in terms of equivalent units.

3 Determine total costs to be accounted for.

4 Determine unit costs of production.

5 Account for both total costs and units.

Physical Flow of Production

To understand process costing fully, we must first be able to visualize the physical flow of production through a factory. Physical flow may be expressed in terms of both units and costs; hence, we should be aware of where the units come from and where they go as they progress through the manufacturing operations and also where the costs come from and where they go as they flow through the accounts.

Use of Flow Charts The physical flow of production is frequently clarified by the use of flow charts depicting the various processes and departments through which the units flow as well as the accounts through which the costs flow. The chart that follows illustrates a situation in which units are processed through two departments, incurring costs for material, labor, and overhead in both.

Flow Chart

Work in Process Account Whereas flow charts present an overall view of the physical flow of production, the flow of costs can even more readily be followed by examining the individual accounts, particularly the Work in Process account. The Work in Process account for the month of June, 19___, constructed from our illustration of the cost of production report on pages 656 and 657 would appear in T-account form as follows:

Work in Process—Department B

Beginning balance (1,200 units)	5,200	Transferred out (3,000 units)	24,100
Transferred in (2,800 units)	5,600	Ending balance (1,000 units)	4,500
Material added	2,800		
Labor added	6,000		
Overhead added	9,000		
	28,600		28,600
Beginning balance (1,000 units)	4,500		

The relationship between the cost data in the Work in Process account and the cost of production report in our illustration may be summarized as follows:

Work in Process Department B		Cost of Production Report	
Beginning balance	$ 5,200 ——————→ Transferred out_		$ 5,200*
Transferred in	5,600 ⟨ ——————→ Transferred out_		3,600*
	→ Still in process_		2,000
Material added	2,800 ⟨ ——————→ Transferred out_		1,800*
	→ Still in process_		1,000
Labor added	6,000 ⟨ ——————→ Transferred out_		5,400*
	→ Still in process_		600
Overhead added	9,000 ⟨ ——————→ Transferred out_		8,100*
	→ Still in process_		900
Total cost	$28,600		$28,600
Transferred out	(24,100)*		(24,100)*
Balance (still in process)	$ 4,500		$ 4,500

*$5,200 + $3,600 + $1,800 + $5,400 + $8,100 = $24,100

Equivalent Units of Production (EUP)

In order to allocate properly the costs incurred in a department or process during a period between the units completed during the period and those still unfinished at the end of the period, we must express the production in terms of whole units. To do this, we must reduce the number of units in process as of the beginning and end of the period to the equivalent of completed units and add the result to the number of units that were completely processed (started and finished) during the period.

When there are no unfinished units in process at either the beginning or end of a period, the equivalent units of production are, of course, simply the number of units completed. However, when a department or process has either (1) a beginning inventory of work in process, (2) an ending inventory of work in process, or (3) both beginning and ending inventories of work in process, the degree of completion must be estimated in order to reduce the number of partially completed units to the equivalent of completed units. For example, 200 units in an ending inventory estimated to be 50 percent complete would be the equivalent of 100 completed units; 400 units in an ending inventory estimated to be 25 percent complete would be the equivalent of 100 completed units. Thus, if 1,000 units were put into production during the month, with 600 being completed and the remaining 400 estimated to be 25 percent complete, the equivalent units of production for the month would be 700 units $[600 + \frac{1}{4}(400)]$. The following data and computations illustrate the procedure for computing equivalent units:

CASE 1 No beginning or ending inventory of work in process; 4,000 units were started and finished.

CASE 2 No beginning inventory of work in process, but 1,000 units were estimated to be 40 percent complete as of the end of the period; 4,000 units were started.

CASE 3 No ending inventory of work in process, but 1,200 units were estimated to have been 30 percent complete as of the beginning of the period; 4,000 units were started.

CASE 4 A beginning inventory of work in process of 1,000 units was estimated to have been 40 percent complete as of the beginning of the period, and an ending inventory of 1,200 units was estimated to be 20 percent complete as of the end of the period; 4,000 units were started.

Equivalent Units of Production

	Case 1	Case 2	Case 3	Case 4
Units in beginning inventory of work in process___	—	—	840[3]	600[4]
Units started and finished_____	4,000	3,000[1]	4,000	2,800[5]
Units in ending inventory of work in process_____	—	400[2]	—	240[6]
Equivalent units of production _____	4,000	3,400	4,840	3,640

[1] 4,000 − 1,000 = 3,000   [4] 1,000 × 60% = 600
[2] 1,000 × 40% = 400   [5] 4,000 − 1,200 = 2,800
[3] 1,200 × 70% = 840   [6] 1,200 × 20% = 240

When we say that the units in process at the beginning or end of a period are estimated to be completed to a certain degree, it should be recognized that this is merely an estimated average stage of completion and does not necessarily mean that each unit in process is completed to precisely that degree. Typically, units in process at inventory time will be "strung out" throughout the department with some nearing completion and others just beginning to be processed. In addition, as is the case in our cost of production report, units in process at inventory time may have received all their material, thereby incurring all their material costs. However, since the materials are only partially converted into finished products, only part of their conversion costs (labor and overhead) have been applied. When computing EUPs in such cases, we may have one EUP for material and another for conversion costs. For example, in our illustration the EUP for material is 2,800 units (the number of units started), whereas the EUP for labor and overhead is 3,000 units.

In addition to the possibility of having different EUPs for material and conversion costs in a given department or process, it is not unusual to have more than one EUP for material. For example, the production process may require that one type of material be added at the beginning of the process, another type added uniformly throughout the process, and yet another type added at the end of the process. To illustrate, let us assume the basic data used in our cost of production report on pages 656 and 657, that is, 1,200 units approximately 25 percent complete in the beginning inventory of work in process, 2,800 units started during the period with 1,800 of them being completed during the period, and the remaining 1,000 approximately 30 percent complete at the end of the period. In addition, for illustrative purposes let us assume that three different materials are used: Material A is added at the beginning of the process, Material B is added uniformly throughout the process, and Material C is added at the end of the process. The EUPs for material would be determined as follows:

Equivalent Units of Production

	Material A	Material B	Material C
Beginning inventory of work in process	—	900	1,200
Units started and finished	1,800	1,800	1,800
Ending inventory of work in process	1,000	300	—
Equivalent units of production	2,800	3,000	3,000

Unit Costs of Production

Under process costing, the production costs of a period are spread over the production of the period through the use of broad averages, resulting in an average cost per unit. If all units worked on during a period are completely processed during the same period, the determination of a unit cost is merely a matter of dividing total costs by the number of units processed. If, however, all units worked on are not completely processed during a given period, the various cost elements must be divided by their equivalent units of production; the resulting unit costs per element then must be summed in order that we may arrive at a total unit cost.

(If production flows through more than one department or process, unit costs are ordinarily broken down, again by the use of averages, by department or process.)

In our cost of production report, the $1 unit cost for material was determined by dividing the total cost of material used ($2,800) by the EUP for material (2,800 units). Likewise, the $2 unit cost for labor was computed by dividing $6,000 (the total cost of labor) by 3,000 units (the EUP for labor); the $3 unit cost for overhead was determined by dividing $9,000 (total overhead incurred)[1] by 3,000 units (the EUP for overhead). In summarized form, the computations are:

Unit Costs of Production—Department B

	Total Costs		EUPs		Unit Costs
Material	$2,800	÷	2,800	=	$1.00
Labor	6,000	÷	3,000	=	2.00
Overhead	9,000	÷	3,000	=	3.00

When units are transferred out of a department or process, the average unit cost is determined simply by dividing the total costs associated with the units by the number of units involved. For example, in our cost of production report for June (see pages 656 and 657) a unit cost of $8.03\frac{1}{3}$ would be determined by dividing $24,100 by 3,000 units.

Process Cost System Illustrated

To illustrate the process cost system more fully, let us continue our illustration for the month of July. In addition to studying the operations of Department B for the month, we shall also study Department A. For Department B we shall use the basic data from our previous illustration; you will recall that one unit of material—let us call it Material Z—is added at the beginning of the process for each unit of production, and 1,000 units approximately 30 percent complete with an accumulated cost of $4,500 were in process as of the end of June.

In regard to Department A, let us assume that one unit of Material X is added at the beginning of the process for each unit of production; one unit of Material Y is added at the end of the process for each completed unit; and as of the end of June, 800 units approximately 60 percent complete with an accumulated cost of $1,200 were still in process.

In summary form, the transactions related to the manufacturing operations of Departments A and B for the month of July were:

---

[1] In process costing, overhead may be applied to production as it is incurred or by the use of a predetermined rate, as is ordinarily done in job order costing. In organizations where the physical flow of production is not only continuous but also relatively stable from period to period, the application of the actual overhead incurred is usually satisfactory, since the regularity of production tends to normalize the amount of overhead applied to production from one period to another. However, in organizations where the physical flow of production is not constant from period to period, it is generally preferable that overhead be applied to production by the use of a predetermined rate.

1 Raw materials purchased:

	Number of Units	Unit Cost	Total Cost
Material X	5,000	$ .90	$ 4,500
Material Y	5,000	.10	500
Material Z	5,000	1.00	5,000
			$10,000

2 Direct materials requisitioned and used:

	Number of Units	Unit Cost	Total Cost
Material X	4,000	$ .90	$ 3,600
Material Y	3,000	.10	300
Material Z	3,000	1.00	3,000
			$ 6,900

3 Direct factory labor incurred:

Department A	$ 1,512
Department B	5,945
Total	$ 7,457

4 Factory overhead incurred:

Department A	$ 2,268
Department B	8,410
Total	$10,678

5 Units completed and transferred:

Department A	3,000
Department B	3,000

Units still in process as of July 31:

	Number of Units	Percentage of Completion
Department A	1,800	70
Department B	1,000	20

6 The 3,000 units produced in June and 2,000 units from the July production were sold on open account at $12 per unit. Sales are costed out of the Finished Goods Inventory account on the FIFO basis.

With the journal entries in general journal form and postings shown in T accounts, the manufacturing operations for July would be recorded and posted as follows:

(1)

Raw Materials Inventory	10,000	
Accounts Payable (Vouchers Payable)		10,000

To record the purchase of raw materials.

(2)

Work in Process—Department A	3,900	
Work in Process—Department B	3,000	
Raw Materials Inventory		6,900

To record direct materials used in production.

(3)

Work In Process—Department A	1,512	
Work in Process—Department B	5,945	
Accrued Payroll Payable		7,457

To record direct labor incurred in production.

(4)

Work in Process—Department A	2,268	
Work in Process—Department B	8,410	
Factory Overhead		10,678

To record the application of overhead to production.

(5)

Work in Process—Department B	6,000	
Work in Process—Department A		6,000

To transfer production costs from Department A to Department B. (See the July cost of production report for Department A on pages 666 and 667.)

Finished Goods Inventory	23,865	
Work in Process— Department B		23,865

To transfer production costs from Department B to the Finished Goods Inventory account. (See the July cost of production report for Department B on pages 667 and 668.)

(6)

Accounts Receivable	60,000	
Sales		60,000

To record the sale of 5,000 units at $12 per unit.

Cost of Goods Sold	40,015	
Finished Goods Inventory		40,015

To record the cost of sales.

Composition of Cost of Sales

June production: 3,000 units	_____	$24,100
July production: 1,000 units	_____	7,965*
	1,000 units _____	7,950†
		$40,015

*Units in process at beginning of period. (See the July cost of production report for Department B.)
† From current production. (See the July cost of production report for Department B.)

General Ledger

Work in Process—Department A

Beginning balance	1,200	Transferred to Dept. B		6,000
Material added	3,900	Ending balance		2,880
Labor added	1,512			
Overhead added	2,268			
	8,880			8,880
Beginning balance	2,880			

Work in Process—Department B

Beginning balance	4,500	Transferred to Finished Goods		23,865
Transferred in	6,000	Ending balance		3,990
Material added	3,000			
Labor added	5,945			
Overhead added	8,410			
	27,855			27,855
Beginning balance	3,990			

Finished Goods Inventory

Beginning balance	24,100	Cost of sales	40,015
Transferred in	23,865		

Cost of Goods Sold

40,015	

The cost of production reports for the month of July for both Department A and Department B are shown on pages 666 to 668.

Costing By-products and Joint Products

When more than one kind of product is obtained from a single manufacturing process, the problem arises of how to allocate the costs of manufacturing to the

DEPARTMENT A
Cost of Production Report
For the Month Ended July 31, 19__

Part A

Units to be accounted for:
Units in process at beginning of period	800
Units started (or transferred in) during period	4,000
Total units to be accounted for	4,800

Disposition of units:
Units completed	3,000
Units in process at end of period	1,800
Total units accounted for	4,800

Costs to be accounted for:
Costs in process at beginning of period	$1,200
Costs added during period:	
Material X (4,000 units @ $.90 per unit)	3,600
Material Y (3,000 units @ $.10 per unit)	300
Labor (3,780 units @ $.40 per unit)	1,512
Overhead (3,780 units @ $.60 per unit)	2,268
Total cost to be accounted for	$8,880

Disposition of costs:
Transferred to Department B		$6,000*
Work in process at end of period:		
Cost from previous process or department	—	
Material added this period (1,800 units of material X @ $.90 per unit)	$1,620	
Labor added this period (1,800 units × 70% × $.40)	504	
Overhead added this period (1,800 units × 70% × $.60)	756	2,880
Total cost accounted for		$8,880

*See notes and computations.

Part B

Notes:
   Material X is added at the beginning of processing.
   Material Y is added at the end of processing.
   Work in process at the beginning of the period: approximately 60% complete.
   Work in process at the end of the period: approximately 70% complete.

Equivalent units of production:
Work done on beginning inventory (800 units × 40%)	320
Work done on units started and finished (4,000 units − 1,800 units)	2,200
Work done on ending inventory (1,800 × 70%)	1,260
Equivalent units of production	3,780

Cost added per unit in department:
Material X ($3,600 ÷ 4,000 units) .... $ .90
Material Y ($300 ÷ 3,000 units) .... .10
Labor ($1,512 ÷ 3,780 units) .... .40
Overhead ($2,268 ÷ 3,780 units) .... .60
    Total cost added per unit $2.00

Cost of units transferred to Department B:
Units in process at beginning of period:
  Costs in process at beginning of period $1,200
  Costs added this period:
    Material X (none added) .... —
    Material Y (800 × $.10) 80
    Labor (800 × 40% × $.40) 128
    Overhead (800 × 40% × $.60) 192
Units started and finished:
  Costs transferred in .... —
  Costs added this period:
    Material X (2,200 × $.90) 1,980
    Material Y (2,200 × $.10) 220
    Labor (2,200 × $.40) 880
    Overhead (2,200 × $.60) 1,320
Cost of 3,000 units transferred to Department B $6,000

DEPARTMENT B

Cost of Production Report

For the Month Ended July 31, 19___

Part A

Units to be accounted for:
Units in process at beginning of period 1,000
Units started (or transferred in) during period 3,000
    Total units to be accounted for 4,000

Disposition of units:
Units completed 3,000
Units in process at end of period 1,000
    Total units accounted for 4,000

Costs to be accounted for:
Costs in process at beginning of period .... $ 4,500
Costs transferred in from Department A (3,000 units @ $2 per unit) 6,000
Costs added during period:
  Material Z (3,000 units @ $1) 3,000
  Labor (2,900 units @ $2.05) 5,945
  Overhead (2,900 units @ $2.90) 8,410
    Total cost to be accounted for $27,855

Disposition of costs:

Transferred to finished goods inventory —————————————————— $23,865*

Work in process at end of period:

Cost from previous department (1,000 units @ $2 per unit) ————— $2,000

Material added this period (1,000 units @ $1 per unit) ————— 1,000

Labor added this period (1,000 units × 20% × $2.05) ————— 410

Overhead added this period (1,000 units × 20% × $2.90)————— 580　　3,990

Total cost accounted for ———————————————————— $27,855

*See notes and computations.

Part B

Notes:

Material Z is added at the beginning of processing.

Work in process at the beginning of the period: approximately 30% complete.

Work in process at the end of the period: approximately 20% complete.

Equivalent units of production:

Work done on beginning inventory (1,000 units × 70%)————————— 700

Work done on units started and finished (3,000 units − 1,000 units) ——— 2,000

Work done on ending inventory (1,000 units × 20%)————————— 200

Equivalent units of production ———————————————— 2,900

Cost added per unit in department:

Material Z ($3,000 ÷ 3,000 units)————————————————— $1.00

Labor ($5,945 ÷ 2,900 units) ————————————————— 2.05

Overhead ($8,410 ÷ 2,900 units) ————————————————— 2.90

Total cost added per unit ———————————————— $5.95

Cost of units transferred to finished goods:

Units in process at beginning of period:

Costs in process at beginning of period————————————— $4,500

Costs added this period:

Material Z (none) ————————————————————— —

Labor (1,000 × 70% × $2.05) ———————————————— 1,435

Overhead (1,000 × 70% × $2.90) ————————————— 2,030　$ 7,965

Units started and finished:

Costs transferred in (2,000 × $2) ———————————————— 4,000

Costs added this period:

Material Z (2,000 × $1)—————————————————— 2,000

Labor (2,000 × $2.05) ——————————————————— 4,100

Overhead (2,000 × $2.90)—————————————————— 5,800

Cost of 3,000 units transferred out ————————————————— $23,865 various products. For accounting purposes such products are classified either as by-products or joint products.

The distinction between the two is a relative matter, frequently more practical than theoretical. Generally, **by-products** are minor products having comparatively small value which are produced simultaneously with major products of greater value. Examples are buttermilk, a by-product in the production of butter, and coal tar, a by-product in the conversion of coal into coke. **Joint products,** on the other hand, are products of comparable value which are produced simultaneously from the same raw material. Gasoline, fuel oil, and lubricants in the petroleum industry and ham, pork loins, and bacon in the meat-packing industry are examples of joint products.

The basic difference in accounting for the costs of by-products and joint products relates to the costs incurred prior to their separation from the main product or other joint products. This point is commonly called the **split-off point,** or the **point of separation.** In the case of joint products, all costs incurred prior to the point of separation must be allocated to the separate products. Such costs ordinarily are not allocated to by-products, but instead are treated in their entirety as costs of the main product.

Accounting for By-products There are several methods of accounting for by-products. Theoretically, one of the better ways would be to determine the net realizable value (sales value less estimated cost of disposal) of the by-product and then deduct it from the cost of producing the main product. From a practical standpoint, however, based on expediency and materiality, the revenue received from the sale of a by-product is usually handled either as miscellaneous income or as a reduction of the cost of the main product. If we assume by-product sales of $100, the following entries are illustrative of the practical approach:

(1)

| Cash | 100 | |
| Miscellaneous Income | | 100 |

To record by-product sales (revenue from by-products considered as miscellaneous income).

(2)

| Cash | 100 | |
| Work in Process | | 100 |

To record by-product sales (revenue from by-products considered as cost reduction).

Accounting for Joint Products When accounting for joint products, we must allocate common costs to the individual products. The two principal bases for allocating such costs are (1) quantities produced and (2) relative market (selling market) values.

The quantities produced method requires the use of a common unit of measurement, such as pounds, gallons, or tons, for all products. The relative market value method is based on the premise that common costs should be allocated to joint products in proportion to the revenue earned by each product. When joint products incur additional costs of processing beyond the point of separation, such costs are deducted from the gross revenue of each product in order that net market values at the point of separation may be obtained.

The relative market value method is applicable for practically all types of joint products, whereas the quantities produced method is acceptable only when its results are substantially the same as those which would be obtained if the relative market value method were used. To illustrate both methods, let us assume that 10,000 units of Product A and 20,000 units of Product B were produced jointly at a total cost of $90,000. In addition, let us assume that Product A had a sales value of $2 per unit and Product B a sales value of $5 per unit. As can be observed in the following computations, the $90,000 cost is assigned to Products A and B in different amounts, depending upon the method used.

Quantities Produced Method

Products	Units Produced	Computations	Costs Assigned
A	10,000	10,000/30,000 × $90,000 =	$30,000
B	20,000	20,000/30,000 × $90,000 =	60,000
	30,000		$90,000

Market Value Method

Products	Market Values	Computations	Costs Assigned
A	$ 20,000*	20,000/120,000 × $90,000 =	$15,000
B	100,000†	100,000/120,000 × $90,000 =	75,000
	$120,000		$90,000

*10,000 units @ $2 per unit.
†20,000 units @ $5 per unit.

SUMMARY

Although numerous variations and combinations of cost systems exist in accounting practice, there are essentially only two major ones: the job order cost system and the process cost system. Under the job order system, costs are accumulated for each separate lot, or job, manufactured. Thus, it is a prerequisite of this system that the separate lots of production be readily identifiable.

Under the process cost system both manufacturing costs and quantities of production are accumulated by process or department rather than by the specific job.

QUESTIONS AND PROBLEMS

24-1 Accountants ordinarily use the idea of "equivalent units of production" when computing unit costs in organizations utilizing process cost systems.

(1) Define equivalent production.

(2) Explain why it is used in the computation of unit costs.

(3) Determine the equivalent units of production for Department B, assuming that it had 1,000 units estimated to be 40 percent complete in its beginning inventory of work in process, received 5,000 units from Department A during the period, and had 2,000 units estimated to be 80 percent complete in its ending inventory of work in process.

24-2 Using the following data, which pertain to a month in which both of the departments involved turned out 8,000 units of finished product, compare the equivalent production of Department B with that of Department A.

| | Beginning Inventory | | Ending Inventory | |
	Units	% complete	Units	% complete
Department A	1,000	80	600	90
Department B	600	90	1,000	80

24-3 What is the basic difference between a **by-product** and a **joint product?**

24-4 By-products are often accounted for by assigning to them a value of zero at the point of separation and crediting cost of production with the revenue derived from their sale. (1) Justify this treatment, and (2) discuss its possible shortcomings.

24-5 **Instructions** Prepare a flow chart for the Beta Company, which manufactures two principal products known commercially as AOK and BOK. Incidental to the production of these products is the production of a by-product known commercially as BYPO. The company has three producing departments which it identifies as Departments 101, 201, and 301. Raw materials A and B are put into production in Department 101. Raw materials C and D are added at the end of processing in Departments 201 and 301, respectively. Labor and overhead are incurred in each department. Upon completion of processing in Department 101, one-fifth of the output is transferred directly to BYPO inventory, one-third of the remaining output is transferred to department 201 where it is converted into AOK, and the other two-thirds goes to Department 301 where it becomes BOK.

24-6 The Gamma Manufacturing Company uses a job order cost system. The following data pertain to the month of June, the company's first operating month:

1 Raw materials used on:

Job No. 101	$2,200
Job No. 102	1,900
Job No. 103	1,700
Job No. 104	1,600
	$7,400

2 Direct labor incurred on:

Job No. 101	$ 4,500
Job No. 102	2,000
Job No. 103	2,100
Job No. 104	1,900
	$10,500

3 Factory overhead is applied to production at the rate of 125 percent of direct labor costs.

Instructions Assuming that factory overhead amounted to $13,300 during the month and that Jobs No. 101 and 102 were completed during the month and billed to customers at a markup of 20 percent on cost:

(1) Journalize the June operations.

(2) Determine the balance in the Work in Process account as of June 30.

(3) Determine the amount of over- or underapplied factory overhead for the month.

*24-7 The H Manufacturing Company is engaged in manufacturing items to fill specific orders received from its customers. While at any given time it may have substantial inventories of work in process and finished goods, all such amounts are assignable to firm sales orders which it has received.

The company's operations, including the administrative and sales

*AICPA adapted.

functions, are completely departmentalized. Its cost system is on a job order basis. Direct materials and direct labor are identified with jobs by the use of material issue tickets and daily time cards. Overhead costs are accumulated for each factory service, administrative, and selling department. These overhead costs, including administrative and selling expenses, are then allocated to producing departments, and an overhead rate is computed for each producing department. This rate is used to apply overhead to jobs on the basis of direct labor hours. The result is that all costs and expenses incurred during any month are charged to work in process accounts for the jobs.

Instructions

(1) Compare the H Company's cost system, as it affects inventory valuation, with the usual job cost system.

(2) Criticize the system as it affects inventory valuation and income determination.

(3) State any justification which you see for the use of H Company's system.

24-8 Instructions The production of Product X requires the use of one unit each of Material A, Material B, and Material C. Determine the equivalent units of production for each type of material in each of the following cases, assuming that (1) Material A is added at the beginning of the process, (2) Material B is added uniformly throughout the process, and (3) Material C is added at the end of the process.

	Case 1	Case 2	Case 3	Case 4
Units in beginning inventory of work in process	1,000	1,000	2,000	1,000
Units started	10,000	10,000	9,000	9,000
Units in ending inventory of work in process	2,000	2,000	1,000	2,000
Stage of completion: Beginning inventory of work in process	50%	25%	70%	40%
Ending inventory of work in process	50%	25%	30%	60%

24-9 Instructions From the following data, which pertain to the conversion costs associated with Product A in Process Z, determine (1) the number of units started during the period and (2) the equivalent units of production for the period, assuming that the conversion costs were incurred uniformly throughout the process.

	Case 1	Case 2	Case 3	Case 4
Units in beginning inventory of work in process	3,000	5,000	4,000	3,000
Units completed	14,000	14,000	10,000	—
Units in ending inventory of work in process	5,000	3,000	6,000	8,000
Stage of completion:				
Beginning inventory of work in process	30%	80%	10%	20%
Ending inventory of work in process	60%	20%	30%	90%

24-10 Instructions Given the following information, and assuming that the company values its inventories on the FIFO basis, determine the total amount of cost to be assigned to the units completed during the period.

1 All materials are put into production at the beginning of the process.

2 Inventory of work in process at the beginning of the period: 2,000 units estimated to be 50 percent complete and with an assigned value of $22,000.

3 Material cost per unit for the period: $10.00.

4 Conversion cost per unit for the period: $4.50.

5 Units finished during the period: 10,000.

24-11 Instructions Assuming that Company R produces a product known as MOP in a process known as Process R, and that each completed unit of MOP contains one unit of Material M, one of Material O, and one of Material P, fill in the correct amounts on the credit side of the following T account:

Process R

Beginning inventory	—	Ending inventory (500 units) 40%	
1,000 units of M	5,000	finished, (100 units past 75%	
1,000 units of O	4,000	stage)	??
1,000 units of P	3,000	Finished 500 units	??
Conversion cost	14,000	Material M _____ units .	??
		Material O _____ units	??
		Material P _____ units	??

Material M—Put in at beginning of process.
Material O—Added uniformly during process.
Material P—Added at 75% stage on the basis of one unit for each unit of M.

24-12 Instructions From the following data, which pertain to the operations of Process A for the month of June, determine the:

(1) Unit cost for material

(2) Unit cost for labor

(3) Unit cost for overhead

(4) Value to be assigned to the units remaining in the process at June 30

(5) Value to be assigned to the units transferred out of the process during June

Statement of Costs and Production

Beginning inventory	$ 1,728.00
Direct material	7,560.00
Direct labor	5,676.00
Factory overhead	1,980.00
Total	$16,944.00

Units completed from beginning inventory	4,800
Units completed from current production	8,400
Units uncompleted in ending inventory	3,600
Total	16,800

Material is added at the beginning of the process. The units in process at June 1 were estimated to be approximately 50 percent complete. Those in process at June 30 were estimated to be approximately two-thirds complete.

24-13 The Ace Cycle Company uses a process cost system. Production flows progressively through departments A, B, and C. The following data pertain to the month of June:

Production Costs	Departments A	B	C	Total
Material	$36,150	$ 1,750	$ 3,740	$ 41,640
Labor	4,240	27,140	5,661	37,041
Overhead	7,810	13,210	2,923	23,943
	$48,200	$42,100	$12,324	$102,624

There were no cycles in process as of June 1. During the month production was started on 400 cycles. On June 30 there were 60 unfinished cycles in Department C, estimated to be 50 percent complete as to labor and overhead, all material having been added. There was no unfinished work in either Department A or B at the end of the month.

Instructions

(1) Determine the cost per unit of production in Department A.

(2) Prepare the journal entry necessary to transfer production costs from Department A to Department B.

(3) Determine the cost per unit of production in Department B.

(4) Prepare the journal entry necessary to transfer production costs from Department B to Department C.

(5) Determine the unit cost associated with the units transferred from Department B to Department C.

(6) Determine the cost per unit of production in Department C.

(7) Prepare the journal entry necessary to transfer production costs from Department C to the Finished Goods Inventory account.

(8) Prepare the journal entry or entries necessary when 100 cycles are sold for cash at $400 per cycle.

(9) Determine the value of the work in process in Department C at June 30.

*24-14 The LaBreck Company's common, or joint, cost of producing 1,000 units of Product A, 500 units of Product B, and 500 units of Product C is $100,000. The unit sales values of the three products at the split-off point are Product A, $20; Product B, $200; Product C, $160. Ending inventories include 100 units of Product A, 300 units of Product B, and 200 units of Product C.

Instructions Determine the amount of common cost that would be included in the ending inventory valuation of the three products, assuming that common costs are assigned to joint products (1) on the basis of their relative sales value, and (2) on the basis of physical units produced.

*24-15 During 19X1 the Juno Chemical Co. started a new division whose operation consists of processing a mineral into commercial products A, B, C, and D. Each product passes through identical processing operations. However, Product D is classified as a second or reject and is sold at a lower price. The following information is available regarding the new division's operations for 19X1:

*AICPA adapted.

Sales (including Product D)					$24,480
Production costs					49,769
Selling costs allocated to division					1,224

		Products			
	Total	A	B	C	D
Quantity (tons)					
Beginning inventory	—	—	—	—	—
Production	634	305	137	22	170
Sales	285	132	83	10	60
Ending inventory	349	173	54	12	110
Sales price per ton	—	$100	$100	$100	$33

Instructions   Assuming that the division's selling prices were constant throughout the year, that the company considers Products A, B, C, and D to be joint products, and that the company allocates production costs by using the relative market value method, determine the:

(1) Cost per ton of producing Products A, B, C, and D

(2) Value to be assigned to the ending inventory, assuming that the company values its inventories at the lower of cost or market using the individual item basis

*24-16 The Biltimar Company manufactures gewgaws in three steps or departments. The Finishing Department is the third and last step before the product is transferred to finished goods inventory. All material needed to complete the gewgaws is added at the beginning of the process in the Finishing Department. The company uses the FIFO cost method in its accounting system and has accumulated the following data for July for the Finishing Department:

	Units
Production of gewgaws:	
In process, July 1 (labor and overhead three-fourths complete)	10,000
Transferred from preceding departments during July	40,000
Finished and transferred to finished goods inventory during July	35,000
In process, July 31 (labor and overhead one-half complete)	15,000
Cost of work in process inventory, July 1:	
Costs from preceding departments	$ 38,000
Costs added in Finishing Department prior to July 1:	
Materials	21,500
Labor	39,000
Overhead	42,000
Cost of work in process inventory, July 1	$140,500

*AICPA adapted.

Costs, assigned from preceding departments, of gewgaws transferred to
the Finishing Department during July _____ $140,000

Production costs incurred during July:
Materials_____ $ 80,000
Labor _____ 175,000
Overhead _____ 140,000
Total _____ $395,000

Instructions Determine:

(1) The cost of gewgaws transferred to the finished goods inventory during
July

(2) The cost to be assigned to the work in process inventory at July 31

*24-17 The Incredible Gadget Company manufactures a single product. Its
operations are a continuing process carried on in two departments—the
Machining Department and the Assembly and Finishing Department.
Materials are added to the product in each department.

During the month of May, 75,000 units were put into production in
the Machining Department. Of these units, 60,000 were completed and
transferred to the Assembly and Finishing Department with the other
15,000 being left in process, having picked up all of their materials but
only one-third of their labor and overhead.

Of the units transferred to the Assembly and Finishing Department,
50,000 were completed and transferred to the finished goods stock room
with the other 10,000 being left in process, having picked up 95 percent
of their materials but only 60 percent of their labor and overhead.

Cost records showed the following charges for the month:

	Materials	Labor	Overhead
Machining Department _____	$120,000	$ 87,100	$39,000
Assembly and Finishing Department _____	41,650	100,800	61,600

Instructions Assuming that there was no production in process as of the
beginning of the month in either department, prepare in good form:

(1) A statement showing unit costs for the month of May

(2) A schedule showing the details of the inventory of work in process as
of the end of May

*24-18 The Walsch Company manufactures a single product, a mechanical device
known as Klebo. Material K, a metal, is stamped to form a part which

*AICPA adapted.

is assembled with a purchased part, X. The unit is then machined and cleaned, after which it is assembled with two units of a purchased part Y to form the finished device known as Klebo. Spray priming and enameling is the final operation.

Time studies indicate that, of the total time required for the manufacture of a unit, the first operation requires 25 percent of the labor cost, the first assembly an additional 25 percent, machining and cleaning 12.5 percent, the second assembly 25 percent, and priming and enameling 12.5 percent. Factory overhead is considered to follow the same pattern, as does labor.

The following data are presented to you as of the end of the first month of operation:

Material K purchased—100,000 pounds	$25,000
Part X purchased—80,000 units	16,000
Part Y purchased—150,000 units	15,000
Primer and enamel used	1,072
Direct labor—cost	45,415
Factory overhead	24,905

	Unit Quantity
Units finished and sent to finished goods warehouse	67,000
Units assembled but not primed and enameled	5,000
Units ready for second assembly	3,000

Inventories at the end of the month:	
Finished units	7,500
Material K (pounds)	5,800
Part X (units)	5,000
Part Y (units)	6,000
Klebos in process (units)	8,000

Instructions Assuming that the company has a process cost system in operation, prepare for the first month of operation:

(1) A schedule showing the equivalent units of production for labor

(2) A schedule showing the cost per unit for:
    (a) Each kind of material
    (b) Labor
    (c) Factory overhead

(3) A schedule showing in detail the amounts of material, labor, and overhead costs assigned to the units left in process as of the end of the month

*24-19 The MCB Corporation produces one principal product designated Main-Line.   Incidental to this production two additional products result—Co-Line and By-Line.   Material is started in Process No. 1; the three products come out of this process.   Main-Line is processed further through Process No. 2; Co-Line is processed further through Process No. 3, while By-Line is sold without further processing.   The following data for February are available:

1 Material put in process No. 1, $12,000.

2 Conversion costs: Process No. 1, $8,000; process No. 2, $4,000; process No. 3, $300.

3 There were no beginning or ending in-process inventories.

4 Production and sales data:

	Quantity Produced	Quantity Sold	February Average Sales Price	Market Price at End of February
Main-Line	5,000	4,000	$6.00	$6.00
Co-Line	3,000	2,000	1.00	0.90
By-Line	1,000	900	0.50	0.55

5 Selling and administrative expenses vary proportionally with the quantity sold.   During February they amounted to:

Main-Line	$2,000
Co-Line	800
By-Line	36

6 Standard net profit on Co-Line is 10 percent of sales.

7 No profit or loss is realized on By-Line sales.

Instructions   Assuming that the selling and administrative expenses vary during the next period in the same proportion as they did in February, compute:

(1) The value to be assigned to the By-Line inventory as of the end of February and the costs transferred from Process No. 1 to By-Line units during the month

(2) The value to be assigned to the Co-Line inventory as of the end of February and the costs transferred from Process No. 1 to Co-Line units during the month

*AICPA adapted.

*24-20 The organization for which you work has recently purchased facilities for the production of a new product. The following data, based on studies made by your staff, have been made available to you:

Estimated annual sales		24,000 units

Estimated costs:	*Amount*	*Per Unit*
Direct material	$ 96,000	$4.00
Direct labor	14,400	.60
Factory overhead	24,000	1.00
Administrative expenses	28,800	1.20
Total	$163,200	$6.80

Instructions Assuming that selling expenses are to amount to 15 percent of sales and that a profit of $1.02 per unit is desired:

(1) Determine the selling price per unit.

(2) Prepare a projected income statement for the year.

(3) Compute the break-even point both in (a) dollars, and (b) units, assuming that factory overhead and administrative expenses are fixed and that all other costs are variable.

*AICPA adapted.

25
Budgeting and Standard Costs

Earlier chapters of this text have been devoted primarily to accounting tools and techniques used in planning and controlling business operations in general. In this chapter we shall discuss two accounting tools which are especially useful in the planning and controlling of manufacturing operations: budgets and standard costs.

Simply stated, a **budget** is an estimated plan of operations for the future expressed in financial terms; a **standard cost** is a predetermined cost intended to serve as a yardstick, or standard of performance. In golfing terms, both provide management with "pars" to "shoot at." Although one may be utilized without the other, maximum benefits are ordinarily realized when the two are employed together. This is particularly true if they are interlocked, that is, if the budget is based upon standard costs and standard costs in turn are based upon the budget. Since both budget preparation and the setting of standards require a thorough analysis of the cost functions of an organization, the processes themselves often disclose deficiencies, thus tending to force management to plan efficient and economical operations.

Standard costs and budgets are particularly valuable to management because their use emphasizes variations between preset standards and actual performance. This, of course, is most compatible with the "management by exception principle."[1]

BUDGETING

The idea of budgeting is not new. Budgets have been used at least since the beginning of recorded history. Today they are employed not only by profit-oriented business organizations but also by nonprofit concerns such as churches, school districts, and governmental units, as well as by individuals.

Budgeting generally embraces the entire field of management in a business organization; as a consequence all supervisory and executive personnel are involved, to varying degrees, in the preparation and execution of the organizational budgets. With the aid of all available information, management must determine how the organization can best attain its desired goals, and in so doing it must prepare detailed plans for reaching these goals. The planning phase is known as **budgeting;** the written plans, expressed in financial terms, constitute the **budget.** In large, complex organizations it often becomes necessary to employ a master budget in which all plans are summarized; the details are then "spelled out" in various departmental and specialized budgets, which in turn may be supplemented by supporting schedules.

Budgeting Illustrated

In order that effective budgeting may be accomplished with a minimum of time and effort, it is important that management set standard operating policies and procedures tailored to the particular organization. Clear-cut policies should be established, for example, regarding the:

1 Responsibility for budget preparation and administration

2 Length of the budget period

3 Order in which the different budgets are to be prepared

Each department head is customarily responsible for the preparation and administration of his departmental budget. The responsibility for overall budgeting, however, is commonly centralized in one of the organization's top financial executives such as the controller, the treasurer, or the financial vice-president. His office acts as a control agency for the collection of data and the preparation and administration of all budgets.

---

[1]The management by exception principle, which is more or less fundamental to the study of management, is based upon the assumption that performances which meet a preset standard are satisfactory and that only those which vary from standard require management's attention.

Most organizations utilize a budget period which they have determined to be best suited to their particular needs. This may be a month, quarter, year, or occasionally 13 periods of 4 weeks each, in which the year is merely broken down into 13 equal time periods.

There is no set order in which the various budgets are prepared. In profit-oriented organizations, however, budgeting ordinarily starts with a sales forecast (estimated sales for the budget period), and operating plans for all segments of the organization are then developed. Thus, the usual procedure is to start with the sales budget and plan the other budgets around it. In addition to the sales budget, at this time we shall examine the production budget and the cash budget, two of the more common budgets employed in manufacturing organizations.

Sales Budget Although there are a number of methods of making sales forecasts, most of them are based upon a projected **sales volume** and a projected **sales price,** and these in turn are normally based upon an analysis of:

1 Past sales performances

2 Present and prospective general business conditions

3 Relative status of competitors

To illustrate the preparation of a sales budget, let us assume that Company B manufactures and sells products X, Y, and Z. During 19X1, Company B sold 10,000 units of product X at $25 each, 1,000 units of product Y at $600 each, and 100,000 units of product Z at $1 each. After a careful analysis of past sales performance, present and prospective general business conditions, and the relative status of its competition, Company B decides to raise the price of product X by 20 percent and the price of product Y by 30 percent, and at the same time to lower the price of product Z by 5 percent. According to this new price list, the company expects to sell 10 percent fewer units of product X during 19X2 than during 19X1, 5 percent fewer units of product Y, but twice the number of units of product Z. Based upon these actions and projections, the sales budget for 19X2 would be:

COMPANY B
Sales Budget
For the Year Ending December 31, 19X2

Product	Volume (units)	Sales Price	Total Sales
X	9,000[1]	$ 30.00[4]	$ 270,000
Y	950[2]	780.00[5]	741,000
Z	200,000[3]	.95[6]	190,000
			$1,201,000

[1] 10,000 − (10% × 10,000) [4] $25.00 + (20% × $25.00)
[2] 1,000 − (5% × 1,000)   [5] $600 + (30% × $600)
[3] 2 × 100,000   [6] $1.00 − (5% × $1.00)

Production Budget The major purpose of the production budget, which is predicated upon the sales budget, is to assure the continuous availability of finished goods in an amount sufficient to meet the demands of the sales department and at the same time to maintain the inventory at its proper level. If the amount of finished goods on hand becomes too small, there is a danger of losing sales because the goods are not available; if the amount becomes too large, a financial loss could result from such factors as deterioration, spoilage, obsolescence, and excess storage and handling costs.

To illustrate the preparation of a production budget, let us assume the basic data used in the preceding illustration. In addition, let us assume that the finished goods inventory as of December 31, 19X1, was composed of 2,000 units of product X, 100 units of product Y, and 40,000 units of product Z, and that Company B's plans call for having on hand 2,500 units of product X, 75 units of product Y, and 50,000 units of product Z as of December 31, 19X2. As you can see in Schedule A, in order to meet both the sales and inventory requirements, Company B must produce 9,500 units of product X, 925 units of product Y, and 210,000 units of product Z during 19X2.

SCHEDULE A
Production in Units
For the Year Ending December 31, 19X2

	Product X	Units Product Y	Product Z
Planned sales	9,000	950	200,000
Desired ending inventory	2,500	75	50,000
Total units needed	11,500	1,025	250,000
Less: Beginning inventory	2,000	100	40,000
Units to be produced	9,500	925	210,000

If we assume that Company B has a standard cost system in operation and that the standard cost per unit of product is as shown in Schedule B, Company B's production budget for the year ending December 31, 19X2, would appear as on page 686.

SCHEDULE B
Standard Cost per Unit of Product
For the Year Ending December 31, 19X2

	Product X	Product Y	Product Z
Material	$ 4.00	$ 38.00	$.25
Labor	12.00	300.00	.15
Overhead	1.75	90.00	.30
Total	$17.75	$428.00	$.70

COMPANY B
Production Budget
For the Year Ending December 31, 19X2

Product	Quantity*	Standard Cost†	Total Costs
X	9,500	$ 17.75	$168,625
Y	925	428.00	395,900
Z	210,000	0.70	147,000
			$711,525

*See Schedule A.
† See Schedule B.

Cash Budget In our study of the statement of source and disposition of cash in Chapter 20, it was pointed out that a knowledge of cash flow is fundamental to the effective utilization of cash. At that time we were looking at cash flow from a historical point of view and attempting to answer two questions: (1) Where did the cash come from? and (2) What did the organization do with it?

Although analyses of past cash flows are of considerable value to management, there is probably no more important aspect of planning for the future than that concerned with the management of future cash flows. Effective cash planning requires that management not only make provision for having adequate cash available to meet needs as they arise, but also that it formulate plans for effectively utilizing any excess cash as it becomes available. The questions then become: (1) Where is the cash to come from? and (2) How is it to be used? It is the purpose of the cash budget to provide answers to these questions. Although cash budgets may be prepared for any period of time, they are usually set up on a monthly, quarterly, or yearly basis.

To illustrate the preparation of a quarterly cash budget, let us assume that as of January 1, 19X2, Company B's Cash account has a $50,000 debit balance and, for simplicity, that its Accounts Receivable account has a zero balance. In addition, assume the data given directly in the budget and in Schedule C, both shown on page 687.

Flexible Budgeting

Because they are based on estimates for specific volumes or levels of activity, the budgets that have been discussed and illustrated thus far are commonly known as **fixed** or **static budgets.** Our sales budget, for example, was based on a specific volume of sales and our production budget on a given level of production. When the volume of an organization's activities can be very closely estimated, the fixed budget is, as a rule, satisfactory for planning and control purposes. Modern business, however, is dynamic rather than static; as a consequence, management may find it very difficult to forecast precisely such activities as sales and produc-

COMPANY B
Cash Budget
For the Year Ending December 31, 19X2

	First Quarter	Second Quarter	Third Quarter	Fourth Quarter
Beginning balance	$ 50,000	$ 77,000	$147,500	$190,000
Estimated receipts:				
Cash sales	160,000	170,400	185,000	205,200
Collections on receivables*	50,000	85,000	111,200	132,420
Sale of machinery		7,600		
Issuance of bonds			48,800	
Total cash available	$260,000	$340,000	$492,500	$527,620
Estimated disbursements:				
Payment of current payables	$180,500	$190,000	$220,000	$210,500
Retirement of mortgage				250,000
Purchase of equipment			80,000	
Payment of dividends	2,500	2,500	2,500	2,500
Total cash disbursements	$183,000	$192,500	$302,500	$463,000
Ending balance	$ 77,000	$147,500	$190,000	$ 64,620

*See Schedule C.

SCHEDULE C
Collection of Accounts Receivable
For the Year Ending December 31, 19X2

			Collections*		
	Credit Sales	First Quarter	Second Quarter	Third Quarter	Fourth Quarter
First quarter	$100,000	$50,000	$30,000	$ 19,000	
Second quarter	110,000		55,000	33,000	$ 20,900
Third quarter	118,400			59,200	35,520
Fourth quarter	152,000				76,000
	$480,400	$50,000	$85,000	$111,200	$132,420

*Collections on credit sales are generally made as follows:
During quarter of sale — 50%
During first subsequent quarter — 30%
During second subsequent quarter — 19%
Uncollectible — 1%

tion. In organizations where this is the case, it is common practice to employ what are known as flexible or variable budgets.

Flexible budgets are composed of a number of individual budgets that have been prepared for different levels of activity. For example, a flexible production budget may consist of separate budgets prepared for each 10 percent level of activity ranging from the 60 percent level to the 100 percent level. Thus, budgets of this kind reflect what costs should be at different levels of activity, rather than at one specific level.

A knowledge of cost behavior is fundamental to a sound understanding of flexible budgeting. As you recall from our study of break-even analysis in Chapter 22, costs behave in different ways, but as a general rule may be categorized as either fixed or variable. Fixed costs, synonymously called fixed expenses, do not change in response to changes in activity, whereas variable costs or expenses change proportionately with changes in activity. Since fixed costs are constant in total, the amount of fixed cost associated with each unit of output will vary depending upon the number of units produced, whereas the amount of variable cost associated with each unit will remain the same. Although somewhat condensed, the following budget is illustrative of the general idea underlying flexible budgeting.

COMPANY A

Production Budget

For the Year Ending December 31, 19X2

Production in units	7,000	8,000	9,000	10,000
Material costs	$ 35,000	$ 40,000	$ 45,000	$ 50,000
Labor costs	49,000	56,000	63,000	70,000
Fixed overhead costs:				
Depreciation on plant	30,000	30,000	30,000	30,000
Insurance	2,000	2,000	2,000	2,000
Supervision	5,000	5,000	5,000	5,000
Taxes	1,000	1,000	1,000	1,000
Variable overhead costs:				
Depreciation on machinery	7,000	8,000	9,000	10,000
Heat, light, and power	10,500	12,000	13,500	15,000
Indirect labor	3,500	4,000	4,500	5,000
Supplies	1,400	1,600	1,800	2,000
Total cost of production	$144,400	$159,600	$174,800	$190,000
Cost per unit	$20.63*	$19.95	$19.42*	$19.00

*Rounded off.

Flexible Budgeting Personalized To illustrate the concept of flexible budgeting on a personal level, let us assume that you drive your automobile within a range of 1,000 and 2,000 miles a month. The cost of operating the automobile, of course, includes both fixed and variable elements, for example, typical fixed expenses of insurance and taxes, and typical variable expenses of gas and oil. If we assume that your costs amount to $80 a month when you drive 1,000 miles and $110 a month when you drive 2,000 miles, we can arrive at a variable cost per mile of 3 cents [variation in total cost ($30) divided by variation in total mileage (1,000 miles)].

If the variable cost per mile is 3 cents, the fixed expenses per month will be $50, determined as follows:

	1,000-mile Month	2,000-mile Month
Total cost	$80	$110
Less variable expenses (3 cents per mile)	30	60
Fixed expenses	$50	$ 50

Your personal flexible budget for the operation of your automobile could be set up as follows:

Flexible Budget Monthly Operation of Personal Automobile			
Number of Miles	*Fixed Expenses*	*Variable Expenses*	*Total Costs*
1,000	$50	$30	$ 80
1,200	50	36	86
1,400	50	42	92
1,600	50	48	98
1,800	50	54	104
2,000	50	60	110

If your total costs amount to $100 in a month in which you drive your automobile 1,600 miles, a quick check of the budget will warn you that you are exceeding it by $2 ($100 as compared to $98). However, if your total costs are $100 in a month in which you drive your automobile 1,800 miles, you are "beating the budget" by $4 ($100 as compared to $104).

As you can see from the following schedule, the more mileage you put on your automobile in a month, the lower your fixed cost per mile becomes, and therefore the lower your total cost per mile.

Flexible Budget **Monthly Operation of Personal Automobile** **Schedule of Cost per Mile**						

Miles driven	1,000	1,200	1,400	1,600	1,800	2,000
Fixed expenses	$50	$50	$50	$50	$ 50	$ 50
Variable expenses	30	36	42	48	54	60
Total cost	$80	$86	$92	$98	$104	$110
Fixed cost per mile	$.05	$.0417	$.0357	$.0313	$.0278	$.025
Variable cost per mile	.03	.03	.03	.03	.03	.03
Total cost per mile	$.08	$.0717*	$.0657*	$.0613*	$.0578*	$.055

*Rounded off.

Flexible Budgeting and Overhead Application   Flexible budgeting is particularly useful in the analysis and control of factory overhead costs.   This is especially true when an organization employs a standard cost system.   (Standard costs are covered in the next section of this chapter.)

When we discussed in general the application of factory overhead to jobs and products in Chapter 23, we used a predetermined overhead rate based upon an estimated level of activity.   In situations where the actual amounts of overhead and production closely coincide with the estimated amounts, this approach is ordinarily satisfactory.   However, at times management may find it difficult to estimate overhead and production with any degree of accuracy.   If actual production turns out to be more or less than the estimated production, or if the actual and the estimated costs differ to any extent, comparisons of such data may not be too useful.   For example, the results obtained by comparing costs estimated for an output of 10,000 units with those actually incurred for an output of 8,000 units would be of limited value.   The significant comparison is one that relates budgeted and actual costs to the same level of activity.   Flexible budgeting provides a means whereby this may be accomplished.

To illustrate the importance of flexible budgeting to the application of overhead costs, let us assume that a predetermined overhead rate of $2 per unit is arrived at by dividing $20,000 of estimated overhead by 10,000 units of estimated production.   If actual production is 10,000 units and the actual amount of overhead incurred is $20,000 as was estimated, we have no problem.   Let us assume, however, that actual production is only 8,000 units and the actual amount of overhead incurred is $17,000.   If we use the approach illustrated in Chapter 23, $16,000 of overhead will be applied to production (8,000 units × $2 per unit), resulting in a $1,000 underapplied overhead variation.   Using flexible budgeting, however, and assuming a variable cost per unit of $1.50 (any amount under $2 per unit could be assumed), we find that in reality no variation is involved.   This may be illustrated as follows:

Flexible Budget
Factory Overhead

Production in units ———————————	7,000	8,000	9,000	10,000
Fixed expenses* ———————————	$ 5,000	$ 5,000	$ 5,000	$ 5,000
Variable expenses*———————————	10,500	12,000	13,500	15,000
Total cost———————————	$15,500	$17,000	$18,500	$20,000
Fixed cost per unit ———————————	$ .714	$ .625	$ .556	$ .50
Variable cost per unit———————————	1.50	1.50	1.50	1.50
Total cost per unit ———————————	$2.214	$2.125	$2.056	$2.00

*Since the variable cost per unit was given as $1.50 and the total cost incurred at the 10,000 unit level is $20,000, the amount of fixed overhead is $5,000 [$20,000 minus the variable overhead of $15,000 (10,000 units at $1.50 per unit)].

As can be deduced from the budget, the $1,000 difference between the actual amount of overhead incurred ($17,000) and the amount applied to production ($16,000) was the result of fixed expenses being charged to production at the rate of $.50 per unit (the amount chargeable at the 10,000-unit level) instead of $.625 (the amount that should be charged at the 8,000-unit level). The $.125 per unit difference ($.625 − $.50), when multiplied by 8,000 units (the actual production), is equal, of course, to the $1,000 difference between the actual and the applied overhead.

STANDARD COSTS

Standard costs are forecasts of what costs for products or services should be under specified conditions. They are generally determined as a result of detailed engineering studies, time and motion studies, and other analyses of cost and production relationships.

Cost control through the use of standards is usually accomplished in manufacturing organizations in three basic steps:

1 Standards are established for each element of cost (material, labor, and overhead).

2 Actual costs are compared with the established standards.

3 When necessary, investigative and corrective action is taken.

When the actual cost incurred for material, labor, or overhead differs from the standard amount allowed, the difference is known as a **variance.** If the standard cost is greater than the actual cost, the variance is said to be favorable, whereas if the actual cost exceeds the standard amount, an unfavorable variance results.

The analysis of variances is an essential element of cost control. It is important that deviations between actual and standard costs be reported to the person or department responsible for the incurrence of the actual costs in order that corrective action may be taken. Although variances may be stated in terms of physical units, they are ordinarily expressed in dollar amounts in order to emphasize their significance. At this time we shall examine the establishment of standards for material, labor, and overhead, as well as the analysis of applicable variances.

Materials Standards

Cost standards for materials are composed of two basic factors: (1) the quantity of material that should be used to produce the desired end product, and (2) the price that should be paid for the material used. Thus, two major variances are possible, one related to the *quantity* of material used, and the other related to the *price* paid for the material. To illustrate briefly, let us assume that the standards established for product X allow for 10 units of material A at a standard price of $2 per unit. If production of product X requires 11 units of material A, the quantity standard will be exceeded by one unit. Likewise, if the actual price paid for the material used is only $1.90 per unit, it will be 10 cents per unit under the price standard.

Materials Quantity Standard and Variance The standard quantity of material required to manufacture a unit of product is generally determined from standard materials specifications developed by the organization's engineering department.

The dollar value of the materials quantity variance is determined by multiplying the difference between the actual quantity of material used and the standard quantity allowed for the production by the standard price. Stated as a formula, letting MQV equal materials quantity variance, AQ equal actual quantity, SQ equal standard quantity, and SP equal standard price, we have:

$$MQV = (AQ - SQ) \times SP$$

or

$$MQV = (SQ - AQ) \times SP$$

For example, a standard quantity of 2,000 units of material Z is allowed for the production of 1,000 units of product A. The standard price for material Z is $2 per unit. Materials requisitions for the production of 1,000 units of product A show that 1,920 units of material Z were requisitioned and used. The materials quantity variation of $160 would be computed as follows:

$$MQV = (SQ - AQ) \times SP$$
$$MQV = (2,000 - 1,920) \times \$2$$
$$MQV = 80 \times \$2$$
$$MQV = \$160$$

Since the actual quantity of material used was less than the standard quantity allowed for the production, the $160 figure constitutes the dollar value of a favorable quantity variance. If the actual quantity of material used had exceeded the standard quantity allowed for the production, the variance would have been unfavorable.

Materials Price Standard and Variance The standard price for material is ordinarily determined as the result of collaboration between the accounting and purchasing departments. It should reflect current market values, vendors' contract prices, and optimum lot purchases.

The dollar value of a materials price variance is determined by multiplying the difference between the actual price incurred and the standard price by the actual quantity of material used. Stated as a formula, using our previous abbreviations and letting *MPV* equal materials price variance and *AP* equal actual price, we have:

$$MPV = (AP - SP) \times AQ$$

or

$$MPV = (SP - AP) \times AQ$$

For example, assume the data used in our previous illustration, that is, that 2,000 units of material Z with a standard price of $2 per unit were allowed for the production of 1,000 units of product A, and that 1,920 units of material Z were requisitioned and used. In addition, assume that the actual price of material Z was $2.10 per unit. The materials price variation of $192 would be computed as follows:

$$MPV = (AP - SP) \times AQ$$
$$MPV = (\$2.10 - \$2.00) \times 1,920$$
$$MPV = \$.10 \times 1,920$$
$$MPV = \$192$$

Since the actual price of material used exceeded the standard price, the $192 figure constitutes the dollar value of an unfavorable materials price variance. If the actual price had been less than the standard price, the variance would have been favorable.

Recapitulation of Materials Variances The following data are presented to review the computations involved in the determination of the two materials variances and also to show the combined effect of the variances.

Actual cost of material used (1,920 units @ $2.10 per unit)	$4,032
Standard cost of material that should have been used	
(2,000 units @ $2 per unit)	4,000
Net unfavorable variance	$ 32

The net unfavorable variance of $32 was the result of:

Unfavorable price variance (1,920 units @ $.10 per unit)	$192
Favorable quantity variance (80 units @ $2.00 per unit)	160
Net unfavorable variance	$ 32

Material variances may be analyzed graphically. The following illustration, which is purposely not drawn to scale, is indicative of the procedure:

Graphic Analysis of Material Variances

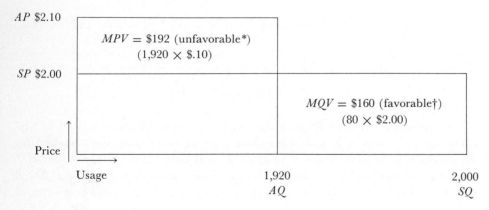

*Unfavorable because the actual price exceeds that allowed by the standard.
†Favorable because the actual quantity is less than that allowed by the standard.

Labor Standards

Cost standards for labor, like those for materials, are composed of two basic factors: (1) the amount of labor that should be utilized to produce the desired end product, and (2) the price that should be paid for the labor. Thus, again, two variations are possible, one related to the *quantity* of labor used, and the other related to the *price* paid for the labor.

To illustrate, let us assume that the standards established for product X allow for 2 hours of labor per unit at a standard price of $5 per hour. If production of product X requires only $1\frac{1}{2}$ hours of labor per unit, it will be $\frac{1}{2}$ hour per unit under the quantity standard. Likewise, if the actual price paid for labor is $5.25 per hour, the price standard will be exceeded by $.25 per hour.

Labor Quantity Standard and Variance The labor quantity standard relates to the amount of time required to produce a unit of product; it can be compared with the quantity standard for materials. Quantity standards for labor are generally established by time study personnel or by industrial engineers who are specialists in the area.

The dollar value of the labor quantity variance is determined by multiplying the difference between the actual amount of time required for production and the standard time allowed by the standard price. Stated as a formula, using our previous abbreviations and letting LQV equal labor quantity variance, we have:

$$LQV = (AQ - SQ) \times SP$$

or

$$LQV = (SQ - AQ) \times SP$$

For example, a standard quantity of 4,000 hours of direct labor at a standard price of $3 per hour is allowed for the production of 1,000 units of product A. However, labor records for the production of 1,000 units of product A show that 4,200 hours of direct labor were actually incurred. We then have:

$$LQV = (AQ - SQ) \times SP$$
$$LQV = (4,200 - 4,000) \times \$3$$
$$LQV = 200 \times \$3$$
$$LQV = \$600$$

Since the actual amount of labor used exceeded the standard quantity allowed for the production, the $600 figure constitutes the dollar value of an unfavorable labor quantity variance. Had the amount of labor been less than the standard quantity allowed, the variance would have been favorable.

Labor Price Standard and Variance The labor price standard relates to the rate paid for labor; it can be compared with the price standard for materials. Labor price standards are ordinarily based upon standard base rates of pay which are established for each type of operation performed in the production process. In many organizations the standard is based on rates that have been established by collective bargaining.

The dollar value of the labor price variance is determined by multiplying the difference between the actual price incurred and the standard price by the actual quantity of labor performed. Stated as a formula, using our previous abbreviations and letting *LPV* equal labor price variance, we have:

$$LPV = (AP - SP) \times AQ$$

or

$$LPV = (SP - AP) \times AQ$$

For example, assume the data used in our labor quantity illustration, that is, that 1,000 units of product A require 4,000 hours of direct labor at a standard price of $3 per hour, and that 4,200 hours of direct labor actually were performed to produce 1,000 units of product A. In addition, assume that the actual price of direct labor was $2.95 per hour. We then have:

$$LPV = (SP - AP) \times AQ$$
$$LPV = (\$3.00 - \$2.95) \times 4,200$$
$$LPV = \$.05 \times 4,200$$
$$LPV = \$210$$

Since the actual price of the labor was less than the standard price allowed, the $210 figure constitutes the dollar value of a favorable price variance. Had the price of the labor been more than the standard price allowed, the variance would have been unfavorable.

Recapitulation of Labor Variances   The following data provide a review of the computations involved in the determination of the two labor variances, and at the same time show the combined effect of the variances.

Actual cost of labor used (4,200 hours @ $2.95 per hour)	$12,390
Standard cost of labor that should have been used	
(4,000 hours @ $3 per hour)	12,000
Net unfavorable variance	$ 390

The net unfavorable variance of $390 was the result of:

Unfavorable quantity variance (200 hours @ $3 per hour)	$600
Favorable price variance (4,200 hours @ $.05 per hour)	210
Net unfavorable variance	$390

Overhead Standards

Our discussion of factory overhead in Chapter 23 applies equally well here, with one major exception which pertains to the determination of the overhead rate.

In developing predetermined overhead rates, which are commonly used to apply overhead to production by organizations not employing standard cost systems, we divided estimated overhead costs by estimated production. However, when standard costs are used, overhead is applied to production on the basis of a **standard overhead rate,** which is determined by dividing standard overhead costs by standard production. Stated as a formula, letting *SOR* equal standard overhead rate, we have:

$$SOR = \frac{\text{standard overhead costs}}{\text{standard production}}$$

Standard Overhead Costs Standard overhead costs are determined by establishing standards for each item of overhead expense. These standards are based on what costs should be under specified conditions rather than on what they were in the past or are expected to be in the future.

Standard Production When establishing overhead standards, management must decide on the level of production at which the standards should be set. Although there are many variations in practice, standard production is often stated in terms of **normal capacity,** which in turn is ordinarily expressed in direct labor hours per month or year, machine hours per month or year, or units of production. Other terms used synonymously with normal capacity include normal activity, normal production, normal volume, average activity, average capacity, average volume, and simply, standard production.

In establishing normal capacity, management must make allowances for a normal amount of unavoidable work stoppage due to lack of sales orders, delays in delivery of materials or supplies, breakdown in machinery and equipment, labor shortages and absenteeism, and other like factors.

Overhead Variances

Since the standard overhead rate per unit is determined by dividing standard overhead costs by standard production, a deviation between the actual overhead incurred and that applied to production during a specific period may result from differences between:

1 Standard overhead allowed and actual overhead incurred

2 Standard production and actual production

3 A combination of (1) and (2)

Up to this time, we have assumed that fixed expenses for a given period of time and a specified range of output do not change in response to changes in volume, and that variable expenses change more or less proportionately in response to changes in volume. While our assumption regarding fixed expenses is reasonably sound, it does not always hold true in regard to variable expenses. They often tend to be somewhat "sticky," and therefore seldom vary in exact ratio to variations in volume. As a consequence, deviations between actual and standard overhead result primarily from:

1 Incurrence of variable expenses in an amount other than that called for by the standard

2 Spreading of fixed expenses over more or fewer units than called for by the standard

3 A combination of (1) and (2)

We can visualize the two basic deviations if we study the cost behavior schedule shown below. Assume that actual production for a given period is 40,000 units, normal capacity is 50,000 units, and the actual variable expenses incurred amount to $32,000. As you can see on the schedule, the variable expenses at the 40,000-unit level should be only $30,000; thus, there is an unfavorable deviation of $2,000. Similarly, when the standard overhead rate of $1.75 per unit, based on normal capacity of 50,000 units, is employed, only $1 of fixed expense per unit is applied to production; at the 40,000-unit level, however, $1.25 per unit should be applied if all the fixed expenses are to be charged to production. Since $10,000 of the fixed expenses [40,000 units $\times$ ($1.25 − $1.00)] would not be charged to production, we would have another unfavorable deviation.

Cost Behavior Schedule					
Production (Units)	20,000	30,000	40,000	50,000 (NC)*	60,000
Overhead costs:					
Fixed expenses	$50,000	$50,000	$50,000	$50,000	$50,000
Variable expenses	15,000	22,500	30,000	37,500	45,000
Total	$65,000	$72,500	$80,000	$87,500	$95,000
Overhead cost per unit:					
Fixed expenses	$2.50	$1.667	$1.25	$1.00	$ .833
Variable expenses	.75	.75	.75	.75	.75
Total	$3.25	$2.417	$2.00	$1.75 (NC)*	$1.583

*Normal capacity.

The deviations associated with the variable expense elements of overhead are commonly known as **controllable variances,** and those associated with the fixed expense elements are referred to as **volume variances.**

Controllable Overhead Variance   The controllable variance is determined by comparing the actual amount of variable expense incurred with the standard amount that should have been incurred for the level of production attained.   Stated as a formula, letting SVE equal standard variable expenses and AVE equal actual variable expenses, we have:

$$\text{Controllable variance} = SVE - AVE$$

or

$$\text{Controllable variance} = AVE - SVE$$

For example, assume the basic data in our cost behavior schedule and also assume that $82,000 of overhead is incurred during a period in which 45,000 units are produced.

$$\text{Controllable variance} = SVE - AVE$$
$$\text{Controllable variance} = \$33,750^* - \$32,000\dagger$$
$$\text{Controllable variance} = \$1,750$$

*45,000 units @ $.75 per unit for variable expenses.
† $82,000 − fixed expenses of $50,000.

Since we assume that the fixed expenses are rigidly fixed, we can also determine the controllable variance in another way, that is, by comparing the total amount of overhead incurred with the total standard amount that should have been incurred for the level of production actually attained.   Using this approach and letting STO equal standard total overhead and ATO equal actual total overhead, we would have:

$$\text{Controllable variance} = STO - ATO$$
$$\text{Controllable variance} = \$83,750^* - \$82,000\dagger$$
$$\text{Controllable variance} = \$1,750$$

*$50,000 fixed expense plus $33,750 variable expense (45,000 units @ $.75 per unit).
† As given in the basic data.

As the actual variable expenses incurred were less than the standard amount allowed for the production, the $1,750 figure constitutes the dollar amount of a favorable controllable variance.   If the actual variable expenses were to exceed the standard, the variance would be unfavorable.

Overhead Volume Variance   The volume variance is determined by comparing the amount of fixed expense incurred with the amount applied to production. This is accomplished by multiplying the difference between actual and standard production by the fixed expense element of the overhead rate.   Stated as a formula, letting *ACP* equal actual production, *STP* equal standard production, and *FOR* equal the fixed expense element of the overhead rate, we have:

$$\text{Volume variance} = (ACP - STP) \times FOR$$

or

$$\text{Volume variance} = (STP - ACP) \times FOR$$

For example, using the basic data in our cost behavior schedule and the additional data in our preceding illustration, we would determine a volume variance of $5,000 as follows:

$$\text{Volume variance} = (STP - ACP) \times FOR$$
$$\text{Volume variance} = (50,000 - 45,000) \times \$1*$$
$$\text{Volume variance} = \$5,000$$

*Fixed expense element of the standard overhead rate.

Since actual production was less than standard production, the $5,000 figure constitutes the dollar amount of an unfavorable volume variance. If the actual production were to exceed the standard, the volume variance would be favorable.

Recapitulation of Overhead Variances The following data provide a review of the computations involved in the determination of the overhead variances, and at the same time show their combined effect.

Actual overhead (given)	$82,000
Applied overhead (45,000 units @ $1.75 per unit)	78,750
Net unfavorable variance	$ 3,250

The net unfavorable variance of $3,250 was the result of:

Unfavorable volume variance (5,000 units @ $1* per unit)	$5,000
Favorable controllable variance (standard variable expenses of $33,750 — actual variable expenses of $32,000)	1,750
Net unfavorable variance	$3,250

*Fixed expense element of the standard overhead rate.

Standard Costs in the Accounts

Standard costs may be recorded in the accounts by one of three methods. All three ordinarily credit the Work in Process account for standard costs, but they differ regarding the amounts to be charged to the account. One method charges the Work in Process account with actual quantities at actual prices; a second method charges the account with actual quantities at standard prices; and a third charges the account with standard quantities at standard prices. The differences are illustrated in T-account form as follows:

First Method

Work in Process

$AQ \times AP$	$SQ \times SP$

Second Method

Work in Process

$AQ \times SP$	$SQ \times SP$

Third Method

Work in Process

$SQ \times SP$	$SQ \times SP$

Although the end results are the same (production is costed at standard cost), under the first method all variances are reflected in the Work in Process account; under the second method **price variances** are determined before the costs are transferred to the Work in Process account; and under the third method **all variances** are determined before the costs are transferred to the Work in Process account.

When variances are determined before the costs are transferred to the Work in Process account, as in the second and third methods, they are ordinarily recognized in the accounts as they occur. For example, a material price variance would be recognized at the time of purchase rather than at the time of use. Each method has advantages and disadvantages, but because of the simplicity and economy of operation of the first method, we shall use it in the illustration that follows.

Standard Cost System Illustrated

To illustrate the standard cost system more fully, let us assume that the Arcat Company employs standard costs when accounting for its principal product, Arcat. Standard specifications per unit of Arcat are:

Material A: 2 units @ $10 per unit

Material B: 3 units @ $6 per unit

Direct labor: 100 hours @ $3 per hour

Overhead: 100 hours @ the standard overhead rate

The Arcat Company's standard overhead rate is based on normal capacity of 10,000 direct labor hours per month and standard costs of $4,000 and $5,000 for fixed and variable expenses, respectively.

The actual costs and production of Arcat during the month of June were:

Material A: 188 units @ $9.95 per unit

Material B: 274 units @ $6.04 per unit

Direct labor: 8,980 hours @ $3.06 per hour

Overhead: $10,920

Units of Arcat produced: 90

The Arcat Company's manufacturing operations for June would be recorded and posted as follows:

(1)

Work in Process	1,870.60	
Raw Materials Inventory		1,870.60

To record the cost of Material A used in production (188 units @ $9.95 per unit).

(2)

Work in Process	1,654.96	
Raw Materials Inventory		1,654.96

To record the cost of Material B used in production (274 units @ $6.04 per unit).

(3)

Work in Process	27,478.80	
Accrued Payroll Payable		27,478.80

To record direct labor incurred in production (8,980 hours @ $3.06 per hour).

(4)

Work in Process	10,920.00	
Factory Overhead		10,920.00

To transfer factory overhead to the Work in Process account.

(5)

Finished Goods Inventory	38,520.00	
Work in Process		38,520.00

To transfer standard production costs from the Work in Process account to the Finished Goods Inventory account (90 units @ a standard cost of $428* per unit).

*The standard cost of a unit of Arcat is:

Material A: 2 units @ $10 per unit	$ 20.00
Material B: 3 units @ $6 per unit	18.00
Labor: 100 hours @ $3 per hour	300.00
Overhead: 100 hours @ $.90† per hour	90.00
Standard cost per unit	$428.00

†Standard overhead rate $= \dfrac{\text{standard overhead costs}}{\text{standard production}}$

Standard overhead rate $= \dfrac{\$4{,}000 \; FE + \$5{,}000 \; VE}{10{,}000 \text{ direct labor hours}}$

Standard overhead rate $= \$.90$ per direct labor hour

To illustrate the entries involved when a sale is made by an organization employing a standard cost system, let us assume that the Arcat Company sold 50 units of Arcat during the month of June at $600 per unit.

Accounts Receivable	30,000.00	
Sales		30,000.00

To record the sale of 50 units of Arcat at $600 per unit.

Cost of Goods Sold	21,400.00	
Finished Goods Inventory		21,400.00

To record the cost of sales (50 units @ a standard cost of $428 per unit).

General Ledger

Work in Process

Material A (actual)	1,870.60	Material A (standard)	1,800.00[1]
Material B (actual)	1,654.96	Material B (standard)	1,620.00[2]
Labor (actual)	27,478.80	Labor (standard)	27,000.00[3]
Overhead (actual)	10,920.00	Overhead (standard)	8,100.00[4]
Actual costs incurred	41,924.36	Standard cost of work done	38,520.00
		Variances from standard	3,404.36
	41,924.36		41,924.36
Variances from standard	3,404.36*		

*See Schedule A on page 704.
[1] $(90 \times 2 \times \$10) = \$1,800$
[2] $(90 \times 3 \times \$6) = \$1,620$
[3] $(90 \times 100 \times \$3) = \$27,000$
[4] $(90 \times 100 \times \$.90) = \$8,100$

Finished Goods Inventory

38,520.00	21,400.00

Cost of Goods Sold

21,400.00	

Disposition of Variances When monthly or other interim statements are prepared, variances from standard costs are ordinarily carried forward on the balance sheet, with net unfavorable variances being classified as deferred charges and net favorable variances as deferred credits. Year-end variances, however, are generally closed out. This may be accomplished in one of two ways. Theoretically, each variance should be closed proportionately to the Cost of Goods Sold account and the pertinent inventory accounts. Practically, however, based on expediency and materiality, a variance is usually closed in its entirety directly to the Revenue and Expense Summary account.

Schedule A
Analysis of Variances from Standard
For the Month of June

Material Variances

Material A:	Quantity variance [(180 − 188) × $10]	$ (80.00)	
	Price variance [($10 − $9.95)] × 188	9.40	
	Net unfavorable variance	$ (70.60)	$ (70.60)
Material B:	Quantity variance [(270 − 274) × $6]	$ (24.00)	
	Price variance [($6 − $6.04) × 274]	(10.96)	
	Net unfavorable variance	$ (34.96)	(34.96)

Labor Variances

Labor quantity variance [(9,000 − 8,980) × $3]	$ 60.00	
Labor price variance [($3 − $3.06) × 8,980]	(538.80)	
Net unfavorable variance	$ (478.80)	(478.80)

Overhead Variances

Controllable overhead variance [(90 × 100) × $.50*] − ($10,920 − $4,000) or [$4,000 + (90 × 100 × $.50*)] − $10,920	$(2,420.00)	
Overhead volume variance [(9,000 − 10,000) × $.40†]	(400.00)	
Net unfavorable variance	$(2,820.00)	(2,820.00)
Total variation from standard for the month of June		$(3,404.36)

*Variable expense element of the standard overhead rate (variable expenses of $5,000 divided by the normal rate of production of 10,000 direct labor hours per month).
† Fixed expense element of the standard overhead rate (fixed expenses of $4,000 divided by the normal rate of production of 10,000 direct labor hours per month).

To illustrate the two methods, let us assume the same operating data as in our Arcat illustration, and also assume that the data are for the year ended June 30, 19X1, rather than only for the month of June. In addition, for purposes of simplicity, let us assume that the only other Arcat income activities of the year were the incurrence of $2,000 of selling expenses and $3,000 of administrative expenses. As you study the illustrations on the following page note that when the variances are closed to the Revenue and Expense Summary account, they appear as deductions from gross margin before selling and administrative expenses are deducted. It should also be noted that the difference of $1,513.05 between the two reported net income figures ($1,708.69 and $195.64) is equal to the amount of the variances allocated to the finished goods inventory ($\frac{4}{9}$ × $3,404.36). This, of course, is the amount of the variances prorated to the 40 units that were produced but not sold.

ARCAT COMPANY

Income Statement

For the Year Ended June 30, 19X1

(Variances prorated)

Sales	$30,000.00
Cost of goods sold (at actual cost)	23,291.31*
Gross margin	$ 6,708.69
Less: Selling expenses _____ $2,000.00	
Administrative expenses _____ 3,000.00	5,000.00
Net income	$ 1,708.69

*Standard cost	$21,400.00
Plus $\frac{5}{9}$ of the variances from standard ($\frac{5}{9} \times$ $3,404.36)	1,891.31
	$23,291.31

ARCAT COMPANY

Income Statement

For the Year Ended June 30, 19X1

(Variances closed directly to R & E Summary)

Sales		$30,000.00
Cost of goods sold (at standard cost)		21,400.00
Gross margin (based on standard costs)		$ 8,600.00
Adjustments for standard-cost variances:		
Material quantity variance ($80 + $24)	$ 104.00	
Material price variance ($10.96 − $9.40)	1.56	
Labor quantity variance	(60.00)	
Labor price variance	538.80	
Overhead controllable variance	2,420.00	
Overhead volume variance	400.00	3,404.36
Gross margin—adjusted		$ 5,195.64
Less: Selling expenses	$2,000.00	
Administrative expenses	3,000.00	5,000.00
Net income		$ 195.64

SUMMARY

Budgets and standard costs are two of the accounting tools most useful to management in planning and controlling manufacturing operations. Budgets are forecasts of business operations expressed in monetary terms, and standard costs are pre-determinations of what costs should be under a given set of conditions. Both are useful to management in that they facilitate the spotlighting of variations between actual performance and the expected or predetermined performance. By empha-sizing variations, they assist management in the application of its "management by exception principle."

QUESTIONS AND PROBLEMS

25-1 (1) Define what is meant by **standard costs.**

(2) List what you consider to be the more important advantages of a standard cost system.

25-2 (1) Define the terms **quantity variance** and **price variance** as they are used with regard to direct materials.

(2) Illustrate their application to the following data:

Standard: 1,000 units @ $12
Actual: 950 units @ $13

25-3 What is the price variance situation in a case where actual price equals $12 per unit, standard price equals $10 per unit, actual quantity equals 14,000 units, and standard quantity equals 13,000 units?

25-4 What is the quantity variance situation where actual quantity equals 1,100 units, standard quantity equals 1,200 units, actual price equals $1.30 per unit, and standard price equals $1.25 per unit?

25-5 From the following data, which pertain to the Johnson Manufacturing Company's operations for the month of August, determine (1) the control-lable variance and (2) the volume variance:

Normal capacity	30,000 units
Actual production	27,000 units
Actual overhead	$29,200
Fixed expense element of the standard overhead rate	$ .60*
Variable expense element of the standard overhead rate	$ .45*

*Per unit.

25-6 From the following data, which pertain to the Hartford Company's opera-tions for the month of September, determine (1) the controllable variance, and (2) the volume variance:

Normal capacity	20,000 units
Actual production	20,400 units
Actual overhead	$40,800
Actual variable overhead	$ 8,800
Standard overhead rate per unit	$ 2.00

25-7 Instructions Assuming that an organization's fixed factory overhead is budgeted at $60,000 and that the variable expense element of its overhead rate is budgeted at $1 per unit:

(1) Prepare a flexible overhead budget depicting production at the 10,000-, 15,000-, 20,000-, and 25,000-unit levels.

(2) Assuming that overhead is applied to production at the rate determined in (1) above for the 10,000-unit level, and also assuming that 12,500 units are produced and that $73,000 of overhead is actually incurred, determine the amount of over- or underapplied overhead.

(3) Assuming that overhead is applied to production at the rate determined in (1) above for the 20,000-unit level, and also assuming that 16,000 units are produced and that $78,000 of overhead is actually incurred, determine the amount of over- or underapplied overhead.

25-8 Instructions Assuming that an organization's fixed expenses are rigidly fixed and its variable expenses are strictly variable, and that its total factory overhead amounts to $80,000 at the 50,000-unit level and $66,000 at the 30,000-unit level:

(1) Prepare a flexible overhead budget depicting production at the 30,000-, 40,000-, 50,000-, and 60,000-unit levels.

(2) Assuming that overhead is applied to production at the rate determined in (1) above for the 40,000-unit level and that actual production amounts to 42,000 units, determine the amount of over- or underapplied overhead.

(3) Assuming that overhead is applied to production at the rate determined in (1) above for the 60,000-unit level and that actual production amounts to 58,000 units, determine the amount of over- or underapplied overhead.

25-9 When establishing its standard overhead rate, the ABC Manufacturing Company used the following flexible budget:

Percentage of Capacity	Estimated Factory Overhead
100 (normal capacity)	$400,000
90	372,000
80	334,000
70	316,000

Instructions Assuming that during a period in which 9,000 units (90 percent of capacity) were produced, the actual factory overhead incurred amounted to $404,000, determine the amount of (1) the controllable variance and (2) the volume variance.

25-10 The Century Company uses a standard cost system. The following data summarize certain of its operations for the month of June:

Material	Standard Cost per Unit	Actual Cost per Unit	Standard Usage, Units	Actual Usage, Units
A	$1.50	$1.48	2,000	2,100
B	1.60	1.55	1,000	980
C	1.70	1.78	1,500	1,700
D	1.80	1.76	1,600	1,600
E	1.90	1.80	1,800	1,900

Instructions Determine the (1) net, (2) quantity, and (3) price variances for each type of material.

25-11 The Eastern Company uses a standard cost system. The following data summarize certain of its operations for the month of July regarding its use of direct labor:

Product	Standard Cost per Hour	Actual Cost per Hour	Standard Usage, Hours	Actual Usage, Hours
AA	$3.75	$3.80	1,000	1,100
BB	3.80	3.84	2,000	1,950
CC	3.90	3.79	2,200	2,000
DD	4.00	3.95	2,500	2,520
EE	4.10	4.00	2,400	2,460

Instructions Determine the (1) net, (2) quantity, and (3) price variances for labor for each product.

25-12 The Western Company uses a standard cost system. The following data summarize certain of its operations for the month of July regarding its incurrence and use of factory overhead:

Product	Standard Rate per Hour	Actual Overhead	Standard Hours for the Month	Actual Hours Worked
1	$2.00	$ 4,620	2,000	2,200
2	2.20	8,710	4,000	3,900
3	2.10	9,340	4,400	4,000
4	2.30	11,592	5,000	5,100
5	2.40	11,400	4,800	4,920

Instructions Assuming that the variable expense element of the overhead rate is equal to $1 in each instance, determine the (1) net, (2) controllable, and (3) volume variances for each product.

25-13 The standard cost of a unit of Product Q, based on normal production of 100,000 units per month, is as follows:

Materials ($\frac{1}{2}$ pound)	$ .50
Labor ($\frac{1}{4}$ hour)	.70
Variable overhead	.20
Fixed overhead	.10
Total	$1.50

The following costs apply to the month of March (a month in which 104,000 units were produced):

Materials (52,300 pounds @ $ 98 per pound)	$ 51,254
Labor (25,800 hours @ $2.83)	73,014
Variable overhead	20,600
Fixed overhead	10,000
Total	$154,868

Instructions To the extent possible, determine the:

(1) Material quantity variance
(2) Material price variance
(3) Labor quantity variance
(4) Labor price variance
(5) Controllable overhead variance
(6) Overhead volume variance

*25-14 The Dearborn Company manufactures Product X in standard batches of 100 units. Management has noted that actual costs per batch frequently deviate somewhat from standard costs per batch. The standard costs per batch are as follows:

Raw materials (60 pounds @ $.45 per pound)	$ 27.00
Direct labor (36 hours @ $2.15 per hour)	77.40
Overhead (36 hours @ $2.75 per hour)	99.00†
	$203 40

† Includes a fixed expense element of $33 per batch.

Production for the month of April amounted to 210 batches. The relevant statistics follow:

Standard output for the month of April	24,000 units
Raw materials used	13,000 pounds
Cost of raw materials used	$ 6,110.00
Direct labor cost	16,790.40
Overhead cost	20,592.00
Actual overhead rate per hour for April	2.60

Instructions Compute the following variances for the month of April:

(1) Net material variance

(2) Material quantity variance

(3) Material price variance

(4) Net labor variance

(5) Labor quantity variance

(6) Labor price variance

(7) Net overhead variance

(8) Controllable overhead variance

(9) Overhead volume variance

25-15 The Smith Company uses a standard cost system. The standards are based on projected budgeted operations for the current period.
Current standards for material and labor are as follows:

Materials:

Material A	$1.20 per unit
Material B	2.60 per unit
Direct labor	2.05 per hour

*AICPA adapted.

Finished products (content of each unit):

	Special Widgets	De Luxe Widgets
Material A	12 units	12 units
Material B	6 units	8 units
Direct labor	14 hours	20 hours

The overhead budget and operating data for the month of August were as follows:

Overhead budget:

Projected direct labor hours	9,000
Fixed factory overhead	$ 4,500
Variable factory overhead	13,500

Operating data:

Sales:

500 special widgets	$52,700
100 de luxe widgets	16,400

Purchases:

Material A	8,500 units	$ 9,725
Material B	1,800 units	5,635

Material requisitions:

Issued from stores:

	Material A	Material B
Standard quantity	8,400 units	3,200 units
Over standard	400 units	150 units
Returned to stores	75 units	—

Direct labor hours:

Standard	9,600 hours
Actual	10,000 hours

Wages incurred:

500 hours @	$2.10 per hour
8,000 hours @	2.00 per hour
1,500 hours @	1.90 per hour

Expenses incurred:

Manufacturing	$20,125

Instructions Using the above data and assuming that material price variances are recognized in the accounts at the time of purchase rather than at the time of use, determine the:

(1) Quantity variance for Material A

(2) Price variance for Material A

(3) Quantity variance for Material B

(4) Price variance for Material B

(5) Quantity variance for labor

(6) Price variance for labor

(7) Controllable variance for overhead

(8) Volume variance for overhead

*25-16 The Du-Rite Company, established in 19X3, manufactures a single product which passes through several departments. The company has a standard cost system. The company's inventories at standard cost, as of December 31, 19X3, are as follows:

Raw material	—
Work in process:	
Material	$ 75,000
Labor	7,500
Overhead	15,000
Total	$ 97,500
Finished goods:	
Material	$ 60,000
Labor	20,000
Overhead	40,000
Total	$120,000
Total inventories	$217,500

Part of the company's preliminary income statement for the year ended December 31, 19X3, prior to any year-end inventory adjustments, follows:

Sales		$900,000
Cost of goods sold:		
Standard cost of goods sold:		
Material	$300,000	
Labor	100,000	
Overhead	200,000	
Total	$600,000	
Variances:		
Material	$ 25,400	
Labor	25,500	
Overabsorbed overhead	(16,500)	
Total	$ 34,400	634,400
Gross margin		$265,600

Instructions Prepare a schedule showing the actual cost of goods manu-

*AICPA adapted.

factured. Your schedule should provide for a separation of costs into material, labor, and overhead costs.

*25-17 The H. G. Company uses a standard cost system. The standards are based on budgeted monthly production of 100 units per day for the usual 22 working days per month. Standard cost per unit for direct labor is 8 hours at $3 per hour. Standard cost for overhead was set as follows:

Fixed overhead per month	$29,040
Variable overhead per month	39,600
Total budgeted overhead	$68,640
Expected direct labor cost	$52,800
Overhead rate per dollar of labor	$ 1.30
Standard overhead per unit	$ 31.20

During the month of September the plant operated only 20 days, producing 2,080 units while incurring the following costs:

Direct labor, 16,430 hours @ $3.04	$49,947.20
Fixed overhead	29,040.00
Variable overhead	39,325.00

Instructions For the month of September, determine the:

(1) Net labor variance

(2) Labor quantity variance

(3) Labor price variance

(4) Net overhead variance

(5) Controllable overhead variance

(6) Overhead volume variance

*25-18 Instructions The Metals Products Company manufactures three different models of a single product. From the following data, which pertain to the upcoming year:

(1) Prepare a schedule showing the dollar amount available for covering the budgeted nonvariable cost per unit of each model.

(2) Determine the number of units of each model which must be sold in order to enable the company to cover its budgeted nonvariable costs.

(3) Determine the required sales in dollars for each model necessary to enable the company to cover its budgeted nonvariable costs.

*AICPA adapted.

Budgeted Sales Data			
Model Number	Annual Sales Budget, Units	Budgeted Unit Sales Price	Budgeted Sales Allowances for a Year
100	30,000	$15.00	$1,260
200	16,000	18.00	480
300	10,000	25.00	410

Budgeted Cost Data				
	Quantity Budgeted for		Cost per Unit	
Model Number	Production	Total	Variable Cost	Nonvariable Cost
100	30,500	$15.072	$ 9.871	$5.201
200	15,000	17.335	10.250	7.085
300	10,000	23.756	15.436	8.320

*25-19 Normal capacity of the ABC Company is regarded as 180,000 units per year. Standard variable manufacturing costs are $11 per unit. Fixed factory overhead is $360,000 per year. Variable selling expenses are $3 per unit and fixed selling expenses are $252,000 per year. The unit sales price is $20.

Instructions

(1) Assuming no variances from standard, determine ABC's break-even point in (a) units, and (b) dollars.

(2) Assuming no variances from standard, determine the number of units which must be sold in order to earn a net income of $60,000 per year.

(3) Assuming no variances from standard, determine the number of units which must be sold in order to earn a net income equal to 10 percent of sales.

(4) Assuming that no variances from standard existed other than a possible volume variance, that the beginning inventory for the year 19X1 contained 10,000 units, and that 160,000 units were produced during the year with 150,000 units being sold, prepare income statements for the year under (a) full costing, and (b) variable costing.

*AICPA adapted.

(5) Briefly account for the difference between the net incomes determined in requirement (4).

*25-20 Instructions From the following data, which pertain to budgeted operations of The Appliance Business for the upcoming 6 months, prepare a cash budget by months, with appropriate supporting schedules, which will summarize cash receipts, cash disbursements, and additional cash investments required to comply with the terms of the bank loan.

Budgeted Sales

	Units
January	100
February	160
March	180
April	220
May	380
June	360

Each appliance will be sold for $200. It is anticipated that 25 percent will be sold for cash and the balance on an installment contract. The installment contract requires a down payment of 10 percent and 10 monthly payments of $20 each, which include the finance charge. The finance charge is assumed to be earned in proportion to the collections on installment contracts.

The appliances cost $125 each. Their purchase can be financed by paying 20 percent down with a non-interest-bearing note for the balance. This balance must be paid at the end of the month in which the appliance is sold. An average inventory of 200 units should be maintained. The same purchase terms will be available for all replacements.

The installment contracts will be pledged as collateral for loans of 60 percent of the unpaid balance. These loans will be reduced, monthly, by 60 percent of all installment collections received. The Appliance Business agrees to maintain a minimum bank balance of $15,000.

Salesmen will be allowed a commission of $20 per unit, to be paid the month of the sale. Other variable expenses will be approximately $30 per unit sold. Other fixed expenses are estimated at $1,200 per month. Interest expense on bank loans will be 6 percent per annum on loans outstanding at the end of the previous month.

Assume that payments to the manufacturer and monthly advances from the bank will be consummated on the last day of each month. Bank interest will be payable monthly following the date the loan is received. For budgeting purposes, all computations should be rounded to the nearest $10.

*AICPA adapted.

Part Eight
Mathematics of Accounting

26
Mathematical Techniques Essential to the Accounting Process

The modern accountant works in a mathematical world. In order to be able to measure properly the economic phenomena with which he deals and thus provide adequate information to those responsible for making decisions based upon accounting data, it is imperative that he have a thorough understanding of basic mathematics.

When the mathematical approach is applied to the accounting process, much of the guesswork in developing information upon which business decisions are based can be eliminated or, at the least, greatly reduced. Mathematics generally makes possible more precise descriptions and affords a better comprehension of facts than can be achieved simply by reliance upon experience, judgment, and general knowledge. A typical example of its value may be seen in the area of inventory management, where the main objective is to have the right inventory item in the right place at the right time in the right quantity.

In this final chapter, we shall review some of the more important mathematical techniques fundamental to the accounting process. It is not the purpose of the chapter to provide a complete coverage of mathematics, nor to teach the subject "from scratch," but rather to present a memory refresher for those who may require it.

Each technique discussed here can be employed manually, or it can be mechanized via the computer. Obviously, when computerized, mathematics becomes a significantly more valuable tool, because of the speed with which computations can be made. Our review will cover (1) basic arithmetic, (2) basic algebra, and (3) probability theory.

BASIC ARITHMETIC

When we first began our study of accounting and the management process in Chapter 1, the maxim "knowledge is power" was stressed. Like a building, knowledge is only as strong as the foundation upon which it rests. So it is with mathematics. Our mathematical knowledge is weak and unreliable unless it is founded upon a strong understanding of the underlying principles. Therefore, a review of mathematics must necessarily begin with the fundamentals of arithmetic. In this section we shall review (1) basic arithmetic operations, (2) powers and roots, and (3) logarithms.

Basic Arithmetic Operations

As you no doubt recall from your grade school days, arithmetic is the science of numbers, a number being a concept of quantity. In arithmetic the symbol for the value of a quantity is a numeral or its equivalent, for example, a bead position on an abacus or a light position on a computer.

The four fundamental operations of arithmetic (and, incidentally, of all the mathematical sciences) are addition, subtraction, multiplication, and division. All mathematical techniques, regardless of the degree of complexity or sophistication, eventually "boil down" to one or more of the four basic operations. Since you are thoroughly familiar with these operations, this brief review should be considered merely as a terminology refresher.

Addition Addition is the process of uniting two or more quantities into one. The result obtained by adding is called the **sum.** The numbers added are called **addends.** Thus, in the computation $10 + 10 = 20$, the 10s are addends and the 20 is the sum.

Subtraction This is the process of finding the difference between two quantities. The result obtained by subtracting is called the **difference,** or **remainder.** The quantity subtracted is called the **subtrahend** and the quantity from which the subtrahend is subtracted is called the **minuend.** Thus, in the computation $30 - 10 = 20$, 30 is the minuend, 10 is the subtrahend, and 20 is the difference, or remainder.

Multiplication Multiplication is the process of adding a quantity to itself as many times as is indicated by another quantity. The result obtained by multiplying is called the **product.** The quantity to be added to itself is called the **multiplicand,** and the quantity specifying how many times the addition is to be performed is called the **multiplier.** Thus, in the computation $6 \times 8 = 48$, 6 is the multiplicand, 8 is the multiplier, and 48 is the product.

Division This is the process of finding how many times one quantity is contained in another quantity. The result obtained by dividing is called the **quotient.** The quantity that contains the other is called the **dividend,** and the quantity contained in the dividend is called the **divisor.** Thus, in the computation $60 \div 4 = 15$, 60 is the dividend, 4 is the divisor, and 15 is the quotient.

Powers and Roots

Many arithmetic computations require the repetitive use of one or more of the basic operations. For example, accountants frequently need a product obtained by multiplying a given quantity by itself several times. Similarly, it is often necessary to obtain a quantity which when multiplied by itself a certain number of times produces a given quantity. Computations such as these are greatly expedited by the use of powers and roots.

Powers of Numbers The **power** of a number is the product of that number multiplied by itself a designated number of times. The number is called the **base.** For example, 32 is a power of the number 2 (the base) and is equal to $2 \times 2 \times 2 \times 2 \times 2$. However, instead of writing $2 \times 2 \times 2 \times 2 \times 2$, we can simply use the notation 2^5, which means 2 multiplied by itself 5 times.

Exponents The figure placed to the right and slightly higher than the base, which shows how many times the base is to be multiplied by itself, is known in mathematical terminology as an **exponent.** The exponent is used whenever possible in mathematical methodology in order to conserve time and space. For instance, a number such as one hundred million (100,000,000) will consume considerably less space and can be written in less time in its exponential form, 10^8.

A number written without an exponent is assumed to have an exponent of 1, thus, $2 = 2^1$. **Negative exponents** are used to express powers that are less than 1. A microsecond (a one-millionth part of a second), for example, is ordinarily expressed in mathematical terms as 10^{-6}. Similarly, a hundredth part of a microsecond ($1/100 \times 1/1,000,000$) is expressed as 10^{-8}. To find the power indicated by a negative exponent, we merely change the sign of the exponent from minus to plus and write the resulting term as the denominator of a fraction whose numerator is 1, thus: $10^{-6} = 1/10^6 = 1/1,000,000$. Similarly, $10^{-8} = 1/10^8 = 1/100,000,000$.

Multiplication of Numbers with Exponents When numbers with exponents have the same base, multiplication is accomplished simply by adding the exponents and then raising the number to the power that is the sum of the exponents. For example, $2^2 \times 2^3 = 2^{2+3} = 2^5 = 32$. When numbers with exponents have different bases, they may be multiplied in one of two ways: They may either be converted into numbers having the same base and then multiplied by adding their exponents, or they may be converted into numbers with exponents of 1 and multiplied in the usual way. For example, $4^3 \times 2^2$ may be multiplied by converting 4^3 into 2^6 and multiplying, thus: $4^3 \times 2^2 = 2^6 \times 2^2 = 2^8 = 256$; or by converting the numbers into numbers with exponents of 1, as follows: $4^3 \times 2^2 = 64 \times 4 = 256$.

Division of Numbers with Exponents Division of numbers with exponents is accomplished, when they have the same base, simply by subtracting the exponent of the divisor from the exponent of the dividend and then raising the number to the power indicated by the difference. For example, $2^5 \div 2^3 = 2^{5-3} = 2^2 = 4$. If the exponent of the divisor is greater than the exponent of the dividend, the law of negative exponents applies, thus: $2^3 \div 2^5 = 2^{3-5} = 2^{-2} = 1/2^2 = 1/4$. As in multiplication, numbers with exponents having different bases may be divided in one of two ways: They may be converted into numbers with the same base and then divided by subtracting their exponents, or they may be converted into numbers with exponents of 1 and divided in the usual manner. To illustrate, $2^9 \div 4^3$ may be divided by converting 4^3 into 2^6 and dividing thus: $2^9 \div 2^6 = 2^{9-6} = 2^3 = 8$; or by converting the numbers into numbers with exponents of 1, as follows: $2^9 \div 4^3 = 512 \div 64 = 8$.

In certain cases, the division of numbers with exponents will result in a number having an exponent of zero. A number having an exponent of zero has a value of 1, thus: $2^0 = 1$. Therefore, if we convert 4^2 to 2^4, $4^2 \div 2^4$ will result in a quotient of 1, as follows: $4^2 \div 2^4 = 2^4 \div 2^4 = 2^{4-4} = 2^0 = 1$. The end result, of course, would be the same if we were to convert 2^4 to 4^2, thus: $4^2 \div 2^4 = 4^2 \div 4^2 = 4^{2-2} = 4^0 = 1$.

Power of a Power A number with an exponent can itself be raised to a power. This is accomplished by multiplying the exponents and then raising the number to the power indicated by the product of the exponents. For example, 15,625, the power of $(5^2)^3$, is determined as follows: $(5^2)^3 = 5^{2 \times 3} = 5^6 = 15,625$.

Roots of Numbers In contrast to the power of a number, which is the product of that number multiplied by itself a given number of times, the **root** of a number is that number which, when multiplied by itself a specified number of times, will equal the given number. Thus, 32 is the fifth power of 2, whereas 2 is the fifth root of 32; similarly, 16 is the fourth power of 2, and 2 is the fourth root of 16.

The extraction of a root of a number is ordinarily indicated either by a radical sign ($\sqrt{}$) placed in front of the number or by the use of a fractional exponent. When the radical sign is employed, a small figure called the **index** of the root is placed at the left of the radical sign to show what root is indicated. If the index is omitted, the **square root** is indicated. For example:

$$\sqrt{9} = 3, \text{ the square root of } 9$$
$$\sqrt[3]{64} = 4, \text{ the cube root of } 64$$
$$\sqrt[4]{625} = 5, \text{ the fourth root of } 625$$

When a fractional exponent is used to indicate the root of a number, the numerator of the exponent is always 1, and the denominator shows what root is indicated. Thus:

$$9^{1/2} = 3, \text{ the square root of } 9$$
$$64^{1/3} = 4, \text{ the cube root of } 64$$
$$625^{1/4} = 5, \text{ the fourth root of } 625$$

Roots of Numbers with Exponents On occasion, the root of a number with an exponent may be required. If the radical sign is used to indicate the extraction of a root, its index is first divided into the exponent of the number and the problem is then solved in the usual way. When the fractional exponent is employed, the exponent of the number is first multiplied by the fractional exponent and the problem is then solved in the usual way. Thus, the cube root of 2 to the sixth power may be determined in either of the following ways:

$$\sqrt[3]{2^6} = 2^{6/3} = 2^2 = 4$$

or

$$(2^6)^{1/3} = (2^{\overset{2}{\cancel{6}}})^{1/\cancel{3}} = 2^2 = 4$$

In like manner, the twelfth root of 4 to the sixth power may be determined as follows:

$$\sqrt[12]{4^6} = 4^{6/12} = 4^{1/2} = \sqrt{4} = 2$$

or

$$(4^6)^{1/12} = (4^{\cancel{6}})^{1/\cancel{12}} = 4^{1/2} = \sqrt{4} = 2$$

Tables of Powers and Roots Powers and roots of numbers may be found by arithmetic processes or by the use of reference tables. If reference tables are readily available, they may prove to be the best source; they are, however, usually quite limited in their coverage. Table 1 on page 724 gives squares, square roots, cubes, and cube roots.

Table 1 Powers and Roots

No.	Square	Square Root	Cube	Cube Root	No.	Square	Square Root	Cube	Cube Root
1	1	1.000	1	1.000	51	2,601	7.141	132,651	3.708
2	4	1.414	8	1.260	52	2,704	7.211	140,608	3.733
3	9	1.732	27	1.442	53	2,809	7.280	148,877	3.756
4	16	2.000	64	1.587	54	2,916	7.348	157,464	3.780
5	25	2.236	125	1.710	55	3,025	7.416	166,375	3.803
6	36	2.449	216	1.817	56	3,136	7.483	175,616	3.826
7	49	2.646	343	1.913	57	3,249	7.550	185,193	3.849
8	64	2.828	512	2.000	58	3,364	7.616	195,112	3.871
9	81	3.000	729	2.080	59	3,481	7.681	205,379	3.893
10	100	3.162	1,000	2.154	60	3,600	7.746	216,000	3.915
11	121	3.317	1,331	2.224	61	3,721	7.810	226,981	3.936
12	144	3.464	1,728	2.289	62	3,844	7.874	238,328	3.958
13	169	3.606	2,197	2.351	63	3,969	7.937	250,047	3.979
14	196	3.742	2,744	2.410	64	4,096	8.000	262,144	4.000
15	225	3.873	3,375	2.466	65	4,225	8.062	274,625	4.021
16	256	4.000	4,096	2.520	66	4,356	8.124	287,496	4.041
17	289	4.123	4,913	2.571	67	4,489	8.185	300,763	4.062
18	324	4.243	5,832	2.621	68	4,624	8.246	314,432	4.082
19	361	4.359	6,859	2.668	69	4,761	8.307	328,509	4.102
20	400	4.472	8,000	2.714	70	4,900	8.367	343,000	4.121
21	441	4.583	9,261	2.759	71	5,041	8.426	357,911	4.141
22	484	4.690	10,648	2.802	72	5,184	8.485	373,248	4.160
23	529	4.796	12,167	2.844	73	5,329	8.544	389,017	4.179
24	576	4.899	13,824	2.884	74	5,476	8.602	405,224	4.198
25	625	5.000	15,625	2.924	75	5,625	8.660	421,875	4.217
26	676	5.099	17,576	2.962	76	5,776	8.718	438,976	4.236
27	729	5.196	19,683	3.000	77	5,929	8.775	456,533	4.254
28	784	5.292	21,952	3.037	78	6,084	8.832	474,552	4.273
29	841	5.385	24,389	3.072	79	6,241	8.888	493,039	4.291
30	900	5.477	27,000	3.107	80	6,400	8.944	512,000	4.309
31	961	5.568	29,791	3.141	81	6,561	9.000	531,441	4.327
32	1,024	5.657	32,768	3.175	82	6,724	9.055	551,368	4.344
33	1,089	5.745	35,937	3.208	83	6,889	9.110	571,787	4.362
34	1,156	5.831	39,304	3.240	84	7,056	9.165	592,704	4.380
35	1,225	5.916	42,875	3.271	85	7,225	9.220	614,125	4.397
36	1,296	6.000	46,656	3.302	86	7,396	9.274	636,056	4.414
37	1,369	6.083	50,653	3.332	87	7,569	9.327	658,503	4.431
38	1,444	6.164	54,872	3.362	88	7,744	9.381	681,472	4.448
39	1,521	6.245	59,319	3.391	89	7,921	9.434	704,969	4.465
40	1,600	6.325	64,000	3.420	90	8,100	9.487	729,000	4.481
41	1,681	6.403	68,921	3.448	91	8,281	9.539	753,571	4.498
42	1,764	6.481	74,088	3.476	92	8,464	9.592	778,688	4.514
43	1,849	6.557	79,507	3.503	93	8,649	9.644	804,357	4.531
44	1,936	6.633	85,184	3.530	94	8,836	9.695	830,584	4.547
45	2,025	6.708	91,125	3.557	95	9,025	9.747	857,375	4.563
46	2,116	6.782	97,336	3.583	96	9,216	9.798	884,736	4.579
47	2,209	6.856	103,823	3.609	97	9,409	9.849	912,673	4.595
48	2,304	6.928	110,592	3.634	98	9,604	9.899	941,192	4.610
49	2,401	7.000	117,649	3.659	99	9,801	9.950	970,299	4.626
50	2,500	7.071	125,000	3.684	100	10,000	10.000	1,000,000	4.642

Logarithms

While the mathematical determination of powers or roots of numbers with relatively small exponents or indexes is generally a simple matter, you may recall from your previous studies that such is not the case when the exponents or indexes are relatively large. For instance, the raising of 2.510 to the fourteenth power, or the extraction of the eleventh root of 5,250, requires a certain degree of mathematical sophistication.

The mathematics involved in the determination of powers or roots of numbers containing large exponents or indexes can be greatly expedited by the use of logarithms. The mathematical procedure for raising a number to a power, for example, is reduced by the use of logarithms to the much less complex operation of multiplying the logarithm of the number by the exponent of the power. Similarly, the mathematics of extracting the root of a number is reduced by the use of logarithms to the simpler operation of dividing the logarithm of the number by the index of the root. In addition to their value in solving problems which deal with powers and roots, logarithms are also quite useful in the multiplication and division of numbers which contain numerous digits.

Concept of the Logarithm   A **logarithm** (generally abbreviated simply to **log**) is an exponent that indicates the power to which a fixed base must be raised in order to produce a given number. Although logarithms can be devised using any positive number except 1, unless otherwise stipulated the term refers to the so-called **common logarithm,** which uses 10 as a base. Thus, in the equation $10^3 = 1,000$, the exponent 3 is the common logarithm of the number 1,000; in the equation $10^4 = 10,000$, the exponent 4 is the common logarithm of the number 10,000.

We learned in our study of the powers of numbers that to find the power indicated by a negative exponent we merely change the sign of the exponent from minus to plus and then write the resulting term as the denominator of a fraction whose numerator is 1; for example, $10^{-3} = 1/10^3 = 1/1,000 = .001$. Thus, in the equation $10^{-3} = .001$, the exponent -3 is the common logarithm of the number .001, and in the equation $10^{-4} = .0001$, the exponent -4 is the common logarithm of the number .0001.

By combining the definition of a common logarithm with our knowledge of positive and negative powers of 10, we can readily see that:

1 is the common logarithm of 10.

2 is the common logarithm of 100.

3 is the common logarithm of 1,000.

4 is the common logarithm of 10,000.

and that

−1 is the common logarithm of .1.

−2 is the common logarithm of .01.

−3 is the common logarithm of .001.

−4 is the common logarithm of .0001.

A study of the foregoing data will reveal that the common logarithm of a whole number which is a multiple of 10 is always 1 less than the number of digits in the number. For example, 4, the common logarithm of 10,000, is equal to 1 less than the number of digits (5) in the number. We can also see from the data that the common logarithm of a decimal which is a multiple of 10 is always equal to the number of places to the right of the decimal point in which the first significant digit (any digit other than zero) occurs. For example, −4, the common logarithm of .0001, is equal to the number of places (4) to the right of the decimal point in which the first significant digit occurs (1 being in the fourth place).

It should also be apparent from the data that the logarithm of a number between 10 and 100 is "something" more than 1 and less than 2; thus, it must be 1 plus a fraction. Likewise, the logarithm of a number between 100 and 1,000 is more than 2 and less than 3, and thus must be 2 plus a fraction. A generalization of this observation follows:

The log of 6   = 0."something."

The log of 16   = 1."something."

The log of 160   = 2."something."

The log of 1,600 = 3."something."

and

The log of .6   = −1."something."

The log of .016   = −2."something."

The log of .0016 = −3."something."

The log of .00016 = −4."something."

Although it is possible to determine by simple inspection the common logarithm of a number that is a multiple of the base 10, this is not the case when the numbers are not multiples of 10. We can determine quite easily that the logarithm of 252 is 2."something," but most of us would find it very difficult to determine by mere inspection that the logarithm of 252 expressed to the fifth decimal place is 2.40140. However, easy-to-use tables are available for the determination of logarithms in such cases.

Characteristics and Mantissas You probably noticed in the preceding discussion that the logarithm of a number is ordinarily composed of two separate elements, one being to the left of the decimal point and the other to the right. The part to the left of the decimal point is called the **characteristic,** and the part to the right, the **mantissa.**

The characteristic of a logarithm of a number is determined by the location of the first significant digit of the number. If this digit is to the left of the decimal point of the number, the characteristic is positive and is 1 less than the number of digits to the left of the decimal point. If this digit is to the right of the decimal point, the characteristic is negative and is equal to the number of places to the right of the decimal point in which the digit occurs. Although characteristics may be either positive or negative, mantissas are always positive, and their values are determined by the digits in the number, irrespective of the position of the decimal point. For example, the logarithms of .252, 2.52, 25.2, and 252 all have the same mantissa, 40140. Whereas characteristics are determined by inspection, mantissas are determined from logarithm tables.

Construction and Use of Log Tables Logarithm tables of numbers contain only two things: mantissas and numbers. If we have the number, we can obtain the mantissa, and vice versa.

Log tables are constructed with varying degrees of accuracy. Six and seven-place tables, for instance, are more accurate than five-place ones, but the general principles of construction and use apply equally well to all tables. The excerpt on pages 728 and 729 is from a five-place table.

Upon examination we can see that the table is composed of numbers and mantissas. The first three digits of numbers are listed in the column headed N, and the fourth digits are listed as column headings 0 to 9. The mantissas are arranged so that the first two digits (first two decimal places) are tabulated in the column headed 0, and, in order to save space, they are not repeated in subsequent columns. The next three digits (third, fourth, and fifth decimal places) of the mantissas are listed in the columns 0 to 9. For example, the mantissa of the number 2500 is .39794, the mantissa of the number 2505 is .39881, and the mantissa of the number 2563 is .40875.

When, in obtaining a mantissa from a log table, we encounter an asterisk (*), this means that the first two digits (first two decimal places) of the mantissa are to be taken from the next two-digit entry appearing in column 0. For example, the first two digits of the mantissa of the number 2512 are 40, whereas the first two digits of the mantissa of the number 2511 are 39. Thus, the mantissa of the number 2511 is .39985, and the mantissa of the number 2512 is .40002.

To determine the digits of an unknown number from a known mantissa, it is necessary to use the table in the reverse order of that described above. First, find the page in the table containing the first two digits of the mantissa. Next,

Table 2   Logarithms of Numbers

(an excerpt)

N		0	1	2	3	4	5	6	7	8	9
200	30	103	125	146	168	190	211	233	255	276	298
01		320	341	363	384	406	428	449	471	492	514
02		535	557	578	600	621	643	664	685	707	728
03		750	771	792	814	835	856	878	899	920	942
04		963	984	*006	*027	*048	*069	*091	*112	*133	*154
05	31	175	197	218	239	260	281	302	323	345	366
06		387	408	429	450	471	492	513	534	555	576
07		597	618	639	660	681	702	723	744	765	785
08		806	827	848	869	890	911	931	952	973	994
09	32	015	035	056	077	098	118	139	160	181	201
210		222	243	263	284	305	325	346	366	387	408
11		428	449	469	490	510	531	552	572	593	613
12		634	654	675	695	715	736	756	777	797	818
13		838	858	879	899	919	940	960	980	*001	*021
14	33	041	062	082	102	122	143	163	183	203	224
15		244	264	284	304	325	345	365	385	405	425
16		445	465	486	506	526	546	566	586	606	626
17		646	666	686	706	726	746	766	786	806	826
18		846	866	885	905	925	945	965	985	*005	*025
19	34	044	064	084	104	124	143	163	183	203	223
220		242	262	282	301	321	341	361	380	400	420
21		439	459	479	498	518	537	557	577	596	616
22		635	655	674	694	713	733	753	772	792	811
23		830	850	869	889	908	928	947	967	986	*005
24	35	025	044	064	083	102	122	141	160	180	199
25		218	238	257	276	295	315	334	353	372	392
26		411	430	449	468	488	507	526	545	564	583
27		603	622	641	660	679	698	717	736	755	774
28		793	813	832	851	870	889	908	927	946	965
29		984	*003	*021	*040	*059	*078	*097	*116	*135	*154
230	36	173	192	211	229	248	267	286	305	324	342
31		361	380	399	418	436	455	474	493	511	530
32		549	568	586	605	624	642	661	680	698	717
33		736	754	773	791	810	829	847	866	884	903
34		922	940	959	977	996	*014	*033	*051	*070	*088
35	37	107	125	144	162	181	199	218	236	254	273
36		291	310	328	346	365	383	401	420	438	457
37		475	493	511	530	548	566	585	603	621	639
38		658	676	694	712	731	749	767	785	803	822
39		840	858	876	894	912	931	949	967	985	*003
240	38	021	039	057	075	093	112	130	148	166	184
41		202	220	238	256	274	292	310	328	346	364
42		382	399	417	435	453	471	489	507	525	543
43		561	578	596	614	632	650	668	686	703	721
44		739	757	775	792	810	828	846	863	881	899
45		917	934	952	970	987	*005	*023	*041	*058	*076
46	39	094	111	129	146	164	182	199	217	235	252
47		270	287	305	322	340	358	375	393	410	428
48		445	463	480	498	515	533	550	568	585	602
49		620	637	655	672	690	707	724	742	759	777
250		794	811	829	846	863	881	898	915	933	950
N		0	1	2	3	4	5	6	7	8	9

Table 2   **Logarithms of Numbers** (cont'd)

(an excerpt)

N		0	1	2	3	4	5	6	7	8	9
250	39	794	811	829	846	863	881	898	915	933	950
51		967	985	*002	*019	*037	*054	*071	*088	*106	*123
52	40	140	157	175	192	209	226	243	261	278	295
53		312	329	346	364	381	398	415	432	449	466
54		483	500	518	535	552	569	586	603	620	637
55		654	671	688	705	722	739	756	773	790	807
56		824	841	858	875	892	909	926	943	960	976
57		993	*010	*027	*044	*061	*078	*095	*111	*128	*145
58	41	162	179	196	212	229	246	263	280	296	313
59		330	347	363	380	397	414	430	447	464	481
260		497	514	531	547	564	581	597	614	631	647
61		664	681	697	714	731	747	764	780	797	814
62		830	847	863	880	896	913	929	946	963	979
63		996	*012	*029	*045	*062	*078	*095	*111	*127	*144
64	42	160	177	193	210	226	243	259	275	292	308
65		325	341	357	374	390	406	423	439	455	472
66		488	504	521	537	553	570	586	602	619	635
67		651	667	684	700	716	732	749	765	781	797
68		813	830	846	862	878	894	911	927	943	959
69		975	991	*008	*024	*040	*056	*072	*088	*104	*120
270	43	136	152	169	185	201	217	233	249	265	281
71		297	313	329	345	361	377	393	409	425	441
72		457	473	489	505	521	537	553	569	584	600
73		616	632	648	664	680	696	712	727	743	759
74		775	791	807	823	838	854	870	886	902	917
75		933	949	965	981	996	*012	*028	*044	*059	*075
76	44	091	107	122	138	154	170	185	201	217	232
77		248	264	279	295	311	326	342	358	373	389
78		404	420	436	451	467	483	498	514	529	545
79		560	576	592	607	623	638	654	669	685	700
280		716	731	747	762	778	793	809	824	840	855
81		871	886	902	917	932	948	963	979	994	*010
82	45	025	040	056	071	086	102	117	133	148	163
83		179	194	209	225	240	255	271	286	301	317
84		332	347	362	378	393	408	423	439	454	469
85		484	500	515	530	545	561	576	591	606	621
86		637	652	667	682	697	712	728	743	758	773
87		788	803	818	834	849	864	879	894	909	924
88		939	954	969	984	*000	*015	*030	*045	*060	*075
89	46	090	105	120	135	150	165	180	195	210	225
290		240	255	270	285	300	315	330	345	359	374
91		389	404	419	434	449	464	479	494	509	523
92		538	553	568	583	598	613	627	642	657	672
93		687	702	716	731	746	761	776	790	805	820
94		835	850	864	879	894	909	923	938	953	967
95		982	997	*012	*026	*041	*056	*070	*085	*100	*114
96	47	129	144	159	173	188	202	217	232	246	261
97		276	290	305	319	334	349	363	378	392	407
98		422	436	451	465	480	494	509	524	538	553
99		567	582	596	611	625	640	654	669	683	698
300		712	727	741	756	770	784	799	813	828	842
N		0	1	2	3	4	5	6	7	8	9

find the row and column containing the last three digits of the mantissa. In the left column of the table (headed N) opposite the last three digits of the mantissa, read the first three digits of the number. Find the fourth digit of the number at the top of the column containing the last three digits of the mantissa. For example, the digits of a number with a mantissa of .39933 are 2508; the digits of a number with a mantissa of .40071 are 2516; and the digits of a number with a mantissa of .47480 are 2984.

As you undoubtedly noticed, we have not pointed off the numbers found by the use of mantissas. In order to do so, we need the entire logarithm, which includes both the mantissa and the characteristic.

When a known logarithm is used to determine an unknown number, the number is referred to as the **antilogarithm,** or more simply as the **antilog.**

Determining the Logarithm of a Known Number In sum, to determine the logarithm of a known number using a five-place table similar to Table 2, we must:

1 Determine the characteristic of the logarithm by examining the number.

2 Find the page in the table that contains the series of digits that make up the number.

3 In the column headed N, find the line that contains the first three digits of the number.

4 In the numbered columns, locate the column that contains the fourth digit of the number.

5 Determine the last three digits of the mantissa. These are located at the intersection of the line containing the first three digits of the number, determined in (3) above, and the column containing the fourth digit of the number, determined in (4) above.

6 Determine the first two digits of the mantissa from the column headed 0. [Remember that if an asterisk (*) is encountered when you are obtaining a mantissa from the table, the first two digits of the mantissa are to be taken from the next two-digit entry appearing in column 0.]

Utilizing our earlier discussion on characteristics and mantissas and Table 2, determine, for practice, the following:

Log of 2500   = 3.39794
Log of 25.02 = 1.39829
Log of 251.4 = 2.40037
Log of 29550 = 4.47056
Log of 298.34 = 2.47471*

*Because a five-place log table lists mantissas of four-digit numbers only, we must interpolate in this case. Straight-line interpolation provides only an approximation, but it is close enough for our work at this time. Thus, the mantissa of .47471 was determined by taking 40 percent of the difference (.00015) between mantissas .47465 and .47480 and adding the resulting .00006 to the lower mantissa (.47465).

Log of .2990 = −1.47567

Log of .0299 = −2.47567

Log of .0025 = −3.39794

Determining the Antilogarithm (Number) of a Known Logarithm The procedure for determining an antilogarithm (the number corresponding to a given logarithm) is the reverse of that for determining a logarithm. Thus, in sum, to determine the number corresponding to a known logarithm, using a five-place table, we must:

1 Find the page in the table that contains the first two digits of the mantissa. (Remember, these digits are located in column 0.)

2 Locate the line containing the last three digits of the mantissa.

3 In the column headed N, opposite the line containing the last three digits of the mantissa as found in (2), determine the first three digits of the number.

4 In the numbered column containing the last three digits of the mantissa, determine the fourth digit of the number.

5 Determine the location of the decimal point based upon the value of the characteristic of the logarithm.

For practice, by following our discussion on characteristics and mantissas and using Table 2, determine that the:

Antilog of   1.39950 = 25.09

Antilog of   2.40603 = 254.7

Antilog of   3.40054 = 2515

Antilog of   4.47451 = 29820

Antilog of −1.40841 = .2561

Antilog of −2.39829 = .02502

Antilog of −3.46850 = .002941

Antilog of   2.47150 = 296.14*

Mathematical Computations Using Logarithms In mathematical computations involving complex problems of multiplication, division, raising to powers, and extracting roots, logarithms can be used to great advantage, because they simplify the operations involved. Since logarithms are exponents, all logarithmic operations follow the exponential concepts developed in the preceding section of this chapter.

---

*Again, we must interpolate because the five-place log table lists mantissas of four-digit numbers only, and we have a five-digit number. Since a five-digit number with a mantissa of .47144 is 29610, and one with a mantissa of .47159 is 29620, one with a mantissa of .47150 is 29614 ($\frac{6}{15}$ of the way between 29610 and 29620).

Therefore, when logarithms are used, multiplication becomes a problem of addition, division becomes a problem of subtraction, raising to a power becomes a problem of multiplication, and extracting a root becomes a problem of division.

To **multiply** two or more numbers using logarithms, we merely add the logarithms of the numbers and then determine the antilog of the sum. For example, a product of 4,237,800 would be determined logarithmically by multiplying 33 × 1,499 × 85.67 as follows:

$$\begin{aligned}
\text{Log of } 33 &= 1.51851 \\
\text{Log of } 1499 &= 3.17580 \\
\text{Log of } 85.67 &= \underline{1.93283} \\
\text{Antilog of } 6.62714 &= 4,237,800
\end{aligned}$$

For practice, using Table 2, determine logarithmically that the:

Product of 2.131 × 22.41 × 23.51 × 24.61 = 27,630

Product of 28756 × 29.634 × 2.7412   = 2,336,000

Product of 29670 × .00293 × 2.8653   = 249.100*

Division is accomplished logarithmically by subtracting the logarithm of the divisor from the logarithm of the dividend and then obtaining the antilog of the difference. For example, a quotient of 189.025 is obtained by dividing 68,655 by 363.2, as follows:

$$\begin{aligned}
\text{Log of } 68655 &= 4.83667 \\
-\text{Log of } 363.2 &= \underline{2.56015} \\
\text{Antilog of } 2.27652 &= 189.025
\end{aligned}$$

For practice, determine logarithmically that the:

Quotient of 22580 ÷ 28.65 ÷ 2.734 = 288.274

Quotient of 203.55 ÷ 27.66 ÷ 2.54 = 2.8973

Quotient of 22.18 ÷ .2984 ÷ 2.65   = 28.05†

To **raise a number to a required power** logarithmically, multiply the logarithm of the number by the exponent of the power and then determine the antilog of the product. For example, 101,625,000,000, the fifth power of 159 (that is, 159^5) is determined as follows:

*When you solve for this product, your final log should be 2.39636.

† When you solve for this quotient, your final log should be 1.44791.

$$\text{Log of } 159 = 2.20140$$
$$\frac{5}{\text{Antilog of } 11.00700} = 101,625,000,000$$

For practice, determine logarithmically that:

$$280^3 = 21,952,500$$
$$22.4^4 = 251,767$$
$$2.90^{14} = 2,975,786*$$

To **extract the root of a number** logarithmically, divide the logarithm of the number by the index of the root to be extracted and then determine the antilog of the quotient. For example, 2.1787, the eleventh root of 5,250 (that is, $\sqrt[11]{5250}$), is determined as follows:

$$\text{Log of } 5250 = 3.72016$$
$$3.72016 \div 11 = .33820$$
$$\text{Antilog of } .33820 = \underline{2.1787}$$

For practice, determine logarithmically that:

$$\sqrt[4]{21.37} = 2.15005$$
$$\sqrt[6]{264} = 2.53278$$
$$\sqrt[12]{21865} = 2.29958\dagger$$

BASIC ALGEBRA

Arithmetic, the language of numbers, has been the traditional language of accounting. However, many of the advances in accounting methodology in the recent past have been based upon algebra, the language of symbols. Obviously, if this trend is to continue, and it appears very probable that it will, the accountant of the future must be well-versed in the fundamentals of algebra. As in our review of arithmetic, we shall cover here only the more basic and useful principles of algebra.

---

*When you solve for this power, your final log should be 6.47360.

†When you solve for this root, your final log should be .36165.

Algebraic Concepts of Signs, Symbols, and Numbers

A review of algebra logically begins with a review of its operating signs, its symbolic use of letters in place of numbers, and its underlying concepts of numbers.

Operating Signs While the operating signs $(+, -, \times,$ and $\div)$ carry the same meaning in algebra as they do in arithmetic, algebra utilizes some additional ones. For example, the center dot $(\cdot)$, parentheses, and sometimes no sign at all are used to indicate multiplication. Thus, a multiplied by b may be written as $a \times b$, $a \cdot b$, $a(b)$, or simply as ab. Although the usual arithmetic sign for division $(\div)$ is employed in algebra, division may also be indicated by placing a dividing line between the dividend and the divisor as is done in common fractions. Thus, a divided by b may be written as a/b, and $a + b$ divided by $c + d$ as $(a + b)/(c + d)$.

Symbolic Use of Letters Letters are used symbolically in algebra in two ways: (1) to represent numbers that have known values, and (2) as symbols for numbers whose values are to be found. Galileo's classic law regarding the effect of gravity on a free-falling object, when stated symbolically, is illustrative of both. The law, as you remember, states that the distance traveled by a free-falling object is equal to one-half of the product of the acceleration of gravity and the square of the elapsed time. Stated algebraically, the law reads: $d = \frac{1}{2}gt^2$, with d being the distance traveled, g the acceleration rate, and t the elapsed time in seconds after the start of the fall. Since g, as you recall, is a constant 32 feet per second, if we know t, we can find d, and vice versa.

Algebraic Concept of Numbers Certain quantities are capable of existing in opposite directions. For example, air temperature may be above or below zero; in mechanics there are actions and reactions; and in financial transactions there are gains and losses. Opposite quantities of this nature exist in algebra in the form of positive and negative numbers. The idea underlying such numbers may be depicted graphically on a number line as follows:

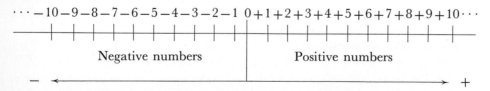

Positive numbers are either preceded by a plus $(+)$ sign or have no sign at all, while negative numbers are always preceded by a minus $(-)$ sign. As you study the algebraic operations in the following pages, remember that the **absolute value** of a number is its measured magnitude regardless of its sign; as related to the number line, it is the distance from the zero point to the number, regardless of the direction. Thus, the absolute value of $+8$ is 8, and the absolute value of -8 is also 8.

Algebraic Operations

The basic mathematical operations of arithmetic and algebra are essentially the same, except that in algebra letters are frequently used as symbols for numbers, and numbers may be either positive or negative.

Algebraic Addition To add two algebraic numbers with **like** signs, add their absolute values and prefix the result with their common sign. The following are examples:

$+5$	-4	$+3a$	$+a$
$+3$	-2	$+2a$	$+b$
$+8$	-6	$+5a$	$+(a + b)$

To add two algebraic numbers with **unlike** signs, subtract the smaller number from the larger and prefix the result with the sign of the larger. The following are examples:

-5	$+4$	$+3a$	$+a$
$+3$	-3	$-2a$	$-b$
-2	$+1$	$+1a$	$+(a - b)$

Algebraic Subtraction To subtract one algebraic number from another, change the sign of the subtrahend and add the subtrahend and the minuend. The following are examples:

$+5$	-4	$-3a$	$+a$
$+3$	-2	$+2a$	$-b$
$+2$	-2	$-5a$	$+(a + b)$

Algebraic Multiplication To multiply two algebraic numbers with *like* signs, multiply their absolute values and prefix the result with a positive sign. The following are examples:

$+5$	-4	$+3a$	$+a$
$+3$	-2	$+2a$	$+b$
$+15$	$+8$	$+6a^2$*	$+ab$

*As you will recall from our review of exponents, the exponent in the product is the sum of the exponents in the multiplier and the multiplicand. Thus, when we multiply a times a, we get a^2.

To multiply two algebraic numbers with *unlike* signs, multiply their absolute values and prefix the result with a negative sign. The following are examples:

$$
\begin{array}{r} -5 \\ +3 \\ \hline -15 \end{array}
\qquad
\begin{array}{r} +4 \\ -2 \\ \hline -8 \end{array}
\qquad
\begin{array}{r} +3a \\ -2a \\ \hline -6a^2 \end{array}
\qquad
\begin{array}{r} +a \\ -b \\ \hline -ab \end{array}
$$

Algebraic Division   To divide two algebraic numbers with *like* signs, divide their absolute values and prefix the result with a positive sign. The following are examples:

$$(+15) \div (+5) = +3$$
$$(-15) \div (-5) = +3$$
$$(+ab) \div (+a) = +b$$
$$(-ab) \div (-b) = +a$$
$$(+a^5) \div (+a^2) = +a^{3}*$$

To divide two algebraic numbers with *unlike* signs, divide their absolute values and prefix the result with a negative sign. The following are examples:

$$(+15) \div (-5) = -3$$
$$(-8) \div (+2) = -4$$
$$(+ab) \div (-a) = -b$$
$$(-ab) \div (+b) = -a$$
$$(+a^5) \div (-a^2) = -a^3$$

Order of Operations   The order in which the basic algebraic operations are performed in a given problem depends upon the operations and groupings involved. When the problem contains only addition and subtraction, the operations may be performed in any order desired. However, when multiplication and division operations appear in the same problem with addition and subtraction operations, the multiplication and division must be performed first.

When you are solving a problem containing grouping signs such as parentheses ( ), brackets [ ], and braces { }, the operations within the grouping signs must be performed first. When grouping signs are enclosed within other grouping signs, the operations within the innermost grouping signs are to be performed first.

Algebraic Determination of Unknown Quantities

Equations may be defined as statements that two expressions are equal in value; in algebra we use them to solve for unknown quantities. Algebraic equations are employed by accountants in many areas. For instance, as we saw in Chapter 22, they are fundamental to break-even and marginal analysis; they also are useful

*Remember that when exponents are involved in division, the exponent in the quotient is equal to the difference between the exponents in the dividend and the divisor.

in solving problems dealing with such things as profit-sharing bonuses, income taxes, cost allocations, and the economic order quantity for inventory purposes.

The algebraic procedures for the determination of unknown quantities are clear cut. First, we must write the problem as an equation, letting a letter such as x represent the unknown quantity. We then systematically arrange all the terms involving the unknown quantity on one side of the equation—usually the left side—and the known quantities on the other side. We next combine and reduce both sides of the equation by symbolic arithmetic until there remains only a single letter representing the unknown on one side and a known number on the other. This, of course, is the answer. Thus, in solving an algebraic equation, we want to find the value of an unknown quantity, which is expressed in the equation in terms of a lettered notation. In the equation $x - 4 = 5$ we are solving for the value of x.

Algebraic Axioms While it is readily determinable simply by inspection that in the equation $x - 4 = 5$ the value of x is 9, the value of an unknown quantity in many instances may not be determined so easily. On the contrary, the solution of many algebraic equations may become quite difficult or even impossible unless certain fundamental principles, often called **axioms of equality,** which you undoubtedly recall from your previous study of algebra, are understood and utilized. You will remember that equal quantities may be added to, subtracted from, multiplied by, or divided into both sides of an equation without destroying the equality, provided that no divisor is zero. In addition, it is possible to shorten the process of adding to or subtracting from both sides of an equation by **transposition,** which is accomplished simply by shifting a term from one side of an equation to the other and changing its sign. Thus, in the equation $x - 4 = 5$, we can add 4 to both sides merely by transposing the 4 from the left side to the right and getting $x = 5 + 4$. Similarly, in the equation $x + 4 = 6$, we can deduct 4 from each side by transposing the 4 from the left side to the right side and getting $x = 6 - 4$.

Equation-solving Procedure While equations such as those in the preceding paragraph can be solved in one or two simple operations, others often require that the equation be put into a succession of forms, thus involving application of several operations. The following routine provides a useful step-by-step procedure from given equation to final solution:

1 Clear the equation of fractions, if any, by multiplying each term by the lowest common denominator (LCD).

2 Remove any grouping signs by performing the indicated operations.

3 Collect terms by transposing the unknown terms to the left side of the equation and the known terms to the right side.

4 Finally, combine similar terms and divide both sides of the equation by the numerical coefficient of the unknown term.

To solve the equation

$$\frac{x}{3} + \frac{4x}{6} = 3 - \frac{1}{4}(x - 5)$$

we would proceed as follows:

1 Clear the equation of fractions by multiplying each term by 12 (the LCD). Thus:

$$12 \cdot \frac{x}{3} + 12 \cdot \frac{4x}{6} = 12 \cdot 3 - 12 \cdot \frac{1}{4}(x - 5)$$

$$\overset{4}{\cancel{12}} \cdot \frac{x}{\cancel{3}} + \overset{2}{\cancel{12}} \cdot \frac{4x}{\cancel{6}} = 12 \cdot 3 - \overset{3}{\cancel{12}} \cdot \frac{1}{\cancel{4}}(x - 5)$$

$$4x + 8x = 36 - 3(x - 5)$$

2 Remove the parentheses by multiplying the enclosed terms $x - 5$ by the -3 which precedes the first parenthesis.[1] Thus:

$$4x + 8x = 36 - 3x + 15$$

3 Collect terms by transposing the unknown terms to the left side of the equation and the known terms to the right side. In this case transfer the $-3x$ from the right side to the left side, changing the sign so that it reads $+3x$. Thus:

$$4x + 8x + 3x = 36 + 15$$

4 Combine similar terms and divide both sides of the equation by the numerical coefficient of the unknown term, as follows:

$$15x = 51$$
$$x = \underline{\underline{3.40}}$$

We can verify our result by substituting 3.40 for x in the original equation and solving as follows:

$$\frac{x}{3} + \frac{4x}{6} = 3 - \frac{1}{4}(x - 5)$$

$$\frac{3.40}{3} + \frac{4(3.40)}{6} = 3 - \frac{1}{4}(3.40 - 5)$$

$$1.133 + 2.267 = 3 - .85 + 1.25$$

$$\underline{\underline{3.40}} = \underline{\underline{3.40}}$$

---

[1] You should recall from your previous study of algebra that in terms of symbols of addition and subtraction $-(+3)$ acts the same as -3.

Linear Equations   Algebraic equations such as those used to illustrate the equation-solving procedure involve only the first power of an unknown and are called **first-degree,** or **linear,** equations.   Many everyday business problems can be stated as linear equations; thus, the ability to solve them is considered fundamental to the management process.   Although they contain no power of the unknown higher than the first, linear equations may contain any number of unknowns.

Linear Equations with One Unknown   To illustrate the practical use of linear equations containing one unknown, let us examine their application in the area of profit-sharing bonuses.   When an organization's profits are shared between the employers and employees in such a way that the employees receive shares in the profits of the business in addition to their regular wages or salaries, these shares are known as **profit-sharing bonuses.**   Such bonuses may or may not be considered as expenses in the determination of the amount of profits upon which the bonuses are based.

Let us assume a situation in which an organization has profits of $100,000, subject to an agreement whereby one-seventh of the profits are to be distributed among designated employees in the form of bonuses.   If the bonuses are not considered as expenses, the total bonus can be computed very simply as one-seventh of $100,000.   If, however, the bonuses are considered as expenses that must be deducted before the profits upon which the bonuses are to be based can be determined, we have a different problem.   The $100,000 will then have to be reduced by the total amount of all the bonuses before the amount of profits upon which the bonuses are to be based can be arrived at; or, stated another way, the total bonus to be distributed will be equal to one-seventh of $100,000 less the bonus. If we let B equal the bonus, we can state and solve the problem algebraically, using linear equations, as follows:

$$
\begin{aligned}
B* &= \tfrac{1}{7}(\$100{,}000 - B) \\
7B &= \$100{,}000 - B \\
8B &= \$100{,}000 \\
B &= \$12{,}500
\end{aligned}
$$

We can verify our result by substituting $12,500 for B in the original equation and solving as follows:

$$
\begin{aligned}
B &= \tfrac{1}{7}(\$100{,}000 - B) \\
\$12{,}500 &= \tfrac{1}{7}(\$100{,}000 - \$12{,}500) \\
&\qquad\quad \$12{,}500 \\
\$12{,}500 &= \tfrac{1}{7}(\$\cancel{87{,}500}) \\
\$12{,}500 &= \$12{,}500
\end{aligned}
$$

*The letters $x, y,$ and z are commonly used in algebra as notations for unknown quantities, but in some cases it is more practical to use the first letter or letters of the unknown quantity.

Linear Equations with Two or More Unknowns   When two or more independent
linear equations, each containing two or more unknowns, can be satisfied by the
same set of values for the unknowns, they are called **simultaneous equations.**   For
example, the set of values $x = 4$ and $y = 3$ is the simultaneous solution to the
following pair of equations:

$$4x + 3y = 25$$
$$5x + 4y = 32$$

We can verify the set of values $x = 4$ and $y = 3$ by substituting in the equations
as follows:

$$4(4) + 3(3) = 25$$
$$5(4) + 4(3) = 32$$

When linear equations with two or more unknowns are solved simultaneously,
the values of the unknowns are ordinarily found by combining the equations into
a single equation containing only one unknown.   Although the equations may
be combined in various ways by using the previously reviewed axioms of equality
as they pertain to addition, subtraction, and multiplication, one of the easiest
approaches is to state one of the equations in terms of one of the unknowns and
substitute this value in the other equation.   This latter equation is then solved
and the value obtained is substituted in the other equation; the value of the other
unknown is then obtained.

To illustrate, let us assume the data used in our bonus illustration except that
the income figure of $100,000 is determined without consideration being given
to either the bonus or to income taxes.   In addition, let us assume that the terms
of the profit-sharing agreement provide for the deduction of both the tax and the
bonus when the net income figure upon which the bonus is to be based is determined.   Thus, the bonus would be equal to one-seventh of $100,000 less income
taxes less the bonus.   If we assume a tax rate of 50 percent and let T equal the
tax, we can state and solve the problem algebraically, using simultaneous equations, as follows:

$$B = \tfrac{1}{7}(\$100{,}000 - B - T)$$
$$T = .50(\$100{,}000 - B)$$

If we substitute the value of T, as indicated in the second equation, for T in the
first equation, we get:

$$B = \tfrac{1}{7}[\$100{,}000 - B - .50(\$100{,}000 - B)]$$
$$7B = [\$100{,}000 - B - .50(\$100{,}000 - B)]$$
$$7B = \$100{,}000 - B - \$50{,}000 + .5B$$
$$7.5B = \$50{,}000$$
$$B = \$6{,}667$$

By substituting the $6,667 value for B in the second equation above, we can readily determine the tax T to be $46,667, as follows:

$$T = .50(\$100,000 - B)$$
$$T = .50(\$100,000 - \$6,667)$$
$$T = \$46,667$$

We can verify our results by substituting back into the original equations as follows:

$$B = \tfrac{1}{7}(\$100,000 - B - T)$$
$$\$6,667 = \tfrac{1}{7}(\$100,000 - \$6,667 - \$46,667)$$
$$\$6,667 = \tfrac{1}{7}(\$46,667)$$
$$\$6,667 = \$6,667$$

and

$$T = .50(\$100,000 - B)$$
$$\$46,667 = .50(\$100,000 - \$6,667)$$
$$\$46,667 = \$46,667$$

Although common fractions were utilized in the preceding bonus formulas, decimal fractions could also have been employed. To illustrate, let us assume the same data except that the bonus is to be 50 percent rather than one-seventh and the applicable tax rate is 40 percent instead of 50 percent. For comparative purposes both the common fraction and the decimal fraction approaches are illustrated.

Common Fraction Approach

$$B = \tfrac{1}{2}(\$100,000 - B - T)$$
$$T = .40(\$100,000 - B)$$
$$B = \tfrac{1}{2}[\$100,000 - B - .40(\$100,000 - B)]$$
$$2B = [\$100,000 - B - .40(\$100,000 - B)]$$
$$2B = \$100,000 - B - \$40,000 + .4B$$
$$2.6B = \$60,000$$
$$B = \$23,077$$

Decimal Fraction Approach

$$B = .50(\$100,000 - B - T)$$
$$T = .40(\$100,000 - B)$$
$$B = .50[\$100,000 - B - .40(\$100,000 - B)]$$
$$B = .50(\$100,000 - B - \$40,000 + .4B)$$
$$B = \$50,000 - .5B - \$20,000 + .2B$$
$$1.3B = \$30,000$$
$$B = \$23,077$$

PROBABILITY THEORY

Modern accounting is becoming increasingly more probabilistic and less deterministic. This is only logical because we live in a world of uncertainty; few aspects of our lives elude the touch of chance. An unpredictable grouping of genes, for example, determines our physical makeup, and an unplanned encounter may decide our choice of a mate.

Unable to control chance, man does the next best thing. He tries to evaluate the likelihood of the occurrence of a particular event. As an example, we have the "friendly weatherman" with his 40 percent chance of rain, 90 percent probability of snow, and similar forecasts. In the business world we hear such statements as: "We have an excellent chance of making the sale;" "Our prospects of collecting from him are very poor at best;" or, "There is about a fifty-fifty possibility that we will be able to hire him." Although each statement refers to a situation the outcome of which is uncertain, it nevertheless expresses some degree of confidence that the evaluation will be reliable. Probability theory provides a mathematical framework for scientifically evaluating such likelihoods.

Mathematics of Probability

Mathematically, the probability of the occurrence of a particular event may be expressed as a ratio, a fraction, or a percentage. The probability of a coin tossed into the air falling "heads," for instance, may be stated as one in two, one-half, or 50 percent. Conversely, the probability that the coin will fall "tails" is also one in two, one-half, or 50 percent.

Probability can be expressed mathematically in terms of either success or failure. The probability of success is often indicated by the letter P and the probability of failure by the letter Q. The sum of the two, of course, is always equal to 1 and may be stated mathematically as follows:

$$P + Q = 1$$

or

$$P = 1 - Q$$

or

$$Q = 1 - P$$

The mathematical development of the theory of probability, as you may recall from your previous studies, originated as the result of inquiries from gamblers seeking inside information to assist them in games of chance. Although the theory now has numerous practical applications in both the physical and social sciences, a review of the premises underlying it is perhaps still best approached by the use of examples taken from games of chance.

Independent Events The rolling of dice can serve to illustrate the probability of the occurrence of an independent event. For example, there are six different ways that a rolled die can turn up. Thus, it follows that the probability of any of the numbers 1 through 6 turning up on a single roll is $\frac{1}{6}$.

If we let m equal the number of ways that an event can succeed and n equal the number of ways that it can fail, the probability of success can be stated mathematically as $P = m/(m + n)$ and the probability of failure as $Q = n/(m + n)$.

To illustrate the use of the formula, let us assume that one ball is drawn from a box containing four red balls and 12 white balls. The probability of a red ball being drawn is $\frac{1}{4}$, determined as follows:

$$P = \frac{m}{m + n}$$

$$P = \frac{4}{4 + 12} = \frac{4}{16} = \frac{1}{4}$$

Two or More Independent Events Two or more events are said to be *independent* of one another if the outcome of one in no way affects the outcome of the other. For example, no matter how many times a coin is tossed into the air, the probability of it turning up "heads" on any given throw is $\frac{1}{2}$.

To find the probability of the occurrence of a combination of two or more independent events, we multiply their separate probabilities. For example, the probability of a 5 turning up on two consecutive rolls of a die is $(\frac{1}{6} \times \frac{1}{6})$ or $\frac{1}{36}$, and on three consecutive rolls is $(\frac{1}{6} \times \frac{1}{6} \times \frac{1}{6})$ or $\frac{1}{216}$.

Dependent Events If two or more events are so related that the outcome of each affects the outcome of the other or others, the events are said to be *dependent*. To find the probability of the occurrence of a sequence of dependent events, we must determine the separate probabilities in sequence and then multiply them. For example, the chance of drawing a spade from a deck of cards on both the first and second draws is $\frac{13}{52} \times \frac{12}{51}$. (Note that after the first spade is drawn, only 12 spades and 51 cards remain to be drawn from.) Thus, the probability that a spade will be drawn on the second draw decreases from $\frac{13}{52}$ to $\frac{12}{51}$. The probability of a third spade appearing on a third draw, of course, would be $\frac{11}{50}$.

Mutually Exclusive Events If the occurrence of one event makes it impossible for another event to occur, the events are said to be *mutually exclusive*. For example, if one number turns up on the roll of a die, this event excludes the possibility that any other number can turn up at the same time. To find the probability of the occurrence of either of two mutually exclusive events, we add the separate probabilities. Thus, the probability of either a 4 or a 5 turning up on a single roll of a die is $(\frac{1}{6} + \frac{1}{6})$ or $\frac{1}{3}$.

Statistical Probability

Although probability theory still bears the marks of its sporting origin, it does have more practical uses. It is a major factor in the science of statistics and plays an important role in various aspects of business. For instance, in the insurance field it aids in the determination of rate structures, and in manufacturing organizations we frequently find both quantity and quality control devices based upon it. However, there is a decided difference between the way probability theory is employed in games of chance and its more useful business applications.

The probability of all possible outcomes can be predicted precisely when the theory is applied to the rolling of dice and the drawing of cards; however, when business predictions are made, all the cards in the deck are seldom known in advance. As a consequence, when employing statistical probability as an aid to making business decisions, management must take experimental samples and assume that they are representative of an entire group. In the same way that an apple grader judges the quality of a basket of apples by examining only a few of the apples, or a wine grader judges the quality of wine by tasting only a small portion, the accountant may judge the quality of an organization's inventory or its receivables by examining only a few of the items and accounts involved. If statistical probability is to be properly employed, those using it must have not only an understanding of the mathematics of probability but also some knowledge of the measures of central tendency and dispersion.

Measures of Central Tendency Central tendency may be defined as the inclination of large groups of data to "bunch up" at one general point or central value. It is often used by accountants to determine the general characteristics of a group of data.

Three of the more important measures of central tendency are (1) the arithmetic mean, (2) the median, and (3) the mode. The **arithmetic mean** is the sum of the values of the various items in a group of data divided by the number of items in the group. The **median** is the middle value in a given sequence of values, and the **mode** is that value which occurs most frequently in a group of data. In the following group of data, the arithmetic mean is 84, the median is 85, and the mode is 87.

$$
\begin{array}{l}
96 \\
91 \\
\left.\begin{array}{l} 87 \\ 87 \end{array}\right\} \text{Mode} \\
85 \quad \text{Median} \\
80 \\
78 \\
77 \\
75 \\
\hline
9\,\lfloor 756 \rfloor\ 84 \quad \text{Arithmetic mean}
\end{array}
$$

Measures of Dispersion Although measures of central tendency give the analyst a general idea as to the nature of his data, in many cases accountants need more information. This is particularly true with regard to the **dispersion,** or **scatter,** of the values in the data. For example, two groups of data may have exactly the same arithmetic means, medians, and modes and yet be quite dissimilar in other respects because of dispersion.

Dispersion can be measured in several ways, with two of the more important measures being (1) the interquartile range, and (2) the standard deviation. Quartiles divide data into four equal parts; therefore, the two middle quarters of the data constitute the **interquartile range.** The **standard deviation** is the square root of the quotient resulting from the division of the sum of the squared deviations from the arithmetic mean by the number of items in the data. As a general rule, about two-thirds of a large group of data will fall within one standard deviation of the arithmetic mean, about 95 percent within two standard deviations, and practically all within three standard deviations. If we let:

σ = the standard deviation

Σ = the symbol for the "sum of"

d = the algebraic deviation of each item from the arithmetic mean

N = the number of items in the data

the formula for computing the standard deviation may be expressed as follows:

$$\sigma = \sqrt{\frac{\Sigma(d)^2}{N}}$$

In the following group of data, the interquartile range runs from 75 to 87, and the standard deviation is 7.385.*

		d	d^2
96		+14	196
91		+ 9	81
87		+ 5	25
87		+ 5	25
85		+ 3	9
80		− 2	4
78		− 4	16
77		− 5	25
75		− 7	49
75		− 7	49
71		−11	121
11 $\overline{)902}$ 82	Arithmetic mean		600

$*\sigma = \sqrt{\dfrac{\Sigma(d)^2}{N}}$

$\sigma = \sqrt{\dfrac{600}{11}}$

$\sigma = 7.385$

MATHEMATICS APPLIED TO INVENTORY MANAGEMENT

Up to this time we have touched only briefly on the practical applications of mathematical techniques to business problems. In this section we shall examine some ways in which they may be applied to a specific area, inventory management.

Mathematical techniques applicable to inventory management have been recognized for several years, but little use of them was made prior to the advent of automatic data processing. At present, considerable attention is being directed toward two of the more important of these procedures, namely, the determination of the economic order quantity and the reorder point.

Economic Order Quantity (EOQ)

The **economic order quantity** is the optimal amount of an inventoriable item to be ordered at a given time, the quantity to be ordered which will not only meet inventory requirements but will also result in the lowest total annual cost. Because ordering creates procurement costs (order processing, etc.) and possession involves carrying or holding costs (insurance, storage, taxes, obsolescence, interest, etc.), the lowest total annual cost generally corresponds to the point where the **cost to order** is equal to the **cost to hold.** Let:

Q = the economic order quantity, in dollars

A = the annual value of the usage of the item

C = the cost to order, in dollars

H = the cost to hold, expressed as a percentage per year on the average inventory investment

Then the mathematical formula for computing the economic order quantity may be expressed as follows:

$$Q = \sqrt{\frac{2AC}{H}}$$

To illustrate the use of the formula, let us assume that the cost to place an order for item A is $2.50, the holding cost is 10 percent per year, and annual usage is $1,800. Thus:

$$Q = \sqrt{\frac{2AC}{H}}$$

$$Q = \sqrt{\frac{2(\$1,800)(\$2.50)}{10\%}}$$

$$Q = \sqrt{\frac{\$9,000}{.10}}$$

$$Q = \sqrt{\$90,000}$$

$$Q = \$300$$

Mathematics of the EOQ The value of using an algebraic approach to an EOQ problem may be emphasized if we work the same problem arithmetically as follows. (Note that although the answers are the same, the algebraic approach greatly reduces the amount of work involved.)

	Economic Order Quantity (determined arithmetically)					
Months' Supply	*Orders per Year*	*Value per Order*	*Average Inventory*	*Cost to Hold*	*Cost to Buy*	*Total Cost**
12	1.0	$1,800	$900	$90.00	$2.50	$92.50
11	1.1	1,650	825	82.50	2.75	85.25
10	1.2	1,500	750	75.00	3.00	78.00
9	1.3	1,350	675	67.50	3.25	70.75
8	1.5	1,200	600	60.00	3.75	63.75
7	1.7	1,050	525	52.50	4.25	56.75
6	2.0	900	450	45.00	5.00	50.00
5	2.4	750	375	37.50	6.00	43.50
4	3.0	600	300	30.00	7.50	37.50
3	4.0	450	225	22.50	10.00	32.50
2	6.0	300	150	15.00	15.00	30.00
1	12.0	150	75	7.50	30.00	37.50

*Cost to hold plus cost to buy.

As you study the EOQ table, note that the EOQ of $300 in our example corresponds to the point where the cost to buy ($15) and the cost to hold ($15) are equal. This is also the point at which the total cost ($30) is the lowest. You should also bear in mind that an EOQ stated in dollars may be readily stated in terms of units simply by the division of the dollar amount by the cost per unit. Thus, if we assume a unit cost of 50 cents, an EOQ of $300 could also be stated as an EOQ of 600 units.

Graphic Presentation of the EOQ The relationships of the cost to buy, cost to hold, and cost to both buy and hold to the EOQ expressed in units may be illustrated graphically as follows:

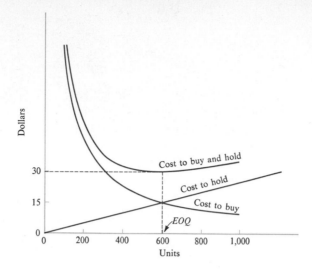

Reorder Point (ROP)

The **reorder point** is that quantitative point at which an inventoriable item should be reordered so that sufficient stock will be continuously available to meet requirements and thus avoid sales losses in merchandising organizations or production stoppages in manufacturing organizations. Whereas the EOQ is an indicator of *how much to buy,* the ROP is an indicator of *when to buy.*

Mathematics of the ROP Mathematically, the reorder point is the sum of (1) the delivery lead time quantity, and (2) the safety level quantity.

The **delivery lead time quantity** is the amount of an inventoriable item that is needed to fulfill inventory requirements from the time an order is initiated until delivery is accomplished. This quantity is ordinarily based upon normal usage and normal delivery times. For example, if normal usage of item A is 12 units per day and 20 working days are normally required for delivery, the delivery lead time quantity would be 240 units (12×20).

The **safety level quantity** is the amount of an inventoriable item needed to ensure continued operations during the procurement period in the event that delivery time is longer than normal or usage is greater than anticipated. Although there are numerous variations, for purposes of simplicity the safety level quantity is often based upon maximum usage, while the delivery time is assumed to be relatively constant. For example, if in the above illustration the maximum daily usage that reasonably can be anticipated is 18 units, the safety level quantity will be 120 units [20 working days $\times$ (18 units $-$ 12 units)].

If we let ROP equal the reorder point, *DLTQ* equal the delivery lead time quantity, and *SLQ* equal the safety level quantity, we can compute a reorder point of 360 units as follows:

$$ROP = DLTQ + SLQ$$
$$ROP = 240 \text{ units} + 120 \text{ units}$$
$$ROP = \underline{\underline{360}} \text{ units}$$

Graphic Presentation of EOQ and ROP The following illustration, based upon the data that were employed in our ROP and EOQ illustrations, depicts graphically both the concept of the reorder point and its relationship to the economic order quantity.

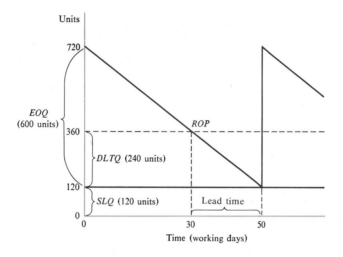

ROP and Probability Theory If usage and delivery times during the procurement period could be forecast with certainty, the determination of the reorder point would be a simple matter; we would need to know the delivery lead time quantity only, and no safety level quantity would be required. However, although delivery times can ordinarily be determined with a certain degree of accuracy, the precise amount of usage is seldom known in advance. As a consequence, management may be faced with a problem that perhaps can be solved best by the employment of probability theory.

The "when to buy" (ROP) decision is essentially a safety level decision, which in turn is an "acceptable level of customer service" decision. If the possibility of running out of stock is completely unacceptable to management, ROP computations would have to be based upon rates of usage and delivery times that could not possibly be exceeded. Needless to say, an inventory policy of this nature could result in excessively high carrying costs. Therefore, instead of trying to guard against all possible stockouts, management ordinarily assumes some degree of stockout risk by establishing an acceptable level of customer service at something less than 100 percent. The level accepted in any given situation, of course, should be the result of sound decisions regarding the possible loss of profits due to stockouts as opposed to the cost of carrying additional safety stock in order to avoid or reduce the possibility of stockouts.

If we assume the term **normal** to be synonymous with **average,** a reorder point based solely upon normal usage (containing no safety stock provision) provides a 50 percent probability of no stockouts occurring during the procurement period. Therefore, if an inventoriable item is ordered six times a year and the possibility of three stockouts a year constitutes an acceptable level of customer service, there is no need for a safety stock provision. If, however, management wishes to maintain a higher level of customer service, a safety stock provision is necessary. For instance, if an item is ordered six times a year and management decides that only one stockout a year is acceptable, a sufficient quantity of safety stock should be included in the reorder point formula to provide for stockout protection in five of the six times yearly that actual usage during the procurement period is likely to exceed normal usage. In other words, management wants an $83\frac{1}{3}$ percent assurance that stockouts will not occur.

To illustrate the use of probability theory in ROP computations, let us assume the data employed in our ROP illustration, that is, that normal usage of item A is 12 units per day and that 20 working days are normally required for delivery. We based our safety level in the ROP illustration on the maximum usage that could reasonably be expected during the procurement period, while the delivery time was held constant. Let us now assume that there is one chance in 10 that usage may be as high as 22 units per day, and one in 20 that it may be as high as 25. If management protects against the one in 10 chance, it has a 90 percent assurance that no stockout will occur during the procurement period; if it protects against the one in 20 chance, it has a 95 percent assurance. If management accepts the one in 10 odds, the reorder point will be 440 units, determined as follows:

$$ROP = DLTQ + SLQ$$
$$ROP = (12 \times 20) + [20 \times (22 - 12)]$$
$$ROP = 240 + 200$$
$$ROP = \underline{\underline{440}} \text{ units}$$

If management accepts the one in 20 odds, the reorder point will be 500 units, determined as follows:

$$ROP = DLTQ + SLQ$$
$$ROP = (12 \times 20) + [20 \times (25 - 12)]$$
$$ROP = 240 + 260$$
$$ROP = \underline{\underline{500}} \text{ units}$$

SUMMARY

The modern accountant must have a thorough understanding of basic mathematics if he is to function adequately in today's business climate.

All mathematical techniques are based on one or more of the four fundamental operations of arithmetic: addition, subtraction, multiplication, and division. The employment of powers and roots expedites computations requiring the repetitive use of one or more of the basic operations. Logarithms simplify the determination of powers or roots of numbers containing large exponents or indexes.

Equations are used in algebra to solve for unknown quantities. Linear equations are particularly useful in the accounting process.

Probability theory provides a mathematical framework for scientifically evaluating the likelihood of the occurrence of particular events. It is useful in many areas of business, one of which is inventory management.

QUESTIONS AND PROBLEMS

26-1 Using Table 2 on pages 728 and 729, determine the logarithms of the following numbers:

(1) 29,654   (6) .22233
(2) 2,373.5   (7) .02367
(3) 263.45   (8) .00245
(4) 27.366   (9) .00026
(5) 2.4623   (10) .00003

26-2 Using Table 2, determine the antilog of the following logarithms:

(1) 4.43136   (6) -1.45301
(2) 3.46352   (7) -2.42586
(3) 2.43600   (8) -3.39094
(4) 1.42111   (9) -4.36173
(5) .44162   (10) -5.30103

26-3 Using Table 2, determine logarithmically the product of:

(1) $21.31 \times 224.1 \times 2.356 \times 246.7$
(2) $28.756 \times 2.9634 \times .27412$

(3) $2.9670 \times .0293 \times 28.653$
(4) $29.634 \times 283.1 \times .00246$
(5) $274.12 \times .00213 \times .00022 \times 211$

26-4 Using Table 2, determine logarithmically the quotient of:

(1) $20,355 \div 2.766 \div 254$
(2) $2,218,000 \div 2,984 \div .0265$
(3) $2,773,125 \div 233.6 \div 2.24 \div 2.20$
(4) $2,810,600 \div 201.2 \div 2.90 \div 20.202$
(5) $2,423,500 \div 290.75 \div 2.047 \div .2009$

26-5 Using Table 2, determine the value of:

(1) 290^3
(2) 22.2^4
(3) 2.94^5
(4) 2.541^6
(5) 2.208^7

26-6 Compute the value of 251^6 (1) arithmetically, and (2) logarithmically, using Table 2. Comment on the computations from the standpoint of time.

26-7 Using Table 2, determine the value of:

(1) $\sqrt[3]{22.2}$
(2) $\sqrt[4]{29.91}$
(3) $\sqrt[5]{225.5}$
(4) $\sqrt[6]{202.3}$
(5) $\sqrt[7]{2039}$

26-8 Solve for x in the following equations:

(1) $4x - \frac{7}{3}x + \frac{1}{7}x = 10$
(2) $\frac{2}{6x} + \frac{3}{8} = \frac{3}{2x} + \frac{1}{12}$
(3) $\frac{1}{5}x - \frac{19}{15} = \frac{4}{9}x - \frac{2}{3}x$
(4) $\frac{1}{6}(4 + x) - \frac{7}{24}(1 - 5x) = \frac{3}{16}(1 + 2x) - \frac{5}{32}(2 - 3x)$
(5) $\frac{x}{4} - \frac{5x}{12} = 2 - \frac{1}{18}(x - 2)$

26-9 A single card is drawn from an ordinary 52-card deck. What is the probability that the card is:

(1) A spade?

(2) Red?

(3) An ace?

(4) A king or queen?

(5) Not a jack?

26-10 Two cards are drawn from an ordinary 52-card deck. The first card drawn is not replaced in the deck before the second card is drawn. If the first card drawn is the ace of spades, what is the probability that the second card drawn is:

(1) Another spade?

(2) Black?

(3) Another ace?

(4) The two of spades?

(5) Not another ace?

26-11 The Coda Cosmetics Company is considering the possibility of a bonus arrangement with its president, B. Coda. The arrangement, if instituted, is to be based on the earnings of the company.

Instructions Assume that the earnings of the company for a given year, before either the provision for income taxes or the bonus is deducted, amount to $252,000. Compute the amount of bonus Coda would receive if the bonus is:

(1) Ten percent of the earnings before the provision for income taxes or the bonus is deducted.

(2) Ten percent of the earnings after the bonus is deducted but before the provision for income taxes is deducted.

(3) Ten percent of the earnings after both the provision for income taxes and the bonus are deducted. (Assume that the tax rate is 50 percent and that the bonus is deductible for tax purposes.)

*26-12 A meteorological report reveals that during the past 10 years a particular area has been fogbound 250 times for one day and that fog continued 100 times for a second consecutive day, 40 times for a third consecutive day, 20 times for a fourth consecutive day, and 10 times for a fifth consecutive

*AICPA adapted.

day. Occasions and length of fog were both random. Fog never continued more than 5 days and there were never two separate occurrences of fog in any 6-day period.

Instructions Assuming that fog *first* occurs on a particular day, determine the probability that:

(1) The next day will be foggy.

(2) The next day will be clear.

(3) The next two days will be foggy.

(4) The third day will be clear.

(5) The next three days will be foggy.

(6) The fourth day will be clear.

(7) The next four days will be foggy.

(8) The fifth day will be clear.

*26-13 The Commercial Products Corporation has requested your assistance in determining the potential loss on a binding purchase contract which will be in effect at the end of the corporation's fiscal year. The corporation produces a chemical compound which deteriorates and must be discarded if it is not sold by the end of the month during which it is produced.

The total variable cost of the manufactured compound is $25 per unit and it is sold for $40 per unit. The compound can be purchased from a competitor at $40 per unit plus $5 freight per unit. It is estimated that failure to fill orders would result in the complete loss of eight out of ten customers placing orders for the compound.

The corporation has sold the compound for the past 30 months. Demand has been irregular and there is no sales trend. During this period sales per month have been:

Units Sold per Month	Number of Months†
4,000	6
5,000	15
6,000	9

Instructions

(1) Determine the probability of sales of 4,000, 5,000, or 6,000 units in any one month.

*AICPA adapted.

†Occurred in random sequence.

(2) Prepare a schedule showing marginal income if sales of 4,000, 5,000, or 6,000 units are made in one month and 4,000, 5,000, or 6,000 units are manufactured in the same month. (Assume that all sales orders are filled regardless of the circumstances.)

(3) Prepare a schedule showing the average monthly marginal income the corporation might expect over the long run if 5,000 units are manufactured every month and all sales orders are filled.

26-14 Instructions Find the (1) median, (2) arithmetic mean, and (3) standard deviation of the following group of data: 74, 76, 77, 79, 82, 85, and 87.

26-15 Instructions Find the (1) mode, (2) median, (3) arithmetic mean, and (4) standard deviation of the following group of data: 73, 75, 77, 77, 78, 81, 82, 83, and 85.

26-16 Instructions Determine the EOQ (economic order quantity) for each of the following items:

Item	Annual Usage in Units	Unit Cost	Cost to Hold, %	Cost to Buy
A	40,000	$ .10	20	$4.00
B	2,000	2.00	5	4.00
C	200	11.25	20	4.00
D	10,000	.25	5	2.50
E	10,000	1.35	10	3.00

26-17 Instructions Determine the ROP (reorder point) for each of the following items:

Item	Normal Delivery Time, Days*	Normal Daily Usage, Units	Maximum Daily Usage, Units†
A	10	10	14
B	12	20	29
C	15	30	38
D	16	40	46
E	20	50	64

*Stated in terms of working days.
† Based on maximum daily usage that reasonably can be anticipated.

26-18 Normal usage of item A is 30 units per day and 14 working days are normally required for delivery. Based on experience, however, there is one chance in five that usage may be as high as 35 units per day, one chance in ten that it may be as high as 37 units, one chance in 20 that it may be as high as 40 units, one chance in 25 that it may be as high as 45 units, and one chance in 40 that it may be as high as 50 units.

Instructions Compute the ROP (reorder point) for item A, assuming that management wants:

(1) An 80 percent assurance of no stockouts

(2) A 90 percent assurance of no stockouts

(3) A 95 percent assurance of no stockouts

(4) A 96 percent assurance of no stockouts

(5) A $97\frac{1}{2}$ percent assurance of no stockouts

*26-19 There are ten men working as a group on a particular manufacturing project. When the weekly production of the group exceeds a standard number of pieces per hour, each man in the group is paid a bonus for the excess production in addition to his wages at hourly rates. The amount of the bonus is computed by first determining the percentage by which the group's production exceeds the standard. One-half of this percentage is then applied to a wage rate of $2.50 to determine an hourly bonus rate. Each man in the group is paid, as a bonus, this bonus rate applied to his total hours worked during the week. The standard rate of production before a bonus can be earned is 200 pieces per hour. Production for the past week was as follows:

Production Record		
	Hours Worked	*Production*
Monday	72	17,680
Tuesday	72	17,348
Wednesday	72	18,000
Thursday	72	18,560
Friday	71.5	17,888
Saturday	40	9,600
Total	399.5	99,076

Instructions   Based on the production record, compute the:

(1) Applicable bonus rate for the week

(2) Total dollar value of the bonus earned by the group during the week

*AICPA adapted.

(3) Total earnings of Allen, who worked 40 hours at a base rate of $2 per hour, and of Knoll, who worked $39\frac{1}{2}$ hours at a base rate of $3 per hour

*26-20 The cost accountant of the Stangren Corporation wants your opinion of a technique suggested to him by a young accounting graduate he employed as a cost analyst. The following information was furnished you for the corporation's two products, trinkets and gadgets:

Exhibit A				
	Daily Capacities in Units			
	Cutting Department	*Finishing Department*	*Sales Price per Unit*	*Variable Cost per Unit*
Trinkets _____	400	240	$50	$30
Gadgets _____	200	320	$70	$40

The daily capacities of each department represent the maximum production for either trinkets or gadgets. However, any combination of trinkets and gadgets can be produced as long as the maximum capacity of the department is not exceeded. For example, two trinkets can be produced in the Cutting Department for each gadget not produced and three trinkets can be produced in the Finishing Department for every four gadgets not produced.

Material shortages prohibit the production of more than 180 gadgets per day.

Exhibit B is a graphic expression of simultaneous linear equations developed from the production information given above in Exhibit A.

*AICPA adapted.

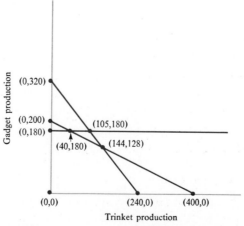

Exhibit B.

Instructions

(1) Comparing the information in Exhibit A with the graph in Exhibit B, identify the graphic locations (coordinates) of the:
    (a) Cutting Department's capacity
    (b) Finishing Department's capacity
    (c) Production limitation for gadgets because of material shortages
    (d) Area of possible production combinations of trinkets and gadgets

(2) (a) Compute the contribution margin per unit for both trinkets and gadgets.
    (b) Compute the total contribution margin for each of the points of intersections of lines bounding the possible production area.
    (c) Identify the best production combination of trinkets and gadgets.

Index